THE DUKE

Philip Guedalla

"I have been much exposed to authors"
WELLINGTON TO MRS. NORTON

WORDSWORTH EDITIONS

To
JOHN FORTESCUE
GRATEFULLY

This edition published 1997
by Wordsworth Editions Limited
Cumberland House, Crib Street, Ware,
Hertfordshire SG12 9ET

ISBN 1 85326 679 5

Printed and bound in Great Britain
by Mackays of Chatham plc, Chatham, Kent.

HOW many English streets, squares, monuments, and licensed premises bear the name of Wellington? His title has become one of the commonplaces of urban, and even Imperial, topography. He has his thoroughfares and schools and clubs and institutions; obelisks and open spaces still take their names from him, though he has vanished from the bootmaker's. Yet his memory, in spite of all these verbal honorifics, seems a trifle faded. He cast so large a shadow once. All Europe was his province, and no public act was quite complete until the Duke approved. There was no other Duke; how could there be?

But he survives to later memory as little more than the instrument of a single victory and the gruff hero of a dozen anecdotes; and one is left reflecting on the contraction of that vast achievement to so meagre a residue. It was inevitable, perhaps, that his Indian career should be forgotten, since silence is posterity's one repartee to Anglo-Indian reminiscences. But seven years of patient and brilliantly successful warfare in the Peninsula, by which the British expeditionary force was brought from a beach in Portugal to the recovery of Spain and a victorious invasion of Napoleonic France, are less easily mislaid. Yet such a steady march to victory was, perhaps, a shade inimical to his chances of lasting popularity in England. For a kindly nation seems to prefer its heroes slightly unsuccessful; its mind dwells more readily upon a last stand or a forlorn hope than upon the unchivalrous details of a crushing victory; and if it is to be allowed to choose, its favourite event will always be after the pattern of Rorke's Drift, its chosen hero in the manner of Sir John Moore. Judged by these sentimental tests, Wellington's career in Spain was far too successful to be really appealing. A second factor inter-

vened to wither his Peninsular laurels, since British tradition is predominantly maritime and loves to murmur, with Admiral Mahan, that " those far-distant, storm-beaten ships, upon which the Grand Army never looked, stood between it and the dominion of the world." It is profoundly flattering to an island race to view sea-power as the deus ex machina *of war; and the Blue Water view of history is so picturesque. Besides, it substitutes for adoration the sprightlier figure of Nelson who, though victorious, at least atoned for his success by falling in the hour of victory. But it is hardly just to those British soldiers whose efforts actually won the war, which sea-power alone was impotent to win.*

And Waterloo? That, surely, cannot have been forgotten. Hardly; though a century of French assertion, combined with a steadily increasing Napoleonic cult, seems to have imposed the odd belief that Waterloo was lost by the Emperor rather than won by Wellington. His years of peace slide still more easily towards oblivion, since a generation with peace-treaties of its own is scarcely impressed by authors of earlier peace-treaties; though it might well spare a glance for a system which effectually silenced the guns of Europe for half a century and for a soldier who inspired such universal trust that the whole problem of Reparations was left by common consent in his hands.

His subsequent career in politics has done more, perhaps, than any other influence to efface his memory, since it provoked the Whigs. By a peculiar division of labour British history, quite considerable parts of which have been made by Tories, has been very largely written by Whigs; and Whig historians are a little apt to dispose summarily of Tory reputations. Viewed by such eyes, the Duke became a stiff-necked conqueror trailing an unwelcome scabbard into civilian assemblies. It was even feared that his faith in democracy was imperfect, that he did not trust the people. Why should

*he ?   Half his life had been devoted to a war against the
French Revolution ; and it was hardly likely that he would
find revolution any more congenial because it happened to
be English.   Crowds had no sanctity for him—he had seen
far too many—and the purely arithmetical basis of democracy
failed to impress the Duke.   Shocked by this revelation, the
Nineteenth Century tended to belittle his entire achievement.
Perhaps the Twentieth may feel inclined to number it among
his merits.*

*At any rate, his portrait richly deserves to hang in the
great gallery of English prose.   But it is not there yet, though
it is nearly eighty years since the Duke died.   Stevenson,
who was once to paint it for a series of Andrew Lang's,
fingered the brushes for a little while.   Many hands have
sketched his long career (and I am indebted to almost all
of them) ; but when Waterloo is passed, they nearly always falter, and the story dies away in a desultory stream of
anecdote.   I have tried to follow its whole course ; and when
novelists devote a quarter of a million words to the records of
persons who did nothing in particular, I make no apology
for requiring three-quarters of that quantity to describe the
Duke of Wellington.   Indeed, his career might even entitle
him to the full ration customary for the portrayal of a
thoughtful bank-clerk or an introspective commercial
traveller.   But in this case brevity has a real value, since his
reputation seems to lie buried under the immense cairn of
printed matter which posterity has raised in his honour.
His correspondence has been printed in thirty-four volumes ;
and those 20,000 pages are the foundation of this book.
I have done my best to supplement them by exploring the
vast literature of his age and by using a mass of unpublished
MS. material.   The richest treasury of documents is, of
course, at Apsley House ; and the generosity of the Duke of
Wellington in giving me full access to the papers has been
of inestimable value.   For the rest, the magnitude of the*

undertaking has laid me under so many obligations for unpublished material, illustrations, and other assistance that I am forced to tabulate my acknowledgments.

DUKE OF WELLINGTON, K.G. .	Apsley House Papers and portraits.
MARQUESS OF LANSDOWNE . .	Wellington–Russell letter.
EARL BEAUCHAMP, K.G. . .	Walmer MSS.
EARL CAMDEN	Camden Papers.
EARL OF LONGFORD . . .	Wellington–Pakenham letter.
VISCOUNTESS GOUGH . . .	Pakenham information.
LORD GERALD WELLESLEY . .	Mornington–Fortescue letters.
HON. SIR JOHN FORTESCUE and	
MESSRS. MACMILLAN & CO. .	Maps from *History of the British Army*.
MISS LOWRY COLE . . .	Lowry Cole Papers.
HON. MRS. MAURICE GLYN . .	Wellington–Grosvenor letters.
F. M. GUEDALLA, ESQ. . .	Wellington–Flint correspondence.
C. HAMILTON, ESQ. . . .	Hamwood Papers.
P. HENRY, ESQ. . . .	Books from the Broadley Collection.
C. A. OLIVER, ESQ. . . .	Wellesley–Gordon correspondence.
THOMAS U. SADLEIR, ESQ. . .	Irish researches and information.
M. G. DE LA VILLEBIOT . .	Angers information.
OFFICE OF ARMS, DUBLIN CASTLE	Mornington Declaration.
PIERPOINT MORGAN LIBRARY, NEW	
YORK	Wellington–Russell correspondence.
BRITISH MUSEUM . . .	Portrait by Goya.
NATIONAL PORTRAIT GALLERY .	Portrait by Heaphy.
ROYAL UNITED SERVICE MUSEUM	Waterloo Model.

But though my thanks are tabulated, my gratitude is not. One further source of information has been explored, since places are frequently as informing as documents. I have, therefore, so far as possible, studied the Duke's career on the spot. Whilst I make no pretence to supplement the military historians, numerous journeys to Spain and Portugal have familiarised me with the Peninsula; and I have made detailed studies of the ground at Salamanca, Talavera, Burgos, San Sebastian, and the Lines of Torres Vedras. I have visited such points of minor interest as the Duke's school at Angers, and the scenes of his early life in Ireland. The kindness of the Duke of Wellington enabled me to conduct the greater part of my documentary researches in my subject's own library at Apsley House; and I am indebted to the Marchioness Douro for a sight of

Stratfield Saye and to Earl Beauchamp for a thorough exploration of Walmer Castle. But I cannot conclude my thanks without particular acknowledgment of the sustained and various assistance which I have received from Lord Gerald Wellesley, who has made many of these expeditions possible, taken part in some of them, furnished unpublished documents, and given every aid to my undertaking.

The writing of this book, though it is founded upon much earlier reading and travel, was begun in 1928 ; and since that date it has extinguished all other interests (and almost all other occupations) for me. I feel bound to thank all who have borne with me during that time—and one dear person in particular.

1931 P. G.

The authorities, published and unpublished, on which the text is founded are fully cited in the notes grouped at the end of the volume. References to these notes (of which more than 1,600 have been necessary) appear in the margin of the text ; and it is hoped that this system provides the necessary aids to scholarship without defacing the narrative page with footnotes or interrupting sentences with small, imprisoned numerals.

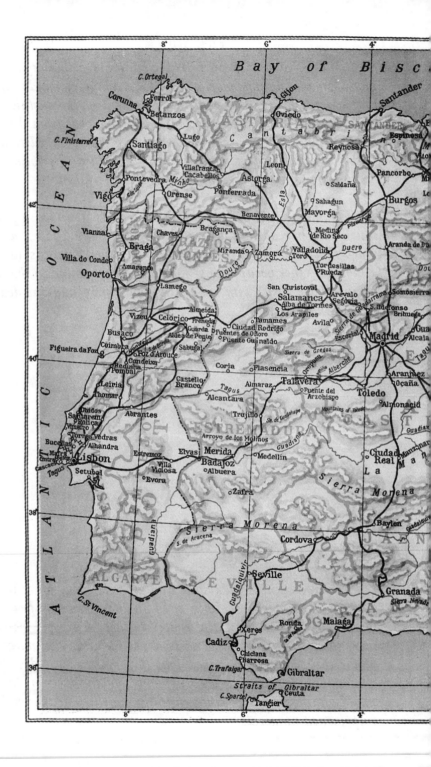

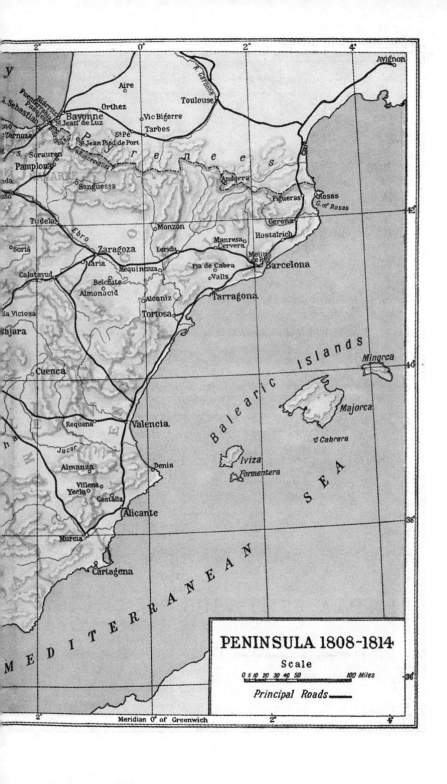

PENINSULA 1808-1814

Scale

0 5 10 20 30 40 50   100 Miles

Principal Roads

Meridian 0° of Greenwich

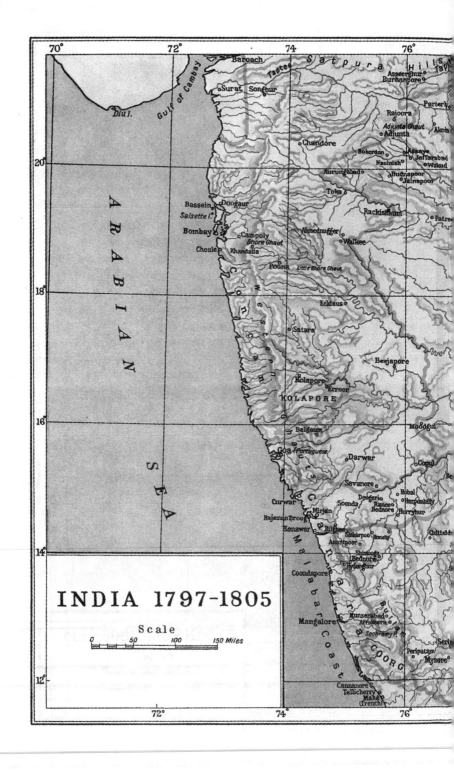

INDIA 1797-1805

Scale

0   50   100   150 Miles

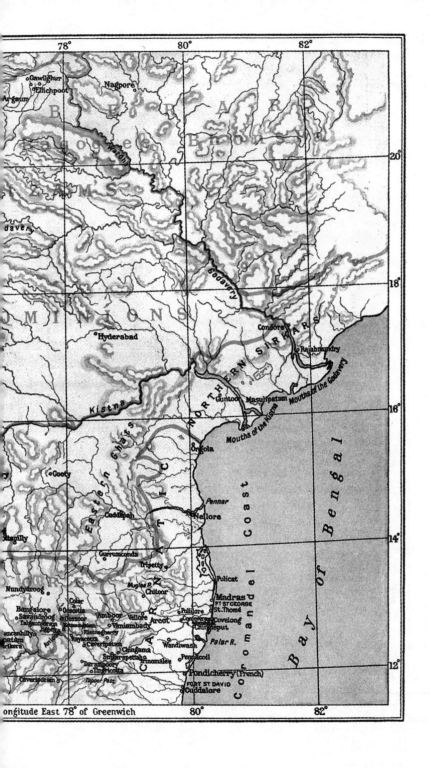

78°　　　　80°　　　　82°

BERAR

Gawilghur
Ellichpoot
Argaum
Nagpore

NIZAM'S

davery

Wardha

20°

DOMINIONS

Godavery

18°

Hyderabad

Condore
Rajahmundry

NORTHERN SIRKARS

Kistna

Eastern Ghats

Guntoor
Masulipatam
Mouths of the Godavery

16°

Gooty

Mouths of the Kistna

Ongole

Cuddapah

Pennar
Nellore

Coromandel Coast

Bay of Bengal

14°

Sitapilly

Gurrumconda

Tripetty

Nundydroog

Mugloo R.
Chittor

Pulicat

Bangalore
Savandroog
Colar
Ooscotta

Ambor
Vellore
Arcot

Madras
FT.ST.GEORGE
St.Thomé
Pollilore
Conjeveram Covelong
Chingleput

Talgautdroog
Jessoor
Sevendroog
Vaniambady
Arunconlilya
patam
Krikera
Rayacota
Kistnaghorry
Caveripatam

12°

Arny
Chengama
Singarapettah
Darrampoory
Tingricotta

Wandiwash
Palar R.

Chinnamalee
Permacoil

Caveriporam
Tapoor Pass

Pondicherry (French)
FORT ST DAVID
Cuddalore

THE DUKE

La gloire des grands hommes se doit mesurer aux moyens qui ils ont eus pour l'acquérir.—LA ROCHEFOU-CAULD.

I

I

CASTES mark their children deeply ; and as a caste the English gentry resident in Ireland were pronounced. Every conquest leaves a caste behind it, since conquerors are always apt to perpetuate their victory in superior social pretensions. Had not the Romans been the noblemen of Europe ? Even a Norman raid became an aristocracy in England ; and in Ireland the Anglo-Norman conquest left a similar deposit. Such castes are frequently absorbed, assimilated by their subject populations. But where race combines with religious differences and recurrent insurrection to keep the two apart, the schism is absolute and the conquerors remain an alien caste. Such castes, where they survive, are aristocratic by necessity, since their *hauteur* is less a mannerism than the sole condition of their survival. For without a sinful pride the conqueror will vanish, merged in his subject population—the Norman turned Englishman, the Anglo-Irish a mere Irishman, and the Anglo-Indian ' gone native.' But while their pride remains, the little garrisons live on.

Generations of secluded life amongst an alien and subject population breeds aristocrats. For the perpetual proximity of inferiors is a rare school of high demeanour. Anglo-Irish magnates knew themselves observed by long, resentful rows of Irish eyes ; and what conqueror would condescend before such an audience ? The silent watchers made and kept them prouder than ever ; and in the last half of the Eighteenth Century the Anglo-Irish magnate was indisputably *grand seigneur*. The visitor from England might stare at occasional crudities—at oxen roasted whole, at fourteen meat dishes for dinner, at a host who *1* sat before his claret half the day and all night long, lord of " vast but unproductive " acres, dispensing in a mansion " spacious but dilapidated " hospitality that was " lavish but inelegant." The Irish *ton*, perhaps, was sometimes a shade barbaric. There was an awkward contrast between the Duke of Leinster's guests at Carton and the little houses of Maynooth huddled at its gates, *2* while behind the big façade the house-party breakfasted to the

3

sound of French horns off chocolate and honey and an immense
table of " hot bread—cold bread—brown bread—white bread—
green bread, and all coloured breads and cakes." A chasm
yawned between the classes, as it yawned between Versailles and
France. But safe on the hither side the gentry lived their lordly
lives, drank claret, toasted the " glorious, pious, and immortal   *1*
memory," ran races, and matched fighting-cocks. Their very
differences wore an aristocratic colour, since they adored the point
of honour ; and Dublin duellists met behind Lucas' coffee-house   *3*
near the Castle with more than contemporary gusto. Even their
rivalries were lordly. As their rents rode ever higher on the
mounting tide of Irish population, they scattered their argosies
(and mortgaged their remotest prospects) in the lordliest game of
all. For they built as recklessly as kings. The trim Palladian   *4*
façades rose gracefully in every Irish county ; tall windows looked
down innumerable avenues of trees towards the ornamental
water ; obelisks defined the prospect ; and Grecian temples
ornamented the demesne with hints of the antique. Outbuilding
neighbours afforded even richer sport than horse-racing ; and a
light-hearted gentry built with an increasing fervour, since rents
could never fall while tenants swarmed in every cabin. Besides,
borrowing was always easy ; and the cheerful landlords sat
before their wine in the new glories of their mansions, an aristocracy indeed.

They bore themselves, besides, with the immense patrician
dignity that comes from superposition on a foundation of slavery.
For the native Irish, even in the last years of the Eighteenth Century, were not far removed from slavery. The lash, the penal
laws, the casual assault arouse misgivings in the onlooker. Misgivings turn to suspicion, when an English visitor notes that " a   *5*
landlord in Ireland can scarcely invent an order which a servant,
labourer, or cotter dares to refuse to execute. . . . Disrespect,
or anything tending towards sauciness, he may punish with his
cane or his horse-whip with the most perfect security. . . .
Knocking down is spoken of in the country in a way that makes
an Englishman stare." Suspicion deepens, as the same eye
observes the strings of little Irish cars along the winding Irish
roads " whipped into a ditch by a gentleman's footman, to make
way for his carriage " ; the " spalpeen broker," shipping his gangs   *6*
of barefooted mountaineers to work in English fields, confirms it.

It met the observant eye of Arthur Young a few years later—
" Speaking a language that is despised, professing a religion that
is abhorred, and being disarmed, the poor find themselves in
many cases slaves even in the bosom of written liberty." And
when a Lord-Lieutenant writes that " the poor people in Ireland
are used worse than negroes by their lords and masters, and their
deputies of deputies of deputies," the whole unpleasing truth
appears.

For the nearest social parallel to rural Ireland was to be found
three thousand miles away in the cotton-fields of Carolina.
There, too, a little caste lived on its acres.   The grace of Southern
manners on the white-pillared porches of Colonial mansions
matches the ease of Irish country-houses.   There is the same
profusion, the same improvidence against the same background
of slavery.   The same defects recur.   Even the fighting-men and
gamesters of the Irish countryside, who " kept miserable packs
of half-starved hounds, wandered about from fair to fair and
from race to race in laced coats, gambling, fighting, drinking,
swearing, ravishing, and sporting, parading everywhere their
contempt for honest labour," are reproduced in every unprepossessing detail on Mississippi levées.   Ireland, it seems, had
Southern wastrels as well as Southern charm.   For who can fail
to recognise the meaner types of Southern life in " the class of
little country gentlemen, . . . bucks, your fellows with round
hats edged with gold, who hunt in the day, get drunk in the
evening, and fight the next morning " ?   Small wonder, then,
that a mild critic finds the Irish upper classes " exposed to all the
characteristic vices of slaveholders, for they formed a dominant
caste, ruling over a population who were deprived of all civil
rights and reduced to a condition of virtual slavery.   They were
separated from their tenants by privilege, by race, by religion, by
the memory of inexpiable wrongs."   The fires of religious persecution had burned low, since persecution connotes an enthusiastic faith ; and enthusiasm was the last defect of an Irish
Churchman in 1769.   For a thoughtful Deist could hardly be
expected to derive unlimited satisfaction from the spectacle of
his brother-Deist at the stake.   But though persecution had
almost vanished, its legacy of social inequality remained.   There
were still serfs and, not less deeply caste-marked, " Protestant
Bashaws."   Slavery survived, and the vast dignity that marks

slaveholders. For such a caste does not part lightly with the lordly faith that some are born to rule and some to serve. Elsewhere the same soil put out the stiff blossoms of Washington and Lee ; and something, perhaps, of that unbending quality in war and statesmanship which grows in cotton-fields was latent in Ireland's Virginian gentry.

But though their aristocracy was real enough, the temptation (always strong) to view eighteenth-century life as a protracted costume play is nowhere stronger than in Ireland. Not that it was a genteel comedy of wigs and patches, devised by stage costumiers and laboriously played with carefully flirted handkerchiefs and dutifully taken snuff. The Dublin round—*ridotto*, dinner, dance, Italian opera, charity concert, Drawing-room—was natural enough. For one lived as other people lived in 1769, when all life in its more elegant forms had a faint air of *bal travesti*. But if the whole prevailing air was slightly unreal, still greater unreality hung on the air of Dublin, until it almost seemed a masquerade. Indeed, it was—a light-hearted masquerade where pleasant, slightly insignificant persons wore the impressive costumes of great officers of state. It was a little parody of England—Court, judges, bishops, Lords, and Commons—played out upon the stage of Dublin and watched with scared indifference by rows of Irish eyes. The stage was crowded ; Lord Chancellors elbowed Masters of the Rolls ; Privy Councillors nodded on every side to major-generals ; bishops abounded ; and there was a glorious profusion of Hereditary High Treasurers, Chief Barons, Remembrancers, and every known variety of public dignitary, with functions and without. The *rôles* were awe-inspiring ; but the maskers often seem a shade inadequate under their dominoes. For lawyers, whose merits might reasonably have escaped detection in the Temple or Lincoln's Inn, appear in ermine on the Irish bench ; and estimable clergymen, designed at best to fill a quiet canonry, inhabit vast episcopal palaces and preach to hushed cathedrals. It was the Irish masquerade, a delectable charade in which a little group of English families played at the government of Ireland upon a high and lighted stage in Dublin.

Dublin, in the spring weather of 1769, was never more Dublin. Somewhere beyond the hard, blue waters of St. George's Channel the Irish packets found a city where the ordered elegance of pagan ornament proclaimed the Eighteenth Century. For it was

eighteenth-century indeed.   Grilles, cornices, and porticoes
10 attested it.   Flambeaux announced the fact with iron tracery ;
door after door insisted blandly with a delicious fanlight and a
pair of elegant pilasters ; it echoed from painted walls where the
discreet festoons wandered from urn to urn ; unnumbered
chandeliers nodded assent with every gleaming prism ; and where
ceilings were an exquisite blend of stucco and mythology, marble
deities reclined in bas-relief on innumerable mantelpieces.
Murmuring (in heroic couplets) the last enchantment of the
Eighteenth Century, Dublin sat decorously true to type beside
its river.   Other capitals might falter in their allegiance.   In
London the steady pulse of the century, shaken dangerously by
the disordered tramp of Mr. Wilkes' supporters, wavered a little ;
it throbbed faintlier now in Paris under an ageing king ; and,
ingenious Mr. Townshend aiding with a tax on tea, tempers rose
in Boston to a most inelegant pitch.   Perhaps the Eighteenth
Century might not last for ever.   Boston rioters and Middlesex
electors almost seemed to suggest a doubt.   But could it ever end
in Dublin ?   Dimly conceivable elsewhere, the notion there
became wholly unthinkable.   Every doorway seemed to deny it ;
each modish column barred the way ; and carved divinities
looked down in bland denial, refused the extravagant surmise
with every attribute held in their marble hands or poured from
their cornucopiæ and, the wild thought dismissed, resumed their
allegories.   So Flora's altar smoked again with stony clouds of
incense, Ceres renewed her sheaves, and Endymion his slumbers.
Behind the porticoes of Dublin it would always be the Eighteenth
Century.   For the stamp of its century was unmistakably on
Dublin.

      And on its people, too.   It was not easy to be born in Dublin,
where every wall exhaled it, and escape the Eighteenth Century.
Had not Mr. Walpole informed Pitt's sister Anne a few years since
11 that " all the spirit or wit or poetry on which we subsist comes
from Dublin " ?   At the Castle on spring nights in 1769 loyal
ladies dropped their curtseys to Lord Townshend by Viceregal
candlelight, while their lords said hard things about him in the
Irish House of Commons with a watchful eye upon the pension
list.   Perhaps the face of politics was slightly unprepossessing.
12 Even Mr. Walpole had enquired a trifle acidly, " Pray, sir, how
does virtue sell in Ireland now ? "   Placemen filled places, pen-

sioners drew pensions, and in a dim perspective beyond Dublin
landlords collected rent. Something, perhaps, was stirring on
those shadowy hills where flitting figures burned outbuildings,
houghed cattle, or cropped Protestant ears, as the Irish pipes
wailed out *The Lad with the White Cockade*. Rebellious   13
Whiteboys were matched by Oakboys no less outrageous and
even by Steelboys, while distracted soldiers shot impartially at
either. But Dublin went on as usual. Ladies poured tea in
Sackville Street ; their lords fingered decanters ; and Signora
Cotilloni, fresh from her triumphs in " a neighbouring kingdom,"   14
begged leave of the *Dublin Mercury* to acquaint the nobility and
gentry of her arrival and of her intention to open a Dancing
Academy, and even to perfect her female pupils " in all the necessary manœuvres of coquetry, to manage the eyes to advantage,
to smile a man into hopes or frown him into uncertainty, to deny
favours without offending, and grant them with grace," the whole
concluding with the loyal (and not untimely) sentiment, *Honi soit
qui mal y pense.*
     That week Lord Mornington, lately removed from Grafton
Street, was with his countess at their new town house. They were
in treaty with Lord Antrim for the lease ; but the house seemed   15
to be theirs already. Built in the latest mode, it stood in Merrion
Street, and the two stately flambeaux were not unworthy to   16
enlighten guests in search of Mornington House. Their ceilings
were a graceful medley. Urns, shells, and garlands graced the
new dining-room, where convivial Irish gentlemen might finger
convivial Irish glass, while the ceiling in the drawing-room was a
more womanish affair of birds and flower-baskets. But these new
glories failed to engage Lady Mornington, since she lay upstairs
in the big bedroom at the back. It looked across a little garden
to the open space of Merrion Square. A harassed doctor
called ; the apothecary from Dawson Street brought round a
soothing draught ; and then a child—her sixth—was born on   17
May Day, 1769. They called him Arthur, and the Dublin round
was undisturbed. Fine gentlemen fought duels ; coaches went
up and down the street ; ladies stepped out of chairs ; wits
rhymed ; and the long tide crept slowly round the bay from
Dalkey to the hill of Howth.

THE happy father was an earl. He was, besides, Professor of Music at Trinity College, Dublin. For he was an earl of parts. Earldom itself, indeed, was something of a novelty, since it was barely nine years old. Lord Mornington was a Wesley of Dangan, son of the first Lord Mornington who, born a Colley of Castle Carbury, had inherited both name and fortune from his cousin, Garrett Wesley, whose mother had been a Colley. The name of Wesley accompanied the money ; and the same generous impulse had once suggested to the wealthier Wesleys a frustrated interest in Charles Wesley, then passing through Oxford on the long road to Methodism. The Colleys, emerging from the English Midlands in the later Middle Ages, had retained their English purity through three centuries of life in Ireland. No single Irish name adorns their pedigree ; and when Richard Colley, as his cousin's heir, assumed in 1728 the no less English name of Wesley, they were still Anglo-Irish squires.

The Wesley fortune eased affairs. There was an ampler air ; the family was moved to the big house at Dangan, and its new master entered the Irish House of Commons for the adjacent and well-disciplined borough of Trim. He planned improvements in the grounds, planted considerably, and dwelt upon the pleasing theme of ornamental water. There were to be canals that ships might ride on, lakes with islands in them, and a sufficiency of temples. It was an easy, cheerful home where everyone assembled in the hall for breakfast, shuttlecock, a little dancing, draughts, and family prayers, or strolled about the grounds and visited the temples. Apollo, Neptune, and Diana each received due honour in their shrines, and the company paraded gravely, bearing white staffs inscribed with their " Parnassus names " and complaining slightly that it made them look " like the sheriff's men at the assizes." For hospitality at Dangan extended even to the supply of classical allusions, and lady visitors were gratified by the *rôles* allotted them in Mr. Wesley's mythological charades. A delighted guest informed her correspondent

that she was " nothing less than Madam Venus," whilst one belle   *3*
united in her lovely person all three Graces, and their host was
a trifle apt to nominate three rival goddesses and to reserve for
the master of the house the arch *rôle* of Paris.   He had an organ
in the hall, and there was always a good deal of music.   They
often breakfasted to the harpsichord, to say nothing of a simultaneous game of shuttlecock.   For bewildered guests found the
Wesleys equal to the contrasted charms of drinking chocolate, the
battledore, and counterpoint in the big hall at Dangan, all at
once and without apparent interference with the enjoyment of
either.   Their picnics were invariably to music.   Even on a little
run from Dublin they hesitated to rely upon the unaided powers
of " cold fowl, lamb, pigeon pye, Dutch beef, tongue, cockells,   *4*
sallad, much variety of liquors, and the finest syllabub that ever
was tasted."   But the Muses were invoked, a lady placed at the
harpsichord jangled a little, and afterwards Mr. Wesley's violin
kept time to his daughters' dancing.   For, as a courtly ear observed, he " played well (for a gentleman) on the violin."   Some-   *5*
times, indeed, they essayed the grander pleasures of a water-   *6*
concert on the canal at Dangan where, their flag hoisted on " a
very pretty boat," they rowed harmoniously between the listening
fields of Meath.

So, music and the classics aiding, the years passed pleasantly.
An heir appeared ; Mr. Wesley, presently ennobled as Lord
Mornington, passed to the Irish House of Lords ; the big house   *7*
was burnt and sumptuously rebuilt.   Mythology reigned in the
grounds ;   the temples multiplied, and seats for exhausted
worshippers graced every alley ; obelisks abounded ; and each
sacred grove displayed the gracious gleam of statuary.   Presently
a visiting godmother found a small Garrett Wesley, whose one
desire was to celebrate her arrival with an artillery salute.   For
he was governor of a tiny fort, as well as lord high admiral of a
considerable fleet that rode on the canal, comprising the yawl
Fanny and the barge *Pretty Betty*, the whole commanded by the   *8*
flagship *Caroline*, a model of the King's yacht, carrying a battery
of guns and a complement of two, destined originally for presentation to a royal duke and acquired by some happy accident for
Dangan.   But when the honour of a salvo was declined politely,
his instinct for military courtesies was satisfied by hoisting all
his flags at once.

8   The boy was musical. Indeed, one feels that unless he had been, life at Dangan with an organ in the hall and the harpsichord at breakfast would have been unbearable. But while the first Lord Mornington played well (for a gentleman), his heir stood in no need of such genteel allowances. For he approached proficiency of a more plebeian order. In fine, he was a prodigy. Almost from birth the infant marvel intimated his enjoyment of his father's performances by beating time ; and as the air changed pace, awed onlookers saw the tiny hands alter their beat. Nor did his growth belie the promise of these talented gesticulations. The dawn of taste even preceded speech. For when a guest essayed to take the violin from his father, the infant interposed ; and the transfer could only be effected while the small, indignant hands were held. But the visitor proving to be no less than the celebrated Dubourg, the fastidious infant, having once heard that virtuoso, was with difficulty persuaded to permit the noble amateur to resume his instrument. Indeed, when Dubourg was in the house, the child, with rare (if scarcely pious) discernment, would never let his father play. At nine he scraped a bow himself, rendering *Christ Church Bells* and *Sing one, two, three, come follow me*, and shortly afterwards played second violin in Corelli's Sonatas, an experience to which connoisseurs attributed that lifelong steadiness in time which never, it was said, deserted him. Then, pricked by the emulation which stirs musicians to their greatest efforts, he turned composer. For a local clergyman, having won considerable applause with a country dance of his own composition, Master Wesley responded with a minuet marred by a slight excess of fifths, and shortly afterwards achieved a duet for French horns and an *Andante*. His gifts survived the discouragements incidental to membership of a large and cheerful family, since his sisters drove him continually from the harpsichord in a sisterly opinion that he spoiled the instrument. But he played by stealth ; and when an organ was installed in the chapel at Dangan, he startled the family by playing an impromptu fugue at the organ-maker's. His studies progressed ; and though he lacked formal instruction, compositions flowed from his pen with such happy consequences that when he consulted Rosengrave and Geminiani, those masters modestly replied that they could not be of the least service to one who had already mastered the science.

The gentle youth grew up ; and his godmother found him at
thirteen " a most extraordinary boy," almost unnaturally good at   7
lessons and playing the violin at sight. His varied accomplishments extended to shipbuilding and fortification as well as
music ; and their diversity was almost equal to her own somewhat
injudiciously assorted passions for conchology, gossip, fossils, and
every form of petrifaction. For she was no less than Mrs.
Delany. At twenty-two he stepped sedately into the family
borough, and uneventfully represented Trim in the Irish House of
Commons. In the next year his father died, and he succeeded
to the title. The exacting dowager found him a trifle lacking in
" the punctilios of good breeding." Perhaps a nobleman required   9
a thought more polish than the organ and Trinity College, Dublin,
had power to impart ; and when he chose a wife, her disapproval
grew more pointed. His first choice was admirable. Lady   10
Louisa Lenox was a duke's daughter ; and all was smiles, until
Mr. Conolly, of Castletown, offered his ampler means. The rival,
as a loyal godmother confessed, had " double his fortune (and
perhaps about half his merit)." But even dukes are human ; and
Lord Mornington was blandly informed that " the young lady had
an insurmountable dislike to him." The wounded lover reeled ;
for the ducal alliance was not without its savour. But his wounds
were promptly assuaged by Miss Hill, of Belvoir. Her father,
though he had once kept a bank in Dublin, was younger brother
to a viscount. Perhaps his manners were a shade excessive, since   11
he was always apt to give a slightly unconvincing rendering of the
fine gentleman. But, manners apart, he was agreeable, " with a   12
little pepper in his composition," which might enliven the mild
Wesley stock. The bride was turned sixteen, a fine young woman
in Mrs. Delany's estimation, although " rather a little clumsy, but
with fine complexion, teeth, and nails, with a great deal of modesty
and good-humour." These charms prevailing, the young Lord
Mornington paid his addresses. Mr. Hill was gallantly informed   13
that the eager bridegroom asked no fortune, was even prepared
to make a settlement himself ; if the bride had any fortune, he
chivalrously " desired it might be laid out in jewels for her." So
all was smiles again. The clothes were bought ; the settlements
were drawing up ; and Lord Mornington was seen at the play in
Dublin, looking a little solemn.
     They were a happy pair, though his exacting godmother still

had her moments of uncertainty as to how far her qualities would remedy his defects. He was "a very good young man on the
14   whole," if slightly lacking in punctilio ; but Anne Mornington herself lacked finish, although she made shell flowers. (Yet even then she seemed wanting in distinction ; for when she furnished Mrs. Delany with a shell or so for her endless decorations, they were nothing rare.) Unclouded by these mysterious defects, their life opened happily enough. They lived at Dangan or in Grafton Street. An heir was born in Dublin, and a grateful press recorded
15   " the great joy of that noble family." King George II died ; and the new reign brought Mornington a step in the Irish peerage. A pleasing fancy traces his earldom to the new sovereign's interest in music ; but it had a likelier connection with the exigencies of Irish government, since the fountain of honour played steadily upon obliging Dublin legislators, and the next dozen years enriched the Irish nobility with thirty-three barons, sixteen viscounts, and twenty-four earls.

The new Earl of Mornington had his own interests. For the Muses followed him to Dublin, where he initiated a Musical Academy and supported burlesque productions in opposition to
16   the Italian burletta of a rival theatre. It was an age of musical
17   refinement, when Irishmen proudly recorded that " the god of music had taken a large stride from the Continent over England to this island . . . and it has been observed that Corelli is a name in more mouths than many of our Lord-Lieutenants." Respectful instrumentalists played Handel to listening cathedrals ; and when Lord Mornington essayed a charity concert, an orchestra of noblemen and gentlemen obeyed his *bâton*. A Lord-Lieutenant's daughter sang ; there was a peer among the flutes ; a noble clergyman bowed diligently above his 'cello. The Italian taste prevailed ; and one vocalist recalled to a disgusted ear Mingotti's " trills and squalls." But these ardours did not check Morning-
18   ton's melodious pen, which ran mostly to Church music, with a strong predilection for full harmony and the minor third, but had its lighter moments. For he could even stoop to glees, and grateful glee-singers rendering *Here in cool grot* and *Come, fairest nymph* acknowledged a noble author. *'Twas you, Sir*, was his work as well, to say nothing of *By greenwood tree* and *Gently hear me, charming maid*. Small wonder, then, that Trinity College conferred a Doctorate of Music and even advanced the earl to be

professor. For music had quite vanquished his earlier leanings towards naval architecture and the principles of Vauban.

Meanwhile his family increased. They had named the heir Richard after the first Lord Mornington ; and the happy infant bore the title of Viscount Wellesley, a prouder, mediæval form of Wesley. The second was called Arthur after her father ; but he did not survive, and the first Arthur Wesley died in childhood. Then came a third son, named William, followed by a short-lived Francis, and a daughter, whom they christened Anne after Lady Mornington. The sixth child, born at the new house in Merrion Street, was a boy. They called him Arthur, too. So he got her father's name and perhaps (who knows ?) something of her father's pepper.

III

LIFE opened for the child in Dublin ; and as they brought him
down the big staircase lit by its one tall, pillared window for his
first outing in Merrion Street, the bland, unhurried days followed
each other. Not that the times were bland. It was a wild
decade, that opened (in Mr. Walpole's pained enumeration) with
1 "no Government, no police, London and Middlesex distracted,
the Colonies in rebellion, Ireland ready to be so, and France
arrogant, and on the point of being hostile." Crowds had an
ugly tendency to roar *God save great Wilkes our king*, and public
men were in a flutter—" Lord Bute accused of all and dying in a
panic ; George Grenville wanting to make rage desperate ; Lord
Rockingham, the Duke of Portland, and the Cavendishes thinking we have no enemies but Lord Bute and Dyson, and that four
mutes and an epigram can set everything to rights ; the Duke of
Grafton like an apprentice, thinking the world should be postponed to a whore and a horse-race ; and the Bedfords not caring
what disgraces we undergo, while each of them has £3,000 a year
and three thousand bottles of claret and champagne." That
summer—Arthur Wesley's first—London was alarmed by a
terrific *revenant*. For at St. James's men heard the blind tapping
of a familiar crutch across the palace floor, looked nervously
behind them, and saw the tormented eyes under the peak of a
great wig which were all that remained of Chatham. The old
2 man had come to Court again, "himself" (as Mr. Walpole
tittered) "*in propriâ personâ*, and not in a strait-waistcoat";
and his sovereign's eyes protruded more than ever, as that
imperial nose descended with tremendous deference to meet those
ailing knees. Overseas the angry quaver of Mr. Samuel Adams'
voice hung on the air of Boston ; lion and unicorn still ramped
cosily upon the State House ; but who could say how long they
would remain there with an angry voice insisting that taxation
was slavery, that Rome was never better than when it had no
king, that thirty thousand men with bayonets and knapsacks
would infallibly spring from the soil of Massachusetts. It was a

15

flurried age, when Mr. Walpole feared the worst and England
lived uneasily under the mosaic ministry of Burke's inimitable
apologue ; and in the wings Lord North was waiting for his turn.
    But these discontents scarcely reached Mornington House.
Burke wrote a pamphlet ; and Lord Mornington composed a glee.
The angry *Junius* strained the limits of invective ; and that
gentle nobleman made a mild addition to the English hymnal.
Mobs roared ; and he was seen, a little puffy now, bending a
dark, shaven chin above deft fingers at the keyboard. As
America flamed into civil war, his peaceful *bâton* waved imperturbably above the busy violins of Dublin gentlemen at a charity
concert. His calm was perfect—almost, it would seem, too
perfect for his countess, since Mr. Walpole breathed to Lady   *3*
Ossory a wicked "history of Lady Mornington," asking with
finished malice " where should bawds and bishops pay court but
to youthful hypocrisy ! Could her Ladyship apprehend a cold
reception where Lord Pembroke is a Lord of the Bedchamber ? "
Once, indeed, his calm was interrupted, when a Dublin footpad   *4*
named Murphy stopped his sedan-chair, let off a pistol, and
removed his lordship's gold watch with all his money. But the
rogue was apprehended and left to dangle in a halter on the mound
at the corner of St. Stephen's Green.
    Sometimes they breathed the calmer air of Dangan ; and
from the big windows of his country home the small Arthur
Wesley saw Meath rolling gently into the distance. They sent
him to the little school at Trim just down the road, where his
brother Wellesley had displayed his early promise. That promise
was, indeed, their pride. For Richard, their eldest, was exceptionally gifted ; the other children lived in awe, and a loyal family
prepared to applaud the rise of Richard Wellesley. He rose,
whilst Arthur played at home with William and Anne, to Harrow.
But Harrow failed to hold the aspiring youth for more than
eighteen months, since a school riot, occasioned by the appointment of an Etonian headmaster, claimed him. Marked by these
prejudices as a born Etonian, he was removed and sent to Eton.
His faculties reviving in that nobler air, he became a prodigious
Latinist and a considerable Grecian. They were all in England
now ; for the family (increased by the addition of a small Gerald,
a still smaller Henry, and a tiny Mary Elizabeth) had let the
Dublin house and moved to Knightsbridge. Lord Mornington   *5*

was heard at the harpsichord one night at Lady Stamford's, where a distinguished amateur played first violin and a lady vocalist rendered *Dové sei* so sweetly that one grateful member of her audience " slept better than for many nights before."

Transplanted from his native island, the small Arthur Wesley studied the rudiments at Brown's seminary (later dignified as Oxford House Academy) in King's Road, Chelsea ; and the splendid Richard passed on to Christ Church.   That was the year that British armies laboured heavily through Carolina, while the mature intelligence of Lord George Germaine was busy organising defeat at the War Office.   King George's guns thudded without conspicuous success in almost every hemisphere.   The fires of victory burned low, and every tent was full of disappointed paladins.   Gage was at home forgetting Bunker's Hill ; Burgoyne was back in Hertford Street explaining Saratoga ; and Howe was polishing his *Narrative.*   Even the fleet, at war with France and Spain and heavily outnumbered, rode insecurely ; and for a summer week of madness the mob ran wild for " No Popery " and Lord George Gordon, while the dull glare of burning houses glowed on the London sky.   Small wonder that the harassed North begged to resign ; but his inexorable sovereign pointed implacably to duty and the unique (though sadly underrated) perfection of the British constitution.

Like his afflicted country, Lord Mornington was not without his troubles.   For the subsequent finances of infant prodigies are often far from cheering.   His married life had opened with the rich prospect of eight or ten thousand pounds a year.   But twenty years devoted to the Muses (at what cost the Muses only knew) had darkened the financial prospect.   Few orchestras enrich their patrons ; Musical Academies are rarely remunerative ; and his man of affairs in Dublin surveyed a mournful landscape. For his later airs were pitched, like so many of his youthful compositions, in a minor key.   Their migration to London, though hardly well-conceived as a measure of economy, had been in the nature of a retreat.   They were rather stinted now, " not able to appear in any degree as we ought," though he still kept his coach.   But lodgings in Knightsbridge were a sad decline for the noble *maestro* ; and at the prospect of a continued effort to live on £1,800 a year Lord Mornington grew positively rebellious. There was so much to be provided—Richard's allowance, and the

2

six younger children's education, to say nothing of the costly array of masters requisite if Anne's accomplishments were to be perfected with due elegance. One estate was already deeply mortgaged ; but his dreams in Knightsbridge were haunted by an unpleasant sum of £16,000 that had to be raised somehow. Richard, of course, might join with him to raise it. But would he ? After all, that eminent young man would shortly come of age ; and he might not consent. Then, was it altogether wise to remove his property from his own power ? For he had dismal recollections of too trusting parents sadly ill-treated by their unnatural offspring. It was a depressing problem, for which the hopeful earl found a solution in an ingenious scheme for raising £3,000 a year, rising in a yet more hopeful postscript to the cheering theme of lottery tickets—" If you will send me ten numbers I shall take two and give each of my Children and my Lady one, but don't let these numbers run all in order, but different thousands if possible." Such expedients are not unfamiliar in the after-lives of patrons of the arts.

Nor was the brilliant Richard, trailing a nobleman's gold tassel from his cap at Christ Church, untouched by these melancholy concerns. His allowance was a family problem, since their touching faith persisted that he was " likely to make a figure in the world from his great abilities," and such prospects plainly called for at least four hundred pounds a year. But graver themes engaged him in the very moment of his triumph as Chancellor's prizeman for 1780 with a Latin ode on Captain Cook. His father was unwell, and a prudent counsellor in Dublin reviewed the unpleasing prospect. There was the mortgage, and the debts, and the eternal £16,000 that had to be raised somehow. If the earl recovered, he would really have to live at Dangan. If not, his heir must sell the Dublin house and travel. His adviser, having lived abroad himself and been twice to Italy, grew almost eloquent on travel. The sapient Richard was, he felt, unlikely to indulge in " any of the fashionable vices and follies wch ruin so many young Men," but touched with a nobler aspiration " to bring home a knowledge of the different Constitutions & Policy of the several States he visits," a sober programme, with the additional advantage of being vastly cheaper. For his adviser added with justice that " the flowers of travelling may be gathered at a moderate expense, they ornament Character. The weeds

are costly, they poison the mind & are a canker in the fortune."
In fine, when he succeeded, the young gentleman would be well
advised to economise abroad.   His choice came all too soon.
For Lord Mornington died in May, 1781, and the Madrigal Society
lost their most zealous member.   Music apart, he had always
been a shade inadequate : Mrs. Delany had foreseen as much.
And if she had foreseen his sons, what else could she expect ?
For fame reserves no niche for the father of the Gracchi.

So Richard became an earl at twenty, and Arthur at twelve had
lost his father.   They buried him with seemly state, and more
than eighty pounds of Richard's inheritance vanished in the pious
outlay—fourteen mutes with black gloves and truncheons ; cloaks
and crape hat-bands for the little party of eight mourners ; and
black gloves for the Knightsbridge landlady, to say nothing of a
stupendous canopy (the undertaker's pride), nodding with sable
plumes, and hired for the sad occasion.   Two coaches followed
him ; and for once a Wesley outing lacked its music.   Something
of him, perhaps, lived on in Arthur's violin.   For the small boy
played ; and if he remembered anything of his father, it was the
pleasant, slightly ineffectual figure conjured up for him three-
quarters of a century later by the Muse of *Jeames de la Pluche :*

> " His father praps he sees,
> Most musicle of Lords,
> A-playing madriggles and glees
> Upon the Arpsicords."

IV

THE little family bore their bereavement. Now there were only eight of them—Lady Mornington, the fine young woman of Mrs. Delany's distant recollection, a dowager at thirty-nine; the incomparable Richard; William just turned eighteen; and Arthur, a boy of twelve, with two small brothers and a pair of sisters. The young earl came down from Oxford and assumed his mournful post as head of the family. Mournful in more ways than one, since family finance in 1781 was uninviting. A thoughtful cousin had, it is true, reduced their burdens by leaving an estate in Queen's County to William (together with the name of Pole). But something must be done for his mother, to say nothing of five children all waiting for expensive educations and his own career. Besides, there were the debts. It was all highly disagreeable for a rising man. He came of age in June, and the next month he was in Dublin raising mortgages on the Meath lands. *1* But the further programme of an inexpensive Continental tour failed to attract him, since foreign spas afford few opportunities for statesmanship, and Richard was resolved to be a statesman. Taking his seat at the long table of the Irish House of Lords, he quickly shewed that mild temper of rebelliousness which is the surest path to office. But the family were not sacrificed to this brilliant opening. For that very year two of his brothers went to Eton.

The autumn mists of 1781 crept up from a Virginian river, and the British guns were flagging behind the crumbling works of Yorktown, when Arthur Wesley went to boarding-school. The trap closed on Cornwallis three thousand miles away, as the two small brothers stared round at Eton. For there were two of them. He took Gerald with him; and this pair of Daniels (though one of them was only nine) kept one another in countenance among the lions of their new abode. Lions, indeed, abounded. For Eton, in the spasmodic reign of Jonathan Davies, was a marked advance upon Brown's academy at Chelsea. Numbers alone were terrifying, since three hundred boys were quite

enough to alarm two newcomers from Knightsbridge. Had not
the formidable Chatham confessed that " he scarce observed a
boy who was not cowed for life at Eton ; that a public school
might suit a boy of turbulent forward disposition, but would not
do where there was any gentleness " ?   But, turbulent or not, the
two small Wesleys survived this stern initiation. Lower boys
were scarcely disturbed by their vociferous headmaster. That
slightly indecorous figure was almost as remote as royalty itself,
which was always riding past the Long Walk with empty, staring
eyes, or buttonholing stray promenaders on the terrace with his
" Well, well, my boy, when were you last flogged, eh, eh ? " or,
more searchingly, " What's your name ? who's your tutor ?
who's your dame ? " concluding with the invariable reassurance
of, " *Very* good tutor, *very* good dame " from royal lips. The two
small brothers were largely untroubled by these high matters.
But the long ritual of lessons, ' absence,' chapels without number, and still more lessons, all to be performed under three
hundred pairs of watching eyes, was quite sufficiently alarming.

They boarded at Naylor's, played in the muddy garden of the
Manor House, and shared rooms with strangers. Decorum did
not always reign, since Arthur fought a battle—his very first—
with a schoolfellow named Smith, provoked by being stoned
while bathing, for whom fate reserved the still more mournful
destiny of being brother to a wit (even a thrashing from Arthur
Wesley may well have been more palatable than a lifelong course
of Sydney's brightest sayings) ; and there were schoolboy jokes
about the maids, who slept in a room just off the kitchen, termed,
with exaggerated courtesy that stayed in Arthur's memory for
forty years, the " Virgins' bower." Far more sedate was their
scholastic progress. Not theirs the lofty destinies of Richard,
whose declamations had drawn tears from royal eyes and compliments from Garrick ; no statesmen, lured by their promise, drove
down from London to enlist their gifts. For they were not, were
very far from being their unnaturally gifted school-fellow George
Canning ; and no Mr. Fox stopped at their door. Early promise
was the last thing about them. Breasting the slope together,
they had advanced within the year to ' Upper Greek,' where they
toyed with Ovid, Terence, and the Vulgate. By the next Easter
they were both deep in the recesses of the Fourth Form, sustained
upon a sober diet in which, though Ovid still predominated, there

were nutritious extras in the way of Cæsar, Æsop, and Greek **6**
Testament. It was depressing to observe how close his younger
brother trod to Arthur's heels ; for if Wesley *ma.* sat fifty-third
out of seventy-nine, Wesley *mi.* came fifty-fourth, the hounds of
spring keeping assiduous company with winter's traces. The fact
was not without its consequence for Wesley *ma.*, since he was
shortly afterwards withdrawn from Eton. School bills were
heavy, and Richard was moving up into the costlier arena of
British politics. Besides, there was a third brother now in the
abysses of the Lower Remove ; and with Wesley *minimus* to pay
for, the ant-like pace at which Wesley *ma.* scaled Parnassus
scarcely rewarded outlay. So early in 1784 his brief rearguard
action with the classics ended.

Its effects remain slightly mysterious. For the classical
attainments, with which Eton equipped her sons for public life,
were not for him. He once prescribed his rules of public speaking
—" One is, I never speak about what I know nothing, and the **7**
other, I never quote Latin "—a wise abstention, since his quantities
were always uncertain. Did not the nation's hero, in the full
robes of Oxford Chancellor, once alarm the Sheldonian Theatre
with a *Jacobus* whose second syllable was short, hastily atoned for
by a *Carolus* whose second (and still more fatal) syllable was
long ? Yet, however impervious to Ovid, no Etonian could
possibly escape a sense of the indisputable truths of revealed
religion, since these were publicly rehearsed with impressive and
even wearisome regularity. What else he learned is more
obscure. Scarcely, it seems, a genius for friendship. Nor was he
formed upon the playing-fields. Indeed, the playing-fields were
hardly formed themselves. Cricket and fives were practised ;
but the remaining catalogue of Eton games varies between the **8**
infantile and the purely occult. It is not easy to believe that
hoops and hop-scotch developed valuable qualities ; few statesmen owe their eminence to early marbles ; nor do the martial
virtues thrive upon a simple diet of peg-top and battledore. The
civic lessons of Bally Cally, Conquering lobs, and Hunt the
dark lanthorn must remain enigmatic ; but the heartening
presence of Puss-in-the-corner may be felt to indicate that the
stern reign of pure athletics was still far distant. Nor was
Arthur's own recollection less unheroic. For revisiting the place
in later years, he stared into Naylor's (then Ragueneau's) garden, **4**

and enquired affectionately for a broad, black ditch he used to leap over, adding that in his own belief he owed his spirit of enterprise to the tricks he used to play there.   The tribute may be found unsatisfying by athletic purists and a shade disappointing even to Etonians, since their playing-fields appear only in the attenuated form of a ditch in a dame's garden.   But, such as it was, he paid it.

The next instalment of his education took him abroad.   For, taste coinciding with finance, his mother chose to travel ; and Arthur travelled with her.   Not that they travelled far.   For their brief journey ended in a town with which he was to have a fuller acquaintance, since they lay at Brussels.   The cheerful, slightly equivocal little capital of the Austrian Netherlands lived uneventful days in 1784, only slightly complicated by the unlikely spectacle of a reforming Kaiser.   For the solemn Joseph II, who ranked among the best-travelled men in Europe (since he had visited almost all his own dominions), suffered from the fatal illusion that he was a man of his times and—yet more fatal impulse—resolved to move with them.   But the times, at any rate in Belgium, were sadly immobile ; for the best intentions of Teutonic persons are often wasted upon Belgium, and his most progressive gestures were coldly received by a community that was still obstinately mediæval.   To this accompaniment Lady Mornington and Arthur took up their residence in Brussels.   It lasted for a year—the year that saw the last of Dr. Johnson and the first of Palmerston, that heard Mr. Pitt denouncing Mr. Fox above the lively uproar of the Westminster election, that saw the *Tragic Muse* begun and the *Decline and Fall* nearly ended. Arthur, perhaps, fell something short of her ideal.   The retreat from Eton had not been altogether to his credit.   And then he was fifteen.   Few boys, whatever their moral excellence, are seen to the best advantage at fifteen : an excess of limb scarcely lends charm to an unaccustomed gruffness.   Small wonder, then, that Lady Mornington vowed to God she did not know what she should do with her awkward son Arthur.   Really, with Richard winning golden opinions in Parliament, William in the Irish House of Commons, Gerald destined for the Church, and Henry still too young to think about, Arthur's future began to be something of a problem.   Meanwhile, it could do him no harm to learn a little French, if only with a Belgian accent.

French, it appears, was almost all he learned at Brussels. Their obliging landlord dispensed vague draughts of learning. But a fellow-pupil remembered Arthur Wesley mainly for his devotion to the violin. For the Muse was easier to woo in foreign lodgings than at Eton. So the world glided into 1785 ; and he played on, as the slow days went by in Brussels. Ste. Gudule struck the hours ; the light slanted from the west across the uneventful fields by Hougoumont ; and in a Brussels room an awkward boy was playing on the violin.

That year his education moved him on once more. Lady Mornington went home to England. But two years of Eton and twelve months of casual tutoring in Brussels being judged insufficient, he must go somewhere to be ' finished ' ; and since his range included little in the way of manly accomplishments, he was consigned to Angers, where the fifth of a dynasty of riding-masters presided over a celebrated academy. It stood behind a noble grille of iron-work—such iron-work as Marie Antoinette, the Queen, passed through each time her coach rumbled discreetly off to Trianon and turned into the tiny drive before her tiny palace. But at Angers the shapely modern work was gracefully disposed under the very hulk of the Middle Ages, where King René's castle lay—striped, blackened, and truncated—like a grounded leviathan. The tall Academy behind the grille was modern too—trim angles of white stone, a rounded hall, and at the back a flight of stately little steps descending from the tall façade, where art had carved a sheaf of palettes, French horns, and books, contrasted decorously opposite a panoply of arms, such armour, baldricks, and cuirasses as classical hero never wore. Its educational resources consisted mainly of a riding-school. But the curriculum included dancing lessons, together with a course in fencing. This happy blend was customary in such establishments, when dancing was apt to start at dawn, followed by riding, fencing, and a little grammar, with mathematics in the afternoon and a final dancing class to close the happy day. It was an age of elegance, when *haute école* and foils were felt to lack something if unaccompanied by Terpsichore. These studies, vaguely military in intention, were often followed by young gentlemen in search of a more general finish ; and for about a year, his destiny being still uncertain, Arthur pursued them, walking the streets of Angers, seeing King Louis' soldiers in their white, or pounding round the riding-school in strict accordance with the rules of horse-manship. But the niceties of *haute école*, even when expounded with hereditary fervour by M. de Pignerolle, were scarcely more attractive than construing Ovid ; and his attention often wandered. It was far pleasanter to pass the time playing with his dog or dining with the local gentry. He was often at the Duc de Brissac's, where the wine was poor and there was not much to eat, although their host had been an ornament of Versailles, under Louis XV. The old nobleman kept open house, though Pignerolle's cadets were a little apt to make themselves unpleasant to injudicious guests.

He saw a good deal of the French. There was one of them who had a brother in the Church named Talleyrand ; and one day at the Duc de Praslin's table he met an Abbé Sieyès, full of vague politics designed for the new Assembly of Notables and preparing to astound the world with his conundrum, *Qu'est-ce que le Tiers État ?* He even retained a dim (and, most likely, unfounded) recollection of meeting Chateaubriand, then a wild-eyed subaltern in the King's army. But his most congenial world was a small English set known, by the pleasing Continental practice of promiscuous ennoblement, as the *groupe des lords.* For more than one young gentleman of quality was sent to Angers, and among them a real lord or so. One pair, who lived in lodgings in the town and kept a famous cook, saw a good deal of Arthur. It was a cheerful world, where Pignerolle's cadets tried their very hardest to be manly, lose money at the tables, run into debt, and pick really grown-up quarrels (*bourgeois* French parents were mildly shocked by the establishment, because " *elle n'était remplie que de seigneurs Français ou Anglais, et . . . l'on ne connaissait pas de pays, où le libertinage, le jeu, le ton querelleur soient poussés plus loin que dans cette ville* "), although their manliest efforts were occasionally contradicted by the school confectioner's advertisements of sweets.

Arthur, staring up in the big round bastions of the castle or watching the gaitered infantry go stiffly by in their three-cornered hats, was seventeen. He had been two years abroad ; and it was time for him to find a calling. They found one for him, since his mother had announced without enthusiasm that he was " food for powder and nothing more." Richard must use his influence and try to get him a commission. The rising man (he was in the ministry now, one of Mr. Pitt's Junior Lords of the Treasury) approached the Lord-Lieutenant ; and that potentate was presently informed of " a younger brother of mine, whom *13* you were so kind as to take into your consideration for a commission in the army. He is here at this moment, and perfectly idle. It is a matter of indifference to me what commission he gets, provided he gets it soon." Dangan was mortgaged, and *14* there was not much to spare for the support of younger brothers. But Richard's nonchalance was less uncritical than might appear, since there was at least one variety of commission which he felt to be unsuitable for Arthur. For he declined the artillery, feeling *15* perhaps that Arthur's birth (no less than Arthur's education) unfitted him for service in the learned arm. Such scruples were not universal. Watched by another family, another widow's son born the same summer and educated at another French academy was with his battery already. The pinched young subaltern, just seventeen and newly-joined, was deep in his gunnery. The guns attracted him ; he even found a charm in mortars ; and the frayed uniform grew dirtier than ever on the shadeless polygon of Valence. But then Lieutenant Bonaparte was not a Wesley, was not quite (as Arthur afterwards observed) a gentleman. Such ardours are not for Etonians. For Arthur's reading eschewed Rousseau ; less ardent, he composed no novelettes of passion ; and at no moment of his life was he capable of five perusals of *Werther*. More equable, he waited for the Lord-Lieutenant, through the good offices of Richard, to do something for him. And in due course he did. For on March 7, 1787, Arthur Wesley received the King's commission as Ensign in the Seventy-third. It was a Highland regiment ; and, better still, it was in India, where there was not the slightest need for him to join it.

V

HE was gazetted Ensign just in time for his eighteenth birthday. It was the year of Mr. Pitt's *Entente Cordiale* and Hastings' impeachment. Mr. Burke was tuning up the deeper notes of his invective ; Boswell was writing hard ; and Mr. Gibbon, busy with his final volume, enjoyed the prospect of his lake. The century seemed at high noon, though the shadows fell a little longer as the sun, that decorously gilded sun, declined towards its last decade. Its melody was fuller than ever. *Don Giovanni* was heard that year, and Gluck's melodious shepherd mourned his Eurydice. Boucher was gone ; but Fragonard still scattered rose-leaves. Countesses simpered for Gainsborough, and the cloaked Venetian maskers looked their most mysterious for Guardi. But they were all simpler (if a thought sweeter) now. For the sad tale of *Paul et Virginie* left no dry eyes that season, and the Queen of France was watching duchesses milk cows under the trees at Trianon, when Arthur Wesley first put on the red coat he was to wear, with impressive variations, half-way into the next century.

He had a calling now, though scarcely a profession, since he could hardly live upon an Ensign's pay ; and their main anxiety was to find means of preventing him from following his unit to the East upon a pittance. Not that he shared their hesitations. The calling seemed to interest him and, as he said in later years, he " was not so young as not to know that since I had undertaken a profession I had better try to understand it." His curiosity, which Latin elegiacs had singularly failed to stir, began to move ; and in a laudable pursuit of knowledge he had a Highland private weighed in full marching-order. But the family curtailed these barrack-yard experiments. For something better must be found for Arthur than bare regimental prospects ; and hope gleamed, as usual, from Dublin Castle. That autumn there was a new Lord-Lieutenant, and Lady Mornington promptly asked him to do something for her boy. His reply was more than charming. For the obliging man made him an aide-de-camp the very instant

that he had his own appointment. Meanwhile, there was his
leave to be arranged, his small belongings to be purchased, and
(had he not been an Ensign for eight months ?) something in the
way of promotion. Advancement came to him through an
ingenious series of exchanges rather than from any vulgar exercises in the barrack square. For the younger brother of a rising
man found military life less arduous than a lonely gunner at
Valence ; and, after flickering uncertainly through the Ninth
Foot, by Christmas he was a Lieutenant in the Seventy-sixth.

There was so much to be contrived for him, and his mother
worked her very hardest. Now she was prouder of him. For
Angers had done wonders for her awkward son. He had not
learnt to dance for nothing, and the Duc de Praslin's table was a
rare school of manners. Besides, the awkward age was over.
He was eighteen ; Eton was all forgiven now ; and the grace
acquired in French provincial *châteaux* quite effaced any shortcomings in his Latinity. So it was all written off to her two
inseparable friends in Wales, and the " Dear Ladies " at Llangollen learned at becoming length from Lady Mornington how
extremely obliging the Lord-Lieutenant had been, and how
" there are so many little things to settle for *Arthur* who is just   2
got into the army and is to go to Ireland in the capacity of Aid
De Camp to Lord Buckingham, and must be set out a little for
that, in short *I must* do *every thing* for him and when you see him
you will think him worthy of it as he really is a very charming
young man, never did I see such a change for the better in any
body he is wonderfully lucky, in six months he has got two steps in
the army and appointed Aid De Camp to Lord Buckingham which
is ten shillings a day." Her pride in him was almost breathless ;
and there was still much to be arranged. For his new regiment
had been raised for service in India ; and if Dublin Castle was to
see its latest aide-de-camp, he must exchange again. So she was
busier than ever on his account (with the added torment of an
intolerable bout of toothache)—" I have so much to get settled   3
for Arthur, that I am sure it will not be done in the time. The
King has given him leave to go to Ireland only upon condition
of making an exchange into another regiment, as the one he is in
is destined for the East Indies, and it cannot go without its full
compliment of officers ; this will cost some money and take some
time to effect it ; but at all events he will be a gainer." She

seemed to grudge him nothing now ; and it was all safely engineered at last.   For in the first weeks of 1788 he got his transfer
to the Forty-first ; and, the laborious penury of foreign service
thoughtfully eluded, the new aide-de-camp was packed off to
Dublin.   On the road he stopped to pay a call.   For as they drove
through Wales, he looked in upon the Ladies at Llangollen and
earned the commendation of his mother's friends—" Lady
Dungannon and Arthur Wesley arrived.   A charming young
man.   Handsome, fashioned tall, and elegant.   He stayed till
two, then proceeded to Ireland."

So he was back in Ireland, his formal education ended.   It
had been a strange affair.   Two years of Latin elegiacs, followed
by two years of—what ?   Of French, of *haute école*, of ballroom
deportment, of dinner at the Praslins'.   Yet he had managed
somehow to profit by it, though the virtues that won his mother's
unexpected praise were rather social than military.   His seat
upon a horse was secure, if unattractive ; his French was fluent,
though he mastered it rather by vigorous assault than by more
insidious methods (someone remarked in later years that he
spoke French as he fought them—*bravement*) ; and in some
mysterious way he had acquired a habit of private reading.
But Dublin was unfriendly to studious habits, and Dublin
resumed him—the cheerful, rather factious Dublin of 1788, where
Lord Buckingham kept his Court and Mr. Grattan made his
speeches.   Chariots turned out of Dame Street, passed the Castle
sentries, and set down before the Lord-Lieutenant's door ; and
lights shewed in windows, where gentlemen were losing money
at the tables or Dublin hostesses received.   The aide-de-camp
was seen at parties—not always to his advantage.   For somebody
refused an invitation to a picnic until she was assured that " that
mischievous boy " would not be there ; and one heartless beauty,
upon whom his company had palled, went home alone and left
him stranded to get back as best he could with the musicians.
The bright Viceregal world enveloped him and, Dublin completing
what Angers had begun, he learned to point a toe and turn a
compliment.   He played as well and naturally lost ; and, these
diversions straining a yearly stipend of £172 9s. 3d., he was
occasionally left to stare disconsolately at the Liffey from his
windows on Lower Ormond Quay.   But his landlord, a sympathetic bootmaker, relieved the young gentleman's more pressing

needs on loan, and was rewarded by full repayment and a place. Not all his rescuers were so fortunate. For a friend of his agent's brother, who advanced £100 to Lieutenant Wesley in 1789, was repaid by Major-General Sir Arthur Wellesley in 1806.   *9*

He had his duties too. For aides-de-camp were expected to ride out with the Lord-Lieutenant or to take their turn at Vice-regal ceremonies among the gilded pillars of St. Patrick's Hall ; nor was it quite without significance that when Lieutenant Wesley first saw the world, he saw it from behind a throne. Besides, his brother Mornington, busy with his own career at Westminster, was always giving him estate business to do. So he had quite enough to think about in Dublin—his debts, his duties, and his violin ; for he still played. He had a change of uniform as well, though without promotion. But it was a convenience for him to get a regiment that was stationed in Ireland. Since no acute professional interests attached him to the infantry, a fresh exchange transferred him to the cavalry ; and he was now Lieutenant Wesley of the Twelfth Dragoons. Within the month a mob went roaring against the Bastille, and the first heads were bobbing through the Paris streets on the first pikes. Mr. Fox was in ecstasies ; but Dublin (and the Eighteenth Century) went on. The ladies danced ; their masters dined ; the aides-de-camp rode out as usual, though Arthur's sister Anne enquired in some agitation of the Ladies of Llangollen, " A'n't you sorry for poor   *10* dear France, I shall never see Paris again " ; and as the echoes died away, Lieutenant Wesley was putting on his new cavalry uniform.

A graver initiation waited, since he was nearly of age. Richard, the rising man in London, marshalled his forces. His brother William sat for their Irish borough. The post was not exacting ; and, with Arthur growing up, William might very well be transferred to Westminster, while the young Castle aide-de-camp relieved him in the Irish House of Commons. So an English seat was found for William, and Arthur at twenty stood on the edge of Irish politics. Irish politics in 1790 were full of an uneasy stir. For there was positively an Irish question. Perhaps it had been answered at Bunker's Hill. Had not Mr. Flood announced that " a voice from America had shouted to   *11* liberty " ? Napper Tandy might even be the voice of the people (which France was now so busy proclaiming to be divine) ; and

conceivably the truth might be with that ecstatic commentator
who had recently distilled an apocalyptic nationalism from the
Book of Revelation and heartened the Lord-Lieutenant in well-
doing by the coincidence between the harps, the sea of glass, the
linen robes of Holy Writ and Ireland's coat of arms and leading
manufactures.   But borough-owners were largely untroubled by
these lofty problems.   For Castle politics in the age of Lord
Chancellor Fitzgibbon were mercifully simple, consisting mainly
in the humbler arts by which majorities are managed.   Trim,
represented by a Castle aide-de-camp, would be a unit in the
Crown's majority ; but before he could perform these simple
evolutions, Arthur must qualify to represent it.   First he became
a Freemason, being initiated into Lodge 494, of Trim, co. Meath.
Then he ran his first political errand.   It was a matter of some
delicacy that brought him into Trim one March day in 1790.
For the Corporation, it seemed, was about to confer its freedom
upon Mr. Grattan, a proceeding that could scarcely be congenial
to the Castle.   The family was bound to oppose it ; and before
an audience of eighty Lieutenant Wesley made his first recorded
public speech.   According to his own report, he " got up and said
that the only reason given why Mr. Grattan should get the freedom of the corporation was his respectability, that really if we
were to admit every man because one or two people said he was
respectable, the whole community would belong to the corporation, that *he* could never be of any use to us and never would
attend, and that I would certainly object, however great my
respect for him."   This was sensible enough.   Then the orator
grew more ingenious : " I said I should always vote for three
sorts of people, those who were made to repel a party striving to
turn the old family interest out of the borough," for a lawyer who
might be serviceable upon election business, and for local residents.   The meeting adjourned.   But the young emissary was not
inactive during the adjournment, since " I told my friends that
it was a question of party, that they must stick by me " ; and
under this strenuous leadership the opposition carried the previous
question in triumph.   On the same eventful day he announced
his candidature, and was promptly buttonholed by an elderly
voter, who declined to promise until he knew what Lord Mornington proposed to do about a bond for £70.   This was extremely
awkward ; and the candidate, with rare discretion, " said I would

have nothing to do with it, as in case of a General Election such a transaction would entirely vitiate my return." The simple appetites of eighteenth-century electors stirred on every hand ; but the youthful politician, though considerably embarrassed, was not unskilful : " I was in the most difficult situation I ever experienced, and only got out of it by sticking up manfully to what I first said. I must say that, although I was plagued with requests of all kinds and totally unable and disinclined to make any promise . . . they behaved as handsomely as people could do. . . . They are all fine fellows."

Such was his first engagement. It ended in a modest triumph and a gratified despatch to Richard. But politics, it seemed, drew him as little as soldiering, since a postscript added that, " I am still of the same opinion with regard to your going abroad, and hope you will accept my offer to accompany you." Richard, however, stayed in England; and Arthur's duty called, however faintly, in Ireland. For, his regiment apart, the assault on Trim was promptly followed up ; the Irish Parliament dissolved that spring ; and Arthur was returned in 1790 for the family borough. There was some fear of a petition ; for malice had been heard to whisper that the young gentleman was not quite of age when Trim elected him. These apprehensions kept him busy. He left his regiment in June, and posted to Dublin for   14 grave consultations with the Lord Chancellor and the Attorney-General. But his constituency was not neglected, since that summer he subscribed five guineas to the local races. The House   15 met in July, and the petition was set down for hearing. But the   16 petitioners failed to proceed ; and, all apprehensions set at rest, Lieutenant Wesley was beyond dispute Member of Parliament for Trim.

If contact with the Trim electors was an imperfect education in democracy, the Irish House of Commons was unlikely to impress its new recruit with the virtues of Parliamentary government. Two-thirds of that assembly owed their election to less than a   17 hundred borough-owners ; one-third were in receipt of salaries or pensions from the Crown ; their collective appetites absorbed almost one-eighth of the Irish revenue ; and it was not surprising that they rarely deviated from an inveterate conviction that the King's government must be carried on. Such was the first assembly in which Arthur Wesley learned to legislate.

Not that he legislated with any undue fervour. The rafters
rang with the eloquence of Mr. Grattan ; and he served modestly
on a committee. Dublin repeated the latest sally of Sir Boyle
Roche ; and the Castle aide-de-camp was inconspicuously jobbing
supporters into small places. His zeal enriched the public service
with a deputy barrack-master, whilst another suppliant was safely
lodged in the Lottery. But as the voices rose and fell behind the
portico on College Green, Arthur Wesley's never vied with the
solemn note of Sir Hercules Langrishe ; and for two years after
his election he remained discreetly mute, a boyish-looking figure
with a high colour, a red coat, and a large pair of epaulettes,
sitting among the silent cohorts genially termed by Wolfe Tone
" the common prostitutes of the Treasury Bench." He was a
Captain now, promoted in 1791 to command a company in the
Fifty-eighth Foot on the Irish establishment, and regimental duty
sometimes took him as far as Cork ; though he soon turned
cavalryman again, exchanging into the Eighteenth Light
Dragoons in the next year. But he was mostly to be found in
Dublin, on duty at the Castle, or strolling to the House of Commons
from his rooms in Grafton Street, or else at Dangan deep in new
tenancies, ejectments, renewals, and all the fierce joys of estate
management. That noble property was a sad trial to them now.
There was the mortgage interest to be found. And for what ?
The big iron gates were always waiting, their tracery etched on
the ragged skies of Meath ; and the long drive still led down the
hill and over the bridge across the ornamental water. But they
never seemed to go there. No organ-music woke the hall ; the
still canal heard no more water-concerts ; and the garden gods
waited forlornly in their temples. Besides, the intrepid Richard
needed cash for his assault on Westminster. His ties with
Ireland were always of the slightest (did he not live to resent his
own Irish marquessate as a " double-gilt potato " ?), and he had
turned his back on Dublin. There was the seat at Trim, of course ;
a vote on College Green was not without its uses ; and it would
be as well for them to keep their hold on Castle favours through
the family borough. But Arthur could look after that. There
was no need for Dangan, though. Richard had never cared for
it. What did a rising man in London want with a mortgaged
Irish mansion ? Mr. Pitt could surely see his worth without that
to set him off. His discreetly orthodox opinions on the Regency

3

question were even approved by Majesty itself, now happily   23
restored to reason ; and when Windsor smiled, Dangan was
surely far behind him.   So before 1792 was out, the place was for   24
sale.

While Richard spread his wings in London for these impressive
flights, obedient Arthur stayed behind in Ireland.   His brother's
deputy (and Irish patriots found hard things to say of " the petty   25
pilfering, jobbing, corrupting tricks of every deputy of a deputy
of an English minister "), he cultivated Meath electors, subscribed   26
ten guineas to the Corporation plate, and earned Mornington's
slightly condescending praises for his management of Trim,
" where by his excellent judgment, amiable manners, admirable   27
temper, and firmness he has entirely restored the interest of my
family."   Versed in these unobtrusive arts, he even made a
maiden speech, rising to second the Address one January day in
1793.   It was a fluttered world, in which the French—wild-eyed
and shouting unfamiliar songs—threatened by turns to conquer
Holland and behead their king, and an exuberant Minister of
Marine promised his countrymen the added joys of a descent on
England with the pleasing objects of depositing fifty thousand
caps of liberty, planting its sacred tree, and holding out fraternal
hands to the groaning subjects of King George.   Small wonder,
then, that Captain Wesley, seconding the Address on College
Green, hazarded the blameless sentiment that " at a time when   28
opinions were spreading throughout Europe inimical to kingly
government it behoved us, in a particular manner, to lay before
our gracious Sovereign our determination to support and maintain the constitution," with more (but not much more) to the
same effect.   Taking a wider survey he " reprobated, in very
severe terms, the conduct of the French towards their king, and
their invasion of the territories of foreign princes, and their
irruption into the Austrian Netherlands."   Then, returning
homewards, he particularly approved a faintly liberal allusion to
the Catholic question in the Speech from the Throne—" He had
no doubt of the loyalty of the Catholics of this country, and he
trusted that when the question would be brought forward,
respecting that description of men, that we would lay aside all
animosities, and act with moderation and dignity, and not with
the fury and violence of partizans."   It was a theme on which
fuller reflection brought him worse counsel.

But Catholic Emancipation in 1793 was, by a queer inversion, the policy of sound reactionaries. Pitt was propitious ; Burke could not forget that he was an Irishman ; Popery itself grew daily more congenial to all who ranged themselves with Catholic allies against the godless excesses of Paris ; and even the Castle gave a sulky acquiescence. Its drilled majority, sometimes a little out of step, obediently passed a Catholic Relief Bill, which conferred the franchise and removed the major disabilities, excepting the exclusion of Catholics from Parliament. That must be maintained ; for who would lay an impious finger on the palladium of Protestant ascendancy ? Not Arthur Wesley, since he was positively chosen as the Castle spokesman to resist the bold amendment. It was his second speech in Parliament ; and since his first the whole world was changed. For a king's head had fallen in Paris, and England was at war. The fact, though he might not suspect it, concerned him intimately. It concerned, indeed, his whole generation and Anglo-Irish younger sons more than most. For the bland decorum of the Eighteenth Century was sharply interrupted by a new age, which the fantastic calendar of Paris did well to date from the Year One. Elegance went out of fashion ; and young gentlemen who trailed a graceful scabbard after the Lord-Lieutenant were a thought behind the mode. A stir was in the air, as Europe drifted into its long duel with the Revolution ; and the war, of which a Castle aide-de-camp watched the opening from Dublin, came closer to him until, a little grey about the temples, he observed its final scene from the saddle above Hougomont.

But as the drums began to sound in February, 1793, he was speaking in the Irish House of Commons. This time he managed to abstain from general reflections. His tone, though unsympathetic to the full Catholic claims, was reasonable. For having voted for the Catholic franchise, he " had no objection to giving the Roman Catholics the benefits of the constitution." But there were plainly limits ; and a Parliament of Papists seemed to exceed them. When both sides were satisfied with a more gradual measure, the cautious young gentleman declined to " agitate a question which may disturb both." Not that he was a Protestant alarmist. His common-sense scouted the orthodox dismay at visions of enfranchised Papists voting solidly behind their priests

—" Have not Roman Catholics, like Protestants, various interests and various passions by which they are swayed ? The influence of their landlords—their good or bad opinion of the candidates—their own interests—and a thousand other motives ? It appeared to him that they would not vote in a body, or as had been supposed, if the bill should pass in its present form ; but if the motion of the honourable gentleman should be adopted, then indeed they would undoubtedly unite in support of Roman Catholic candidates." This was a fair sample of moderate opinion from a young gentleman on the Castle list whose brother wished to stand well with Mr. Pitt. In that judicious mood much might have been done for Ireland. But it was the year 1793 ; and it is the fate of Irish hopes to be dashed by European wars.

The world was stirring around him. But his interests seemed all to lie in Ireland. His seat in Parliament, his place at Court kept him in Dublin ; affairs occasionally called him to Dangan ; and regimental duty took him no farther than an Irish barrack. There were other interests as well. For Lord Longford had a sister ; Kitty Pakenham had a pair of bright eyes ; and Captain Wesley often called at Rutland Square. Vows were exchanged ; but what are vows without a competence ? Longford, considering his sister's prospects on a Captain's pay, was stern. Plainly the couple could not marry. But Arthur might find out a way—there was no need for him always to be a Captain. Richard must manage something for him. So that spring he wrote to Richard ; ³¹ the purchase money was advanced ; and before April was out, he was a Major in the Thirty-third. But it was not enough to be a Major. If Kitty was to be achieved, he must rise in his profession. Cards had betrayed him more than once ; and card-playing was ³² promptly forsworn. He had a deeper passion, though, which seemed to stand between him and promotion. For music (was he not his father's son ?) absorbed his leisure ; and a violin was often in his hand. Music had brought his father almost to poverty, and a little grimly he resolved to break the charm. Besides, it would never do for a promising young officer to indulge in secret orgies of the violin. To say the least, it was not martial. Brass, perhaps ; or even wood-wind (Frederick the Great had played the flute) ; but scarcely strings. His head, if it was ever to wear laurels, must be filled with drill-ground evolutions, not with the

adorable intricacies of counterpoint or the sweet wail of strings.
33 So one day in that eventful summer of 1793 he burned his fiddle.
He never touched another, though the taste lived on in him. For
34 dinner-parties years away were carried off from Apsley House to
hear the Ancient Concerts ; their host's preference was understood to lie with Handel, and even with Corelli, though the
severity of the programme was somewhat mitigated by his invariable seat upon a special sofa between two handsome women. He
could still take pleasure in a lady's touch upon the harp, and was
assiduous at the Opera, when Jenny Lind was singing ; his wrist,
although he only used it now for carrying the Sword of State
upright in the House of Lords, remained supple as a violinist's ;
35 and once in later years, when Madame Lieven played some
waltzes on the pianoforte, he supported her (an executant once
more) upon the triangle. There was always a thin strain of
music in him. But the charm was broken now. His father's fate
had warned him ; and when Major Wesley, in hopes of Kitty
Pakenham, resolved to be a soldier, the flames licked a broken
violin in Dublin. Perhaps an artist died. He never cared to
have it spoken of.

VI

THAT summer, as the Queen of France sat waiting in her prison, the storm broke. It had climbed slowly up the sky ; and as it climbed, the light died out of Europe. There was a hush, and the familiar sounds came plainly over the still air—the tap of heels, the rustle of polite society, the scratch of rhyming pens, the buzz of coffee-houses, and even the level voice of Mr. Pitt assuring the hopeful Commons that " unquestionably there never was a time   *1* in the history of this country, when, from the situation of Europe, we might more reasonably expect fifteen years of peace than at the present moment." His hope died on the silence, and the dainty world began to lose its colours. For a cloud had swung across the sun, and a long shadow seemed to fall across the trim parterres. Even Mr. Pitt could see it now. " The war," he   *2* observed, with a singular change of heart, " is not only unavoidable, but, under the circumstances of the case, absolutely necessary to the existence of Great Britain and Europe." The skies were leaden ; and Burke raved in the gathering gloom, while Gibbon with grave elaboration begged leave to agree with him— " I admire his eloquence, I adore his chivalry, and I can almost   *3* excuse his reverence for church establishments." The century, the eternal Eighteenth Century, had turned to bay ; and all its children—positive, polite, and sceptical—took up their places for the conflict. For the storm broke that summer ; and the thunder which had muttered above Paris rolled halfway round the world. There was a sudden gleam of bayonets ; and Europe marched, as the French rallied round the great voice of Danton. But before the stiff battalions of the Monarchies could reach their stations, France dashed to meet them, breaking like surf along the frontiers. Austrians pounded the northern fortresses ; the Prussians barely held along the Rhine ; Spain moved deliberately in the sunshine of the Pyrenees ; and half the west was up in the King's name, while Britons resolved with loud huzzas to—

> "stand by the Church, and the King, and the Laws ;   *4*
> The old Lion still has his teeth and his claws ;
> Let Britain still rule in the midst of her waves,
> And chastise all those foes who dare call her sons slaves."
>
> *Derrydown.*

38

The surf rose higher now ; a wilder melody hung on the air above its charges. But the seventh wave was still delayed. Perhaps it lurked among the shallows, where a lean captain of artillery trailed dustily along a road near Avignon in charge of sixteen gunners and two guns. It was his first command. For Captain Bonaparte was an apprentice, the long form of Carnot sprawled in the dust of office floors across his maps to shift the candles with his armies, and the heads were falling fast in Paris, when Major Wesley took to soldiering.

But soldiering in such a season meant rather more than the punctual performance of regimental duties in Irish barrack squares. It was not quite enough for him to jingle spurs in Dublin corridors behind the Lord-Lieutenant ; and that summer he was writing once again to Richard, desiring him " to ask Mr. Pitt to desire Lord Westmorland to send me as Major to one of the flank corps. If they are to go abroad, they will be obliged to take officers from the line, and they may as well take me as anybody else. . . . I think it both dangerous and improper to remove any part of the army from this country at present, but if any part of it is to be moved, I should like to go with it, and have no chance of seeing service except with the flank corps, as the regiment I have got into as Major is the last for service." He must see service, if he was to rise in his profession. But his application, if it was ever made, was disregarded—fortunately, perhaps, since the flank companies despatched that year from Ireland went off to die of yellow fever in Martinique. So Arthur Wesley eluded the crowded cemetery at Fort Royal, to say nothing of the more dreadful fate that waits upon returned heroes of Colonial warfare. For their conversation, a just object of alarm, abounded in the tedium of concealed enemies and cocoa trees—" Here stood the enemy . . . and here, my love, are my fellows : there the cocoa trees. . . ." How the delicious Harriette learned to dread that opening in later years. But whatever else Miss Wilson had cause to fear from Arthur, it was never that.

The Thirty-third still kept the peace in Ireland ; and the assiduous Major drilled his men, as the world reeled through the stupendous calendar of '93. His century, with all that Arthur Wesley lived for—Dublin Castle, Dangan, and the King's uniform —was assailed that year. *93 est la guerre de l'Europe contre la France et de la France contre Paris. . . . De là l'immensité de cette minute épouvantable, 93, plus grande que tout le reste du siècle.* He missed the rhapsody, perhaps, but caught a little of the uproar.   For his countrymen were shouting Dibdin's chorus :

> " Thus in famed Ninety-three   9
>   Britons all shall agree,
> While with one heart and voice in loud chorus they sing,
> To improve ' Ça ira ' into ' God Save the King ! ' "

That summer, as the armies swayed along the frontier, Paris raved.   There was a fever of eloquence, a rash of tricolour cockades, a frenzy of citizenship.   Voices rose shriller now on the still air above the stifling city ; the big knife clanked down at briefer intervals in the great square beyond the Tuileries ; and France, beside herself, shewed the pale face of the Terror like a Medusa's head to the oncoming battalions of the invasion.   Marat died in those hot weeks and Charlotte Corday ; and a young man stood muttering, as the cart went by, that it were beautiful to die with her.   But Arthur Wesley was still drilling redcoats in the soft Irish sunshine.   He went to England in the autumn.   For Dangan had found a purchaser at last ; and when Richard signed away the big square house, Arthur witnessed his signature.   10 They had no ornamental water now ; the garden gods knew other owners ; and the family, their castle gone, depended solely upon Richard and his soaring prospects.   That day the guns were opening above Toulon, watched by a " short, taciturn, olive-   11 complexioned young man, not unknown to us, by name Buona-parte," ranking now as Lieutenant-Colonel.

Arthur was soon promoted too ; and as the gunfire echoed round the hills behind Toulon, Lieutenant-Colonel Wesley went back to Ireland to command the Thirty-third. (From Ensign to Lieutenant-Colonel in less than seven years was creditable going—more creditable, perhaps, to influence and army-brokers than to military science.   But there was little need for a   12 Lieutenant-Colonel to blush at twenty-four, when Kitty Paken-ham's brother was a Major at seventeen, and Cotton had a regiment at twenty-one and Lowry Cole at twenty-two.)   As the leaves fell, the crisis deepened.   Disordered tides of war raced round the coasts of Europe ; a Paris court-room heard the unpleasant voice of Fouquier-Tinville denounce a hunted woman, grey-haired at thirty-eight, as a Messalina, a Medicis, a Merovingian tyrant ; the French infantry went roaring up the slope

through the October mist at Wattignies ; in Paris the knife fell
and rose again and fell ; and Arthur Wesley still sat on in
Dublin, busy with regimental accounts. Late in the year, though,
there was a vague hint of active service. For the strategy of
British ministers is normally composed of a vast number of
divergent gestures ; and finding their commitments in Flanders,
Provence, and the West Indies palpably insufficient for an army
of 20,000 men, they gaily contemplated a descent on Normandy.
A force was fitting out at Portsmouth for the French coast, and
there was a notion that the Thirty-third would sail with it.
Sudden departures are no less disturbing to gentlemen of honour
than to their creditors, and Arthur made careful dispositions to
discharge his Dublin debts, his income being assigned to an
obliging tradesman who undertook to pay them off. But Moira's
expedition started down-Channel on its aimless cruise without the
Thirty-third ; and as the year went out, Colonel Wesley was left
standing in the wings, still waiting for his cue.

Dublin retained him, as a fresh year opened and the echoes of
a world at war floated across St. George's Channel. They were
still there in February. Spring came, the dreadful spring of
'94, when Revolution, thirsting still and gorged with its enemies,
turned unnaturally upon its own children. The Girondins had
gone already, gone singing down the narrow street that ended in
the waiting crowd, the planks, the angular machine. He was in
Cork, still striking regimental balances the month a big, square-
shouldered form came up against the evening sky in Paris and
stared across a packed and silent square muttering, " Danton, no
weakness." May found him there as well, still signing army
forms. But the next month they got their orders ; and Colonel
Wesley prepared to take his first battalion on his first active
service. It fell, by the symmetry of fate, in Belgium.

The skein of war was slightly tangled. Rarely without com-
plexity for Allies and always apt to yield its richest tangles to
Austrian fingers, it bore extensive witness to the welter of cross-
purposes which was the Allied substitute for strategy. Soldiers
of European standing did their solemn best to conduct a war as
wars should be conducted. Having learnt their profession fighting against or under Frederick the Great, they took measures
admirably calculated to outmanœuvre a Prussian army of 1760.
But the delicate precision of their military minuet somehow failed

of its effect upon the coarser fibre of French *Demi brigades* in 1793.
Fashions, perhaps, were changing ; and at Hondschoote the prim
tactics of the Eighteenth Century met the untutored onslaught
of the Nineteenth with all the *gaucherie* of last year's fashions at
a dress-parade. Besides, there was the Revolution. It appeared
to affect them in the oddest manner, so that troops, which by
every rule were off the board, insisted upon scrambling to the
attack without a vestige of formation, shouting the most unusual
songs. It was all highly disconcerting. Military science was
almost wasted on such adversaries. For armies threatened with
complete (if theoretical) disaster by the loss of a strategical point
failed from sheer ignorance to notice it, and pressed obstinately
forward. The best military minds had learnt to play at war as
other men at chess ; but chess is rarely satisfactory with an
opponent who declines to learn the rules and is more than a little
apt to spill the board. So the stiff *Kaiserlicks* tramped dutifully
in all directions, and nothing came of it. White-coated infantry
faced with cerise, with mauve, with green, with every colour in the
Imperial spectrum moved in strict obedience to orders ; gunners
in grey tilted their big tricornes and served little guns ; pre-
posterously hatted units threw pontoon bridges across slow-flow-
ing Flemish rivers ; while, furred and frogged, hussars of every
shade—Kaiser in blue, Barco in blue and green, Wurmser in
green and scarlet—jingled off, watched by respectful villages, or
dismounting stiffly from red saddle-cloths with the big Hapsburg
cipher trailed their long scabbards over the Flemish cobblestones.
It was a brave display ; but nothing came of it. For the skein
of war was tangled. Wound by the Emperor, the King of
Prussia, the *Reich*, King George, the Cabinet, the Duke of York,
and half the *Almanach de Gotha*, it abounded in sudden turns
that led nowhere, and was generously involved with every knot of
European policy. (Few campaigns are less rewarding than
those directed by Foreign Office strategy.) For in '94 the
crusading march of outraged Europe upon Paris had degenerated
sadly. Checked at Mauberge the year before, it declined after
Tourcoing to a precarious defensive strung awkwardly along the
Belgian frontier. France gathered strength in front of them, and
the invaders halted in a mood of dull bewilderment, resolved
apparently to await its impact in the impressive posture of a
sanitary cordon. But the dispositions convenient to frontier-

guards in dealing with infected persons will not usually avail to
check a nation in arms.

Somewhere towards the right of this depressed array a British
contingent, shaken at Tourcoing and more than a little jaded by
the endless series of aimless withdrawals and attacks that were
not followed up, stood waiting in the Flanders plain. Waiting,
indeed, appeared to be their leading occupation. For, apart from
one major (and distinctly unsatisfying) engagement and a few
dashing encounters, their derisive countrymen had summarised
their operations with tolerable accuracy :

> "The rare old Duke of York,
> He had ten thousand men ;
> He marched 'em up to the top of the hill,
> And he marched 'em down again."

The Duke, indeed, was young ; his command was in the neighbourhood of thirty thousand ; and there were no hills in sight.
But, these facts conceded, there was little fault to find with the
disrespectful *précis* of their position and prospects. Vaguely
alarmed, the Cabinet sent reinforcements. For Ostend was palpably in danger. It has been observed that Belgian ports hold a
peculiar power of fascinating English statesmen ; and their heads
are sadly affected by names which, in the case of Queen Mary,
were harmlessly engraved upon the heart. Ostend, like Antwerp,
had the fatal charm. So the Thirty-third were moved at last :
they sailed from Cork in the first week of June ; and after nineteen days at sea Colonel Wesley landed his regiment at Ostend.

He was on active service now. Had not an elderly Colonel of
the Guards warned him of its approaching trials—" You little
know what you are going to meet with. You will often have no
dinner at all. I mean," the horrified Guardsman had added,
" literally no dinner, and not merely roughing it on a beefsteak
or a bottle of port wine." The forecast was correct. For the
Duke's army lacked almost everything. There was even a
shortage of generals ; and their exiguous supplies reached the
dejected redcoats through the intermittent activities of the new
Waggon Train, known (from their origins and tunic) as the
' Newgate Blues.' Once more a British army swore terribly in
Flanders. For it was a continuation of Marlborough's wars
conducted with much of Marlborough's equipment and lacking
only Marlborough to complete the resemblance. But Arthur

Wesley and the rest of Moira's reinforcements were still among
the sand-hills of Ostend.   The Colonel found himself commanding
a brigade of three battalions ; and when Moira marched away to
join the main Allied army, Wesley's brigade was left as rearguard
" to settle matters at Ostend " (the French, including a young   22
Colonel named Murat, were getting near) " and then to come on
as quick as I could."   Ostend was promptly evacuated ; and
preferring a short sea voyage to a dangerous flank-march in face
of an advancing enemy, he re-embarked his men, put them on
shore again at Antwerp, and reached the Duke of York's position
before the leading files of Moira's force which had come overland.
So his first minor operation comprised a deft retreat and a neat
use of the ubiquity conferred by sea-power on British expeditionary forces.

     There was an agonised succession of Allied conferences, while
the line still held uneasily in front of Brussels.   They met at
Braine-l'Alleud ; they met again, by a felicitous choice, at Waterloo.   But with Austrians to line it, that position was scarcely at
its best.   The French tide was running strongly across Belgium ;
and finally each Ally went his way.   For the last strand of Allied
strategy had almost parted.   The Austrians trailed off towards
the east, while the Duke of York, receding slowly northwards,
still undertook to keep the French out of Holland by the united
efforts of the Dutch, his own little army, and a few German troops
in British pay.   Then the retreat began.   There was a small
affair at Boxtel in Dutch Brabant one September day, when
Arthur Wesley took his battalion into action under the eye of
Abercromby.   The Thirty-third were competently handled,
holding their fire in face of the oncoming French until their
Colonel ordered a volley.   The old General (whose bushy eyebrows gave one, as someone said, " the idea of a very good-   23
natured lion ") called a few days later to convey " the Duke of   24
York's thanks and his to the Thirty-third for their good conduct
on the 15th."   But these laurels failed to dazzle him, since the
same letter which conveyed the news to Richard announced that
he would be back in Ireland before the winter was out.   There
was the usual trouble with their Irish tenants ; and as he lay in
front of Nijmegen, Arthur's mind was full of small practical
expedients of estate-management in Ireland.   Not that his eye,
as it turned homewards, was blurred by sentiment ; for as he

offered slightly contradictory counsels, he added tartly, " This is
Irish language, but not less true for that country of scoundrels."
     The winter deepened round them, and the retreat went on
through the dreary landscape and grotesque nomenclature of the
Netherlands. They stood along the Waal ; and Arthur, whose
health was none too good, lived in a perpetual rearguard action.
Now he commanded a brigade, and acted in virtual independence
—" I was on the Waal, I think, from October to January, and
during all that time I only saw once one General from the headquarters." But the young Brigadier, haunted by thoughts of
leave, commanded without especial gusto. Hope gleamed a little,
as the French hung on the edge of winter-quarters—" I think it
impossible for any troops (even the French) to keep the field in
this severe weather. As soon as their intentions are decided I
intend to go to England." The French, alas ! were ignorant of
these refinements, and frankly disinclined to treat campaigning as
a seasonal occupation. Besides, the season, however unpleasant,
was particularly propitious for their offensive, since the frost
eliminated water-lines which must otherwise have served as
strong defences. So the war flickered along his outposts through
the black nights of a Dutch winter—" We turn out once, sometimes twice every night ; the officers and men are harassed to
death. . . . I have not had my clothes off my back for a long
time, and generally spend the greater part of the night upon the
bank of the river." By day the enemy were entertaining enough,
" perpetually chattering with our officers and soldiers," and ready
to oblige on request with lively performances of the *Carmagnole.*
But as he watched the ice-packs grinding in the Waal or wrote
out his endless regimental accounts, he still thought of leave—
" I intend to go to England in a few days, that is to say, if the
French remain quiet, and if the regiment is relieved from the
advanced post upon the river Waal, where it has been for above
six weeks." The French, however, with republican discourtesy
resumed the offensive ; and in the last week of the year the
Thirty-third cleared a Dutch village with the bayonet.
     The year went out on his discomfort, on a winter land of
freezing polders and ice-bound canals, on a ragged army straining
precariously to defend a country which had not the least wish to
be defended. For the Dutch found the French invasion more congenial than their Allied champions. The countryside was frankly

hostile, and there were even dark suspicions of the Dutch army.
Arthur was once instructed to escort a Dutch officer through his   *15*
lines for a secret interview with Pichegru. Watched by the
Colonel, two muffled figures met on the ice ; and shortly afterwards (it seemed a little sinister) the French were in Utrecht.
The Dutch defences broke in all directions ; there was a brief
resistance in front of Arnhem, when the Thirty-third performed
once more ; then the retreat went miserably on in the short
winter days. With the French in the Dutch ports and solemn
Dutchmen dancing round trees of liberty in Amsterdam, there was
no way to England for the retreating army except across the
frozen heaths that lay between the Zuider Zee and the North
German ports ; and their line of march slanted towards the east.
It lay across an endless plain of white under the dark winter sky.
Trying at first, the retreat soon deepened into tragedy. For the
army was practically unclothed ; a few units had great-coats
purchased by public subscription over a year before, and the
remainder owed the small comfort of a flannel waistcoat to the
private charity of officers. An arduous winter on the long road
from Antwerp to the north of Holland had left them in rags ; and
as the iron frost gripped these pitiable scarecrows, they died along
the frozen tracks. The last semblances of discipline almost
vanished in its grip ; for having no supplies they looted, and
having no enemy to fight they fought one another. All the   *29*
torments of 1812 were let loose upon them in one dreadful week
of January, 1795. The white plain lay behind them now ; but
it was marked with broken waggons, with frozen pack-horses,
with silent heaps that had been marching yesterday, even with
women. The worst was over then. They reached the Ems at
last ; and a rueful General reported to the Duke of York, " Your
army is destroyed ; the officers, their carriages, and a large train
are safe, but the men are destroyed. . . ." Life was easier now ;
discipline returned, and Brigade Orders began to abound in   *30*
prohibitions of promiscuous shooting of all edible forms of game.
A Hanoverian unit (Jägers in more than name) having found
someone's deer quite irresistible, the sporting instincts of the
British were restrained by a threat of court-martial for any soldier
" detected in using his firelock except when on Duty." The
winter turned to spring, and they dragged their way to the quay-
sides of Bremen. A period of endless embarkation returns set in.

But Colonel Wesley, his duty in the field once done, eluded the confusion. They reached the port in March ; and before the month was out, he was in London. His regiment was still abroad. Transports slid up the German river to fetch them home ; and one Monday morning (it was April 13, 1795) the remnants of the Thirty-third were marched on board. The long campaign was ended.

Ended for Arthur Wesley also. Another chapter of his education closed, he was in England. It had been arduous— more arduous than the old Guardsman's forecast. But it had been instructive too. He said of it in later years that he had " learnt what one ought not to do, and that is always something." Few campaigns, indeed, were more admirably designed to perform the functions of the awful warning. The least attentive mind could hardly miss its lessons. It has been frequently observed that British armies are at their finest in retreat. But the higher command seemed almost over-anxious to display these qualities. Arthur himself was most unfavourably impressed by the limpness of headquarters, which left regimental officers in virtual independence—" We had letters from England, and I declare that those letters told us more of what was passing at headquarters than we learned from the headquarters themselves. . . . The real reason why I succeeded in my own campaigns is because I was always on the spot—I saw everything, and did everything myself." Not so the Duke of York and his headquarters. Besides, what they did was almost certain to be wrong—" There was a fellow called Hammerstein, who was considered the chief authority in the army for tactics, but was quite an impostor ; in fact, no one knew anything of the management of an army, though many of the regiments were excellent." But, excellent or not, authority left them to freeze and frequently to starve ; for it had yet to dawn upon the martial mind that orders on the day of battle are of far less importance than regular meals upon the intervening days. The lesson was not lost on Arthur. Nor, perhaps, the disastrous consequences of indiscipline upon retreating troops, or the effect of a judicious volley from British infantry in line upon the scrambling columns of the French. It was a dozen years before he saw their blue uniforms again, and the interval taught him the art of war. But he had learnt some of it in Holland through that dreary winter.

VII

RETURNED, but not conspicuously laurelled, the Colonel of the Thirty-third resumed the problem of his own career. The years were passing (he was twenty-six that spring), and so much remained to be achieved—promotion, Kitty Pakenham, even a competence. For the most devoted younger brother could hardly be expected to live for ever upon Richard's prospects ; and, these apart, Arthur had really not much more to live on. Five hundred pounds a year, perhaps, comprised the total of a Lieutenant-Colonel's pay with the allowances of a Castle aide-de-camp. One could not cut a figure in the world on five hundred pounds a year. Indeed, it was distinctly doubtful if that income would suffice to meet the cost of past appearances. For Dublin and his creditors were waiting, and the returning warrior faced the bleakest of financial prospects.

He faced it with resource ; for Irish patronage was always a resource to those with friends at Dublin Castle. There was no need for him to go to Dublin, though. The new Lord-Lieutenant was in London ; and Arthur promptly waited on Lord Camden ¹ with a modest intimation that he should take some opportunity of stating the claims which he conceived himself to have upon the Government of Ireland. But Pitt's latest Lord-Lieutenant had more to think about than a remunerative place for Colonel Wesley. There was the rest of Ireland to be considered ; and Ireland in 1795 stood in need of full consideration. For whilst Arthur Wesley had been countermarching on by-roads in Holland, Lord Fitzwilliam had been countermarching with no less vigour upon Catholic Emancipation. Camden was to succeed that unhappy strategist ; the whole country was in a lively uproar ; and with all his problems still unsolved the new Lord-Lieutenant went off a little grimly to take up his residence in Dublin. The faithful aide-de-camp, still close to the Viceregal ear, followed his chief and paced the Castle yard again. Dublin had drawbacks for him, too. His tradesmen lived in Dublin ; ² but a trifle of fourteen pounds to settle with a clothier was not to be thought of—was, in fact, suspended until the hero of Assaye, returning as a Major-General, paid the account twelve years away. The spring of 1795 grew bright above these cares. He lived in quarters now more advantageously than in his former lodgings. Catholics, United Irishmen, Defenders, Peep of Day Boys all pressed on Camden ; but none pressed so hard as Arthur Wesley. The Thirty-third, returned from Germany, were peacefully encamped in Essex. But their determined Colonel traced his parallels and laid his mines, as he besieged the Lord-Lieutenant. That dignitary was evidently disinclined to be taken by storm ; the March reconnaissance in London had shown that. So Arthur settled down in Dublin to a siege *en règle.* All April he was in the trenches. He spoke discreetly to His Excellency "upon a certain object of mine in this Country " ; he spoke of it again ; he wrote a note enclosing—here he unmasked his batteries —a letter from Lord Mornington in Richard's most majestic manner. That nobleman informed the Lord-Lieutenant, as one earl to another, of his happiness at news of Camden's civility to Arthur—" You may easily believe how happy this account has made me, and how strongly I feel these proofs of your friendship for me." (A helping hand to Arthur was, it seemed, a mere form of courtesy to Richard.) But more might yet be done—" My Brother tells me, that the situation of Secretary at War . . . is likely to be opened soon "—and what more suitable to Arthur, more gratifying to Richard, or more convenient to the public service ? The note concluded with a scornful word or so on " His *çi-devant* Excellency," Fitzwilliam, and the sage reflection (familiar to belligerents in need of consolation) that the French " are very nearly exhausted even by their victories."

This bold attack encountered an insurmountable defence from the besieged Lord-Lieutenant, which wrung from Arthur the slightly rueful admission that " I see the manner in which the Military Offices are filled, and I don't wish to ask for that which I know you can't give me." Plainly his next assault must take another road. But before the storming-party left his trenches, he prepared their way with slightly touching ingenuity. He was still in Parliament ; and if only he could be of service to the Castle, perhaps the Castle might be less impregnable. His chance arrived one night in May, when angry gentlemen denounced a

4

former Lord-Lieutenant for the high misdemeanour of denuding
Ireland of troops. The voices rose ; Lord Westmorland was
sadly trounced ; and when Curran had dealt scornfully with
" 6,000 clowns, without shoes, and with ribbands in their hats,"
Grattan rose to a *crescendo*. Soaring at once into his loftiest
manner, he spoke boldly of impeachment, of a Lord-Lieutenant
convicted of the very act for which King James had been deposed
—" How can we otherwise dispose of him ? here are the laws which   5
contain the covenant, and here are the army returns which contain the breach of it—can we connive with Lord Westmorland,
and combine and confederate with him against the law—against
the Revolution—against the Declaration of Rights—against
. . ." His lightnings played about the absent peer ; and the
official answer—that recruits had been raised to fill the gaps
created by withdrawals—sped dancing like a dead leaf down the
gale of his eloquence. " The new levies . . . the suggestion of
an evasion, not of a defence, it is the suggestion of a trick—of an
impostorship—of a fraud ; it is not a bad defence, but a scandalous
prevarication—a sort of clerk-like dexterity—but so clumsy, so
miserable, and so glaring—that it does not keep within the letter
of the act, whose object it professes to defraud, and of whose
provisions it professes to cheat the public." His closing sentence
dropped a challenge—" It is a striking circumstance, that in a
debate where the conduct of Lord Westmorland towards the Irish
army has been so publicly and so loudly arraigned, no one veteran
of the army, nor any old officer, has ventured to defend him."
The challenge confidently made by Grattan was promptly
accepted. For Colonel Wesley rose to follow him. He had not
spoken for two years ; and even then he spoke without *éclat*.
But the intrepid Colonel was prepared to follow Grattan in
debate : men have earned medals for acts of lesser heroism.
Not that he failed in the encounter. For as he spoke, the chilling
voice of common-sense fell on the listening chamber. " What did   6
the act require ? 12,000 men for the national defence : Were they
or were they not in the country ? It was admitted that the public
service demanded troops to send abroad, and an addition was
therefore made to the establishment by parliament. Was it the
new levies just recruited that were to be sent abroad to meet an
enemy, or the disciplined soldiers ? The question answered
itself, and justified sending the old regiments out of the Kingdom,

and retaining new corps." That cleared Lord Westmorland ;
but he remained upon his legs a moment longer to deal faithfully
with a previous speaker who had described the new recruits as
ragamuffins. " He congratulated that hon. baronet on his
military sagacity, who would send ragamuffins upon foreign
service ; but he assured the hon. baronet that however he might
treat the new levies with contempt, they were not objects of contempt to the enemies of their country." It was an adequate
performance ; and few acts in his military career were more
courageous than the prompt reply to Grattan's challenge.

The House rose in the first week of June ; and he went off
to Trim to think about his own affairs. They owned no castle
now, and Arthur had a bachelor's refuge—rectangular refuge of
a bachelor growing slightly rectangular himself—among the trees
at Fosterstown. The Lord-Lieutenant must be stormed again ;
and this time he launched a fresh assault against another face of
the Viceregal fortress. His tone was not so lofty now :

> " I assure you nothing but the circumstances under which I
> labour would induce me to trouble Your Excellency's Government
> at any time and the Offices to which Lord Mornington has desired
> me to look are those at the Revenue and Treasury Boards and con-
> sidering the persons who are at present at these Boards, and those
> it is said are forthwith to be appointed to them, I hope I shall not
> be supposed to place myself too high in desiring to be taken into
> consideration upon the first vacancy at either of them. If Your
> Excellency and Mr. Pelham are of opinion that the Offices at those
> Boards are too high for me, of course you will say so ; and as I am
> convinced that no man is so bad a judge of the justice of a claim as
> he who makes it. . . .
> " You will perhaps be surprised at my desiring a civil instead of
> a military Office. It certainly is a departure from the line which I
> prefer ; but I see the manner in which the military Offices are
> filled, and I don't wish to ask you for that which I know you can't
> give me. Although the necessities under which I labour from
> different circumstances have nothing to do with the question
> whether I have a claim to the Offices I have mentioned, I again
> repeat that nothing but them should induce me to trouble Your
> Excellency's Gov't at any time."

Always his wretched circumstances. They haunted him that
year. It was June now ; and as he sat waiting for the Lord-

Lieutenant's answer in his little house at Trim, he faced a cheer-less outlook. After all, a place in the Irish Revenue would mean security; and he might even sell the King's commission for the price of a home with Kitty Pakenham. For there had been little in his Dutch campaign to kindle military ardour. Strange that the summer, which saw Arthur Wesley contemplate civilian life, witnessed the stranger spectacle in Paris of General Bonaparte applying for transfer to the Turkish army.

But Arthur's manœuvre failed completely; and as the summer turned to autumn, he launched his last attack supported by his invariable heavy gun, Lord Mornington. The Lord-Lieutenant was informed discreetly that the incumbent of an Irish post would shortly be resigning; that there was " the best reason in the world why he should "; that someone in England would have a grievance if he did not ; that, in fine, a vacancy might be expected in the eligible place of Surveyor-General of the Ordnance for Ireland; and that Arthur " should prefer to have that office to any of those which I mentioned in my letter to you." He would not for the world have pressure put on the incumbent to resign. For one thing, he was an uncle of Kitty Pakenham. Besides, place-hunting has its etiquette : one does not forcibly create the vacancy that one desires to fill. But Camden, still obdurate, resisted every assault. Foiled by the long defence, Arthur drew off his forces and, resigned at last to military life, raised the long siege of Dublin Castle : sieges would never be his *forte*.

That autumn he was with the Thirty-third once more. They were in England still, waiting for the tangential strategy of Mr. Pitt to dispose of them. The regiment lay near Southampton under orders for the West Indies ; and their Colonel wrote to inform the Lord-Lieutenant that he proposed to go with them. The Earl, relieved from his besieging aide-de-camp, was distinctly gratified. He was, as courtesy required, " very sorry we are likely to lose you next winter," but could not but " approve of your determination to accompany your reg't to the West Indies, as I am convinced that a profession once embraced should not be given up. I shall be very glad if I can make some arrangement satisfactory to you against you come back, but if a vacancy should happen in the Revenue Board I fear the Speaker's son must have the first." That written, he turned again to a distracted Ireland,

and Arthur went about his regimental duties. He was not well
10 that autumn, seemed slightly feverish, and consulted a physician.
His Dutch winter might well have left its mark. Besides, a touch
of fever was the right preparation for a soldier's grave in St.
Domingo. So he lived once again in the shadow of Miss Harriette
Wilson's dreaded cocoa trees. They were ordered to Barbados
first, and then to capture the Dutch islands ; for the Cabinet,
11 having singularly failed to rescue Holland, had resolved upon the
more prudent course of rescuing the Dutch colonies. Meanwhile
they waited near Southampton, as autumn turned to winter and
the Channel grew daily less inviting. They sailed at last ; and
as the fleet of transports with the tall ships of their convoy swept
with all sails set past Weymouth one November day, men
crowded to the shore to watch. But the November day was
followed by a November night. A gale went screaming over
12 Portland ; and in the morning seven wrecks were grimly aligned
along the wind-whipped Chesil Beach. The rest put back to
Portsmouth, sailed once more in the first week of December, and
more venturesome than ever tempted the Channel in the teeth of
a mid-winter gale. It blew for seven weeks, blew one of them
clean past Gibraltar to the Spanish coast, scattered a hundred into
the unknown until they dropped weeks later, one by one, into
West Indian harbours, and blew thirty—Arthur's amongst their
number—back to the sheltering Solent after seven vivid weeks
of crowded maritime adventure. So the Thirty-third saw
England once again ; and their Colonel completed an unpleasant
spell of duty, which had comprised one storm at sea and seven
weeks of gale. But few gales have ever done more useful service.
For it spared him a campaign in the West Indies and (most likely)
the West Indian grave that generally followed. " It's very hard,"
as the redoubtable *Major Monsoon* informed *Charles O'Malley*,
" to leave the West Indies if once you've been quartered there,"
since " what with the seductions of the coffee plantations, the
sugar-canes, the monsoons, the brown skins, the rainy season, and
the yellow fever, most of us settled there."

The voice of duty called, though not quite so raucously, in
the first weeks of 1796. Restored to their unwilling country,
the storm-tossed regiment reposed at Poole. They passed the
winter there in the deep calm of Wessex. Meanwhile, their
destinies were altered ; for Whitehall, which had proposed them

for the Western hemisphere, consigned them to the Eastern.
Now they were under orders for India and sailed in April. But
their Colonel was not well enough to go with them. He was still
convalescent in Dublin. There was so much to be arranged
before he could leave Ireland—a paper to be written for his   *13*
successor on the management of Trim electors, his post as aide-
de-camp to be resigned, his brother's interests, estate affairs, to
say nothing of his own. These dismal occupations filled the
spring days in Dublin, as a ragged army swept through the passes
into Italy and the names of Bonaparte's first victories—Lodi,
Montenotte, Mondovi—were sounded upon silver trumpets.
But Colonel Wesley, getting back his health, went patiently
about his business. He was full Colonel now. The Castle was
still vaguely benevolent, assured him of its continued sympathy,   *14*
and murmured something indistinct about a future prospect of
the Revenue Board, adding to Richard that it felt "so much   *15*
the propriety and spirit of Col. Wesley's conduct in going to
the E. Indies that I should be very happy to relieve his mind
from the embarrassment it feels on account of some pecuniary
arrangements which he was obliged to leave unsettled when he
left England. He mentioned these circumstances to me "—and
His Excellency, it seems, had vanished in a haze of insubstantial
promises of profitable places. So Ireland slipped behind him,
rattling miserably down towards the melancholy rapids of '98
in a froth of violence, night drilling, and informers, with the fatal
miasma of rebellion "creeping" (in Grattan's words) "like a   *16*
mist at the heels of the countryman."
    In June he was in London, lodging at 3 Savile Row, and
wafted on his way by the good wishes of an agent, who could not
quite suppress an anxious hope that he would leave express   *17*
instructions to Lord Mornington to pay, should the worst happen,
£955 4s. 8d. of outstanding bills. He did his final shopping at a
bookseller's in Bond Street; and before the month was out, he
was at Portsmouth waiting for a wind. The Thirty-third had   *13*
sailed in April; but a fast cruiser should overhaul them before
they passed the Cape. And so, his trunks packed, his lot decided
now, he waited on the Hard. Among his baggage a large corded
trunk contained the last additions to his library. Now, men will
frequently buy books with the simple object of display, but
rarely when the books are to be their sole companions in distant

countries. Such libraries are more revealing. Arthur's was newly bought from Mr. Faulder, the bookseller in Bond Street, whose corner shop became that very year the background of Gillray's agreeable record of Lord Sandwich's encounter with a more than usually bouncing barrow-wench. The bookseller's account survives with its particulars of solemn quartos, of barely sprightlier octavos, of Oriental phrase-books and forbidding pamphlets, down to the corded trunk itself :—

HONBLE. COL. WESTLEY

June 6, 1796.   *B^{ot} of R. Faulder.*

	£	s.	d.
Crawfurd's Sketches of the Hindoos		6	6
Dow's History of Hindostan. 3 vol. 8vo	1	1	
Verelst's Bengal. 4°		7	6
Vansittart's Narrative. 3 vol.		18	
Bolt's India Affairs. 3 vol.	1	11	6
Scrafton's Reflections on Bengal		3	
Holwell's Historical Events with other Tracts		6	
Cambridge's War in India		6	
Dirom's Campaigns. 4°	1	1	
Monro's Narrative	1	1	
Mackenzie's Campaigns. 2 v.	2	2	
Fullarton's Account of India. 8°		6	
Scott's History of the Dekkan. 2 vol.	2	2	
Analysis of British India. 3 v.		18	
Plans for the Government of India. 4°	1	1	
Hastings' Memoirs of Bengal		3	6
History of Hyder Ali Khan. 2 v.		5	
Rennel's Map and Memoir	2	2	
D'Herbelot, Biblotheque Orientale	1	18	
Richardson's Persian Dict_y. 2 vol.	12	12	
Hadley's Persian Grammar		7	6
Moises Persian Interpreter. 4°		16	
Halhead's Bengal Gram^r.	1	1	
Account of the Siege of Mangalore		6	
Jones' Hist. de Nadir Shah		18	
Fraser's History of Kati Jehan		3	6
Volney's Egypt. 2 vol.		16	
Savary's Egypt and Greece. 3 vol.	1	1	
Cæsar's Commentaries		4	6
Plutarch's Lives. 6 vol.	2	2	
Locke's Works. 9 vol.	4	4	
Paley's Works. 5 vol. gilt	5	5	6

	£	s.	d.
Blackstone's Commentaries. 4 vol.	1	16	
Smith's Wealth of Nations. 3 vol.	5	5	
Ainsworth's Dictionary. 8°		10	6
Tableau de l'Histoire Moderne. 3 tom.		10	6
Bolingbroke's Works. 4 vol.		3	3
Swift's Works. 24 vol.		2	10
Voyage de Bernier. 2 tom.		5	
Russell's Laws of the India Company	2	2	
„ Hist. of the India Company		5	
Trunk, Cord, &c.	1	11	6
	£58	2	6

His programme of reading was severe, but salutary. For nearly half his acquisitions were palpably designed to equip him for the East with a substantial grasp of its history, language, and administration. His purchases were strong upon the late wars with Tippoo ; excepting Cæsar, all his new military works were purely Indian ; nor was current Indian controversy disdained. It was plain from these elaborate researches that Colonel Wesley destined himself for a long stay in India, since officers in quest of quick promotion and the first passage home scarcely require such full documentation. Dublin was fading from his vision now. As Richard wrote of him in the next year, " If Arthur has good luck, he will be called to act on a greater stage than dear Dublin." His stage, it seemed, was India ; and the bookseller's bill shewed that he meant to learn his part. It was his chance in life—the very first that had come his way. For Dublin Castle had been little more for its anxious aide-de-camp than an expensive pastime ; and military reputations were scarcely to be made in Holland. But India was different. Richard, a student of Indian affairs, could see that " the Station is so highly advantageous to him, that I could not advise him to decline it." For India might make something of him—and he of India. At any rate, he meant to try. So much was plain from the forbidding volumes in his trunk.

The rest were no less arduous—Cæsar to be attempted with a Latin dictionary and vague memories of Eton afternoons ; Plutarch (in English) ; the foundations of belief to be explored with Locke and Paley, the mysteries of commerce with Adam Smith, of law with Blackstone, and of Toryism with Bolingbroke.

One item only amongst his new purchases was for recreation—a
set of Swift. Arthur, it seemed, was just a shade sardonic in his
tastes. Besides, what amateur of Irish politics could fail to savour
Swift ? There was a link between them, too ; for Laracor, the
little church near Dangan, had been a living of the Dean's as well
as Wesley property. So Swift, in twenty-four small volumes, was
packed in Arthur Wesley's trunk for India.

He had other books, of course. His London purchases did
not compose the whole of Colonel Wesley's library, though they
formed almost half of it ; since a later list survives in his own
writing, which includes his recent acquisitions together with
books that manifestly came from his rooms in Dublin :—

LIST OF BOOKS
No. 1

Vols.

	Vols.		
2	Richardson's Persian Dictionary	2	Volney's travels
		1	Howell's Events
2	Herbelot's Bibliotheque Orientale	24	Swift's works
		13	Hume's History of England
3	Reports Secret & Select Committees	8	Smollett's Continuation
		9	Woman of Pleasure
1	Harleian Miscellany	10	Faublas
15	Œuvres du Roi de Prusse		

No. 2

Vols.		Vols.	
4	Blackstone's Commentaries	1	Hastings' Trial
1	Verelst India Affairs	1	Account of the Siege of Mangalore
3	Bolt's India Affairs		
3	Orme's Indostan	1	War in Asia
2	Edward's West Indies	1	Walpole's Answer to Bolingbroke
1	Petit Neptune François		
9	Locke's works	3	British India Analysed
5	Paley's works	1	Moore's Narrative of Little's Detachment
1	Graves' regulations		
3	Smith's Wealth of Nations	1	Sketches of the Hindoos
7	Raynal's Histoire des Indes		

No. 3

Vols.

1 Manufactures and Commerce of Bengal
1 Dirom's Narrative last campaign
1 Plans for British India
1 Russell's India
1 Statutes relative to E. In. Company
2 Scott's Deckan
1 Persian Grammar
1 Account of 1st June
1 Memoir and Map of Indostan
2 McKenzie's War in Mysore
1 Proceedings of Com^ee of Officers at home
1 Munro's Letters on ye last war
3 Dow's Indostan
3 Voltaire Fables
1 Hastings' memoirs
4 German dictionary
1 Jones' Persian Grammar

Vols.

1 Arabick Grammar
1 Universal politician
1 Hadley's Grammar
1 Papers on Maroon War
1 Hadley's Persian Grammar
2 Savary's letters
1 Savary Greece
1 Nadir Shah
1 Memoires Marshall Saxe
1 Abregé Chronologique Histoire de France
1 Chapman Venereal disease
1 Transactions in India
1 McIntosh Vindiciæ Gallicæ
1 Cambridge's War in India
1 Cæsaris Commentaria
3 Vansittart's Narrative
1 Reynell's Marches of the B. Armies
1 Clarendon's Irish Affairs

No. 4

Vols.

1 Johnson's dictionary
1 Ainsworth's dictionary
2 Memoirs Baron de Tott
1 German Grammar
3 Gazetteer of France
3 Loyd's War in Germany
1 Dundas Quarto
Proceedings of Officers
Map of France
Bengal Army List
Roads of Bengal
1 Fullarton's India
1 Scrafton's reflections
1 Robertson's Historical Disquisition

Vols.

1 Dundas Cavalry Tacticks
1 Dumourier's campaign in Flanders
Pamphlets
3 Dumourier's life
2 Histoire d'Hyder Ali
2 Bernier
1 Crebillon 2nd Vol.
1 Leonora
9 Royal register
Pamphlets
Allan's views of Hill Forts, &c.
7 Nouvelle Heloise
8 Robertson's works

This library was evidently formed before he left for India, though more than half of it consists of volumes that do not appear in Faulder's bill. The Colonel's list was made (for packing purposes, no doubt) on the occasion of his move from Calcutta to Madras in August, 1798. But one can hardly doubt that almost all the books had come with him from Europe. More than a hundred of the volumes had been bought in Bond Street just before he sailed ; and the rest were palpable survivors from his Dublin library, since it was barely thinkable that Clarendon's *Sketch of the Revenue and Finances of Ireland* (sad relic of his vain designs upon the Irish Revenue Board) was bought for reading in Calcutta, and two items—*Papers on the Maroon War* and Edwards' *History, Civil and Ecclesiastical, of the British Colonies in the West Indies*—had manifestly been acquired when the Thirty-third were destined for that theatre of war. Besides, he had a habit of reading and was unlikely to discard his entire library in favour of the new books from Faulder's shop : a man, whose interests impel him (at a moment of financial stringency) to spend fifty pounds on books, inevitably has more books at home. So the list represents his choice of books at a decisive moment ; and men reveal themselves in their selection of reading for a sea voyage of six months and a long residence abroad.

What does his library disclose ? A military man of rather solemn tastes, whose books were almost all for use. There were no flourishes. His latest purchases reveal his concentration on India ; for India filled his horizon. But there was more than India among his books. He was inclined to history and (the East apart) took out no less than thirty volumes, distributed between the venerated, if slightly alarming, names of Hume, Robertson, and Smollett. Nor were his thoughts confined to Britain, since French history was included. Even the Revolution engaged him, and from an unexpected angle. For he possessed a copy of Mackintosh's *Vindiciæ Gallicæ*, that judicious answer to Mr. Burke's fevered denunciations of French excesses. The Revolution was by far the most conspicuous fact in Europe ; but one would expect a British Colonel to examine it (if he examined it at all) through the congenial medium of a hostile publication— unless, of course, he were genuinely concerned to ascertain what could be said in favour of it. But in that case he would be a most unusual Colonel. Perhaps he was. His literary tastes, indeed, might seem to show as much. For his light reading, apart from a new set of Swift, comprised two foreign authors who were, to say the least, unusual in military circles. King George's officers were seldom to be found with Rousseau in their hands. Yet seven volumes of his *Nouvelle Héloïse* accompanied the Colonel ; and Arthur's sensibility could thrill with the melting *Julie* and enjoy the exquisite delineation of an English nobleman in *Mylord Édouard Bomston*. Voltaire, his second choice, displayed a more astringent quality that might well commend itself to a reader of Swift. But the combination of Voltaire with Rousseau on Arthur Wesley's shelves is undeniably intriguing. That he was not unacquainted with French literature in its naughtier moods is evident from his inclusion of an odd volume of *Crébillon*—with the appended note, touching to bibliophiles, " 2nd vol." Apart from these, his literary tastes, though French, were almost commonplace. For he endured, it would appear, nine volumes of the *Woman of Pleasure,* to say nothing of ten more containing Louvet's interminable *Aventures du Chevalier de Faublas*, and a translation of the latest German romance, *Leonora.* An odd volume of the *Harleian Miscellany* kept eccentric company with these sparks and nymphs, serving the Colonel, it would seem, for intellectual recreation between the lilies and languors of Louvet and the roses and raptures of Rousseau.

His military reading was of a graver cast. Upon the present war in Europe he was content with the writings of the refugee Dumouriez. Dundas supplied a meagre textbook of drill and tactics. But Arthur's choice of masters in the art of war was more significant. Frederick the Great in fifteen small volumes, Marshal Saxe in quarto, and Lloyd's *History of the late War in Germany between the King of Prussia and the Empress of Germany and her Allies* formed his equipment. Frederick was plainly to be studied at full length in his own *Histoire de Mon Temps* and *Histoire de la Guerre de Sept Ans.* (It may be justly doubted how far the studious Colonel penetrated the last ten volumes of that monarch's works, where the dust gathers on his odes, his rhymed epistles, and his endless correspondence with the *coryphées* of French philosophy.) But Frederick, however instructive in military practice, rarely theorised upon the art of war. More theory, as well as sound correctives of undue subservience to Prussian views, was to be found in Major-General Lloyd's volume of *Reflections on the General Principles of War*, with which his narrative concluded. Slightly obsessed by the eighteenth-century delusion that wars could be won without battles by the simple (and magic) occupation of decisive points, and that " if you possess these points, you may reduce military operations to geometrical precision, and may for ever make war without ever being obliged to fight," the General was fairly sound on strategy. His tactics, in spite of an eccentric predilection for the pike, were more suggestive, since he departed from the Frederician line, and proposed to meet cavalry attacks with infantry formed into squares :

21   " I will join the four companies, and form a complete square ; can they break this ? No ; they will not say they can : for, exclusively of the musket, lances, and pikes, I will venture to say that no body of horse, with any degree of velocity, is able to break through a body of infantry of sixteen ranks, because the quantity of action produced by a horseman on full gallop (for one only shocks at a time) is not equal to the resistance of sixteen men placed behind each other, so near as to support in a mass the shock of the horseman.
        " I conclude that, armed as I propose, a battalion of infantry will beat in the open field twice the number or indeed any number of horsemen formed and armed as they are at present."

This was strange reading in 1796; but after Waterloo, perhaps it did not read so strangely.
        The thoughtful Lloyd was equally inclined for change in his extended use of *tirailleurs*. Light infantry was to operate on a
22 wide front before the troops in line.

        " The fire of our two light companies will alone produce a greater effect than that of the enemy, for this obvious reason, that our light infantry acts where and how they please, aims at their leisure, crosses their fire along the enemy's whole front, goes upon their flanks, &c. ; in short, it acts with all the advantage of real and expert chasseurs."

For these new purposes he recommends that their numbers should be expanded to one-fifth of each battalion :

23   " The number of the latter may appear too great ; and in fact it is so, if they are confined to that kind of service only in which they are now employed. . . . But according to our plan, they will perform all the duties commonly done by light troops ; and likewise in a day of action, they shall be employed in such a manner, as will enable them to render more real service than the heavy infantry."

24   Here, in his little library of 1796, was the germ that may have led an officer in 1809 to attach a rifle company to each brigade of

his command in the Peninsula, to form Portuguese infantry
brigades with one battalion to every five—Lloyd's exact proportion—trained and equipped as *Caçadores*, and to put out a line
of skirmishers whose fire could invariably hold the French
voltigeurs. So perhaps his country's debt was greater than it
ever knew to Major-General Lloyd, late of the Austrian army, and
variously denominated by a choleric historian of Frederick
" Epimetheus Lloyd," " surly sagacious Lloyd," and " a man of
great natural sagacity and insight ; decidedly luminous and
original, though of somewhat crabbed temper now and then ; a
man well worth hearing on this and on whatever else he handles."
    Arthur's last military instructor was no less suggestive. For
Marshal Saxe survived in his *Reveries* as a singularly active mind,
busy with every topic from the desirability of body-armour to
the endowment of motherhood. Inclined by nature to an excessive ingenuity in details of equipment that faintly recalls the
preparations of the White Knight for active service, that accomplished soldier was severely practical upon the theory of war.
The soldier's health engaged him ; he was strong for vinegar as
the secret of Roman vigour, and insists in detail upon care of the
feet. He was admirable upon the leg—" *Le Principal de l'Exer-
cice sont les jambes & non pas les bras : c'est dans les jambes qu'est
tout le secret des manœuvres, des combats, et c'est aux jambes qu'il
faut s'appliquer.*" (One almost catches, in this firm abstention
from heroics, the ring of a later voice.) Not that he failed to
explore the higher regions of the military art. He was sagacious
on the merits of reserving fire till the last moment—" *Le quel
emportera l'avantage, de celui qui s'est amusé à tirer ou celui qui
n'aura pas tiré ? Les gens habiles me diront que c'est celui qui aura
conservé son feu, et ils auront raison* "—a salutary lesson which the
French, omitting to absorb it from Saxe, had ample opportunities
of learning on Peninsular battlefields. The villainy of army
contractors roused his invective ; he was emphatic on the value
of light infantry ; and his whole survey of warfare was conducted
with the cold gaze of a realist.
    Such, if he read them, were Colonel Wesley's first masters
in the art of war. Saxe, Frederick, Dundas, Dumouriez, and
Lloyd hung like fairies, good or bad, above his professional cradle
to bestow their gifts. Not that war bulked largely in his library.
For, India apart, it accounted for barely twenty of his two

hundred volumes. India was his main interest; almost a quarter of his books related to the East. Yet he was disinclined to think of India as a mere battlefield. For India had civil problems, which were included in his studies. He could even refer them to first principles, finding his politics in Bolingbroke, his law in Blackstone, and his economics in the *Wealth of Nations*. It was a statesman's library in miniature—but all designed for use, and none to awe visitors.

His purchases revealed him, as another library, bought two years later for another soldier, revealed its owner. For General Bonaparte, just leaving for the East and scrawling a list of purchases for Bourrienne in '98, entered the same confessional. The list was more impressive. It was analytical and erudite. It had an air.

30

BIBLIOTHÈQUE DU CAMP

1° *Sciences et arts.*
2° *Géographie et voyages.*
3° *Histoire.*
4° *Poésie.*
5° *Romans.*
6° *Politique et morale.*

Sciences et Arts

	Vol.
Mondes de Fontenelle	1
Lettres à une princesse d'Alle-	
magne	2
Le Cours de l'École-Normale	6
Aide nécessaire pour l'artillerie	1
Traité des Forlifications	3
Traité des Feux d'artifice	1

Géographie et Voyages

Géographie de Barclay	12
Voyages de Cook	3
Voyages français de La Harpe	24

Histoire

Plutarque	12
Turenne	2
Condé	4
Villars	4
Luxembourg	2
Duguesclin	2
Saxe	3
Mémoires des Maréchaux de	
France	20

	Vol.
Président Heinault	4
Chronologie	2
Marlborough	4
Prince Eugène	6
Histoire philosophique de Indes	12
D'Allemagne	2
Charles XII	1
Essai sur les mœurs des nations	6
Pierre le Grand	1
Polybe	6
Justin	2
Arrien	3
Tacite	2
Tite-Live	
Thucydide	2
Vertot	4
Donina	8
Frédéric II	8

Poésie

Ossian	1
Tasse	6
Arioste	6
Homère	6
Virgile	4
Henriade	1
Télémaque	2
Les Jardins	1
Les chefs-d'œuvre du Théâtre-	
Français	20
Poésies légères (choisies)	10
La Fontaine	

Romans	*Vol.*	*Politique*	*Vol.*
Voltaire	4	*Le Vieux Testament.*	
Héloïse	4	*Le Nouveau.*	
Werther	1	*Le Coran.*	
Marmontel	4	*Le Vedam.*	
Romans anglais	40	*Mythologie.*	
Le Sage	10	*Montesquieu.*	
Prévost	10	*L'Esprit des Lois.*	

There were pretensions here. Besides, the General had ten [31]
thousand francs to spend, compared with Arthur's fifty pounds.
So he bought three times as many volumes. Yet how few of all
their purchases appeared in both selections. Both owned a set of
Frederick the Great ; each bought the *Reveries* of Saxe ; they
both agreed in reading Voltaire and the *Nouvelle Héloïse* ; and
both sailed with Plutarch in their baggage. That was the mode, of
course ; and the coincidence of choice scarcely argues a taste in
common. Born the same year and living in the last decade of
the Eighteenth Century, they could scarcely hope to escape
Plutarch. But it is pleasant to discover a classical allusion
shared between these two admirable subjects for a Plutarchian
diptych.

What else do the two trunks reveal ? Arthur's was full of
his resolve to master India, to learn Indian warfare and administration. But there was little about Egypt in Bonaparte's. He
preferred to soar with *Orlando Furioso*, to explore the deeps of
melancholy with *Werther*, or to draw a gentler sigh over the
destinies of *Manon*. Even his military works ranged every age
and nation ; his classics were impressive ; and his collection of
travels qualified him rather for the conquest of the world than for
an exact knowledge of the Syrian Desert. In fine, it was a gentleman's library in perfect miniature—perhaps a shade too perfect to
be quite a gentleman's. " You find me," he could exclaim to
callers, " among my books." Arthur's were far less universal.
But then the Colonel of the Thirty-third would not have to sustain
exhausting conversations with French *savants* on the voyage out.
Neither was he inclined to class the Bible as *Politique et morale* ;
but then, perhaps, he did not need to buy one for the journey.
Heroic poems had no charms for him ; life would, it seemed, be
tolerable for Arthur without the Iliad ; he took no tragedies in
verse. Indeed, had fate exchanged their trunks, one doubts how

much of Bonaparte's he could have endured. Voltaire undoubtedly, and Rousseau, and the military history. But the sardonic amateur of Swift must have jettisoned almost all the other's lighter reading. For his choice was more austere. But then austerity is frequently the note of books selected by intending travellers. How many of them get a reading, how few survive the journey, are dark questions rarely answered. In Arthur's case, however, the later list remains to show how many of his purchases of '96 were still by him in '98. Swift survived ; but Bolingbroke alas ! had vanished. He had Locke and Paley with him still ; his *Wealth of Nations* kept its charm, his Blackstone too. But though Cæsar was retained, the classics lost their hold on him. For the six volumes of Plutarch no longer darkened his bright Indian horizons. But as he waited for his passage out, his trunk was full of them, and he of a high resolve to read them.

He was at Portsmouth still in the last week of June, 1796, waiting for a wind for India to take himself, his sword, and the light baggage of his education ten thousand miles from England. For he was twenty-seven, his education ended now. It had been a singular affair from start to finish. His family, perhaps, had taught him least of all. They saw so little of him. Besides, their interest was always centred on Richard's bright ascent— Richard's success would surely atone for all his backward brothers. But if he learnt little from his family, had Eton taught him more ? Angers, perhaps, imparted polish and a notable distinction of manners. And Dublin ? Dublin and Trim had been his university, where he learned all the arts of management, the shifts of personal finance, Viceregal deportment, and the under-side of Parliamentary affairs. That had been his civilian education. As to his profession, had he not studied it in the sombre academy of his Dutch winter ? Formed by a varied past, he waited for the wind at Portsmouth. A wind sprang up ; the frigate sailed and Europe faded into the summer haze behind him.

5

SEPOY GENERAL

*Contra la mar salada conpezo 'de
guerrear
A oriente exe el sol e tornos a esa
part.*
                    POEMA DEL CID.

A TEDIUM inseparable from the professional recollections of retired administrators broods impenetrably above the brightest
pages of Anglo-Indian history. Besides, there are so many of
them, and almost uniformly bright. That glorious circumstance,
perhaps, contains the secret of their tedium ; since bright surfaces
repel protracted contemplation. Viewed by posterity, there is a
lack of vicissitudes about them that is almost distressing. That
lofty destiny, those prescient forerunners, and the long roll of
their inevitable victories sweep past like a political speech to its
foregone conclusion. We see the goal ; we note the all too
steady progress ; and our starved dramatic sense cries out for a
hitch somewhere. But it cries in vain ; and our ingratitude
almost forgets that no victory is inevitable until it has been won.
Familiar in its outline, the story seems to pall by reason of its
very grandeur. For a continent subdued is vastly less exciting
than a city saved or an election barely won. It has all the un-
impressive vastness of astronomical dimensions, and fails as
dismally of its effect upon our fainting comprehension. Eastern
history is often disappointing to the Western mind. Did not
1   Macaulay,in a famous Minute,expose to impolite derision "history
abounding with kings thirty feet high and reigns 30,000 years
long, and geography made up of seas of treacle and seas of
butter " ? Something, perhaps, of those staggering proportions
survived to haunt the latest phase of Indian history, to infect the
conquerors themselves, and touch the annals of the British conquest with Oriental tedium.

Yet India in the first stages of the British conquest was far
from tedious. Familiar objects of the Anglo-Indian horizon
were not yet conspicuous or existed only in the most rudimentary
forms. Not yet the grave Civilian ; not yet his lady. The
stupendous flood of Indian reminiscence was a modest rill, still
near its source. No voice rehearsed the endless anecdote of how,
2   " when we were at Dumdum in '36, we ate some colt. Don't you
remember Jubber's colt—Jubber of the Horse Artillery,

69

General ? "   For India was still a land of promise, gleaming with
faint allurement over the edge of the world. But Eldorado
draws livelier company ; and India, though less improving, was
distinctly brighter. For it was Hastings', Francis', Impey's,
Hickey's India, where a cheerful world, pleasantly redolent of
factors, writers, and supercargoes, defied the climate upon claret
or withdrew sedately to more dignified repose beneath a Latin
tag in a Calcutta graveyard. The scene was bright with powdered   3
heads, with gentlemen in white, with smiling ladies who could
smile the brightlier for a comforting knowledge that " the men
are out of all proportion to the female world." They rode ; they
danced ; sometimes they danced themselves into a decline. They
strolled at sunset on the Fort or aired themselves in more adventurous mood upon the water.   Oars dipped, as families reclined
in pinnaces and bands of music floated by. For the Eighteenth
Century, disinclined to pine in exile, viewed the waters of Babylon
rather as an invitation to a water-concert than as a signal to hang
up its harp.   It was a masculine society, where life was planned
delectably for male diversions ; and the lively exiles ate the bread
of affliction with a certain gusto.   They ran wild for masquerades
and supped heroically off oysters, while gentlemen amateurs un-
endingly rehearsed the parts that they could never get by heart.
Life was inalterably eighteenth-century, as though Bengal had
been a sultrier Bath and the Great Tank reflected the Piazza at
Covent Garden.   Did not the pen of *Asiaticus* deplore in a Calcutta journal the sad decease of a young lady " celebrated for her
poetry and misfortunes," who—cruel to relate—had " died of
pure sensibility " ?   How clear it rings, the authentic voice of
the Eighteenth Century, speaking quite unmistakably with bland,
familiar accents in its unusual surroundings.   Europe might have
its moments of uncertainty, as the harsh voices of the Revolution
fell on its ear.   Europe, perhaps, was changing now ; something
was stirring in the air of Europe that might mean a change of
season, and the Eighteenth Century was putting on its wraps.
But, whatever hour the clocks might chime in Paris, it was still
the Eighteenth Century in India. A traveller would find it there
and, once landed at Calcutta, need never leave his comfortable
century.   Indeed, the journey would prolong it, as summer is
prolonged for travellers who follow summer round the world.
     One traveller found it indubitably so, obtaining by his timely

exile a prolongation of the Eighteenth Century, a reprieve for that delicious prisoner of Time, who lay in Europe under sentence. Born at its height behind a Dublin fanlight, he had passed his youth in it ; for what was more *dix-huitième* than a Viceregal world and Dublin Castle ? But as the glow began to fade from Europe, he passed on to India, where the world still walked by its unwavering light. Splintered at home, the mirror of the Eighteenth Century was still intact in India. The judicious traveller could point a toe in its smooth surface and survey himself still framed by its gracious gilding. For the century enclosed him still ; there was no need for him to leave it yet. Had he not followed its summer round the world to India ? He had always lived in its easy weather ; and in India, it seemed, he would live in it still. Indeed, he would find it far from pleasant to en-counter other seasons : they were unthinkable for him. Perhaps he would resist them, when they came.

I

The ship sailed on. Portsmouth was far behind them now, and the dim headlands of the Spanish coast. The road to India led southward down the broad sea-lanes of the Western Ocean, and Teneriffe stood up out of the summer sea to watch them pass. The summer turned to autumn, as they made the long haul past St. Helena to the Cape. Those were the days when travellers paused at the Cape to taste its wine and eat its grapes and stretch their legs with a ride to Constantia and a scramble up Table Mountain. But now the Cape was more congenial than ever, since British enterprise had lately rescued it from the unworthy Dutch. For though the French might overrun the Netherlands and indulge the antics of their preposterous Batavian Republic, they should never have the Cape : the sheltering arm of Britain would secure it from the dread contagion. Indeed, it had just done so, finding the rescue of Dutch colonies less arduous (and more rewarding) than that of Holland. So Colonel Wesley found himself ashore in the very latest British garrison. He found the Thirty-third as well, and resumed his regimental duties in the inter-vals of paying his respects in Cape Town to two young ladies, fresh from school in Bloomsbury and on their way to India. Miss Jemima Smith was gay, satirical, and enterprising ; but Miss

Henrietta, aged seventeen, conquered the Colonel with her more
retiring manners, to say nothing of a " pretty little figure and
lovely neck." And a caller at the house found him " all life   5
and spirits " and the very image of John Philip Kemble. His
blue eye was clear ; his nose was large ; his speech was rapid,
" with, I think, a very, very slight lisp " ; and a beard of obstinate
growth placed him under the distressing necessity of shaving
twice a day. Before they sailed, he wrote in the interests of his
career to the Governor of Madras. Then they sailed on to India,
enduring " a most tedious passage " in the *Princess Charlotte*   6
East Indiaman. Even the composition of a second letter to Lord
Hobart failed to relieve the tedium. He had his regiment ;
he had his box of books ; he had his thoughts. But the bright
spaces of the Indian Ocean stretched endlessly away, and India
still lurked somewhere behind the haze. A line of coast appeared
at last. The sea became the Roads ; the Roads dwindled to the
Hooghly ; the Hooghly turned to Garden Reach ; and halfway
through February, 1797, the Colonel landed at Calcutta.

Once safe ashore, he had his duties. For there was the
Governor-General to be called upon. There was not a notion yet
that Richard might be summoned to fill that lofty throne. When
Arthur sailed, Lord Mornington was deep in politics at home with
every expectation of staying there ; and Sir John Shore sat
modestly in Warren Hastings' seat. That potentate recalled
(after a fitting interval) his first prophetic estimate of Arthur.
For the discerning Governor-General observed that if Colonel   7
Wesley should ever have the opportunity of distinguishing himself, he would do it. He even found in the young man " a union
of strong sense and boyish playfulness." Both would find scope
in India. Indeed, his playfulness seemed likely to be called upon
before his sense. For one muggy night in March Mr. Hickey
found him presiding at the Calcutta dinner for St. Patrick's Day   8
and doing the duties of the Chair with peculiar credit to himself
—and in matters of conviviality Mr. Hickey's standards were
exacting. Now he was in the cheerful world that went for morning rides, paid calls, and made its bow at the Governor-General's
levée. It was Dublin Castle over again, but Dublin Castle with a
difference. For the Calcutta *ton* was often quite inseparable   9
from its hookah, drew fragrant puffs between the hands of cards,
or smoked discreetly in the back of theatre boxes. A mob of pipe-

bearers sometimes came in with the dessert, and furtive devotees
had been occasionally known to snatch a sly cheroot in guest-
rooms. Even the fair could not escape the strange infection.
(Here was a novelty for Arthur, a variation upon Dublin Castle.)
For long years before the Nineteenth Century could draw its first
emancipated whiff, pale ladies in Calcutta tasted smoke. But
when they stooped to smoke, they smoked with grace ; since
eager beaux approaching with the pipe put a fresh mouthpiece
on, uncoiled the snake, and offered it respectfully to the fair
novice. Once that spring he went up the river to Chinsurah and
stayed with Mr. Hickey and a men's party. The house was new,
the company select ; after mornings pleasantly divided between
horse exercise and billiards they sat down twelve to table ; and
having dined, a cheerful company " pushed the claret about very
freely," while somebody obliged with a song. He was there again
in June. They rode races every morning, and the King's birthday
was celebrated with loyal ceremony. For the convivial Hickey
had procured a turtle and some venison, to say nothing of the
very best champagne, hock, claret, Madeira, and " an eminent
French cook " imported from Calcutta for the occasion. Small
wonder that they fell to glees and catches, and a General rendered
The British Grenadiers with the utmost spirit. But these
diversions failed to distract the Colonel. His mind still ran on
Indian campaigns ; and when the General invited his opinion
upon the introduction of light artillery, he could respond with a
wealth of technicality, though not " regularly bred to artillery,"
in a paper citing the late wars in Mysore, the defects of recent
operations, and the scarcity of horses in India. For he had read
to some purpose his forbidding library of Indian history.

That summer a hope of active service dawned. For Spain
having rashly entered the war on the French side, the British
formed a sage resolve to appropriate the Spanish colonies in the
Pacific. The Philippines were most inviting ; so were the Dutch
establishments in Java ; and a combined attack from India was
freely talked of. While the expedition was deliberately fitting
out, there was a chance that Arthur might be given command
of the Bengal contingent. He was alert at once, drew plans for
submission to the Governor-General, and displayed a terrifying
intimacy with monsoons, the defences of Batavia (" surrounded
by a slight brick wall, which has no defence. It has on

the eastern side of it a citadel, which stands close to the bay,
but which, however, is not within shot of the artillery-ground. . . .
In the rear of the town, at some distance, are two redoubts ;
in which, however, as I am informed, there are no guns "), and the
comparative merits of Malay harbours. The Colonel was unusually thorough ; and he wrote hopefully to Richard on his pros- ·
pects of the command:

> " I desired the person who communicated his wishes to me to   *14*
> decline it in my name, and to propose Doyle. If any thing should
> prevent Doyle . . . I intend to accept of it ; taking the chance
> that the large force they intend to send, the known pusillanimity of
> the Enemy, and my exertions will compensate in some degree for
> my want of experience. I hope to be at least as successful as the
> people were to be to whom Hobart wishes to give the command.
> . . . Of course the Chief Command of this expédition would make
> my fortune ; going upon it at all will enable me to free myself from
> debt."

The prospect was alluring ; but the offer, alas ! was not renewed.
His initial gesture of abnegation had been successful—more
successful, possibly, than he intended—and he sailed with no
higher rank than that of Colonel commanding the Thirty-third.
But before the expedition left, he had a touch of fever. India,   *15*
perhaps, seemed less attractive now—" I have not yet met with
a Hindoo who had one good quality, and the Mussulmans are
worse than they are. Their meekness and mildness do not exist."
Cruelty, deceit, and perjury formed a depressing background ;
and he began to feel a little lonely, having " no news from England
since I left it, which is extraordinary, considering that that was
in June '96." Now it was July '97 ; and almost wistfully he
asked his brother to " let my mother, &c., know that I am well."

But within a fortnight a mail arrived with the sublime intelligence that Richard was to come out to India as the next
Governor-General. So that bright promise was to be fulfilled at
last, and Richard awaited with serenity its rich fulfilment. Imperial attitudes had always suited him, and his new appointment
would enable him to strike the most imperial of all. For what
spoke plainlier of Rome, what more reminiscent of the legions and
the eagles, than a proconsul ? Not that the prior associations of
the office were conspicuously proconsular. His countrymen had

strikingly declined to award the civic crown to Warren Hastings ; few warrors were less adapted to the pallium than Lord Cornwallis ; and the judicious qualities of Sir John Shore—" a good man, but cold as a greyhound's nose "—were scarcely of the order that cries out for bronze to be their record. But these predecessors could not conceal its rich possibilities from the discerning Richard. It was, he could see that it was " the most distinguished situation in the British Empire after that of Prime Minister of England " ; and he was modestly prepared to discharge its functions. Meanwhile (since Roman dignities were often followed by a Roman triumph) it would be just as well to think about a marquessate, if one should come his way. For Mornington was quite resolved to be Marquess Wellesley ; and Ulster King of Arms, in his secluded room at Dublin Castle, was kept busy with Richard's eager enquiries upon heraldic points— had he the right to quarter Cusack, Geneville, and De Lacey with Wellesley ? who married Walter Cowley of Castle Carbury in the reign of Henry VIII ? and what was known about a shadowy ancestor traditionally thought to have been standard-bearer to Henry II and feudal holder of some lands near Wellington in Somerset ? These lofty themes engaged him, as the new Governor-General prepared to enter on his splendid province. But he had living relatives as well, whose prospects might be gilded as Richard's luminary rose in the skies of patronage to become, in Burke's splendid image, ' lord of the ascendant.'

Richard, it seemed, had other views, though his brother Henry went with him as secretary. For his Roman qualities appeared to include the austerer forms of Roman virtue ; and one hopeful applicant received the chilling answer that a young gentleman, for whom his favour was desired, would receive—

" every encouragement and assistance ; and if he deserves it (not otherwise) I will take care that he shall rise as quickly as the Regulations of the Company's Service, and the attention due to the merits of others will permit ; more I will not do for my own Brother ; nor would I accept this high station, unless I were assured of my possessing firmness enough to govern the British Empire in India without favor or affection to a human being either in Europe or Asia. The integrity of my own character in such a government is the best provision which I can make for any branch of my family ; and if this were not good policy, as well as morality, I have vanity enough

to be resolved to sacrifice every consideration (but the public
interest) to the preservation of a just and well-founded fame."

This was austerity indeed ; for it was the golden age of
patronage, and India was almost sacred to nepotism. But
Arthur was not unprepared for Richard's Roman virtues, since
his reception of the news of the great appointment concluded
with an almost formal offer of " service to you in your Government " and the rueful supplement that " such are the rules   20
respecting the disposal of all patronage in this country, that I
can't expect to derive any advantage from it which I should not
obtain if any other person were Governor-General." It gratified
him, though. Had he not pressed his brother to entertain the
appointment within a month of his own arrival in India ? He
even offered reasoned consolations for Richard's approaching
separation from his domestic hearth, though " I acknowledge
that I am a bad judge of the pain a man feels upon parting from
his family." For the twelve months' absence of a line from home
still seemed to rankle.
    Meanwhile, with Richard brushing up his quarterings at
home, Arthur went soberly about his duties, untroubled by
heraldic problems or the lands once held by spectral ancestors
near Wellington. What was Wellington to him ? They would
be sailing for Manilla soon ; and the Colonel plagued Government   21
for mess allowances and a prompt amendment of the system by
which ships' surgeons were to be made responsible for his soldiers'
health at sea—" It takes out of my hands entirely the superintendence and control over the management of the sick. . . .
I shall be deprived of that part of the superintendence over my
corps which is most gratifying to me when they are embarked,
and by exercising which I can render most service to the soldiers."
For he was strong upon their health (had he not watched an army
die in Holland ?) ; and his regimental orders for the voyage were   22
a judicious code of hygiene that included frequent fumigation of
the decks, daily exercise with dumb-bells, and the sterner prescription that " the men should be made to wash their feet and legs
every morning and evening, and occasionally water should be
thrown over every man ; every day if possible." The new
practitioner did not disdain such unheroic aids to war.
    Not long before they sailed, he had a word with Mr. Hickey

on a loftier theme.   The Thirty-third, it seemed, were unprovided
with a chaplain ; a friend of Mr. Hickey's had a nephew ; and the
Colonel " in the handsomest manner " promptly appointed him.
The appointment, it must be confessed, disclosed a somewhat
languid interest in their spiritual health, since the new chaplain
was " a young clergyman of very eccentric and peculiarly odd
manners," whom he had met at Hickey's house.   They sailed in
August ; but the ships were barely three days out from land
before the new regimental chaplain disgraced himself completely.
For this unaccountable young man became intolerably drunk
and gave a public exhibition of extreme impropriety.   Then,
seized with contrition, he refused all nourishment and stayed
secluded in his cabin.   The captain's consolation failing, Colonel
Wesley came on board and plied the penitent with kindly arguments—" that what had passed was not of the least consequence,
as no one would think the worse of him for the little irregularities
committed in a moment of forgetfulness : that the most correct
and cautious men were liable to be led astray by convivial society,
and no blame ought to attach to a cursory debauch."   But all in
vain.   The unhappy clergyman continued to repent, drooped for
a week or so, and died.   Meanwhile, the little fleet pursued its
way through the still summer days, until they reached ' the
shallow sea that foams and murmurs on the shores of the thousand
islands, big and little, which make up the Malay Archipelago.'
For the first stage was ended in the long journey to Manilla ; and
Arthur Wesley walked ashore among the palms that overlook
Penang.

That region of romance, of Malays and Chinamen, ' of shallow
waters and forest-clad islands, that lies far east, and still
mysterious between the deep waters of two oceans,' was more
mysterious still in 1797.   But the Colonel seemed impervious
to mystery and, Malays and palm-trees notwithstanding, wrote
sturdily to Dublin ordering some Irish linen for his back.   His
tone was reassuring—" I don't think that people get quite so
rich in India as it is imagined in England that they do, but I
must say that I am richer now than I ever was & I hope in the
course of 4 or 5 months to have it in my power to send you home
at least a sufficiency to pay 2 years Interest on my debts."   Here
was good news for an anxious agent, and the cheerful Colonel
breathed the soft Malayan air more lightly for its despatch.   But

before their first attack was launched across the Straits upon the unsuspecting Dutch in Java, an impulsive Government recalled the little force. The French, it seems, commanded by the atrocious Bonaparte, had lately made the most disquieting progress in Italy. Besides, the peace of India itself was vaguely threatened ; and for these somewhat occult reasons it was thought well to concentrate the British forces in the East. So the expedition to Manilla sailed home again from Penang, and Arthur never walked the shadowy stage of romance, where silent rivers creep mysteriously past Malay stockades and drums throb in vast, unlistening forests.

Indeed, he resolutely declined to see its mystery and instead composed a memorandum on the material advantages of holding Penang. Its defences, garrison, and revenue were minutely esti- mated ; and the treatment of commercial problems seemed to shew that his Adam Smith was not unopened. This freight of views returned with him to India, where he was seen again at dinner with his mess or dining with a brother officer at Alipore. Hickey was with them more than once and found " eight as strong- headed fellows as could be found in Hindostan." After the cloth was off, they despatched twenty-two toasts " in glasses of con- siderable magnitude " ; then discipline relaxed, the Chair con- siderately ruling that gentlemen might drink as little as they choose ; but a cheerful company persisted bravely with the task until they staggered out to find their carriages and palanquins a little after two, leaving Mr. Hickey to enjoy an excruciating head- ache, which lasted forty-eight hours and extorted the impressive tribute that " a more severe debauch I never was engaged in in any part of the world." This was high praise indeed. Such relaxations aiding, Arthur resumed his regimental life. Not that his interests were exclusively military, since he still had his books and composed a lengthy memorandum in refutation of someone's heretical *Remarks upon the Present State of the Husbandry and Commerce of Bengal.* This malcontent had assailed the British connection through the East India Company, and the resourceful Colonel offered a detailed defence. His economics were self- taught ; he ventured boldly on the sugar question and devised an ingenious naval argument in support of Great Britain's preferen- tial tariffs in favour of West Indian produce by insisting upon the necessity of the Atlantic trade as a school of seamanship. The

Colonel was growing positively encyclopædic ; and he improved his Indian knowledge with a visit to Lord Hobart at Fort St. George, where he found the little world of ' hum-drum Madrassers ' and the more pressing problems of a Presidency which dwelt in uncomfortable proximity to the unrestful Tippoo. But he was back in Calcutta on the May day in 1798 that Richard— dapper, aquiline, and stately—made his auspicious landing. The frigate which had brought him out was so " encumbered " (to the irreverent eye of the *Morning Chronicle*) " with stores, carriages, and baggage, that should the rencontre of an enemy make it necessary to prepare for action, Lord Mornington will inevitably suffer from clearage in the course of six minutes a loss of at least £2,000." Such were Richard's imperial paraphernalia.

Lord Mornington was still an Irish earl ; but, halfway to his goal already, he was Lord Wellesley in the English peerage now. They called his brother Henry by the new name of Wellesley, too. Richard had always seemed to prefer the fuller version, writing their surname, with a faint contempt for its abbreviated form, " Wellesley, otherwise by corruption Wesley." It had an ampler air ; and since the family must do their loyal best to live up to Richard, Arthur felt bound to make the change as well. For it would never do for Colonel Wesley to persist, when the foremost name in India was Wellesley. So Arthur made the change ; and within two days of Richard's landing he signed his first letter in the more impressive style of ' Arthur Wellesley.'

II

HE was a person of importance now, with Richard safely installed in Warren Hastings' seat and Henry, his younger brother, at the new Governor-General's elbow as private secretary. What could be of better augury for Arthur than these highly-placed relations ? Not that their influence would waft him straight into preferment. For Calcutta was not Dublin Castle ; and the cruder forms of patronage were checked effectively by the Company's regulations, to say nothing of Richard's stern resolve to play the Roman parent. But Richard, however, lofty, was still Richard. Had he not always been the architect of Arthur's career, brought him into Parliament for Trim, advanced the purchase price of his promotion, even supported him in the vain pursuit of Irish places ? His principles might indispose him to endow his brother as an Indian placeman ; but Lord Mornington was not reluctant to use him for the public service.

The new proconsul was inclined by nature to become a thunderbolt of war. But the technique of war presents an obstacle that even the most high-spirited of civilians find awkward ; and Arthur was welcome to his brother in the capacity of technical adviser. The post was strictly unofficial. But since the Company omitted to supply their Governor-General with a military cabinet, that enterprising potentate proceeded to repair the omission by employing Arthur Wellesley as an informal chief of staff. Unofficial or not, the post was real enough ; and Colonel Wellesley was kept busy writing memoranda for the ^{1} Governor-General upon a forward policy in Mysore, troop movements in the Carnatic, supply, fortifications, professional grievances in the Company's army, and the defences of the north-west frontier. His detail (he was always strong on detail) was abundant ; he projected forts without omitting to estimate their armament, and " said nothing about Dindigul, as I have not seen ^{2} it, and don't understand anything relating to it." Supply engaged him quite as deeply as strategy ; and, always disinclined to soar, he kept his feet firmly on the ground of practicable operations—" It is impossible to carry on a war in India without ^{3}

bullocks. . . . Order that the collectors of the different districts
under the Company's Government should endeavour to ascertain
the number of bullocks they have in their districts, and what
number they could collect without doing much injury to the
cultivation of the country." This was the prose of war ; and
few officers were better fitted to dispense it than Lord Mornington's unofficial chief of staff.

But Arthur Wellesley still remained a regimental officer. He
was a Colonel still. Not quite an ordinary Colonel, though. He
had his books ; and in a list of them he made that summer there
was abundant evidence of reading that was far from habitual
with Colonels in 1798. He had discarded little of the library that
had come out with him two years before. His irony still fed on
Swift ; Paley and Locke still guided him towards the eternal
verities, Blackstone and Adam Smith towards a just apprehension
of earthly problems ; and India still formed the staple of his
library. Cæsar, Saxe, Lloyd, and Frederick were still his coun-
sellors upon the art of war. Indeed, he found his Cæsar curiously
relevant to Indian military problems ; for he confessed in later
years how much he learned from him, " fortifying my camp every
night as he did," and borrowing Cæsar's methods of crossing rivers
by basket-boats. But Bolingbroke had gone. Was it not Mr.
Burke who had uttered the scandalised enquiry, ' Who now reads
Bolingbroke ? ' Not Arthur Wellesley, it would seem ; and the
attempt on Plutarch was abandoned—or, his six volumes read,
a triumphant reader had discarded them. He even weeded his
light reading ; and a judicious pen was drawn through *Faublas*
and the *Woman of Pleasure*, as he made his list of books for packing. For he was ordered south that summer, and Mr. Hickey
was deprived of the society of the Thirty-third. They sailed in
August for Madras, and reached port after an arduous four weeks
of navigation, that comprised collision with a reef outside Calcutta,
a leak, a spell of pumping, and a supply of drinking water that
spread dysentery on board. Arthur was not immune himself,
lost fifteen men, and was left reviling the commissariat for its
shortcomings—" I conceive it to be very inconsistent with the
principles of the Christian religion to give people bad water when
he had notice of the probability that it would be so. . . . A
Gentile could not have done worse than give us a bottle of good
rum by way of muster, and fill the casks with the worst I ever

6

saw." The convalescent was still fuming a month later—" It   *7*
is unpardonable, as I warned him of it, and I am afraid that I
must make a public complaint of him."

Now he was in Madras, where officers took evening rides on
the Mount Road acknowledging profound salaams from the old
Nabob of Arcot, as he rode, turbaned and long-bearded, in a   *8*
venerable English chaise behind his black postilions. But, his
regiment apart, Colonel Wellesley was in Madras on special duty.
His enterprising brother at Calcutta was inclined for war with
Mysore. Somewhat unduly shocked by an egregious gesture of   *9*
the French, Lord Mornington fingered his thunderbolts. For a
flurried Frenchman at Mauritius had produced a sonorous
proclamation calling for volunteers and reciting that Tippoo was   *10*
only waiting for French aid to drive the British out of India.
Such ill-considered eloquence is habitual with revolutionaries.
But Mornington jumped almost fiercely to conclusions ; and
exasperating visions of ' Citizen Tippoo ' planting trees of
liberty, while grateful Mysoreans performed the Carmagnole,
danced angrily before his eyes. The French were everywhere ;
they were in Egypt now ; a draggled shipload of them had even
reached Mysore ; and with India in danger would not a prescient
Governor-General be wise to strike before worse happened ?
Besides, prompt action would enable him to settle the ancient
reckoning with Tippoo. Arthur, consulted on his policy, was less
inflammable and wrote a chilling memorandum. The French
alliance with Mysore appeared to leave him singularly calm.
While Richard's fancy kindled with the dreadful prospect of
Tippoo allied with the Republic, One and Indivisible, Arthur was
coldly counting heads—" the consequence of that alliance has   *11*
been an addition to the forces of Tippoo of 150 men at most."
And even if the French should send a force from Europe, he
estimated that it could not exceed 3,000 men, who must first
elude the British squadrons at the Cape and in Indian waters
before they could appear in Mysore. Once there, a chain of
causes lovingly enumerated would reduce their efficacy by three-
quarters. In fine, the Colonel was not alarmed by the alliance
and concluded that " if it be possible to adopt a line of conduct
which would not lead immediately to war, provided it can be
done with honour, which I think indispensable in this Government, it ought to be adopted in preference to that proposed in

the conversations. . . . Let the proclamation be sent to Tippoo
with a demand that he should explain it and the landing of the
troops. Don't give him reason to suppose that we imagine he has
concluded an alliance with the objects stated in the proclamation ;
and finding he has derived so little benefit from the alliance, there
is every probability that he will deny the whole, and be glad of an
opportunity of getting out of the scrape. In the meantime we
shall believe as much as we please, and shall be prepared against
all events." This was the wisdom of the serpent. His chief of
staff declined to soar with Richard ; for soldiers are sometimes
less given to military moods than spirited civilians. The Colonel's
view received abundant confirmation and, to his brother's deep
regret, prevailed. The *rôle* of Mars postponed, Lord Mornington
prepared his plans, organised allies, and waited for his moment.

Colonel Wellesley's mission in Madras was closely connected
with these preparations. He brought instructions to the Commander-in-Chief, expounded Richard's strategy, wrote freely in
cipher to Calcutta commenting on his seniors, and exercised
unwearied pressure to secure a degree of military readiness. His
major task, more delicate, was to ensure co-operation by the
Governor of Madras. Lord Clive was difficult and dull, cast in
the mould that Nature favours to obstruct the bold designs of
clever men. His speech was slow, but easily kept pace with his
thought ; and the resulting compound formed an unlikely partner
for the leaping Richard, who angrily enquired of a colleague,
" How the Devil did he get there ? " Arthur, a shrewder judge,
was doubtful " whether he is so dull as he appears, or as people
here imagine he is." So the judicious Colonel took the slow-
spoken peer in hand. Scarcely articulate themselves, such types
are frequently impervious to the spoken word. But Arthur's
diplomacy prevailed ; indeed, he was so far successful that there
was even a danger of his being almost permanently attached to
this uninspiring duty, " merely because there is a chance that
endeavours may be made to set Lord Clive against the measures
which the Supreme Government have thought necessary."
Meanwhile, his backward pupil made gratifying progress, and was
presently discovered by Mornington to be " a very sensible man
. . . on the most intimate and cordial footing." It was Arthur's
first diplomatic triumph.

But his diplomacy found more strenuous exercise in im-

portuning languid authorities to move the siege-train nearer to
the frontier of Mysore, to have a plan of operations, to locate
supplies " upon the line which it may be intended to follow," and
to substitute effective commissaries for " the vague calculations
of a parcel of blockheads, who know nothing, and have no data."
His efforts, though extremely trying to the temper, were successful. But the success left him unsatisfied. He was still uncon-
vinced that Richard's dashing policy was sound, and urged that
Tippoo should not be pressed too far—" Nothing should be
demanded which is not an object of immediate consequence. . . .
I would confine the demand to his receiving an ambassador
from us." Besides, his personal position as Richard's legate *in
partibus infidelium* was particularly awkward ; and his embarrassments were confided to his brother Henry with strict
injunctions to say nothing of them to Mornington. They had
a more material side as well. For his situation in Madras denied
him all chances of obtaining a command elsewhere ; and though
his tone was highly disinterested—" whether I return £500 richer
in consequence of having been in a command, or poorer in consequence of having been in Fort St. George, is a matter of indifference to me "—it was not surprising that his eye wandered
in the direction of an impending vacancy in Ceylon, " if there be
no war." But even if there were, his mood was curiously cool.
It would, he felt, be long and doubtful ; and he appeared to view
with calm his own recall to Europe whenever seniority should
make him a Major-General. Even when Mornington obligingly
proposed him for the Staff in India, he acquiesced without marked
enthusiasm, preferring European service, but conceding gloomily
that " as I am obliged to serve in some part of the world, however
disagreeable this country is, I don't know whether I may not as
well remain here as go to any other place. I have been perfectly
well in India, and I don't much care about being in a disagreeable
place."

The drums of war, it seemed, scarcely made music in his ears.
Meanwhile he struggled dutifully on, pestering supine officials
and mitigating his exile with a shipment of delicacies from the
Governor-General's *maître d'hôtel* and the more graceful *rôle* of
witness at Belle Johnston's wedding. The tone of Richard's
correspondence with Mysore began to deepen ominously. Tippoo
was still profuse in his desire for " gladdening letters notifying

16
17

18

19

20
18

19

21

15

22

23

your welfare " ; but Mornington, past compliments, responded
grimly (and with a creditable mastery of Oriental idiom) that
" dangerous consequences result from the delay of arduous
affairs." His correspondent countered with an exasperating
rigmarole rich in allusions to Jamshyd, the major constellations,
and his continuing anxiety for further intelligence of Richard's
health, concluding with the unhelpful information that " being
frequently disposed to make excursions and hunt, I am accordingly proceeding on a hunting expedition," adding however that
a British envoy " slightly attended (or unattended) " would not
be unwelcome. Lord Mornington, his moment come, permitted
himself the luxury of impatience ; and Tippoo was informed that
24　　further negotiations would be conducted by the Commander-in-
Chief of the British army in the field. Richard, it seemed, was
going hunting too. Indeed, he wrote almost savagely to England
25　　that " I have had the satisfaction to succeed completely in drawing the Beast of the jungle into the toils . . . our own army is
the finest which ever took the field in India ; and by dint of
scolding and flattering I have equipped it within a period of time
perfectly astonishing to the old school." Much of the scolding
had been Arthur's.

26　　　　The Colonel's preparations for the field included a soup-tureen
and dishes for a mess of twelve. He was still deep in questions
of supply and earned the unusual tribute from the Commander-
27　　in-Chief that " the judicious and masterly arrangements in respect
to supplies . . . were no less creditable to Colonel Wellesley than
advantageous to the public service, and deservedly entitle him to
my thanks and approbation." Small wonder that this adept
28　　viewed with profound disgust " two Company's officers ; one of
them . . . so stupid that I can make no use of him, and the other
such a rascal that half of my occupation consists in watching
him. . . . Besides this, they neither of them understand one
syllable of the language ; have never even been in a camp, much
less on service." His own experience was scarcely extensive ;
but the young Colonel (he was close on thirty now) began to know
his mind. Before they took the field, however, a trying incident
engaged him. Consulted by an angry Colonel who was deep in
an aimless wrangle with subordinates over a minor point of regimental accounting, Arthur advised him to abstain from issuing
an irritating order. But since good advice is rarely welcome, his

incensed colleague insisted, and Arthur (always eminently practical and excusably a trifle ruffled) enquired, " Then why, if you   29
had made up your mind to do so, consult me on the subject ? "
The injudicious order issued, the inevitable duels followed between the Colonel and his juniors ; and the unhappy man, after
a death-bed interview with his " dear Arthur," expired, another
melancholy instance of the degree to which a trying climate can
exalt the sense of honour, as well as of the prevailing taste—high-
spirited, but how uncalled for—of British officers for avoidable
casualties.

The war was ready to begin. Arthur, who had been in temporary charge of the whole army, commanded a division of native
allies with a slight stiffening of English troops, consisting (in his
own enumeration) of " the 33rd, six excellent battalions of the   30
Company's sepoys, four rapscallion battalions of the Nizam's,
which, however, behaved well, and really about 10,000 (which
they called 25,000) cavalry of all nations, some good and some
bad, and twenty-six pieces of cannon "—a respectable command,
its nucleus being formed by the Nizam's contingent, whose presence in the field was largely due to Mornington's acceptance of   31
Arthur's earlier advice to eliminate French influence at Hyderabad
by a prompt *coup de main*. The Colonel had been reading his
Dumouriez—" You have read Dumourier's account of his organis-   32
ing the Poles ; I am employed in a business of much the same
kind. My Poles fight too, and that not badly, I assure you."
The " ponderous machine " moved slowly up towards the high-   33
lands of Mysore, and Arthur viewed without elation the prospects
of the war. His misgivings were sharply accentuated by an
enquiry from Madras whether Richard should take the field
himself. Arthur's negative was prompt and unqualified—" All   34
I can say upon the subject is, that if I were in General Harris's
situation, and you joined the army, I should quit it." Such
frankness was, perhaps, a trifle more than brotherly ; but
Richard, to his credit, took it extremely well, adding his satisfaction at the general praise of Arthur's management—" I wish to
God the whole were under your direction ; but even as it is, I
think our success is certain." Arthur did not. His mood was
notably subdued. Henry was warned that " our war cannot be   35
successful in one campaign " ; and he was at extreme pains to
water Richard's wine more liberally than any stranger would

36   have dared—" I am glad that you are prepared for a failure. . . .
My despondency goes thus far, and no farther. . . . I think I
have done better to make it known to you, than to tell you that
it was impossible that we should not succeed. It is better to see
and to communicate the difficulties and dangers of the enterprise,
and to endeavour to overcome them, than to be blind to everything but success till the moment of difficulty comes, and then
to despond."

His spirits rose a little as they penetrated deeper into Mysore
37   —" There is not *now* a doubt but that we shall bring that monstrous equipment to Seringapatam, and, in that case, we shall
certainly take the place." They had a brush with the Mysoreans
in the last week of March, and the Thirty-third charged with the
38   bayonet. His tone was higher now—" We are here with a strong,
a healthy, and a brave army, with plenty of stores, guns, &c., &c.,
and we shall be masters of his place before much more time passes
over our heads." But Arthur's health was slightly affected.
His trying spell of duty in Madras left him a little low ; and the
heat of Mysore in April combined with bad water to bring on
38   dysentery, " which did not confine me " (so Richard was informed), " but teased me much. I have nearly got the better of
it, and I hope to be quite well in a few days." Before it left him,
though, he was tried harder than is entirely good for any man with
dysentery. For on the very night he wrote about his health to
Richard, the Colonel was in charge of a small column engaged in
39   clearing the approaches to Seringapatam. The night was " dark
as pitch *forward*, and in the *rear* towards our camp the fires and
lights burnt brilliantly, which increased the darkness in front."
40   The column stumbled through the night into a little wood, which
nobody had reconnoitred. Entangled in the darkness, they were
heavily fired on and lost formation ; the gloom filled suddenly
with shots and shouting ; a spent ball struck him on the knee ;
somewhere in front the leading files were captured in the night ;
and as confusion deepened, the Colonel—a trifle unaccountably—
left them to report his failure. Shaken and unwell, he reeled
back to camp. It was not far from midnight ; and the exhausted
man, his nerves all frayed, flung himself face down across the
mess-table to sleep. Attacking in the morning, he retrieved himself and carried the position ; but the nightmare of the little wood
41   had left him with the bitter flavour of defeat—" mad," as an

officer recorded, " with this ill success "—explaining ruefully to
Richard his " determination, when in my power, never to suffer   *42*
an attack to be made by night upon an enemy who is prepared
and strongly posted, and whose posts have not been reconnoitred
by daylight."   And forty years away he could still draw a sketch-   *40*
map in explanation of the affair at Sultanpettah Tope.   For the
unpleasing night lived in his memory.   Such lapses are occasionally final.   Arthur's, happily, was not.   That icy rigour of control,
it seems, which led his countrymen to an unkind suspicion that
nerves had been omitted from his composition, came to him only
by degrees.   He was not born, but made himself, the unmoving
soldier of later years ; and learning his lessons as they came,
he learned some of them (since night attacks are a rough school
of war) that night at Sultanpettah.

The siege was duly opened with the becoming ritual of parallels
and breaches ; and Arthur found himself one evening in charge
of a successful operation against an outlying work.   But on the   *43*
day of the assault he was in reserve, commanding in the trenches,
while General Baird enjoyed the unusual treat of storming a
fortress in which he had once been a prisoner.   Baird's part was
played to perfection ; his sword was drawn ; his big voice roared,
" Then forward, my lads " ; a flag fluttered in the breach ; and
panting Englishmen scrambled into Seringapatam.   But when
they found Tippoo's body, Colonel Wellesley was at the eager   *44*
General's side, and Arthur's careful hand assured them that no
life remained.   The captured fortress was a problem, since it
contained vast quantities of treasure and a scared native population.   The situation plainly called for skilful handling by the
command ; and the heroic Baird was scarcely likely to display
the requisite touch.   Had not his mother, hearing years before
that he was chained to a fellow-captive at the tail of one of
Tippoo's guns, gaily exclaimed, " I pity the mon wha's tied to   *45*
ma Davie."   And Arthur's portrait of him, drawn in later years,
was no less distinct—" a gallant hard-headed, lion-hearted   *46*
officer ; but he had no talent, no *tact* ; had strong prejudices
against the natives ; and he was peculiarly disqualified from his
manner, habits, &c., and it was supposed his temper, for the
management of them.   He had been Tippoo's prisoner for years.
He had a strong feeling of the bad usage which he had received
during his captivity."   This was unpromising for the prospects

of good government in Seringapatam ; and Baird received a
morning call from Colonel Wellesley. He disliked the Colonel,
since he had always resented Arthur's command of the Hyderabad
contingent, overlooking the fact that Arthur was almost wholly
responsible for its existence and that the Nizam's son had asked
expressly for the Governor-General's brother to be appointed.
47 Seated at breakfast with his staff in the palace, he heard the
Colonel say, " General Baird, I am appointed to the command of
Seringapatam, and here is the order of General Harris." The
angry General rose, turned to his staff, and said, " Come, gentlemen, we have no longer any business here." But Arthur, upon
whom rhetoric was invariably wasted, politely added, " Oh, pray
finish your breakfast."

Such was Arthur Wellesley's entry on his first responsible com-
48 mand. His fiery senior departed in a blaze of protests, wrote
angrily to the Commander-in-Chief, and received no vestige of
satisfaction. For General Harris was not disposed to vary his
selection, though he let Richard know that the appointment had
occasioned comment. But Richard could reply with perfect
49 justice that he had " never recommended my brother to you, and,
of course, never suggested how or where he should be employed."
He added, though, that Arthur was " the most proper for that
service " ; and Arthur's own reflections after thirty years con-
46 firmed his verdict—" I must say that I was the *fit person* to be
selected. I had commanded the Nizam's army during the campaign, and had given universal satisfaction. I was liked by the
natives." The choice, at any rate, was not his brother's. Arthur
had earned the prize from the Commander-in-Chief ; and if, as
he declared in later years, " it is certainly true that this command
afforded me the opportunities for distinction, and then opened
the road to fame," he owed it to himself.

THE new Governor of Seringapatam succeeded at an awkward moment, with half his subjects actuated by a strong desire to plunder the other half. Indeed, for a brief interval the army enjoyed a spell of looting, in which gold ingots changed hands for a bottle of brandy and one judicious Scot acquired the Sultan's *1* jewelled armlets at a modest price from an impulsive private. Meanwhile the Colonel sent grimly for the provost-marshal, and " by the greatest exertion, by hanging, flogging, &c., &c., in the *2* course of that day I restored order among the troops." Four of the criminals were hanged and confidence returned to the scared population, though the new commandant's embarrassments were not diminished by the hungry presence of the late Sultan's collection of live tigers. Colonel Wellesley held himself responsible for Tippoo's subjects, and urged with emphasis that " General *3* Harris ought to go away as soon as he can, as the plunderers of his army and that of the Nizam still occasion great confusion and terror among the inhabitants, and tend to obstruct our settlement of the country." He seemed to pride himself that he had " gained the confidence of the people." For his mind was busy with civilian problems ; and Richard was advised at length upon the future of Mysore. He still kept his independence though, insisting with his former clarity that Richard should not act the *rôle* of conqueror in person—" Many persons in camp . . . are exceed- *3* ingly anxious that you should come here to settle everything. I am (as I was upon a former occasion) of a different opinion." The conquered state was duly partitioned, surviving under British influence in a diminished form, while the Company shared its remaining territories with Richard's native allies. Freely consulted on the settlement, Arthur advised with all his shrewdness— " I recommend it to you not to put the Company upon the *4* Mahratta frontier. It is impossible to expect to alter the nature of the Mahrattas ; they will plunder their neighbours, be they ever so powerful. . . . It will be better to put one of the powers in dependence upon the Company on the frontier, who, if plundered, are accustomed to it, know how to bear it and to retaliate, which we do not."

Richard, the war successfully concluded, prepared to bind his sheaves. The Cabinet was promptly informed that a marquessate, or else the Garter, would be acceptable. But the fountain of honour was distant, and mails were slow. Meanwhile the conquering army offered him the insignia of St. Patrick tastefully composed of Tippoo's jewels. Richard at first declined the gift ; but the Company overbore his coy refusal, adding an offer of £100,000. Once more the Governor-General had scruples, whereupon his Board with sound commercial instincts substituted an annuity of about half the value. The news of victory reached England and elicited the thanks of Parliament ; the fountain of honour began to play, and Richard's sovereign was pleased to advance him in the peerage as Marquess Wellesley. It was his marquessate at last ; but the marquessate, alas ! was Irish. His disgust was eloquent. A letter home was signed " Mornington (not having yet received my double-gilt potato) " ; and the angry nobleman declared that " as I was confident there had been nothing Irish or pinchbeck in my conduct or in its results, I felt an equal confidence that I should find nothing Irish or pinchbeck in its reward." What now remained but for them to " dispatch the overland express ; and for God's sake bring me home, home, home ; home first, home last, home midst " ?

Remote from these impassioned outcries, Arthur sedately governed Seringapatam. He had his troubles too, though the prize-money seemed to afford a brighter prospect. Richard was promptly advised that " my share . . . will enable me to pay the money which you advanced to purchase my lieutenant-colonelcy, and that which was borrowed from Captain Stapleton on our joint bond." But Mornington refused the offer with the utmost chivalry. Arthur was still embarrassed, though. Campaigning with a staff (and without increased allowances) had proved a heavy burden ; his present post was quite as costly ; and he concluded gloomily that " I am ruined." Yet he was disinclined to leave it. For when Richard proposed that he should go home with the trophies of Seringapatam, he made an unconvincing gesture of consent, " if it is thought that I can be of any use." But his pen was busy with reasons for remaining in Mysore. Had he not " the most respectable and the best situation for me that

I could have in India " ?   Besides, the thought of his successors
filled him with alarm—Baird was impossible, and Generals were
" generally so confoundedly inefficient." So, if the choice were
left to Arthur, he should prefer to stay ; he might " render service
to the public " ; and as the year wore on, he was confirmed in
command of the Company's forces in Mysore.

He was a satrap now, immersed in local administration and
native grievances. How seriously he took the last appears from
his anxiety to be dissociated from a somewhat ill-considered order
of the Commander-in-Chief, which outraged local feelings by a
search of Tippoo's zenana for hidden treasure—" I had nothing to   8
do with it excepting that I obeyed the General's order, and . . .
I took every precaution to render the search as decent and as
little injurious to the feelings of the ladies as possible." Indeed,
before the year was out, he gave still stronger proof of his respect
for native customs. For when the redoubtable Abbé Dubois,
labouring in the Indian mission-field for a revival of native
Christianity, demanded the return of two hundred Christian
women from the late Sultan's zenana, Arthur reluctantly declined,
" although the refusal is unjust, because, the Company having   9
taken this family under its protection, it is not proper that anything should be done which can disgrace it in the eyes of the
Indian world, or which can in the most remote degree cast a shade
upon the dead, or violate the feelings of those who are alive."
The limit of his concessions was to demand a census of the
Christian women, which would enable the eager missionary to
re-marry any members of his flock whose wives had died behind
Tippoo's purdah ; the Sultan's heirs must be assured that " it is
not intended to ask for a single woman," though warned that
refusal to comply would involve a reference to Government, which
might be followed by unpleasant consequences, since " I am by
no means certain that if the matter came before Government they
would not be obliged to give up every woman of them. Justice
and all our prejudices and passions are on the side of the Chris-
tians. . . . If the Princes and the family here carry *their* prejudices so far as to refuse compliance . . . the result will then be
most probably, that Government will give orders not only that
every Christian woman, but every woman detained in the Zenana
against her consent, may be allowed to depart." How many
colonels in 1799 would have declined to liberate the Christian

captives of a defeated Moslem ? This was moderation with a
vengeance. Not that his temper was un-Christian, since he submitted an official request for a chaplain, so that the garrison of
10   Seringapatam might "have the advantage of regular divine
service, and other duties which a clergyman could perform." But
he administered an awkward province with a due sense of native
rights ; and when he authorised a lengthy code of regulations for
11   the re-establishment of native justice, he sanctioned separate
tribunals for Hindu and Moslem law (together with short forms of
pleading and a compulsory reference to arbitration before trial)
in terms that reflected equal credit on his Blackstone and his
Indian library.

The Colonel laboured to restore his province. The battered
12   city was rebuilt under a watchful eye—" This morning I was
there at half-past ten, and the people who mix up the chunam were
then coming to work, in number about 12, and there were no other
persons near the work "—and calm gradually returned to Seringapatam. But the country districts were disturbed, and the
remaining months of 1799 passed in the strenuous pursuit of an
elusive enemy. The *terrain* was uninviting, since *guerrilla* warfare
in the jungle is hardly favourable to the higher flights of strategy ;
and Arthur found few openings for Frederician manœuvre, though
the ingenuities of Saxe were not without their lesson. Such
operations (rendered acceptable to tender European consciences
by the term ' pacification '), which are the aftermath of every
conquest, normally abound in opportunities for minor misadven-
13   ture. But Arthur pacified with skill, distributing his force in
flying columns with defined objectives and orders that were invariably distinct and detailed. He took the field himself and toured
his frontier posts, enjoining a respect for native feelings on troops
engaged in punitive operations, and stigmatising exactions from
14   the villagers as a departure from " the first principle of a soldier,
which is fidelity to the trust reposed in him." He was still deep
in the absorbing task of pacification when Richard offered him a
15   new command. The unworthy Dutch were now to be relieved of
Batavia ; the operations would be light, the credit ample, and the
prize-money more than rewarding. This lucrative excursion was
proposed to Arthur, " provided you can safely be spared from
Mysore." But Mysore, alas ! had claims upon him. Madras
16   was loud with outcries at the prospect of his departure ; Lord

Clive grew almost eloquent upon the impossibility of replacing the
energetic Colonel ; and he regretfully put by the chance—" I do   *17*
not deny that I should like much to go ; but . . . my troops are
in the field "—assured consolingly by Richard that " you could   *18*
not quit Mysore at present.   Your conduct there has secured your
character and advancement for the remainder of your life, and
you may trust me for making the best use of your merits in your
future promotion."

Promotion tarried in the most provoking way ; and Richard,
who detected an affront to his own dignity in any check to Arthur,
fumed over the fate of " Colonel Wellesley not only unnoticed but   *19*
his promotion protracted so studiously, that every Intriguer here
believes it to be delayed for the express purpose of thwarting me."
A Colonel still, he took the field again in 1800 to remove the last
reproach of insurrection from his province.   One *insoumis* still
stained the bright horizon of Mysore, where Dhoondiah Waugh
hung on the northern border, wearing the slightly excessive title
of ' King of the Two Worlds.'   Arthur, more modestly concerned
with only one, resolved on " the destruction of this man," and   *17*
moved against him in force.   His correspondence—a protracted
litany of bullocks and road-making—shewed how completely he   *20*
had mastered the lesson that transport is the key of war ; and he
was disinclined to linger on the awkward problem of Dhoondiah's
precise status—" he either belongs to the Mahrattas, or he does   *21*
not : if he belongs to the Mahrattas, they ought to remove him
to a greater distance, as no state has a right to assemble on the
frontier of another such a force as he has on ours ; if he does not
belong to the Mahrattas, and he is there contrary to their inclination, they ought to allow us to drive him away, and to join with
us in so doing."   In May he started from Seringapatam ; in June   *22*
he was one hundred and fifty miles to the north in an exasperating
region where rivers rose and fell at precisely the wrong moments ;
in July he was storming forts in the Mahratta country and, these
obstacles removed, prepared for the agreeable *finale* of rounding
up his adversary.   But as the operation entered on its closing
phase, the elusive Dhoondiah was far from passive in the hands of
fate, and Indian rivers almost uniformly failed to co-operate with
Wellesley's time-table.   In August the hunt turned eastward
towards Hyderabad ; the pursuing columns converged ; and as
the net was drawn round him, Dhoondiah dashed at its meshes,

encountering Colonel Wellesley and his cavalry. They met on a September day in 1800, and Arthur enjoyed the exhilarating luxury of leading a cavalry charge. Four regiments in line behind him drove at the enemy who broke, leaving the monarch of the Two Worlds (expelled with violence from one) to explore his other kingdom. The campaign had lasted fifteen weeks—the summer weeks of 1800, in which Bonaparte, First Consul now, dazzled the Austrians by the consummate swordsmanship of Marengo. Arthur was rounding up a robber-chief ; and if his later exploits were a somewhat doubtful progeny of Eton playing-fields, the pursuit of Dhoondiah derived more obviously from hide-and-seek in Naylor's garden. For the Colonel had achieved a business-like triumph over a shadowy foe and the unmanageable facts of Indian climate and geography, leaving his brother to announce with sober exultation that " we have now proved (a perfect novelty in India) that we can hunt down the lightest footed and most rapid armies as well as we can destroy heavy troops and storm strong fortifications." The novelty and the proof were alike Arthur's.

The disturber of its peace removed, he was engaged once more in the settlement of Mysore. Land tenure, flying columns, and the incalculable proceedings of native potentates absorbed him. One night a dismissed favourite from Hyderabad poured endless grievances into his ear during the cheerful uproar of a nautch ; and as duty kept him on the advancing frontier of Richard's empire, he surveyed the new problem of the Mahratta confederacy, where Scindia threatened to achieve " that which we learn that all our policy ought to be directed to prevent, viz. one man holding and exercising nearly all, if not all, the power of the Mahratta empire." Not that he favoured the heroic sur-gery of preventive war—" one country has no right to commence a war upon another because at some time or other that other may form an alliance with its enemy. . . . The question of peace or war is not, and cannot be, only the probability of success, but must depend upon other circumstances, and in this country must depend upon the prospect of being attacked by the power with which it is proposed to go to war." Late in the year these specu-lations were sharply interrupted by an order transferring him from Mysore, and a fresh prospect opened. For Richard's war-like eye, sweeping the western skies, observed the French to be more menacing than ever. Were they not still in Egypt ?

Besides, Marengo had been fought that summer. A British force was concentrating in Ceylon with the spirited design of making trouble for the French ; and Colonel Wellesley was to lead it, though Richard was perfectly aware that " great trouble will [28] arise among the general officers in consequence of my employing you ; but I employ you because I rely on your good sense, discretion, activity, and spirit ; and I cannot find all those qualities united in any other officer in India who could take such a command." So he departed from his province, leaving behind a [29] military testament of impressive detail, which enlightened his successor on the topography of Mysore, together with exhaustive notes upon supplies, civil government, and lines of operation ; and for a time Seringapatam knew him no more.

IV

Before the year was out, the Colonel was at Trincomalee (with six cases of claret, six of Madeira, and six of port), deep in demands for vinegar, tea, sugar, beef, Staff officers, and rum. Their destination was a trifle vague. It seemed to oscillate between Mauritius and a voyage through the Red Sea to take in rear the French whom Bonaparte had left marooned in Egypt. Mauritius was their first objective ; and Richard offered the agreeable prospect that " if you should succeed in taking the Isles of France and Bourbon, I mean to appoint you to the government of them, with the chief military command annexed." Arthur was then to choose between this novel eminence and a return to his command in Mysore. Meanwhile he cross-examined likely informants on the approaches to Mauritius, the French defences, tides, landing-places, and the unfamiliar problems of amphibious war. His little army waited in Ceylon. But, the customary dislocation prevailing between the services, the fleet was nowhere to be found ; and its delays ended all hope of a surprise attack upon the islands. Early in 1801 the Colonel warned his brother of the altered prospect ; the Admiral, a distant voice in the Straits of Malacca, declined (from Penang) to attack Mauritius without an order from the King ; his muffled protest was decisive, and the expedition was diverted.

Richard's next notion, since Batavia was always tempting, was to send them to attack the Dutch in Java. But before the plan matured, orders from England changed their direction once again. Egypt was now their goal ; the waiting forces in Ceylon were destined for a protracted spring across the Indian Ocean, past Aden and the bald Arabian littoral of the Red Sea, and on to the Egyptian coast. Once there, they might reach Suez, or a desert march from Kosseir would take them into Upper Egypt. But Arthur's part in this amended programme was sadly diminished. For the angry Generals had prevailed, and Colonel Wellesley was to sail (as Colonels should) as second in command— and second in command, by an unhappy dispensation, to the most

trying of his seniors, Major-General Baird. Before this intimation reached him, he had gathered up his force, put it on board
the transports, and shipped it to Bombay *en route* for Egypt.
The blow fell while he was still at sea. Letters from the embarrassed Richard broke the news as best he might, that poten-   5
tate, in a rare mood that bordered on apology, explaining almost
timidly to Arthur that the postponed attack upon Mauritius
should be reserved as a tit-bit for him, that he could not have had
the command in Egypt without a breach of every service regulation, that Baird should prove to be a charming colleague who was
quite sure to listen to his views, that Richard would not feel
offended if Arthur chose to return to Mysore, though he should
much prefer him to remain with Baird. But Richard's prefer-
ences were Arthur's last concern. He was exceedingly annoyed.
For this supersession seemed to his angry eye to ruin his professional prospects ; and the indignant Colonel rained resentful   6
letters on his brother Henry, who sent consoling answers but
discreetly kept the correspondence from the Marquess. Here he
was—" at the top of the tree in this country " and trusted   7
equally by two Presidencies—degraded suddenly, without stated
cause, from an attractive command. The General might be his
senior ; but Richard had no right to raise his hopes, to make use
of him for the preliminary drudgery, and—least of all—to give
no public explanation of the sudden change : " I have not been
guilty of robbery or murder, and he has certainly changed his
mind ; but the world, which is always good-natured towards
those whose affairs do not exactly prosper, will not, or rather
does not, fail to suspect that both, or worse, have been the occasion
of my being banished, like General Kray, to my estate in Hun-
gary." This was a novel tone for Arthur, since he grew almost
shrill at the thought of the affront, of all his wasted efforts in
Ceylon, of his subordinates misled into an unpleasant trip with
Baird, of his own career in danger.

     That was a novel thought. Arthur—the patient, rather list-
less Arthur—had a career. He had not seemed to think so in the
bleak discomfort of his Dutch campaign six years before, when
his mind ran mainly upon prospects of leave. Had he not done
his best on his return to Dublin to become something in the
Irish Revenue ? And even in India he seemed almost indifferent
as he balanced the prospects of a return to Europe against an

Indian career—" I don't know whether I may not as well remain
here as go to any other place." His tone had mounted slightly,
when he announced his preference for staying at Seringapatam ;
and now the angry Colonel, raging round Bombay in an unen-
viable mood, was anything but indifferent to his prospects.

His first impulse was to stay in India, to sulk anywhere in
preference to serving under Baird. Before the month was out,
however, his mood changed. News came in March that Abercromby was already striking at Egypt from the north ; and if
the Red Sea expedition was to serve any purpose, it must move
at once. Baird had not yet arrived, and Arthur resolved to sail
immediately and make a start in Upper Egypt—" my former
letters will have shown you how much this will annoy me ; but
I have never had much value for the public spirit of any man who
does not sacrifice his private views and convenience, when it is
necessary." This was more soldierly. Not that Arthur was
unconscious of his own virtue, since he wrote later of his " laudable
and highly disagreeable intention." But the gesture was frustrated ; for he was promptly taken ill. His illness was anything
but diplomatic, since he was assailed after a touch of fever by
an unpleasing malady termed the Malabar itch. The drastic
therapeutics of Bombay plunged the sufferer into nitrous baths,
which positively burned his towels ; and as his cure progressed,
the expedition sailed with Baird. The Colonel, partly reconciled
by an unusual display of manners on the part of his chief, col-
laborated loyally with a voluminous memorandum on Egyptian
warfare ; he had been studying local politics, the desert, and the
Nile and gave Baird the benefit of his researches. But Egypt in
1801 was not his destiny. Richard restored him to the command
in Mysore, and he returned with evident relief to Seringapatam.
The incident almost parted the brothers. For Arthur's "My
dear Mornington " cooled instantly to " My Lord," reverted
momentarily to " My dear Mornington," and was succeeded by
an awful silence. The brothers ceased to correspond ; and, this
breach apart, the *imbroglio* of the Egyptian command revealed
the interesting fact that Arthur had ambitions.

V

THAT summer he returned with sober elation to his province. The ₁
voyage south was uneventful ; but once ashore the convalescent
travelled at breakneck speed, lending interest to the long ride
up-country by leaving his little escort far behind, and remarking
cheerfully to a young captain, " If we are taken prisoners, I shall ₂
be hanged as being brother to the Governor-General, and you will
be hanged for being found in bad company." A day was spent
en route in courtesies to a native ruler, of which Arthur's Persian
stood the strain admirably, even rising to corrections of the Com- ₃
pany's interpreter. Then he resumed the dash to Seringapatam.
On the road they heard of a promotion of Colonels to be Major-
General ; he brightened at the news and called for an Army List ;
but when he found that he was not included, he wistfully exclaimed, " My highest ambition is to be a Major-General in His ₄
Majesty's service."

A Colonel still, he entered on his little kingdom once again,
assured by a consoling friend that honour and wealth awaited
him at Seringapatam and by Henry that he was " still at the top ₅
of the tree as to character . . . I have never heard any man so
highly spoken of, nor do I know any person so generally looked
up to. Your campaign against Dhoondiah . . .'' His lot was
enviable enough, though his grievances still haunted him and he
hinted darkly to Henry that " I have some thoughts of going ₆
home in the next winter if I don't see some prospect of being
actively employed in India." But this was little more than a
brotherly *boutade*, since he lived in a happy whirl of local administration and cheerful company. They sat down eight or ten to
dinner in the old palace, the Colonel opposite his saddle of mutton.
He ate well, though his recipe for health in India was " to live ₇
moderately, to drink little or no wine, to use exercise, to keep the
mind employed, and, if possible, to keep in good humour with
the world. The last is the most difficult, for, as you have often
observed, there is scarcely a good-tempered man in India."
Arthur was one of them, however ; for roast mutton was his chief

8   indulgence. He rarely took more than four or five glasses beyond
his pint of claret ; and such abstinence seemed almost total in
9   an age when military manners prescribed officially a monthly
ration of fifteen bottles of Madeira as the bare limit of necessity,
with such extras as beer and spirits and water by way of luxuries.
Not that the abstemious Colonel was a gloomy host. For he was
always gay at his own table, talking in his quick way of his past
successes in the field (a meagre theme for Wellesley in 1801), of
intrusive seniors—" we want no Major-Generals in Mysore "—
and of commissariat iniquities, which moved him to inform the
mess one day that if he ever commanded an army of his own,
he should not hesitate to hang a commissary. So the lively
Colonel talked the afternoons away over his mutton and claret at
10   Seringapatam. He was just thirty-two, a little grey already about
the temples ; but that was a mere legacy of fever, since his
brown hair (he wore it cropped and disapproved of powder on
hygienic grounds) still crowned a young man's face. Sometimes he got a game of billiards ; and occasionally they went
after antelope with Tippoo's hunting leopards, the Colonel
following the hunt in his own howdah. They had feminine
society as well. For wives were not excluded ; and Arthur
shewed a distinct partiality for wives. A brother-officer
11   recalled him as the wearer of " a very susceptible heart, particularly towards, I am sorry to say, married ladies." A
prudish aide-de-camp was shocked ; an interfering lady interfered ; but if eyes were bright and husbands negligent, who
could blame the Colonel ? He might, perhaps, have thought
of Kitty Pakenham. But Kitty Pakenham was ten thousand
miles away.

With these agreeable mitigations he laboured at his oar,
writing innumerable letters about public works and army stores
10   and the illimitable theme of transport bullocks, or taking the
garrison's salute after an early morning parade in a cocked-hat,
long coat, white pantaloons that ended in Hessians and spurs,
and an impressive sabre with a big silver hilt. His official life
from ten to four was mainly filled with a supremely distasteful
12   enquiry into the malversation of large quantities of stores. It
ended, after dragging him through " scenes of villainy which would
disgrace the Newgate Calendar," in stern sentences upon the
guilty officers. But though the Colonel's duty was performed

down to its most unpleasant particular, he was still capable of
pity, writing to the Governor of Madras :

> " I take the liberty of addressing your Lordship in favour of an   13
> old man, (the late) Lieutenant-Colonel ——, whom I have lately
> been the means of convicting of very serious crimes before a general
> court-martial ; and I do so, not from any doubt that I entertain of
> the reality of his guilt, but from a conviction of his former good
> conduct as an officer, and of the extreme poverty and distress to
> which he has been reduced in consequence of the sentence of the
> general court-martial. I understand that when he will have paid
> the Company the sums which are due to them in consequence of
> that sentence, he will be left entirely destitute ; and, without
> attempting to justify any part of his conduct, I may safely say that
> he becomes an object of charity.
> " Allow me, therefore, to entreat your Lordship to give him some
> small pension to enable him to support himself, or that you will
> recommend him for some provision to the Court of Directors on
> account of his long services and his present reduced situation."

Few causes have been better pleaded.   For Arthur, incapable of
false sentiment, was genuinely moved to pity.

His other interests survived.   He resumed the never-ending
struggle to secure respect for native rights and customs, though
he had few illusions as to native virtues, writing acidly that
" every native who gets a paper signed by the name of a person   14
having any power makes a bad use of it and generally contrives by
its means to extort something to which he has no right."   But he   15
shielded villagers from requisitions ; insisted on behalf of Tippoo's
zenana that " the greatest attention may be paid to their prejudices and customs. . . . Keep everybody at a distance from
them, and prevent all intrusion upon them, which can be occasioned only by a desire to gratify a vain curiosity " ; and even
promulgated a sentence on an army surgeon for maltreating
natives with the stern comment that the prisoner " ought to have
known that he is a part of a body of troops placed in this country
to protect the inhabitants, and not to oppress them."   He had
little taste for the strong hand—" I long for the return of the civil   16
government.   Although a soldier myself, I am not an advocate
for placing extensive civil powers in the hands of soldiers merely
because they are of the military profession, and I have always
opposed the idea excepting in cases of necessity."   His corre-

17 spondence, though, was not uniformly official. A colleague was assured that " I shall send to Mrs. Stevenson in two days some cabbage and celery plants, and in about a week her rose-trees."

18 He was a gardener himself, sent cuttings to his friends, and quite early in his residence at Seringapatam made judicious use of

19 creepers on unsightly walls. Sometimes he enclosed drawings of native monuments with notes on Jain theology ; and once the Governor of Bombay received from Arthur a letter that was positively arch. A young lady, it seems, had sent him a portrait

20 of himself ; this tribute elicited the grim comment that " the two or three glances which you mention made very little impression upon the fair artist, as the picture is as like anybody else as it is to the person for whom it is intended." This was ungrateful. But the Colonel's chivalry was equal to the occasion, since he proposed to write to her himself, " to tell her that I am glad to find that those few glances made an impression upon her memory so exceedingly favourable ; and I have employed a gentleman here to draw the picture of a damsel in the character of a shepherdess, which I shall also present as the effect of the impression made upon my memory by the fair artist." Here was the Colonel in a graceful mood.

21 He had other moods as well. An awful silence still prevailed between him and Richard, and he seemed to view with equanimity his brother's possible recall to England in 1802. His tone with Baird was friendly ; the rough General seemed to have won him in Bombay, and Arthur wrote him all the news of India to brighten his campaign in Egypt. He took the field himself quite soon in order to dispose of an insurgent rajah in the west. This time,

22 early in 1802, he undertook the complexities of forest warfare ; and the campaign in Bullum was a neat and punctual operation by three converging columns. The leading rebel was run to earth and hanged in pursuance of Arthur's grim determination on " *the suspension* of the Rajah " ; and the whole salutary process was concluded in three weeks. The expedition appeared to leave him with few illusions on the subject of British authority in India, since he wrote that year on the necessity of military power

23 " for a government which exists only by the sword." But he rarely generalised ; the news from Europe elicited little beyond gruff disapproval of Addington's limp pacificism—" There is too

24 much moderation and candour for these bad times. . . . I see

that they have submitted to abuse from the opposition, and
instead of retorting it according to the good old custom, they have
deprecated it "—and he was soon back at Seringapatam, lost
in the familiar jungle of timber contracts, errant subordinates
on whom he sometimes turned a slightly indulgent eye—" He
has a wife and family (who in my eyes cover a multitude   25
of sins, &c.) "—and mess disputes that drew from him the sage
opinion that " a drunken quarrel is very bad, and is always   26
to be lamented, but probably the less it is inquired into the
better." A small godson engaged him, receiving kisses in
the postscript of official letters ; and Arthur, with a sense of   27
duty rare among god-parents, was at pains to have his name-
sake submitted to the mysteries of vaccination for the cowpox.
He had lighter interests too. For that year the Colonel's
mess was swept, if one may judge from Arthur's bills, by a
passion for theatricals ; and his purchases of plays appear
among dozens of Madeira, casks of ale, lamp-glasses, and
potatoes. Some remain enigmatic ; for his acquisition of " 1   28
Book plays " and " 8 plays " reveal little of the station's taste
in drama. But Schiller's *Robbers* shewed them in a tragic
mood ; though a sprightlier taste appeared in his purchase of
Sheridan (though no particular play was specified), no less than
of Davies' *Plays written for a Private Theatre.* The last, published
in 1786, had just attained the degree of staleness appropriate to
amateur performance, though no record survives to shew whether
Arthur played *General Blunder, M.P.,* in *News the Malady.*
The same account records his literary diversions, which consisted of a complete set of *The Novelist's Magazine* and a French
novel. Duty was tempered by these mild alleviations. Promotion came at last ; gazetted in April, 1802, the news reached
him in December ; and the world heard at length of Major-
General Wellesley, commanding the troops in Mysore, Malabar,
and Canara.

Whilst Arthur loyally hewed regimental wood and drew
provincial water, Richard—a Marquess now—surveyed imperial
horizons. The little autocrat was more august than ever. Seated
majestically in the stately replica of Kedleston that rose at his
command (to exasperate his parsimonious Directors with its
" style of Asiatic pomp and display " and to direct the juvenile   29
attention of a successor to India, implanting " the ambition, from

an early age, to pass from a Kedleston in Derbyshire to a Kedleston in Bengal "), Lord Wellesley held the gorgeous East in fee with peculiar enjoyment of the fact that it was gorgeous. " The drums and banners, the turbans and the flowing robes, the spears, the silver maces, the elephants with their canopies of State " entered his splendid repertory, as he " elevated " (in a successor's envious phrase) " the spectacular to the level of an exact science." His taste for grandeur found appropriate expression in an expanding Body Guard which, fifty strong at his accession, rose to two hundred in a year or so, mounted in two years more to three hundred men and two guns, and twelve months later reached the impressive total of four hundred men, two guns, and a band. Small wonder that Cornwallis was a little staggered on his arrival to succeed this Cæsar ; the old soldier lost himself in endless corridors, was startled by Richard's innumerable sentries—" If I show my head outside a door, a fellow with a musket and fixed bayonet presents himself before me "—and the embarrassed veteran ended by ordering this galaxy of martial state back to the guard-room. Not that Richard's splendour was all for show. It was easy to ridicule " the sultanised Englishman " ; but even Mr. Hickey, always a trifle fretful, could not withhold a tribute to " the pompous though undoubtedly able little Knight of St. Patrick." For he transformed " a little patchwork of crimson spots on the map of the Indian Continent " into an Indian empire. This process was observed with growing horror by an ungrateful Company. Leadenhall Street breathed its concern into the ear of Westminster ; the Board of Control transmitted softened versions to the Governor-General ; and that dignitary, resolved that India should be " ruled from a palace, not from a counting-house ; with the ideas of a Prince, not with those of a retail-dealer in muslins and indigo," and mounting

> " the high horse he loved so well to ride,"

became increasingly impatient of restraints. His resignations grew in frequency, since he was by nature ill-adapted to a system of government based rather on the principles of ventriloquism than upon those of Montesquieu ; and even Arthur, scarcely a sympathetic witness now, was moved to resentment of " the corrupt and vulgar interference of Leadenhall Street in the operations of his government." He felt for Arthur too, when an ill-

timed economy curtailed his allowances for the Mysore command ;
for official disregard of Arthur's claims seemed to the angry
Richard to " have offered me the most direct, marked and dis- *38*
quieting personal indignity." Their paths converged again,
since he had work for Arthur now.

The last stage in Lord Wellesley's strenuous conversion of
" a British Empire *in* India " into " the Empire *of* India " was *39*
the extension of British influence to the vast territories of the
Mahratta confederacy. As usual, action was preceded by a
preliminary phase of diplomacy. Arthur was not consulted
upon this stage, since the brothers' intimacy was still interrupted
by their Egyptian misunderstanding. But Richard's finger,
vigorously thrust into the rich compound of Mahratta jealousies,
drew out the unquestionable plum of a treaty with the Peshwah, *40*
that dignitary engaging to submit to British influence in exchange
for restoration to his throne. Arthur was promptly notified that *41*
his force in Mysore would be required to take the necessary action.
The order was not unexpected, since he had composed a paper in
the previous year on the subject of operations against the Mahrattas ; and he plunged with gusto into his customary prepara- *42*
tions. Bullocks and rice became the burden of his official correspondence, because " if I had rice and bullocks I had men, and if *43*
I had men I knew I could beat the enemy." His strategy was
simple :

> " It is obvious that the intentions of the British government *44*
> regarding the affairs of the Mahratta empire cannot be carried into
> execution unless Holkar's army is either defeated or dissipated. The
> object of the campaign must therefore be to bring him to a general
> action at as early a period as possible. . . . If it be our intent to
> bring Holkar to a general action, it is his to avoid it ; and it may be
> depended upon that he will avoid it as long as possible.
>
> " His army is light, and chiefly composed of cavalry. The whole
> composition of our armies is heavy . . . Holkar, therefore, will have
> not only the inclination but the means of avoiding the result which,
> I take it for granted, can alone bring the war to a conclusion. . . .
> Therefore I conclude that, after a certain period for which our stock
> of provisions will have been provided, we shall be obliged to return
> to our own country for a fresh supply.
>
> " There are but two modes of carrying on this war by which we
> may avoid this disagreeable result : one is to place the seat of it in
> a country . . . near our own resources . . . ; the other is to keep

up our communication with our own country, whatever may be the distance from it of the seat of war. In regard to the first, viz., to command the seat of war, I have to observe that we shall no more be able to do that than we shall be able to command its operations. . . .

" The second mode then is that alone by which we can succeed. By this mode we shall always supply ourselves ; the enemy may protract his defeat, but sooner or later it must happen."

This was clear-eyed. It was to be a commissariat war ; and, omitting all heroics, General Wellesley waded ankle-deep in questions of supply. He called for beef ; he called for sheep ; he called for forage ; he was meticulous upon the packing of his provisions, specifying gunny bags for his rice, kegs for his salt beef, and casks " with iron hoops of four gallons each " for his arrack. Depots were stocked in northern Mysore adjacent to the Mahratta border ; and though operating from the south, he conceived the unusual project of an advanced base somewhere along the western coast, to which he could transfer his communications on reaching the region of Poona—" by this arrangement we should carry on the war at Poonah . . . with the resources of Bombay ; and we should shorten our line of communication many hundred miles." (The same manœuvre was to shift a later army's base from Lisbon to the north coast of Spain, as they worked northwards into the Pyrenees.) For months he lived in an ecstasy of preparation ; and though the breach with Richard was not yet bridged by a single letter, Arthur's feelings were a shade kinder now, since he urged him indirectly to come south to Madras on the ground that " nothing but Lord Wellesley's presence can keep the government of Madras in the direct line." The army moved in February, 1803 ; in March they crossed the border ; and at the moment of invading Mahratta territory Arthur broke the long silence with a letter to the Governor-General (though he was still " My Lord "), expressing some uncertainty as to his own future in Mysore. Richard responded with a whole-hearted testimonial to " his approved talents, firmness, temper, and integrity," concluding with a vigorous insistence on his retention in the Mysore command. These powers at peace once more, the war proceeded smoothly. The long march was almost uneventful, and in April General Wellesley rode into Poona after a final dash of sixty miles with four hundred cavalry.

His dealings with the Mahrattas were almost uniformly satisfactory, and in the view of one highly competent observer this
easy progress had been largely due " to the admiration which the   *50*
Mahratta chiefs entertain of that officer's military character, and
the firm reliance which the inhabitants place on his justice and
protection."

With the Peshwah safely restored to his throne at Poona, the
first stage of the war was over.   Richard was promptly notified
of the success in terms which made it plain that Arthur approved   *51*
his policy and would deal faithfully with the " croaking " of his
brother's critics ; the family alliance was almost reconstituted
now, the General resenting with exemplary warmth the latest
slight upon the Governor-General—" the letter from the Court   *52*
of Directors to the Governor of Fort St. George is shocking.   I
hope that you do not propose to stay in India longer than the
end of this year.   Such masters do not deserve your services."
At first it seemed unlikely that there would be any further need
of military operations.   Mahratta bands were still at large in the
northern provinces, and for these his strategy was shrewd and
practical :

> " Press him with one or more corps capable of moving with   *53*
> tolerable celerity. . . . The effect produced by this mode of
> operation is to oblige him to move constantly and with great celerity.
> . . . He cannot venture to stop to plunder the country, and he does
> comparatively but little mischief, at all events ; the subsistence of
> his army becomes difficult and precarious ; the horsemen become
> dissatisfied ; they perceive that their situation is hopeless, and they
> desert in numbers daily ; and the freebooter ends by having with
> him only a few adherents, and he is reduced to such a state as to be
> liable to be taken by any small body of country horse."

But he wrote cheerfully of his " great hopes . . . that the   *54*
combination of the northern Chiefs will end in nothing. . . .
I think that, although there will be much bad temper and many
threats, there will be no hostility."   He made his preparations,
though, his mind running on pontoons as a means of obtaining
superior mobility by crossing rivers that remained impassable for
native armies.   His correspondence soon abounded in five-inch   *55*
cables, anchors, graplins, and measurements of boats ; and as
the work advanced, he discovered an increasing disrespect for
native allies who " think that when once they have put the seal   *56*

to a treaty with us, they have nothing to do but to amuse themselves and sleep." (In a long experience of allies Arthur was generally disappointed.) The summer months of 1803 passed slowly by ; and he was still detained in Poona by an endless web of Mahratta diplomacy. He was not altogether easy, since he seemed to have his doubts of Richard's eternal forward policy—

57 " One bad consequence of these subsidiary treaties is, that they entirely annihilate the military power of the governments with which we contract them. . . . In my opinion we ought to withdraw from Poonah, and leave some chance that the principal chiefs may have the power of the state in their hands ; . . . I would preserve the existence of the state ; and guide its actions by the weight of British influence." The General was disinclined to war, if war could be avoided. He could still write in June, as interminable *pourparlers* proceeded with the Mahratta chiefs,

58 that " my object is the preservation of peace " ; in July he was a shade more sceptical—" If there be any truth in a Mahratta

59 durbar, we shall have peace." Taking a hand himself in the negotiations (Richard presently conferred full powers on him in the most complimentary terms), he bluntly challenged Bhonsla and Scindia to withdraw their forces, still clinging gallantly to

60 his conviction that peace was " very probable." But he wisely fixed no date for the expiry of his ultimatum from a practical

61 desire " to keep in my own breast the period at which hostilities will be commenced ; by which advantage it becomes more probable that I shall strike the first blow, if I should find hostile operations to be necessary." Then, as the last skein of procrastination wound slowly off the reel, he grimly informed his incorrigible correspondents in the first week of August that he had offered

62 " peace on terms of equality, and honorable to all parties : you have chosen war, and are responsible for all consequences."

63   His first movement was a swift attack on Ahmednuggur. The place was stormed with a precision which elicited the rueful compliment that " these English are a strange people and their General a wonderful man. They came here in the morning, looked at the pettah-wall, walked over it, killed all the garrison, and returned to breakfast." This capture deftly covered Poona from the Mahrattas. Then he moved north to find them, crossing the Godavery in full flood by means of his precious basket boats.

64 His plan was simple—" I do not expect that we shall be able to

bring the enemy to an action, but we must try to keep him in movement, and tire him out." He was at peace with Richard now, writing that month to " My dear Mornington " once more ;   65
and his main preoccupations consisted of dealings with the natives, in which he lived up to an exacting standard (" If we   66
lose our character for truth and good faith, we shall have but little to stand upon in this country "), and the eternal problem of military hygiene—" I consider nothing in this country so valuable   67
as the life and health of the British soldier." After an interlude of countermarching to the east and back again, he moved north and stumbled on his enemy, a day earlier and in considerably greater force than he anticipated, at Assaye.

The *rencontre* on September 23 was unexpected, since his intelligence was far from perfect. Nearly half his force had been   68
detached to follow by another route, and the men with him had marched twenty miles that morning. The odds were serious, since the enemy had 40,000 men in line to his own 7,000 ; and the situation was uninviting, as they were strongly posted in the angle formed by two rivers. Plainly he must attack at once, since his little force was manifestly unequal to sustaining the weight of an attack by an enemy of six times their numbers. Success depended on a double gamble. If the enemy would have the courtesy to keep reasonably still, he might cross their front and reach their flank ; once there, if only they would oblige by still continuing to face in the same direction, he might roll them up. His flank march across their front was uninterrupted, and the first perilous throw succeeded. Guessing at a ford, he got his force across one river, and drew it up with 40,000 men in front and two rivers behind. This seemed a trifle reckless, although the gamble might succeed, if an unwieldy enemy continued to expose an unprotected flank to his impending blow. But the enemy, less unwieldy than Wellesley had hoped, changed front with admirable precision and faced his little force in its perilous peninsula. Then his attack was launched, and the result was " one of the most   69
furious battles that has ever been fought in this country." With little scope for tactics, he handled the attacking units well, led infantry charges against guns, and had two horses killed under him. The Mahrattas were well drilled and amply provided with artillery ; they broke at last, however, leaving Wellesley in possession of the ground and ninety-eight of their guns. But he

was almost spent ; and that night Wellesley sat motionless among the casualties, his head between his knees. His gay strategy—
70 "Dash at the first fellows that make their appearance, and the campaign will be ours "—was justified, but at a singularly heavy price. Richard received the news with stately raptures. He had
71 observed their march " with much solicitude for the success of our operations on public grounds, and with every additional anxiety, which affection could inspire " ; and now the watcher had been gratified in " all my affection and all the pride of my blood." He had foreseen it all—" It was not more than was expected from you "—and a majestic hand waved Arthur forward to his niche in a blaze of Ciceronian commendation. Arthur was melted visibly ; and, until lately satisfied with a bare " Believe me, &c.," he now
72 became ever Richard's most affectionately. Meanwhile, the army bound its wounds, assisted by a dozen of the General's own
73 Madeira for every tent of casualties, and moved off in pursuit. Two months of marching, to an accompaniment of dilatory
74 negotiations (and a touch of fever for the General), ended in a second encounter with the Mahrattas at Argaum on November 29. Unlike Assaye, this was premeditated ; and the affair pro-
75 ceeded with perfect regularity, though Arthur personally checked a panic of his native infantry. He wheeled his cavalry into position, riding sedately at their head, and presided calmly over an inexpensive victory. The last stage of the war was the storm of Bhonsla's fortress of Gawilghur. Arthur directed the attack
76 against both faces of the place, riding a daily circuit of fifty miles. It duly fell ; and the year ended with a pair of peace-treaties which satisfied even Richard's exacting notions of conquest, and left him
77 in ecstasies over " a brilliant point in the history of this country, and a noble termination of your military glory."

By comparison, the next year was almost restful. Indeed,
78 after three years in tents the General began to need a rest ; for early in 1804 he found himself " much annoyed by the lumbago." But his repose was interrupted by a minor operation, in which he moved five regiments sixty miles in thirty hours and wrote
79 exultantly that " we now begin to beat the Mahrattas by the celerity of our movements." Had he not once insisted to a
80 colleague that " time is everything in military operations " ? Then he returned to Poona and received a presentation from his officers. The triumph continued at Bombay, where he rode

through crowded streets, received addresses, made sedate replies, dined at the theatre (confronted by " an elegant transparency " of his own coat of arms), and " had much conversation with mercantile gentlemen there." Even his correspondence took a gentler turn ; a Colonel's lady in Bombay was asked to procure

" some pickled oysters, and I wish you to prepare some and send *82* them here. You must lose no time, as I understand that the oysters at Bombay become best when the rains commence.

" Don't send them by Coleman, as he will eat more than his share before he reaches camp ; nor by any of your great eaters, or I shall get none of them. . . .

" Tell Colonel Gordon that I see that all the offices of subordinate Collector in Malabar are filled up, and that his brother-in-law has no chance. But as a recommendation from a *great Man* is always a good thing I write this day to Lord Wm. Bentinck to recommend Captain Watson to him."

Arthur, it seems—unlike the stately Richard—could positively jest about his greatness. His next letter was no less familiar, since it announced with relish that

" the oysters were excellent ; everybody likes them. . . . *83*

" As for your susceptible youths, I consider three days full enough for them at Bombay, particularly when I want them elsewhere. But whenever you have a mind to detain one of my champions as you call them, you have my permission to do so, and I shall not be the ' Deaf Adder ' of the reasons which you will give for detaining them, provided that you don't allow them to marry. After that they would not answer my purpose."

This was no grim disciplinarian. The sprightly General even pressed his correspondent to visit them in camp :

" We get on well, but we want you to enliven us. Allow me to prevail upon you. If you'll come I'll go and meet you with my Servts. at the top of the Ghaut, so that you will only have 24 miles to travel in palanqueen.

" There is excellent galloping ground in the neighbourhood of camp, and the floor of my tent is in a fine state for dancing and the fiddlers of the Dragoons and 78th and Bagpipes of the 74th play delightfully."

Here was a charming mood. His proximity to Bombay enabled him to replenish his library as well ; and purchases of books appear among sword-belts, expensive saddlery, pale ale, York hams, and Gloucester cheeses. His taste for drama still prevailed ; for Bell's Shakespeare (in nineteen volumes) and the *British Theatre* (in thirty-four) entered his library that year. Dow's *History of Hindostan* (to replace, perhaps, a missing copy, since he had brought out a set from England), together with a work on Egypt followed the line of his earlier reading, though the purchase of Gentz's survey of *The State of Europe before and after the French Revolution* showed plainly that his thoughts were turning homeward. A sheaf of pamphlets—*Brief Answer . . , Cursory Remarks . . , Substance of a Speech . . , Report of the Cause . .* —kept him abreast of current affairs. He bought some military books—two volumes of French tactics, Smirke's *Review of a Battalion of Infantry,* and Porter's *Military Instructions,* to say nothing of a *Summary Account and Military Character of the several European Armies that have been engaged during the late War.* For Arthur was beginning to envisage other theatres of war than Mysore and other enemies than contumacious rajahs. This work (which chilled its latest reader with the depressing observation that "an English general, who returns from India, is like an Admiral, who has been navigating the Lake of Geneva ") surveyed the European armies. French methods were well summarised ; the Austrians were sternly judged ; and no reader could retain illusions as to the military efficiency of Spain after reading its choleric verdict—"a Spanish regiment . . . looks like an assemblage of beggars. . . . During a siege, they have been known to destroy the trenches . . . in order to steal the earth bags, and sell them for a few pence." A terrifying appendix warned readers of the *Parallel of the Policy, Power, and Means of the Ancient Romans and Modern French ; shewing the real Designs of the latter against the Independence of Europe ; particularly of Great Britain and Ireland.*

Not that Arthur's reading was exclusively professional. For at the same time he bought the *Sporting Magazine* for 1802–3, together with some odd numbers of the *Universal Magazine.* His latest acquisitions—dramatic, military, and miscellaneous—were added to the General's little library ; and one work, a shade more unexpected than the rest, appeared in his bookseller's account.

8

He positively bought a copy of Dr. Priestley's *Socrates and Jesus Compared*, and Arthur Wellesley faced that slightly condescending examination of the enlightened pagan. But his purchases were not invariably literary in design or male in destination. For " 1 Brilliant hoop Ring and 2 pearl guards to ditto, 150 Rs." reveal a gentler mood. He was not easy, though, contemplating an early return to Europe and pressing Richard to resign before an ungrateful Company dismissed him. But Lord Wellesley, fairly launched on his career of conquest, was disinclined to stop. Fresh provinces beckoned him on to further wars ; and Arthur wrote ruefully that " the system of moderation and conciliation by which, whether it be right or wrong, I made the treaties of peace . . . is now given up," His own principles were plain :

> " I would sacrifice Gwalior, or every frontier of India, ten times over, in order to preserve our credit for scrupulous good faith, and the advantages and honor we gained by the late war and the peace ; and we must not fritter them away in arguments, drawn from over-strained principles of the laws of nations, which are not understood in this country. What brought me through many difficulties in the war, and the negociations for peace ? The British good faith, and nothing else."

Small wonder that the questionable ingenuities of Richard's later diplomatic manner left him " dispirited and disgusted . . . beyond measure." War was resumed, with Arthur as a gloomy commentator. He watched the operations from a distance ; but this time there were few victories, and the epitaph of the campaign was written in his grim comment that he did not " think that the Commander-in-Chief and I have carried on war so well by our deputies as we did ourselves." For Lake and Wellesley had made 1803 glorious by Laswaree and Assaye ; but Monson's retreat and Lake's failure at Bhurtpore clouded 1804.

Arthur was growing restless now. Had he not " served as long in India as any man ought, who can serve any where else ? " There was " a prospect of service in Europe, in which I should be more likely to get forward." (This seemed a trifle selfish ; but his distaste for Richard's policy hardly increased the hold of India upon him.) Besides, his rheumatism would not be improved by another rainy season under canvas. The course of operations in 1804 rendered him almost superfluous ; and after setting his

administrative house in order, he withdrew to Calcutta, where he
91   sat to Home for a head-and-shoulders at the modest price of 500
rupees, and assisted the Governor-General with a steady stream
of memoranda, including a lengthy vindication of the earlier
92   phases of his Mahratta policy. Calcutta had its softer side as
well, attested by the purchase of a pearl necklace with some
93   bracelets and a " silk worked shawl." But Monson's " retreat,
defeats, disgraces, and disasters " (Arthur was not indulgent to
these " woful examples of the risk to be incurred by advancing
too far without competent supplies ") recalled him to the south
94   again, more convinced than ever that " against the Mahrattas in
particular, but against all enemies, we should take care to be sure
of plenty of provisions." Before the year was out, he was back at
Seringapatam. The atmosphere was peaceful now ; and the
95   Colonel's lady from Bombay was informed of his " great dinners
daily " and a sufficiency of dances, together with the General's
gallant wishes for her return to Bombay " in high health and
beauty to be again its ornament."
96   He was quite clear about his destination now—" I certainly
do not propose to spend my life in the Deccan ; and I should not
think it necessary, in any event, to stay there one moment longer
than the Governor-General should stay in India." The clouds
were gathering round Richard—some foreshadowing resignation,
others shaped perilously like dismissal ; and Arthur foresaw " a
variety of subjects in discussion, relating to this country, upon
which some verbal explanation is absolutely necessary. I conceive, therefore, that in determining not to go into the Deccan,
and to sail by the first opportunity for England, I consult the
public interests not less than I do my own private convenience
and wishes." India, he felt, had been a hard mistress, from whose
penurious Directors he " had never received any thing but injury.
. . . I am not very ambitious ; and I acknowledge that I have
never been very sanguine in my expectations that military services
in India would be considered in the scale in which are considered
similar services in other parts of the world. But I might have
expected to be placed on the Staff in India. . . ." This was a
standing grievance with him. Besides, British India was not in
danger—had it been, he " should not hesitate a moment about
staying, even for years "—and he concluded almost angrily that
" these men or the public have no right to ask me to stay in India,

merely because my presence in a particular quarter may be
attended with convenience." His plans were definite in the first   *97*
days of 1805 ; he should resign, if quiet continued on the northern
borders of Mysore. Richard consented ; and the General promptly
notified the authorities. A Madras official was advised of his
desire to secure a passage home—" I am not very particular about   *98*
accommodation, and I would take any rather than lose the opportunity . . . and I don't care a great deal about the price. I
should prefer, however, either half a round house or the starboard
side of a quiet cabin ; and I don't much care who the captain is,
or what the ship." This was almost precipitate. But his departure was delayed by endless complications—official business to   *99*
be wound up, his staff to be provided for, portraits distributed to
friends, and the safe bestowal of two elephants presented to the
departing traveller by a devoted rajah at the last moment. Before he started, he found time for an unusual act of kindness.
Years before, when he defeated Dhoondiah, the dead man's son
was captured ; Arthur had taken the boy under his own protection ; and on leaving India he settled a sum of money on him,   *100*
taking steps at the same time to assure his future. Whilst he
was waiting at Madras (and very far from well), he received a
pleasant piece of news which he passed on to Richard :

> " A fleet arrived from England this morning ; it sailed on the   *101*
> 4th of Septr. I enclose a paper of the 3^d. containing an extract of
> the Gazette of the 1st Septr. by which it appears that General Lake
> is made Lord Lake of Delhi and Laswaree, and I a Knight of the
> Bath. I have heard no other news, excepting that Captain Fitz-
> gerald of the 34th informed me that the fleet had spoken a Ship
> which left England the 27th Sept^r., the Captain of which ship
> informed them that there was every probability of war between
> France and the Northern Powers. He did not recollect the name of
> the ship, or of the Captain, or where he saw the Ship."

So the world heard for the first time of Sir Arthur Wellesley,
though the recipient's sense of his new honour appeared to be
almost effaced by his contempt for Captain Fitzgerald's inexacti-
tude of mind. A passenger who went on board ten days later to   *102*
find his own luggage informed Sir Arthur that there was a box
" kicking about the *Lord Keith*," which contained his insignia.
Then he prepared to start for home. His final purchases com-

prised a selection of reading-matter for the voyage ; and it is pleasant to observe a marked deterioration in the severity of Sir Arthur's tastes. Nine years before the Colonel had acquired a library which would not have disgraced a public institution. But Major-Generals need relaxation, and his choice of books in 1805 would have given entire satisfaction to a girls' school. *Love at First Sight* (in five volumes) was matched by *Lessons for Lovers* (in two) ; his fancy wandered from *Illicit Love* to *Filial Indiscretion or the Female Chevalier.* His bookseller supplied him with a dazzling array of the most brilliant popular successes in recent fiction, which appeared (if their titles could be trusted) to concentrate upon family complications. For the eager traveller was regaled with four volumes of *The Rival Mothers* and three of *The Supposed Daughter*, to say nothing of *The Disappointed Heir* and the wider horizons suggested by *Fashionable Involvements* and *The Fairy of Misfortunes.* In all, he bought twenty-six novels by authors ranging from Madame de Genlis to Mrs. Gunning. Almost the sole exception to his prevailing thirst for fiction was *Beauties of the Modern Dramatists*, a purchase which appeared to shew that his theatrical interests survived exile from the dramatic circle in Seringapatam. Nor was an earlier allegiance overlooked in his acquisition of Crébillon's *Letters of Madame de Pompadour.* The spirit of Crébillon almost seemed to haunt another entry in the same account, which debited Sir Arthur, homeward-bound, with ten pairs of ladies' shoes—small gifts of Oriental elegance for Western wearers.

The last farewells (including a convivial evening with the field officers and captains of the station, which " passed off with great harmony " and ended in a young gentleman's inexcusable refusal to sing and the arrest in error of a completely innocent captain by an inebriated Town Major) were safely said and due answers returned to the grateful addresses of Madras, Seringapatam, and his own Thirty-third. They sailed in March, Sir Arthur with a comfortable conviction that " in India at present there is not, or will not in a short time, be anything for a military man to do." But he had Richard's business to transact at home—" Send me all your commands to England ; I shall have nothing to do excepting to attend to them, and I will exert myself to forward your views." Richard was still his chief ; though Arthur, who was nearly thirty-six, had learnt his trade and, in his own later judgment, " under-

stood as much of military matters as I have ever done since."
Once more the breeze sprang up ; a frigate sailed ; and India
faded behind him.

At midsummer an island stood up out of the sea ; and Arthur
Wellesley went ashore at St. Helena. His health, in spite of
mal de mer, was better now ; and he found " the interior of the   *108*
island . . . beautiful, and the climate apparently the most
healthy that I have ever lived in." (Richard confirmed his view
a few months later, deriving satisfaction from " its singular
beauty and delightful climate," as well as from a congenial
atmosphere of deference, and testifying to its beneficial effects
upon a delicate young man, whose " health is restored by this
climate.") Sir Arthur stayed there for three weeks, rode into
Jamestown for a christening, and derived peculiar enjoyment from   *109*
a Governor of antique cut—" a good man, but a quiz, of a description that must have been extinct for nearly two centuries. I
never saw anything like his wig or his coat." The General lodged
at The Briars ; the house (it had another lodger later) lay   *110*
pleasantly among the trees in a deep valley close by the road to
Longwood. The names were unfamiliar to Sir Arthur—and still
more so to an eager man, who waited in those summer weeks of
1805 for news of a fleet that he had flung halfway round the world
to set a trap for Nelson, whilst his bugles rang upon the hills
above Boulogne. But for three weeks in 1805 a malicious fate
enjoyed the brief paradox of Napoleon at large and Wellington
at St. Helena. Then, in July, Sir Arthur Wellesley sailed on to
Europe : the island waited.

DUBLIN CASTLE

> *One of Ireland's many tricks is to fade away to a little speck down on the horizon of our lives, and then to return suddenly in tremendous bulk, frightening us.*—AVE.

I

THE ship sailed home across the summer seas of 1805. Their course was northward now; and as the bright Atlantic waves danced before *Trident*, Sir Arthur Wellesley sat writing in his cabin. His pen was busy with a paper upon Indian famines, in which he wrote learnedly of irrigation and native agriculture; and he replied at length to a proposal of Lord Castlereagh's for the employment of Indian troops in the West Indies and the substitution in India of West Indian negroes. Though strong upon the sepoy's virtues—" I have tried them on many serious occasions, and they have never failed me "—he was sceptical of the experiment, and suggested that Malays might answer better, whilst he was more than doubtful about garrisoning India with negro slaves.

There was a pause in Europe; and as *Trident* brought Sir Arthur home, the world was waiting. London, a little anxious, waited for news of Nelson, last heard of halfway to America in pursuit of phantom Frenchmen; the big hills above Boulogne waited to pour two hundred thousand men across the Channel into Kent; Sir Robert Calder waited doggedly off Finisterre to bar the road to England; and in a little room behind Boulogne the Emperor was waiting for a fleet that never came. *Trident*, in company " with about forty sail of Indiamen and Chinamen," sailed decorously homeward up the broad avenues of the Atlantic. Far to the west Nelson, eager and miserable in his feverish pursuit of Villeneuve, hunted the French towards their ports; and in those summer weeks of 1805 Nelson and Wellesley both rocked to the Atlantic swell. The General was nearing Europe now. Portugal heaved slowly out of the sea as they sailed by, and the Spanish mountains stood ranged behind the mists. But nothing stirred in the Peninsular sunshine. They passed the coast of France; but all the hutted alleys of Boulogne were emptying. For the Emperor had changed front abruptly, turned a scornful back on the derisive cliffs of Dover, and flung himself angrily against Vienna. Eastwards across the world obedient Russians in the last of Mr. Pitt's despairing Coalitions moved stiffly forward to the tap of their monotonous drums, and Austrians fumbled with their arms, as the Emperor's *berline* rolled into Germany. Gold-braided Marshals in stupendous collars tilted hats of panto- mime proportions ; the French cavalry jogged eastwards through the blinding summer dust in the full coquetry of sabretache and dolman under a nodding avenue of busbies, shakoes, and immense brass helmets with plumes, with crests, with horse-hair tails, with strips of leopard-skin, with great imperial ciphers, as the long lines of bayonets wound across France behind their clanging bands to write Austerlitz upon their eagles.

Sir Arthur read his novels, walked the deck, and wrote notes to fellow-passengers. They reached England in September, and the General set off for London to lay siege to ministers in Richard's interests. One day he had a strange encounter in " the little   *4* waiting-room on the right hand " of the old Colonial Office in Downing Street. Another visitor was waiting there already—a sad-eyed little man, " whom from his likeness to his pictures and the loss of an arm " Sir Arthur promptly recognised as Nelson, home from the sea and happy in a few weeks of Emma Hamilton and " dear, dear Merton." The Admiral began to talk and, as Wellesley recollected drily, " entered at once into conversation with me, if I can call it conversation, for it was almost all on his side and all about himself, and in, really, a style so vain and so silly as to surprise and almost disgust me." (Sir Arthur was unlikely to be captivated by the manner which, when expressed in an excess of stars and ribbons, had elicited from John Moore the pained comment that their wearer seemed " more like the Prince   *5* of an Opera than the Conqueror of the Nile.") Then, suspecting something, the sailor left the room, learnt the identity of the spare military man, and came back transformed. All that the General " had thought a charlatan style had vanished, and he talked of the state of this country and of the aspect and probabilities of affairs on the Continent with a good sense, and a knowledge of subjects both at home and abroad, that surprised me equally and more agreeably than the first part of our interview had done ; in fact, he talked like an officer and a statesman." So the French marched to Austerlitz, and the first broadsides of Trafalgar came faintly up the wind, as Nelson and Wellesley sat talking one September day in a room off Whitehall. Lord Castlereagh was

busy ; and they talked above half an hour. The talk stayed in
Sir Arthur's memory ; and after thirty years he judged that " I
don't know that I ever had a conversation that interested me
more," adding the shrewd reflection that " if the Secretary of
State had been punctual, and admitted Lord Nelson in the first
quarter of an hour, I should have had the same impression of a
light and trivial character that other people have had, but
luckily I saw enough to be satisfied that he was really a very
superior man ; but certainly a more sudden and complete meta-
morphosis I never saw." They never met again.

All that autumn he besieged ministers with rare assiduity.
His first assault was on Lord Castlereagh. Born the same year,
they had seen something of each other in Dublin as young
members of the Irish House of Commons. The other's legislative
triumphs as Chief Secretary and pilot of the Act of Union through
the muddy shallows had fallen in Sir Arthur's absence. But as
Pitt's understudy Castlereagh now assisted another pilot to
weather a severer storm, and the Secretary for War and President
of the Board of Control took for his province the whole world
(including India). Wellesley was soon correcting his Indian
opinions, submitting memoranda, reading draft despatches, and
setting Richard's proceedings in the most favourable light. He
saw Lord Camden too, and told him bluntly that the Prime
Minister's support of Richard left much to be desired. Pitt
promptly sent for Sir Arthur ; and, deep in Indian affairs, they
rode slowly into town together—two noses of rare quality jogging
comfortably side by side down the long road from Wimbledon.
Then he was off to Cheltenham for a rest. Not that his visits
were confined to ministers ; for on the way he stopped at Stowe
to prospect the Opposition. The Whigs were full of promises,
pressed Richard to return to his old political friends, and to
remember above all that the Prince of Wales was younger than
the King. The shrewd General surveyed an unfamiliar problem,
took counsel with his brothers, and reached the sage conclusion
that Richard would be well advised " to remain neutral for some
time and observe the course of events." This was judicious
strategy.

His own prospects were slightly obscure. The Duke of York
was gracious, and ministers shewed a mild tendency to make use
of his advice on military questions. He met them all that

autumn, when he was staying in Lord Camden's house at Chisle-
hurst. They rode twenty miles a day ; and Mr. Pitt's invalid
refreshment of steak and bottled porter was sent on ahead ; then
they rode home again to Camden Place, changed their splashed
clothes, and held a Cabinet on how to foil the French. (A strange
irony sent the last Emperor of the French to die in the same house
three-quarters of a century later.) Once or twice Sir Arthur was
consulted upon proposals for Continental expeditions. At one
moment it was hoped that Prussia could be induced to take the
Emperor in rear ; and the notion commended itself to Mr. Pitt,
whose strategy consisted less in striking blows than in making
agitated passes above the map of Europe. But this slightly
feverish prestidigitation scarcely commended itself to Wellesley,
who predicted grimly that the Prussians could not be " raised,
equipped, and on the Danube in less than three months " ; and
the event proved him correct. These consultations left Sir
Arthur with a less favourable impression of Mr. Pitt than Mr.
Pitt's of him. For while the soldier gauged the civilian defects of
the Prime Minister—" the fault of his character was being too
sanguine . . . he conceived a project and then imagined it was
done, and did not enter enough into the details "—the admiring
statesman found that Sir Arthur " states every difficulty before
he undertakes any service, but none after he has undertaken it."
This was a blessing, after the querulous paladins with whom Pitt
was normally condemned to work.

The autumn passed away. The sagacious Mack marched
twenty thousand Austrians into the iron trap of Ulm ; Nelson lay
murmuring in the half-darkness of the cockpit ; and one November night Sir Arthur at a table in Guildhall heard the Prime
Minister returning thanks in two immortal sentences " for the
honour you have done me ; but Europe is not to be saved by any
single man. England has saved herself by her exertions, and will,
as I trust, save Europe by her example." One of the cheering
voices was Sir Arthur Wellesley's. He soon had an opportunity
to display the quality of uncomplaining service which had impressed Mr. Pitt. For in December, 1805, he was appointed to
command a brigade in a Continental expedition affording the
most ample grounds for complaint. A Hanoverian officer, who
bore the slightly unpromising name of van der Decken, had proposed to plant a British army in Hanover with the laudable

design of worrying the French; the Cabinet complied; and through the winter months of 1805 an aimless stream of reinforcements was maintained. An infantry brigade of three battalions was commanded by Sir Arthur Wellesley. He was a week at sea, passed an unpleasant Christmas Day in a gale among the sands of Heligoland, and landed below Bremen, seeing once more the unpleasing levels of the winter landscape which Colonel Wesley of the Thirty-third had left behind in '95. They saw the rain; they saw the unpleasing news of Austerlitz; they never saw the French. As the stricken Pitt dragged home from Bath to die, orders were sent to bring them home again; and Sir Arthur's second taste of European warfare—six uneventful weeks in the neighbourhood of Bremen—had been scarcely more inspiring than his first.

Returned to England in February, 1806, he subsided equably into the modest dignity of a brigade at Hastings, " in command of a few troops stationed in this part of the coast, the old landing place of William the Conqueror." The post, since all danger of invasion had perished with the French navy at Trafalgar, was not conspicuously exacting. But when someone asked how he endured it after his greater days in India, his answer was impressive—" I am *nimmukwallah,* as we say in the East; that is, I have ate of the King's salt, and, therefore, I conceive it to be my duty to serve with unhesitating zeal and cheerfulness, when and wherever the King or his government may think proper to employ me." Besides, the Whigs were in and Castlereagh was out; as Sir Arthur wrote to a friend in India, " *we* are not actually in opposition, but we have no power "; and it was hardly likely that professional plums would fall into his lap. Not that his situation was unfavourable; he was gazetted to the Staff as well as to the lucrative dignity of the colonelcy of his old regiment, and he wrote comfortably that these appointments " have made me rich."

Perhaps he needed to be rich in 1806. At any rate, he assumed at least one fresh liability that year. For in the spring he married. It was in some ways the most obscure of all his actions. There are no maps of such affairs; the heroine herself confessed that there were no love-letters; and the surviving facts barely suffice to indicate the meagre anatomy of his unpromising romance. He had loved at twenty-four, when the bright vision of Kitty Pakenham first danced before his eyes. Because he loved, his violin lay smouldering in a Dublin grate, and he resolved to be a soldier. That was in '93. A taste of soldiering in Holland almost cured him of military views. But love survived ; and at twenty-six, a lover still, he set his modest hopes in '95 upon a civilian situation under the Irish Revenue and a home in Dublin. What felicity for Kitty Pakenham, designed by Providence to be his little Dublin wife. But Providence unkindly omitted to provide her with a Dublin husband. For in '96 the quays, the Castle, and the Custom House receded ; and for nine years he walked an ampler stage under a deeper sky. At thirty-six the East restored him. Was he her lover still ? If so, he had been unusually passive. For they never wrote. This singular departure from romantic ritual was confessed upon the highest author-ity. Kitty attested it herself in answer to the Queen ; for when *16* she went to Court, the royal couple beamed approval. Her Majesty was pleased to be inquisitive—

" I am happy to see you at my court, so bright an example of constancy. If anybody in this world deserves to be happy, you do. But did you really never write *one* letter to Sir Arthur Wellesley during his long absence ? "

" No, never, madam," answered Kitty.

" And did you never think of him ? "

" Yes, madam, very often."

But fortunately his enquiring sovereign never asked Sir Arthur how often he had thought of Kitty. Hardly, it would seem, with embarrassing frequency. Never when writing letters ; nor at the jeweller's. Yet during their nine years of separation he both wrote to ladies and bought jewellery—but not, it would appear, for Kitty, since she never wrote to thank him for it.

Was he her lover, then ? If he was, he scarcely seemed to know it. But her world appeared to think so. Perhaps it was not, at first sight, the sort of world that might be expected to carry weight with Sir Arthur. For it was the slightly high-pitched world of Dublin beaux and Longford belles, where young ladies romped and languished in provincial mansions or flushed and paled in Merrion Square over matrimonial prospects. Their skies were filled by her Excellency the Lord-Lieutenant's wife, the Castle season, and the latest breath of London fashion ; and when little Miss Edgeworth of Edgeworthstown distilled her

17 raptures over "sweet Kitty Pakenham," she drew an air that was nothing if not provincial. But it was not unfamiliar to Sir Arthur. (How long was it since Captain Wesley, a stiff Castle aide-de-camp, made his first awkward bows in Dublin ?) So he
18 was not surprised to hear a Dublin voice one day at Cheltenham, as General Sparrow's lady greeted him. She was a daughter of Lord Gosford's ; besides, he had seen something in the East of her brother-in-law, Lord William Bentinck, the Governor of
19 Madras. But the Sparrow twittered ; and Sir Arthur heard with more surprise her sudden assurance that Kitty Pakenham's sentiments towards him were still unchanged. What, the startled gentleman enquired, did she still remember him ? And did the Sparrow think he should renew his offer ? If so, he was prepared to. The chivalrous reply did credit to his self-command ; and chivalry combined with Lady Olivia Sparrow to seal his fate. For Arthur Wellesley found himself Prince Charming unawares, hero (or victim) of a one-sided romance.

The next step was easy ; for if Dublin drawing-rooms expected him to marry, what other course was open to a Castle aide-de-camp ? His dignity (to say nothing of the lady's feelings) seemed to demand it. Besides, her attitude was distinctly flattering ; and, his family apart, Sir Arthur was a little lonely. His friends were all in India, and the Longfords were a respectable connection. So he laid siege to Kitty in due form. Sieges were never his strong point ; but it was the most successful of his sieges, though perhaps the fortress fell just a thought too easily. For Kitty Pakenham, at thirty-three, surrendered at discretion ; Sir Arthur won his prize ; and in the spring of 1806 he went to Ireland to bring home his bride. Pretty ? Perhaps. Young? Well, not quite so young as she had been in Dublin. Devoted ? Ah, devotion was her *forte*.

20 They married at St. George's, Hill Street ; and every *amateur* of romance in Dublin thrilled with delight at the lovers parted for long years, the maiden's vigil, her knight in peril overseas, the hero's homecoming, and then a leap into his arms, rapture, and
21 wedding-bells. Miss Edgeworth plied a gleeful pen over " one of those tales of real life in which the romance is far superior to the generality of fictions," hoped ecstatically that " the imagination of this hero and heroine have not been too much exalted, and that they may not find the enjoyment of a happiness so long

wished for inferior to what they expected," and asked with fervour what Sir Arthur looked like. An unreliable observer at the Castle informed her that he was " handsome, very brown, quite bald, and a hooked nose." But though he retained an admirable head of hair, he fell lamentably short of his romantic *rôle.* For his Irish wedding-trip was accomplished inside a week ; and when he sailed for England, he travelled by himself. True, he had overstayed his leave to be with her. That was a saving touch of romance. But was it kind to leave the bride to travel after him " under the care of his brother, the clergyman " ? It almost seemed to lend substance to the dreadful whisper that when the couple drove home from the honeymoon, a startled world beheld the bride inside the carriage, the bridegroom on the box. And yet, perhaps, she found it a relief : she was always scared of him.

So Prince Charming, contrary to precedent, came home alone ; and the bride followed later in charge of a relation. This was a shade discouraging ; but when his hands were full, Sir Arthur was not easily discouraged, and at the moment he had other things to think of. There was his brigade at Hastings, which occupied him with agreeable problems of coast-defence ; he read stimulating papers on the Rye inundations and the military virtues of Winchelsea Castle. Besides, that summer he went into Parliament. His motive for the step was not ambition or any appetite for politics, but the defence of Richard. For, loyalty apart, the family viewed Richard's fame as their main asset. Resigned at last, the splendid Marquess was back in England, draped in the dignity peculiar to returned proconsuls. But his attitude, though always regal, was not wholly free from uneasiness. A pertinacious Anglo-Indian named Paull had dogged him spitefully for years. This mischief-maker had succeeded in entering the House of Commons, and was now engaged in a series of manœuvres unpleasantly suggestive of impeachment. Impeachment was the mode that year. Lord Melville was already well on the road to Westminster Hall ; and if Paull had his way, Lord Wellesley seemed likely to follow him. (Such persecution seemed, if he might judge from the dismal precedent of Warren Hastings, the customary reward of Indian service.) If Pitt had been alive, the Marquess might perhaps afford to disregard his persecutor. But Pitt was gone ; the obnoxious Paull had Whig connections ; and it was doubtful how far Whig ministers would undertake Richard's defence. Slightly alarmed, he mobilised his little cohort. Henry was busy on official doorsteps ; William was in the House already ; and in April Arthur was returned for Rye.

The campaign was not exacting, since the Rye electors listened more closely to their proprietor than to any candidate. Their simple appetites appear in his election accounts :

	£	s.	d.
Wine &c. &c. at the Meeting at the Court Hall	3	8	o
Supper for Corporation at Nomination	37	10	o
Cold Collation day of Election	15	8	o
Election Dinner Tea Supper &c.	123	o	6
do. do. for Freemen Wives & Families	88	12	6
Town Clerk's Fees &c. &c.	26	5	o
Serjeant's Fees	13	2	6
Ringers	5	5	o
Waiters at the Inn	5	5	o
Donation to the Poor in lieu of Garlands &c. &c.	50	o	o
	£367	17	o

The freemen dined ; the corporation supped ; the ringers rang ; the waiters waited ; the poor of Rye were richer by fifty pounds in lieu of wearing Wellesley's colours ; and on these reasonable terms the obliging borough sent Sir Arthur to the House of Commons.

9

II

HE took his seat in April, 1806, when politics were complicated
by the strange ministerial interlude of ' All the Talents,' and the
gunpowder muzzle of Charles Fox hung like a benevolent
thundercloud over the Treasury Bench. Before the month was
out, he was at grips with Paull, challenging his brother's assailant   1
to state his charges ; and Mr. Secretary Fox, who spoke in the
debate, discovered a diminished taste for India impeachments in
distressing contrast with his robust appetite when in Opposition.
A few days later Mr. Paull launched his First Charge rather   2
inaudibly, and only found a seconder after a most embarrassing
pause. Sir Arthur followed with a fervent hope that the House
would " consider the feelings of his noble relative, and come to
such decision as would lead to a speedy and full discussion of the
whole case " ; and William testified with deep emotion to his
respect for Richard. Unmoved by this affecting spectacle, the
persevering Paull retorted in the subsequent debate that " the   3
hon. but indiscreet Knight of the Bath was an accessory to many
of the facts," eliciting from Sir Arthur the curt answer that " as
to the observation that he himself was implicated in some of the
proceedings, his short reply was, that what he did in India was in
obedience to the orders he had received ; and for the manner of
that obedience, and its immediate result, he was ready to answer,
either to that House, or to any other tribunal in the realm."
It was adroit of Arthur to appear as Richard's leading
advocate. The laurels of Assaye formed a becoming ornament
of the defence ; and all through the summer, his days divided
between rooms in Clifford Street, the House of Commons, and an   4
uneasy feeling that he ought really to be back with his brigade
at Hastings, he laboured at his forensic oar. He harried Mr.
Paull with a zest once savoured in the pursuit of Mahratta chief-
tains, pressing him for specific charges, moving for papers, and   5
scrambling over discovery of documents with a professional gusto
worthy of the Temple. In July he made a Parliamentary appearance on a large scale, though India was still his theme ; for he   6

exercised himself at length upon the Indian Budget, chosen
hunting-ground of all sun-dried legislators, with a wealth of figures
and a grasp of public finance highly creditable in a soldier. He
7 spoke once on army matters in favour of increased rates of pay for
junior officers. Then the House rose, and he escaped from
Westminster.

Not that he found his *rôle* particularly congenial. The company was stupid ; and two sporting members, deep in discussion
8 of their books, were vastly entertained when the General, who sat
between them, asked gravely to what books they alluded. He
9 informed a friend in India that " I am in Parliament, and a most
difficult and unpleasant game I have to play in the present extraordinary state of parties." For it was not easy, even for a skilled
tactician, to align all parties in support of Richard, though the
egregious Paull ably seconded his efforts. Besides, there was his
own profession and the brigade at Hastings. After midsummer
the General resumed his military avocations in the plain little
town, still innocent of attractions and parades, where a green
10 haze of tamarisks hung about every street. But even there his
pen was busy with a long vindication of Richard's policy ; and
they still corresponded upon Parliamentary business. Sir Arthur
was managing the St. Ives election for him, securing the return
of two members at the slightly exorbitant rate of £3,500, payable
within fourteen days after the meeting of Parliament. But
11 Westminster was plainly not his own destination. Sir Arthur
was growing restless, and his brother was informed that " it is
such an object to me to serve with some of the European Armies
that I have written to Lord Grenville upon the subject ; & I
hope that he will speak to the Duke of York." His eyes had
strayed from Mr. Paull to more interesting horizons. For the war
in 1806 was more widespread than ever, with the French slowly
bearing down on Prussia, a British army in the toe of Italy, and
12 unlikely Russians on the Adriatic. A military friend in Calabria
sent him a full account of the victory at Maida, which confirmed
13 his own impression that the French column could be beaten by
British infantry in line. There was even a vague notion of send-
14 ing a small force to Portugal. Surely employment could be
found somewhere in the world for the Hastings brigadier.

Since his experience of active service was confined to Europe
and Asia, ministers consulted him exclusively upon operations

in America. The war with Spain had opened vast colonial per-
spectives ; and delirious enterprises swam constantly before
their eyes. Nine hundred bayonets, four guns, and six dragoons   15
were hopefully consigned into the vast spaces of the Argentine to
capture Buenos Ayres ; five battalions were entrusted with the
flattering mission of rounding Cape Horn, occupying Chile, and
crossing the Andes ; and the same lofty disregard of time and
space dictated a third project, which verged on the sublime.
Two forces starting in two separate hemispheres were to converge
on Mexico. One, based upon Jamaica, had the relatively simple
task of striking at the Atlantic sea-board ; but the other, destined
for a simultaneous attack on the Pacific coast, was to travel by
a route devised in Bedlam. Embarking at Madras, it was
expected to proceed to Mexico by way of Singapore, the Philippines, and Botany Bay. The tedium of its voyage would be
relieved by capturing Manilla on the way ; and having sailed
halfway round the world, it should arrive punctually in Mexico
to co-operate with the contingent from Jamaica. This promising
command was offered to Sir Arthur, " if Lord Grenville can ar-   16
range it for me, & if upon the examination of the papers in the
Secretary of State's office, & upon a conversation with the persons
who have been in that Country I should think the plan likely to
succeed, & Gov^t. should still be of opinion that it is desirable to
obtain possession of Mexico." (The papers, it appeared, were
being studied at the moment by a Colonel Robert Craufurd,
destined by Government for another *rôle* in their South American
extravaganza, with whom Sir Arthur was to be better acquainted.)
The General conferred with the Prime Minister on the egregious
project, and even wrote a paper in which it was examined with per-   17
fect gravity, arguing with painstaking lucidity that the time-table
was wholly impracticable, that a garrison of one thousand men
could not maintain themselves with any comfort on an island with
a population of two millions, and that if Mexico was to be attacked
at all, the attack had better start from Jamaica without Pacific
complications.

Small wonder that he turned almost with relief to Richard's
politics, urging him to bow to the spirit of the age and seek
journalistic allies—" It appears that the Newspapers have at last   18
made such progress in guiding what is called publick opinion in
this Country, that no Man who looks to publick station can attain

his objects, without a connection with & assistance from some of the Editors." Even editors and politicians might well seem preferable to Cabinet strategy ; and in the autumn he expressed his own readiness to come into Parliament again and even to contribute to his brother's party fund. (That week the Emperor struck once again at Jena, and Prussia crumbled into dust.) The enterprising Richard hoped to mobilise a group of eight members with a total outlay of £7,000, which Sir Arthur judged to be " certainly cheap." He was prepared to sit with them himself, and to give £1,500 ; for his finances were distinctly brighter, and old Dublin debts began to melt before the rising sun of unaccustomed affluence. Not that he was reconciled in any way to a career as a back-bencher. His battalions were being steadily withdrawn for active service, and he was anxious to go with them—" and I don't care in what situation. I am only afraid that Lord Grenville does not understand that I don't want a Chief Command if it cannot be given to me ; and that I should be very sorry to stay at home when others go abroad, only because I cannot command in Chief." This was a very different tone from the indignant outcries with which he had once refused to go to Egypt as second in command to Baird. But now all the world was in the field—John Moore and Lowry Cole in Sicily, Beresford on the River Plate, and even Craufurd off to some eccentric destination—and it would never do for Wellesley to remain in command of a few martello towers at Hastings.

The Cabinet detained him still with South American enquiries. He wrote copiously upon the coast of Mexico, and was condemned to the exasperating company of political exiles, spies, and noblemen with bright ideas. His views were shrewd, and on one vital point his grasp of Mexican realities was quite surprising :

" The French gentlemen who have turned their thoughts to this subject have recommended that one of the French princes should be established as king in New Spain, and the English and Spanish writers have recommended an independent government, without specifying of what nature it should be. None, however, have pointed out in what manner the government recommended to be established in that country should be kept in existence, carried on, and supported after the revolution should have been effected, particularly against the attempts which might be made upon it by the United States."

Such foresight, exercised two generations later, might have saved

Maximilian and Bazaine ; and uttered by Sir Arthur Wellesley in
1806, it came near to prophecy.   But though vague on the political
prospects, he was prepared to conquer Mexico with eleven
thousand men and listed the requisite supplies with admirable
precision.   A sounder instinct than the French displayed in 1861
dictated that " the object . . . upon the arrival and disembarka-   22
tion of the troops in Mexico must be to remove them from the low
countries on the coast to the higher and more healthy parts
inland.   I have asked for horses, mules, and pioneers, with a view
to this object principally."   But the mirage of Mexico dissolved ;
and he was left at Deal, writing stray paragraphs for Richard
against the outrageous Paull.

That winter he returned to Parliament, elected in the first
weeks of 1807 for a Cornish borough which lurked obscurely under   23
the *aliases* of St. Michael and Michael Midshall, otherwise Mitchell.
He had a house in Harley Street ; and in February, as the French
felt their way across the snow to Eylau, a child was born there.
He still favoured ministers with his opinions on Central America,   24
commenting shrewdly that their high-minded action in abolishing
the slave trade would scarcely enlist the enthusiastic support of
the slave-owners of Venezuela.   The defence of Richard was   25
resumed in Parliament ; and once at least Sir Arthur left his
heir's cradle in Harley Street to get some hunting at Hatfield.   26
But before March was out, these agreeable exercises were sharply
interrupted by a change of Government   A threat of toleration
for his Catholic subjects aroused the sleeping dragons of King
George's conscience, and Whig ministers were abruptly consigned
to outer darkness.   Pitt's heirs returned in force ; Lord Castlereagh resumed the War Department, while Mr. Canning took the
Foreign Office, and the Duke of Portland inspired general confidence as Prime Minister in time of war by the twin circumstances
of being seventy years of age and in failing health.   Sir Arthur
Wellesley was invited to accept the post of Chief Secretary for
Ireland.   The offer marked him as a Tory.   But the Tories had
befriended Richard ; and he accepted.   His reasons, which were
transmitted with unusual delicacy to the late Prime Minister, were
almost wholly governed by the exigencies of his brother's position.
As this manifestly demanded a Tory connection—

" the only doubt I had . . . was whether I should accept a civil office   27
the duties of which might take me away from my profession.   I have

consulted the Duke of York upon this point, & he has told me, that he approves of my acceptance of the office, & that he does not conceive that it ought to operate to my prejudice ; & the Ministers have told me that they consider me at liberty to give up the office in Ireland whenever an opportunity of employing me professionally will offer, & that my acceptance of this office, instead of being a prejudice to me in my profession, will be considered as giving me an additional claim to such employment."

A minister on this unusual tenure, he left his infantry brigade ; and in March, 1807, his career as a back-bencher ended, Sir Arthur Wellesley was Chief Secretary for Ireland.

III

DUBLIN resumed him in the third week of April, 1807. It
was ten years since he had lived there ; and both of them were
changed. His haunt was still the Castle. But the Castle aide-
de-camp living a shade precariously on credit was now a Major-
General, K.B., and Chief Secretary at the eccentric salary of
£6,566. He was the great Sir Arthur now. And Dublin ? [1]
Dublin had waned a little. For the slow poison of the Act of
Union was working. There was no Parliament to meet on College
Green ; coaches were rarer now in Dame Street ; and fewer gentlemen kept up their houses in Merrion Square. The city's pulse
was slower. But Ireland was more feverish than ever. For deprived by Union of the traditional leadership of its resident
gentry, an impatient country turned from its natural leaders to
more exciting substitutes. The new Chief Secretary lost his
illusions rapidly. Within a month he was assuring ministers
that " no political measure which you could adopt would alter [2]
the temper of the people of this country. They are disaffected
to the British Government ; they don't feel the benefits of their
situation ; attempts to render it better either do not reach their
minds, or they are represented to them as additional injuries ;
and in fact we have no strength here but our army." Relief for
Catholics scarcely promised a solution, since he retained in later
years a strong conviction that " Ireland has been kept connected [3]
with Great Britain by the distinction between Protestants and
Catholics since the Act of Settlement. The Protestants were the
English garrison. Abolish the distinction and all will be Irishmen
alike, with similar Irish feelings. Shew me an Irishman and I'll
shew you a man whose anxious wish it is to see his country independent of Great Britain. . . . I was astonished when I was in
office to find the degree in which the opinion had grown that
Ireland could stand alone as an independent country among
gentlemen of property, persons in office, and connected with
government. The connection with Great Britain has decreased
in popularity since the Union, the abolition of jobs, the curtail-

ment of the patronage of the Crown. . . ." Small wonder that
as he paced a little square in Portugal, he once proclaimed his
belief that " independence is what the Irish really aim at, and he
is therefore for giving no more, but proceeding upon King
William's plan to keep them down by main force, for he thinks
that they have too much power already, and will only use more
to obtain more, and at length separation."

So Dublin Castle taught him to be a Tory. There are few
better schools ; and Sir Arthur was a likely pupil. For the
accident of his career had kept him in the East for nine decisive
years between 1796 and 1805. In those years the movement of
ideas at home sent many thoughtful men to study unfamiliar
topics, and the principles that underlay the Revolution were
viewed by calmer eyes than Burke's. Soldiers were not exempt
from such reflections ; John Moore was something of a Whig ;
and Wellesley himself had owned a copy of *Vindiciæ Gallicæ*.
But whilst the leaven of the Revolution was working in English
minds, he was governing Mysore. He stepped ashore again in
1805, quite untouched by any questionings. The accident of
Richard's grievances aligned him with the Tories ; the Tories
sent him to Dublin Castle ; and the Castle made a Tory of him.

Landed in Dublin after a most unpleasant crossing, he plunged
into his duties ; and before the month was out, he was knee-deep
in patronage, dispensing promises with easy grace and draping
refusals with profound regrets. The dissolution of Parliament
doubled his work, since the Chief Secretary acted as head organ-
iser for Government in all the Irish seats, and he was soon desiring
the Whips' office in London " to make me acquainted with the
price of the day." Some borough-owners were reported to sell
to the highest bidder ; others were more amenable, responding
to a timely hint of Church preferment for a brother. But in some
lively instances his martial instinct was rewarded by the tumultuous delights of a contested election ; and he reported gleefully
upon the prospects of ' beating out,' and even ' kicking out,'
an Opposition candidate. An Irish contest had a rare flavour,
affording ample scope for military attainments since, in *Charles
O'Malley's* cheerful recollection—

" the adverse parties took the field, far less dependent for success
upon previous pledge or promise made them, than upon the actual

stratagem of the day. Each went forth, like a general to battle, surrounded by a numerous and well-chosen staff; one party of friends, acting as commissariat, attended to the victualling of the voters, that they obtained a due, or rather undue, allowance of liquor, and came properly drunk to the poll; others again broke into skirmishing parties, and, scattered over the country, cut off the enemy's supplies, breaking down their post-chaises, upsetting their jaunting cars, stealing their poll-books, and kidnapping their agents. Then there were secret service people, bribing the enemy and enticing them to desert; and lastly, there was a species of sapper-and-miner force, who invented false documents, denied the identity of the opposite party's people, and, when hard pushed, provided persons who took bribes from the enemy, and gave evidence afterwards on a petition."

Duels abounded; the military were present in force " which, when nothing pressing was doing, was regularly assailed by both parties "; and " the man who registered a vote without a cracked pate was regarded as a kind of natural phenomenon." Sir Arthur's bulletins recorded that Tipperary mobs, " parading through the country with green flags and feathers," had broken up conveyances taking electors to the poll; that the dragoons were out; and that a Wexford candidate had killed his opponent in a duel, adding a little grimly that " as this is reckoned fair in Ireland, it created no sensation in the country." He pressed reluctant voters, reproached placemen whose support of Government left something to be desired, suggested skilful arguments " on the ground of the Protestant interest and on Talbot's revolutionary speech on the first day of the election," and generally proved himself a worthy manipulator of the electoral machine. The experience was scarcely calculated to increase his respect for representative institutions. But the Irish elections of 1807 were, perhaps, the most remarkable (and not the least successful) of Wellington's campaigns.

His own electoral career was less adventurous. Relinquishing his Cornish seat on grounds which may be surmised from its earlier history (St. Michael had cost Clive so much that he was driven back to India and glory on the field of Plassey), Sir Arthur stipulated that its successor must be inexpensive, rejected Ipswich, and with admirable simplicity " directed Justice Day to return me for Tralee." That luminary complied; though Sir Arthur was

simultaneously returned for Newport, Isle of Wight, for which
he subsequently elected to sit. His fellow-member was a fresh-
faced young gentleman just down from Cambridge, who had
succeeded recently as Viscount Palmerston. Till the House met,
work kept him at his desk in Dublin. He was housed comfortably
at the Chief Secretary's Lodge in Phœnix Park, left his bow-
fronted home each morning, and rode across the Park with the
Lord-Lieutenant's daughters. They parted at the gate (as yet
unshadowed by any Wellington Testimonial) ; and he rode slowly
down the quays towards the Castle. His work was waiting on the
table in the Chief Secretary's room ; and through the summer
days he sat writing courteous letters to his official correspondents.
His correspondents all had wishes ; and with rare unanimity their
wishes seemed to run in one direction. For they invariably
coincided in a disinterested anxiety to see deserving friends
accommodated at the public expense. A bland Chief Secretary
was " concerned that he cannot adopt this opportunity of gratifying your wishes," politely indicated obstacles " which may, and
indeed must, retard the accomplishment of your wishes," and
confessed how happy he should have been " in being instrumental in forwarding your wishes." The gentle sibilant ran, like
a mild refrain, through all his correspondence. But he could still
be firm, refuse a pension to a peeress, and write firmly to his
sister that there was no vacancy in the Dublin packets, and that
if there were, " it may be expected that the Duke of Richmond
or I, who have been all over the world, have naval friends of
merit, but not rich, to whom we may be desirous of giving such
a provision." Matters of larger policy occasionally interrupted
the absorbing business of distributing loaves and fishes. He
wrote wisely on the defence of Ireland, dismissed martello towers
in favour of mobile naval defence, and assumed judiciously that
" Ireland, in a view to military operations, must be considered
as an enemy's country." But he was capable of moderation, and
could refuse leave for a Yeomanry celebration of the events of
'98 upon the admirable ground that " it appears impossible to
celebrate the victory at Vinegar Hill without recalling . . . the
persons over whom that victory was gained, and all the unfortunate circumstances of the times which concurred to bring about
that state of affairs which rendered that battle and victory
necessary. His Grace cannot believe that those who wish to

commemorate their military achievement are desirous to hurt
the feelings of others, however blameable and guilty they may
have been ; and he does not suppose that they can wish to perpetuate the memory of the unfortunate circumstances which led
to the contest in question." For long memories, the standing
curse of Ireland, were best discouraged ; and a wise Chief Secretary checked the throb of Orange drums.

Indeed, his ears were tuned that summer to the sound of other
drums. For a rumour reached him of an expedition to the
Baltic, and he was soon pressing Castlereagh to release him from
his desk—" It will be understood and said that I had avoided or   *15*
had not sought for an opportunity of serving abroad in order to
hold a large civil office. As I am determined not to give up the
military profession, and as I know that I can be of no service in
it unless I have the confidence and esteem of the officers and
soldiers of the army, I must shape my course in such a manner
as to avoid this imputation. If, therefore, you send the expedition, I wish you would urge Lord Hawkesbury to fix upon a
successor for me, as I positively cannot stay here whether I am
to be employed with it or not." But, for the moment, duty
called at Westminster, and Sir Arthur's eye surveyed civilian
ranks. For the House met in June ; an Irish relative was gaily
informed that " we must get our troops over by the 22nd of this   *16*
month . . . and I think your presence here in the next week to
hurry the fellows away might have good consequences " ; and
before the month was out, he sailed for England. As they left
Dublin, his observant eye was caught by a defective pier, and he   *17*
learned something on the passage about the grievances of packet
captains. Kitty was left behind in Phœnix Park. For she was   *18*
his little Dublin wife ; and, instinctively perhaps, she stayed
behind in Dublin. But Sir Arthur was back at Harley Street,
deep in correspondence upon Church patronage or speaking in
the House of Commons on an Irish sinecure. He was still pressing   *19*
the egregious Paull to state his charges against Richard ; and the
Chief Secretary found himself introducing a Coercion Bill inherited from his predecessor. In the best Castle style he proposed
a duration of seven years, and experienced the unpleasant sensation of being thrown over in the debate by the Chancellor of the
Exchequer. He was heard once again—this time on Indian
finance—wrote countless letters about military loaves and

ecclesiastical fishes, pressed a young sailor's claims upon the
First Lord of the Admiralty with the dry commendation that
20 they were " founded upon his being the favourite son of his
mother, who was a favourite of yours about thirty years ago,"
and did his best to govern Ireland from his room in Harley Street,
opining tartly that " it would be best to take no further notice of
the trees of liberty at Tipperary " because " Lord Landaff will be
tired of furnishing trees as often as those planted will wither."
One day in June, as the slow waters of a northern river mirrored
a barge on which two Emperors shared out the world, Sir Arthur
21 Wellesley was busy writing dutiful injunctions about a Castle
informer.

Small wonder that he turned with evident relief to his own
professional prospects. For the vague expedition to the Baltic
had now a less uncertain outline. A descent on Denmark was
suddenly projected ; and in the last week of July ministers
acceded to Sir Arthur's application to serve with the expedition—
22 " I don't know, and I have not asked, whether I am to return to
my office when this coup-de-main will have been struck or will
have failed." Indeed, he scarcely seemed to mind. For war was
23 his profession ; and " no political office could compensate to me
the loss of the situation which I hold in the army, and nothing
shall induce me to give it up." They gave him a division ; and,
Chief Secretary still, the strange pluralist posted from Harley
Street to Sheerness and sailed in the *Prometheus* fire-ship for
Copenhagen.

IV

In the Danish expedition of 1807 Great Britain's policy against Napoleon became, for the first and last time, Napoleonic. A friendly neutral was curtly summoned to give up its fleet. True, there was reason to suppose that France was on the point of seizing it herself. Besides, Great Britain undertook to hold the ceded warships as a "sacred pledge" until the war was over. But Albion, rarely perfidious, seemed suddenly resolved to earn her title. An unaccustomed ruthlessness transformed those amiable features ; scruples were hastily discarded by the vivacious Canning ; King George appeared in the aggressor's *rôle* ; and this departure was rendered still more shocking by its complete success.

The expedition to the Baltic was hastily diverted from its random exploration of seaside resorts and strongly reinforced. Sir Arthur took command of the reserve, though he did not owe the appointment " to any favour or confidence from the Horse Guards. . . . In the first place, they thought very little of any one who had served in India. An Indian victory was not only no ground of confidence, but it was actually a cause of suspicion. Then because I was in Parliament, and connected with people in office, I was a politician, and a politician never can be a soldier. Moreover, they looked upon me with a kind of jealousy, because I was a lord's son, ' *a sprig of nobility*,' who came into the army more for ornament than use . . . they thought I could not be trusted alone with a division. . . . When the Horse Guards are obliged to employ one of those fellows like me in whom they have no confidence, they give him what is called a *second in command* —one in whom they have confidence—a kind of *dry nurse*." Sir Arthur's nurse, a thoughtful brigadier named Stewart, was admirably chosen ; and half his command came from the infantry training-camp at Shorncliffe, where John Moore forged the Light Brigade. They sailed in summer weather, and he went ashore in the first week of August beneath the battlements of Elsinore. His professional custodian was discreetly helpful at every turn—" during the embarkation, the voyage out, and the disembarkation General Stewart did everything. I saw no kind of objection to anything he suggested, and all went *à merveille.*" His command landed with "one simultaneous and tremendous cheer" in the summer dawn to the north of Copenhagen. The city was invested; and when a Danish force that had been left at large shewed a disturbing tendency to interrupt, Sir Arthur was detached to deal with it. His plan was simple: whilst he attacked the enemy in front, a second force was to sweep round and take them in rear. But chance, a broken bridge, and somebody's mishap denied him the complete success; and though he found the Danes at Kioge on August 29, attacked with spirit, and destroyed them, he was left lamenting that " not a man would have made his retreat if [General Linsingen] had carried into execution his part of the plan; but, as it is, they have been sufficiently beat to prevent their assembling again." It was a neat performance, and the credit was all his own. For when the helpful Stewart began to make suggestions, " I stopped him short with ' Come, come, 'tis my turn now.' I immediately made my own dispositions, assigned him the command of one of the wings, gave him his orders, attacked the enemy, and beat them. Stewart, like a man of sense, saw in a moment that I understood my business, and subsided with (as far as I saw) good humour into his proper place."

The British forces could dispose of Copenhagen at their leisure now. It was to be bombarded, though Sir Arthur felt a strong distaste for this form of coercion and would have preferred to starve the city. But the guns played on it, whilst he ranged the open country and exchanged chivalrous correspondence with defeated Danes. He met a gentleman named Rosencrantz, and resisted, as he afterwards confessed, a strong temptation to ask him after Guildenstern; a General conveyed his gratitude in imperfect English " for your human and generous conduct . . . it is a great pitty that political views should counteract the private feelings of the individuals "; one grateful Dane thanked him " sincerely and of my heart for the protection you have given me in these days your troops have laid in my neighbourhood "; and an indignant Princess, whose property had been tampered with, was so far mollified by his courtly apologies and its prompt restoration as to offer a shy gift of fruit—" *pleignant seulement qu'ils ne*

soyent pas meilleures"—and to invite Sir Arthur, " *comme le Chevalier est amateur de chasse,*" to shoot her coverts. These amenities lasted into the autumn. The city fell ; and in recognition of his services at Kioge Sir Arthur was detailed to negotiate   10
the terms of its capitulation. Then he recalled that he was still Chief Secretary for Ireland, and that the days were drawing in— " the *long nights* are approaching fast, and if I am to have any   11
concern in the government of that country, it is desirable that I should be there."   So he was given leave at once and sailed home, shortly followed by the surrendered Danish fleet. His sole memento of the expedition was a likely colt named " Copen-   12
hagen."

V

THE world was more than usually out of joint that autumn ; and England seemed to run before the gale under bare poles. How proudly she had sailed with Mr. Pitt for pilot and all the sails of Coalition set. But now the last shreds of her allies had vanished, as gust after gust swept across Europe from the west. Austerlitz had carried Austria away ; Jena took off the Prussians ; and the inconstant Czar, shaken at Eylau, went dancing down the wind of Friedland. There were no allies left for England excepting a mad King of Sweden, who was too mad even to change sides. Small wonder that the Emperor, parading Europe with a troupe of kings and dealing continents like cards, shared half the world with Alexander on the barge at Tilsit. For the world obeyed him now. His writ ran from Naples to the Baltic ; and the Pope was a mere bishop—one of his bishops. He could make dukes like wild flowers (he made twenty-six that year), give laws to the whole Continent, leave England starving on its island, its goods shut out by his *douaniers* from every port. For every port seemed to be his. True, Portugal still kept a narrow doorway on the Atlantic. If so, then Portugal must take his orders ; and when the Emperor commanded, who could deny him ?

Sir Arthur Wellesley sailed sedately home from Copenhagen,
1 landed at Yarmouth, and was stopped at a country house in Suffolk to confer with Castlereagh. There was a notion of sending him back to Denmark to continue the negotiations, but
2 Lord Hawkesbury demurred. The traveller reached London " in high spirits." For the brush at Kioge stood to his credit, and ministers appeared to value him. Had not Lord Castlereagh
1 written that " we shall want him for Flushing " ? But fate spared him Walcheren ; and he returned to Dublin, the Castle, and his Lodge in Phœnix Park. Not that he meant to stay there, since he assured a friend in India that he was even ready to return to
3 the East, though " I don't think it probable that I shall be called upon . . . men in power in England think very little of that country, and those who do think of it feel very little inclination

that I should go there. Besides that, I have got pretty high upon
the tree since I came home, and those in power think I cannot
well be spared from objects nearer home." So Canning was
informed that " I shall be happy to aid the government in any   *4*
manner they please, and am ready to set out for any part of the
world at a moment's notice." Meanwhile he governed Ireland.
His problems varied. There was still, there was always the
multitude waiting to be fed ; and the Chief Secretary performed
his daily miracle from a diminishing supply of loaves and fishes.
Tithes engaged him deeply ; and that adaptable intelligence
produced a system of reform which even included " a law to   *5*
compel the residence of the clergy in their benefices." (Junot's
men were winding through the passes into Spain.) His busy
mind ran on Irish education ; and though Sir Arthur valued the
curriculum less highly than public order—" I believe it will turn   *6*
out that there are more schools in Ireland, and more people taught
to read and write, than in England. We want discipline, not
learning "—he was still capable of writing with sudden enlighten-
ment that " in my opinion the great object of our policy in Ireland   *7*
should be to endeavour to obliterate, as far as the law will allow us,
the distinction between Protestants and Catholics, and that we
ought to avoid anything which can induce either sect to recollect
or believe that its interests are separate and distinct from those
of the other. I would apply this principle to the education which
you intend to propose to the Board." (The marching columns of
the French had left Spain behind them now.) Sir Arthur wrote   *8*
respectfully to the Lord Primate of Ireland enclosing a return of
private schools to be filled up by his clergy ; and that day Junot's
ragged infantry limped into Lisbon.

With the French in Portugal, official minds began to fear a
raid on Ireland, though Sir Arthur predicted wisely that the
invader " must make up his mind to the loss of his communication   *9*
with France for every purpose excepting that of intelligence."
His plan for its defence was drawn upon the sage assumption that
" no position will be safe excepting where the troops will be " ;
and quite unruffled, he returned to tithes and education. One
hopeful clergyman sent him a play to read, which he undertook
to " send and recommend to the manager of the playhouse, but   *10*
you must be aware that no recommendation of that sort can ensure it success " ; and as the year went out, he was opining that

11   " Ireland is not a country on which the experiment of sudden and rapid reforms of abuses can be tried. However enormous the latter may be, they are too inveterate and of too long standing to bear the sudden application of the former ; but I know that neither the abuses which exist, nor the reforms which can be applied to them, have been lost sight of since I have been in this country." How many tenants of the Chief Secretary's Lodge have stared across the Park and murmured the same good intentions towards the Wicklow mountains ?

As 1808 came in, the Emperor pervaded Europe, and Sir Arthur Wellesley was signing departmental letters in a room at Dublin Castle. He would be forty soon ; and Alexander had conquered the world at thirty-one. But as the *rôle* of Alexander seemed adequately filled at present, Sir Arthur was confined to writing lucidly upon the government of Ireland. His task was modest, since it scarcely amounted to more than the preservation of an English bridgehead on a hostile island. For Ireland, once a little parody of England, was barely more in war-time than a mere parody of Ireland. French agents flitted up and down ; informers in back streets composed incredible reports or crept mysteriously to the Castle ; the Tipperary mails were robbed ; there was an argument about Maynooth ; innumerable busy-bodies asked for official favours ; and the Chief Secretary presided imperturbably over the simple operations of unrepresentative government upon a countryside whose leading crop was a luxuriant nobility. It was a singular employment for Sir
12   Arthur, who gave no signs of impatience. His second son was born in January ; and before the month was out, he left for England to attend the House of Commons. (He was unwell, and
13   asked the Lord-Lieutenant to keep the news from Kitty " as it is only making a piece of work out of nothing.") Business was
14   unexciting. One afternoon he sat demurely in his place to listen to the Speaker's thanks for the Copenhagen expedition and managed a becoming answer. He was still capable of an injured speech upon the eternal charges against Richard ; and when the virtuous Whitbread attacked the conduct of the troops in Denmark or grudged Lake a pension, he replied. Perhaps the predestined futility of all war-time Oppositions helped to make a thorough Tory of him. But he could navigate the vexed waters of a debate upon religious education with the rational complaint

that the Catholics instructed Irish children out of textbooks
calculated " to breed them up in a fixed and rooted hatred to   *15*
Protestants," to say nothing of the dreaded writings of Tom
Paine.

But he had other interests. For Castlereagh employed him to
advise once more on operations in America. The vague design of
raising insurrection in the Spanish colonies persisted ; and he conferred at length with General Miranda, whose company was not
congenial. The revolutionary shocked him—" I always had a   *16*
horror of revolutionising any country for a political object. I
always said, if they rise of themselves, well and good, but do not
stir them up ; it is a fearful responsibility." Besides, he could not
bear Miranda's symmetrical constitutions " of a Republican form,   *17*
and too regularly constructed ever to answer any practical good
effect. . . . All the old institutions in the country ought in the
first instance to be maintained, and to be changed and amended
only as time and experience would point out what would suit both
people and country better." For Sir Arthur was still Chief Secretary ; and it would never do to concede in South America the very
principles which he was combating in Kerry. But he wrote careful memoranda on the prospects of a descent on Venezuela and
made detailed estimates of army stores.

As 1808 wore on, Sir Arthur seemed to be the military maid-of-
all-work of a bewildered Cabinet—" considered here very much in   *18*
the light of the *willing horse*, upon whose back every man thinks
he has a right to put the saddle." His views were asked for on a   *19*
Swedish expedition entrusted to John Moore ; and when France
and Russia appeared to contemplate a combined attack on India
by way of Persia, he supplied ministers with the lines of a defen-   *20*
sive campaign. But his official skies were filled with Ireland.
There was still a full budget of outrages ; he was deep in a scheme
for providing Dublin with a police force ; and favours were asked   *21*
for daily, though he was learning to be stern with applicants,
regretting his inability to oblige even the Duke of Kent. One   *22*
night he confessed to the House of Commons in defence of an
unduly sectarian appointment that " his own opinion was, that   *23*
without distinction of religion, every man ought to be called upon
to do service to the state, where he was particularly qualified to
do that service " ; and he was even capable of drafting regulations
positively countenancing the attendance of Catholic soldiers at   *24*

mass. But that week a longer shadow fell across his office table.
25 For " the Government have lately been talking to me about taking
the command of the corps destined for Spain, which is to be
assembled at Cork " ; and 1808 moved to a livelier measure.
The air, as airs are apt to be in New Castile, was minor, the
performers odd. King Charles of Spain—high-nosed for Bourbon
and strongly, too strongly chinned for Hapsburg—performed an
uncertain bass, Ferdinand his heir a piercing treble. Two voices
rendered the melody—the Queen with amorous *roulades*, and
Manuel Godoy, Prince of the Peace, with romantic *brio*. For
Queen and Prince were lovers, son and father enemies. A deeper
note intruded on this discord at Aranjuez as,

> " Cannon his name,
> Cannon his voice,"

Napoleon sounded the dominant fifth. The voices were unfairly
matched ; and the part-song became a solo. For it was barely
human to pit the ruthless purity of that Canova profile against the
collective imbecility of a Bourbon family group by Goya. The
26 sharp voice at Fontainebleau offered a principality in Portugal to
Godoy, a French princess to Ferdinand, and in a swift aside called
27 Joseph, King of Naples, to Bayonne. His troops were moving now.
The marching columns wound through the pale winter sunshine
of 1808 down the long road towards Madrid ; Junot was safe in
Lisbon ; and Murat, furred and frogged, jingled through Burgos.
The air quickened suddenly in March, as King Charles pronounced
his abdication and, watched by incredulous French troopers,
Ferdinand succeeded. The uneasy vocalists were summoned to
Bayonne ; and the sharp voice resolved their discords. One night
in April King Ferdinand, who shambled in before the rest,
received a message after dinner that the House of Bourbon had
better cease to reign. (Sir Arthur Wellesley was busy with his
papers, and wrote a few days later to the Lord-Lieutenant that
28 " there is nothing new.") Before the month was out, the caste
assembled at Bayonne for the strange harlequinade—the old King
as Pantaloon, Godoy a sadly dishevelled Harlequin, and his
devoted Queen an indomitable Columbine. The Emperor surveyed his troupe ; and the charade began. (In the House of
29 Commons Sir Arthur Wellesley was harmlessly augmenting the
stipends of Irish curates.) Charles abdicated first, then Ferdinand

—and Spain was his to dispose of. King Joseph waited for his cue. But Spain was not so passive. For beyond the mountains Murat's cavalry was sabring the *Madrileños*, and the dull volleys of his firing-parties rolled across Madrid : it was the first gun-fire of the Peninsular War. (That day Sir Arthur wrote about a pier   *30* in Meath.) Then, their *rôles* concluded, Clown, Harlequin, and Pantaloon shuffled off the stage ; the Emperor turned happily to other matters—to Italy, to Poland, to the little son just born to Hortense (they had better name him Charles-Louis-Napoléon), to the defences of Ancona, to the fleet, to canals in Lombardy, to Marmont's defalcations in Dalmatia and the prospects of a French mission to Morocco ; while Sir Arthur Wellesley thought of Church affairs and entertained the House of Commons with the   *31* innocent theme of first-fruits.

VI

THAT summer England heard the news from Spain. A little force
was fitting out at Cork for a raid on Venezuela ; and Sir Arthur
Wellesley, just promoted Lieutenant-General and deep in preparations for his expedition, was quick to see the chance. Some
months before he had sent out a spy to Spain " to pick up what he
can find out." But when the news came in May, he wrote
ministers a paper. For if Spain was really in revolt, " this would
appear to be a crisis in which a great effort might be made with
advantage ; and it is certain that any measures which can distress
the French in Spain must oblige them to delay for a season the
execution of their plans upon Turkey, or to withdraw their
armies from the north." He proposed to divert the Venezuela
expedition to Gibraltar and to employ it in raising Spain against
the French or organising a general exodus of Spaniards to South
America upon the model of the loyal Portuguese, who had left
Lisbon for Brazil. The notion was experimental—" one month
would probably be sufficient to ascertain the chances of advantage
to be derived from the temper of the people in Spain "—and if
none appeared, the expedition could proceed to South America
according to its former plan. But the chance of distracting the
Emperor by a diversion in Spain appealed to him—" the manner
in which his armies are now spread in all parts of Europe, each
portion of them having great objects and ample employment,
which cannot be given up without injury to his affairs, afford (sic)
an opportunity which ought not to be passed by." This simple
conception, born in May, 1808, somewhere between the Irish
Office and his house in Harley Street, brought seven years of war
to the Peninsula, and raised on the smooth surface of the Empire
the ' Spanish ulcer' (in Napoleon's unpleasing image) which
ultimately drained its strength.

Ministers were more than usually receptive ; and on June 1
Sir Arthur wrote in greater detail of " the plan of operations
at present in contemplation," enumerating with precision the
quantities of stores required for its two objectives. By June 4

ministers were talking of Wellesley for the command ; and two   6
days later the plan had been officially espoused by Castlereagh.
Two lions waited in his path—Kitty's wifely tears and the disappointed hopes of General Miranda. Both were alarming ; and
Sir Arthur handled both with rare discretion, postponing Kitty
with a warning to the Lord-Lieutenant—" Don't mention this   5
subject, as I don't write it to Lady W. till it be positively determined "—and, by a wise precaution, breaking the unpleasant
news to the Venezuelan patriot in a London street " to prevent   7
his bursting out. But even there he was so loud and angry, that
I told him I would walk on first a little that we might not attract
the notice of everybody passing. When I joined him again he
was cooler." But until he cooled, Sir Arthur was followed
down the street by Spanish curses. " You will be lost," the disappointed patriot informed that trim, retreating back, " nothing
can save you ; that, however, is your affair ; but what grieves me
is that there never was such an opportunity thrown away."
Yet Venezuela's loss was Spain's, Portugal's, and ultimately
Europe's gain.

It was decided, then. They were to try their chance in Spain
en route for Venezuela ; and if they made anything of Spain (the
first month or so would show), Sir Arthur Wellesley must win his
laurels elsewhere than on the Orinoco. At any rate, there would
be laurels to win, since he had got a command. For on June 14   8
Majesty traced its large, uncertain signature in the top, left-hand
corner of a commission appointing him to command a force
" employed on a particular service." That evening Mr. Croker   9
dined with them in Harley Street ; Kitty, who had come to town,
was there as well. Their guest was to take charge of Irish business
in the House of Commons while the Chief Secretary was abroad ;
and there was some conversation after dinner upon the rousing
theme of the Dublin Pipe Water Bill. Mr. Croker was inclined
to argue, and suggested that his host should write him on the
subject. " No, no," Sir Arthur said in his quick way, " I shall
be no wiser to-morrow than I am to-day. I have given you my
reasons : you must decide for yourself." Then his attention
seemed to wander. He fell silent ; and for a time nothing was
said in the dining-room at Harley Street, until his guest enquired
what he was thinking of. " Why, to say the truth," Sir Arthur
told him, " I am thinking of the French that I am going to fight.

I have not seen them since the campaign in Flanders, when they were capital soldiers, and a dozen years of victory under Buonaparte must have made them better still. They have besides, it seems, a new system of strategy which has out-manœuvred and overwhelmed all the armies of Europe. 'Tis enough to make one thoughtful ; but no matter : my die is cast, they may overwhelm me, but I don't think they will outmanœuvre me. First, because I am not afraid of them, as everybody else seems to be ; and secondly, because if what I hear of their system of manœuvres be true, I think it a false one as against steady troops. I suspect all the continental armies were more than half beaten before the battle was begun. I, at least, will not be frightened beforehand." Thoughtful but unafraid, he soliloquised to Mr. Croker, and sat thinking in his chair in Harley Street of British infantry in line waiting for the French columns of attack.

¹⁰ At any rate, he would get back to his profession now. He had piloted the Dublin Police Bill through Committee, and politics were palling on him. For the Opposition intoned an endless and ¹¹ repetitive litany of fault-finding, and even ministers seemed to fail lamentably in unanimity—the first duty of ministers, as viewed by Sir Arthur. Not that his tenure of the new command was quite secure. For the veiled deities of the Horse Guards were adverse. In those discriminating eyes he was still a novice and (what was worse) a politician. Venezuela, perhaps, might be entrusted to such hands with safety ; but the command in Spain appeared excessive for the youngest Lieutenant-General in the ¹² Army List. Ministers, of course, might feel a natural partiality for the Chief Secretary. But while they did their best, the Duke ¹³ of York had other views, and Majesty itself was understood to frown. The Horse Guards, by the customary device, gave him a ¹⁴ second in command ; Sir Arthur dutifully visited Windsor ; but the outraged gods were still unappeased.

¹⁵ In the third week of June he went off to Ireland to prepare the embarkation of his new command. He was seen driving down ¹⁶ Whitehall in a post-chaise and four, spent the evening at Coombe Wood with Lord Liverpool, and slept at his married sister's. On ¹⁷ the road to Holyhead he stopped to see some old friends of his mother's at Llangollen ; and the inseparable Ladies made a peculiar addition to his equipment. For they supplied a Spanish prayer-book, from which Sir Arthur " learnt," as a grateful

inscription testified, " what he knows of the Spanish language."
Armed with this unusual *vade mecum*, he prepared to start for the
Peninsula. His actual destination was uncertain, since Spain was
in an uproar. The cold voice of history, wiser than usual after
the event, may diagnose " the Spanish revolution, like a leafy   18
shrub in a violent gale of wind, greatly agitated but disclosing
only slight unconnected stems." But to contemporary eyes
Spain in the early summer of 1808 was a more heartening scene,
where province after province assembled an indignant *Junta*,
declared its independence and rose. The French, thrown suddenly
on the defensive, fumbled a little ; fortresses as old as time,
armed with museum pieces, failed to surrender at their summons ;
and bewildered Generals faced the incalculable prospect of an
endless war against an unforgiving population. The infection of
revolt spread to the Portuguese, and Junot was forced back on
Lisbon. Great Britain, until recently so friendless, had her allies
now. A pleading delegation from the north of Spain appeared in
London ; even the Whigs, unmoved by monarchs in distress, were
melted by the anguish of a nation struggling to be free ; and
ministers enjoyed the rare and pleasurable experience of hearing
their noble sentiments echoed by Opposition speakers, when they
announced a crusade in the Peninsula. Its precise destination,
though, was still obscure. Sir Arthur was not unduly sanguine—
" I think the whole question depends upon whether the Junta   19
of Andalusia had been assembled. If they had, and had submitted to the French Government, the game appears to be over."
It had not ended yet. Indeed, it had not quite begun, with the
French staring helplessly into Saragossa and Dupont groping
among the hills of northern Andalusia. Sir Arthur's orders were
to drive Junot out of Portugal. He was to concentrate on that   20
objective, though he might look in at Vigo or Corunna on his
passage out ; and in a cheerful whirl he made his preparations for
departure. Old habits revived ; he gave directions for the troops   21
at Cork to be landed frequently from their transports, as " it will
tend much to the health of the men, and will make them feel
less unpleasantly the heat and confinement " ; he wrote with   22
eloquence on the superior convenience of " small tin kettles " ;
and in utterances that recalled all the bullocks of Mysore he   23
made desperate endeavours to secure sufficient transport. The
troops were ready now ; and he lay waiting for a wind at Cork.

24 Lord Castlereagh desired him to go straight to Portugal, detaching
someone to report on conditions in the north of Spain. But Sir
Arthur thought better of it, and preferred to see the Spaniards for
25 himself, since " it appeared to me that the intelligence which I
should receive here might decide on the expedition, and that I
could trust no person excepting myself with such a decision." He
was not trustful. For it was his way to see for himself : his
strength lay in the fact—and, perhaps, something of his
weakness also. So he should sail ahead in a fast frigate, touch
at Corunna, and rejoin the expedition before they came in sight
of Portugal.

Through the first days of July, 1808, he lay waiting for the wind
to set from Ireland towards Spain. He was to fight the Frenchmen whom he had not seen since Flanders ; and what else had life
formed him for, if not for fighting Frenchmen ? For their unholy
challenge threatened his whole tradition. His eyes had opened
to the tap of heels on Dublin floors under the marble eyes of
drawing-room divinities ; his first games were played among the
garden gods at Dangan ; and he learned manners at the silken
knees of the Eighteenth Century. Its sad, tinkling melody had
filled his ears at home, at Dublin Castle, on College Green, at
Westminster, in the Chief Secretary's lodge. The age enfolded
him ; and, inalterably eighteenth-century, he walked its minuet.
But France turned violently from the Eighteenth Century and
with an impious hand waved Europe on towards the witches'
cauldron of the Nineteenth. The harsh challenge of the Revolution broke in upon the ordered dance. Hoarse voices called
outside ; there was a glare of torches, a sudden hammering on the
doors. They splintered ; and as the intruders flooded in with
wild eyes and snatches of discordant song, the mounting numbers
of the *Marseillaise* rose on the air. For the scared violins had
fallen silent. The dance had stopped. They were not dancing
now. But frightened ladies huddled into corners, and their angry
partners confronted a new age with drawn swords. What other
course but fighting Frenchmen was open to a gentleman ?

Besides, it was his trade. He was by choice a soldier ; and
he found it more than usually congenial to fight in such a cause.
For it engaged him as deeply as a duel engaged other men, since
the issue of the war was, in its way, a duel. His home, his origins,
his life, his century had all been challenged by the French ; and

now he was to meet them on the four-square ground of the Peninsula. The trim duellist of the *ancien régime* stepped smartly
forward, measured the distance with a steady eye, tested his
sword against the turf, and waited. A wind sprang up on July 12;
he put to sea at last ; and by the divine inconsequence of British
institutions the Chief Secretary for Ireland sailed in a cruiser
named *Crocodile* to deal a death-blow to the French Empire.

PENINSULAR

Devers Espaigne vei venir tel bruur,
Tanz blancs osbercs, tanz elmes
flambïus !
Icist ferunt nos Franceis grant irur.
CHANSON DE ROLAND.

HE was at sea once more ; and as the big Biscayan rollers staggered beneath a creaking ship, Sir Arthur crossed the Bay. It was past midsummer, 1808, and the Peninsula was waiting. That was where he was to fight the Frenchmen ; and it was a noble theatre of war. For there would be room to fight in the Peninsula. Portugal, perhaps, was slightly cramped between the mountains and the sea. But Spain lay beyond ; and he would find room enough in Spain. Those wide horizons would give him back the freedom of manœuvre that he had once known in India. For Spain, where interminable uplands stretched endlessly away to tall sierras, was the most spacious country in Europe—perhaps the only one (Russia alone excepted) where there was really room to fight. Vast, inhospitable distances lay between dead cities strung at intervals on crumbling roads ; grey olives marched interminably across red, rounded, and unlikely hills; and discouraged rivers wandered aimlessly with shrunken waters past fantastic cliffs or died away in the wide spaces of immense, unwelcoming plains. It was all singularly baffling to Marshals trained on trim South German pastures or in the neatly chequered fields of Italy. For as they entered Spain, they passed beyond the certainties of Europe ; Africa received them now ; and they were left to stray disconsolately across an unfamiliar stage, where cues were missed, and the scenery was ill-adapted to the triumphant tableaux of Napoleonic warfare. But to eyes accustomed to the East, the Spanish scene was less bizarre ; Indian experience might serve his turn in the Peninsula ; and there would be room enough to fight.

There was one drawback, though. For it was an empty land ; and to fight (he knew it well) one must indubitably feed. But armies left at large to wander down the broad corridors of Spain were lamentably apt to starve. They could not hope to live in the French style upon the country, since the country barely lived itself. Great armies could support themselves in Central Europe by wayside requisition ; but in Spain they must transport their

food. A war of transport and supply waged across starving
provinces was novel to the French ; but to a soldier of the East
India Company it was the most familiar mode. He was accustomed to intone an endless litany of commissariat bullocks, and
had mastered the eternal truth of Indian warfare that " if I had   *1*
rice and bullocks I had men, and if I had men I knew I could beat
the enemy." So if it was to be the bullocks of Mysore over again,
it was as well, perhaps, to be a Sepoy General.

I

He was a week at sea. *Crocodile* was a fast sailer ; Ireland
faded into the haze behind them ; and in the third week of July,
1808, the sterner outline of Corunna stood up out of the summer
sea. The Spaniards in the north, supported on a heady diet of non-
existent victories, were most encouraging ; and Sir Arthur, whose
credulity was still undimmed by intimacy (or any great command
of Spanish), reported happily that " the accounts of these suc-   *2*
cesses, although credited, are only private ; but I credit them."
Then he wrote a note to the Lord-Lieutenant about the Clare   *3*
election and sailed to meet his transports off Cape Finisterre.
He left the fleet again and landed at Oporto. The Portuguese
were slightly lacking in enthusiasm ; but a startled bishop
undertook to send five hundred mules to meet his force when it   *4*
was landed. Sir Arthur sailed again, rejoined his transports,
and coasted southwards. They were to land at the mouth of the
Mondego and move on Lisbon. Meanwhile, he found a moment
for a line to the Home Secretary about some Customs patronage   *5*
at Cork. Then he turned happily to more immediate problems.
There was strange news from Spain. Far to the south Dupont
and eighteen thousand Frenchmen stumbling through the Andalusian glare, where mud roads wander circuitously towards white
villages, had walked into a trap. Leaving Andujar in the plain,
its brown towers aligned between the broad Guadalquivir and the
green sierra, and groping uncertainly towards the hills, he found
across his road to safety a Spanish army under a Swiss commander with the unlikely name of Reding. The Swiss, the
Spaniards, and the French fought through a blazing summer day.
The Frenchman failed to clear Reding from his road ; Castaños
with more Spaniards lay in his rear ; and Dupont was trapped

at Baylen. The trap closed in due form with a capitulation;
and when Dupont surrendered, it dawned upon a pleased and
startled world that the tricolour, in spite of eagles, Emperor, and
6 *Marseillaise*, was not invincible—gratifying intelligence for a
General hanging off the coast of Portugal with orders to drive it
from the Peninsula.

His news from home was less exhilarating. For the veiled
divinities of the Horse Guards had prevailed, and he was to be
superseded in command of the expedition. Ministers had done
their best for a colleague; but, as the austere Moore recorded,
7 " he was so young a Lieutenant-General that the Duke had
objected to it." Age would be served; the Cabinet succumbed;
and as " the King and the Duke of York objected to him," something more venerable than Wellesley must be found to drive the
French out of Portugal. For it would never do to win a battle
with a junior Lieutenant-General. Greybeards abounded in the
8 Army List; and a greybeard in command would at least save
them from John Moore. For that Galahad was home from
Sweden. His troops were added to the expedition; he had a
perfect right to follow his command to the Peninsula; and if he
went, he would command as Wellesley's senior. This prospect
was distasteful to the Cabinet, exasperated by his Scottish recti-
tude, a slightly Whiggish flavour, and an unhappy aptitude for
being very nearly always right. (Few qualities are less rewarding,
since Cabinets, so apt to err themselves, prefer a saving touch of
human frailty in their instruments.) It was resolved to irritate
John Moore into resignation by a familiar artifice. For he was
curtly informed that if he went to the Peninsula, he went as
junior to Sir Hew Dalrymple and Sir Harry Burrard. These
paladins, both Guardsmen, were of unquestionable seniority;
one had served against Washington with Howe; and both now
enjoyed the dignified repose reserved for governors of fortresses,
Sir Hew residing in the flowered shades of the Convent at Gibraltar,
and Sir Harry exercising a less arduous tutelage of Calshot Castle.
The Cabinet, rendered aware of their existence by research (mitigated in the case of Sir Hew by some activity in his relations with
the Spanish insurrection), decreed that they should take command
in Portugal. This was a studied insult to John Moore, who was
expected to throw up his *rôle* and go off to mutter in the wings.
But though the fuse was lit, no explosion followed; for the tire-

11

some man possessed, in addition to his other qualities, the virtue of long-suffering. Besides, he was determined not to miss a chance of active service. So he drove off to Portsmouth after a snappish interview with Castlereagh ; and one more General was added to the lengthening list of Wellesley's seniors in the field.

The unpleasing news reached him as they lay off the Mondego. The blow was tempered by a note from Castlereagh assuring him that the Secretary of State had " made every effort to keep in *9* your hands the greatest number of men, and for the longest time that circumstances would permit." For the Cabinet still favoured him ; and Wellesley was commended to his new commander as " an officer of whom it is desirable for you, on all accounts, to *10* make the most prominent use which the rules of the service will permit." This was promising. But with Sir Hew, Sir Harry, and Sir John each on his way to Portugal, Sir Arthur's days of command were numbered. He had a second in command as well ; but " I came to an immediate explanation with him ; I *11* told him I did not know what the words ' *Second in command* ' meant, any more than third, fourth, or fifth in command ; that I alone commanded the army, that the other general officers commanded their divisions ; that if anything happened to me, the senior survivor would take the command ; that in contemplation of such a possibility I would treat them, but him in particular, as next in succession, with the most entire confidence, and would leave none of my views or intentions unexplained ; but that I would have no *second in command* in the sense of his having anything like a joint command or superintending control ; and that, finally and above all, I would not only take but insist upon the whole and undivided responsibility of all that should happen while the army was under my command." This was plain : until Sir Harry or Sir Hew appeared, Sir Arthur would command.

As time was short, he prepared to land his force ; and Portugal was told that her allies were fighting " for all that is dear to man— *12* the protection of your wives and children ; the restoration of your lawful Prince ; the independence, nay, the very existence of your kingdom ; and for the preservation of your holy religion." This was strange language from a Chief Secretary. But he was always tender of native customs (had he not kept a missionary out of Tippoo's zenana ?) ; and in a General Order that would

have scandalised Dublin Castle he prescribed a code of manners
for the use of Protestant soldiery in a Catholic country :

13

" It is almost essential to the success of the army that the
religious prejudices and opinions of the people of the country should
be respected, and with this view the Lieutenant-General desires the
following rules may be observed :

" 1st. No officer or soldier belonging to the army is to go to any
place of religious worship, during the performance of Divine service
in such places, excepting with the permission of the officer commanding his regiment, and the General officer commanding the
brigade to which he belongs.

" 2nd. When an officer or soldier shall visit a church, or any
other place of religious worship, from motives of curiosity, at periods
when Divine service is not performed, he is to remain uncovered
while in the church.

" 3rd, When the Host passes in the streets, officers and soldiers,
not on duty, are to halt and front it ; the officers to pull off their
hats, and the soldiers to put their hands to their caps. When it
shall pass a guard, the guard will turn out and present arms ; when
a sentry, the sentry must present arms."

This was the statesmanship by which Mysore had once been
governed.   Indeed, it shewed a little more than judicious tenderness for local prejudices ; for his little code concealed an ingenious measure of toleration for the Catholics in his command.
As he wrote twelve months later,

14

" The soldiers of the army have permission to go to mass, so far
as this : they are forbidden to go into the churches during the performance of divine service, unless they go to assist in the performance
of the service. I could not do more, for in point of fact soldiers
cannot by law attend the celebration of mass excepting in Ireland.
The thing now stands exactly as it ought ; any man may go to mass
who chooses, and nobody makes any inquiry about it.   The consequence is, that nobody goes to mass, and although we have whole
regiments of Irishmen, and of course Roman Catholics, I have not
seen one soldier perform any one act of religious worship in these
Catholic countries, excepting making the sign of the cross to induce
the people of the country to give them wine."

But his preparations were not entirely spiritual, since another
order specified with his old precision the loads of pack-mules
and bullock-waggons.   For he was eternally the Sepoy General.

The surf that thunders along Portuguese beaches was roaring in their ears, as they landed in the first week of August. That *15* was the ground-bass, audible ten miles out to sea and uncomfortably evident inshore in the form of drowned men and broken boats. They landed fifteen thousand strong ; Sir Arthur came ashore ; and presently the leading *motif* of his Peninsular symphony fell on their ears. For the dusty air filled with the shriek of solid wheels revolving slowly under bullock-carts. That shrill *falsetto* creaked its unchanging melody above all other noises ; newcomers to the country always caught it first ; the squealing axles were even audible to dashing Light Dragoons ; and to the *16* more delicate sensibilities of a German commissary " the scratching of a knife on a pewter plate is like the sweet sound of a flute beside them." With this music in their ears they toiled southward through the dust to find the French. They found them *17* first across the road to Lisbon near Obidos on August 15. A scuffle ensued ; and the French fell back upon an admirable position at Roliça, against which Sir Arthur two days later *18* launched a serious attack. The ground was difficult, and he preferred to impose retreat upon his enemy by the persuasive method of outflanking rather than by the brutal (and costly) insistence of a frontal attack. But an impulsive Colonel compromised his plan, and it cost Sir Arthur close on five hundred casualties to dislodge the French from Roliça.

His southward thrust brought the French swarming out of Lisbon like angry wasps. Junot gathered thirteen thousand *19* men and moved north to meet him. Sir Arthur's numbers were increasing now, as two more brigades from England had anchored off the coast ; and he took post on the hills above Vimeiro to cover their landing. Unhappily they were accompanied by one of Wellesley's seniors. For Sir Harry Burrard was in the *Brazen* sloop ; and his arrival automatically relieved Wellesley of the command. That afternoon (it was August 20), just as Sir Harry's boat was ordered to land him, Sir Arthur came on board. He was inclined to advance ; but his senior, more cautious, favoured a waiting game ; and Sir Arthur dutifully cancelled his orders for a fresh offensive, writing disconsolately to Castlereagh that " this determination is not in conformity with my opinion, *20* and I only wish Sir Harry had landed and seen things with his own eyes before he had made it." Sir Harry did not land ; like

every traveller, he had letters to write ; another night on board
his sloop seemed preferable to the dubious hospitality of a
Portuguese beach ; and Wellesley remained in charge for a few
hours longer. Perhaps it was as well. For the French moved
that night ; and two days later he could write gleefully to the
21   Lord-Lieutenant that " as I am the most fortunate of men,
Junot attacked us yesterday morning with his whole force, and
we completely defeated him." Sir Harry landed in the morning,
rode hurriedly inland to the sound of guns, and found the action
22   in progress at Vimeiro. Sir Arthur " in few words explained to
me the position occupied by the Army, and the steps taking to
beat the enemy. . . . I had reason to be perfectly satisfied with
his disposition, and the means he proposed to repulse them, and
I directed him to go on with an operation he had so happily and
so well begun." So, thanks to Sir Harry, Wellesley had his
chance.

It was a simple affair. The French in their white summer
uniforms came on in columns of attack, and the British waited on
the ridge in scarlet lines. The columns panted uphill in the hot
August sunshine, and the long lines received them with a volley
and then the bayonet. As he recalled with a grim smile in later
23   years, they came on " with more confidence, and seemed to *feel
their way* less than I always found them to do *afterwards*. I
received them in line, which they were not accustomed to."
The columns broke ; and this simple process having been repeated
several times at various points, the shattered French drew off.
Sir Arthur turned to his exiguous cavalry with a lift of his cocked
hat and " Now, Twentieth, now is the time." He turned to
Burrard too, who sat beside him on an indifferent mount, and
watched proceedings through his glass, observing, " Sir Harry,
now is your time to advance. The enemy are completely beaten,
and we shall be in Lisbon in three days." But the rules of war
lay heavy on Sir Harry. He was a pardonably cautious man ;
for his professional experience was almost limited to unsuccessful
expeditions. So he resolved to wait once more ; and once again
delay was fatal to his own chances of distinction. For in the
24   morning Sir Arthur, early on the beach, observed a fresh arrival
and reported to Sir Harry, not without glee, that he was superseded in his turn by the appearance of Sir Hew Dalrymple. That
thunderbolt of war was even less inclined to sudden action, since

his last (and sole) experience of active service had been in Flanders
fourteen years before with the Duke of York.   He, too, preferred
to wait on events.   What could Sir Arthur do ?   His seniors
chose to waste his victory, and he was irritably helpless.

Not that his victory was altogether wasted.   For the French,
with a somewhat juster appreciation of the consequences of
Vimeiro, surrendered.   Their action caused a flutter, since an
impulsive Portuguese vedette had diagnosed the approach of a
dismal little group, consisting of two squadrons of dragoons with
a white flag and a French General with a slight grasp of English,
as a French offensive.   But when its nature was disclosed, Sir
Hew received the emissary.   A long afternoon of negotiation
ensued—" from about halfpast two till near nine at night, with   25
the exception of the short time we sat at dinner "—in the hot
little room at Vimeiro.   Sir Harry and Sir Arthur were both
present, though the latter was uneasy with his new commander   26
and disliked the terms of the armistice.   As he wrote to Castlereagh on the next day, " I beg that you will not believe that I   27
negotiated it, that I approve of it, or that I had any hand in
wording it.   It was negotiated by the General himself in my
presence and that of Sir Harry Burrard ; and after it had been
drawn out by Kellermann himself, Sir Hew Dalrymple desired me
to sign it."   Wellesley dutifully complied, with the comment
that it was an extraordinary paper, promptly silenced by his   26
superior's retort that it did not contain anything that had not
been settled.

He was extremely uncomfortable—" my situation in this   27
army is a very delicate one.   I never saw Sir Hew Dalrymple till
yesterday ; and it is not a very easy task to advise any man on
the first day one meets him.   He must at least be prepared to
receive advice."   Sir Hew was not.   Advice from Wellesley was
the last need he felt ; and the veteran was not rendered more
receptive by Castlereagh's expressed desire that he should make   10
of Sir Arthur the most prominent use permitted by the rules of
the service.   For, as he testified, " those rules, and my own   28
feelings of what was due to myself, and to the distinguished
Officers senior to Sir Arthur Wellesley . . . would not allow of
my making any extensive use of the talents of that General after
my whole force was assembled."   Small wonder that Sir Arthur's
letters grew almost plaintive—" I should prefer going home to   27

staying here. However, if you wish me to stay, I will : I only beg that you will not blame me if things do not go on as you and my friends in London wish they should." Things undeniably did not. The imperfect armistice became a still more imperfect Convention ; the French were to evacuate Portugal ; but as the precious weeks before the autumn rains went by, the British hung uncertainly about the outskirts of Lisbon. Wellesley was more uncomfortable than ever. Slighted by Dalrymple, he found consolation in defiant presentations and addresses from his military colleagues and in angry letters home—" I am sick of all that is going here, and I heartily wish I had never come away from Ireland, and that I was back again with you." That might be compassed ; but before he went, he made a singular approach to Moore. Drawn to him by a generous letter of congratulation after Vimeiro, Sir Arthur was still more attracted by Moore's chivalrous attitude : " I have told both Sir Hew and Sir Arthur that I wished not to interfere ; that if the hostilities commenced, Sir Arthur had already done so much, that I thought it but fair he should have the command of whatever was brilliant in the finishing. I waived all pretensions as senior. I considered this as his expedition. . . . I should aid as far as I could for the good of the service, and, without interference with Sir Arthur, I should take any part that was allotted to me." These feelings were reciprocated on Sir Arthur's side by a positively mutinous determination to secure the substitution of Moore for Dalrymple in command of the expedition. He wrote to him at length, offering to press the Cabinet in this direction ; they talked the matter over ; but John Moore, always impeccable, replied a shade severely that he " could enter into no intrigue upon the subject." He was frankly disinclined to save ministerial faces by making " a submission, or anything that tended to it, which I thought unbecoming," though he admitted stiffly that he should be obliged to Wellesley or to any other friend who might remove the unfavourable impression that he had made upon the Cabinet.

There was no more for him to do in Portugal. He had declined a fatuous proposal of Sir Hew that he should go to Madrid upon a diplomatic mission ; and he was equally unenthusiastic about a scheme of Castlereagh's for sending him to report upon the north of Spain—" I am not a draftsman, and but a bad hand at description. . . . I have told Sir Hew Dalrymple that I was not able to perform the duty in which you had desired I should be employed ; that I was not a topographical engineer, and could not pretend to describe in writing such a country as the Asturias." He grasped the problem, though. Where soldiers like Moore irritably denounced Cabinet strategy as " a sort of gibberish which   35 men in office use and fancy themselves military men," Sir Arthur helped ministers towards a plan.   Before he sailed from Portugal, he wrote a luminous survey of Spanish prospects.   His estimate showed few illusions as to his country's allies :

> " I doubt not that, if an accurate report could be made upon   36
> their state, they want arms, ammunition, money, clothing, and
> military equipments of every description ; and although such a
> body are very formidable and efficient in their own country, and
> probably equal to its defence, they must not be reckoned upon out
> of it ; and in any case it is impossible to estimate the effect of their
> efforts.   In some cases equal numbers will oppose with success the
> French troops ; in others, 1,000 Frenchmen, with cavalry and
> artillery, will disperse thousands of them, and no reliance can be
> placed on them in their present state."

He was prepared to contemplate the conduct of combined opera-tions with these allies by a British force of 15,000, which " should advance from Portugal, to which Kingdom it would be in the mean time a defence."   But he drew a great distinction between the risks that could properly be taken with this relatively small British contingent and the bulk of the expeditionary force :

> " The next consideration is the employment of the remainder
> of the army now in Portugal, amounting by estimate to about
> 10,000 men, with an additional corps of 10,000 men assembled and
> ready in England, and some cavalry.   I acknowledge that I do not
> think the affairs in Spain are in so prosperous a state as that you
> can trust, in operations within that kingdom, the whole disposable
> force which England possesses, without adopting measures of pre-
> caution, which will render its retreat to the sea coast nearly certain.
> Besides this, I will not conceal from you that our people are so new
> in the field, that I do not know of persons capable of supplying, or,
> if supplied, of distributing the supplies, to an army of 40,000 men
> (British troops) acting together in a body.   Even if plenty could be
> expected to exist, we should starve in the midst of it, for want of
> due arrangement.   But the first objection is conclusive.   We may
> depend upon it that whenever we shall assemble an army, the French

will consider its defeat and destruction their first object, particularly
if Buonaparte should be at the head of the French troops himself ;
and if the operations of our army should be near the French frontier,
he will have the means of multiplying and will multiply the numbers,
upon our army in such a degree as must get the better of them.   For
the British army, therefore, we must have a retreat open, and that
retreat must be the sea. . . .

" The only efficient plan of operations in which the British troops
can be employed, consistently with this view, is upon the flank and
rear of the enemy's advance towards Madrid, by an issue from the
Asturias.   If it be true, as is stated by the Asturian deputies in
London, that their country is remarkably strong, and that it is
secure from French invasion—if it be true that the ports of Santander
and Gijon, the former particularly, are secure harbours in the
winter—and if the walls can give to both, or either, the means of
making an embarkation, even if the enemy should be able to retreat
through the mountains—the Asturias is the country we should
secure immediately, in which we should assemble our disposable
forces as soon as possible, and issue forth into the plains, either by
Leon or the pass of Reynosa.   The army could then have a short,
although probably a difficult communication with the sea, which
must be carried on by mules, of which there are plenty in the
country. . . ."

Meanwhile the British striking force of 15,000 might join the
Spaniards farther to the south.   Their lot, he granted, would be
more precarious ; but he was prepared to face the risk.

" First, I conceive that there is a great deal of difference between
the risk of the loss of such a corps as this, and that of the loss of the
whole of the disposable force of Great Britain.   Secondly, it does
not follow that, because the whole British army could not make its
retreat into Portugal, a corps of 15,000 could not. . . .   I conclude,
then, that although this corps might be risked, and its retreat to the
sea should be considered in some degree *en l'air*, that of the whole
disposable force of Great Britain ought to be, and must be, saved."

These bold designs differed completely from the prevailing
character of British operations.   For sea-power, which kept
an easy line of retreat permanently open behind every British
expedition, had largely atrophied strategical conceptions ; and
most contemporary soldiers were satisfied with " our old style
of expedition,—a landing, a short march, and a good fight, and
then a lounge home again."   Even John Moore had once made

use of the disastrous term, ' a littoral warfare.' But this innocuous form of military ' tip-and-run ' was unlikely to modify the
European situation. For in 1808 the French Empire was broad-
based upon its undefeated armies. The last word of sea-power
had been spoken at Trafalgar ; and if the world was ever to be
freed, the victory must be won on land. Baylen had shewn the
way ; Vimeiro followed ; and Sir Arthur saw the long road that
lay before his country.

Meanwhile, there was no prospect of immediate operations.
The French were gone ; the rains were imminent ; a high official
at Dublin Castle had just died ; and he applied for leave. He
scarcely seemed to mind what prospect offered, so long as Dalrymple did not darken it, since he wrote to Castlereagh that " it
is quite impossible for me to continue any longer with this army ;
and I wish, therefore, that you would allow me to return home
and resume the duties of my office, if I should still be in office,
and it is convenient to the Government that I should still retain
it ; or if not, that I should remain upon the Staff in England ; or,
if that should not be practicable, that I should remain without
employment." For Dublin Castle, the Horse Guards, or half-pay
were preferable to an endless farce with a cast consisting almost
wholly of preposterous veterans—of an old gentleman who habitually alluded to the Thames when he meant the Tagus, and the
less endearing figures of Sir Harry and Sir Hew, who lived on in
his exasperated memory as ' the Gentlemen.' So he turned an
indignant back on Portugal, and went down to the water-front at
Lisbon. A ship received him ; the brown forts of Cascaes slid
by ; the tall hills above Cintra receded in the autumn mists ; and
he was homeward-bound once more.

II

His homecoming was not triumphal—quite the reverse. For the people of England, always a trifle irresponsible on military matters, had decided to resent the Convention under which the French evacuated Portugal. Opinion settled down with gusto to a noisy hunt for scapegoats, and from the accident that Dalrymple's despatch enclosing the Convention was dated from Cintra,

1   " Britannia sickens, Cintra! at thy name."

This temper was excusable, since the treaty was a bitter disappointment. A defeat would have been easier to bear ; for defeats were usual. But to be starved of victory for fifteen years, to thrill with the glad tidings of Vimeiro, to wait on tip-toe for a crowning triumph, and then to learn that the defeated enemy were to be shipped comfortably home was beyond bearing. The mild eyes of Mr. Wordsworth flashed fury at the outrageous
2   thought of " turning the British Lion into a beast of burthen, to carry a vanquished enemy, with his load of iniquities, when and whither it had pleased him." Small wonder that, in *Childe Harold's* memory,

3   " Pens, tongues, feet, hands combined in wild uproar ;
        Mayors, Aldermen laid down the uplifted fork ;
        The Bench of Bishops half forgot to snore ;
        Stern Cobbett, who for one whole week forbore
        To question aught, once more with transport leapt,
        And bit his devilish quill agen, and swore
        With foes such treaty never should be kept,
      While roared the blatant Beast, and roared, and raged and—slept ! "

The explosion was universal and ranged the whole gamut of abuse from shrill invective in newspapers with funeral borders and angry caricatures of the three Generals wearing white feathers or dangling from gallows to Canning's bland announcement that he should in future spell ' humiliation ' with a ' Hew.'

These clouds were mounting in the sky, as Wellesley sailed for England. He reached Plymouth on October 4 and gathered his *4* forces to resist the onslaught. His strategy was deft, since he promptly wrote a friendly letter to a leading member of the Whig *5* Opposition. As he had written to John Moore, " I am no party *6* man " ; and at such moments there was something to be said for a slight cultivation of the mammon of unrighteousness. Not that he was afraid. For his sturdy temper appeared in the note he sent to Richard upon reaching Harley Street once more :

> " I arrived here this day, and I don't know whether I am to be *7* hanged drawn & quartered ; or roasted alive. However I shall not allow the Mob of London to deprive me of my temper or my spirits ; or of the satisfaction which I feel in the consciousness that I acted right."

The Wellesley clan was mobilised in his defence—William at the Admiralty, Henry at the Treasury, and Richard in the solemn shades where returned proconsuls await the summons (often long delayed) to high office—whilst angry Whigs confessed themselves " not sorry to see the Wellesley pride a little lowered," and *8* Cobbett railed against " the arrogance of that damned infernal family." The family, indeed, was veering slightly. For their hopes, so long pinned upon Richard, were positively turning to Arthur. Their mother, with a slight lapse of tact, congratulated him on his younger brother's victory—" upon the glorious *9* success of our Beloved Hero ! God Bless him . . ."—and Richard was left brooding darkly on the fate reserved for the brothers of great men. But he was still head of the family ; and Kitty, sometimes a little apt to gush, poured out her troubles to him after Vimeiro.

> " Even the Hopes with which the Newspapers are filled are too *10* agitating not to give great uneasiness. But I am a Soldier's Wife and the husband of whom it is the pride of my life to think shall find that he has no reason to be ashamed of me. All promises well, the Cause is a glorious one, and Please God we shall see our friends return safe and successful. My Boys are well and lovely."

Arthur's first errand was to Castlereagh, where he did his best for Moore and reported to Sir John that " I am placed under your *11* command, than which nothing can be more satisfactory to me. I will go to Coruña immediately, where I hope to find you." They never met, though ; for a postscript added that he must first appear in the enquiry to be held into the Portuguese *imbroglio*. Tempers were rising ; and when he asked Castlereagh to drive him to the Levée, the cautious statesman " hemmed and hawed, and said that there was so much ill-humour in the public mind that it might produce inconvenience, and, in short, he advised me not to go to the levée."

Sir Arthur had an answer ready. " When I first mentioned it," he said, "I only thought it a matter of respect and duty to the King ; I now look upon it as a matter of self-respect and duty to my own character, and I therefore insist on knowing whether this advice proceeds in any degree from His Majesty, and I wish you distinctly to understand that I will go to the levée to-morrow, or I never will go to a levée in my life."

Sir Arthur went.

His sovereign, who had faced mobs himself, was uncommonly civil ; and whilst he was at Court, the General enjoyed the spectacle of the Corporation of London petitioning for an enquiry into the Convention and being royally snubbed. But no Government could resist the public pressure indefinitely, and a military tribunal was appointed to inquire "into the late Armistice and Convention concluded in Portugal, and into all the circumstances connected therewith." Meanwhile Sir Arthur went to Ireland, saw Kitty once again, and steadily refused to take part in the public controversy. Friends were informed that " I will publish nothing, nor will authorise the publication of anything by others " ; strangers who volunteered assistance in the press were faced with a polite refusal to furnish material or correct their text ; and the obliging Croker, who had laid his pen at the Chief Secretary's feet, learned that Sir Arthur had " not read even one, much less all, the calumnies which have been circulated against me during my absence in Portugal." Not that he was inactive. For he corresponded with his Whig connections, read interminable arguments in his defence composed by William, and returned to London in November, when the Board was ready to sit.

It was a strange tribunal. Solemnly convened at Chelsea Hospital by royal warrant, the Board of General Officers met under the tall windows of the Great Hall. There were seven of them—three peers, a baronet, two commoners, and a knight. But the knight presided, since Sir David Dundas was blest with seniority compared with which Sir Hew Dalrymple was a school-boy. Had he not served on one of Chatham's expeditions in the Seven Years' War ? The War of Independence found him deep in military erudition ; he wrote profusely upon tactics ; at sixty he commanded a brigade in Colonel Wesley's first campaign ; and now at seventy-three, known with affectionate derision as ' Old Pivot,' he presided in the court by which Sir Arthur and his seniors were to be tried. The other members, a galaxy of minor talent with reminiscences of Bunker's Hill and Pitt's less successful expeditions, presented an array of martial eminence less formidable in the field than in White's window. Sir Hew, Sir Harry, and Sir Arthur were summoned to their bar in the Great Hall at Chelsea, where they sat before mellow panelling not yet ennobled by the names of Sir Arthur's victories. These instruments of justice moved with becoming deliberation. They called for bales of correspondence ; disdaining hasty study, they listened patiently whilst a clerk recited it *vivâ voce* ; they summoned witnesses and, with all eternity before them, invited written narratives. Sir Hew disclosed his spite against Sir Arthur at the first opportunity, complaining of newspaper attacks " for the purpose of rescuing a   17 more favoured Officer from the unlooked for unpopularity of a measure he most certainly approved." Wellesley retorted with a comprehensive denial of complicity in any press campaign and blandly admitted his concurrence in " the principle of the measure, viz. that the French should be allowed to evacuate Portugal," adding that he " did not think it proper to refuse to sign the paper on account of my disagreement on the details." (That day the Emperor beneath the spires of Burgos watched his marching columns flooding southwards across Old Castile ; for the *Grande Armée* was bearing King Joseph back to his capital.) Sir Arthur's narrative was put in evidence, and he met a written cross-exami-nation with bare, but convincing, references to the correspondence. He was at pains to spare Sir Harry " not only out of regard to   18 him, but because I think it fatal to the public service to expose officers to the treatment which I have received, and to punish-ment for acting upon their own military opinions." His whole difference was with Dalrymple, and his defence was plainly stated :

" It is perfectly true that I advised the principle of the arrange-   19 ment, that I assisted the Commander-in-Chief in discussing the different points with General Kellermann ; and that I gave him my opinion when he asked it, and when I thought it desirable to give it him. But I was not the negociator, and could not be, and was not so considered, the Commander of the Forces being present in the room, deciding upon all points, and taking part in all discussions. If indeed, the Commander of the forces had given me instructions to negociate this instrument, and I had then negociated it, I might have been responsible for its contents ; or at all events, for the manner in which it was drawn up ; but as it is, my signature is a mere form."

This was plain enough ; and as the case went on, he called his witnesses. (The French were still in flood ; Polish lancers cantered against entrenchments in the throat of a Spanish pass ; and the Emperor breasted the mountains that look down on Madrid.) Sir Arthur was still answering questions beneath the picture of King Charles II, who caracoled across a wall in Chelsea resisting the discreet allurements of a whole bevy of feminine mythology. His closing speech was lucid and assured. The Board took three meetings to consider its Report, one more to draft it, and a final assembly for signature. It was December now. The French were marching north again. For John Moore, emerging warily from Portugal, had thrust into Leon " bridle in hand ; for if the bubble bursts, we shall have a run for it." The run was just beginning ; for the Emperor had divined the threat to the long road that wound behind him towards France and turned sharply north to meet the challenge. The hunt was up ; John Moore edged northwards ; and his pursuer crossed the Guadarrama in the teeth of a midwinter storm, tramping angrily among the freezing, cursing files with the snow driving in his face.

That day the Board at Chelsea Hospital signed their Report. It was a cautious document, less actuated by an overwhelming sense of justice than by a professional desire to spare everybody's feelings. It found the facts, praised Wellesley for Vimeiro, arrived at no decision on the sole point to be decided, and concluded in a mood of hazy benevolence that " no further military proceeding is necessary on the subject." The Duke of York perused it and unkindly pointed out the evasion, writing with unseasonable sharpness on Christmas Day that the Convention of Cintra " has been altogether omitted." Faced with the unpleasant necessity of making a decision, the Board (while Moore's rearguard were breaking bridges on the long road to the sea) had one meeting more and approved the armistice by six votes to one and the Convention by a narrower majority of four to three.

This terminated the proceedings, though the public mind continued to be exercised. Mr. Wordsworth, writing at some disadvantage from his retreat at Grasmere, explored the larger issues in the *Courier*. He quoted Milton and the Georgics and ransacked the outer regions of Petrarch and Dante for damaging quotations. But though he tramped up the bare shoulder of Dunmail Raise   *23* to meet the post, polemics at long range were far from easy ; and when his noble lucubrations were expanded into ' the last great example of a Miltonic tract ' and (De Quincey aiding with the proofs) put out in a pamphlet, few of the five hundred copies were sold, though Walter Scott agreed with his sentiments. But   *24* while disapproving of the treaty, Scott was very far from disapproving of Sir Arthur—" I would to God Wellesley were now   *25* at the head of the English in Spain. His late examination shows his acute and decisive talents for command ; and although I believe in my conscience that when he found himself superseded, he suffered the pigs to run through the business, when he might in some measure have prevented them—

> ' Yet give the haughty devil his due,
> Though bold his quarterings, they are true.' "

But the haughty devil was relegated for the moment to the lowlier duties of Chief Secretary for Ireland and, as 1809 came in, sat modestly behind his writing-table at Dublin Castle. Moore's men, vowed unforgettably to " glory, disgrace, victory, and   *26* misfortune," were reeling through the snow to Lugo, as Sir Arthur fingered official tape once more. Ireland was quite unchanged. The same gentlemen still asked for the same favours, and the same Yeomanry pursued the same offenders. But Wellesley was indisposed to govern it indefinitely. " I shall go to England for   *27* the meeting of Parliament, and mean to join the army as soon afterwards as I shall be allowed to go." His martial inclinations were encouraged by loyal tributes from Londonderry and Limerick ; and Castlereagh was duly advised of his intention to   *28* " join the army if it should remain on service in Spain within a limited time." Meanwhile Sir Arthur wrote to the Lord Mayor   *29* of Dublin upon street improvements, and Moore turned to bay on the jagged hills above Corunna.

The House met in January, 1809 ; and he was in his place to receive the thanks of Parliament for Vimeiro. Kitty gave a parting ball in Dublin and followed him to England. When his own pluralism was challenged by the Opposition, he undertook to resign his civil office upon being appointed to another command ; and to accelerate, perhaps, this welcome event he spoke in defence of the Duke of York, now labouring in sad disgrace by reason of unkind suggestions, the sprightly Mrs. Clarke, and the list of promotions pinned to the royal bed-curtains. There was a long debate on the Convention ; and when Tarleton spoke against it, Sir Arthur assured that dashing relic of the War of Independence that he " would much rather follow his example in the field than his advice." On the next day he testified before the Clarke committee to the excellence of the Duke of York's work for the army ; and before March was out, the House of Commons heard him on the blessings that canals would confer on Irish agriculture. It was his swan-song. For on April 7 he resigned his seat.

There was more work for him abroad ; and he escaped from Westminster with obvious relief. All Spain was now submerged by the French tide ; and as the rising waters flooded into Portugal, Cradock, who had succeeded John Moore, waited uneasily near Lisbon. The Cabinet (as Cabinets will in times of military doubt) looked in two directions. For Canning fixed a fascinated stare upon Cadiz and thought hard of campaigns in Andalusia, while Castlereagh's mind ran on Portugal. The latter still relied on Wellesley for military advice. Sir Arthur had not lost his confidence ; his brother Charles still wrote to Castlereagh from the Peninsula, " Would to God we had the hero of Vimeiro at our head now " ; and in March Wellesley wrote a paper for the Secretary of State on the Defence of Portugal. His views were simple :

> " I have always been of opinion that Portugal might be defended whatever might be the result of the contest in Spain ; and that, in the mean time, the measures adopted for the defence of Portugal would be highly useful to the Spanish in their contest with the French. My notion was that the Portuguese military establishments, upon the footing of 40,000 militia and 30,000 regular troops,

12

ought to be revived, and that, in addition to these troops, his Majesty ought to employ an army in Portugal, amounting to about 20,000 British troops, including about 4,000 cavalry. My opinion was that, even if Spain should have been conquered, the French would not have been able to overcome Portugal with a smaller force than 100,000 men ; and that, so long as the contest should continue in Spain, this force, if it could be put in a state of activity, would be highly useful to the Spaniards, and might have eventually decided the contest. . . .

" The first measures to be adopted are to complete the army in Portugal with its cavalry and artillery, and to horse the ordnance as it ought to be. As soon as this shall be done, the General and Staff officers should go out. . . ."

They took him at his word. For when Canning's Andalusian designs went thoroughly astray, Castlereagh prevailed and the Cabinet submitted Wellesley's name for the Portuguese command. Their tone, in writing to the King, was diffident. For " your Majesty's servants have not been unmindful of the in- [37] convenience that might arise, in case of any considerable increase of this force, from Sir Arthur Wellesley's being so young a Lieutenant-General. But, as any material increase of the army in Portugal cannot be at present looked to as probable . . . they humbly conceive that your Majesty's service (without prejudice to the claims of the distinguished officers in your Majesty's army who are his seniors) may have the benefit of Sir Arthur Wellesley's being employed where he has had the good fortune of being successful, and that it will remain open for your Majesty's future consideration to make a different arrangement of the command, if, under all the circumstances, it shall appear to your Majesty proper to confide it to a general officer of higher rank." This oddly apologetic tone served his turn ; Majesty concurred ; and Wellesley was appointed.

It was the end of March, 1809 ; and he was free to go. Ireland receded now (though there was still time for a note to the Irish [38] Office upon Mr. Croker's attitude towards the Dublin Paving Bill) and, his seat and office gleefully resigned, he made his preparations. As the Lodge in Phœnix Park was given up, Kitty would want a place in England. The Lord-Lieutenant offered obligingly to let them a small house near Goodwood ; but Sir [39] Arthur thought she would be going to Malvern when the weather

got warm enough. Then he went down to Portsmouth and waited for a wind. Before sailing he called for a complete print
38 of " the Spanish & Portuguese papers, including Mr. Frere's correspondence with Sir John Moore," together with a volume of evidence on Indian patronage for lighter reading in Portugal.
40 He felt some scruples about superseding Cradock and, with a lively recollection of his own embarrassments after Vimeiro, declined to do so " if he had been in any manner successful " ; for Sir Arthur was disinclined to play the *rôle* of Sir Hew. For days he stared across the Solent, waiting for a wind ; and when it blew, it blew a gale. *Surveillante* sailed ; and as they pitched down-Channel in the roaring darkness, the despairing captain
41 thought of running them ashore on the Isle of Wight. It was just bedtime, when an excited aide-de-camp informed Sir Arthur that it would soon be all over with them. " In that case," his studiously undramatic chief replied, " I shall not take off my boots."

III

I⊤ was the month of April, 1809, when he sailed once again for
the Peninsula. Each time the curtain rose on a new scene to
the same overture. For each chapter of his life appeared to open
with the same interlude at sea. The boatswain piped, blocks
creaked, the waves went dancing by, and the sea-wind sang in
the halyards. Sometimes it was the Dublin packet taking a
small boy to England, sometimes a transport ferrying an anxious
Colonel to his first campaign ; tall East Indiamen carried him
round the Cape and up the Hooghly to Calcutta or, more respectful of their passenger, sailed up-Channel homeward bound with
a tanned General. It was not long since *Crocodile* had stood
across the Bay, taking an eager man to Portugal ; and now he
sailed in the same track for the last time. For five busy years
he knew the sea no more, since the Peninsula was waiting, its
mountains ranged behind the mists ; and his road wound endlessly across the bare hillsides, past empty towns and dim
cathedrals, until the folded mountains lay all behind him and he
could look back to Spain. France lay before him then, mile
after mile, spread out below the Pyrenees. When he next
stepped on board ship (it was at Calais), a Duke came up the
gangway and a discarded Emperor sat idly in the sunshine of
1814, watching the summer waves that broke on Elba. But now
it was mid-April, 1809 ; and the long road still lay before him,
winding all the way from Lisbon to the Pyrenees.

He would be forty in a week or so ; and Alexander, he could
still reflect, had conquered the world at thirty-one. But then, had
Alexander governed Mysore or sat in the Chief Secretary's room
at Dublin Castle ? These odd preliminaries of conquest had filled
Sir Arthur's life. (Perhaps they taught him lessons Alexander
never knew.) Besides, Sir Arthur took his time. Rarely impulsive, he proceeded with a measured tread ; and now his sober
pace took him once more to Portugal. If fighting Frenchmen was
his business in life, there were Frenchmen in abundance to be
fought in the Peninsula. Life, indeed, seemed to hold little else for

him. For he was not leaving much behind. There was always Kitty, to be sure. Poor, fluttered Kitty did her best to be ' a Soldier's Wife.' He was her pride—the slightly alarming object of her veneration. But what was she to him ? When England dropped below the horizon, Kitty, one feels, dropped with it. His fancy was unvisited by images of Kitty ; or if they came to him, they wore a slightly exasperating aspect—of Kitty with her frightened manner running into debt, or sitting in the big barouche with her face hidden in a book. He hated debts ; he had seen debts enough when he was young ; but Kitty could never manage money and was too shy to tell him until she had fallen into arrears. And then she always read a book when she drove out, because she was dreadfully short-sighted. For Kitty could never recognise the bowing figures in the myopic haze along the pavement and sought refuge in her book—unworthy artifice for the wife of a coming man. Small wonder that, as he rose steadily, she lagged a little. For she was born to be his Dublin wife ; and as Dublin receded, Kitty—short-sighted, muddled about accounts, and a little scared—receded with it. She was uneasy, too ; for at the news of his next victory, her brother expressed without undue confidence a hope that " it may ultimately produce as much comfort to his family as honour to his Country." It evidently had not brought much comfort yet.

So Kitty waited for the news in Harley Street, and the ship sailed on, taking Sir Arthur back to the Peninsula. He was not leaving much behind. Perhaps the thought made him a little hard when other men applied for leave. Perhaps the dusty distances of Spain dried up some spring within him. At any rate, the void at home left him free to concentrate upon his problems. His plan was formulated on paper within two days of his arrival at Lisbon :

" I intend to move towards Soult, and attack him, if I should to able to make any arrangement in the neighbourhood of Abrantes, which can give me any security for the safety of this place during my absence to the northward.

" I am not quite certain, however, that I should not do more good to the general cause by combining with General Cuesta in an operation against Victor ; and I believe I should prefer this last, if Soult were not in possession of a part of this country which is very fertile in resources and of the town of Oporto, and if to concert the operations with General Cuesta would not take time which might be profitably employed in operations against Soult.

" I think it probable, however, that Soult will not remain in Portugal when I shall pass the Mondego : if he does, I shall attack him. If he should retire, I am convinced that it would be most advantageous for the common cause, that we should remain on the defensive in the north of Portugal, and act vigorously in co-operation with Cuesta against Victor. . . .

" I am convinced that the French will be in serious danger in Spain only when a great force shall be assembled which will oblige them to collect their troops ; and this combined operation of the force in this country, with that under General Cuesta, may be the groundwork of further measures of the same and a more extended description."

The design was simple—a thrust at Soult in northern Portugal, followed by a joint Anglo-Spanish attack upon the French in central Spain. He made his customary preparations, assembled bullock-carts, called loudly for horse transport, and reviewed in detail the supply arrangements of his Portuguese allies. His flank was shielded from the French in Spain by the simple-minded expedient of collecting all the boats in which they might have crossed the flooded Tagus. Then he moved northwards against Soult. One novelty was introduced into his command. For he attached a company of riflemen to his infantry brigades—a memory, perhaps, of early reading in Lloyd's *History of the late War in Germany* (purchased by Colonel Wesley in 1796 before his voyage to India), assisted by his observation of the French columns of attack at Vimeiro. A strange interlude engaged him, when a French Captain of Dragoons appeared mysteriously in the British lines. His story was obscure. Soult, it appeared, assuming royal airs at Oporto, encouraged crowds of Portuguese to shout for ' King Nicholas.' After all, if Murat was King of Naples and Joseph Bonaparte of Spain, there could be no impropriety in Soult's becoming King of Northern Lusitania. Crowns were in fashion ; but some of his brother-officers, either from envy or revolutionary austerity, resented the new mode and were prepared to kidnap the aspirant, if Wellesley would oblige with a timely offensive. Furtive interviews with mysterious strangers were not Sir Arthur's *forte* ; nature had not designed him for a conspirator. But he saw Argenton and

picked up some useful information upon Soult's dispositions,
though he retained his determination that he " should not wait
for a revolt, but shall try my own means of subduing Soult."
His visitor returned one night. They met over a camp-fire
beside the road ; and Argenton repeated his incitements,
obligingly presenting Wellesley with a paper upon Soult's line of
retreat. But Sir Arthur persisted in his endeavour to eject Soult
from Portugal by fair means, leaving Argenton to a feverish
career of hairbreadth escapes that was ended, before the year was
out, by a French firing-party at Grenelle.

His march towards the French continued through days bright
with flowers showering from grateful windows and nights thrilling
with false alarms and the never-ending song of frogs. Soult was
still waiting for him at Oporto, sweeping the seaward sky for a
first glimpse of his sails. But Sir Arthur was ashore and marching
north. True, the broad Douro, flowing beneath its cliffs, glinted
between his marching columns and the town ; but had not
fording Indian rivers formerly been one of his accomplishments ?
Some barges were discovered ; the bank was quite unguarded ;
and one morning he launched a surprise attack with the unobtrusive recklessness of his gruff " Well, let the men cross." The
astounding throw succeeded ; and the French, surprised in broad
daylight, were hustled out of Oporto on May 12 at a cost of one
hundred and twenty British casualties. Soult, headed off from
every practicable road, plunged miserably off in driving rain into
the hills towards the north. His guns, his bullion, and his stores
were sacrificed ; and after a week of arduous retreat by winding
tracks that hung precariously above terrifying gorges a starving,
tattered mob, that had once been the Army of Portugal, staggered
to safety in the first Spanish town. Sir Arthur's opening move
was a complete success, though he wrote home resentfully that
" if the Portuguese troops had been worth their salt," his adversary " would have been hard pressed and probably could not have
escaped." A fortnight had sufficed him to manœuvre Soult out
of Oporto, and in less than four weeks from his landing he had
cleared Portugal.

Then he turned south again to carry out the second part of
his design and deal with the French in central Spain, writing
briskly to a colleague that " as you have seen Soult out, you might
as well see what we can do with Victor." Much might be done

with Victor. For the operations of the French were unco-ordin-
ated beyond Sir Arthur's wildest dreams. King Joseph hunted
his rebellious subjects with a divergent pack of Marshals, who
bayed in all directions—Junot and Mortier in Aragon, Ney in
Galicia, St. Cyr in Catalonia, and Sebastiani among the dust and
windmills of La Mancha. At intervals King Joseph sounded an
ineffectual horn ; and at longer intervals the post brought
Imperial rescripts full of detailed instructions in the familiar
staccato manner, months out of date and hopelessly inapplicable
to Spanish conditions. The Emperor, deep in another war,
was off again in Central Europe ; and the sharp voice came
faintlier now from bivouacs along the Danube—from Eckmühl,
from Ratisbon, and at length from the echoing corridors of
Schönbrunn. Left almost to themselves, the Marshals plunged
about Spain a little wildly, and Sir Arthur had an unequalled
opportunity to interrupt their gambols. Far to the north Soult
irritated Ney ; Ney reviled Soult ; their officers fought duels
freely ; and a Marshal's sword was positively drawn upon a
brother-Marshal. Small wonder that their operations lacked
unity of purpose, and that the King of Spain was left to learn the
news of Soult's eviction from Oporto by the circuitous route of
a despatch from Paris. Victor, in this strategic whirlpool, had
essayed an isolated thrust almost up to the Portuguese frontier ;
and if the riposte were swift, much might be done with Victor.

    But Sir Arthur had allies, and the delights of combined
operations with a Spanish army were new to him. He was
already equal to the shaggy geniality of up-country *guerrilleros*,
all side-arms and moustaches ; but grave-eyed generals by Goya,
whose elaborate courtesy almost invariably ran to full uniform
and decorations but rarely kept appointments, were a more
serious affair. His present collaborator was Don Gregorio de la
Cuesta, Captain-General of Estremadura. This paladin, now
rising seventy, was less menacing as an adverary than as an ally ;
for he looked back upon an uninterrupted record of sanguinary
(and frequently avoidable) defeat. Composed in equal parts
of pride and failing health, he was the embodiment of Spain at
its very worst—old, proud, incompetent, and ailing—and Sir
Arthur could hardly hope to have a more instructive object-lesson
in the joys of allied operations. With his illusions strong upon
him he moved southward, while Cuesta proffered imbecile

suggestions for a combined attack on Victor, which rested on the
rosy hypothesis that Victor would oblige by keeping absolutely
still while they annihilated him at leisure. But Victor, who had
not been trained in Cuesta's school, fell back. Sir Arthur was
not altogether easy, though for the moment the causes of his
uneasiness were domestic. For his army gave him grave reason
for dissatisfaction. Discipline left much to be desired. As he
wrote, " we are not naturally a military people ; the whole
business of an army upon service is foreign to our habits . . .
particularly in a poor country like this." He hated looting and
wrote angrily that " I have long been of opinion that a British
army could bear neither success nor failure, and I have had
manifest proof of the truth of this opinion in the recent conduct
of the soldiers of this army. They have plundered the country
most terribly. . . ." The Government was pouring its best
troops into the thirsty levels of Walcheren ; and perhaps Sir
Arthur got more than his share of Irish units. At any rate his
complaints ended in a grim announcement : " the army behave
terribly ill. They are a rabble who cannot bear success any
more than Sir John Moore's army could bear failure. I am
endeavouring to tame them. . . ." Besides, supplies were short
(these were the days when he assured a ruffled commissary that
if a General had really threatened to hang him, he would keep
his word) ; and Mr. Huskisson at the Treasury was slow in meeting
his demands for currency.

But he moved slowly forward, writing cheerfully that " the
ball is now at my foot, and I hope I shall have strength enough to
give it a good kick." In the last week of June they left Abrantes ;
on July 3 they passed the frontier into Spain ; and for ten days
they lay at Plasencia. Then he reviewed the Spanish army and
knew the worst. He reviewed it, owing to a slight lapse of
Spanish staff-work, at night ; but even by torch-light the aspect
of his allies was far from reassuring, and their commander's
scarcely more so. For Cuesta, whose cavalry escaping hastily
from his last defeat had ridden over him, was in the habit of commanding from a coach, though he had been hoisted for the occasion
on to a horse, where he was precariously maintained by pride and
two assistants. He had already impressed Sir Arthur in correspondence with being " as obstinate as any gentleman at the head
of any army need be," and he was no easier in conference, where

his refusals to comply with his ally's suggestions were filtered through an English-speaking Chief of Staff named (with a friendly reminiscence of Dublin) O'Donoju. Victor was waiting for them near Talavera by the slow waters of the Alberche. When they came up with him, Cuesta was lifted from his coach, deposited upon its cushions, and invited by Sir Arthur to co-operate in an attack ; but the chance was missed. The French fell back once *21* more ; and his enemy having withdrawn, Cuesta became unnaturally enterprising. Faint but pursuing in his coach, he pressed after them across the endless plain that rolled dustily towards Madrid, leaving Wellesley at Talavera darkly resolved to go no farther. Cuesta grew " more and more impracticable every *22* day. It is impossible to do business with him, and very uncertain that any operation will succeed in which he has any concern." Besides, he could not move without supplies ; the Spaniards fed *23* themselves and left their allies to starve. So he resolved to halt and, if necessary, withdraw from Spain. Meanwhile, the impulsive Spaniards in full cry towards Toledo and Madrid, stumbled into forty thousand Frenchmen with Marshal Jourdan and King Joseph at their head and hastily fell back towards Sir Arthur. He watched them streaming in and begged his colleague to retreat a little farther. The Spaniards, he conceived, would not be at their best, if they engaged the French with a river immediately in their own rear. So he sought Cuesta ; but his ally was invisible. It was a July afternoon, and the old General was (not *24* unpardonably) sleeping off his retreat. Sir Arthur interrupted his prolonged siesta and found him more than usually obstinate. For if it was bitter to have lost the bright vision of Madrid, whose gleaming towers had danced before his eager eyes during the brief advance, would it not be galling beyond words to watch his ragged, scared battalions trailing back under the cold eyes of a contemptuous ally ? Sir Arthur pleaded, argued, coaxed, and positively knelt to the exacting mummy to whom fate had bound him as an ally. Then the old *hidalgo's* pride was satisfied ; and he consented to fall back a little farther. The British were to stand on the green hills that shoulder their way towards the plain of Talavera. The mules of Cuesta's coach jingled incon- *25* gruously by ; and as the old gentleman sat in the shadow of a cross on the roadside, his staff scandalised a German commissary by standing round with cigarettes. There was a scuffle, as the *26*

French passed the Alberche ; Sir Arthur galloped to the front and was almost caught among their skirmishers. Then he rode off to rally the agitated Spaniards in the dusty plain between Talavera and the green hills that climbed towards the tall sierra. Their officers appeared to have abdicated ; and the Sepoy General, who was not unaccustomed to fluttered auxiliaries, took charge himself.

That night (it was July 27–28) his command was roughly aligned to the north of Talavera facing eastwards, and the brook Portiña crawled along their front. The position—half hillside, half dusty levels—had nothing very much to commend it. But at least his troops were all assembled there, and the French, it seemed, would be good enough to attack. They were ; indeed, they did so in the night. They attacked again at dawn ; and through the heat of a long summer day they flung themselves against the scrubby sides of the Portiña gorge or streamed across the plain. Sometimes there was an interval, when panting men crept to the little stream between the armies and gulped its uninviting pools. But Wellesley cantered up the line or sat watching on the green hill that looks across Talavera and its brown towers to the carved cliffs beyond the Tagus. Once a spent bullet bruised his chest. But the day faded, and the French attacks died down. King Joseph saw his armies fail ; and in the night they marched away. Judged by the strictest tests, it was a muddle. For Sir Arthur insisted upon doing everything himself ; and as he could not be everywhere at once, there were imperfections. But a muddle ending in the retreat of forty thousand French before twenty thousand British was a victory.

He was more hopeful now, "after two days of the hardest fighting I have ever been a party to." For in the morning Robert Craufurd brought up the Light Brigade (which later years swelled to the Light Division), having marched to the sound of the guns and covered forty-three miles in twenty-two hours at Moore's celebrated quickstep of three paces at a walk alternating with three paces at a run. Small wonder that Sir Arthur wrote that day, " We shall certainly move towards Madrid, if not interrupted by some accident on our flank." But his instinct was sound enough. The accident occurred, since the next day brought news that the French had come down from the north behind him and were threatening his homeward road to Portugal.

The pack of Marshals were all baying in the same direction now, Jourdan and Victor in front of him, and Ney and Soult behind. So there was nothing for it but retreat. That, indeed, would probably have been imperative even without the French. For if he stayed much longer in the parched valley of the Tagus, he was faced with a prospect of starvation. In the first week of August he wrote grimly that it was " almost impossible " for him to stay ³⁰ in Spain—" a starving army is actually worse than none. The soldiers lose their discipline and their spirit. They plunder even in the presence of their officers . . . and with the army which a fortnight ago beat double their numbers, I should now hesitate to meet a French corps of half their strength." This was unpleasing ; and their situation was not improved by their allies, who were apparently content to let them starve. Sir Arthur's pen poured acid in all directions. Lisbon was informed that " we are ³¹ starving, and are ill-treated by the Spaniards in every way. . . . There is not a man in the army who does not wish to return to Portugal " ; Lord Castlereagh learnt that " we want everything ³² and can get nothing ; and we are treated in no respect as we ought to be ; and I might almost say not even as friends " ; and Spanish statesmen were naturally aghast at his resolve to leave the country.

" I am fully aware of the consequences which may follow my ³³ departure from Spain. . . . But I am not responsible for these consequences, whatever they may be. Those are responsible for them who, having been made acquainted with the wants of the British army more than a month ago, have taken no efficient measures to relieve them ; who have allowed a brave army, that was rendering gratuitous services to Spain, that was able and willing to pay for every thing it received, to starve in the centre of their country, and to be reduced by want almost to a state of inefficiency ; who refused or omitted to find carriages to remove the officers and soldiers who had been wounded in their service, and obliged me to give up the equipment of the army for the performance of this necessary duty of humanity."

Now he had no illusions left about his allies and wrote bitterly to Castlereagh that " the information which I have acquired in the ³⁴ last two months has opened my eyes respecting the state of the war in the Peninsula." The sole accomplishment of Spanish troops appeared to be rapid dispersal followed by " reassembly in

a state of nature " ; and his angry litany was echoed in the shrinking ears of the Junta by a majestic voice. For Richard had
consented to appear in Seville as Ambassador Extraordinary.
It was a strange reversal. For he was Arthur's armour-bearer
now. There were odd visitors to the Peninsula that summer.
Lord Byron walked the quays of Lisbon, admiring " Cintra's
glorious Eden " and noting how

        " Fandango twirls his jocund castanet,"

meditated freely upon history, legend, and current politics, and
passed on to meditate at appropriate points along the Mediter-
ranean and to carve his name upon selected fragments of the
antique. But Lord Wellesley was a stranger visitor, running
civilian errands in Seville, whilst Arthur won his battles. His
family, which had no tact, was always congratulating him on
Arthur's latest triumphs ; and here he was, a mere second on
the field of honour, writing dutiful reports to Canning in place
of Mr. Frere. That adept at light verse had vanished ; and, the
sublime succeeding the ridiculous, Lord Wellesley occupied his
post. But the requisite diplomacy was quite to Richard's taste,
since his leading duty was to make the Spanish Government feel
small. This feat was well within Lord Wellesley's range. Indeed,
it was his *forte*. He echoed Arthur's strongest invectives to the embarrassed Spaniards and derived unlimited satisfaction from informing one of them with stately vehemence that he " would not
trust the protection of a favourite dog to the whole Spanish Army."
    But strong language could not mend Sir Arthur's case or feed
his troops ; and he retreated sulkily, slanting south-west towards
the Portuguese frontier on the Guadiana. His mind was quite
made up—" I have fished in many troubled waters, but Spanish
troubled waters I will never fish in again." There were to be no
more combined operations, and he lay irritably at Badajoz. But
there were compensations. For Cuesta, worn out at last—or
shocked by his unaccustomed participation in a victory—had a
stroke. Besides, Talavera brought recognition to Sir Arthur.
The Spaniards gave him presentation chargers and the rank of
Captain-General (of which he declined the pay, refusing " to
become a burden upon the finances of Spain during this contest
for her independence ") ; the House of Commons voted him
£2,000 a year for three years ; and his sovereign was moved to

elevate him to the peerage. He was to be a Viscount ; and the problem of his title raised questions of rare delicacy which William handled for him, while Kitty and her boys were by the sea at Broadstairs. He could not well include Talavera in Arthur's style without Spanish consent ; and if he made any reference to Wellesley, what would Richard say? Some feudal ancestor, it seemed, had held lands near Wellington. So much was safe ; and William risked the rest. The General should become Baron Douro of Wellesley and Viscount Wellington of Talavera ; and in the autumn of 1809 Sir Arthur vanished in the new glory of Lord Wellington.

IV

THE leaves of 1809 were falling, as the last addition to the Peerage waited in Estremadura with his back to Portugal. He signed his new name for the first time on September 16 to the usual letter about biscuit and cash balances (for Lord Wellington was very like Sir Arthur), adding a modest application to the Portuguese for leave to shoot a royal covert across the frontier. (His prayer was granted, and subsequent advices record his prowess with ball cartridge among the Braganza deer.) But though Sir Arthur was unchanged, the scene was changing round him. For the French wound homewards from Vienna with the name of Wagram on their eagles. Now there was time for them to think of Spain once more. Berthier was to be Chief of Staff there ; a hundred thousand men were on the march for the Pyrenees ; and as his cavalry jogged southward once again and booted Marshals in their blue and gold tilted enormous hats and muttered about Spain, the Emperor spoke of going with them. But he stayed behind that autumn, detained in Paris by an ageing, pretty woman who trailed about the Tuileries holding her head low so that they might not see how red her eyes were ; and as Josephine dragged miserably towards divorce, his armies surged into Spain once more.

The English, waiting for their impact, were a shade distracted by the news from home. True, the new Viscount received the comforting intelligence that his brother Henry was to be Minister at Lisbon, prompting Lord Byron to the ribald enquiry

> " How many Wellesleys did embark for Spain,
> As if therein they meant to colonise ? "

But the family *bloc*—Arthur at Badajoz, Richard at Seville, and Henry at Lisbon—was soon dislocated. For the Government collapsed with the resonance peculiar to governments in war-time. The Duke of Portland, who was still Prime Minister (if only people could remember it), was taken ill. That did not matter much. But his surviving colleagues failed to agree on a successor. The Foreign Secretary refused to serve under the Chancellor of the Exchequer ; the Chancellor returned the compliment ; the

Secretary of State for War resigned and (better still) fought a
duel with the Foreign Secretary; the Prime Minister, who had
been quite forgotten in the scuffle, resigned as well; and with
these agreeable preliminaries his startled country passed to the
rule of Mr. Spencer Perceval, K.C. This modest figure (one
contemporary termed him with friendly disparagement an
" honest little fellow ") assumed the disconcerting task of forming
a Cabinet in circumstances strongly reminiscent of Casabianca's.
Canning and Castlereagh, the duellists of Putney Heath, had
gone; but since the pressing needs of war and foreign policy had
not gone with them, Perceval adopted the expedient of bringing
Richard Wellesley home from Seville to the Foreign Office and
giving the War Department to Lord Liverpool and the rosy-
cheeked young Palmerston (who thought it "suited to a   6
beginner "). This was grave for Wellington, since Castlereagh
had always been his sponsor at the War Office, and he wrote to
him in grateful terms :

> " It would appear that your friendship for me, of what I believe   7
> in the instance referred to I ought more properly to call your sense
> of what was just to me and others, was the original cause of the
> dissatisfaction of your colleague. . . .
> " I have experienced many acts of friendship and kindness from
> you. If I had been your brother you could not have been more
> careful of my interests than you have been in late instances, and on
> every occasion it has always appeared to me that you sought for
> opportunities to oblige me and to mark your friendship for me ; of
> all which I assure you that I am not forgetful."

The scene was changing fast. He had new masters now ; that
was a novel (and not particularly reassuring) circumstance in
Wellington's rear. For who could tell how far Lord Liverpool
would share Castlereagh's enlightened taste for Peninsular
adventures ? True, Richard could answer for his brother in
Cabinet. But since Walcheren had failed, overseas expeditions
were a trifle out of favour. In front of him the change was almost
as disconcerting, since the French flood was gathering. The
tramp of marching feet came nearer ; the Young Guard were
filing through the passes of the Pyrenees ; and he could almost
catch the sharp orders of the Emperor. There was one consolation, though : the Spaniards remained almost wholly unaltered.
For they passed the autumn in their customary pastime of

8   superfluous defeats, engaged, as he wrote bitterly, in " doing Bonaparte's business for him as fast as possible " ; and after Tamames and Ocaña Wellington occupied the position of an allied General with the unusual advantage that his allies had been annihilated.

But there was still Portugal ; and while Portugal remained, he had his plan. So early as the month of August, in the hot weeks that followed Talavera, he faced the problem :

9   " The next point in this subject is, supposing the Portuguese army to be rendered efficient, what can be done with it and Portugal, if the French should obtain possession of the remainder of the Peninsula ? My opinion is, that we ought to be able to hold Portugal, if the Portuguese army and militia are complete.

" The difficulty upon this sole question lies in the embarkation of the British army. There are so many entrances into Portugal, the whole country being frontier, that it would be very difficult to prevent the enemy from penetrating ; and it is probable that we should be obliged to confine ourselves to the preservation of that which is most important—the capital.

" It is difficult, if not impossible, to bring the contest for the capital to extremities, and afterwards to embark the British army. . . . However, I have not entirely made up my mind upon this interesting point. I have a great deal of information upon it, but I should wish to have more before I can decide upon it."

A sound instinct told him that when the French arrived in force, " their first and great object will be to get the English out " ; and as the autumn passed, his mind was busy with his plan for a defensive. As usual he must see the ground for himself ; and in October he slipped away to Lisbon. Twelve months before, in the exasperating days that followed Vimeiro, he had tried to break into Lisbon, while Junot lay among the big hills in front of Torres Vedras. He would see Torres Vedras once again ; for Torres Vedras might serve his purpose now. So he spent half October riding in and out among the great green hills that climb along the sky ; the square ruin of a Moorish keep above the little town watched him go by ; and before he left, he had composed a

10 Memorandum of twenty-one precise instructions for his Engineers. He saw more besides ; for that watchful eye detected a mule-cart

11 which a Major of Light Dragoons had appropriated for his own baggage, and a visit to a Lisbon theatre inspired the acid com-

13

ment that " officers who are absent from their duty on account   *12*
of sickness might as well not go to the playhouse, or at all events
upon the stage, and behind the scenes."
The plan was clearer now. He should not stand upon the
frontier—" the line of frontier of Portugal is so long in proportion   *13*
to the extent and means of the country, and the Tagus and the
mountains separate the parts of it so effectually from each other,
and it is so open in many parts, that it would be impossible for an
army acting upon the defensive, to carry on its operations upon
the frontier without being cut off from the capital." He should
stand nearer to the sea, because (as he wrote later) " when we do   *14*
go, I feel a little anxiety to go, like gentlemen, out of the hall door,
particularly after the preparations which I have made to enable
us to do so, and not out of the back door, or by the area." So he
prepared the hall, devising for his adversary an impenetrable blend
of field fortification and mountain warfare ; and bewildered Portuguese were set digging on the tumbled sky-line above Torres Vedras.
Then he was back at Badajoz, posted to Seville, saw Richard   *15*
off to England from Cadiz, and returned to his command once
more. A busy winter lay before him. For if he had resolved on
making Portugal a fortress, someone must organise the Portuguese.
Their army and militia, vigorously drilled by British officers and
re-equipped in a fair semblance of British uniform, were slowly
coming into shape under Beresford. For Wellington had little
faith in patriotic emotion as an unaided instrument of national
defence and passed a shrewd judgment on the French :

> " As to the enthusiasm, about which so much noise has been   *16*
> made even in our own country, I am convinced the world has
> entirely mistaken its effects. I believe it only creates confusion
> where order ought to prevail . . . and I fancy that, upon reflection,
> it will be discovered that what was deemed enthusiasm among the
> French, which enabled them successfully to resist all Europe at the
> commencement of the revolution, was force acting through the
> medium of popular societies and assuming the name of enthusiasm,
> and that force, in a different shape, has completed the conquest of
> Europe and keeps the continent in subjection."

At any rate, the Portuguese (unlike the Spaniards) were to wear the
strait-jacket of British discipline ; and, to do them justice, they
wore it with some credit. A sterner test awaited them, since his
reading included a " *Mémoire de la Campagne en Portugal, l'an*   *17*

1762," and " Correspondence relative to the War in 1762," and
he had resolved to use their ancient weapon of the *Ordenanza.*
As an historian of the Spanish war of 1762 had written, the King
of Portugal commanded " his subjects to fall upon the invaders,
and the national hatred always excites them to execute the
' Ordinance.' As the Spanish army pushes on, the villages are
depopulated, and the inhabitants fall back on the capital." That
was the plan—an exodus before the French, leaving an empty
countryside in front of them. For starvation was to be the glacis
of his fortress.

His mood was almost cheerful now, since the plan stood
clearly in his head. That autumn he got " pretty good sport "
after the red deer near Badajoz ; and the new Cabinet agreed
with his conviction " not only that we cannot in good policy give
up the Peninsula, but that we may be able to continue the contest
in Portugal with success, and that we shall finally bring off our
army." That was the comforting reflection which lay behind
his forecasts of the next campaign : their retreat was safe. For
the new Lines at Torres Vedras would, in the last resort, ensure a
sheltered embarkation ; and if they had to go, he meant to take
the Portuguese, though " I shall not have a single ton for a
Spaniard." The campaign, of course, would have to be defensive ; there would be a dearth of brilliant deeds ; and he should
" be most confoundedly abused, and in the end I may lose the
little character I have gained." But that would not greatly
matter, though he paid a shade more attention than usual to
Opposition attacks upon him, welcoming Mr. Croker's heroic
poem upon Talavera and forwarding a narrative of the campaign
of 1809 to a correspondent with an unaccustomed warning : " If
it is desired to publish anything upon the subject founded upon
the enclosed, pray let it be so disguised that it cannot be supposed
to come from me. I think, however, that a publication might
be of some use." He was inclined to view his English critics with
philosophy—" You see the dash which the Common Council of
the city of London have made at me ! I act with a sword hanging over me, which will fall upon me whatever may be the result ;
but they may do what they please. I shall not give up the game
here as long as it can be played."

He saw clearly now, as the last weeks of 1809 went by, how he
meant to play it. The ground was chosen. For they turned

their backs on Spain before the year was out ; and as 1810 came
in, they were waiting for the French among the piled and tumbled
rocks of Beira.   Best of all, he wrote with gleeful underlinings   *24*
that he had " *an unanimous army.*" They were not perfect (he
complained to Liverpool that " if I succeed in executing the ardu-   *25*
ous task which has devolved upon me, I may fairly say that I had
not the best instruments, in either officers or men, which the
service could have afforded ") ; but at least they did not argue
with him. Indeed, they trusted him—not yet, perhaps, with the
blind confidence of later years. But Lowry Cole, who had come
out to take command of a Division, bore striking testimony :

> " I never served under any Chief I like so much, Sir J. Moore   *26*
> always excepted, as Lord W. He has treated me with much more
> confidence than I had a right or could be expected from anyone.
> Few, I believe, possess a firmer mind or has, as far as I have heard,
> more the confidence of the Army."

Cole's good opinion was, it would appear, reciprocated ; for his
commander wrote to him that week, " I have got two dozen of   *27*
excellent port for you, which I do not know how to send you."
(There were some compensations for making war in Portugal,
though Lord Wellington's anxieties sometimes included the   *28*
delivery of his tea.)

     The weeks went by ; and he was waiting " in a situation in   *29*
which no mischief can be done to the army, or to any part of it ;
I am prepared for all events ; and if I am in a scrape, as appears
to be the general belief in England, although certainly not my own,
I'll get out of it."   He slipped off to Lisbon in the winter for a   *30*
final look at his new works ; and from the orders that he left
behind, in case the French attacked in his absence, it was plain
that he had already chosen ground near Busaco for an action.   *31*
Then he returned to his position just inside the Portuguese
frontier, waiting, like any duellist, for some invisible second to
give the signal. This time his duel was to be fought with
Masséna. He was ascending in the scale of Marshals ; and it
was fitting that—with Junot, Soult, and Jourdan already to his
credit—he should be matched with Masséna. The Prince of
Essling was, at fifty-two, a shade past his prime, with a weakness
for feminine society in its more portable forms ; but he was extremely able—in his adversary's judgment, " the ablest after   *32*
Napoleon." He was a little tired, perhaps. But he brought

nearly 80,000 Frenchmen into play against Wellington's 25,000 British (with the dubious addition of the Portuguese) ; and the long columns wound towards Portugal under the wide horizons of western Spain. Somewhere behind the blue distances Lord Wellington was waiting with his sober " doubt whether they can bring that force to bear upon Portugal without abandoning other objects, and exposing their whole fabric in Spain to great risk. If they should be able to invade it, and should not succeed in obliging us to evacuate the country, they will be in a very dangerous situation ; and the longer we can oppose them, and delay their success, the more likely are they to suffer materially in Spain." That was his purpose now ; that was the meaning of the Lines. There might be a battle, " if the enemy should invade this country with a force less than that which I should think so superior to ours as to create the necessity for embarking." But his taste for battles was very far from insatiable—" I am not so desirous as they imagine of fighting desperate battles ; if I was, I might fight one any day I please. But I have kept the army for six months in two positions." Small wonder that impatient men grew more impatient, that the Staff gossiped and preferred " writing news and keeping coffee houses " to their own business, and positively croaked out their gloomy predictions, while their irritable chief expressed his displeasure with the doubters by continuing to entertain the meanest opinion of his instruments, professing to be " apprehensive of the consequence of trying them in any nice operation before the enemy, for they really forget every thing when plunder or wine is within their reach," and informing William (who was now Chief Secretary for Ireland) that " the army was, and indeed is still, the worst army that was ever sent from England." Nerves were a little strained by the long wait for Masséna. Sometimes, indeed, his outcries verged upon somewhat boisterous comedy :

" I have received your letter announcing the appointment of Sir William Erskine, General Lumley, and General Hay to this army. The first I have generally understood to be a madman. . . . Really when I reflect upon the characters and attainments of some of the General officers of this army, and consider that these are the persons on whom I am to rely to lead columns against the French Generals, and who are to carry my instructions into execution, I tremble ; and, as Lord Chesterfield said of the Generals of his day, ' I only hope that when the enemy reads the list of their names he trembles as I do.' Sir William Erskine and General Lumley will be a very nice addition to this list ! However, I pray God and the Horse Guards to deliver me from General Lighthume and Colonel Sanders."

But he did not despair. For he retained a sound conviction that he knew best—better than his subordinates, and far better than Masséna. Besides, the new Government appeared to trust him ; and Majesty itself positively vouchsafed a favourable opinion of him before a final lapse into insanity. Kitty was well ; his little boys were over their whooping-cough ; and he waited briskly for the French.

They came slowly on, as summer mounted in the sky. He fell back before them, curbing Robert Craufurd's inconvenient apti- tude for expensive rearguard actions. For that eager warrior was ill-attuned to Fabian exercises ; and, as he disregarded orders, his blue chin projected farther than ever above the high peak of his saddle. But he found Wellington indulgent ; for " if I am to be hanged for it, I cannot accuse a man who I believe has meant well . . . although my errors, and those of others also, are visited heavily upon me, that is not the way in which any, much less a British army, can be commanded." Craufurd meant well enough ; but his alacrity marred the smooth perfection of their withdrawal from the Coa. Then ill-luck took a hand ; and a stray French shell sent up the powder-magazine of Almeida in thunder—" a great and unexpected misfortune. I had hoped that the place would have detained the Enemy for some time, and that I might have relieved it if circumstances had favoured me." But its guns were silent now, and they fell back upon the deep windings of the upper Mondego. The French came slowly after them through a jumble of fir-clad hills across the heather towards Busaco. The ground was almost perfect for defence, and he stood to fight them on the tall ridge. It was September 27 ; 60,000 Frenchmen faced 50,000 Allies, half of whom were Portuguese ; but through an autumn day Masséna launched forty-five battalions against his twenty-four and failed to dislodge them. The British fought according to their custom, and the Portuguese with a new vigour. Their stout defence surprised Masséna ; but that autumn Masséna was not spared surprises. For a fortnight later, as he followed Wellington's receding columns towards Lisbon and the sea, the big hills of Torres Vedras climbed slowly up the sky, and he was faced by that inspired introduction of the broad facts of geography into the art of war. A nervous Staff excused itself for its omission to report upon the Lines by explaining apologetically that Lord Wellington had made them. " *Que diable,*" the Marshal snapped, " *Wellington n'a pas construit ces montagnes.*"

They loomed stolidly in front of him, from the great bulk of São Vicente to the rectangular green slopes that curve away towards the gleaming reaches of the lower Tagus, where the Dutch sails of wherries seem to drift through the water-meadows. The whole foreground was full of mountains ; and the mountains were all full of guns and Englishmen and Portuguese. It was most disconcerting. And that, though Masséna did not know it yet, was not the worst ; for behind the Lines that filled his grey horizon a second line of field-works stood waiting for him on the big, bare hills beyond Mafra, and even a third traced in the dusty plain between the river and the Cintra hills. That was the triple keep of Wellington's enormous fortress, the citadel of Portugal.

It was October now ; and the clouds hung low above the Lines. The autumn rain drove down, and the French were raking a dun wilderness of scrub for food. To Wellington's intense annoyance, they found a little. For the Portuguese, though improved out of all knowledge, had failed to rise completely to his Fabian conception of an evacuated desert (perhaps it is impracticable to play Roman *rôles* without a Roman Senate) ; and the Regency had left gaps in the projected glacis of starvation, which impelled their exasperated ally to fish at intervals in the muddy waters of Portuguese politics and even to the impassioned outcry that " if Principal Souza is to remain either a member of the Government, or to continue at Lisbon . . . he must quit the country or I shall." But the French lay hungrily before the Lines, hesitating to attack with a lively recollection of Busaco, and hoping with increasing fervour that Wellington would sally out. That wary fighter, finding himself " in sight of a very numerous but starving Army, which has been in our front now for ten days, and does not appear to like to attack us," looked down one day from a redoubt and thoughtfully remarked, " I could lick those fellows any day, but it would cost me 10,000 men, and, as this is the last army England has, we must take care of it." So he took care of it in the Lines. As he had written to Mr. Arbuthnot of the Treasury, " they won't draw me from my cautious

system. I'll fight them only where I am pretty sure of success."
Besides, what need was there to fight a battle, when Masséna
chose to starve himself ? The " sure game " was best, and   *47*
Wellington preferred to play it. He watched them starving in
the plain, as autumn turned to winter. But one November night,
as the fog lay in banks along the Lines, the French slipped off.
Their hungry columns groped northwards through the mist
towards Santarem, and he followed warily—" Feeling, as I do, all   *48*
the consequences which would ensue from the loss of a battle,
and the risk which I must incur, in the existing situation of
affairs, if I should fight one, I have determined to persevere in my
cautious system, to operate upon the flanks and rear of the
enemy with my small and light detachments, and thus force them
out of Portugal by the distresses they will suffer, and do them all
the mischief I can upon their retreat. Masséna is an old fox, and
is as cautious as I am ; he risks nothing." With an uneasy feeling   *49*
that he " could not attack them without incurring the risk of
placing the fate of the Peninsula on the result of a general action,
in which the advantage of ground would be much in favor of the
enemy," Wellington remained almost stationary when Masséna
halted for the winter. The old fox had gone to ground, and a
wary huntsman was content to wait.

As 1810 went out, the French were still in Portugal. But so
was Wellington. That was the miracle. The Emperor had put
reinforcements into the Peninsula to the surprising tune of
100,000 men ; but by some strange perversity the British still
maintained their 25,000 there, and their commander wrote
proudly home that " I am at the head of the only army remaining   *50*
in the Peninsula—or, I believe, in Europe—that is capable and
willing to contend with the French." Small wonder the delighted
Lowry Cole wrote that " the ability displayed by Lord Wellington   *51*
is universally acknowledged and I hope the good folks in England
will do him equal justice. He certainly is in the literal sense of
the word a fine fellow with the best nerves of anyone I ever met
with." Busaco and the Lines had added Masséna to his bag of
Marshals. Better still, a British army had faced the Empire at
its widest, when a man could walk from Genoa to the Baltic on
French soil, and had stared it out of countenance. The slow tide
was turning ; and though the Peninsular War was not yet won,
after Torres Vedras it could not well be lost.

V

THE military problem of the Peninsula was almost maddeningly simple. The French objective, from which the Marshals were intermittently distracted by the allied lures of loot and side-shows, was to find and destroy the British expeditionary force. It was two years since the Emperor had announced, with a slightly hysterical blend of heraldry and natural history, that ' the Leopard ' would shortly be driven into the sea. That was the essence of French strategy. And the British problem was just as simple. For it presented two objectives—to avoid expulsion and then, resuming the offensive, to expel the French. The first goal was reached when Masséna, with the whole weight of the Empire behind him, turned back from Torres Vedras. It was plain from that moment that Wellington could not be driven out of the Peninsula. But could he drive out the French ? That was his second problem, and in 1811 it was still unsolved. Its elements were simple, too. For the French occupation of Spain hung by one precarious chain—the great road from Bayonne to Madrid. If that were snapped, their armies must recoil from every province, since they could not maintain themselves with a British force across the road to France. If it were threatened, they must all come swarming north to safety. (Had not John Moore touched them on that nerve-centre in 1808 and seen the Emperor whip round towards him like an animal upon whose tail an unexpected foot had trodden ?) If Wellington could get across their road to Paris, the game was won. That was the short way with the French. So he must thrust eastwards out of Portugal across Old Castile and break the road to France somewhere between Madrid and the Ebro. There was one point at which an angle of the road brought it nearer to him ; the angle was at Burgos. That must be his goal, as it had once been John Moore's. But this time there would be no sudden dash for Burgos. For it was no part of his programme to make a gallant raid into Spain and scramble on board his transports at Corunna. The judicious Wellington was indisposed to risk

himself beyond the shelter of his mountains, unless the gates of
Portugal were safely held behind him. He must be free to move
decorously out of Portugal and to re-enter it at will ; and this
privilege would not be his unless he held the gates. So Badajoz
and Ciudad Rodrigo must be his first objective ; and, these once
secured, he might make his decisive thrust towards the road to
Paris.

I

As 1811 opened, the deadlock on the Tagus held. Masséna's
men starved at Santarem with a will that impressed their adversary as " an extraordinary instance of what a French army can   *1*
do. It is positively a fact that they brought no provisions with
them, and they have not even received a letter since they entered
Portugal. With all our money, and having in our favour the
good inclinations of the country, I assure you that I could not
maintain one division in the district in which they have maintained not less than 60,000 men and 20,000 animals for more
than two months." That was written in December ; by the first
week of March their transport was a shadow, their shoes a memory,
and their supply the stray outcome of marauding forays across a
chilly waste of empty villages. Then, with Junot wounded and
Ney frankly mutinous, Masséna turned to go. Withdrawing
deftly, he slipped off towards the north with Wellington shepherding him on his way a trifle gingerly. For he was disinclined to
risk unnecessary battles, when it was far simpler to preside over
the inevitable disintegration of the French from a safe distance.
Had he not in his charge the last army of England ? Defeated,
it would let the tide of war surge into Britain—" then would His   *2*
Majesty's subjects discover what are the miseries of war, of which,
by the blessing of God, they have hitherto had no knowledge ; and
the cultivation, the beauty, and prosperity of the country, and
the virtue and happiness of its inhabitants would be destroyed,
whatever might be the result of the military operations. God
forbid that I should be a witness, much less an actor in the
scene. . . ." But victorious, it might be the instrument to end
the interminable European war—" I am equally certain that if   *3*
Buonaparte cannot root us out of this country, he must alter his
system in Europe, and must give us such a peace as we ought to
accept." He saw the goal ; and in his marching redcoats he
saw the means to reach it. For he had more work for them to do

than winning rearguard actions against Masséna. His mind was
ranging eastward now towards the Spanish frontier ; the gates
of Portugal began to gleam on his horizon ; and he preferred " to
keep my own army entire, rather than to weaken myself by fighting them, and probably be so crippled as not to have the ascendant
over the fresh troops on the frontiers. Almeida and Badajoz are
to be retaken."
    They were to be his next objective. Meanwhile, he followed
warily as Masséna struggled back to Spain. They scuffled on
the road at Pombal and again at Redinha, while Ney displayed
the sombre aptitude for rearguard actions that was soon to light
a larger army down a longer, darker road. (That month the guns
in Paris flashed and boomed for an heir born to the Emperor :
all that remained was to retain an Empire for him.) Masséna's
ragged columns wound slowly through the mountains after a
running fight at Foz d'Aronce ; their road was littered with discarded transport, and they left a growing legacy of weary, bare-
foot men to be gathered in by their pursuers. The spring rains
were falling now ; Ney had gone raging off under virtual arrest,
when the army of Portugal, enlivened by the *feux de joie* for the
small King of Rome, fought a confused engagement in the fog at
Sabugal, which only served to strengthen Wellington's conviction
that " these combinations for engagements do not answer unless
one is on the spot to direct every trifling movement." (Had he
not been his own " general of cavalry and of the advanced guard,
and leader of two or three columns, sometimes on the same day,"
throughout the long pursuit ?) Then Masséna crept out of
Portugal, leaving behind 8,000 prisoners and 17,000 dead, while
Wellington proudly informed the Portuguese that the French
invasion was at an end.
    The first phase was over ; and it remained to batter in the
gates of Portugal. For the French still held Almeida (which
guards the vestibule of Ciudad Rodrigo) and Badajoz ; and
Wellington directed simultaneous blows at both. Leaving
Almeida in the grip of an investing force, he rode south to survey
Badajoz, covering 135 miles in three April days, killing two
horses, writing endless letters on the road, and losing two dragoons
of his escort in a torrent. He reconnoitred Badajoz in person and
drew up a detailed code of instructions for Beresford, who was
to besiege the fortress ; in case the French attempted to relieve

it and Beresford resolved to fight, he was recommended to concentrate at Albuera. Then Wellington returned to the north.
The French were on the move again ; for Masséna, his gaps
repaired with fresh troops, came marching to the rescue of
Almeida. They faced him one May morning at Fuentes de
Oñoro on the upland which parts the high prairies of western Spain
from the tumbled rocks of Beira. All that day and the next the   *9*
struggle swayed along the slopes. Then Masséna, groping round
the British right, launched his attack on May 5. French cavalry
charged British infantry in squares ; the squares held (it was a
lesson that Wellington observed) ; and whilst his infantry stood
firm, his cavalry heavily outnumbered were ridden off the field,
and two British guns by the supreme paradox of war charged and
broke through a whirlpool of French horse. But, with his right
in danger, Wellington swung it back with Frederician deliberation ; and when the long day ended, his 37,000 men still lay
between Almeida and its 47,000 rescuers. But he felt little
pride in the achievement, writing to William that " Lord Liver-   *10*
pool was quite right not to move thanks for the battle at Fuentes,
though it was the most difficult one I was ever concerned in.
We had very nearly three to one against us engaged ; above four
to one of cavalry ; and moreover our cavalry had not a gallop
in them ; while some of that of the enemy was fresh and in excellent order. If Boney had been there, we should have been beaten."
But Boney was not there ; and in his absence it might be permissible to take occasional liberties with the art of war.
     Its fate duly sealed by the battle at its gates, Almeida fell.
But to Wellington's acute annoyance the garrison escaped, and
he was left reviling " the most disgraceful military event that has   *11*
yet occurred," reaching the grim conclusion that " there is
nothing on earth so stupid as a gallant officer." (Indeed, one
unhappy object of his displeasure shot himself.) The spring
campaign in the north had cleared the way to Ciudad Rodrigo
and incidentally closed Masséna's career ; for an ungrateful
Emperor rewarded him with summary retirement, and Marmont
commanded in his place.
     But news from Badajoz drew Wellington's attentions south
again. For Soult had pounded Beresford at Albuera—" a
strange concern," as Wellington wrote. " They were never   *10*
determined to fight it ; they did not occupy the ground as they

ought ; they were ready to run away at every moment from the time it commenced till the French retired." Yet dogged gallantry prevailed ; and Soult learned reluctantly, in Napier's eloquent rhapsody, " with what a strength and majesty the British soldier fights. . . . Nothing could stop that astonishing infantry . . . and fifteen hundred unwounded men, the remnant of six thousand unconquerable British soldiers, stood triumphant on the fatal hill ! " But such heroic exploits were not to Wellington's taste ; and he was left writing grimly that " another such battle would ruin us." Meanwhile, the summer was before him ; and he made a rush at Badajoz before the French could return in force to relieve the fortress. But ample time is the essence of successful sieges, and time was wanting. They were too quick for him ; and he drew off to safety, falling back once more to a strong position just inside the Portuguese frontier. At midsummer the armies faced one another in Estremadura. But the deadlock held ; and the war drifted north again along the frontier. For Wellington was still knocking at the gates of Portugal ; and having failed at Badajoz, he turned briskly to Ciudad Rodrigo. That red-tiled fortress with its big brown church and vaguely Mexican aspect was waiting in a broad green valley ; and in August he encircled it in preparation for a siege. But Marmont came up in force to its relief ; there was a scuffle on September 25 at El Bodon ; once more a British square held off the charging French ; and Wellington again withdrew—without conspicuous assistance from the impulsive Craufurd. He made a point of it on parade next morning.

" I am glad to see you safe, General Craufurd," he observed with elaborate irony.

" I was never in danger," his rash subordinate replied.

" Oh ! I was," said Wellington tartly.

" He's damned crusty this morning," muttered his unabashed lieutenant.

His designs on Ciudad Rodrigo postponed, Wellington fell back with loving deliberation to a strong position on the Coa ; but Marmont lay watchfully in front of him and made no attack. The war was over for the season now ; and 1811 went out upon Wellington among the rocky hills of Beira. It had been a fruitful year. He had cleared Portugal and broken Masséna, and the gates of Portugal gleamed hopefully before him. His business now lay with the frontier fortresses ; and whilst they lay waiting for his onslaught, the initiative had passed to him. Better still, he had transformed the war ; as he wrote to Liverpool, " we have certainly altered the nature of the war in Spain ; it has become, *15* to a certain degree, offensive on our part. The enemy are obliged to concentrate large corps to defend their own acquisitions ; they are obliged to collect magazines to support their armies (Marmont says he can do nothing without magazines, which is quite a new era in the modern French military system) ; and I think it probable, from all that I hear, that they are either already reduced, or they must soon come, to the resources of France for the payment of those expenses which must be defrayed in money. As soon as this shall be the case, and as soon as the war will not produce resources to carry itself on, your Lordship may be certain that Buonaparte will be disposed to put an end to it, and will submit to anything rather than draw from France the resources which must be supplied in order to keep together his armies. I think it not unlikely, therefore, that peace is speculated upon in France."

Peace flushed the eastern sky, as he looked eastwards out of Portugal. Spain lay before him now, and beyond Spain the long line of the Pyrenees. That was the goal ; his exclamation in a letter pointed it—

" You appear to think it probable that Buonaparte would be *16* inclined or obliged to withdraw from the Peninsula ; and you ask, what would I do in that case ? I answer, attack the most vulnerable frontier of France, that of the Pyrenees. Oblige the French to maintain in that quarter 200,000 men for their defence ; touch them vitally there, when it will certainly be impossible to touch them elsewhere."

It was a lucid vision, and he followed it across his maps on a December day in 1811. He was still in Portugal, and between him and a sight of the Pyrenees lay Marmont, Soult, King Joseph, the French armies, and the long corridors of Spain ; but the Pyrenees were waiting.

2

The war was forming him. Now he was nearly forty-three— high-nosed, clear-eyed, and confident. His nerves were always

steady. That was his secret ; Lowry Cole had pierced it, when he
1 termed his commander " a fine fellow with the best nerves of
any one I ever met with." For the sharp gaze never wavered,
and the upper lip drew tightly down over the slightly prominent
teeth without a quiver. His nerves were admirable ; exercise,
long days in the saddle, and plain fare helped to keep them so.
Did not Alava learn to dread his standing answer to the question
at what o'clock the Staff would move and what there was to be
for dinner ? " At daylight," he invariably replied ; and to the
2 second interrogation, " Cold meat." " *J'en ai pris en horreur,*"
the anguished Spaniard moaned, " *les deux mots* daylight *et* cold
3 meat." But Wellington throve on them. His night's rest varied
between three hours and six ; and for his first four years in the
Peninsula, although he was Commander-in-Chief, he had reverted
to the practice of his Indian campaigns and slept in his clothes.
4 His days were regular ; rising at six, he wrote steadily until
breakfast at nine o'clock. Those quiet morning hours served to
dispose of his enormous correspondence with incredible punc-
5 tuality ; for " my rule always was to do the business of the day
in the day." Then he breakfasted and transacted military business with the Staff. This lasted all the morning, except on hunting days when a gleeful Quartermaster-General records that he
6 " could get almost anything done, for Lord Wellington stands
whip in hand ready to start, and soon despatches all business."
Those were the days that startled Portuguese on lonely hillsides
beheld an unprecedented cavalcade, heard view-halloos and the
sharp note of hounds, and marvelled at the strange proceedings
of their incomprehensible allies. " Here," as *Captain O'Malley*
7 loved to recall, " the shell-jacket of a heavy dragoon was seen
storming the fence of a vineyard. There the dark green of a
rifleman was going the pace over the plain. The unsportsman-
like figure of a staff officer might be observed emerging from a
drain, while some neck-or-nothing Irishman, with light infantry
wings, was flying at every fence before him "—and the Peer him-
8 self followed his hounds in the sky-blue and black of the Salisbury
hunt. Such was the impressive apparatus with which Lord
Wellington toned his nerves in winter-quarters.

His nerves, indeed, were admirable ; and a becoming sense of
who he was and what he had achieved contributed to steady
9 them—" I am the mainspring of all the other operations, but it is

because I am Lord Wellington ; for I have neither influence nor support, nor the means of acquiring influence, given to me by the government." Small wonder that his correspondents never ventured upon a more familiar address than " My dear Lord." Even behind his back he was ' the Peer ' to Generals and ' our great Lord ' to ardent subalterns ; although an intoxicated private once alluded (in the presence of a scandalised staff officer) to " that long-nosed b——r that beats the French," and the army had been known to call him ' Atty.' But such diminutives were rare ; for he kept his distance.

Not that he kept it by conventional distinctions of uniform and entourage. Headquarters, as one observer noted, were " strikingly quiet and unostentatious. Had it not been known for a fact, no one would have suspected that he was quartered in the town. There was no throng of scented staff officers with plumed hats, orders and stars, no main guard, no crowd of con-tractors, actors, cooks, valets, mistresses, equipages, horses, dogs, forage and baggage waggons, as there is at French or Russian head-quarters ! Just a few aides-de-camp, who went about the streets alone and in their overcoats, a few guides, and a small staff guard ; that was all ! About a dozen bullock-carts were to be seen in the large square of Fuente Guinaldo, which were used for bringing up straw to headquarters ; but apart from these no equipages or baggage trains were visible." Perhaps he had seen quite enough of personal magnificence in Richard's case to damp his taste for it. At any rate, his dress was unpretentious. A harassed army might echo *Micky Free's* lyrical complaint to the Fourteenth Light Dragoons :

"Bad luck to this marching,
Pipe-claying and starching ;
How neat one must be to be killed by the French ! "

But such niceties were scarcely to their commander's taste. One subaltern recorded that " provided we brought our men into the field well appointed with their sixty rounds of ammunition each, he never looked to see whether trousers were black, blue, or grey. . . . The consequence was that scarcely any two officers were dressed alike ! Some wore grey braided coats, others brown : some again liked blue ; many (from choice, or perhaps necessity) stuck to the ' old red rag.' " His own opinions were plainly stated to the Horse Guards :

16 "I hear that measures are in contemplation to alter the clothing, caps, &c. of the army.

"There is no subject of which I understand so little ; and, abstractedly speaking, I think it indifferent how a soldier is clothed, provided it is in a uniform manner ; and that he is forced to keep himself clean and smart, as a soldier ought to be. But there is one thing I deprecate, and that is any imitation of the French in any manner.

"It is impossible to form an idea of the inconveniences and injury which result from having anything like them. . . . I only beg that *we* may be as different as possible from the French in everything."

This was severely practical. So was his own costume, which generally ran to grey. His taste for personal reconnaissance in-
17 clined him to the inconspicuous combination of a grey frock-coat worn with a low cocked-hat in an oilskin cover. It bore no plume ; and before long Europe learned to know that austere silhouette. He was not altogether innocent of sartorial vanities, though, fancying the skirts of his coats a trifle shorter than most
18 men's in order (a Judge-Advocate conjectured) to set off a trim figure ; nor was he without strong and individual opinions upon a novel cut of half-boots. But these effects were all contrived in the modest key of grey ; and his entourage was equally inconspicuous. An unpretentious Staff, designed for use rather than ornament, was put to shame by the glory of gold lace and plumes that caracoled in the splendid wake of any Marshal of the Empire. But Wellington had little appetite for millinery. Besides, few Marshals shared his taste for solitary reconnaissance. He had unbounded faith in a strong glass and a fast horse, and often rode beyond his outposts, a lonely horseman in a cloak, with his perpetual desire to see things for himself—the French vedettes would never suspect a single figure in grey. So he dressed modestly below his military station, leaving the foppery of war to gaudier, if less successful, Marshals. Indeed, their master did the same. For Europe held another *redingote grise* : he might be matched against it one day.

Grey-coated, spare, and trim, the bleak figure, sharply outlined against the deep blue of Spanish skies, appears a shade incongruous. He never dressed the part ; indeed, he had little taste for drama. When his advance-guard blundered into the whole

14

French army, he greeted the alarming intelligence with a casual,
" Oh ! they are all there, are they ?   Well, we must mind a little   *19*
what we are about then."   And news that the French were off,
leaving Almeida in his grasp, reached him one morning early
whilst he was shaving.   He lifted the razor from his cheek, remarking " Ay, I thought they meant to be off ; very well " ; the
shave resumed, and nothing more was said.   He specialised in a
form of dry understatement peculiarly unfriendly to heroics.
Who else, addressing a charitable appeal to the Prime Minister
on behalf of a devastated ally, was capable of the sublime exor-
dium :   " The village of Fuentes de Oñoro having been the field of   *20*
battle the other day, and not having been much improved by this
circumstance . . ." ?   Few themes, indeed, moved him to
eloquence except the imperfections of his human instruments.
But there his language often verged on the sublime.   Unwearying
himself, he was unmerciful in his comments upon lack of energy
in others ; and exasperation frequently betrayed him into unpardonable generalisations.   A fixed belief that insufficient in-
ducements were offered to recruits had led him to the conclusion
that " none but the worst description of men enter the regular   *21*
service " ; and from this premise he proceeded to the gravest
disparagements of the men under his command.   " The scum of   *22*
the earth," he termed them, " the mere scum of the earth. . . .
The English soldiers are fellows who have all enlisted for drink
—that is the plain fact—they have all enlisted for drink."   This
tone became habitual with him in later years, as a congenial
antidote to the prevailing cant.   For Wellington could not bear
his hearers to be romantic about soldiers—" people talk of their   *23*
enlisting from their fine military feeling—all stuff—no such thing.
Some of our men enlist from having got bastard children—some
for minor offences—many more for drink ; but you can hardly
conceive such a set brought together, and it really is wonderful
that we should have made them the fine fellows they are."   They
were fine fellows, then.   He was prepared to admit as much ;
and for seven years in the Peninsula he toiled to make them so.
Seven volumes of General Orders, drafted in his own handwriting   *24*
and traced endlessly across the paper with " the short glazed
pens " from Tabart's in New Bond Street, testify to his parental   *25*
care.   ' Crime ' is duly present ; the crackle of illicit pig-shoot-
ing is heard ; bee-hives are purloined ; and the misdeeds peculiar

to military operations in wine-producing countries stalk through
his pages. But camp-kettles, shirts, and brushes haunted him ;
his dreams were full of army biscuit ; and his housekeeping
anxieties are in strange contrast with the grave ablatives absolute
of Cæsar or Napoleon's baroque eloquence. Supply was still the
burden of his severely humdrum song. He still insisted that " it
26 is very necessary to attend to all this detail, and to trace a biscuit
from Lisbon into the man's mouth on the frontier, and to provide
for its removal from place to place, by land or by water, or no
military operations can be carried on, and the troops must starve."
Even his strategy was dominated by the practical consideration
27 that " a soldier with a musket could not fight without ammunition, and that in two hours he can expend all he can carry."
This was admirably unheroic. But in one particular he found
his gallant subordinates more unheroic than himself. Uniformly
indifferent to the risks of battle,

28
> " When, squadron square,
> We'll all be there,
> To meet the French in the morning,"

they failed to share his taste for uneventful winters in the discomfort of up-country billets in the hill villages of Beira. Moved
with a simultaneous passion for the immediate transaction of
urgent business at home, they applied for leave. Such unanimity
was touching. But their commander was untouched ; for leave
was one of Wellington's blind spots. Lisbon leave was one thing.
He could be positively debonair on the subject of Lisbon leave,
29 recording in a sardonic postscript that a subordinate " wants to go
to Lisbon, and I have told him that he may stay there 48 hours
which is as long as any reasonable man can wish to stay in bed
with the same woman." But why gentlemen who had come all
the way to the Peninsula in order, he presumed, to fight the French
should wish to go home again entirely passed his comprehension.
Ill-health might form a valid reason ; but business grounds left
him frankly incredulous. Even Craufurd was grudgingly in-
30 formed that " Officers (General Officers in particular) are the best
judges of their own private concerns ; and, although my own
opinion is that there is no private concern that cannot be settled
by instruction and power of attorney, and that after all is not
settled in this manner, I cannot refuse leave of absence to those
who come to say that their business is of a nature that requires

their personal superintendence.   But entertaining these opinions, it is rather too much that I should not only give leave of absence, but approve of the absence of any, particularly a General Officer, from the army. . . .   I may be obliged to consent to the absence of an Officer, but I cannot approve of it.   I repeat that you know the situation of affairs as well as I do, and you have my leave to go to England if you think proper."   He could contrive a kindly refusal—" I always feel much concern in being obliged to refuse officers who wish to quit the army ; indeed it is the most painful duty I have to perform.   But it must be performed ; otherwise, between those absent on account of wounds and sickness, and those absent on account of business or pleasure, I should have no officers left."   Indeed, he ultimately moved the Horse Guards to confine Peninsular appointments to Generals prepared to make a declaration in advance that they had no private business likely to recall them to England.   More romantic reasons moved him to irony, although a hint from home that one young lady's continued separation from a love-lorn Major might be followed by fatal consequences elicited a kindly, though terrifying, lecture on the course of love : 31 32

"It appears to me that I should be guilty of a breach of dis- 33 cretion if I were to send for the fortunate object of this young lady's affections, and to apprise him of the pressing necessity for his early return to England : the application for permission ought to come from himself ; and, at all events, the offer ought not to be made by me, and particularly not founded on the secret of this interesting young lady.

"But this fortunate Major now commands his battalion, and I am very apprehensive that he could not with propriety quit it at present, even though the life of this female should depend upon it ; and, therefore, I think that he will not ask for leave.

"We read, occasionally, of desperate cases of this description, but I cannot say that I have ever yet known of a young lady dying of love.   They contrive, in some manner to live, and look tolerably well, notwithstanding their despair and the continued absence of their lover ; and some even have been known to recover so far as to be inclined to take another lover, if the absence of the first has lasted too long.   I don't suppose that your *protégée* can ever recover so far, but I do hope that she will survive the continued necessary absence of the Major, and enjoy with him hereafter many happy days."

This was not unkindly. After all, Lord Wellington himself had the best reasons for believing in the capacity for survival of young ladies in love. Had not Kitty borne his own absence for nine years (and very nearly married Lowry Cole in the course of her vigil) ? That, perhaps, was why he was a shade unsympathetic about leave. He had left so little behind him (his brother William was informed that " as for private concerns, I never trouble my head about them "), that home meant little to him ; and why should it mean more to others ?

Not that he was inhuman. He even had his moments of weakness. The day after Somers Cocks was killed at Burgos he came into someone's room, paced it for some time in silence, opened the door to go, and as he left exclaimed abruptly, " Cocks was killed last night." But his emotion was dry-eyed ; how, with his work to do, could it be otherwise ? High command is a supremely lonely business. Yet there were moments when he needed company. At four o'clock on winter afternoons he left his room " and then, for an hour or two, parades with any one whom he wants to talk to, up and down the little square of Frenada (amidst all the chattering Portuguese) in his grey great coat." The talk ran on anything—on India, on Ireland, on Mr. Canning's views about the Catholics—and the trim figure in grey paced up and down the little square among the staring drovers. He could be affable ; and the Headquarters mess grew familiar with his laugh—a terrifying cachinnation " very loud and long, like the whoop of the whooping cough often repeated."

The Peer kept his distance, though. For was it not almost his duty as Commander-in-Chief to be a shade aloof ? Perhaps aloofness came natural to him. At any rate, it was his fate, his rather lonely fate, always to be a little different from his surroundings, his head held a trifle higher than his neighbours'. Had he not been an Englishman in Ireland, an Anglo-Indian in India, a soldier among politicians, and finally a politician among soldiers ? He was invariably in contrast, never in perfect harmony with his assorted backgrounds ; and the spare figure, tightly buttoned in its grey beneath a black cocked-hat, contrasted oddly with the glare of Spain. It was a lonely *rôle* to be Lord Wellington.

VI

THE worst was over now. For it was 1812, and the slow tide of war began to ebb. They had withstood the full force of it since 1810, bearing up against the whole weight of the Empire. In those crucial years—the years of Busaco, of Torres Vedras, Masséna's retreat, and Fuentes de Oñoro—all Europe beyond the Pyrenees had been at peace, its Emperor at leisure to pour the flood-tide of his armies into Spain. But now the tide checked and, called by its unrestful luminary, began to ebb away towards the north, where the French faced about to meet another enemy. For Russian drums were tapping in the mist beyond the edge of Germany ; the Czar's tall grenadiers were stiffly aligned ; and the little Cossack ponies trotted smartly beneath the long lances of their bearded riders. Soon there would be more than Spain to think of. Spain must be held, of course ; but now the Guard had gone, the Poles were going, and there would be no more reinforcements for King Joseph and the fretful Marshals. The tide was ebbing now. The French, evicted three times in four years from Portugal, were scarcely likely to return ; although the Emperor seven hundred miles away in Paris still appeared to regard Lisbon as their objective, and pelted his Marshals with a succession of fantastic orders. These documents, in which Napoleon appears at his least impressive, were uniformly unhelpful, since the facts on which he founded his instructions originated almost exclusively in that powerful imagination, and the resulting orders (which bore no relation to Peninsular conditions) were invariably out of date when they arrived. Indeed, the least harmful to their recipients' chances of success were those which failed to arrive at all.

A fair proportion of these missives were diverted from their lawful destinations by the kindly forethought of *guerrilleros* ; for the military genius of Spain, which had hitherto found infelicitous expression in a disastrous series of pitched battles, was admirably suited to the stealthier operations of the *petite guerre*—the *guerrilla*. Cloaked figures haunted Spanish defiles ; French despatch-riders, ambling inattentively into the throat of some dreadful gully, failed to emerge into the sunlight ; and as the empty road beyond wound dustily across the plain, eager knives were slitting French saddlery in search of correspondence, to be forwarded by faithful hands and lonely tracks and patiently deciphered at Lord Wellington's headquarters. (If official Spain left much to be desired as an ally, few armies have found more effective friends than the Spanish *guerrillero*, who effaced the long French line of communications with grim persistence, rounding up the rumbling convoys, rushing incautious posts, and imposing an escort of 1,800 men upon a French General who wished to reach his destination.) From his perusal of intercepted despatches Wellington might pardonably conclude that, as an adversary at long range, the Emperor was fallible, and from the tone which he habitually employed towards inferiors that Napoleon was distinctly not a gentleman. This, indeed, became one of his fixed convictions. Did he not once inform a house-party of Lord Hertford's that " Buonaparte's mind was, in its details, low and ungentleman-like," a defect which he charitably attributed to " the narrowness of his early prospects and habits " ? His fastidious taste was equally repelled by the Emperor's frequent use of deception—" Buonaparte's whole life, civil, political, and military was a fraud. There was not a transaction, great or small, in which lying and fraud were not introduced. . . . Buonaparte's foreign policy was force and menace, aided by fraud and corruption. If the fraud was discovered, force and menace succeeded." Not that he was convinced of their success—" I never was a believer in him, and I always thought that in the long-run we should overturn him. He never seemed himself at his ease, and even in the boldest things he did there was always a mixture of apprehension and meanness. I used to call him *Jonathan Wild the Great,* and at each new *coup* he made I used to cry out " Well done, Jonathan." . . . As he read his papers at Headquarters, this rich distaste, the full fruit of later years, was slowly ripening.

But a more valuable discovery which emerged from the Emperor's tangential dealings with King Joseph and the bewildered Marshals was that Napoleon could err. Lord Wellington sat in his Portuguese headquarters above a village street and learned that serviceable lesson. Other adversaries encountered the Emperor for the first time on battlefields, and were appropriately awed into helpless immobility. But Wellington first came upon him in the more reassuring form of palpably absurd instructions to his deputies in Spain. " The habit of Napoleon," as Wellington wrote of him later, " had been to astonish and deceive mankind, and he had come at last to deceive himself." He did not fall into the vulgar error of underrating him, retaining salutary belief that " his presence on the field made the difference of forty thousand men." But no student of his interventions in Peninsular affairs could retain in its full perfection the awe in which Europe held the white-breeched, green-coated figure. That, if Wellington was ever to meet him in the field, would be something gained.

Meanwhile, his problem waited. The French were still at large in Spain, and the strong places of the frontier barred his way. But if Ciudad Rodrigo and Badajoz awaited his attack, he enjoyed the rare advantage that he could choose his own moment for attacking them. For the initiative had passed to Wellington. He was at perfect liberty to move his pieces up and down the board, while the French could do little more than pant after him, parrying his blows. The cause was simple : Spain was a desert, and in desert warfare supply and transport are the only wings upon which armies can rise into motion. The Sepoy General had both ; the French had neither.

Endowed with this superior mobility, he made a winter thrust at Ciudad Rodrigo. The January snow was deep in Leon as they moved against the fortress ; and after twelve days in open trenches they stormed it on January 19—" in half the time " (as he wrote Liverpool with a rare note of triumph) " that I told you it would take, and in less than half that which the French spent in taking the same place from the Spaniards." His speed was costly, though ; for the siege cost heavily in casualties, including Robert Craufurd, whose last words of reconciliation evoked the wondering comment that " Craufurd talked to me as they do in a novel." But speed was vital, if they were to snatch Ciudad Rodrigo before Marmont could return to its relief ; and the sudden *coup* secured the northern gate of Portugal, eliciting for Wellington a Spanish dukedom from the grateful Cortes, a marquisate from Portugal, an earldom from the Prince Regent, and an annuity of £2,000 from Parliament.

The new Earl of Wellington and Duque de Ciudad Rodrigo surveyed the frontier with half the winter still before him. Badajoz remained, a rich prize to be seized before Soult from the south or Marmont from the north could intervene to rescue it. Time is the essence of siege-warfare—ample time for the slow ritual of investment, opening trenches, tracing parallels, saps, sorties, siting batteries, mining and countermining, and breaching scarps, the whole culminating in the triumphant *finale* of an assault and escalade. When conducted in due form, it had something of the grave decorum of a minuet (had not the Eighteenth Century once opened trenches to the sound of violins ?) ; or it might be viewed under the guise of courtship—of a singularly formal courtship in which the gallant besieger drew a reluctant fortress with exquisite deliberation into the embraces of his parallels and saps. But time was the essence of this lingering procedure ; and when time presses, besiegers are of necessity crude, hasty, and ungraceful. Wellington's approach to Badajoz was sadly lacking in the graces of unhurried siege-warfare, since his problem was to batter down the last remaining gate of Portugal before its guardians could return to save it. He moved south in February, with an agreeable pretence for the benefit of the French that he was " going to hunt . . . and you might even have a house arranged for the hounds at Aldea de Yeltes." Whilst his exceedingly impromptu siege-train jolted slowly forward towards Badajoz, he corresponded on the agreeable theme of his latest honours, even finding time for lengthy expositions of French finance and Indian army problems. News reached him that his brother Richard, whom the passing years rendered increasingly intractable, had resigned the Foreign Office and elicited the judicious comment that " in truth the republic of a cabinet is but little suited to any man of taste or of large views "—a sentiment of which he was himself to experience the justice later. Richard, indeed, was scarcely suited to republics ; even a not too constitutional monarchy cramped him unduly. But his defection left Arthur as the leading Wellesley, though Henry still toiled patiently as British Ambassador at Cadiz—had laboured there, indeed, since Richard's translation to Downing Street—and now received the recognition of knighthood.

Meanwhile, the French still mounted guard in Badajoz. The siege began in March ; the parallels crept closer ; Easter

went by ; and on a dark spring night (it was April 6) the attack   9
was launched. For two interminable hours it swayed round the
fortress in a glare of port-fires, as each storming column went
roaring forward into failure. When the news came to Wellington,
the colour left his face and his jaw fell ; but he turned to give an
order in that calm way of his, and even apologised with formal
courtesy for giving it to the wrong person. Then a report arrived
that Picton's men were in the fortress ; the Staff hallooed ; but
Wellington was still giving orders in his level voice. Badajoz was
his. Yet, for the moment, it was not Lord Wellington's, but his
army's ; and for three nights and days of unprecedented riot
they celebrated their capture. Discipline dissolved in floods of
wine ; locks were shot open ; looting was universal ; and scared
nymphs (in comb and *mantilla*) fled shrieking down the winding
alleys before reeling fauns (in scarlet tunics). Even the gaunt
silhouette of gallows in the Plaza failed to check the saturnalia,
though their formidable master " fulminates orders and will
hardly thank the troops, so angry is he." But he was sad as
well as angry. For he had purchased Badajoz at a cruel price ;
and when he saw the casualty returns, Wellington (for once not
dry-eyed) wept bitterly.

The first phase of 1812 was over. Badajoz and Ciudad
Rodrigo secured, the gates of Portugal swung open ; and in June
they marched eastwards into Spain, having the red earth under-
foot and on their right a line of snow mountains, until they saw
the heaped brown cupolas of Salamanca piled up against the
eastern sky. That was the first stage on the long road from
Portugal to the Pyrenees. His blow was aimed at Marmont in
Leon rather than at Soult further to the south in Andalusia, for
the simple reason that French movements would be cramped by
starvation (had not hunger just recalled Marmont from a raid
into Portugal ?) until the harvest ripened ; and " the harvest in   10
all the countries north of the Tagus . . . is much later than it is
to the southward. We shall retain our advantages for a longer
period of time in these countries than we should do to the southward." This was the application of supply to strategy with a
vengeance ; and obedient to its dictates Wellington marched on
Salamanca.

The French fell back, leaving a garrison to hold some forts ;
and early one June morning Wellington rode in. The town was

11 roaring ; and he rode slowly through the press, deafened with shrill *vivas*.   Excited women crowded round him with tears, with kisses, with hoarse Spanish voices ; and the still figure, writing orders on a sabretache, was almost pulled from his saddle.   Three armies in four years had jingled spurs under the brown arcades of the Plaza Mayor—Moore's hurried redcoats racing against the Emperor in 1808, then an interminable succession of Frenchmen in blue, and now the redcoats once again.   Some of them marched off to besiege the French remnant in the forts ; the rest took post to the north of the city on the ridge of San Christoval, where Wellington hoped against hope that Marmont would attack him. That position, where he deliberately offered battle on two occasions in the course of 1812, was never fought over.   But as the ideal is always more exquisitely rounded than the real, Wellington's conception of a defensive action is perfectly revealed in the unfought battle of San Christoval.

Exposing to the French a long and easy slope of innocent aspect and a blind skyline, the ridge dropped steeply on its inner face, affording perfect concealment to the defenders until the moment came to reveal them.   For the Wellingtonian defensive had the splendid simplicity of a booby-trap.   Its modest object was to spring unsuspected forces upon surprised attackers ; and San Christoval (like Busaco before it and Waterloo a few years later) was admirably suited to this simple pleasantry.   The attackers would pant uphill towards the blind skyline ; somewhere behind the crest a line of British infantry would crouch, completely sheltered from artillery and waiting happily to fire its volley, utter its huzza, and leap forward with the bayonet. This game, if only Marmont would oblige with an attack, could be repeated three times on three successive ridges of identical conformation, before the French offensive could pierce through to Salamanca.   One afternoon they came quite close to the posi-

12 tion ; and Wellington was heard muttering, " Damned tempting ! I have a great mind to attack 'em."   The French guns opened, and the round shot began to fall among his Staff quite close to

13 where Wellington was standing with a map.   He " moved a few paces, and continued his directions."   But the moment passed ; Marmont thought better of it, and drew off towards the north ; and the battle of San Christoval—the perfect Wellingtonian battle—was never fought.

Twelve hundred miles away the Emperor, a squat figure in a greatcoat, whistled *Malbrouck s'en va't en guerre* and watched his long columns wind slowly across a Polish river into Russia. Their bayonets gleamed in the June sunshine, as the loaded caissons rumbled across the bridges and the *Grande Armée* took the long road for Moscow. Then the dust settled in the plain, and silence fell again behind them. In Spain Marmont and Wellington were groping for one another outside Salamanca. At one moment the deadlock seemed complete, and the Peer miraculously gave leave to a Staff officer, conjecturing that " you have seen the end of it. . . . I shan't fight him without an advantage, nor he me, I believe." There was an interlude of countermarching, in which each followed suit with the precision of chess-players in the opening moves. Marmont was edging round Salamanca towards the road to Portugal. If that were threatened, Wellington must fall back ; and the two armies wheeled against the distant and unchanging background of a tall sierra across a sort of dusty Wiltshire with long, marine horizons—a reddish Wiltshire with tiled villages built of adobe—and this blend of Mexico and Salisbury Plain appropriately evoked a series of precise manœuvres. For they wheeled in full sight of one another, the two armies racing southward side by side for the faint line of trees that marked the Tormes. The air, oddly enough (since it was the third week of July), was fresh, chilled by a biting wind off the sierra ; and Wellington " never suffered more from cold." The focus shifted round the city, as Marmont felt for the road behind his adversary ; and as they swung south of Salamanca, the French seemed to be leading in the race. They could not be quite sure, though, how much of Wellington's command was on the ground ; for he had interposed a slope—one of his favourite long slopes with a blind skyline—and three divisions were concealed behind it. As the French headed for the west, they were strung out a little in the race, gaily unaware that they were marching across the front of Wellington's entire command. The morning of July 22 passed in this agreeable manner, Marmont " manœuvring " (as Wellington wrote) " in the usual French style, nobody knew with what object." But about lunch-time the French lapse became manifest. Wellington was " stumping about and munching " in a little farmyard among the brown cottages of Los Arapiles, lunching apparently off alternate bites of chicken and glances at the

French through a telescope. (The occasion lingered in Alava's memory because, for once, there was not cold meat.) The Peer's lunch was interrupted by a final look towards the French. " By God," he suddenly exclaimed, " that will do "—and scandalised Alava by flinging far over his shoulder the leg of chicken which he had been eating in his fingers. Then he cantered up the hill for a more comprehensive view, and the whole field was spread before him—the red masses of his own command, the still country, and the marching French. The game was in his hands. " *Mon cher Alava*," he said cheerfully, " *Marmont est perdu*," and rode off to launch the attack. For it was not his way to entrust such vital missions to subordinates ; and when he left the stony hill, he galloped across level fields with one companion to give his orders. Edward Pakenham, Kitty's brother, commanded the leading column of attack.

" Ned," said his formidable brother-in-law, " move on with the Third Division ; take the heights on your front ; and drive everything before you."

" I will, my lord," he dutifully answered, " if you will give me your hand."

There was a handshake ; and the attack developed which ' beat forty thousand men in forty minutes.' In the later phases he presided lovingly over each turn of his battle ; as Pakenham informed his mother, " our Chief was every where and Sadly Exposed himself." For he was seen riding forward with the advancing lines of his own infantry ; and when the heavy cavalry went thundering against the French (it was a favourite hallucination of the Prince Regent in later years that he had charged with them), Wellington was close enough to remark to their commander, " By God, Cotton, I never saw anything so beautiful in my life ; the day is *yours*." The day, at any rate, was England's. For Wellington had launched twenty-eight battalions against seventy-eight and sent them reeling eastwards into Castile ; Marmont and Clausel, his second in command and successor, were both wounded ; and the Army of Portugal hurried to shelter with a loss of fifteen thousand men and twenty guns, a solid testimony to Wellington's ability to do something more than defend strong positions of his own choice. Foy termed the battle Frederician ; and there were traces of the King of Prussia's ' oblique order ' in the slanting thrust of Wellington's attack.

Indeed, the victory might have been still more crushing if a Spanish force, which he had posted at a ford behind the French, had been capable of simple obedience. But Carlos de España had decamped from Alba de Tormes, and the French slipped by. Spain was at Alba, though—the sinister, uncomprehended Spain of macabre *Caprichos* and sardonic portraits of egregious Bourbons and preposterous grandees—watching through the sharp eyes of Francisco Goya y Lucientes. For Goya watched him, as he rode in that night from Salamanca, if the note appended to his sketch can be believed ; and the strange drawing, with its unavoidable suggestion of an ascetic interrupted in his cell or a drowning man restored unexpectedly to the surface, records the exhausted victor —unshaven, hollow-eyed, the damp hair plastered to his forehead, a little shaken by the spent bullet which had bruised his thigh— a wild-eyed, unfamiliar Wellington, as Goya saw him on that summer night in a Spanish village.

The long corridors of Spain lay open to him now ; and the French scurried wildly in all directions. Clausel drew off the wreckage of Salamanca towards the north ; King Joseph hung disconsolately round Madrid ; and Soult with infinite deliberation moved out of Andalusia to the rescue. Wellington, whose *forte* was not pursuit, shepherded Clausel warily towards Valladolid and the great road to France. A little artifice, framed to delude King Joseph's outposts, employed legitimate deception—" I shall stay here all day," he advised an officer in command of Portuguese cavalry, " and will act according to the Intelligence which I shall receive from you " ; but an ingenious postscript enclosed " a letter which I beg you to send to the French advanced posts by an officer of the German Cavalry well-mounted with a well-mounted Escort. . . . Tell him to answer no questions and give no information excepting that Marmont's army is totally annihilated as a Military Body ; and to get all the information he can. Desire him to say he does not know where I am, and that I move every day."

A choice, it would appear, was open to him between pressing still farther to the north, where Burgos beckoned at the angle of the road to France, and evicting Joseph from his capital. He chose the latter, very largely for the reason that " I could not go farther north without great inconvenience, and I could at that moment do nothing else." Besides, to send King Joseph scam-

22

23

24

pering out of Madrid would deprive his government of all air of permanence ; and the threat would almost certainly draw the French armies out of southern Spain. (Far beyond hearing now, behind the silence in the north, the long columns of the *Grande Armée* wound through the summer haze across the endless Russian plain. Napoleon was half inclined to reach Smolensk and halt, to check his senseless march deeper and deeper into Russia. But, as Wellington said of him later, " a conqueror, like a cannon-ball, must go on. If he rebounds, his career is over." So he went on into the silence.)

Bound for Madrid, Lord Wellington rode southward from Valladolid under the wide skies of Old Castile. Segovia watched him go by, the Roman arches of its aqueduct stepping serenely across the prostrate town ; he passed the bald Guadarrama in the blazing August days ; and within three weeks of Salamanca he was in the dusty plain below Madrid. King Joseph, a reluctant harbinger, scuttled before him into his capital and out again, bound for the distant security of Valencia with a retreating army and a vast convoy. For that unhappy monarch moved southward like a tribal migration in the choking dust of two thousand vehicles, whilst his capital made cheerful preparations to welcome the approaching British. They marched in on August 12, and found a city in the grip of the splendid dementia of which Southern capitals are occasionally capable. Bells pealed ; the road ran wine and lemonade by turns, became a forest of waving palm-branches, and changed with dream-like ease into a *ballet* of young ladies pirouetting alongside the marching redcoats with offerings of grapes, of sticky sweets, of laurel leaves, and treating their impassive chief to worship that bordered perilously on the divine. For Wellington, high-nosed and silent, rode at the centre of the din with wild brunettes covering his hands, his sword, his boots, even his horse with Spanish kisses, and picked his cautious way across a bright sea of flowered shawls, until King Joseph's palace walls shut out the roaring city ; and the new master of Madrid after this violent apotheosis resumed his problems.

Far behind him a grateful England, ringing with the news of Salamanca, poured out fresh honours. Official England was a little changed that summer, since a crazy pistol-shot had accounted for the inoffensive Perceval. But Liverpool assumed his place, Castlereagh returned to office, and the Government was still in friendly hands. The Peer was to be a Marquess now ; and from his retirement Lord Wellesley, whose sumptuous mind was always apt to run on heraldry, offered the generous suggestion that his victorious younger brother should be permitted to augment his coat of arms with the French eagle. Ministers, consulted on this vital problem, preferred the Union Jack ; and Lord Wellington, who felt that the French emblem " carries with it an appearance of ostentation, of which I hope I am not guilty," concurred in their opinion. The Prime Minister was busy with the purchase of the manor of Wellington on his behalf ; and though cheerfully indifferent to his step in the peerage (he asked someone, " What the devil is the use of making me a Marquess ? "), he took some interest in his new estates, and was not above indicating that his allowances were quite inadequate to his expenses in the field. It was still raining Spanish honours, and his splendid jewellery was augmented by the Golden Fleece.

Meanwhile, there were the French. He hoped to keep them busy in the south with minor operations, whilst he secured the road to France at Burgos. His tone was quite light-hearted— " Matters go on well, and I hope before Christmas, if matters turn out as they ought, and Boney requires all the reinforcements in the North, to have all the gentlemen safe on the other side of the Ebro." (That day the swelling domes of Moscow gleamed under a pale northern sky, and the French dead were piled high round the Great Redoubt at Borodino.) Wellington turned northwards now. Madrid was left behind ; the blind windows of the Escorial stared at the British columns, as they went by towards the north ; the French fell back before them ; and one September day they saw the spires of Burgos and the long saddle of the Castle. That obstacle remained ; and as Wellington saw it rising in tiers above the brown roofs of the town to the crowning defiance of its embrasures, he was inclined to " doubt . . . that I have means to take the castle, which is very strong." (Doubt hung on the autumn air of 1812 ; for while the Peer stared doubtfully at Burgos through his glass, a dreadful doubt hung over Moscow. The bright domes were veiled in smoke ; and as the French marched away, they turned to stare over their shoulders at the red glare on the sky behind them.) He was at Burgos for a month, until the distant mountains were dusted with the October snows. Snow fell in Russia, too—the first drifting flakes that

fluttered harmlessly on the still air, then powdered the interminable plain, until the winter skies were dark above them, and they
toiled endlessly through the white silence. Wellington's three
siege-guns—'Thunder,' 'Lightning,' and 'Nelson' (who had
lost a trunnion)—were banging bravely at the Castle. He was
still hopeful, though his hopes were chastened now—" Time is
wearing apace, and Soult is moving from the south ; and I should
not be surprised if I were obliged to discontinue this operation in
order to collect the army." Headquarters were enlivened by an
opinionated Marine, whom the senior service had consigned to
Burgos to enlighten Wellington with demonstrations of " a new
exercise of the bayonet, which is to render a British soldier equal
to 12 Frenchmen." This bright prospect opened one morning
after breakfast ; whereupon " after Lord W. had looked and listened with some impatience, he gave his orders for the day to the
Adjutant-General, mounted his horse, and galloped to the
trenches." Marines, it would appear, were prodigal of bright
ideas. One had contrived an " artificial hill " for facilitating
reconnaissance ; but his ingenuity faded before that of the
learned Portuguese who " proposed to burn the French army by
means of convex glasses."

Burgos still barred the way ; and impatient men stared from
their batteries at the brown roofs, the pointed spires, the trees
along the river, and the distant roads that wound across the
plain like ribbons. The autumn weeks were passing, and the
French were gathering to north and south of him. His parallels
crept slowly forward ; but the rain drove down, flooding his
trenches. He could not storm the place, " having but little
musket ammunition." Besides, he would not willingly repeat
the slaughter of Badajoz ; when he stood at Cocks' graveside that
autumn, his face was wrung with pain. So he resolved to treat
Burgos a trifle summarily, as he had treated hill-forts in India,
and resorted to half-measures. But in war no half-measure suc-
ceeds. For mining, inadequate bombardment, and small storm-
ing-parties were no substitute for the sustained exertions which
had forced the gates of Portugal ; and the siege failed. As he
wrote later in the year, " I played a game which might succeed
(the only one which could succeed), and pushed it to the last ;
and the parts having failed, as I admit was to be expected," he
faced the consequences. He blamed no one else—" the Govern-

15

ment had nothing to say to the siege. It was entirely my own   *36*
act. . . . That which was wanting . . . was means of transport-
ing ordnance and military stores to the place where it was desirable to use them." Transport, for once, had failed him.

Regretfully he turned to go. Soult and the fluttered Joseph   *37*
were working north towards Toledo ; Madrid was threatened ;
and Wellington could not maintain himself in his advanced position. They must turn back from Burgos, as John Moore had
once turned back from Sahagun on the Burgos road ; but (unlike
Moore) they would not need to run for their transports, since
Portugal was safely held behind them. A grey cathedral watched
them file through the silent streets under the moon ; their wheels
were muffled ; but the Castle guns were silent. Within a week
they were behind the Douro at Valladolid, and November found
them on the familiar heights of San Christoval. The Peer
breathed again, having reassembled his forces without misadventure and "got clear in a handsome manner from the worst   *38*
scrape that he ever was in." Bare countries are like ladders with
few rungs ; and having lost the rung of Burgos, Wellington was
forced to drop to the rung of Salamanca. He hoped to hold it,
though he had scarcely more than fifty thousand men against
ninety thousand. But once more the battle of San Christoval
remained unfought. The French manœuvred round his flank.
Once again the armies wheeled round Salamanca. But, unlike
Marmont, Soult gave no opening; the rain came driving down ;
and Wellington marched his men off to Portugal.

The four final days of retreat were miserable. Supplies went
astray ; starving men ate acorns and shot uncovenanted pigs ; it
rained incessantly ; and an exasperated chief presided over
awkward moments in the rear, confessing that, by God, it was too
serious to say anything. Yet, serious indeed, it was never dangerous ; and he brought off his army " in face of a superior enemy,   *39*
with the deliberation of an ordinary march . . . and the casualties
from the sword under 850 "—a lively contrast with the long
agony of the *Grande Armée*. For Wellington incurred no Beresina,
and did not require a Ney to fight heroic rearguard actions. He
brought his army off ; and long before a pale, furred man in a
sleigh drove hurriedly from Smorgoni towards Paris, he had them
safe in Portugal.

Not that he was content. An angry circular informed sub-

40 ordinates that discipline was lax, that " the officers lost all command over their men " in the retreat, and that this lapse was solely attributable " to the habitual inattention of the Officers of the regiments to their duty." This ungentle document found its way into newspapers, and left a wholly false impression of a grim martinet. His irritation was excusable. For at some points on the long road from Burgos wine had been as plentiful—and almost as destructive—as snow in the retreat from Moscow. But it was all over now ; and they were safe on the windy hills which look down into Portugal after a year in which British arms had secured two vital fortresses, taken twenty thousand prisoners, and cleared southern Spain of the French. Small wonder that the Marquess 35 wrote, " I believe that I have done right " ; while Pakenham 41 reported him " in good health and temper, satisfied with himself." For 1812 was over. The South, the peerless South was free. The Frenchmen with their clanging bands were gone at last ; and Seville throbbed with innumerable strings, while the soft wail of its own music stole through Granada. For the South was free, and Andalusia sang in the sunlight. Twelve hundred miles away the *Grande Armée* was dead.

VII

THE pace was quickening, as 1812 passed into 1813. All Europe was on the move that winter—France falling back across Germany, Russia in ponderous pursuit, the Prussians drilling hopefully, and even Italy stirring a little. The Emperor in Paris created, improvised, decreed, and threatened. He must have fresh armies ; and French drafts went northwards now up the long road towards the Pyrenees. Valladolid and Burgos, long accustomed to their south-bound convoys, watched the changing tide and felt the wind of war set from a new quarter.

Not that Spain was to be left bare ; for 200,000 men remained, *1* of whom nearly 100,000 faced Wellington. Once that winter he left his village street in Beira to visit his allies. His first call was on the Spaniards, who had at last appointed him Commander-in-Chief. This honour was delayed until the Spanish armies had exhausted the possibilities of defeat under their own commanders ; and the Peer accepted the command without enthusiasm. But it might be made to serve as a means of co-ordination and control, and he defined his new authority in a series of precise demands. Then he rode off through winter floods to Cadiz and, enlivened by lumbago on the road, pressed his points in person. This visit has *2* inspired romantic guesses. But his main pursuits during the sixteen days of its duration were far from Capuan ; for he negotiated with the Spanish Regency, addressed the Cortes in bad but energetic Spanish, and wrote stately letters in rather stilted French to his new subordinates. His task, as he defined it to a correspondent, was " to try ' to organise the Poles,' which appears *3* to be a work something of the same kind with that which Dumouriez describes so well in his Life " ; he had used the same comparison fourteen years earlier, when he was organising the Nizam's army before Seringapatam—a testimonial to his thorough reading of a book that had travelled from his Dublin lodgings to Madras in Colonel Wesley's baggage. He judged that he had " made some progress ; but the libellers have set to work, and I am apprehensive that the Cortes will take the alarm." For he

found journalists and Parliamentarians almost uniformly unhelpful. He was prepared, of course, to " fight for Spain as long as
she is the enemy of France, whatever may be her system of
government." But a constitution created " very much on the
principle that a painter paints a picture, viz., to be looked at,"
failed to compel his admiration ; and he was frankly derisive of
" a sovereign popular assembly, calling itself ' Majesty ' . . . and
of an executive government called ' Highness ' acting under the
control of ' His Majesty ' the assembly." He could see the
menace.

" The theory of all legislation is founded in justice ; and, if we
could be certain that all legislative assemblies would on all occasions
act according to the principles of justice, there would be no occasion
for those checks and guards which we have seen established under
the best systems. Unfortunately, however, we have seen that
legislative assemblies are swayed by the fears and passions of
individuals ; when unchecked, they are tyrannical and unjust ;
nay more : it unfortunately happens too frequently that the most
tyrannical and unjust measures are the most popular. Those
measures are particularly popular which deprive rich and powerful
individuals of their properties under the pretence of the public
advantage ; and I tremble for a country in which, as in Spain, there
is no barrier for the preservation of private property, excepting the
justice of a legislative assembly possessing supreme powers."

So he proposed a House of Lords for Spain. Meanwhile, he
" could wish that some of our reformers would go to Cadiz " ; the
lesson, he appeared to feel, might be salutary for Mr. Cobbett.
For Cadiz marked a stage in Wellington's political education,
serving to deepen his distaste for popular assemblies. Apart
from Westminster, he had only known two legislative bodies
intimately—the Irish House of Commons and the Cortes—and
neither was calculated to make a democrat of him.

One ally grounded in the elements of military organisation, he
passed on to his next pupil and rode off to Lisbon. Business was
almost wholly precluded by four days of strenuous celebration.
The anniversary of Ciudad Rodrigo was honoured with a banquet ;
Captain Gurwood, who had commanded the ' forlorn hope,'
arrived a trifle late and was exalted to the skies when his excuses
were greeted with a genial " You were not too late this time last
year." They all went to the Opera, where (for some reason

buried deep in the Portuguese intelligence) doves fluttered in the
cheering auditorium, and one perched on the Peer's box. These
arduous festivities concluded, he rode back to his village in the
hills.

Life at Headquarters was not without its compensations. A
buttoned figure still bent above its papers or tramped the little
square on winter afternoons among the drovers. His hounds
still hunted, and his talk was quite as varied as ever—how Ireland   6
must be held by force, and what a blunder his brother Richard
and Mr. Canning made in taking up the Catholic question ; how
he meant to have twenty-five couples of hounds to hunt next
winter ; and how admirably the Peninsula was suited to warfare,
because there was nothing in it for anyone to damage—" as, for
instance, what is this village worth ? burn it, and a few hundreds
would make it as good as ever with a little labour "—but that he
should be almost sorry to see such a war in Germany. Sometimes
it was play-night in the Light Division, and he rode over to Gallegos
for their theatricals. The programme (printed on War Department   7
paper by the army press at Freneda) announced *The Rivals* with
a cast of Riflemen, a pink subaltern as *Lydia Languish,* and a
small part for Havelock's elder brother—" after which a Variety
of Comic Songs," the whole loyally concluding *Vivat Wellington.*
For the Light Division Theatre was well aware of its position.
But the great occasion was the ball at Rodrigo. That afternoon
he had been working at Headquarters until half-past three ; but   8
he rode the seventeen miles in two hours, dined in his decorations,
danced, took supper, and set off at half-past three for a gallop
home by moonlight. They sat down sixty-five to dinner, and
two hundred guests came to the dance. The ball-room was a
trifle draughty, as the siege had left a large gap in the roof. But
they danced with spirit, though the floor left much to be desired,
and a sentry had to be posted near a hole. Two Spanish couples
obliged with the whirl and flutter of a *fandango* and a *bolero* ; and
a disapproving Judge-Advocate, who failed to relish

> " Fandango's wriggle, or Bolero's bound,"

observed that his allies twirled and handled their partners " a
little more . . . than our fair ones would like at first," but was
inclined to think that on the whole the English practice was for
the best. They drank innumerable toasts—" The next cam-

paign," " Death to all Frenchmen," and " King Ferdinand VII "
—and when the ladies had retired, they taught the Spaniards how
to say " Hip, hip, hip hurra " instead of " *Viva*," and chaired one
another freely until someone dropped a General. Outside the moon
was shining; it was freezing hard; a thoroughbred was clattering up mountain roads at a hand-gallop; and before dawn came
to Ciudad Rodrigo, Lord Wellington was back at Headquarters.

He could be genial, though a snub could still be administered
at need; and a bewhiskered aide-de-camp of the Prince Regent,
appearing on parade in the full glory of a Hussar uniform, received no more from him than two fingers raised to a cocked-hat
at full gallop, followed by a resounding " Grant, if you will dine
with me, I dine at six o'clock." But dinner at Headquarters
had been known to end in a song; and he was apt to call without
undue modesty for the song made in his honour by the Spaniards
after Salamanca. The guitar spoke softly; long fingers plucked
the strings; and, " *Ahe Marmont*," the singer gloated, " *onde vai,
Marmont ?* " Wellington sat listening with composure to the
lift and wail of the *copla*. Indeed, they noticed that he " hears
his own praises in Spanish with considerable coolness "; and
someone termed the song " Lord Wellington's favourite."

But life at Headquarters was not all dinners and fox-hunting.
For there were still his endless papers—letters from ministers,
from grandees of Spain, from half the Army List—all answered
in his swift handwriting. His letters to the Spaniards were a
complete correspondence-course in elementary administration,
enlivened by sardonic comments to his brother Henry on the
unsatisfactory progress of their backward pupils at Cadiz. Then
there were endless courts-martial to be written upon or discussed
with Mr. Larpent, departmental queries from young Lord Palmerston on the inspiring theme of regimental accounts, friendly notes
from the Prime Minister about his new estate at Wellington, the
eternal problem of cash payments, his regular report to the
Secretary of State, and supplies to be collected for the spring
campaign. A more agreeable category related to the fresh
honours which came crowding on him. The Portuguese, not to be
outdone by Spain, made him a Duke under the splendid style of
Duque da Victoria; he became Colonel of the Blues and expressed
his rapture in the shy confession that " there was never so fortunate or so favoured a man "; the Garter was conferred on him,

and he wrote home an anxious query over which shoulder he should wear the blue ribbon.   An enticing offer of Russian troops for the Peninsula flits through his papers ; but Spanish pride was, for some occult reason, offended by the thought ; the offer turned out to be unauthorised ; and, true to their invariable tradition, the phantom Russians never came.

There was no limit to the size, large or small, of the topics submitted to the Commander-in-Chief.   He advised the Cabinet upon European strategy ; and when Lieutenant Kelly of the Fortieth eloped with a young lady, the case received his best attention.   He even interviewed the angry mother and undertook (in Portuguese) to restore the erring child on condition that she should not be ill-treated or consigned to a convent.   Then he directed Lowry Cole to part the lovers.   But Cole, impressed by the mother's menacing aspect, pointed out to the Commander-in-Chief the probable nature of the fair prodigal's welcome.   Besides, the impulsive Kelly (as he reported) was quite prepared to make amends by marriage.   Lord Wellington, more sceptical, could " not but observe that he has it in his power, whenever he pleases, to compensate in that manner the injury which he has done to the family "—and improved the occasion by an impressive homily upon the lamentable tendency of officers and men abroad to commit such outrages as they individually thought fit. But that very day the knot was tied by an army chaplain of Portuguese *Caçadores*.   Propriety had received its due tribute ; and when the outraged parent called at Headquarters, she found a disobliging Wellington who declined to intervene and left his shrill visitor vociferating threats of sudden death for her offspring and transportation for the obliging chaplain.   So romance was satisfied ; and one more frontal attack upon a Wellington position had failed.

England was very far away ; and the distance served to modify his attitude to politics.   He had come out to Portugal as Chief Secretary in a Tory administration, returning from Vimeiro to dispense party arguments from the Treasury Bench without a conscious effort.   But now his view of his position had changed ; and when a Whig correspondent seemed to emphasise the party difference between them, he wrote that " as I have long ceased to think of home politics, it cannot be said that I am of a party different from that to which any other person belongs.   I serve the country to the best of my ability abroad, leaving the Government at home to be contended for by the different parties as they may think proper." In fine, he was Lord Wellington and knew his duty.

Besides, the Peninsula still claimed his full attention. The French were now uneasily aligned on the great road to France; and the French monarchy in Spain was little more than a field-army. The South was up; the Catalans persisted bravely; *guerrilleros* went freely up and down the land; and the shaggy hills behind Bilbao were loud with drumming, as the North marched out to war behind its pipes. A French rearguard still occupied Madrid; but the King's headquarters were already far to the north in Valladolid; and his modest hope was to hold the line of the Douro against the British, who were bound to come marching up from Portugal by way of Salamanca. But were they? Lord Wellington had other views. For he was disinclined to force a passage of the Douro in face of a French army in strong prepared positions. He preferred to cross the river lower down its course, far behind the Portuguese frontier, and to appear in disagreeable force on the French bank. That, he surmised, would be an inexpensive method of dislodging them. So early as the third week of April his design was confided to Beresford:

> "I propose to put the troops in motion in the first days of May. My intention is to make them cross the Douro in general within the Portuguese frontier, covering the movement of the left by the right of the army towards the Tormes. . . ."

This was simplicity itself. At the same time he chose a bold expedient to accelerate his spring towards the north. His base was now at Lisbon; and whilst it might be satisfactory to draw supplies thence so long as he was operating in Leon and Castile, his line of communications would be intolerably lengthened (and the resulting delays increased), if he succeeded in advancing further to the north. So he resolved upon the unusual measure of transferring his base to the north coast of Spain as soon as he should reach the northern sphere of operations. (The same conception appears in the transfer of his base in 1803 from Mysore to the west coast of India.) Before his march began, the Admiral commanding on the station was advised that Wellington thought it "not impossible that we may hereafter have to communicate

with the shipping in one of the ports in the North of Spain ";
and at a later stage his supply ships were definitely ordered to the
great bay of Santander, a striking instance of the superior   17
elasticity conferred by sea-power on land operations.

Now they were ready to advance ; and symptoms of the move
began to appear at Headquarters, where the Peer's claret was   18
reported to be packing. The date was fixed by the ripening of
crops of forage for his horses. But the spring rains were late that
year, and slight delays in the arrival of the bridging-train (he
infuriated the artillery by taking their gun-teams to draw pontoons) deferred his start—fortunately, perhaps, as Wellington was
visited by a devastating cold. They moved before the end of
May ; and as they passed the frontier into Spain, he turned his
horse and, with a rare concession to drama, flourished his hat   19
towards the rear with the apostrophe, " Farewell, Portugal ! I
shall never see you again." He never did.

For the hunt was up that sent the French behind the Pyrenees.
Within a fortnight he had manœuvred them off the Douro ; and
the bells were clashing in Zamora, as a cloaked, grey figure rode
in. He waved away the dishes of an endless lunch ; and dis-   20
appointed Spaniards asked, " Is that Lord Wellington ? The
man who is sitting there so meekly in a grey coat, has only one
officer at his side, and will not eat or drink anything ? Good
God ! " Delighted villages thumped tambourines ; nuns
showered rose-leaves from the security of upper windows ; but
the advance went on, as they moved steadily northwards up the
broad corridors of Old Castile. The Peer was on the move ; and
a hurried glimpse caught him pacing a village street with Beres-   21
ford, whilst his tent was being pitched and the Military Secretary
sat writing orders on his knee under a wall. The French continually fell back, as rung after rung of the long Spanish ladder slipped
from their hands. They stood at Burgos ; but its works were
still unrepaired. He was outflanking them again ; and they fell
back once more, leaving a rearguard to destroy the Castle (and
blow out the glass of the cathedral). The roar of the explosion
reached Wellington, who was on their heels and promptly resolved
to " *hustle* them out of Spain." His first design had contem-   22
plated a formal siege of Burgos. But the French had saved him
the trouble ; and his spirits mounted, as King Joseph's monarchy
dwindled to an army in retreat. " Affairs are somewhat changed,"   23

he wrote, " since the period when the *frightened Leopard* was to
have been driven into the sea.   I think that if the Powers of
Europe chuse it we may now carry on a successful War, or may
force the Tyrant to make a peace which shall give genuine
tranquility to the World, & security to Independant States."
(His spelling seemed to suffer slightly in the swift advance.)   The
French were waiting for him now in the hills south of the Ebro.
It was a strong position, approached precariously by a narrow
road that crawled beneath the wicked spires of Pancorbo.   But
Wellington had little taste for frontal attacks on strong positions ;
and his columns slanted northwards away from the main road to
France by which he was expected.   For he would get behind
the French again.   He was still groping round their right ; and
their route lay by unlikely mountain paths, where he walked his
horse and the guns were man-handled as the teams stepped
gingerly over the boulders.   The French were turned again and
went disconsolately behind the Ebro, the Peer shepherding them ;
and his methods of command were neatly illustrated by three
notes written in a single afternoon to Lowry Cole :

24   " On the heighths near Poder June 19th 1813 ½ past 12 at Noon.
    " I have ordered the Light Division to cross the River, & to get
possession of the Ridge on the Enemy's left ; and you will advance,
& cannonade them in front, & push your Light Infantry across
supporting it by Cavalry & Heavy Infantry.
    " There is a Bridge at the Village, & I understand several fords."

The affair developed, and a second note conveyed his further
wishes :

    " I will make the Light Division continue its march till the
Ridge on your right ends ; & do you follow them up the valley to
the same point.
                    " ¼ before two P.M.
    " Let the Cavalry go with you."

A final scrap torn from his notebook warned the advancing Cole
and left him with a discretion that, from such a source, was both
flattering and rare :

                    2 P.M.   June 19th.
    " Since I wrote to you a quarter of an hour ago I have heard
that the Enemy are in strength on the great Road ; you had better
therefore halt when you will have crossed the River ; & taken up
such Posts as you may think proper."

His great sweep to the north had sent the French behind the
Ebro and placed his own forces between Santander and the enemy.
Now he could draw supplies by a short road from his new base ;
and if the French would fight, he was prepared to fight them.
He had come up with them at last ; and their meeting-place   25
was the great amphitheatre of Vitoria, where the last foothills of
the Pyrenees look out across Castile. The hunted French—an
army fifty thousand strong encumbered with a King, a Court,
large portions of a Civil Service, and an extensive *smala* (someone
irreverently remarked, " *Nous étions un bordel ambulant* ")—lay
across the great road to France. Somewhere behind the hills
Lord Wellington was waiting to attack. It was all a little like
the last phase of a *corrida*, when the trim *matador* steps briskly
sword in hand into the silent ring, watched by a weary bull.
The French waited for the blow, watched by the distant circle
of the hills. The blow prepared by Wellington was a miniature
of the whole campaign, in which he had continually groped round
the French right to place himself between them and their road
to France. His groping left should swing behind them once
again, cut the great road to Bayonne, and encircle them or (at
the worst) deflect them from their natural line of retreat, leaving
them to stumble towards Pamplona and the high passes of the
Pyrenees. That was his plain design, and on June 21 he executed
it. His sole uncertainty was the whereabouts of Clausel's command, which had been hunting *guerrilleros* in the north ; but an
obliging innkeeper rode twenty miles to tell him that Clausel was   26
safely lodged in his *posada*. Lord Wellington had ridden over
the ground ; his troops were up ; and as the guns began to speak
in the mist of a June morning, Vitoria watched from all its
belfries. The Peer, as usual, was everywhere, placing the troops
and riding behind his infantry, as Picton led them into action in
a cloud of blasphemy and a top-hat. Perhaps the full perfection
of his scheme was slightly impaired by Wellington's practice of
ubiquitous intervention, as an orchestral rendering would
scarcely be improved by a conductor unable to restrain his vir-
tuosity from playing half the parts himself. But his blow fell,
though Graham on his left had failed to get behind them ; and
as the shadows lengthened, the French went reeling off towards
the Pyrenees. They had lost all their guns but two, the loot of
Spain, and (worse still) the great road by which they might have

marched back to Bayonne. Behind them in Vitoria excited
27 redcoats were breaking open boxes full of Spanish dollars ; while
Portuguese capered in French Generals' uniforms, and by the light
of flares a great fair was held where the whole *débris* of King
Joseph's monarchy—pictures, books, currency, church-plate, and
tapestry—was auctioned to perspiring men by bawling comrades.
Wellington gave dinner to General Gazan's wife, who had been
left behind. They asked her if another lady in the same plight
was not a General's wife as well. " *Ah, pour cela—non,*" she
answered brightly, "*elle est seulement sa femme de campagne.*" The
lure of loot was almost irresistible ; and the pursuit left something
to be desired, though a Light Dragoon suggested that the cause
28 was rather Wellington's reluctance " to entrust officers with detachments to act according to circumstances, and I am not quite
clear if he approves of much success, excepting under his own
immediate eye."

But the blow had fallen. In just a month from his adieu
to Portugal the French monarchy in Spain had ceased to exist ;
29 and the news rang through Europe. The *Gazette* with Wellington's despatch was printed in French, Dutch, and German and
distributed broadcast ; the unwelcome news was thrust upon
French fishermen in the English Channel ; a Russian *Te Deum*—
the first ever sung for a foreign victory—greeted it ; and the news
sent Stadion running at midnight down the corridors of a
30 Silesian château, knocking at doors and greeting ruffled kings
and ministers with the glad tidings that " *Le roi Joseph est —— en
Espagne.*" The tall Czar was radiant at the news ; the dismal
King of Prussia brightened ; Bernadotte was a more loyal ally
now ; and even Austria veered towards action. For the guns of
Vitoria echoed across the Continent, and Wellington had stepped
from the Spanish to the European stage.

VIII

IT was midsummer, 1813 ; and as they went forward, a long line
of mountains climbed slowly up the sky, where all the folded
Pyrenees stood ranged in order. Beyond them lay the fields of
France. For the long road from Lisbon had brought the marching redcoats all the way from Portugal, across the bare Castilian
uplands, until they saw the last of Spain and the curved skyline
of the Pyrenees. Spain was behind them now with its wide skies
and crumbling cities ; and their road wound upwards, past the
brown belfries of Pyrenean villages and the anfractuosities of
Basque nomenclature, towards the gates of France. King
Joseph was a dejected phantom flitting through the passes to St.
Jean de Luz, his armies a receding line of bayonets winding
beneath the dripping trees through driving rain towards the
frontier. Lord Wellington rode irritably behind them, reviling
the indiscipline of his own troops—" We have in the service the   1
scum of the earth as common soldiers ; and of late years we have
been doing every thing in our power, both by law and by publications, to relax the discipline by which alone such men can be kept
in order. . . . As to the non-commissioned officers, as I have
repeatedly stated, they are as bad as the men. . . ." This angry   2
mood inspired the summary arrest of an unlucky gunner for dis-
obedience. But it soon subsided ; and Pakenham reported him
" vastly well and in high spirits," whilst his indignation grumbled   3
in the distance like a receding storm as he reported to the Horse
Guards that nobody in his army ever thought of obeying an order,
with the rare and generous admission that it was " an unrivalled
army for fighting, if the soldiers can only be kept in their ranks   4
during the battle."

The march went on towards the frontier. They heard the sea
at last in San Sebastian bay and saw the slow tide draw through
the narrows of Pasajes. France lay before them now. For there
was nothing in their path except the garrisons of San Sebastian
and Pamplona ; and they swept past the fortresses, until they
stared through the passes into France and watched the smoke of

French villages across the gleaming Bidassoa. (It was six months before any other European army came in sight of France.) But the Peer was cautious, though civilian correspondents might expect an immediate invasion of France and began to count the days until he should ride into Paris ; yet, as he drily pointed out, " none appear to have taken a correct view of our situation on the frontier, of which the enemy still possess all the strongholds within Spain itself ; of which strongholds, or at least some of them, we must get possession before the season closes, or we shall have no communication whatever with the interior of Spain." Facile ministers might write smooth things about the prospects of his elevation to supreme command of the Allies in Germany (eliciting a dutiful statement that he was the Prince Regent's servant, would do what his masters pleased, but was far better where he was) ; and Prinny himself, to whom he had despatched Marshal Jourdan's *bâton* after Vitoria, responded in a slightly gushing letter that " you have sent me, among the trophies of your unrivalled fame, the staff of a French Marshal, and I send you in return that of England "—a gesture which caused some embarrassment to his advisers, since there was no such thing. But while the Horse Guards did their very best to design one for the occasion—with some misgivings lest the Prince, whom an official acidly denominated " the fountain of taste," might do it for himself—the new Field Marshal, raised at last to the very top of the military tree, obstinately declined to lose his head.

His sole objective, as he saw, was to prevent the French from reaching their isolated garrisons in San Sebastian and Pamplona. Soult was in front of him, selected by the Emperor (who was somewhere in Saxony at grips with half the Continent) as " *la seule tête militaire qu'il y eût en Espagne* "—a warier Soult than the light-hearted Marshal who had waited for Sir Arthur Wellesley at Oporto in 1809. A chastened order now directed all his smaller units to send their eagles back to the depots for safe custody ; for now he had Lord Wellington to deal with. British guns were banging in the sunshine at the roofs of San Sebastian huddled beneath the slopes of Urgull ; and Pamplona would be starving soon. It was time for the French to provide a distraction ; and one morning in the third week of July (the Peer had a slight touch of rheumatism) sharp fighting on the bare hills behind Pamplona brought him to Sorauren. For Soult was thrusting southwards into Spain through Roncesvalles. (Strange how that year's fighting hung about old scenes ; for the Black Prince's men had drawn their bows at Vitoria, and now French bayonets wound through the pass where Charles the King had ridden and the last despairing echoes of Roland's horn once died away.) The French advance was sharply pressed ; and Wellington came up at a gallop, stopping to scrawl a hasty order on the stone parapet of a bridge with the Staff muttering all round him, " The French are coming." But he was off again before they came, the grey figure jolting in the saddle round corners and up mountain paths, until its trim silhouette was seen at the very summit—cocked-hat, frock-coat, and thoroughbred outlined against the summer sky. The Portuguese caught sight of him first ; and their hoarse cries of " Douro " set the whole army roaring, until the cheers ran like a flame along the hillsides and far out of sight. Erect and silent, a trim figure sat its horse above the cheering, as the whole army roared its recognition of " our great Lord," in " that stern and appalling shout " (as Napier termed it in a famous rhapsody) " which the British soldier is wont to give upon the edge of battle." Since Vitoria they called him " the hero of Britain." They knew him now ; and as he said that summer, " they will do for me what perhaps no one else can make them do." He could see the blue and gold of Soult and his staff across the narrow valley ; and the wary Marshal deferred the French attack, spread out his maps, took lunch, and went to sleep, leaving a spirited junior to lean against a tree and positively beat his brow with blind exasperation at the thought of sleep at such a juncture. The attack followed on the morrow ; but by now Wellington's command was comfortably aligned upon a ridge ; and though he termed it " fair *bludgeon* work," the results were satisfactory. It had been a risky business, though (he told someone afterwards that " at one time it was rather alarming certainly, and it was a close-run thing ") ; and he had little taste for mountain warfare, where the nature of the ground prevented him from being everywhere at once—" It is a great disadvantage when the Officer Commanding in Chief must be absent, and probably at a distance. For this reason there is nothing I dislike so much as these extended operations, which I cannot direct myself."

There was an interval, while they were battering San Sebastian into readiness for an assault. The Peer was limping with lumbago (his health gave him unusual trouble that year, with a spring catarrh, his rheumatism, and now his back ; and a misadventure when a chimney at Headquarters caught fire and sent him out to shout directions in the rain with a silk handkerchief over his head had scarcely helped). So when they dined in state for the Prince Regent's birthday, he rose with difficulty for the toasts, though a Spanish commissary rendered his favourite *A he Marmont*. His correspondence now was full of politics—of *haute politique* from Central Europe where a galaxy of Allied monarchs performed a highly complicated dance, and of the usual vexations from Cadiz where an accomplished troupe of Spanish politicians continued to exasperate his long-suffering brother Henry by striking progressive attitudes, when all that the situation called for was a single-minded prosecution of the war. The last evoked from Wellington a promise that he would not "miss a fair opportunity that may offer to give the democratical party a shake " ; he was slightly favourable to an offer of royalist support in France by the plump Duc de Berry ; but he was frankly disrespectful of the Allied sovereigns, whose endeavours to concert a plan of campaign were cheerfully dismissed as " loose conversations among Princes. For my part, I would not march even a corporal's guard upon such a system." His clear intelligence discerned that Allied war-aims must be harmonised before combined Allied strategy could be dreamt of, and he summed them up :

> " The object of each should be to diminish the power and influence of France, by which alone the peace of the world can be restored and maintained : and although the aggrandizement and security of the power of one's own country is the duty of every man, all nations may depend upon it that the best security for power, and for every advantage now possessed, or to be acquired, is to be found in the reduction of the power and influence of the grand disturber."

Meanwhile, he entrenched himself securely at the gates of France. The guns of San Sebastian still boomed ; but on the very day that Soult made another thrust a little nearer to the sea, the place fell. Flames licked its crumbling houses, and the sea swung idly in the bay beneath the silent citadel. The road to France was clear— the long road that they had tramped, mile after mile, since they first heard the thunder of the surf along the beaches and the first creak of loaded ox-waggons in Portugal, six years behind them now. They had seen Lisbon with its straight and sheltered streets,

16

the brown forts along the Tagus, cool hospitals in Belem, and the big hills that guard Torres Vedras, as they tramped through Portugal in the dusty sunshine and watched the cactus writhe silently along the roads. The tall sierras of the frontier, where chilly rivers wind through deep, slaty gorges, had seen them on the march ; and they had passed the empty distances of Spain, until they heard the torrents racing through the shaggy Pyrenees. For those perspiring redcoats in their black shakoes had tramped half the length and breadth of the Peninsula. Choking inside their stocks and loaded with sixty pounds of kit and rations and nine pounds of Brown Bess, they had marched all the way from Portugal to France in scarlet faced with yellow, white, and blue, and heavily cross-belted, through the blinding sunlight of six Peninsular summers. Lord Wellington had formed them, corresponding endlessly about their needs and husbanding them carefully ; for when a French adviser volunteered a wild strategical design, he opined that it " might answer well enough if I could afford, or the British Government or nation would allow of my being as prodigal of men as every French General is. They forget, however, that we have but one army, and that the same men who fought at Vimeiro and Talavera fought the other day at Sorauren ; and that, if I am to preserve that army, I must proceed with caution." Now he was almost proud of them. Army orders might abound with his customary fulminations against irregularity, and he could still ingeminate that " there is no crime recorded in the Newgate Calendar that is not committed by these soldiers, who quit their ranks in search of plunder." But in the privacy of his despatches he informed the Cabinet that " it is probably the most complete machine for its numbers now existing in Europe," adding in a letter to Dumouriez that his command was " *plus en état de faire une campagne d'hiver qu'aucune armée que j'aie jamais vu* " ; and in later years he said proudly that " I could have done *anything* with that army : it was in such splendid order." For he was proud of them ; and they responded with more warmth than he was quite accustomed to, cheering his silent figure for miles along the line at Sorauren and even in camp acclaiming him " not with three times three, or nine times nine, but as long as they could see him."

Now he had brought them to the edge of France ; and in the autumn weeks of 1813 the invasion was ready to begin. France had not been invaded since the wild days of the Republic, when the heads fell in Paris and Colonel Wesley of the Thirty-third beat his disconsolate retreat from the northern fortresses. But now his glass was busy among the red roofs and white walls of Basque villages ; and in the first week of October they slipped across the river below the brown church-tower of Fuenterrabia. (Before the month was out, the Emperor faced a great ring of enemies in front of Leipzig, fought for three days, and trailed off in defeat towards the Rhine.) The strict exigencies of strategy, perhaps, demanded that Wellington, once comfortably established astride of the western Pyrenees, should turn eastwards and drive Suchet from Catalonia. He confessed as much to Dumouriez :

" *La Catalogne m'a donné bien des mauvais momens pendant l'automne, et j'ai bien souvent pensé a y aller.*

" *Peut-être que, si je regardais seulement l'Espagne, ou même si je voyais les affaires sous un aspect militaire seulement, j'aurais du y aller, parcequ' il n'y a pas de doute que Buonaparte tient en Catalogne et tiendra les facilités pour rentrer en Espagne. Je dis peut-être, parceque, dans ce diable de pays, où j'ai fait la guerre pendant cinq ans, j'ai toujours trouvé, comme votre Henri Quatre, qu'avec des petits armées on ne faisait rien, et qu'avec des grandes armées on mourait de faim. . . . D'ailleurs il faut que la vue purement militaire cède à la politique. J'ai vu la marche des affaires en Allemagne, et, malgré les revers très graves qui sont arrivés ; j'ai cru voir des germes des succès très considerables qui sont depuis arrivés.*

" *Si je ne me suis pas trompé, il est bien plus important aux alliés, et à l'Espagne même, que je me porte en avant en France, au lieu de faire une guerre de forteresse en Catalogne. . . .*"

His steady reasoning gleams through the imperfect French ; and he went forward into France. Pamplona fell behind them, and in November they drove the French from the Nivelle, where Soult had hoped to stand behind a miniature version of Torres Vedras. Now they were closing in on Bayonne, and Headquarters moved to St. Jean de Luz, between the blue Biscayan rollers and the carved hills behind. A conversation with a captured Colonel, to whom Wellington gave dinner, informed him of the Imperial *Götterdämmerung*. The Staff plied their unhappy guest with questions ; but the discreet Peer " interfered quietly and whispered to them to let him alone, and that after a good dinner and a few glasses of Madeira our friend would mend." The treat-

ment answered ; and his host adroitly brought the conversation
round to comforts at Headquarters—to the Emperor's recent
experiences in that respect—and then, with the most casual air in
the world, he launched a question.

" *Où était le quartier-général de l'Empereur,*" he innocently enquired, " *d'après les dernières nouvelles ?* "

" *Nulle part,*" the Colonel answered gloomily, " *il n'y a plus de
quartier-général.*"

" *Comment plus de quartier-général ?* "

" *Monseigneur, il n'y a point de quartier-général, et point
d'armée ; l'affaire est finie.*"

But Soult was still in front of him, and the fortress of Bayonne
was formidable. Besides, he had all the novel problems of an
invasion—of French feelings to be handled with his invariable
discretion, angry deputations to be soothed, and proclamations
posted up in Basque. Perfect discipline became more necessary
than ever, and the pardonable inclination of his Spanish troops to
avenge the long French occupation by a carnival of theft and
destruction caused him endless trouble. Indeed, his Peninsular
allies were more than usually trying that season, and he wrote
bitterly that " *le Démon de la discorde se plait à se mêler des*   23
affaires de la Péninsule." Wellington was rarely figurative ; but
the outbreak was not surprising, since he was afflicted with a
Minister of War at Cadiz whom he stigmatised as " that greatest   24
of all blackguards," and he was unusually sensitive to the attacks
of Spanish journalists upon alleged atrocities at San Sebastian.

A new complication threatened his peace, as he faced in his
clear-headed way the problem of the future government of
France. He had been thinking of it ever since he read a *Quarterly*   25
review by Croker in 1811 of a book by some exiled royalist ; he
read the book itself (it was Faber's *Notices sur l'Intérieur de la
France*) and found it highly instructive ; and when two rainy
days confined him with the *curé* at St. Pé and his interlocutor
confirmed his previous impressions of French opinion, he promptly
advised the Government that France was weary, that the pre-   26
vailing hunger was for peace—peace, probably, without the
Emperor. But he found no positive revival of royalist sentiment
and advised peace with Napoleon, if he was inclined to moderation. At the same time he hinted broadly that " if I were a
Prince of the House of Bourbon, nothing should prevent me from

now coming forward, not in a good house in London, but in the field in France ; and if Great Britain would stand by him, I am certain he would succeed." He even sent a message to the same effect to Monsieur ; and the majestic processes of the Bourbon mind, assisted by Wellington's report of his conversations with a village *curé*, evolved the project of despatching the Duc d'Angou-
27 lême to San Sebastian. A grateful letter to Headquarters from Hartwell House even compared Wellington to Marlborough— strange praise from a great-great-grandson of Louis XIV—and advised him of the satisfaction with which Louis XVIII observed his entry into France.

There was a pause in drenching Pyrenean rain ; and two
28 brigades of Guards in scarlet tunics and white pantaloons attended divine worship on the sands at St. Jean de Luz, whilst Lord Wellington in full uniform stood near the drum-head. Then they
29 attacked again, driving the French behind the Nive. But Soult struggled hard, and 1813 went out upon a week of stubborn fighting in the hills behind Biarritz. This year there could be no interlude of peaceful winter-quarters in his village street at Freneda. For the war scarcely halted except for a few weeks of
30 leisure at St. Jean de Luz, when everybody strolled on the sea-wall from four o'clock till six " at a true twopenny postman's long trot," whilst languid Guardsmen (recently arrived and a shade exhausted by their unaccustomed activities) lounged on the parapet, and Lord Wellington himself was seen outraging military sensibilities with his frock-coat and top-hat or the sky-blue and black, no less civilian, of the Salisbury hunt. For he got in his hunting. The little streets were full of vociferating Spanish muleteers and the long strings of jingling mules ; the little shop-windows offered the unaccustomed delights of butter and sar-dines ; and obliging Frenchmen ran the blockade of their own sentries with poultry for their country's foes. For they preferred the invader's ready money (helped out with bags of sugar to which they had been strangers, thanks to the blockade, for seven years) to the less profitable traffic of Soult's requisitions. It had been the invariable practice of French armies to live upon the country ; but when the country happened to be French as well, the practice failed to commend itself, and a shrewd countryside preferred to sell to Wellington's commissaries.

The French prince and his suite arrived, and nobody was

much impressed—"Lord Wellington was in his manner droll   *31*
towards them . . . they bowed and scraped right and left so
oddly, and so actively, that he followed with a face much nearer
a grin than a smile." There were balls at the *Mairie* (where an
adventurous *gendarme* essayed a horn-pipe) and church parade
on Sundays with the Guards in hollow square on the sands against
a sunny background of blue sky and crowded shipping in the
smooth blue bay—"quite," as a rapturous Judge-Advocate   *32*
remarked, "a Vernet." But work crowded on the Peer. His
next enterprise was to encircle Bayonne by bridging the wide
Adour below the town while the February gales were still blowing ;
and someone saw him studying the sea from the sea-wall at half-   *33*
past seven one winter morning. The bold throw succeeded ;
and whilst they made it, Soult was distracted by an attack far
inland, which drove him beyond Orthez on February 27. But
for the first time Wellington was very nearly one of his own casualties. He was standing under fire with Alava, when a wounded
Portuguese limped past, explaining that he was "*ofendido*."   *34*
Something knocked over Alava ; and Wellington was laughing
at him, when he was hit himself. He fell and scrambled to his
feet, remarking with cheerful blasphemy, "By God ! I am
ofendido this time." For a stray shot had driven his sword-hilt
against his hip, bruising it and breaking the skin ; but, though
stiff, he was well enough to ride on the next day.

The French drew off along the Pyrenees ; and the war rolled
eastwards across France. The spring was bitter ; and Lord
Wellington rode after them with the snow driving in his face
(that day his taste for inconspicuous costume selected a white   *35*
cloak). In the north the Emperor was fencing desperately, as
the net slowly tightened round him. The end was coming now ;
and hopeful kings revisited their kingdoms. King Ferdinand
of Spain, more like a Goya than ever, lifted the questionable light
of his unpleasing countenance upon Gerona ; and Wellington
remembered that he had got some pictures of King Joseph's after
Vitoria, which might belong to Ferdinand. They had not im-   *36*
pressed him at the time—not, that is to say, so much as the
Raphaels which they had shewn him in Madrid—and he had
"thought more of the prints and drawings, all of the Italian school,
which induced me to believe that the whole collection was robbed
in Italy rather than in Spain." He sent them home for cleaning,

but was now concerned to learn that they were finer than he had supposed. So Henry Wellesley was instructed to ascertain if they were Spanish royal property, as " I am desirous of restoring them to His Majesty." But he had Bourbons nearer home ; and Wellington, now a convinced royalist on strictly military grounds, pressed the Prime Minister to take a stronger line in favour of the dynasty :

³⁷   " Any declaration from us would, I am convinced, raise such a flame in the country as would soon spread from one end of it to the other, and would infallibly overturn him.

" I cannot discover the policy of not hitting one's enemy as hard as one can, and in the most vulnerable place. I am certain that he would not so act by us, if he had the opportunity. He would certainly overturn the British authority in Ireland if it was in his power. . . ."

Then Angoulême, *incognito* discarded and a Royal Highness once again, rode into Bordeaux in the wake of Marshal Beresford ; and the white cockades came out.

The war rolled slowly east ; and Wellington's paper-work was more than usually exacting. Diplomacy absorbed him now ; he was in the saddle all day long ; and correspondence was reserved for after dinner. But the French were still in front of him. He had a brush with them at Tarbes, a slightly tangled affair with Soult in front and a town amicably bawling " *Vive le roi* " behind. Then he was facing Toulouse in the last week of March, with Soult comfortably ensconced behind the broad Garonne. There was endless trouble with the bridging-train ; and he went reconnoitring in his usual fashion, riding down to the river with an oilskin cover over his cocked-hat and positively chatting with a French vedette. Then he dismounted, strolled about, and having seen the ground rode off. (That week the heavy footsteps echoed in the deserted galleries of Fontainebleau, as Marshals came and went, until a lonely man sat huddled in an empty palace.) An excited note was on its way from Paris, acquainting Wellington that " Glory to God and to yourself, the great man has fallen." But Soult was still in Toulouse ; and on April 10 Wellington's attack was launched. It took liberties that in other circumstances would have been scarcely pardonable, and there were grave vicissitudes. But it succeeded ; Wellington, for once, was playing high for victory ; and Soult, driven from his stronghold, trailed off towards Carcassonne, while the Peer rode

into Toulouse. They cheered him in the streets ; and he had not
been in the place an hour before a Colonel came riding in with   41
news from Bordeaux.

" I have extraordinary news for you."

" Ay," said the Peer, whom nothing could surprise, " I thought
so. I knew we should have peace ; I've long expected it."

" No," said the Colonel, " Napoleon has abdicated."

" How abdicated ? " Wellington replied with cheerful incredu-
lity. " Ay, 'tis time indeed. You don't say so, upon my honour !
Hurrah ! " And the Colonel enjoyed the unprecedented spectacle
of Lord Wellington without his coat on spinning round and
snapping his fingers.

He gave a ball at the *Préfecture* that night ; and they sat
down about forty to dinner. He gave them a new toast as well
—" Louis XVIII "—and someone served out white cockades   42
for them to wear. Then Alava stood up and gave them " *El
Liberador de España*," whilst all the foreigners—French, Germans,
Portuguese, and Spanish—toasted him in their own languages—
" *Liberateur de la France*," " *Liberador da Portugal*," " *Liberateur
de l'Europe*." They shouted for ten minutes ; and then the
embarrassed hero " bowed, confused, and immediately called for
coffee." After that they all went to the play. Their white cockades were stared at ; but when Wellington (who was in the stage-
box with Picton and the Spaniards) laid his hat on the front of the
box to shew the royal colours, the house roared. They played the
royal anthem, too ; and someone recited the new constitution from
a box. The piece was admirably chosen. For it was Grétry's
Richard Cœur de Lion ; and when the band struck up the air, a
vocalist sang the appeal of his devoted Queen disguised as Blondel—

" *Ô Richard, ô mon roi, l'univers t'abandonne . . .*"

and those excited soldiers heard the very air once sung to other
soldiers, as a young Queen at Versailles walked graciously among
them with a sleepy Dauphin in her arms. Dauphin and Queen
were gone ; but the wheel had come full circle. For King Louis
reigned once more in France. Peace came within a week ; Lord
Wellington signed a Convention of Toulouse with less unhappy
consequences than that of Cintra ; and as the firing died away,
the marching columns halted. There was a sudden silence, and
the war was over.

IX

" —— and then all the people cheered again." For it was 1814
—" the year of revelry," as someone called it, with Allied
sovereigns bowing graciously in all directions, and Lord Byron
writing *Lara* whilst undressing after balls and masquerades, and
oxen roasting whole in country market-places, and mail-coaches
bowling along every road in England trimmed with laurel
leaves and rousing sentiments about " the Downfall of the
Tyrant " and bright with transparencies of Lord Wellington.
But Wellington was still at Toulouse. Army business kept him
1 there a few weeks longer, mitigated by more balls at the *Préfec-*
ture and a little hunting ; for within a week of the armistice he
was riding to hounds at five o'clock one morning, and a distinguished soldier enquiring for his whereabouts was scandalised
to learn that the Commander-in-Chief was believed to be somewhere in a forest about eighteen miles away. But his top-hat
2 and blue frock-coat were seen about the streets, as he slipped
unobtrusively out of Angoulême's *levée* on his way back to the
Hôtel de France ; arch whispers even hinted that his residence was
rendered more attractive by the Spanish belle wedded to its
proprietor—" I do not mean to be scandalous," as the Judge-
Advocate primly observed, " but this, perhaps, may have decided
the choice of the house." After all, the war was over. Now they
were all discussing who goes to America ; for " the government,"
3 as someone at the Horse Guards wrote, " have determined to give
Jonathan a good drubbing," and a large detachment of that incomparable army was to see the shining spaces of the Great Lakes,
the flames of Washington, and the endless cane-brakes of Louis-
iana. But Wellington did not go with them. Another duty
called. For Castlereagh invited him to take the British Embassy
4 in Paris, and he accepted with a sober conviction that he " must
serve the public in some manner or other ; and as, under existing
circumstances, I could not well do so at home, I must do so
5 abroad." His acceptance alluded modestly to " a situation for
which I should never have thought myself qualified." But he

was not too old to learn a new trade at forty-five ; besides, six years of dealing with the Spaniards and Portuguese were a respectable apprenticeship in diplomacy, and Henry wrote cheerfully from Madrid that he would find it " very pretty amusement." 6

Then he was off to Paris in the first week of May, arriving just in time to see the Russians march past the Allied sovereigns on the *Quai*. Those exalted personages watched from a window in 7 the Louvre ; and King Louis XVIII sat composedly in an armchair, while the lean Emperor of Austria stood just behind him with the dismal King of Prussia, and the tight-waisted Czar did the honours. Lord Wellington saw the spectacle on horseback, riding between Castlereagh and his brother Charles. But he was quite a spectacle himself ; for all the monarchs craned forward for a sight of him, where he sat his horse almost defiantly civilian in his blue frock-coat and top-hat. They introduced him to old Platow the Cossack ; and when he saw the Russian cavalry, he said in his plain way, " Well, to be sure, we can't turn out anything like this." The Czar called on him that evening, and he looked in at a ball where the company was sublimely mixed—a *galimatias* of reigning princes, Blücher's moustaches, the red head of Ney, and the watchful eyes of Metternich. The Czar waltzed with Maréchale Ney, and Blücher kissed Lady Castlereagh's hand with gusto. Then he was introduced to Wellington and, in default of conversation, " they held each other's hands, and there was a great deal of hearty smiling " ; someone interpreted ; but the old Hussar looked merely puzzled. Wellington was a week in Paris. Whilst he was there, the news arrived that Liverpool and the Prince Regent had given one last turn to the fountain of honour, and so he was to be a Duke. Kitty had it from the Prime Minister himself ; and Richard, who was always strong upon 8 such matters, was duly taken into counsel as to the proper title for him. So Arthur passed him in the race. For Richard was a Marquess still; but Arthur was to be a Duke—the Duke of Wellington. His hands were full ; and it was three weeks before a brotherly postscript acquainted Henry that " I believe I forgot 9 to tell you I was made a Duke."

Before May was out, he was back at Toulouse on the road to Spain, where Ferdinand was rapidly reducing his long-lost subjects to distraction. But it would never do to inaugurate the new golden age with a civil war ; and hopes were entertained that

Wellington's familiar tones might discipline the restive Spaniards
and their unprepossessing king. Castlereagh had thought him
looking well in Paris ; but an observer at Toulouse found him a
little thin and pulled down by a cold. Then he posted off to Spain
at eight o'clock one morning. The long road was familiar ; he
saw Vitoria again, and the tall spires of Burgos ; Valladolid went
by, and once more he came in sight of Madrid. He saw the King,
and thought him " by no means the idiot he is represented."
But his ministers were quite deplorable ; and Wellington discharged a heavy cargo of good advice—that promiscuous arrests
should be followed up by trial or release, or, at the very least, by
some kind of attempt to justify them ; that England would
expect an effort to govern " on liberal principles " ; and that, in
certain circumstances, she might even undertake " to discourage
and discountenance, by every means in our power, the rebellion
in the Spanish colonies." (For the time had not yet come for
calling a New World into being to redress the balance of the Old ;
besides, the Duke of Wellington was not Mr. Canning.) This
business was transacted to an accompaniment of etiquette that
varied between the impressive and the imbecile. He stood with
Ferdinand on a palace balcony and kept his hat on, because he
was a Grandee of Spain ; and when he had his audience, the
simpering San Carlos asked him if he noticed how the guards had
stamped their feet. " That is only done," he added, " for a
Grandee of the first order—you must indeed be a happy man."

He was happy in his way ; for he was fully occupied. His
family displayed a tendency to share his happiness, since William
had brought his household to the Continent and joined him in
Madrid. Soon he would see them all ; for he was on his way to
England now. He stopped a few days in Bordeaux writing farewell epistles, and a final Order was issued to the army :

" 1. The Commander of the Forces, being upon the point of
returning to England, again takes this opportunity of congratulating
the army upon the recent events which have restored peace to their
country and to the world.

" 2. The share which the British army has had in producing
these events, and the high character with which the army will quit
this country, must be especially satisfactory to every individual
belonging to it, as they are to the Commander of the Forces ; and he
trusts that the troops will continue the same good conduct to the last.

" 3. The Commander of the Forces once more requests the army
to accept his thanks.

" 4. Although circumstances may alter the relations in which he
has stood towards them, so much to his satisfaction, he assures them
that he shall never cease to feel the warmest interest in their welfare
and honor ; and that he will be at all times happy to be of any
service to those to whose conduct, discipline, and gallantry their
country is so much indebted."

The debt was honourably acknowledged ; and he was granted
nearly forty years for its discharge—forty years of begging-
letters and hats touched by eager fingers as his horse went by.
There was a loose sovereign ready in his waistcoat pocket for any
old soldier who had served under him. His letter-bag was filled
for nearly half a century with applications for every kind of
favour ; and can he be reproached if his replies more often than
not were in the negative ? Harrowing anecdotes are preserved
of hungry veterans who, dining at his table, filled their pockets
with the broken meats for starving families at home. An angry
officer who had served with him in the East, endorsed his cour-   15
teous confession of inability to find him employment with the
angry query, " Can this Man have a Heart ! ! " Yet the indignant
applicant had voluntarily retired from the service in 1812 ; and
now he was inclined to blame the Duke for not employing him in
1828. (Indeed, his notion of the Duke's utility was even more extensive ; since a note survives in which " the Duke of Wellington
presents his Compliments to Mr. Elers, and is much obliged to
him for his Letter of this day. The Duke has no occasion for a
Newfoundland Dog, and will not deprive Mr. Elers of him.")
Had he a heart ? The contrary is scarcely proved by the
circumstance that he did not grant every favour that was asked
of him. How could he ? It was easy enough for Byron to reel
off indignant stanzas inciting him to

> " go, and dine from off the plate   16
> Presented by the Prince of the Brazils ;
> And send the sentinel before your gate
> A slice or two from your luxurious meals :
> He fought, but has not fed so well of late."

But to become the almoner of fifty thousand men drawn from the
least provident classes of his fellow-subjects, to forward the professional ambitions of half the officers in the Army List, and to

prolong these services into the second generation was utterly impossible. Besides, his hands were often tied by a strong sense of orderly administration. For how could responsible Departments ever do their work if the Duke of Wellington perpetually intervened in favour of innumerable *protégés* ? That was the reason why his correspondents often received an irritating *non possumus*, and concluded angrily that they were forgotten. True, he had every excuse for not remembering them. For whilst they had ample leisure for their reminiscences, Wellington had something more to do than to perfect his recollections of the breach at Badajoz. His life was crowded almost to the end with diplomacy and politics and army administration. New faces and fresh problems perpetually engaged him ; and Larpent once diagnosed his apparent neglect of old associations.

17 " You ask me if Lord Wellington has recollected——with regard ? He seems to have had a great opinion of him, but scarcely ever mentioned him to me. In truth, I think Lord Wellington has an active, busy mind, always looking to the future, and is so used to lose a useful man, that as soon as gone he seldom thinks more of him. He would be always, no doubt, ready to serve any one who had been about him, or the friend of a deceased friend, but he seems not to think much about you when once out of the way. He has too much of everything and everybody always in his way to think much of the absent."

That was excusable ; and if England omitted to make due provision for his soldiers, the fault was not Wellington's, but his country's.

France, from St. Jean de Luz to Calais, flowed past his carriage windows as he posted homewards through the summer days of 1814. He stopped long enough in Paris to transact some army business with the Ministry of War, where Bourbon tact had installed the sleek Dupont ; for that paladin reigned over the army of Austerlitz, wearing the withered laurels of Baylen—a defeat commanding twenty years of victory. Then Calais slipped behind him ; and Wellington came in sight of England, last seen the gusty day he sailed for Portugal in 1809. The little streets of Dover rang with huzzas ; and eager faces pressed against his carriage windows, as he drove through the cheering countryside. Kent and Surrey were one dusty, roaring lane of bawling Englishmen, and London was waiting to take out his

horses. But he drove too fast for them to Piccadilly, where he   *19*
found Kitty and his boys in Hamilton Place—a smiling Kitty,
more short-sighted than ever and a trifle breathless with her
sudden rise from Countess to Marchioness, and now to the last
dizzy empyrean of a Duchess. Besides, she had sustained exhausting conversations with foreign royalties. A crowd was
cheering in the street ; but he escaped by a back way into the
Park, and slipped off to see his mother in Upper Brook Street,
strolled down Oxford Street, met Richard in a cheering crowd,
and went to see his married sister. Then he drove down to Portsmouth, where naval salutes were booming for the Allied sovereigns, and paid his respects to the Prince Regent. Next the protracted triumph—first popular, then royal—took a Parliamentary
turn ; and the new Peer put on his robes to take his seat in the
House of Lords as Baron, Viscount, Earl, Marquess, and Duke.
After the Lords it was the Commons' turn ; and one afternoon he
visited them. They had already voted money for the purchase of
an estate ; as Government proposed £300,000, the Opposition   *20*
outbidding them, as Oppositions will, carried £400,000 with Mr.
Canning and Mr. Whitbread (who had once charged him with
exaggerating Talavera) among the loudest voices. Now he was
coming to the House in person. His voice had not been heard
there since a few words on Irish agriculture and canals five years
before. But now a chair was set for him at the Bar ; the House
rose at his entry, and he sat " for some time covered." The
House was full of uniforms ; the very mace assumed a military
pose, since the Serjeant-at-arms had grounded it and stood
beside him at attention. Then he made them a little speech of
thanks—first to the Commons for their compliment, and then to
the nation for its war-effort.

He was five weeks in England ; and his days were loud with
ceremonial eloquence and bright with presentations, whilst his
evenings were an unending *levée* in the new Field Marshal's
uniform. He went down to Essex, and stayed with William's   *21*
son at Wanstead. The Prince, the royal Dukes, and the whole
Wellesley clan were there ; and the adoring eyes of Lady Shelley
were on him after dinner, when they drank to his father's memory
and the Prince Regent proposed his health. The Duke rose,
smiling broadly, and began :
    " I want words to express . . ."

The Regent promptly interrupted him with royal geniality. " My dear fellow," said Prinny, in his easy way, " we know your *actions*, and we will excuse you your *words*, so sit down." The Duke, always obedient to royalty, sat down " with all the delight of a schoolboy who has been given an unexpected holiday." Then they all drank to Richard, who replied (as might have been expected) at considerable length. After dinner the Duke polonaised ; Blücher performed a country dance ; and old Platow gave a Cossack performance, which convulsed the company and appeared to consist of nodding his head and stamping like a horse.

He was all smiles that summer, savouring his triumph and saying gaily to the lady on his arm, as the crowds outside the Opera parted respectfully before them, " It's a fine thing to be a great man, is not it ? " He enjoyed the incense ; and he could enjoy the general gaiety as well, watching his aides-de-camp all dancing hard at Carlton House and asking cheerfully, " How would society get on without all my boys ? " And someone saw him " in great good humour apparently, and not squeezed to death " at the great masquerade in Burlington House, where Hobhouse went as an Albanian ; Byron was there dressed as a monk, and Caroline Lamb was more outrageous than usual. A *Star* reporter grew rapturously classical, recording that " the company did not separate from the allurements of Terpsichore's court till Sol rose to light them to repose." But there was business to be done—prospective country houses to be viewed with Mr. Wyatt, letters to Henry about Spanish policy, and advice to ministers upon the American war. They consulted him about an expedition to New Orleans, inspired by Cochrane's appetite for prize-money ; but the Duke was full of practical objections. He stated his opinion plainly ; and when the failure had cost heavily in casualties (including Edward Pakenham), he wrote bluntly to his brother-in-law :

22

23

> " We have one consolation, that he fell as he lived, in the honourable discharge of his duty : and distinguished as a soldier & as a man.
>
> " I cannot but regret however that he was ever employed on such a service or with such a colleague.
>
> " The expedition to New Orleans originated with that colleague, & plunder was its object. I knew & stated in July that the transports could not approach within leagues of the landing place, &

enquired what means were provided to enable a sufficient body of troops with their artillery provisions & stores to land, & afterwards to communicate with them.   Then as plunder was the object, the Admiral took care to be attended by a sufficient number of *sharks*, to carry the plunder off from a place at which he knew well that he could not remain.   The secret of the expedition was thus communicated & in this manner this evil design defeated its own end.   The Americans were prepared with an army in a fortified position which still would have been carried, if the duties of others, that is of the Admiral, had been as well performed as that of him whom we lament.

" But Providence performed it otherwise & we must submit. . . ."

Then the cheers died away behind him ; and he was off to the Continent once more.   He did not go direct to Paris, but performed a minor military duty *en route* by reporting upon the defences of Belgium.   This territory was now incorporated in a single kingdom with the Netherlands ; and it was manifestly desirable to render its southern frontier impervious to French invasions.   He reconnoitred for a fortnight, riding round the Belgian villages with three Colonels of Engineers ; and his conclusions were embodied in a memorandum favouring a return to the Barrier line of fortresses.   A brief examination of the country scarcely enabled him to be precise upon the probable course of military operations.   But he indicated " good positions for an army " at various points, of which the last was " the entrance of the *forêt de Soignies* by the high road which leads to Brussels from Binch, Charleroi, and Namur " : it was the ridge of Waterloo.

His reconnaissance concluded, Wellington resumed his new profession and became a diplomat.   It was a pleasant change to bombard the French with arguments about the slave trade and mild remonstrances upon the misdeeds of American privateers.   The French conception of neutrality was frankly scandalous ; and the activities of the *True Blooded Yankee* kept his pen busy.   One ardent privateer, whose appetites appeared to extend to monumental masonry, had even captured a recumbent statue of Queen Louise of Prussia ; and tearful representations were made to Wellington to assist in its recovery for the mausoleum at Charlottenburg.   But a large proportion of his work related to the slave trade. He had been startled whilst in England by " the degree of frenzy " felt in this admirable cause, the Lord Mayor positively hesitating to propose the health of King Ferdinand in the solemn shades of Guildhall in case the company refused the toast. But Paris brought Wellington a closer acquaintance with the problem ; for he was pelted with improving literature, interviewed by Zachary Macaulay and the virtuous Clarkson, and positively satisfied the latter that he had read through his *History of Abolition* and *Impolicy of the Slave Trade*, to say nothing of a little thing by Mr. Wilberforce and all the memoranda from the African Society—strange reading for a conqueror. But his interest was genuine ; and he gave shrewd advice upon the management of French opinion, even volunteering to finance their publications out of public funds. Smaller matters occasionally diversified his work ; once he applied for special library facilities on behalf of a Fellow of Trinity in uncertain health engaged on an edition of Demosthenes ; he argued with some reason in the interests of scholarship that the *Archives* might reasonably raise their ban upon research into the reign of Louis XV ; and that awful eye, before which Generals had shrunk, was turned upon an irritable oculist who had expected every facility for his scientific investigations in spite of a total ignorance of French. Courtesy suggested that he should offer to the King his pack of hounds— " *une meute des meilleures races d'Angleterre* "—a not unflattering description of the assorted hounds behind which he had hunted all the way from Portugal to Toulouse.

Life was a pleasant relaxation—a shade too pleasant, if hostile whispers were to be believed, since a Bonapartist lady circulated stories about a *prima donna*. But Kitty was in Paris now ; his boys were coming out for Christmas ; and if Grassini smiled, who could resist ? Not that his life in Paris was all triumphs and trivialities. Interminable papers brought him accounts of the negotiations at Vienna, and his advice was sought at every turn. He even advised upon the menace of the Regent's wife, suggesting shrewdly that it might be " worth considering whether it is not desirable that every facility should be given to the Princess of Wales to amuse herself abroad, in order that she may not be induced to return to England "—a rich example of the Wellingtonian horse-sense that was requisitioned for the next half century upon every problem from the future of Europe to the disposal of Mrs. Fitzherbert's papers. His own affairs were relatively calm, though a libel in *The Times* moved him to unaccustomed wrath. He could be philosophical enough in general, reminding sensitive acquaintances that " misrepresentation of   *32* facts is the common practice of the writers of newspapers." But this time his patience failed ; and William was instructed to set the Law Officers in motion. His indignation was sublime—

" If I possess any advantages in point of character, I consider   *33* myself bound to set the example to others of a determination to prevent the blackguard editors of papers from depriving us of our reputation by their vulgar insinuations.

" The truth is, I refused to employ a relation of the editor of the ' Times ' in my family, and that is the reason he has accused me of corruption ; but that is no reason why I should bear it."

That autumn ministers discovered a new cause for anxiety. The French were restless ; a stout King in an arm-chair formed an imperfect substitute for an incomparable Emperor on horse-back ; veterans were muttering in corners ; and there were grave fears for Wellington. His life was precious, and a military insurrection might endanger it—or at least detain him in France and deprive the Allies of his services. The official mind was   *34* busy with pretexts for bringing him away. Could he not be sent for to advise the Congress ? Once at Vienna, he need not return to Paris ; and then he could be sent to take command in America. That was their real design. The Regent felt that " nothing   *35* should be neglected to induce the Duke of Wellington to accept of the Chief Command in America as soon as possible, as his name alone will reconcile the whole view & opinion of the Country, & at the same time be the means of obviating as well as removing many difficulties which may afterwards arise." Lord Liverpool concurred, and put it tentatively to the Duke, who felt " no dis-   *36* inclination to undertake the American concern," but demurred on purely European grounds to leaving Paris at the moment. It might, he thought, be possible in March, 1815 ; but at the moment he was strongly inclined to stay. There was no false modesty about his refusal—" I entertain a strong opinion that I *must* not be lost." But the very unrest, which was the reason for his recall, was in itself the strongest argument for retaining him in Europe—" In case of the occurrence of anything in

Europe, there is nobody but myself in whom either yourselves or the country, or your Allies would feel any confidence." Besides, his presence in America would not make much difference, since " that which appears to me to be wanting in America is not a General, or General officers and troops, but a naval superiority on the Lakes " ; without it he could do little more than " sign a peace which might as well be signed now." Then he went on to advise them bluntly to make peace without annexations. The dashing son of solemn Mr. Gallatin, who was negotiating at Ghent, even believed that Wellington, in his eagerness for peace with the United States, corresponded directly with the American delegate, urging him to come to terms and dwelling with some skill on Gallatin's Swiss origin. The effect, if James Gallatin can be believed, was admirable—" Father, I think, was pleased. He is a foreigner and is proud of it." For the Duke's diplomatic accomplishments even included the art of charming that unpleasing type of American whose chief pride is that he is not American. Once he was almost persuaded to leave Paris, though he was still reluctant—" I confess that I don't see the necessity for being in a hurry. . . . I really don't like the way in which I am going away. . . . I don't like to be frightened away." But he admitted the necessity for his recall, though the American command had few attractions. A better plan was found when Castlereagh, recalled to England by his Parliamentary duties, invited Wellington to replace him at Vienna. This was respectable, and he accepted.

The year went out upon a world at peace. For peace was positively signed on Christmas Eve at Ghent between Great Britain and the United States (personified by the pertinacious Adams, Bayard, Henry Clay, and Mr. Gallatin, always comfortably aware of the nobility of his Swiss blood). On the last day of the year Lord Liverpool wrote to the Duke with evident relief about the mission to Vienna and a difficulty with Murat at Naples and his own plans (the Prime Minister was hoping to get down to Bath). Then Europe slept, and midnight sounded from the steeples—from the tall spire above Vienna, from Ste. Gudule at Brussels and Notre Dame (where Paris stirred a little in its sleep) and from the little belfries, where a lonely man counted the hours on Elba—and as the echoes died away, it was 1815.

1815

Waterloo! Waterloo! Waterloo!
morne plaine!
Les Châtiments.

WINTER

EUROPE was under snow. Lord Castlereagh, with something less
than his customary tact, informed an after-dinner audience at
Vienna that " *il commence l'âge d'or* " and was generally understood to have alluded to British subsidies ; the Czar, acutely
conscious of his virtue, was full of noble sentiments and frankly
covetous of Poland ; even the widowed King of Prussia forgot
his mourning in a lively appetite for Saxon territory ; and M. de
Talleyrand limped deferentially among the gilded furniture with
his thin smile. Two carriages rumbled along the miry roads, one
taking Byron and his bride to their uncomfortable honeymoon ;
the Duke was in the other, rolling across the Continent towards
Vienna. Behind him in Whitehall the Horse Guards struggled
with the problem of Peninsular medals ; the Prince Regent was
at Brighton reading official papers and contemplating the Pavilion
domes ; and the Cabinet instructed Wellington upon the future

1   of Corfu. He had a heavy cold when he arrived, and found the
hot rooms of Vienna most exhausting. But it was winter still,
and the hot rooms were full of bowing gentlemen in decorations.
He saw Prince Metternich ; he saw the Swedes ; he saw the Poles.
Life became an endless succession of interviews and drafts—

2   drafts about Switzerland and Frankfort and the Valtelline. The
Czar called one evening with a complicated grievance about the
Danes and Bernadotte and the purchase price of Guadaloupe.
He would be leaving soon for Russia ; but Wellington seemed
doomed to sit for ever manipulating drafts in stifling rooms.
Would the spring never come ?

It came that year a little early. For spring came with the
violets in the first week of March. Prince Metternich had gone

3   to bed at three one morning after a conference. He was not to be
disturbed ; but an officious servant brought in an envelope at
six o'clock. The Prince looked at it and, observing without
interest that it was merely from the Austrian Consul at Genoa,
turned over again. But he failed to sleep ; and about half past
seven he opened it and read that Napoleon was missing from Elba.

Within an hour he saw three sleepy sovereigns ; the Duke, who had a letter to the same effect, was told at ten ; and when Talleyrand predicted that the Emperor would make for Switzerland, the Prince took another view—" *Il ira droit à Paris.*" Metternich was right : the spring had come.

SPRING

There was a sudden stir. The solemn exercises of Vienna were broken off, and diplomacy subsided like an interrupted minuet. Once again there was a sudden rapping on the doors ; the music stopped, the dancers huddled into corners, and angry gentlemen drew swords. The Duke, three Princes, and fourteen assorted noblemen declared in the name of eight governments that Napoleon Bonaparte had forfeited all human rights. It was the dreadful cry once heard from revolutionary lips in Paris, when angry men with starting eyes bawled " *Hors la loi* " and dragged something shrinking to a scaffold. But it rang gravelier now ; for it sounded from the solemn countenances of Wellington and Metternich and Nesselrode and Talleyrand, still wearing his thin smile. The Duke appeared to think at first that the King of France could do the business for himself ; but he could see that Europe might have to intervene, and he was hard at work among the excited Allies—" Here we are all zeal, and, I think, anxious to take the field. I moderate these sentiments as much as possible, and get them on paper. . . ." There was a notion of employing him as a courtly *attaché* to the Czar ; but " as I should have neither character nor occupation in such a situation, I should prefer to carry a musket." There would be ample opportunity, with all Europe marching upon France in a great crescent from the Alps to the North Sea. They gave him the command of an assorted force of Allies, which was to take the right of the line in the Low Countries. His tried battalions were largely in America or in mid-ocean ; and his first instinct, in the absence of that incomparable army, was to call for a contingent of those Portuguese whom he had called its ' fighting cocks.' A soldier once again, he turned briskly from diplomacy and all its drafts—the protocol about the Swiss, the endless chicanery of the Dutch loan, and the Prince Regent's portrait on a diamond-mounted snuffbox to be presented to the Bavarian—and posted across Europe.

7 He was at a party the night before he left Vienna ; and all the
women kissed him, saying gaily that he would conquer Paris and
that in that event he might include them in his conquests. Once
more his carriage rumbled along miry roads ; and at five o'clock
one morning in the first week of April he was in Brussels.
The city was not unfamiliar. He had passed through the
country in the previous summer ; but it was twenty years since
Lady Mornington and her ungainly son had lodged in Brussels,
where he learned French and played his violin. His French was
readier now, and he had manlier accomplishments ; but his
8 mother was once more in Brussels. It was quite fashionable that
winter. The *ton*, denied all opportunities of Continental travel
by twenty years of war, was glad to make a jaunt to Brussels.
The Guards were there ; Mr. Creevey took his wife and girls
(was not *Becky Sharp* seen chattering at the Opera ?) ; and Lady
Mornington, released from Upper Brook Street, was there as well,
until her anxious son arrived and packed her off to Antwerp.
Then the town filled with agitated Frenchmen ; the royalties
9 were all at Ghent ; but Brussels had its share of Marshals—
Marmont at the *Hôtel d'Angleterre*, Victor (with a pleasant echo
of Talavera) at the *Hôtel Wellington*, and Berthier staying with
friends. The Duke was seen at evening parties ; and Mr.
Creevey, who had once crossed swords with him in Indian debates,
10 found him " very natural and good-humoured " and exceedingly
communicative. For Wellington discussed the prospects freely,
and Mr. Creevey was not impressed. Opposition Whips are not
easily impressed by military men ; and when the Duke insisted
that it would never come to war, he left a poor impression of his
perspicacity upon the politician. But there was something to be
said for using peaceful language to members of an Opposition,
which was busy denouncing ministers for hurling Europe wantonly
into another war. So Wellington pained Mr. Creevey by his
unintelligent insistence that the republicans were bound to prevail
in Paris and that in all probability some Brutus would soon make
an end of Bonaparte. Not that he thought so ; for on the very
morning after his tone of stupid confidence shocked Mr. Creevey he
11 wrote to Blücher, " *Je ne serais pas étonné si la partie se trouvait
remise pour quelque temps. Mais nous l'aurons sûrement un jour
ou l'autre . . .*" But it would never do to use that language in
Brussels *soirées*, where every sentence would be promptly echoed

from the Opposition benches. So a military man, for once, was
one too many for an Opposition Whip ; and Mr. Creevey went to
his grave convinced that Wellington had failed to grasp the
gravity of the position in April, 1815.

He made a point of being cheerful, laughed when the *Champ
de Mai* passed off successfully in Paris, and greeted any fresh
desertion of the Emperor as evidence that his house was " tumb-
ling about his ears." He gave innumerable balls and made
everybody dance half the night. For the town was full of eyes ;
and it was just as well that Paris should believe that confidence
prevailed in Brussels. But Brussels, if the truth were known,
was anything but confident. The Duke, indeed, could scarcely
be expected to be in high spirits with a discouraging command in
which foreigners outnumbered British troops by more than two   *12*
to one. His dealings with allies in Spain had made him an expert
in the lukewarm ; but this time their temperature was more
discouraging than usual. His Dutch were poor, his Belgians
unreliable ; even his Hanoverians were hardly more than willing ;
and the King's German Legion alone came up to British standards.
Not that his British troops were an inspiring spectacle. For out   *13*
of twenty-five battalions only six had served in the Peninsula ;
the rest (except the Guards) were neither up to strength nor
standard. His cavalry was tolerably abundant, since there had
been no need for cavalry in America ; but his demand for guns
was answered by a grim intimation from the Ordnance that while   *14*
guns abounded, " men and horses are the only difficulty I have."
Even his Staff depressed him, since he inherited the Staff of a
small army of occupation already in the Low Countries. But
loud protests in his most emphatic manner gradually relieved him   *15*
of them ; the authorities were most obliging, though he complained bitterly of being " overloaded with people I have never
seen before ; and it appears to be purposely intended to keep
those out of my way whom I wished to have " ; and he ended with
a Staff of thirty-three, of whom thirty-one had considerable Staff
experience in the Peninsula. But at the outset it was not surprising that his correspondence rang with indignant outcries.
April found him complaining that the British troops were " not   *16*
what they ought to be to enable us to maintain our military
character in Europe. It appears to me that you have not taken
in England a clear view of your situation, that you do not think

war certain, and that a great effort must be made, if it is hoped
that it shall be short." The month passed in a fever of preparations—of friendly correspondence with the Prussians on his left,
of visits to the French royalties at Ghent, innumerable tangles of
inter-Allied diplomacy, peculiar transactions with foreign potentates for the supply of infantry at a flat rate of £11 2s. a head, and
ingenious rearrangements of the assorted nationalities in his
command until the mosaic gave some promise of stability. But
he could still write in May that he had " an infamous army, very
weak and ill equipped, and a very inexperienced Staff." He was
more hopeful now—" for an action in Belgium I can now put
70,000 men into the field, and Blücher 80,000 ; so that I hope we
should give a good account even of Buonaparte." Besides, the
need might not arise, since he was sometimes tempted to believe
that internal politics might keep the Emperor in Paris. But he
was haunted by his old desire for 40,000 British infantry ; with
them " I should be satisfied, and take my chance for the rest, and
engage that we should play our part in the game."

That thought was in his mind one day, when he met Mr.
Creevey in the Park at Brussels. The pert civilian asked a
question.

" Will you let me ask you, Duke, what you think you will make
of it ? "

The blunt question stopped him in his walk. " By God," the
Duke replied, " I think Blücher and myself can do the thing."

" Do you calculate upon any desertion in Buonaparte's
army ? "

" Not upon a man," said the Duke, " from the colonel to the
private in a regiment—both inclusive. We may pick up a
Marshal or two, perhaps ; but not worth a damn."

Then Mr. Creevey asked him about the French royalists in
Belgium.

" Oh ! " said the Duke, " don't mention such fellows ! No :
I think Blücher and I can do the business."

At that moment his eye was caught by a British private in the
green alleys of the Park ; and as he watched the little scarlet
figure staring at the foreign statues under the foreign trees,
" There," said the Duke, pointing a long forefinger, " it all depends
upon that article whether we do the business or not. Give me
enough of it, and I am sure."

SUMMER

1. *Brussels*

Something was stirring behind the frontier. It was not altogether easy to say precisely what it was, though spies reported copiously and French deserters trickled in with unlikely stories. But secret agents were lamentably apt to enrich the tedium of fact with those livelier circumstances which they wished to happen —or which (better still) they felt that their employers would wish to happen ; and the Duke's writing-table groaned under every form of voluminous misstatement. If his intelligence could be believed, the Empire was becoming momentarily more precarious and the Emperor had developed an uncanny faculty of being in several places at the same time—in Paris, in half the fortresses along the northern frontier, even in Cherbourg on his way to the United States—whilst his regiments appeared to be involved in an endless saraband. They flitted up and down the frontier, were seen drilling in unlikely places, and passed on every road by watchful travellers. But they were plainly coming north. So much was evident. But it was hardly possible to learn more about their strength and movements, since war had not been declared ; and Wellington complained bitterly that " in the situation in which we are placed at present, neither at war nor at peace, unable on that account to patrole up to the enemy and ascertain his position by view, or to act offensively upon any part of his line, it is difficult, if not impossible, to combine an operation, because there are no data on which to found any combination. All we can do is to put our troops in such a situation as, in case of sudden attack by the enemy, to render it easy to assemble, and to provide against the chance of any being cut off from the rest." (This dismal half-measure was the tribute paid to appearances, to the susceptibilities of Opposition speakers who might otherwise have vituperated ministers for being bellicose.) The army waited patiently in Belgian villages, grooming their horses, cleaning side-arms, and counting champagne at 4s. a bottle among their blessings. The Duke was busy with his papers, exchanging memoranda with the Allies upon the impending march of indignant Emperors on Paris timed for the end of June, studying bulky reports on the French army from the lucid pen of

Marshal Clarke, Duc de Feltre (once the Emperor's, and now King Louis', Minister of War at Ghent), and reading fluttered notes from London about the misdeeds of the Opposition which had now been joined, for some inscrutable reason of enlightened views or disappointed pride, by the tangential Richard. Then there were quantities of good advice, and hopeful letters from the War Office promising to hire unemployed post-boys to drive his guns, and indications that it might be possible to call out the Militia by the end of June, a line from Kitty with the news that Lowry Cole was getting married, and a helpful offer from a contractor who was prepared to manufacture howitzers of an entirely new pattern (grimly endorsed " Compliments ; and I do not consider this to be a proper period to alter the equipments of the army or to try experiments "). Slightly inimical to innovations at the moment, he ordered the rocket troop to store its cherished weapons and use ordinary guns instead ; and when someone urged that the change would break their Captain's heart, the implacable reply was, " Damn his heart, sir ; let my order be obeyed."

Sometimes he was out reconnoitring in his usual fashion, riding alone with an orderly dragoon and studying the rolling ground between Brussels and the frontier. They would be moving soon, and he was thinking about the siege of Maubeuge. But he still regretted his lost Peninsular battalions, writing to Lowry Cole how much he wished that he " could bring every thing together as I had it when I took leave of the army in Bordeaux, and I would engage that we should not be the last in the race ; but, as it is, I must manage matters as well as I can." He was still cheerful, though, with an agreeable tendency to crawl about the floor with children. The Duke of Richmond, under whom he had once served as Chief Secretary, had brought out his entire family ; and in his circle Wellington revived old memories of the Viceregal Lodge and morning rides in Phœnix Park. One day he rode to Enghien with one of the girls to see a cricket match. But there is no need to diagnose a sudden taste for cricket, since the Guards were billeted at Enghien and the Duke could have a word with Maitland. For his pleasures were always apt to take a business turn, and the Peer's hounds in Portugal would often take him conveniently near a unit that stood in need of an inspection.

The June days went slowly by ; and when he wrote to Graham accepting membership of a new military club, he added comfortably that the Emperor seemed unlikely to leave Paris at the moment—" I think we are now too strong for him here." But the reports came in—French *feux de joie* were heard at Maubeuge ; Valenciennes was full of troops ; the gates of Lille were closed ; Soult was on the road ; Grouchy had been seen reviewing cavalry ; the Guard was on the march ; the Emperor was everywhere at once. Something was stirring now behind the frontier.

2. Waterloo

The June days went by in Brussels. Late one Thursday carriages were clattering over the cobbles, and a sound of dance-music drifted into the summer night. The Duke was there. *29* He had been working late with Müffling and the Staff ; for he had news that afternoon that the French had passed the frontier opposite the Prussians, and orders had been sent to move the army in the direction of Quatre Bras. But it was just as well to reassure the doubters by shewing up at the ball ; and when he made his bow, Mr. Creevey's girls found him looking as composed as ever ; though one young lady, who shared a sofa with him, thought him quite preoccupied and noticed how he kept turning round and giving orders. More news arrived while they were all at supper ; and he desired the senior officers to leave unobtrusively. He said something civil to his host and slipped off with him to look at a map, remarking when the door closed behind them that Napoleon had *humbugged* him, by God ! and gained twenty-four hours' march upon him. Asked his intentions, he replied that he proposed to concentrate at Quatre Bras—" but we shall not stop him there, and if so, I must fight him "—his thumb-nail traced a line on the map behind Hougoumont and La Haye Sainte—" *here.*" Then he went off to bed. It was a little after two ; and Mr. Creevey, who had stayed at home that evening and heard a deal of hammering on doors along his street, was writing in his Journal,

" *June* 16. *Friday morning,* ½ *past two.*—The girls just returned from a ball at the Duke of Richmond's. . . ."

The marching bayonets went down the empty streets, and in the summer dawn the pipes went by.

He followed them next morning (a gleeful English maid, who *30* caught a glimpse of him as she was opening the shutters, cried,

" O, my lady, get up quick ; there he goes, God bless him, and
he will not come back till he is King of France ! ") ; and before
noon he was staring at the woods beyond Quatre Bras. Then he
rode over to the Prussians and had a word with Blücher. Their
dispositions did not impress him, since they were rather recklessly
aligned (in contrast with his own judicious practice) upon an
exposed slope ; and he said grimly that if they fought there, they
would be damnably mauled. For his ally's benefit he translated
this uncompromising view into the milder sentiment that every
man, of course, knew his own troops, but that if his own were so
disposed, he should expect them to be beaten. His expectation
was not disappointed, since the Emperor shattered them that
evening at Ligny. But Wellington employed the afternoon at
Quatre Bras, where Ney flung four thousand men away in wild
attacks. They heard the guns in Brussels ; and the enquiring
Creevey strolled on the ramparts, while sixteen miles away the
Duke was steadying a line which was often far from steady. It
was a wild affair of French lancers wheeling in the corn and redcoats hurrying up the long road from Brussels. Once Wellington
was almost caught in a flurry of French cavalry far out beyond
his firing-line. The ditch behind him was lined with Highlanders ;
and with a timely reminiscence of the hunting-field he shouted to
them to lie still, put his horse at the unusual obstacle, and cleared
it, resuming a less exciting position of command. And once his
deep voice was heard calling, " Ninety-second, don't fire till I tell
you." For he was everywhere as usual ; while Ney, whose military talents were almost wholly pugilistic, raged up and down the
line watching his cavalry surge vainly round the British squares.
But the price paid was tolerably high, although a great lady in
Brussels cooed consolingly to a friend that " poor Sir D. Pack is
severely wounded, and the poor Duke of Brunswick died of his
wounds. . . . The Scotch were chiefly engaged, so there are no
officers wounded that one knows."

But the reverse at Ligny served to nullify any advantage
gained by the Duke at Quatre Bras ; and he grimly observed that
" old Blücher has had a damned good hiding, and has gone eighteen
miles to the rear. We must do the same. I suppose they'll
say in England that we have been licked ; well, I can't help that."
He took this unpalatable decision early the next morning ; but
(it was typical of him) the retreat was deferred until his men had

cooked a meal. With that inside them they would, he felt, be more equal to the perils of a retirement with Napoleon at their heels. The red columns filed off towards Brussels ; and as they went, the Duke remarked with obvious relief, " Well, there is the last of the infantry gone, and I don't care now." The cavalry, he knew, could look after themselves with a few guns to hold them. He watched the perilous retreat, occasionally sitting in a field and laughing over some old English newspapers or turning his glass on the immobile French. The morning opened brightly ; but as the day wore on, there was a stillness, and a pile of leaden clouds climbed slowly up a sultry sky. The storm broke in floods of rain, as his cavalry were drawing off ; and the thunder drowned the sharper note of guns, while the rockets (in fulfilment of the Duke's most sceptical anticipations) sputtered and fizzed and not infrequently exploded backwards. The rain drove down and the long *pavé* gleamed before them, as they struggled back towards the ridge in front of Waterloo, the French plodding after them across the sodden fields.

There was a night of damp discomfort ; but food was waiting in the British bivouacs. They lit fires, and Peninsular veterans dispensed derisive consolations, observing cheerfully to new-comers, " Oho, my boy ! this is but child's play to what *we* saw in Spain," and " Lord have mercy upon your poor tender carcass. What would such as you have done in the Pyrenees ? " Uxbridge, his second-in-command, came to Wellington and asked what he proposed to do. The Duke countered with a question.

" Who will attack the first to-morrow—I or Buonaparte ? "

" Buonaparte."

" Well," said the Duke, " Buonaparte has not given me any idea of his projects ; and as my plans will depend upon his, how can you expect me to tell you what mine are ? "

Then he rose and, laying a hand upon the other's shoulder, said kindly, " There is one thing certain, Uxbridge ; that is, that whatever happens you and I will do our duty."

For his belief in plans was never strong. He once said pity-ingly of the Marshals that " they planned their campaigns just as you might make a splendid set of harness. It looks very well, and answers very well, until it gets broken ; and then you are done for. Now, I made my campaigns of ropes. If anything went wrong, I tied a knot ; and went on." Blücher had fallen back from Ligny ; so Wellington had tied a knot, conforming with his ally's retreat by falling back to Waterloo. Now he was comfortably established on the ridge ; but who could say what would happen next ? If they attacked him in position, it might be Busaco over again. Or they might know their business better and edge round his right. In that event they might give an opening—and then it would be Salamanca—or they might manœuvre him from Waterloo without a battle. That would cost him Brussels and send the French royalties scampering from Ghent. It was too much to hope that Napoleon would choose a frontal attack, when the manœuvre round his flank promised so richly ; and Wellington inclined to think that he would choose the latter course. So he sat writing in the night—to warn the royalties at Ghent, to suggest that Lady Frances Webster would be wise to leave at once for Antwerp, and to beg someone in authority in Brussels to " keep the English quiet if you can. Let them all prepare to move, but neither be in a hurry or a fright, as all will yet turn out well." And all night long the summer rain drove down on sodden fields ; the trees dripped at Hougoumont ; gleaming pools stood in the little farmyard at La Haye Sainte ; somewhere across the darkness a square figure in a long grey coat was straining eager eyes into the night for a glimpse of Wellington's camp-fires ; and two armies slept in the busy whisper of the rain.

A pale dawn broke over Belgium. The Emperor was breakfasting by eight o'clock. Soult was uneasy ; Ney prophesied that Wellington would slip away again ; but Napoleon swept away all objections.

" *Il n'est plus temps. Wellington s'exposerait à une perte certaine. Il a jeté les dés, et ils sont pour nous.*"

When Soult pressed him to call up reinforcements, he snapped contemptuously, " *Parce que vous avez été battu par Wellington, vous le regardez comme un grand général. Et, moi je vous dis que Wellington est un mauvais général, que les Anglais sont de mauvaises troupes, et que ce sera l'affaire d'un déjeuner.*"

" *Je le souhaite,*" replied the Marshal glumly.

The Emperor sailed before gusts of optimism that morning. Reille, who came in a little later, altogether failed to share his enthusiasm for a frontal attack on Wellington. But then Reille had served in Spain ; even at Quatre Bras he shied nervously from

18

an apparently unguarded position, because " *ce pourrait bien être*   41
une bataille d'Espagne—les troupes Anglaises se montreraient quand
il en serait temps " ; and now the sight of a British line behind
an easy slope made him uncomfortable—he had seen something of
the kind before. But the Emperor was rarely a good listener.
Besides, he meant to have his victory. A victory would mean
so much—the road to Brussels open, France reassured by a
familiar bulletin, King Louis made ridiculous again by further
flight, the British driven into the sea at last, and (who knows ?) a
change of Government in London, the enlightened Whigs in office,
and a world at peace with his tricolour floating peacefully above
the Tuileries. The sky was clearing now ; a breeze sprang up ;
the ground would soon be dry enough for guns to move. He
would have his victory ; and June 18 should take its place among
his anniversaries.

" *Nous coucherons ce soir*," he said, " *à Bruxelles.*"   40
Across the little valley Wellington was waiting on that Sunday
morning in his blue frock-coat and the low cocked-hat that bore
the black cockade of England with the colours of Spain, Portugal,
and the Netherlands. His mixed command was, if anything,
more mixed than ever, since he had left some of his British troops
to guard his right flank and the road to Ostend ; and his foreigners
outnumbered them by two to one. Still, he had got them in
position on a ridge—one of his favourite ridges with an easy slope
towards the enemy and shelter for his men behind its crest. The   42
French outnumbered them ; the Emperor had 70,000 men to the
Duke's 63,000 ; and he had only 156 guns against 266 in the hands
of that incomparable artillerist. But if Blücher was to be
believed, some Prussians would be coming later. The old *sabreur*
had been unhorsed and ridden over at Ligny ; but he dosed himself with a deadly brew of gin and rhubarb (and apologised to a
British officer whom he embraced, observing cheerfully, " *Ich*   43
stinke etwas ") ; and somewhere across the sodden fields his dark
columns wound towards the Emperor's unguarded flank.

The Duke was waiting. As it was showery that morning, he   44
kept putting on a cloak, " because I never get wet when I can help
it." He waited for the French manœuvre to begin ; had not
Marmont manœuvred " in the usual French style " at Salamanca ? But the Emperor made no attempt to manœuvre.
Then it was not to be another Salamanca. For they came plung-

ing straight at the British line in columns of attack, just as he had
seen them when the French columns charged the heights above
Vimeiro and Masséna's men struggled up the slope at Busaco. It
was to be the old style of attack, to which he knew an answer that
had never failed—the waiting line behind the crest, the volley long
deferred, and then the bayonet. (As he wrote afterwards to
Beresford, the Emperor " did not manœuvre at all. He just
moved forward in the old style, in columns, and was driven off in
the old style.") But there were variations ; for the fighting
surged round the outworks of his line at Hougoumont and La
Haye Sainte. Then, the columns foiled, a stranger variation
appeared, as the French cavalry came thundering uphill against
his line. His infantry formed square to meet them, and the
delighted gunners blazed into the advancing target, until they
scampered off to safety in the nearest square bowling a wheel from
each dismantled gun before them, as the bewildered horsemen
rode helplessly among the bristling squares of inhospitable
bayonets. It was a picturesque, but scarcely an alarming, experience. " I had the infantry," as he wrote afterwards, " for some
time in squares, and we had the French cavalry walking about us
as if they had been our own. I never saw the British infantry
behave so well."

The Duke, as usual, was everywhere, fighting his line along the
ridge as a commander fights his ship in action. He rode " Copenhagen " ; and all day long the chestnut carried him along the
lanes of weary men. Each shift of the interminable battle
elicited a gruff comment or an order scrawled on a scrap of parch-
ment. He saw the Nassauers pressed out of Hougoumont and
acidly observed to an Austrian General, " *Mais enfin, c'est avec ces
Messieurs là qu'il faut que nous gagnions la bataille*," put in the
Guards to retake the position with " There, my lads, in with you
—let me see no more of you," and watched Mercer's guns dash
into place between two squares with an appreciative " Ah ! that's
the way I like to see horse-artillery move." When the Life
Guards charged, a deep voice was at hand to say, " Now, gentlemen, for the honour of the Household Troops " ; and when they
rode back, a low cocked-hat was raised with " Life Guards ! I
thank you." At one moment he formed a line of shaky infantry
himself, like any company-commander, within twenty yards of
the flash of an oncoming French column. And as the tide of

cavalry was ebbing down the trampled slope, he asked the Rifles
in his quiet manner to " drive those fellows away."   52
     The light was failing now ; and he rode down the line before
the Guard was launched in the last charge of the Empire.   The
shadows lengthened from the west, as the tall bearskins came
slowly on behind six Generals and a Marshal walking (for it was
Ney) with a drawn sword.   They were still coming on " in the old
style " ; and the waiting line held back its fire in the Peninsular
fashion until the Duke was heard calling, " Now, Maitland !   53
Now's your time."   The volley crashed ; and as the smoke drifted
into the sunset, the Guard broke—and with the Guard the
memory of Austerlitz, of Eylau, Friedland, Jena, Wagram, and
Borodino melted upon the air.   Then the Duke galloped off with
a single officer to order the advance.   The smoke thinned for an
instant ; and a trim, bare-headed figure was seen pointing a
cocked-hat towards the French.   Someone enquired (a shade
superfluously) which way to go ; and the Duke's voice answered
him, " Right ahead, to be sure."   54
     Late that night Blücher met him in the road on horseback and
clasped a weary Duke, exclaiming " *Mein lieber Kamerad* " and   55
exhausting his entire stock of French by adding a trifle inade-
quately, " *Quelle affaire.*"   For the Emperor had shattered his
last army in blind attacks upon the ridge and then crushed it
between Wellington and the Prussians.   A lonely, white-faced
man, he stood in the moonlight waiting in a little wood, waiting
for troops that never came : his cheeks were wet with tears.   Far
to the south the Prussian cavalry were sabring the last remnant
of the *Grande Armée* under the moon. . . .   " No more firing was
heard at Brussels—the pursuit rolled miles away.   Darkness came
down on the field and city ; and Amelia was praying for George,
who was lying on his face, dead, with a bullet through his heart."

     The Duke rode slowly back to Waterloo.   There was no feeling   56
of elation, and they were all exhausted.   Besides, he had a
solemn notion that, where so many had fallen close to him, he
had somehow been preserved by Providence.   " The finger of
Providence was upon me," he wrote that night, " and I escaped
unhurt " ; and he repeated almost the same words in Paris later.
Then they sat down to supper ; the table had been laid for the
usual number, but the Staff had suffered cruelly, and there were

so many empty places. The Duke, who ate very little, kept looking at the door ; and Alava knew that he was watching for the absent faces. When the meal was over, he left them. But as he rose, he lifted both hands saying, " The hand of God has been over me this day." Then he went out and began to write his despatch :

57
"MY LORD,
"Buonaparte having collected the 1st, 2nd, 3rd, 4th, and 6th corps of the French army, and the Imperial Guards . . ."

He asked them to bring in the casualty returns, and slept for a few hours. When he read them by the first morning light, he broke down. Picton, Ponsonby, De Lancey, Barnes, Gordon, Elley . . . it had been worse than Badajoz. Then he took his tea and toast, finished his despatch, and rode sadly into Brussels.

58 He saw Creevey from his hotel window and waved a signal to come in. He was quite solemn still and said that it had been a damned serious business—a damned nice thing—the nearest run thing you ever saw in your life. His mind ran on the losses, and he added grimly that Blücher got so damnably licked on Friday night that he could not find him on Saturday morning and was obliged to fall back to keep in touch with him. Then he walked up and down the room and praised his men. Creevey enquired if the French had fought better than usual.

" No," said the Duke, " they have always fought the same since I first saw them at Vimeiro. By God ! I don't think it would have been done if I had not been there."

3. Paris

In twelve days they were in front of Paris. There was a spectral interlude, in which ghosts walked the Paris streets. For the long figure of La Fayette, last seen when Marie Antoinette was Queen of France, leaned from the tribune ; and men heard a voice of 1790 unmake the Empire. It was as though Mirabeau had spoken. The Emperor, almost a ghost already, haunted the green alleys of Malmaison like an uneasy spirit. The little house among the trees filled with Imperial *revenants*. His brother Joseph came, the shadow of a King of Spain, and Jerome, faint simulacrum of a King of Westphalia ; less shadowy, the indomitable Madame Mère took leave of him ; Walewska came to sob out the last echoes of their love in Warsaw ; and Hortense made a last home for him among her mother's flowers. His tired eyes watched round every corner for the lost figure of an Empress bending above her roses ; for the roses were in bloom at Malmaison.

Uneasy gentlemen flitted in all directions—to safety in the south, to make their peace with the returning King, to Wellington's headquarters with bewildering proposals for an armistice. He had one answer for them all, since in his clear way he discerned the objects of the war. Long before Waterloo he had stated them to Marmont :

" La France n'a pas d'ennemis que je connaisse. . . . Nous 59
sommes les ennemis d'un seul homme, et de ses adhérens. . . . La situation où nous allons nous trouver ne peut pas donc s'appeler un état de guerre contre la France, mais bien une guerre de la part de toute l'Europe, y inclus la France, contre Buonaparte, et contre son armée, de laquelle la mauvaise conduite a donné occasion aux malheurs qui vont arriver, et que nous déplorons tous."

With these opinions it was not surprising that he reminded the invading army that " their respective Sovereigns are the Allies 60 of His Majesty the King of France, and that France ought, therefore, to be treated as a friendly country." But these refinements were far beyond the simple-minded Prussians, who clung to the consoling thought that France, which had so recently dominated Germany, was now defenceless, and behaved accordingly. The Duke, on the other hand, burned with the chivalry peculiar to citizens of uninvaded countries. Even his troops were slightly irked by his tendency to side with the civil population ; and ministers grew almost plaintive over his leniency. " It is quite 61 right," wrote Liverpool, " to prevent plunder of every description, but France must bear a part of the expenses of the war. . . . We do not exactly know what course in this respect the Duke of Wellington has been following. . . . I trust, however, that you will be able to satisfy him that the French nation ought to bear a part of the expense."

Not that his chivalry was mere knight-errantry. For it had a distinct and practical purpose, since he was determined to restore King Louis. His devotion to the Bourbons was anything but sentimental. Long before Waterloo he had described their restoration as " the measure most likely to insure the tran- 62

quillity of Europe for a short time." He recognised that their
cause did not command unanimous enthusiasm, but wrote cheer-
63 fully to Henry Wellesley that " if we are stout we shall save the
King, whose government affords the only chance of peace." After
the victory he moved King Louis into the neighbourhood of Paris
64 on his own authority, because he " wished His Majesty should
be on the spot, or as near it as circumstances would permit." He
65 told the delegates from Paris that he " conceived the best security
for Europe was the restoration of the King, and that the establishment of any other government than the King's in France must
inevitably lead to new and endless wars." With that in view it
was vital to avoid anything that might render him distasteful to
his subjects. It was unhappily inevitable that King Louis should
return *dans les fourgons de l'ennemi* ; but if that enemy were only
reasonably well-behaved, his subjects might forgive his choice of
a conveyance. So the Duke's army orders became a protracted
correspondence-course in good manners, and his command found
that its business with the French had been changed from winning
battles to the more exacting task of winning golden opinions.

Prince Blücher, a devoted partner in the field, was disinclined
to enter this tournament of chivalry. Prussia had bitter memories (as well as natural bad manners), which it was comforting to
gratify by scaring French villagers and devastating French
country houses. So Müffling, duly installed as Governor of
Paris, proposed to apply himself with gusto to the collection of a
fine of 100,000,000 francs. And was it reasonable of Wellington
to discover scruples about blowing up a Paris bridge, whose mere
existence was an affront to his allies, since it was named *Pont
d'Iéna* ? Blücher was strong for it, although the French offered
helplessly to rename the offensive structure *Pont Louis XVIII* ;
and when Wellington still pleaded for the bridge, the old man
66 tartly enquired what would have been the fate of any bridge in
Washington named after Saratoga. But the Duke summarily
closed the discussion by the heroic measure of posting a British
sentry on the bridge; the Prussians, it was thought, would
hesitate to blow up an Allied soldier. But this view was based
upon an under-estimate of their distaste for ill-timed historical
allusions. For, less sentimental, Blücher's engineers promptly
set to work upon the simple problem of destruction ; but though
thoroughly determined, they did not know their business ; and

the bridge, which ultimately survived under the abject name of *Pont des Invalides,* was saved by their complete incompetence rather than by British chivalry.

It was a reasoned chivalry ; for the Duke insisted that " if   67
one shot is fired in Paris, the whole country will rise against us." That would mean a war of conquest for the Allies and a civil war for Louis XVIII. If such disasters were to be avoided, France must be reconciled to the new terms of peace. It was hardly customary to consider the feelings of defeated states ; but the Duke's reasoning rendered this novel course inevitable. It followed that the terms must be of a character that would command French consent ; and this effectually precluded further annexations. As the Duke wrote, " *nous avons raison de croire*   68 *que la France cédera sans grande difficulté sur le système qu'on veut adopter, et que la nation entière s'opposerait à son démembrement.*" The problem was not simple, since *ex hypothesi* France was still a European menace standing in grave need of restraint ; but the restraining measures must be such as would be acceptable to France. Lord Castlereagh devised an ingenious expedient ; but since its character was wholly military, it depended upon Wellington's support. His views were as clear as ever :

" In my opinion . . . the Allies have no just right to make any   69 material inroad on the treaty of Paris, although that treaty leaves France too strong in relation to other powers ; but I think I can show that the real interests of the Allies should lead them to adopt the measures which justice in this instance requires from them. . . .

" My objection to the demand of a great cession from France upon this occasion is, that it will defeat the object which the Allies have held out to themselves in the present and the preceding wars.

" That which has been their object has been to put an end to the French Revolution, to obtain peace for themselves and their people, to have the power of reducing their overgrown military establishments, and the leisure to attend to the internal concerns of their several nations, and to improve the situation of their people. The Allies took up arms against Buonaparte because it was certain that the world could not be at peace as long as he should possess, or should be in a situation to attain, supreme power in France ; and care must be taken, in making the arrangements consequent upon our success, that we do not leave the world in the same unfortunate situation respecting France that it would have been in if Buonaparte had continued in possession of his power. . . .

" If the King were to refuse to agree to the cession, and were to throw himself upon his people, there can be no doubt that those divisions would cease which have hitherto occasioned the weakness of France. The Allies might take the fortresses and provinces which might suit them, but there would be no genuine peace for the world, no nation could disarm, no Sovereign could turn his attention from the affairs of this country. . . . We must, on the contrary, if we take this large cession, consider the operations of the war as deferred till France shall find a suitable opportunity of endeavouring to regain what she has lost ; and, after having wasted our resources in the maintenance of overgrown military establishments in time of peace, we shall find how little useful the cessions we shall have acquired will be against a national effort to regain them.

" In my opinion, then, we ought to continue to keep our great object, the genuine peace and tranquillity of the world, in our view, and shape our arrangement so as to provide for it.

" Revolutionary France is more likely to distress the world than France, however strong in her frontier, under a regular Government ; and that is the situation in which we ought to endeavour to place her.

" With this view I prefer the temporary occupation of some of the strong places, and to maintain for a time a strong force in France, both at the expense of the French Government, and under strict regulation, to the permanent cession of even all the places which in my opinion ought to be occupied for a time. These measures will not only give us, during the period of occupation, all the military security which could be expected from the permanent cession, but, if carried into execution in the spirit in which they are conceived, they are in themselves the bond of peace."

70 He added shrewdly that " the troops of those Sovereigns should be selected for this service who would have the least inclination to remain in possession of the fortresses at the termination of the period."

A later paper neatly summarised the choice before the Allies :

71 " If the policy of the united powers of Europe is to weaken France, let them do so in reality. Let them take from that country its population and resources as well as a few fortresses. If they are not prepared for that decisive measure, if peace and tranquillity for a few years is their object, they must make an arrangement which will suit the interests of all the parties to it, and of which the justice and expediency will be so evident that they will tend to carry it into execution."

Other Allies at the end of other wars have faced the choice
between a negotiated and a dictated peace ; but the alternatives
were not so clearly stated, and the statement did not emanate
from their leading soldier.   The Allied policy of moderation in 1815 owed its main driving-
force to Wellington.   His lucid reasoning served largely to impose
it on a reluctant Cabinet and unenthusiastic Allies ; but his
reasoning prevailed less because it was lucid than because it was
his.   For the Prime Minister referred to it respectfully as " the   72
Duke of Wellington's projet," and its reasonableness was gilded
by the prestige of Waterloo.   Other problems faced him, as the
Allies mounted guard in Paris and irreverent Parisians enjoyed
the unwanted spectacle of redcoats in the Bois and bewildered
Cossacks staring at the Palais Royal, of " Prussian and Russian   73
officers in blue or green uniforms, waists drawn in like a wasp's,
breasts sticking out like a pigeon's ; long sashes, with huge
tassels of gold or silver, hanging halfway down their legs—pretty
red and white boyish faces, with an enormous bush of hair over
each ear ; lancers in square-topped caps and waving plumes ;
hussars in various rich uniforms . . . Austrian officers in plain
white uniforms, turned up with red."   Whilst Europe strolled on
the boulevards in every colour of the rainbow, the Emperor, in
Europe still, admired the coast of Devonshire from *Bellerophon* ;
and the Prime Minister discussed his destination with the First
Lord of the Admiralty.   His presence was embarrassing ; but
Lord Liverpool, stifling a hearty wish that " the King of France   74
would hang or shoot Buonaparte as the best termination of the
business," was prepared, if necessary, to take him into custody.
The Duke, for once, was not consulted ; he had already expressed
a strong distaste for Blücher's bloodthirsty opinions on the subject, stating firmly that " if the Sovereigns wished to put him to   75
death they should appoint an executioner which should not be
me."   And when Napoleon's surrender was announced in Paris,
they heard the Duke say that he must have an interview with him,   76
and that he ought to be imprisoned at Madras.   But Mr. Barrow,
of the Admiralty, recommended St. Helena ; Sir Hudson Lowe
accepted the appointment ; and Lord Bathurst anticipated
comfortably that " Bonaparte's existence will soon be forgotten."   77
Charged with this hopeful mission, *Northumberland* sailed through
the summer days into the south, until the roar of Europe sank

to a distant murmur and the Western Ocean fell silent round them.

In France the Duke of Wellington attended conferences, inspected troops, and drafted inexhaustibly. It was still raining decorations ; his uniform became a gallery of European orders of chivalry, as the long procession of saints and heraldic monsters resumed with St. Andrew of Russia, the Black Eagle of Prussia, and the Elephant of Denmark. The stout King of France detached the ribbon of the Saint-Esprit from his own sacred person, hung it on the Duke, and offered him a park ; though Wellington's good sense preserved him from the *gaucherie* of celebrating a French defeat with an estate in France. The grateful Netherlands, going one better than the rest of Europe, made him a Prince— the Prince of Waterloo. But his own country was a shade embarrassed by the problem of its gratitude, since he had everything already. He was a Duke ; he had the Garter ; so they were reduced to voting him a further £200,000 towards the purchase of an estate. But though the fountain of honour had run dry, the Regent could still gush ; and that royal hand acquainted his dear Wellington that even the consummate skill of the Corsican could not withstand the superior genius of our own hero, and that England once more fulfilled a glorious destiny under the auspices of her transcendent General, adding with condescension that his most sincere friend was George, P.R.

The Duke went cheerfully about his business. The worst was over now. The King of France was on his throne again ; and Wellington, more than any other man, had seated him there. For the second Restoration was the outcome of his prompt initiative after Waterloo and those endless conferences in the Paris suburbs, when Wellington, watched by the narrow eyes of Fouché, imposed the King and (stranger still) imposed a minister upon him who had sent his brother to the guillotine in '93. He had kept uncongenial company, with Talleyrand limping beside him and Fouché's whisper in his ear ; and clever Count Molé thought him so innocent. But Wellington was a deft match-maker ; the King's reluctant hand lodged safely in the old regicide's, the peculiar *mariage de convenance* was successfully contrived ; and King Louis, to the Duke's infinite relief, reigned in France once more. Not that his troubles ended there. For the peace-treaty was still on the anvil. He knew his own mind, which was in complete agreement with Castlereagh ; but there was still the Cabinet to be persuaded, and the Allies had strong opinions of their own. For Allies, once wooed (like Danaë) in a shower of gold, grew sadly independent with no further British subsidies in prospect. The Prussians were stiff-necked by nature ; Metternich was sly ; and the Czar was torn as usual between Russian interests and the Sermon on the Mount. But Russia being largely satisfied, his better self prevailed. Besides, the Duke required a counterpoise to the dead weight of Central European reaction ; and there was less than usual to fear from what he used to term Alexander's " Jacobinical flights." 81

  There were distractions, though ; for the Paris season of 1815 was an endless whirl of balls and reviews. Half London was in Paris to renew the glorious emotions of that unforgettable June evening when a chaise drove up Whitehall with the Waterloo despatch and a French eagle sticking out of each window. Croker was there, rejoiced by the spectacle of " the old Life Guards 82 patrolling the Boulevard last night, as they used to do Charing Cross during the Corn riots " ; Walter Scott came, thrilling with patriotic fire ; and Palmerston prepared to leave the War Department (and Lady Cowper's smiles) for a lounge round Paris. They strolled about the conquered streets, linked arms with friends in uniform, and filled the theatres every night. Not that Paris minded ; for that mercurial city was in raptures over a ballet in which Waterloo was positively mimed and a grateful *ballerina* received her wounded lover from the hands of a noble-hearted Briton. Britons were quite the mode, and kilted High-landers the rage. But though gentlemen abounded, the town seemed to be fuller still of ladies. All the world was there ; white shoulders gleamed in all directions and curls shook at every turn, though Kitty lingered in England, mildly astonished by the ac- 83 curacy of her own presentiment (confided to Scott long before the battle) that when her hero met Bonaparte, he would destroy him at *one* blow. But the bright eyes of half the Continent followed the Duke, as he went briskly about Paris in his blue frock-coat. None followed him more closely than the adoring gaze of Lady Shelley. That devotee was among the earliest arrivals ; and as Lady Granville acidly observed, she and her husband " ran after 84 the great Duke in a very disgusting way, but as they were together, ' sans peur et sans reproche.' " Expanding slightly in the sun-

shine of her simple-minded worship, he talked to her about the
battle, said solemnly, " The finger of God was upon me," and let
her cut off a lock of his hair in the reassuring presence of her
husband. Her sensibility was quite prodigious ; for a *tête-à-tête*
with the Duke was almost too much for her ; and (as she told
someone) it was positively sacrilegious to degrade her adoration
with the coarse name of love. But she drew him out. One day he
shewed her all his gold boxes with the portraits of European
monarchs, and let her watch him answering his letters. He liked
to talk to her about the battle, and tell her what he said to Uxbridge and how experience gave him a pull over other soldiers.
Not that he struck martial attitudes before her. " I hope to
God," he said, " that I have fought my last battle. It is a bad
thing to be always fighting. While in the thick of it, I am too
much occupied to feel anything ; but it is wretched just after."
He told her that next to a battle lost the greatest misery was a
battle gained, and that he was only just recovering his spirits.
(He could write more cheerfully about the losses now—" Never
did I see such a pounding match. Both were what the boxers
call gluttons . . .") Now he looked forward to a cheerful life—
" I must always have my house full. For sixteen years I have
always been at the head of our army, and I must have these gay
fellows round me." Flushed with these confidences, she glowed
with pride in being born an Englishwoman and living in the same
age with this great being, though the sharp eye of Lady Granville
observed the Duke to be a trifle inattentive to her strenuous
pursuit.

The bright round continued, with reviews by day and parties
almost every night. Lady Castlereagh's were dull (though she
did her best to enliven them by wearing her husband's Garter as a
hair-ornament) ; and Wellington preferred more cheerful company. So he was sometimes to be found in a livelier *milieu* than
the grave-eyed world of monarchs and diplomatists. Caroline
Lamb (who startled Paris with a purple riding-habit) amused him
with her outbursts ; and French ladies were a little apt to express
their royalist opinions by embracing him in public. Had not a
roomful of beauty in Vienna offered him a vista of conquests
beyond the dreams of Alexander ? The world whispered (and
even wrote) unseemly things about his friendship with Lady
Frances Webster, though the world knew nothing of the hurried

note which he had scrawled to her in the rainy darkness of the night before Waterloo advising her to remove from Brussels. But Lady Shelley, whose devoted gaze rarely left him, remained quite convinced of their perfect innocence. He seemed so simple and so fatherly. But then Lady Shelley was a goose.

He was the saviour of Europe, just forty-six, with a trim figure and a handsome face. He dressed the part at last ; and an admiring world crowded to watch him bow by candlelight or sit his horse in Field Marshal's uniform with his sword drawn as the long lines of infantry went stiffly by. In the Peninsula they had sometimes called him 'the Dandy '; now he was ' the Beau '; and what is a Beau without his due accompaniment of belles ? Sometimes he rode with Lady Shelley ; and how it thrilled her to hear him say, " Stick close to me." Once she was actually close enough to hear him order an aide-de-camp to " tell that damned adjutant he can't ride : tell him to get off his horse." It positively made her feel as though she could have charged up to the cannon's mouth under her hero's orders. He shewed her how the infantry formed square at Waterloo, and once he told her how much he disliked cheering in the ranks—" I hate that cheering. If once you allow soldiers to express an opinion, they may on some other occasion hiss instead of cheer." They dined at Malmaison one night ; and after dinner she walked in the dark garden with him and explored Josephine's conservatory by the uncertain light of a few candles. Not that their evenings were invariably so restful, since he once polonaised with her all through the house. He let her ride on " Copenhagen " ; and one hot afternoon, as they were sitting in a garden, she watched him playing with a grubby little child—he positively took a bite out of its apple and sat the urchin on his knee. Then they all went off to a fair and rode on the merry-go-round, the ladies cir-culating gaily upon swans and the Duke more suitably accom-modated with a wooden horse.

But there were statelier occasions, when he received his guests. All Europe came ; and the Duke bowed them in—sovereigns, Field Marshals, Allies, Frenchmen, diplomats, and Cossacks. M. de Talleyrand limped up the stairs ; Fouché was there ; and the big double doors flew open, as the footmen bawled, " Sa Majesté le Roi de Prusse." Walter Scott was there as well ; and his eyes filled with tears as he saw Wellington shake hands

89

90

with Blücher. Paris was full of thrills for Scott ; did not old Platow dismount and kiss him in the Rue de la Paix ? Besides, he had been presented to the Czar, wearing his blue and scarlet Selkirkshire uniform ; and royalty, eyeing his lame leg, floored him at once by asking in what affair he had been wounded. The Duke awed him ; he told someone that he had never felt abashed except before the Duke, because Wellington—the greatest living soldier and statesman—possessed every mighty quality of the mind in a higher degree than any other man did or had ever done. But that evening Walter Scott sat down to supper with him and two ladies. The royalties were supping somewhere ; but the Duke apparently preferred the company of Scott and Lady Caroline Lamb, who punctuated their repast " by an occasional scream." There was a bust above his head, which displayed (the house had once belonged to Junot) the marble features of the Emperor ; and two thousand miles away *Northumberland* sailed on into the South Atlantic.

AUTUMN

The ship sailed on below the horizon ; and the leaves fell in Europe. Waterloo was fading into retrospect, and the Duke wrote polite discouragements to eager historians. For he was quite convinced that no true account of it could be written, and that it was just as well.

" The object which you propose to yourself is very difficult of attainment, and, if really attained, is not a little invidious. The history of a battle is not unlike the history of a ball. Some individuals may recollect all the little events of which the great result is the battle won or lost ; but no individual can recollect the order in which, or the exact moment at which, they occurred, which makes all the difference as to their value or importance.

" Then the faults or the misbehaviour of some gave occasion for the distinction of others, and perhaps were the cause of material losses ; and you cannot write a true history of a battle without including the faults and misbehaviour of part at least of those engaged.

" Believe me that every man you see in a military uniform is not a hero ; and that, although in the account given of a general action, such as that of Waterloo, many instances of individual heroism must be passed over unrelated, it is better for the general interests to leave those parts of the story untold, than to tell the whole truth."

He was prepared to help, but added ominously, "Remember, I recommend to you to leave the battle of Waterloo as it is." For he was grimly positive that " if it is to be a history, it must be the truth. . . . But if a true history is written, what will become of the reputation of half of those who have acquired reputation, and who deserve it for their gallantry, but who, if their mistakes and casual misconduct were made public, would not be so well thought of ? " With these opinions it was not surprising that in later years " the Duke entertains no hopes of ever seeing an account of all its details which shall be true." Truth, he believed, might well be damaging ; and he was disinclined to expose brave men to undiluted truth. Besides, he was more indulgent now and even pleaded with the Horse Guards for a delinquent, whom a later age would have diagnosed unhesitatingly as a case of shell-shock :

" Many a brave man, and I believe even some very great men, have been found a little terrified by such a battle as that, and have behaved afterwards remarkably well."

(Had he, one wonders, any recollection of the distant night when a scared young Colonel staggered into camp from Sultanpettah Tope ?) His diagnosis was sympathetic :

" From what I have heard of the case since I received your letter, it appears that, ——— ——— having left the field as wounded, the surgeon of the regiment could not return him in the list of wounded. It will turn, first, upon whether the surgeon was right or wrong ; and, secondly, whether he was not so stunned as to be obliged to quit the field, although not in such a state afterwards as that the surgeon ought to have returned him as wounded."

But now the Duke was busy with a fresh problem. For the Allies, denied any further opportunities of territorial gain, developed a wholly unexpected passion for the fine arts. There were excuses, since France under the Empire had been a connoisseur of comprehensive tastes, appropriating every major work of art from The Hague to Rome, until the Paris galleries came to resemble less a national collection than a complete history of European painting and sculpture. Laocoon writhed in the Louvre ; the horses of St. Mark's stepped decorously on the arch outside the Tuileries ; Apollo Belvedere posed in his niche ; and, far from her native Florence, Venus dei Medici simpered in exile. Art had indubitably followed the eagles, though in the opposite direction ; and the liquidation of this sumptuous collection promised the Allies all the delights of a gigantic jumble-sale where there was nothing to pay. Vast inventories were prepared ; military working-parties took pictures down from walls and handled unaccustomed packages ; Canova came from Rome with an interminable list of Papal property ; there were the Hessian pictures at Malmaison, the Dutch pictures in the Louvre, and the Pope's statuary everywhere ; and Prussia developed a wholly unsuspected wealth of art-treasures. The Venetian horses gave endless trouble, since they were now Austrian property ; but the Austrians, who had no tools, were quite incapable of moving them. They requisitioned British Engineers, lined the Place du Carrousel with a guard of white-coats, and slung the horses down under the watchful eye of Lord Palmerston, who clambered up the arch himself. These exercises somewhat dimmed the lustre of the Duke's popularity in Paris, since the recovery of stolen property is rarely popular among receivers.

Major and minor diplomacy absorbed him ; and he corresponded vigorously upon the composition of the Allied army of occupation for north-eastern France. The Duke was to command it in the name of the Allied monarchs ; and he was full of cares about the British contingent. Ministers, in a sudden access of post-war economy, were demolishing the army, and he advised them gravely that " my opinion is that the best troops we have, probably the best in the world, are the British infantry, particularly the old infantry that has served in Spain. This is what we ought to keep up ; and what I wish above all others to retain." He had his fill of troops that summer ; for it was the season of the great reviews in Paris, when the streets were lined with every colour of the Allied rainbow, and Wellington took the salute in the Place Louis XV beside a King and two Emperors. He watched the Prussians at Grenelle, the Russian Guard at Neuilly, and expounded the superiority of line over column to Palmerston, a fresh-faced young gentleman who had figured in his correspondence as the source of irritating departmental queries. He told the attentive Secretary at War that he had started in the last

19

campaign with the very worst army that was ever got together, fortunately leavened by four or five of his Peninsular regiments. Nothing, he thought, could equal British soldiers in the field. They might not look quite so well as others at reviews, because appearance was, he felt, a trifle underrated. But in the field he was always confident that a detachment would maintain its post against any force until they dropped. So he was proud of them, as he shewed off their paces in the fields beyond Montmartre. It was a replica of Salamanca, faultlessly performed without rehearsals. The Prussians were apt to require two days of preparation for such performances and to peg the ground with finger-posts. But Wellington, who saw the *terrain* for the first time that morning, took it impromptu ; and the watching foreigners were vastly impressed as the long scarlet lines wheeled and deployed with the added (and, in Paris, wholly irresistible) fascination of swinging kilts.

Diplomacy recurred in an unusual form that autumn. For while negotiations for the peace-treaty followed a comparatively normal course, the Czar soared beyond protocols into a region inhabited by the sublime platitudes of revealed religion. This revelation was principally vouchsafed through the ecstatic agency of Baroness von Krüdener, whom Castlereagh described irreverently as "an old fanatic, who has a considerable reputation amongst the few highflyers in religion that are to be found at Paris." Her vein was highly mystical ; she had a Swiss disciple, a private entrance to the Elysée, and a flow of words by which the Czar was frequently reduced to tears. But tears were not enough ; for action was required of a repentant Czar. His noble attitudes had already inspired disrespectful British to term him 'the Magnanimous Dandy' ; but refreshed by nightly draughts from her apocalyptic well, his magnanimity dilated to more than Wilsonian proportions. Not that she led him towards a novel idea ; since he had been vaguely haunted for more than ten years by the nebulous conception of a European union of Christian states, which now emerged, wreathed in sanctimonious garlands of Scriptural allusion. Diplomacy raised polite eyebrows. Prince Metternich concluded that the Romanoff "mind was affected"; Lord Castlereagh agreed that it was "not completely sound"; the Duke was present when the plan was mooted by its Imperial patentee, and experienced some difficulty in keeping a straight

99

face. The Foreign Secretary thought it a " piece of sublime mysticism," and its proposal " what may be called a scrape." But if the Czar derived satisfaction from addressing autograph letters to the Prince Regent inviting him to conduct his policy upon the principles of Holy Writ, it was not easy to refuse him ; and as the October days drew in, they signed the blameless articles of the Holy Alliance in Paris, Alexander glowing with a slightly evangelical pride at the circumstance of their signature in that godless capital.

Far to the south the ship sailed on into the silence. South of the Line an island waited. It was the island where Sir Arthur Wellesley had stayed ten years before on his way home from India. Fate had transposed them now ; for he commanded on the soil of France, while the Emperor descended at the very house where he had stopped on St. Helena in 1805. In those October days a lonely figure paced the garden of The Briars, while kings and emperors in Paris subscribed their august signatures to the Holy Alliance. Europe was growing chilly now ; the year was almost over ; winter had come again.

Nations are never so grateful as their benefactors expect.—WELLINGTON TO CANNING, DEC. 15, 1814.

WAS this the summit ? Field Marshal, Duke—three times a Duke and once a Prince—he had dethroned an emperor and restored a king. His victories had saved Europe, as he had heard Pitt prophesy ten years before, when he sat unrecognised at a long table in Guildhall ; and the greatest soldier in the world had fled before him. Monarchs accepted his rebuke, and respectful nations did as he told them. Cheers were the least part of his incense, although he savoured them. For one summer evening he had stood beside King Louis at a palace window ; candles were set to light their faces ; and when the sea of waiting Frenchmen outside the Tuileries saw their sovereign smiling beside the foreign Duke, they cheered and cheered. The cheers found softer echoes, where adoring ladies flocked after him at evening parties. Aloof from cheering crowds, he was rarely indifferent to ladies' homage ; and it was generously offered. He liked to talk to them about himself ; they listened prettily ; though if they were inclined (like de Staël) to unwomanly accomplishments, he took a manly pleasure in alarming them. For while the wide-eyed Lady Shelley might ask favours freely, he wrote with wicked glee that " I am on proper terms with the Staël—that is, she is confoundedly afraid of me." So the indulgent hero mounted them on " Copenhagen," rode with them in the Bois, took them to boxes at the Opera ; and a skirt generally fluttered among his staff at a review. It was a cheerful picture, although Kitty was not in it. His Duchess was detained in England, since a brief experience of her in the year before had left him disinclined to expose her to the risks of Paris. For her accounts were always in inextricable confusion, and a big establishment was sure to be too much for her. Besides, there were his boys to be looked after. And she was so short-sighted, too ; his vast international parties called for arts of management that lay far beyond her Dublin range. Did not Miss Edgeworth, of Edgeworthstown, write appreciatively, when she called on St. Patrick's Day and found a plate of shamrocks on her table, that " nothing could be more like

Kitty Pakenham " than the Duchess of Wellington ?   So she was
left in England ; and he kept house for himself.   Almost a
widower already, he tasted bachelor delights, was free to choose
his own companions, and walked briskly down the long avenue of
smiling faces.   He was the Duke.   Indeed, he was something more,
since an impressive protocol signed by four Powers appointed him
Commander-in-Chief of an international army of occupation.
Russians, Austrians, Germans, and British presented arms at his
approach ; he reigned in seven Departments from Calais down to
Bâle with 150,000 men ; and an Ambassadors' Conference sat in
Paris to be the vehicle of his communications.   Small wonder
that Miss Berry found that when " talking of the allied sovereigns   *4*
. . . he says *we* found so-and-so—*we* intend such-and-such thing
—quite treating *de Couronne à Couronne.*"   For the Duke of
Wellington had positively become a European Power with his
own army, territory, and diplomatic relations.   Was this the
summit ?

<h1 style="text-align:center">I</h1>

Unpleasant problems faced him before 1815 was out, since Ney,
always injudicious, contrived to get arrested.   A frantic wife   *5*
besieged the Duke with prayers to intercede with the King, and
Ney added something soldierly relying on the general amnesty
embodied in the capitulation of Paris after Waterloo.   The Duke
was disinclined to help, since Ney's treachery to King Louis in
the spring had been exceptionally gross, and settled government
would become wholly impossible in France if such treason went
unpunished.   Besides, the Cabinet were pressing with civilian
sternness for an example to be made in the interests of public
order, and Wellington concurred ; for he was unlikely to lag
behind Liverpool and Castlereagh upon a question of elementary
discipline.   The King apparently expected him to intervene on
behalf of the Marshal, and avoided giving him an audience.
Wellington, who had no such intention, resented the discourtesy
with a tremendous intimation that, as commanding the troops,   *6*
he should remain and do whatever was officially required of him,
but that he was likewise an English gentleman, that the King of
France had insulted him, and that until the insult was atoned for
he should never go near him except on public business.   Meanwhile he made no move in favour of the Marshal, who fell to a

French firing-party ; and angry Bonapartists were convinced that he was a victim to Wellington's jealousy of his military achievement, while lively Radicals in England embraced the martyr's cause and lampooned the Duke for a cold-hearted refusal to interfere with the course of French justice, *Don Juan* ingeminating

7
> " Glory like yours should any dare gainsay,
> Humanity would rise and thunder, ' Nay ! ' "

and adding in a footnote with a grin, " Query, *Ney ?—Printer's Devil.*"

Now it was 1816, and the world began to settle down. The Duke left Paris in the spring and installed his headquarters at Cambrai. There were as many papers as ever on his table— papers about mad Englishmen in Paris who got themselves into scrapes by plotting against the King, complaints from Zieten about the treatment of the Prussians, a polite request that Fouché would discourage the French authorities from their enterprising plan of opening gaming-houses in occupied territory for the benefit of the Allied troops, and a note from Hill who had gone home and found his family in some embarrassment (eliciting the
8 kindly answer that the Duke possessed " a large sum of money which is entirely at my command, and . . . I could not apply it in a manner more satisfactory to me than in accommodating you, my dear Hill, to whom I am under so many obligations "). He wrote judicious letters on French politics to Louis and his minis-
9 ters, pleaded for General Mouton (whose conduct in the Hundred Days, though he commanded a corps at Ligny, had not been actively treasonable), and positively prolonged his residence in Paris at the King's request. How many conquerors have been invited to extend their stay in a conquered capital ? Small wonder that he wrote that " there is not much confidence in anybody either here or in England, excepting myself." Then he was off to The Hague ; the Netherlands were full of problems—French refugees in Brussels, the new fortresses along the frontier, and a growing tendency in Belgian quarters to resent Dutch predominance. In June he was brought back to Paris for a French royal
10 wedding. The Shelleys were there ; and he told her that he was not well and had been recommended to try Cheltenham. He took them to the play and carried her off to drink tea in his favourite social haunts. One evening he gave dinner to the Spaniards, and

she saw him in his Spanish uniform. She had been going on to a reception at the Duchesse de Berry's ; but he pressed her to stay ; and as the royal invitation was for ladies only, she " felt that it would be monstrous dull " and stayed. After the guests had gone, she heard him talking about Spain and about the blunder they had made in abolishing the Inquisition ; someone, it seemed, had proposed it in his time, but he had told them shrewdly, " *Quoi, vous voulez me donner un autre ennemi à combattre ! J'aurai tous les curés de la Castille contre moi. L'Inquisition se meurt d'elle même. Voyez le Portugal ; nous ne l'avons pas aboli là, et cependant elle n'existe plus. Ce sera de même ici. Si vous l'abolissez, elle existera toujours.*" Reformers of abuses have received worse advice.

He gave a ball of his own ; and Lady Shelley, who came a little early, found him by himself moving the chairs about ; for he was always strong on detail. That evening he took in Marmont's wife to supper ; but afterwards he sat with Lady Shelley until he went off to bed at four o'clock in the morning. He told her that he should be going home in a few days—" You must dine with me every day until I go." They rode together, and she talked about her husband's political affairs. " What," said the Duke, " are quarrels to be eternal ? I hate these party squabbles." For he was an indifferent partisan ; and when an injudicious letter from Lord Grey to an arrested Englishman fell into his hands, he returned it unopened to the Whig leader. They had their last ride, and Lady Shelley felt quite sad ; indeed, she was completely overcome that evening by the delicacy of Biggotini's dancing in the affecting ballet of *Nina*. Then he was off at three o'clock one morning, jolting along the road to Calais. The roads of 1816 were full of travellers. That summer Lord Byron swept the Continent again with his sombre regard. It was just seven years since he had meditated on the quays of Lisbon, while Sir Arthur waited for the French at Talavera. Still faithful to Sir Arthur's footsteps, he meditated now in Brussels. He was a trifle patronising with Waterloo (though he compared it favourably with Troy, Mantinea, Leuctra, Marathon, and several other sites of his acquaintance) and, having noted the rare lyric possibilities of a sound of revelry by night, passed on to meditate elsewhere.

II

IT was past midsummer, 1816, when he saw England once again.
The cliffs of Dover gleamed, onlookers cheered, and he drove off
1 to Richard's house not far from Ramsgate. Richard, an enigmatic figure in these days with the air of an imperfectly extinct
volcano that is inseparable from a career of Empire-building, was
getting on for sixty now. Once a master of the art of resignation,
he had nothing left to resign ; but he was still prepared to favour
correspondents and the House of Lords with his unnaturally progressive opinions upon the Catholics and fiscal policy. Besides,
2 there was his toilet ; for Richard was arranged with care. When
Lawrence painted him a few years earlier, he noticed that his
sitter's lips already owed something to art ; and some years later
a malicious eye observed his blackened eyebrows, rouged cheeks,
and awful brow whose lofty pallor, alas ! was not innocent of
artificial aid. The Duke called on this ageing Cæsar and posted
on to London. But London in July was hardly restful. The
3 Regent claimed him for dinner ; he dined out assiduously and
took a hand in a feminine cabal at Almack's against the autocracy
of Lady Jersey. The London round seemed to revive him.
4 Then he was off to Cheltenham for his cure. The spa received
him with triumphal arches and illuminations ; he sipped his
water in Well Walk, gossiped with a few Peninsular acquaintances,
and strolled with Kitty and his boys. She wrote off delighted
bulletins, informing the anxious Ladies at Llangollen that

5 " he for whom all the world is so justly anxious is considerably
better both in looks and spirits since his arrival in England.
" I think I perceive an amendment every day. This happens
to be the time of the holidays of our Boys, and I say with delight
they are as fond of and as familiar with their noble and beloved
Father as if they had never been separated from him. They
accompany him in his walks, *chat* with him, play with him. In
short they are the chosen companions of each other. . . ."

He had always got on well with children, and could get on with
6 these, even if they were his own. Kitty might have her faults ;

299

her trick of admiring him in public was particularly trying. But that summer he was at his gentlest. When someone hinted that he sometimes failed his friends, he defended himself with warmth —" The truth is that for fifteen or sixteen years I have been at the head of armies with but little intermission ; and I have long found it necessary to lay aside all private motives in considering publick affairs. I hope that this practice does not make me cold-hearted, or feel a diminished interest for those I am inclined to love. If I may judge by what I feel, I should say it does not . . ." And judged by what he did, it did not either. For he was busying himself to obtain public aid for Sheridan's impoverished family. His benefactions were often gruff ; and a formal manner some-times left a suitor under the impression that his petition had been dismissed, when it was generously granted. Thus, he reported to a friend of Indian days in search of an appointment that he had spoken for him without success and " I now recommend you to let the matter drop. . . . You may be quite certain that great situations are not obtained in this country by personal exertion and interest. Let a man show that he has talents, integrity, and enlarged views, and he may depend upon it that if employment abroad is his object, he is more likely to obtain it without solicita-tion than by making the most active exertions." The recipient of this homily might be excused for concluding that the Duke had done with his affairs. But without his knowledge Wellington wrote the same day to urge his claims upon the Company, dilating on his zeal, integrity, and talents, and concluding that they could not do better than employ him in a great situation, such as the governorship of Bombay. He always hated to raise hopes or to parade his services ; and they were often rendered under cover of a curt reply.

Another suitor haunted him that season ; for the French were pressing for a reduction of the army of occupation, and its commander was felt to be the likeliest person to view their request with favour. M. de Richelieu had seen him on the subject before he came home on leave ; he advised Castlereagh that there was no danger in the proposed reduction, and gave the French the benefit of his guidance as to the best moment to put forward their demand. His leave was ending now ; the walks with his two boys at Cheltenham were over ; and he was back in London. One afternoon he rode as far as Kensington. For Graham took

him out to Wilkie's studio in Lower Phillimore Place, and he
called on the respectful painter with Lady Argyll and the Duke
and Duchess of Bedford.   The painter had been warned, his
mother and sister posted to watch the great arrival from behind
the parlour curtains, and his works judiciously disposed about
the studio.   The Duke surveyed them and approved, remarking
in his decided tone " Very good " and " Capital."   Then he sat
down to study one of them ; and Lady Argyll began to tell the
artist that Wellington wished him to paint a picture.   The Duke
tilted his chair back and proposed a group of old soldiers outside
a public-house chewing tobacco and telling stories ; he should not
be particular about their uniforms and suggested that the public-
house might be located in the King's Road, Chelsea.   Wilkie
concurred with rapture, adding that the picture only wanted a
story.   Wellington said that perhaps it would do if they were
playing skittles.   Wilkie proposed a reading from a newspaper,
to which the Duke was perfectly agreeable and added that the
sketch might be sent to him abroad.   Then he stood up, took out
his watch, and informed the company that he was dining with
the Duke of Cambridge.   He turned to Wilkie with a bow and
asked when he should hear from him.   The artist answered that
he could not get the picture done for two years.   " Very well,"
replied the art patron, " that will be soon enough for me."   He
went downstairs, bowed once more to his host, saw old Mrs. Wilkie
at the parlour window and bowed to her, mounted his horse, and
then rode off.   The little windows were all full of faces ; two
Guardsmen watched him from the corner ; and as the sound of
hoofs died away down Lower Phillimore Place, they were tying
ribbons on the historic chair which he had honoured.   His leave
was over now ; and before August was out, he was in France
again.

BACK once more in his little kingdom, Wellington resumed the endless correspondence about his troops, about the new Barrier fortresses on the Belgian frontier, about Bonapartist exiles who misbehaved themselves in Brussels, and British officers who misbehaved nearer home in the theatre at Boulogne. Canning *1* passed through on his way back to Lisbon ; and the Duke, whose enthusiasm for abolition had manifestly waned since the days when he discussed slavery with Clarkson in the Paris embassy, disliked his notion of awarding British support to Portugal or Spain according to their respective display of abolitionist virtue— " nonsense and folly " was his brief description of the philan- thropic policy. Then he had his autumn reviews, graced by the *2* royal Dukes of Kent and Cambridge and a due accompaniment of evening parties. The Dukes were hardly to his taste ; as he told Creevey afterwards, " they are the damnedest millstone about the necks of any Government that can be imagined. They have *3* insulted—*personally* insulted—two-thirds of the gentlemen of England." But he had more congenial guests ; for the Duchess of Richmond brought out her girls to stay with him at Cambrai. He had written charmingly to Lady Shelley, telling her how much he missed his ' absent A.D.C. ' at the reviews. But she was far away in Vienna, and now other belles rode " Copenhagen." Georgy Lennox found him a rather trying mount from an un- *4* pleasing mannerism of neighing violently at the sight of troops (an authentic instance of a war-horse laughing ' ha-ha ' to the trumpeters) ; and one day when she found herself inside a square with him, she overheard the ranks remarking, " Take care of that 'ere horse ; he kicks out ; we knew him well in Spain." The house at Mont St. Martin was crowded and cheerful with incessant amateur theatricals and a more violent diversion known as ' riding in the coach,' which appeared to consist of dragging ladies down interminable corridors on rugs. The gentlemen were harnessed ; even the Duke did not disdain this humble office, though he occasionally mounted the rug himself, and Wellington drove through Headquarters behind a team of ladies. A bulletin from his own hand describes the romping :

" We are going on here as usual—' Riding in the coach,' dancing the Mazurka, &c., &c. The house is as full as it can hold. Yesterday was a very bad day, and I went to Cambray, and I understand that they hunted Lord C—— through all the corridors, even that in the roof. At night we had an improvement on the coach. Two goats were brought in and harnessed, but instead of being horses and assisting to draw, they chose to lie down and be drawn. The night before, the ladies drew me the *petty* tour, and afterwards Lord Hill the *grand* tour, but the ' fat, fair and forty,' and M—— were so knocked up that some of us were obliged to go into the harness, although we had already run many stages."

This cheerful horseplay filled his evenings. For he could romp with his own circle, though the outer world found him less oncoming, the indomitable de Staël concluding bitterly that as she had done everything to fascinate him without success, the glacial Duke must be devoid of all " *cœur pour l'amour.*" But he had little taste for clever women. His days were rendered quite sufficiently exhausting by clever men ; and in the evenings he might be excused for preferring something a trifle less exacting.

His days, indeed, were full of problems. He did not spare much attention for the gathering storm at home (which he was inclined to attribute to the sudden "reduction of our war establishments . . . the rage for travelling of all our gentry, which have deprived some of our people of employment, and lastly and principally . . . the idleness, dissipation and improvidence of all the middling and lower classes in England, produced by a long course of prosperity and of flattery of their vices by the higher orders and the government "). His interests were, of necessity, almost entirely Continental ; but in that sphere no problem, however civilian, was beyond his range. He was the guardian of the peace-treaties ; and finance, the inseparable (though often insubordinate) hand-maid of peace-treaties, came within his survey. The French were bound by treaty to pay an indemnity of 700 million francs in five annuities, in addition to the costs of the Allied occupation ; and the Duke picked his way through a morass of foreign loans, of rates of interest, of scrip, of currency, of interviews with Mr. Baring. He favoured the financing of France by an issue of *Rentes* to leading houses in London and Amsterdam, and expressed his view that " unless some arrange-   7 ment of the description proposed is adopted, France will be aground this year, and our settlement of last year will be entirely destroyed." That degree of common-sense in post-war settle- ments was not reached by later generations without years of blundering and controversy. But Wellington could grasp the point. Embodying the wisdom vainly sought by his successors in endless Conferences at unnumbered health-resorts, he saw the bankers for himself and faced the still more tangled problem of French Reparations. He had some experience of finance, since remittances to his army in the Peninsula had always involved complicated banking transactions. But the Reparations question in 1817 was worse than financial, since it included the awkward problem of distribution between hungry Allies as well as that of French ability to pay ; and Wellington was finally enthroned,   8 on the proposal of the Czar, as supreme arbiter of all Allied claims. How many men would rather deal with Napoleon than with Reparations ? But Wellington faced both ; and what is more, he faced Reparations single-handed.

Not that the French were grateful. For nations rarely are; and Paris theatres rang with denunciations of ' *le tyran de Cambrai* '   9 and little jokes on ' *Vilainton*,' whilst he took care never to " go into any blackguard mob or place in which a fellow might insult me with impunity." He went about his business, as the months slipped by, reviewing troops inspecting Belgian counterscarps, discussing Mr. Rothschild's dealings in exchange, and maintaining order in occupied territory. His own affairs scarcely engaged   10 him, though he was still at the Spaniards for a decision about the royal pictures which he had captured at Vitoria ; and when it was suggested that his boys should be educated at the Military College, he was strong for " the education usually given to English   11 gentlemen " in preference to anything more technical. He ran across to England more than once in the course of 1817. On one   12 visit he attended the Prince Regent's inauguration of Mr. Ren- nie's new Strand bridge ; and once he was besieged by James Ward, the Academician, who had just won a prize with his design for an ' Allegory of Waterloo.' This masterpiece, a terrifying composition in which mythology predominated, involved a sitting from the Duke, whose lifelong servitude to painters was just beginning. He saw Mr. Ward and, stifling his objection to being painted by an artist whose leading triumphs had hitherto been achieved in the depiction of bulls, made the valid excuse that he was just off to the Continent.

"My lord," said the determined painter, "I will follow you there."

"Ah, Mr. Ward," the deep voice replied, "a man that has five thousand troops under his command knows not where he may be one day after another. But I will sit to you on my return."

He was back again before the year was out to view another country house. This time it was Lord Rivers' place near Reading; the splendid avenue of trees found favour in his eyes; and the purchase of Stratfield Saye for £263,000 was approved. But his concerns were still wholly Continental; and as 1817 wore on, he was kept busy with a tour of inspection in Alsace, his autumn reviews, and the absorbing business of checking the sporting and pugilistic proclivities of his command in France. Kitty came out to him that autumn; and he wrote sternly to complain that someone had been using in her carriage horses belonging to the pontoon train. He had other pets as well; since a Foreign Office messenger was once charged with a "black and tan dog of the Duke of Norfolk's breed" for the Commander-in-Chief, and Lady Castlereagh recruited his kennels with two boar-hound puppies. But life at Cambrai was not all hunting and house-parties. For French politics were far from reassuring in the first weeks of 1818, and the Duke feared gravely for the dynasty—" I entertain no doubt how this contest will end. The descendants of Louis XV will not reign in France; and I must say, that it is the fault of Monsieur and his adherents . . . I wish Monsieur would read the histories of our Restoration and subsequent Revolution, or that he would recollect what passed under his own view, probably at his own instigation, in the Revolution." Besides, there was the endless wrangle over Reparations; and Wellington reported that "since Baring left me, as I generally spend the greatest part of every morning now with money-changers, Rothschild has been with me." It was not simple to assess the damages resulting from twenty years of European war; and the Duke struggled bravely with the appetites of half the Continent. As he wrote, "my plan is first to ascertain what will really and ought

20

to satisfy each nation . . . I will then, secondly, negotiate with the French government to obtain that sum in the mode which will be most advantageous to the Allies, and least injurious to the other operations of the French government." The goal was plain enough, though it was less readily accessible ; for the intervening region was inextricably tangled with tales of ancient outrages committed by the armies of the First Republic and every exaction of the Empire in its career of conquest. But he laboured on untiringly, and the Allied claims were ultimately reduced by his industry to 240 million francs.

One February night these labours were almost interrupted, as he was driving home in Paris after a party. A shot rang out ; he saw the flash himself and suspected nothing, though he was perfectly aware that his life was threatened ; a sound of running footsteps died away down the dark street, as he got out at his own door and asked the coachman with some heat what he had meant by driving in at such a pace. The coachman answered that he had seen a man fire at his Grace. The news affected Europe variously. Prinny was shocked beyond belief, writing in almost tearful terms to his " dear Friend " and eliciting the courtly answer that if anything could reconcile a man to such attempts upon his life, it was the reception of such letters from one to whom he owed all his success ; old soldiers in French *cafés* muttered in deep moustaches that Waterloo had been avenged ; King Louis fluttered, and his ministers entered with gusto on a series of promiscuous arrests in the best manner of Continental justice ; while poor Kitty sobbed out her relief at his escape in a note to Richard—

" I cannot bear that you should run the hazard of hearing reports so alarming whilst I have the blessing of knowing that he is safe. Thank God, thank God, my dear Lord Wellesley, my Husband is perfectly safe but his life has been attempted as he returned home on Wednesday night at his own door a pistol was fired at him, but he ever was he still continued the special charge of Heaven tho' so close he was not touched neither is there the smallest mark on the carriage why did not the footman seize the varlet for it appears that he stood near the sentry box and that they must have seen him, but he has none but French footmen. . . . My next wish to thanking God for the preservation of the most precious life, is to save you from anxiety."

19

20

21

She was still fluttering, when she wrote to him again :

22   " Tho' still far from well I am so anxious to see you for many
       reasons. . . . I wish to rejoice with you on the success of my dear
       and excellent husband, his very narrow escape which I am not yet
       warrior enough (tho' I have thought myself very valiant) to think of
       it without agitation. . . ."

         While the French police stirred muddy waters by haphazard
23   arrests of Bonapartist malcontents, his own Government ordered
     the Duke to leave Paris forthwith and withdraw to Cambrai.
     He did not relish the retreat and fenced with their command,
     complaining that he had not been consulted in a matter in which
     he was " principally and personally concerned," and politely
     deploring the necessity for disobeying orders. But he disobeyed
     them ; and Wellington's one act of mutiny was concealed in
     a blandly phrased expectation that " the Prince Regent and his
     government will agree with me in thinking that I ought to delay
     to obey His Royal Highness's commands." He even took the
     unusual liberty of examining the desirability of such commands
     being given at all. For why should he be any safer at Cambrai ?
     And if not at Cambrai, why anywhere on the Continent ? In that
     event he would become " the ridicule of the world, and I should
     by this very act deprive myself of the means of serving you in
     future in any capacity." This was unanswerable ; and the Duke
     stayed in Paris.
         There was so much for him to do—French Reparations to be
     settled, French politics to be supervised, and the Allied occupa-
     tion to be brought somehow to an end. His own affair was soon
     disposed of, when they arrested a Bonapartist *bravo* of the name
     of Cantillon, who was manifestly guilty (though a French jury
     subsequently acquitted him). The news reached St. Helena,
     where an ageing, lonely man noted Cantillon's name. Paris
     echoed this unpleasing temper, though King Louis was almost
     tender now, sending the Duke a little present of old Sèvres with a
24   shy intimation that he felt himself " *encouragé dans cette démarche
     par un vieux proverbe que je vais tâcher de rendre dans votre langue :*
     Do little gifts—keep friendship alive." Friendship, alas ! was
     sadly strained by Reparations in 1818. But the Duke persisted,
     revising Allied claims, conferring endlessly with bankers, and
     running backwards and forwards between Paris, Cambrai, and

London. He had a new address in town ; for that spring he
dated his first letter from Apsley House, which he had bought
from Richard. He had a fresh problem, too. For Spain and
Portugal were drifting into war over the rebellious Spanish
colonies in South America. The Duke, it was believed, might
intervene in the commanding character of uncle to the Peninsula ;
but this view reckoned without the towering altitude of Spanish
pride ; and his intervention, when it came, rather resembled the
tentative intrusion of a nephew between two punctilious uncles.
His views were plain enough. No notion of calling a New World
into being to redress the balance of the Old had crossed his mind ;
he was not Canning, and he disapproved of revolutions. Besides,
his main anxiety was lest the United States might seize the
opportunity of recognising infant nations struggling to be free in
South America ; and he pressed the Spaniards to prompt action
in the River Plate before this calamity could supervene.

His hands were full that summer, though life at Cambrai was
still cheerful. Creevey came over and found him riding out to
see a cricket match with two belles from Baltimore. Wellington
talked freely after dinner about the royal Dukes and their bad
manners, and how the House of Commons could not be blamed for
making difficulties about their allowances, as it was their only
opportunity of revenge, and he thought, by God! they were quite
right to use it. This was strange language from a pillar of the
throne to a former Opposition Whip. But the Duke did not see
himself as a strict Tory, and he enquired with friendly interest
about the problem of Whig leadership ; Tierney might do, he
thought, though Romilly was strange to him—but then, the House
of Commons never cared for lawyers. He was less Tory than
ever when he discussed the Regent—" By God ! you never saw
such a figure in your life as he is. Then he speaks and swears so
like old Falstaff, that damn me if I was not ashamed to walk into
a room with him." They dined together again in a French
provincial inn ; and Creevey was quite shocked when two grubby
maids brought in two partridges, a fowl, and a fricassee to set
before six hungry gentlemen. The Duke, who had driven from
Paris on the meagre support of a cold chicken eaten in his
carriage, seemed to enjoy it all. The champagne was poor ; the
tea at breakfast the next morning came out of an enormous coffee-
pot ; there were no saucers ; but when Creevey opined that this

formidable brew was a creditable product for Vitry, Wellington remarked " with that curious simplicity of his " that he had brought it all the way from Paris.   Then Creevey saw his coach driving away at breakneck speed ; for Wellington had got wind of the approaching Duke of Kent, and incontinently bolted.   But the royal Duke caught him up at Valenciennes.   His troubles multiplied, since the new Duchess of Kent accompanied him, to say nothing of a German lady-in-waiting of the most austere appearance.   There was a dinner-party, and Wellington went grumbling round the Staff, enquiring who the devil was to take out the maid of honour.   An anxious silence ended in a flash of in- spiration—" Damme, Fremantle, find out the Mayor and let him do it."   After all, the French had lost the war ; they were in occupied territory ; and the invitation was a mild, but pardon- able, *væ victis*.   They dined ; they danced ; the Duke of Kent amused them all by his new-found solicitude about his lady's health (he positively stroked her cheek after a waltz in order to ascertain if she was overheated) ; and Creevey regaled his host with a sanctimonious saying of the Duke of Kent's about his aged mother's illness.   The delighted Wellington took Creevey by the button and, remarking " God damme ! d'ye know what his sisters call him ?   By God ! they call him Joseph Surface," exploded into one of his tremendous laughs which startled the entire ballroom. But the Duke of Kent always amused him.   Wellington called him ' the Corporal,' from an untidy habit of appearing in undress uniform ; and he could never forget the broad comedy of his con- fessions to Creevey about his royal sacrifices of domestic happiness on the altar of dynastic duty.   He relished simple fun ; and the Duke of Kent afforded ample opportunities, especially when he got them all up at dawn for an inspection, and kept poor Creevey waiting for his breakfast until the shower of royal interrogations had rained itself out.   Wellington advised the starving gossip that it was always wise on such occasions to take his breakfast first and went chuckling round the Staff, pointing at Creevey and repeating with wicked glee, " *Voilà, le monsieur qui n'a pas déjeuné.*"   He liked the little man, savoured his anecdotes, and spoke civilly to him about the Whigs, praising Grey and Lans- downe, and deploring the fact that they were buried in the House of Lords—" Nobody cares a damn for the House of Lords ; the House of Commons is everything in England, and the House of

Lords nothing." And Creevey liked him in return : the Duke's simplicity impressed him—" that curious simplicity of his . . . his comical simplicity . . . the uniform frankness and simplicity of Wellington in all the conversations I have heard him engaged in, coupled with the unparalleled situation he holds in the world for an English subject, make him to me the most interesting object I have ever seen in my life."

His reign at Cambrai was ending now. For the world met once more in conference that autumn to resettle the peace of Europe and to end the Allied occupation. Lord Castlereagh passed through *en route* for Aix-la-Chapelle ; the Czar descended from his distant Sinai ; and the statesmen furbished up their decorations, polished their protocols, and prepared themselves for the invigorating processes of another Congress. He was in Brussels just before it opened, and once more Creevey met him strolling in the Park.

" Well now, Duke, let me ask you, don't you think Lowe a   *28* very unnecessarily harsh gaoler of Buonaparte at St. Helena ? "

" By God ! I don't know. Buonaparte is so damned intractable a fellow there is no knowing how to deal with him. To be sure, as to the means employed to keep him there, there never was anything so damned absurd. I know the island of St. Helena well. . . ."

His view of Lowe was simple—" as for Lowe, he is a damned fool." But one evening when Creevey was at him again at Lady Charlotte Greville's about a newspaper report that he was to join the Cabinet, he answered with a grunt.

Then he was off to Aix-la-Chapelle for the Congress. He and Castlereagh formed the British delegation, and he played his part in the agreeable charade of Continental unity. The Foreign Secretary was " quite convinced that past habits, common glory,   *29* and these occasional meetings, displays, and repledges, are among the best securities Europe has now for a durable peace " ; and if the common past of the Allies was to be recalled, the Duke was a notable exhibit. He gave the Czar a great review, composing for the occasion the libretto of a sham fight which made him feel as if he had been " writing a Harlequin Farce." The ceremonial   *30* round began once more—review, ball, dinner, play—and Palmerston was vastly impressed by the perfection of his manners, " the extreme respect and deference paid by all to the Duke, and, on the other hand, the manly but respectful manner with which he treats the sovereigns." The Prussians, by an odd twist of fate, gave their display at Donchery, outside Sedan, where Prussia was to wait in spiked helmets for the sword of another Emperor. The Duke talked a good deal to Palmerston, telling him all about line and column and how it was his practice to meet French attacks behind the shelter of a little ridge. He pointed at a Prussian column.

"Look how formidable that looks; and yet I defy the French" (the Duke clapped his hands) "to mention any one instance in the whole war in which these masses had made the least impression on our lines."

Then he described the process in detail—the British volley and the scattered reply of the advancing French, the wavering of the attackers, and the odd way in which their columns always frayed out from the rear—"As the French column ran from the rear, one used to see the men huddling together and running to the right and left, just as they saw the means of sheltering themselves behind a body of fellow-fugitives, so that at a little distance they went waddling like ducks." That was his simple picture of the tactics by which the Empire had been broken.

The business of Europe was transacted at Aix-la-Chapelle : the Allied occupation was to end, and Wellington was liberated from his duties in a fresh shower of military honours. For he became a Marshal of the Russian, Austrian, and Prussian armies. At one moment his functions were almost extended beyond Europe, since it was proposed that Wellington should mediate in the name of the Great Powers between Spain and her colonies. But he replied judiciously from the depth of " *mon expérience et ma connaissance intime du caractère Espagnol* " that " *il n'y a pas sur la terre une nation si jalouse que l'Espagne de l'intervention dans ses affaires des Puissances Etrangères.*" Had he not fought a war in the Peninsula to convince the French of that simple truth ? The notion dropped ; and he was left with the less exacting duty of evacuating France. The last time-tables were prepared ; the Allies who had brought down Napoleon parted for the last time ; the bayonets wound homewards across France in opposite directions ; the British sailed ; the Russians and the Germans marched ; and before 1818 was out, Wellington was left alone in

Paris. He went home by way of Brussels, and by Christmas he
was safe at Apsley House.

The long task was over ; but it was unthinkable that Wellington should fade discreetly into private life. He was far too useful ;
and ministers, who had found him a judicious colleague since
1814, still desired his company. Now there was nothing for it but
the Cabinet. They had a notion that he might join without port-   33
folio ; but it was felt to be more appropriate to bring him in as
Master-General of the Ordnance. Lord Liverpool made him the
offer, and he accepted on slightly peculiar terms. Accustomed to
the public service, he was prepared to serve. But he was at
pains to divest his acceptance of all party connotations :

> " I don't doubt that the party of which the present government   34
> are the head will give me credit for being sincerely attached to them
> and to their interests ; but I hope that, in case any circumstances
> should occur to remove them from power, they will allow me to
> consider myself at liberty to take any line I may at the time think
> proper. The experience which I have acquired during my long
> service abroad has convinced me that a factious opposition to the
> government is highly injurious to the interests of the country ;
> and thinking as I do now I could not become a party to such an
> opposition, and I wish that this may be clearly understood by those
> persons with whom I am now about to engage as a colleague in
> government."

In other words, he was prepared to sit with them in Cabinet, but
by no means to go out of office with them, as a good Tory should.
For it was possible that some other Prime Minister might require
his services ; and Wellington plainly viewed himself as a public
servant, not as a Tory politician. It was his sense of public duty,
not party affiliations, that brought the Duke home from France
in 1818 to be a Cabinet minister. For he was still ' *nimmukwallah* '; he had eaten the King's salt and would serve him still,
even among the politicians.

THE CABINET

*And what is a great man ? Is it a
Minister of State ? Is it a victorious
General ?   A gentleman in the
Windsor uniform ? A Field-Marshal
covered with stars ?*—CONINGSBY.

I

IT was 1819, and this handsome, greying man of fifty was home
again. Home would be quite a novelty, since he had been a
wanderer for twenty years. Indeed, it was not easy to recall a
time when he had lived at home. School, Brussels, Angers,
Dublin lodgings, freezing camps in Holland, Dublin once more,
eight years of Indian cantonments, his Irish interlude divided
between the Lodge in Phœnix Park and Harley Street, an endless
succession of Peninsular billets, the Paris embassy, a hotel at
Brussels, Paris again, and then headquarters at Cambrai—it was
a gipsy record ; and home would be a new experience for Wellington. Not that he was unfitted for home life. Quite the reverse ;
since all his inclinations appeared to lie in that direction. For he
liked nothing better than a house full of guests and cheerful evenings in society where all the men were well-connected and nearly
all the women pretty. How he had enjoyed watching his ' boys '
dancing, and confessed to Lady Shelley that he must always have
his house full—" for sixteen years I have always been at the
head of our army, and I must have these gay fellows round me."
The mood recurred with him ; and his house-parties at Cambrai
were an attempt to satisfy it. Perhaps it had been easier for
him to play the smiling host abroad than it would be in his new
mansion at Hyde Park Corner and the big house in Hampshire.
For Kitty would be there as well ; and Kitty seemed to fail him
somehow. Sadly deficient in the arts of household management
(her finances on his return from the Peninsula had been as involved as a French loan), she was afraid of him ; and her fears
were often hidden in an irritating trick of gushing over him in
public. Besides, her eyes were always weak ; and she was quite
unequal to the exacting duty of recognising all London and half
Europe. The Duke could always manage a nod at the right
moment ; but his short-sighted Duchess hid her embarrassment
behind an open book when she drove out. And was she quite so
beautiful as all the smiling faces that had shone like stars on him
in Paris ? Or so intelligent ? He had no taste for bluestockings ;

but when he talked, he liked to be understood. He once defined
feminine ability as " anticipating one's meaning ; that is what a
clever woman does—she sees what you mean." Poor Kitty was
not clever, though ; she never knew what Arthur meant ; and
it was more than doubtful how far home would disappoint him.
    But his own part, if he had leisure, could be played to per-
fection. Trim, handsome, and mature, he was ' the Beau '
indeed, a figure made for admiration. Not that his countrymen
outside Society were particularly ready to admire. For the first
rapture of public worship that succeeded Waterloo had evapor-
ated ; he had not banked its fires by public appearances in England ; and England, in its odd way, had grown slightly indifferent
to the man who won the war. But the wanderer returned to a
cheerful scene ; for London in the last year of the Regency was
nothing if not cheerful. It was the gay arena of *Tom and Jerry*,
where Vestris danced, Grimaldi clowned, the Regent's tilbury
spun through the Park, and Almack's was a nightly galaxy where
the Lieven looked sharply about her and Lord Palmerston
quadrilled with Lady Cowper. The town quoted *Don Juan* ;
Corinthians in vast top-hats boxed uncomplaining watchmen or
strolled through Piccadilly in the tightest garments ; there was a
pleasant buzz about the turf, the masquerade, the ring, and
Tattersall's ; and the *ton* gathered nightly in opera boxes to talk
its Frenchified slang and to exchange the latest wisdom of George
Brummell for the last impudence of Harriette Wilson. Somewhere beyond the town angry provincials tramped to mass-
meetings and stood in rows to stare at banners with exciting
mottoes and listen to the most disturbing speeches. There was
a new stir in the air that alarmed the Cabinet and left county
magistrates bewildered. For misguided men appeared unable
to appreciate that change was anathema, that Waterloo had
been a final victory over change, that change had been exiled to
St. Helena. Why had King George fought the Revolution to
a finish, if his victorious subjects were to be gnawed by revolutionary cravings ? Small wonder that his ministers looked anxious.
For their endless talk about the Sinking Fund and currency
reform concealed deeper misgivings. The Whigs might be too
strong for them. But was that the worst ? Something of graver
menace stirred in the shadows behind the Whigs. No Whig
avowed it ; it was remote from Ricardo's blameless calculations ;

and in their wildest moments Hunt and Cobbett refrained from naming it. But it hung on the dusty air above the lines of sullen Yorkshiremen tramping to meetings. Half seen in the grey skies over Manchester, it struck a distant spark where Shelley, writing by an Italian bay, mouthed his unforgettable

> "I met Murder on the way—
> He had a mask like Castlereagh—
> Very smooth he looked, yet grim ;
> Seven blood-hounds followed him,"

and as his voice rose in the direct appeal of

> "Men of England, wherefore plough
> For the lords who lay ye low ?
> Wherefore weave with toil and care
> The rich robes your tyrants wear ? "

he broke into the marching-song of the English revolution.

Such prospects rendered Wellington a welcome recruit to the harassed Cabinet which, having won the war, found peace a trifle baffling. The glowing memory of *Coningsby* recalled the event—" a Mediocrity, not without repugnance, was induced to withdraw, and the great name of Wellington supplied his place in council. The talents of the Duke, as they were then understood, were not exactly of the kind most required by the cabinet, and his colleagues were careful that he should not occupy too prominent a post ; but still it was an impressive acquisition, and imparted to the ministry a semblance of renown." There was no trace as yet of that pre-eminence which inspired Disraeli's later comment on " the aquiline supremacy of the Cæsars." But the Duke was a valued colleague with interests extending far beyond the somewhat limited concerns of the Ordnance Office ; and it was unlikely that he would be left in peace to rearrange his Paris furniture at Apsley House, stare at King Joseph's pictures on the walls, and hang his latest purchases of the Dutch school. His Parliamentary appearances were, with one exception, slight. But foreign diplomats corresponded freely with him on the prospects of European stability (eliciting the shrewd advice, " *Soyez sûr qu'en politique il n'y a rien de stable que ce qui convient aux intérêts de tout le monde ; et qu'il faut regarder un peu plus loin que soi-même* ") ; and upon foreign policy he was treated by Liverpool and Castlereagh as a member of the inner Cabinet.

His grasp of home affairs was more intermittent, since they came before him mainly in the form of applications by local commanders for Ordnance stores with a view to maintaining public order. He had no doubts upon the subject, since nothing in his previous experience had led him to believe in the divine nature of *vox populi.* Had he not governed Ireland from a room in Dublin Castle ? Few Chief Secretaries are democrats. His long professional career had been an uninterrupted war against French democracy. He was the natural enemy of Jacobins ; and nothing that he had seen of the Spanish Cortes modified his distaste for democrats. His contempt for governments founded upon " *la popularité vulgaire* " was unconcealed. He watched 7 this lamentable tendency abroad—" *Le grand mal en France est, qu'on croit pouvoir gouverner par la popularité, et gagner la popularité en flattant les viles passions de la classe la plus avilie et la plus corrompue de la nation.*" Ignoble abroad, was there the slightest reason to believe that popular appetites in England were any more exalted ? He could see none ; and the Duke diagnosed the objective of the democratic movement as " neither more nor 8 less than the Radical plunder of the rich towns and houses which will fall in their way." This simplified the question. If robbery and arson were in prospect, the Duke knew where he stood. It was just possible, of course, that he misjudged the movement, that it derived its impetus from something nobler than an ill-regulated impulse for destruction. England was deeply moved that autumn ; for 1819 saw the first stirrings of democracy. But democracy was hardly likely to be more congenial to Wellington than arson. For the sanctity of numbers made no particular appeal to him. Less interested in the numerical support for any policy than in its merits, he was no democrat. How could he be ? He had passed a lifetime in the constant endeavour to act wisely ; and in almost every case wise action had been diametrically opposed to a crowd's desires. Indian administration in 1802 was a poor school for democrats ; Dublin Castle was an embodied denial of democracy ; and he was unlikely to absorb its tenets in the Peninsula, since generals in the field are not dependent on securing a majority of votes in favour of next season's plan of operations. Besides, the crowds of his experience had been almost invariably wrong. A London mob had hooted him for the Convention of Cintra ; and as he bled the French Empire to

death in the Peninsula, he had been pursued by Opposition invectives. It was French mobs that had infected Paris with the Terror
and inflicted upon Europe the long nightmare of the Empire ;
even now their sudden fevers were a constant menace to European
peace. Spanish mobs had inspired the ignoble babble of the Cortes
and deepened their country's peril in its darkest hour. And was
there any ground for hope that English mobs would be wiser ?

With these convictions he was single-minded in his resolve
to check the English revolution. Not that he had the slightest
taste for military rule. That might do well enough for France—
9 he told Decazes as much, but added that *" il faut envisager l'armée
en France sous un point de vue tout à fait différent de celui où nous
envisageons l'armée dans ce pays-ci."* England, so far as he could
see, was well served by its civilian institutions ; and he was stout
in their defence. His advice was practical. Local commanders
should keep their forces concentrated and quarter them outside
the towns ; their health should be considered, and it would be
as well to attach a field-gun to each column. The law must be
10 administered—" Don't let us be reproached again with having
omitted to carry into execution the laws. . . . Rely upon it
that, in the circumstances in which we are placed, impression on
either side is everything." The ship rocked a little after Peterloo ;
but the country came safely through the autumn of 1819, and the
11 Duke was writing cheerfully to friends abroad that the crisis had
passed. The return to firm government in the Six Acts raised
his spirits. For he had been thoroughly uneasy in the intervening months before the strong hand was brought into play,
12 writing almost feverishly to Lady Shelley that " if our wise laws
allow 60,000 people to assemble to deliberate, what Government
can prevent it ? If they allow secret societies, having for their
professed object the overthrow of the Establishments, the forging
of pikes, and the training of the people to the use of them, I am
sure there is no Opposition member's wife . . . who would wish
the Government to overstep the law in order to prevent the people
from the exercise of these valuable and useful privileges. Then
every man who attends one of these meetings—whether for the
purpose of deliberation or crime, or for that of secret conspiracy
—thinks, and boasts, that he is performing a public duty ; and it
would be a sin to deprive the people of this gratification." His
irony had the metallic ring of an impatient man who found him-

self a little out of sympathy with his surroundings. But he was heartened in the autumn by a general rally of the propertied classes to the existing order. For he was convinced that the palladium of English liberty reposed mysteriously in the alliance of property with ordered freedom—a blend too subtle for its Continental imitators. As he wrote to Alava,

" On veut notre constitution en Europe ; mais ce qu'on ne veut pas 13 *c'est la sûreté, la conservation des propriétés, que chez nous en fait la base et la force. Observez aussi que c'est cette conservation que nous faisons marcher de front avec nos libertés, et qui en est le garant qui nous rend ennemie toute la classe soi-disant Libérale en France, dans les Pays-Bas, et en Allemagne. Pourquoi ? Parce qu'ils ne veulent que voler, ils ne parlent de liberté qu'avec l'objet d'empocher le bien d'autrui ; et ils ne peuvent pas souffrir un pays où la liberté est établie et fondée sur l'ordre, et sur la sécurité des propriétés."*

His estimate of democratic motives might be unduly low ; but there could be no doubt of his belief in the British compound of private property and freedom. Indeed, his faith in it was almost mystic—and there are few states of mind more perilous than a mystical attachment to any set of institutions. For his fervour inspired him ten years later to an untimely intimation that the human mind could scarcely attain such excellence as the unre-formed constitution—a saying which served to precipitate Reform. His faith was stated in the first week of 1820, when he informed a foreign correspondent that *" grâces à Dieu et à nos* 14 *Institutions miraculeuses "* the danger was, for the moment over, adding shrewdly that *" ce qu'on appelle içi les anciens abus, ce dont les Reformateurs modernes voudraient se defaire et ce que nos voisins et imitateurs liberaux ne veulent pas imiter, sont les circonstances qui nous donnent un appui notable dans toutes nos difficultés."* That month

"An old, mad, blind, despised, and dying king "

faded out of his long dream at Windsor into eternity; and his kingdom passed to George IV. The change was far from sedative, since his domestic infelicity supplied a grateful country with a new form of sport. There was a carnival of indecorum ; and the Queen's virtue became a party question, the Crown challenging and Whigs defending that somewhat battered fortress. Prinny appeared in the unusual *rôle* of an injured husband ; and Opposition speakers, long accustomed to baiting the Prince Regent, found themselves denouncing the sovereign. Attacks upon the monarch were barely distinguishable from attacks upon the monarchy ; and as the coarse fun of the Queen's divorce proceeded, Whiggery itself drifted perilously near to republicanism. The Duke's alignment was inevitable. He was a minister ; he viewed his sovereign (since he was a gentleman) without enthusiasm ; but he kept official company. He had spent Christmas at Stratfield Saye with the Castlereaghs, two foreign diplomats, Mr. Arbuthnot of the Treasury (and his handsome wife), and Mr. Planta of the Foreign Office. Kitty was there, of course ; but an observant Austrian found the house " not very comfortable, the park ugly, the living mediocre, the whole indeed indicating the lack of sympathy existing between the Duke and his Duchess." Poor Kitty's tragedy was known already ; and the Duke went his social rounds without her. Wellington went on to Woburn, where he found the Lievens and the Duke of York. Such company was scarcely likely to make him a *frondeur*.

Besides, the dark forces of disorder were more menacing than ever. There was a plot to murder the Cabinet one night at the Spanish embassy ; but Life Guards cleared the street, and a constable secured a halter thoughtfully provided for hanging Castlereagh on a lamp-post. One evening someone hung about outside the Ordnance Office to stab the Duke, as he walked home across the Park to Apsley House. But that night Fitzroy Somerset happened to meet him in the street ; the two men strolled along arm in arm ; and the pair of friendly backs alarmed an unheroic murderer. Then there were whispers of a dark design to invade the Cabinet at dinner in Grosvenor Square, murder them all, parade Castlereagh's head on a pike down Oxford Street, attack the Bank, break open Newgate, and finish up a crowded evening after the best French precedents by proclaiming the Republic at the Mansion House. Few things are more depressing than the exaggerated deference of English revolutionaries to foreign models ; but their sense of detail was creditable, since a thoughtful butcher had provided two bags for the heads (though the defence contended later that they were destined for the gentler office of carrying off Lord Harrowby's plate). The Cabinet was warned in time ; and the Duke, true to his usual tactics, proposed to await the attack in a favourable defensive position. Ministers, he thought, should take pistols in to dinner with them and await developments. But his civilian colleagues found the proposal unattractive. Indeed, from the civilian point of view it had its flaws ; and they preferred to dine elsewhere, while the Bow Street magistrate rounded up Thistlewood and his associates in a back-street off Edgware Road.

It was a dark, tumultuous time, when Castlereagh carried pocket pistols at the dinner-table ; and the Duke's distaste for democrats deepened excusably. So, it must be confessed, did theirs for him. For the first ecstasy of public admiration had faded before he joined the Cabinet ; he had been cheered at the opening 18
of Parliament the year before ; but in the restive mood of 1820 opinion involved all persons in authority in a common unpopu-larity. Its manifestations were occasionally harmless, as when the roadmenders in Grosvenor Place shouldered their pickaxes 19
and stopped his horse on the way home to Apsley House, insisting that he should say " God save the Queen." The Duke complied.

" Well, gentlemen," he said obligingly, " since you will have it so, God save the Queen—and may all your wives be like her."

In a year of breaking glass his windows were respected. But he was hooted by an English crowd for the first time since 1808. For that autumn Creevey heard them booing him in the 20
Park, though they scattered hurriedly as the Duke reined in. Not that it embittered him against the Opposition, since he could manage a good-humoured nod to the little Whig above the hooting mob and strolled up to him in the Argyle Rooms with a genial " Well, Creevey ; so you gave us a blast last night. . . ." But 21
his contempt for crowds was scored a little deeper—" The mob 22
are too contemptible to be thought about for a moment ! About thirty of them ran away from me in the Park this morning, because I pulled up my horse when they were *hooting* ! They thought I was going to fall upon them and give them what they deserved ! " As the unpleasing scuffle of the Queen's divorce proceeded with its long procession of preposterous and perjured foreigners, his sense of public dignity was gravely offended. His shrewd advice at the beginning of the affair had been to avert 23
the danger by selecting a handsome young diplomat (Fred Lamb, a favourite of Miss Harriette Wilson, struck him as being suitable) and sending him to the Queen's hangers-on abroad with the judicious warning, " You are going to lose your golden eggs—

you are going to kill your goose ! Once in England, and you will
not be able to live with her on your present footing and retain
your present allowances." But the moment passed ; the monumental farce of the royal trial was mounted in the House of Lords ;
and when somebody objected to its effects upon the Crown's
24 prestige, Wellington replied bitterly that the King was degraded
as low as he could be already.

The constant threat to public order filled his mind. He settled
25 routes for cavalry patrols through West End streets with the detail
appropriate to the march of armies, sending six men to Portman
Square, twelve more to Cavendish Square by way of Wigmore
Street, and posting a vedette in Brook Street as though Soult and
all his men had been expected from the direction of Park Lane ;
26 and when the Guards alarmed them all that summer with dangerous symptoms of mutiny, his common-sense evolved the first
proposal of a separate police-force. Not that he had become a
frozen pillar of reaction. For he was quite prepared to recognise
inevitable changes, insisting that the Spaniards could not hope
27 to recover their rebellious colonies—" One would suppose that
the reconquest of their colonies by force of arms would be out of
the question even to them . . . Considering that their colonies
must now be considered as lost. . . ." He was no less positive
upon a policy of non-interference in Spain itself, adducing the
28 whole course of the Peninsular War as evidence that Spain would
never tolerate foreign intervention, and adding generously that
" this result of the war may in part be attributed to the operations
of the Allied Armies in the Peninsula ; but those would form a
very erroneous notion of the fact who should not attribute a fair
proportion of it to the effects of the enmity of the people of
Spain." Even the settlement of 1815 seemed to lose something
of its sanctity for him at times, since he confessed one night at
29 Almack's that he was beginning to doubt how long the restored
dynasties would last ; though when Naples rose, he urged the
Austrians to act promptly, as they could do with 80,000 men now
what they might fail to do with 200,000 later. For he had a
constitutional distaste for revolutions.

He saw a good deal of the Lievens. It was a time when
London society seemed to be full of foreigners ; Allies abounded
in all directions ; Esterhazy and Palmella were seen everywhere ;
Alava told his stories ; and tame Cossacks chattered in opera

boxes. The Duke met the Lievens everywhere, and seemed to
find the unwearied Dorothea agreeable.   There was no accounting
for her triumphs, since a meagre throat surmounted by an indifferent profile formed an inadequate equipment, and malicious
rhymesters were inclined to dwell upon her accessories :

> " *Des broderies, des bouderies,*   30
> *Des garnitures—comme quatre—*
> *Voilà l'Ambassadrice à la façon de Barbarie.*"

But there was no denying her success ; for those curls were shaken
at every magnifico in Europe ; Metternich himself succumbed
at Aix-la-Chapelle ; and lively malice termed her latest child
' *l'enfant du Congrès.*'   This *vivandière* of diplomacy set her
snares for Wellington ; and he yielded so far as to act in country-   31
house charades with her. Indeed, his lifelong renunciation of musical performances was momentarily relaxed, when she played the   32
latest waltzes on the pianoforte ; for the Duke accompanied her
on the blameless triangle.   He talked freely to her and (greatest
test of all) answered politely when she asked him which of his   33
battles he liked best.

   Not that he lived entirely in a world of foreigners. For he
had his English friends. Lady Shelley, home from her travels,
conversed with him at evening parties and found him a little
scared by thoughts of the old age of Marlborough.   They rode   34
together in the Green Park, where he passed an hour most afternoons between office and the House of Lords ; she dined at
Apsley House, where she found Caroline Lamb and Mrs. Arbuthnot, and they saw all his treasures. She loved to hear him talk ;
his friendship was discreet ; and they never knew what dreadful
things " my husband's young kinsman, Percy Shelley, who seems   35
disposed to become a poet " was writing about the Government.
The great day arrived when he came to stay with them in the
country.   Her devotion had roused the countryside, and forty   36
mounted farmers rode beside his carriage ; they took out the
horses and dragged it up the hill ; and as his hostess heard the
cheers, she very nearly fainted. But the Duke's smile revived
her ; even her nervous headache vanished ; and she discharged
her social duties.   He was quite wonderful at dinner, scrawling a
plan of Toulouse upon a scrap of paper (carefully preserved) and
sketching Orthez on the knee of his evening breeches (which were

not available as a souvenir) "with an eagerness and intentness which were quite delightful." She showed him a French account, which he dismissed as "all a lie. The French were much superior to us in force." (His enemies, it may be observed, began about this time to shew a striking tendency to grow in numbers when he discussed his battles.) They talked till midnight, and he entertained them with a full description of the new breakwater at Plymouth and its dimensions. At breakfast the next morning he was quite delightful with her children ; and everything was going *à merveille.* Then they went off to shoot, and Lady Shelley breathed again. Not that she breathed for long; for as a marksman the Duke was anything but commonplace. The terror of his country's foes, he terrified her little girl by letting off his gun in all directions. "What's this, Fanny ? " cried Lady Shelley. "Fear in the presence of the Lord of Waterloo ! Fie ! Stand close behind the Duke of Wellington : he will protect you." Indeed, it was the safest place.

He shot a dog, then a keeper, and finally an aged cottager who had been rash enough to do her washing near an open window.

"I'm wounded, Milady," cried his victim.

"My good woman," she replied, "this ought to be the proudest moment of your life. You have had the distinction of being shot by the great Duke of Wellington ! "

An embarrassed Duke assisted her sense of history with a guinea. But she was not his only bag, since he positively shot a pheasant which his pious hostess had stuffed and added to the museum of Wellingtoniana in her dressing-room, where it stared glassily down upon the coffee-cup which he had used before Waterloo and the chair on which he dined with her in 1814.

They shared a rather schoolgirl joke about Mrs. Arbuthnot and her dominion over him, giggling together over ' *La Tyranna* ' and her uncertain temper, and keeping up the agreeable legend that he lived in abject terror of her and was under the necessity of seizing favourable opportunities to get her leave to visit Lady Shelley. The Duke vastly enjoyed his mythical subordination and was almost kittenish—" I have taken advantage of a favourable moment and have obtained *permission. . . . When the cat's away the mice go and play,* and as she is at her brother's in Lincolnshire, and at her mother's, I have taken leave to ask you to Stratfield Saye. . . ." So Mrs. Arbuthnot's leave, not Kitty's, was the requisite.   Kitty wrote dutifully, sending Lady Shelley news about her boys and farmyard fatalities, and was " quite sorry we are deprived of your company."   But Mrs. Arbuthnot played her part according to their standing joke, writing to Frances Shelley in her most commanding tones that " the slave (poor creature !) has asked my leave to invite you to dinner next Saturday, and, in order to bribe me into compliance, has invited me to meet you and keep watch, in order to prevent any attacks being made upon my legitimate authority.   I have been very magnanimous about it, and I beg you will return me your best thanks.   I have given permission. . . ."   It was a mild diversion ; and the Duke supported his *rôle* admirably with nervous bulletins about his tyrant's moods.   Other news sometimes crept in ; his shooting was improving ; Charterhouse was a better school than Eton (strenuously denied by Kitty) ; he had known so many instances of boys going through Eton without learning anything ; Free Trade in 1821 would mean free, irretrievable ruin ; Bonaparte was printing lies about Waterloo ; but " supposing I *was* surprised : I won the battle ; and what could you have had more even if I had not been surprised ? "

They prattled pleasantly enough, as he went his rounds among the country houses.   Once he was near his mother's old friends at Llangollen, but not near enough to call, though he sent a charming note.   House-parties and official papers filled his life ; and he still had leisure sometimes to give sittings to an artist. Lawrence painted him that year for Robert Peel's collection of notabilities, and he sat without undue protest.   For he was not overwhelmed with business, though he took his position in public life seriously enough.   He was, he knew he was more than Master-General of the Ordnance with a seat in the Cabinet.   For he was the Duke of Wellington ; and when the King displayed an awkward tendency to dismiss the Government, the Duke favoured him with a long memorandum of personal advice.   He had been accustomed to deal with Continental kings and emperors, as someone said of him in Paris, ' *de Couronne à Couronne* ' ; and having managed Louis and Alexander as equals, why should he shrink from George IV ?

Politics were still lively in 1821, though the ferment was dying down.   The ground-swell of revolution, which had menaced 1819, was subsiding now.   But there were still breakers on the surface.

41 For one evening early in the year, when the King risked himself
at Drury Lane, a disrespectful playgoer in the gallery addressed
the royal box with the stentorian enquiry, " Where's your
wife, Georgy ? " But a loyal audience sang *Rule Britannia* and
positively rendered *God Save the King* three times. The crowds
outside the theatre were immense. A slightly officious loyalist
insisted upon making a lane for Wellington, returned into the
crowd, performed the same kind office for Lord Palmerston,
felt in his fob, and then made the disastrous discovery that his
seals were missing. As he had made four journeys through a
crowd within five minutes' walk of Seven Dials, this was not
surprising. But he appeared to think that his loss established
some claim upon the Duke. The Duke, with slightly chilling
42 courtesy, disabused him of the notion. Admitting that he perfectly recollected the incident, he pointed out that " this service,
if it can be so called, was purely voluntary on the part of this
gentleman. The Duke is as well able as any other man to make
his way through a crowd even if there existed any disposition to
impede his progress, which did not appear, and therefore the
assistance of this gentleman was not necessary ; and, moreover,
the Duke's footman attended him." This was unkind ; although
the next paragraph expressed his grateful thanks for the stranger's
courtesy. His sole objection was to the resulting claim for compensation, which he met with a denial of liability that would have
done credit to a solicitor, pointing out that the loss was not discovered until after the journey with Lord Palmerston and,
alternatively, that even if it had been suffered on his journey
with the Duke, the journey was itself wholly superfluous—*volenti*,
in fact, *non fit injuria*. But the Duke did not rest wholly upon
his Common Law rights ; for as the claimant " may be a gentleman in circumstances not able to bear the expense of such a loss,
and as the Duke certainly considered his conduct towards him as
very polite, the Duke feels no objection to assist him to replace the
loss he has sustained," adding the excellent advice " in future to
omit to render these acts of unsolicited and unnecessary politeness
unless he should be in a situation to bear the probable or possible
consequences." The whole effect, it must be confessed, was
chilling ; and the result upon his unknown benefactor's politics
remains unknown. How long did he remain a Tory ? Or did he
go straight home, stopping on the way to buy a pike, and join a

secret society ? Yet Wellington had granted his request for
compensation. Only the kindness had been done, as usual, a
trifle gruffly. For the Duke had been at pains not to create a
precedent. It was a wise precaution, since, after all, he passed
his life in crowds ; he had numerous admirers ; and if it were
known that he was willing to replace all missing jewellery, where
would it end ?

The year wore on with preparations for the Coronation, and
the King plunged with gusto into the details of that sartorial
apotheosis. His ministers struggled with the unholy forces of
economics and the more sanctified obstacle provided by the claims
of Roman Catholics to citizenship. The Duke appeared to hold
a somewhat Dublin Castle view. In former days he used to tell
the Duke of Richmond that " it was nonsense to talk of the
Church and State being in danger ; English influence and connection were in danger if the Catholic Emancipation were ever
carried." But he had spoken on the question in the House of   43
Lords in 1819, arguing with simple-minded emphasis that the
whole question turned upon how far the Protestant Church could
be safeguarded in Ireland, and that in view of the fact that it
had been established " at the point of the sword and by means of
confiscations," the Roman Catholics were quite certain to be
inspired " by the remembrance of the events to which I have
alluded and the idea of unmerited and mutual suffering." These
were generous admissions. But the Duke's conclusion, though
he appeared to realise the whole tragedy of Ireland, was that it
was wholly unsafe to leave the future of Protestantism in the
hands of men who had passed through such fires. For Protestantism must, in his view, come first. Not that he was a   44
bigot, since he declined to become an Orangeman upon the ground
that Roman Catholics were excluded and that, their faith apart,
he had always found them loyal subjects. Besides, that year he   45
began to press Lord Liverpool to take Canning back into the
Cabinet ; and Canning's views on that and other questions were
more advanced. The Duke discerned a useful colleague, though
his own convictions did not incline him further towards respect
for democracy, since he shocked politicians in 1821 by his blunt
statement that, after getting 9,000 signatures to a petition, it   46
was superfluous " to go through the farce of a county meeting."
The Whigs were deeply pained ; but as he regarded it as a national

45   calamity to " give up the Government to the Whigs and Radicals, or, in other words, the country in all its relations to irretrievable ruin," he did not greatly care. This was a very different tone from his non-partisan acceptance of office three years before. But the disorders of 1819, followed by the addiction of democrats in 1820 to the meaner forms of murder, had changed his views; and he was a Tory now.

One day that spring a lonely, dying man was making his will seven thousand miles away. He left 10,000 francs to the *sous-officier* Cantillon, acquitted by a French jury on a charge of attempting to murder Wellington three years before : the Duke had always been convinced that Napoleon was not a gentleman. But Providence designed one of its neatest repartees. For at his funeral (he died within the month) the battle-honours on the colours dipped at the Emperor's grave-side were ' Talavera ' and ' Pyrenees ' : the last word, one feels, was Wellington's. The news came to London in the summer days when the town was buzzing with the Coronation. The great day arrived at last ; and Wellington fitted on his coronet, while Benjamin Robert Haydon hurried round London in an ecstasy of patriotism borrowing the items of his Court suit. The Abbey was a sea of ermine, swayed by the stately tides of the Coronation Service ; although the streets outside witnessed a slight, but farcical, recrudescence of the Queen. Westminster Hall moved Haydon to a page of perfect prose. The royal epiphany was comparable to the sun's—

47   " There are indications which announce the luminary's approach ; a streak of light—the tipping of a cloud—the singing of the lark —the brilliance of the sky, till the cloud edges get brighter and brighter, and he rises majestically into the heavens." Cast for this splendid *rôle*, George IV enraptured his beholder—" A whisper of mystery turns all eyes to the throne. . . . Then three or four of high rank appear from behind the throne ; an interval is left ; the crowds scarce breathe. Something rustles, and a being buried in satin, feathers, and diamonds rolls gracefully into his seat. The room rises with a sort of feathered, silken thunder. . . . As he looked towards the peeresses and foreign ambassadors he shewed like some gorgeous bird of the East." Wellington, in his brightest plumage, figured in this ornamental aviary. As the banquet opened, he walked down the Hall in his coronet, cheered by the Guards, and returned on horseback. He rode up to the

throne and (oh, miracle) backed his horse to the door and out of
it. Next he was seen beside the armoured figure of the King's
Champion. He saw a good deal of the King that summer, since   *48*
he was commanded to go with him as far as Brussels, when he
went abroad. Privileged to escort his sovereign to Waterloo,
the Duke explained the action ; and the lucidity of his explanations doubtless contributed to the King's lifelong belief that he
had fought himself, though Wellington recalled that " His Majesty
took it very coolly ; indeed, never asked me a single question, nor
said one word, till I showed him where Lord Anglesey's leg was
buried, and then he burst into tears."

The year went out upon an increase of Irish anxieties ; and
early in 1822 they had a notion of sending him to Dublin as Lord-
Lieutenant. But his reply was shrewd—" I am ready to go any-   *49*
where you please, but remember my going will attract notice not
only in England but in Europe. Take care that you don't let off
your great gun against a sparrow ! What is it you want me to
do for you ? If you want me to put down *the row*, I will do that
easily enough ; but if afterwards I am merely to continue the
divided system—a Lord-Lieutenant one way and a Secretary the
other—I tell you fairly I don't expect any good from it." So
Richard went instead. He had subsided now into the shadow of
his junior, murmuring to Wyatt, the architect, " Aye ! Arthur
is a much cleverer fellow than I am, you may depend upon it."
Was there a touch of irony ? If so, it might be forgiven ; for
Arthur had passed him in the race. He was the greatest Wellesley
of them all, with Richard's place as head of the family, the dukedom Richard might have had, and even Richard's house at Hyde
Park Corner ; and now Richard went to the Viceregal Lodge
because Arthur would not go. It is a slightly melancholy part
to play Quintus Cicero.

Not that Arthur was devoid of opinions upon Irish matters.
He expressed a healthy appetite for Coercion in the House of   *50*
Lords, though he was equally emphatic on the dereliction of
absentee landlords, who ought to have " gone over to look at their   *51*
properties instead of *brawling* and *balling* in London. . . . A
population of seven millions, increasing in an immense proportion,
without employment, . . . getting in fact nothing for the produce
of their country . . . appears to be a dangerous phenomenon in
political economy. I believe we have not yet seen the last call

of the Irish population on the charity of their English country-men ; and we shall yet have something more to do for them than give charity balls and brawl upon distress. We want in Ireland the influence of manners as well as laws. How we are to get the former in the absence of nearly all the landed proprietors is more than I can tell." This was sensible ; and it shewed a laudable desire to do something more with Ireland than repress it. Other problems faced them, as the summer months of 1822 stole by—resurgent Greece, insurgent Mexico, a restless mood in Italy, Spain ringing with Riego's hymn, and the ferment of revolution working wherever Metternich turned his uneasy eye. There was another Conference in prospect. For the perambulating Areo-pagus was to meet at Vienna in the autumn and dissolve these menaces by the magic of collective wisdom. Castlereagh (he was Lord Londonderry now) was busy on his own Instructions ; and no clouds as yet obscured that " splendid summit of bright

52 and polished frost which, like the travellers in Switzerland, we all admire ; but no one can hope, and few would wish to reach." The Duke took delivery of Wilkie's picture, ordered six years before and now astonishing the Academy with the diversity and liveliness of its Chelsea pensioners.

53 The painter asked £1,260 ; and as the Duke counted out the notes himself, Wilkie suggested that a cheque might be more convenient.

" Do you think," replied his patron, " I like Coutts' clerks always to know how foolishly I spend my money ? "

That summer the Park wall was breached not far from Apsley House ; a shrouded figure trundled through ; workmen

54 were busy on the mound across the road ; and on the anniversary of Waterloo ' Achilles ' was unveiled just outside his library windows. Midsummer passed ; and the candles on Castlereagh's table burned low, as the bowed figure wrote and wrote his in-exhaustible despatches, conjuring an ordered world out of the tumult of 1822. The burden weighed him down ; and the dying light flickered suddenly. For at his farewell audience before

55 leaving for the Continent he scared the King by talking wildly ; his mind was an unhappy whirl of plots ; he started at chance words ; and when the Duke observed it, he warned him with terrible lucidity. The two men were alone. Wellington looked into the white face of Castlereagh and spoke.

" From what you have said, I am bound to warn you that you cannot be in your right mind."

This must be the truth. The Duke would not deceive him. The unhappy man covered his tortured face and answered from the sofa.

" Since you say so, I fear it must be so."

Castlereagh was sobbing bitterly. Wellington offered kindly to stay with him ; but he declined, since the world must not suspect. The Duke warned the doctors—those sagacious doctors whose sole specific was to bleed and bleed. But Castlereagh escaped them all one summer morning, clutching a little knife. A gloating mob outside the Abbey cheered his coffin (the mourners took it to be a cheer for Wellington, since crowds cheered him still) ; and Lord Byron exclaimed with his customary felicity,

> "So *He* has cut his throat at last !—He !   Who ?
> The man who cut his country's long ago."

But Wellington was deeply grieved ; for he had lost his oldest friend in politics.

II

THE age of Castlereagh was over. Who was to succeed him at the Foreign Office ? But there was a more immediate question. Who was to take his place at the impending Conference ? They settled that within a week. For Wellington received the King's command to attend it, and he was writing to assure Metternich " *de ma bonne volonté, et de mon zèle pour consolider l'alliance générale, et le système de l'Europe.*" The choice was natural, since the Duke was now the sole survivor of the diplomatic campaigns of Vienna, Paris, and Aix-la-Chapelle. Besides, he knew everyone in Europe, and everyone knew him ; and Europe, it was to be hoped, had retained its habit of attending to the Duke.

But the main problem still confronted them. Who was to take the Foreign Office ? The choice was difficult, since it was complicated by Parliamentary considerations. For the Government was lamentably weak in the House of Commons, and it was vital to reinforce the Treasury Bench, where Mr. Peel, Home Secretary at thirty-four, withstood the nightly onslaught of the Whigs almost unaided. If they promoted Peel to lead the House, were his lieutenants adequate ? The best was Palmerston ; and Palmerston, in the thirteenth year of his uneventful tenure of the War Department, was scarcely an exciting figure. He had been introducing Army estimates since 1809 ; he wrote a sound official letter ; his defence of flogging was an annual event ; and he had earned from Mr. Croker the doubtful compliment of being judged " as powerful in intellect as Robinson, and much more to be relied on in readiness and nerve." But he was no Rupert of debate ; and, Palmerston apart, the rest was silence. For ability in its more glaring forms was hardly countenanced in Lord Liverpool's administration. There was one possibility, since the first orator in England was Canning ; and Canning was at Liverpool, waiting for his passage to India as Governor-General. It had been a strange career. The favourite disciple, as he liked to think, of Pitt, he had proved a sad embarrassment to Pitt's successors. For he was highly unaccountable. A splendid flourish had proclaimed that his political allegiance lay buried in Pitt's grave ; and it was undeniable that his loyalty resided in no very accessible spot. His course had always been uncertain. Resigning on a deadly feud (and an exchange of pistol-shots) with Castlereagh in 1810, he had hung insecurely in the Parliamentary firmament, until he dropped suddenly like an erratic meteor towards the west. For in 1814 he demobilised his few supporters and departed to the British embassy at Lisbon, content apparently to serve Castlereagh as an official subordinate at an augmented salary of £14,400. Then he returned, rejoined the Cabinet, and administered Indian affairs until his second resignation—this time upon the treatment of Queen Caroline. After an interlude he had accepted the Governor-Generalship of India, consenting, it would seem, to abandon his political ambitions for that opulence which is the last refuge of disappointed politicians. His disappointment was not surprising, since every avenue was closed to Canning in 1822. The King could not forgive his attitude of chivalry towards the Queen, even professing to regard him as her accepted lover ; the Whigs bore too many scars of his corrosive wit ; and Tories sardonically wished him " very well whatever part of the world he might go to." This was a melancholy harvest to reap at fifty-two ; and that summer Canning waited disconsolately for his passage to the East.

The scene was changed suddenly by the tragedy at Cray ; and he was waiting now for Castlereagh's succession. He would take nothing less ; his mind was quite made up ; it must be " the whole heritage "—the Foreign Office with the leadership of the House of Commons—or nothing. Embarrassed Tories hoped to see Peel lead the Commons and the Duke at the Foreign Office. But the Duke had other views. For he had favoured Canning's readmission to the Cabinet since 1821, although it was not easy for him to control the situation now, since he was seriously indisposed. A light-hearted aurist, in a bold attempt to cure his ear-ache, had inserted caustic in the ear, destroyed its hearing, and very nearly destroyed his patient at the same time— a notable achievement for British medicine, which already numbered Castlereagh among its victims for the year. But the King waited on the Duke's opinion. Each found the other slightly trying ; for the King's exuberance jarred on the Duke, and the Duke was apt to differ from George IV on military topics, forcing his sovereign to the painful avowal that " it is not for me to dispute on such a subject with your Grace." But the King knew a loyal adviser, and the Duke knew his duty. Wellington was still in bed ; but a royal emissary was assiduous at his bedside, and the King even deferred his interview with the Prime Minister until he knew the Duke's opinion. Wellington expressed it plainly ; Canning, he felt, was a necessary reinforcement and would prove a loyal minister in spite of his eccentric views upon the Roman Catholic question. As to the King's personal objections, did not the sovereign's honour consist in doing acts of mercy ? This was the height of tact ; and the King's self-esteem expanded in the sunshine of conscious virtue. He positively revelled in his own magnanimity. Indeed, the Duke had almost overdone it ; since the King, borrowing his line from Wellington, summoned Canning to office with an unduly gracious intimation that " the King is aware that the brightest ornament of his crown is the power of extending grace and favour to a subject who may have incurred his displeasure." This was too much for Canning, who was narrowly restrained by Wellington from making a reply. But the Duke, always practical, advised him that " as he intended to accept, he had better take no further notice of the paper." The King and Canning were not his only charges, since his Tory colleagues were a trifle fretful, and he was even compelled to pacify Castlereagh's reproachful widow with a lengthy argument, in which he urged shrewdly that " nothing can be so erroneous as to place any individual of great activity and talents in a situation in which there is no scope for his activity, and in which he must feel that his talents are thrown away. His views must always be directed to disturb rather than to preserve the existing order of things, in order that out of a new arrangement he may find himself in a position better suited to him." This danger was averted now ; Canning was safely installed as Castlereagh's successor ; and the Prime Minister wrote gratefully that without Wellington's assistance " it never might have been brought to such a result."

2

Within a fortnight he was on the Continent, bound for Vienna. He stopped in Paris to confer with French ministers, resumed his journey, and plunged into the latest Congress. For a melancholy

irony compelled Mr. Canning, who had once gleefully announced
that " we shall have no more congresses, thank God ! " to direct   *12*
British policy in a Congress.   But events had an unpleasant trick
of following a course precisely opposite to that laid down for them
by Mr. Canning.   The business before the Congress was highly
variegated—the Greek insurrection, Spanish colonies, the Austrians in Italy, and an awkward tendency on the part of Russia
to claim the coast of British Columbia.   They were to meet at
Vienna ; but the Congress was transferred to Verona, and Byron
welcomed them to Italy with elaborate raillery at

> " Proud Wellington, with eagle beak so curl'd,   *13*
> That nose, the hook where he suspends the world !
> And Waterloo—and trade—and—(hush ! not yet
> A syllable of imports or of debt)—
> And ne'er (enough) lamented Castlereagh,
> Whose penknife slit a goose-quill t'other day—
> And ' pilots who have weathered every storm,'—
> (But, no, not even for rhyme's sake name Reform).
>
> .   .   .   .   .
>
> " Strange sight this Congress ! destined to unite
> All that's incongruous, all that's opposite.
> I speak not of the sovereigns—they're alike,
> As common coin as ever mint could strike ;
> But those who sway the puppets, pull the strings,
> Have more of motley than their heavy kings.
> Jews, authors, generals, charlatans, combine,
> While Europe wonders at the vast design :
> There Metternich, power's foremost parasite,
> Cajoles ; there Wellington forgets to fight ;
> There Chateaubriand forms new books of martyrs ;
> And subtle Gauls intrigue for stupid Tartars ;
> There Montmorenci . . ."

The French delegate played a leading part.   For the chief item
on the agenda was Spain, where the French were shewing awkward
signs of intervening in a civil war.   There was no doubt of British
views upon foreign intervention ; the Duke had made them clear
to Castlereagh six months before ; Castlereagh concurred in his   *14*
disapproval ; and Canning followed suit after knocking impres-
sively at the open door and instructing Wellington " frankly and   *15*
peremptorily to declare, that to any such interference, come what
may, his Majesty will not be a party."   There was no difference
between them, and the Duke did not feel the slightest difficulty   *16*

in conveying that " we had insuperable objections to interfere in the internal concerns of any country " and, more formally, that " to animadvert upon the internal transactions of an independent State, unless such transactions affect the essential interests of his Majesty's subjects, is inconsistent with those principles on which his Majesty has invariably acted in all questions relating to the internal concerns of other countries ; that such animadversions, if made, must involve his Majesty in serious responsibility if they should produce any effect, and must irritate if they should not." The doctrine of non-intervention in Spain was quite congenial to Wellington, since he had argued it at length before Canning came to the Foreign Office ; and now he argued it once more before a highly unsympathetic audience of foreign diplomats. The French were spoiling for a fight against a paralytic enemy ; and the Czar was haunted by a disturbing dream of marching Russian armies across Europe in the sacred name of counter-revolution. The Duke, who diagnosed him shrewdly—" The Emperor would have no objection to a war, but it must be on a stage on which he would have the eyes of all Europe upon him and the applause of the world "—laboured steadily to damp the universal ardour in a modest hope " that we shall get through these difficulties in a creditable manner, and that we may be able to maintain the peace of the world." He had no difficulty in enlisting Austrian apprehensions of the Russian design ; and the danger of a general conflagration was averted by his downright dissociation of Great Britain from common action at Madrid, which immobilised the Alliance. This disposed of Alexander's vision of 150,000 Russians tramping through Austria to Milan *en route* for the Pyrenees. But the uneasy possibility remained that France might intervene alone. Wellington had preached reason on his way through Paris ; but when Villèle disclosed the military details of the French plan for invading Spain, he had not refrained from practical comments. It was his vanity, as a sharp woman guessed, to know " how to do everything, and to do it better than anyone else." The problem of invading Spain interested him professionally. After all, he was the greatest living expert on Peninsular wars ; and he could scarcely be expected to pass by in silence such alluring topics as the line of the Ebro and the military effects of occupying Madrid. Always a strong believer in the virtues of prompt

22

action for the suppression of revolutions (had he not prescribed it   *21*
unofficially in the case of Naples two years before ?), he was
perfectly convinced that " the French will meet with no more   *22*
resistance in marching to Madrid than he does in going to the
Ordnance Office." But it scarcely follows that he told them so.
There is no evidence that Wellington encouraged them to try
the experiment and that, as a learned fantasy suggests, he was   *23*
deliberately false to Canning's policy by privately inciting France
to intervene in Spain. Such treachery was not in his manner.
Besides, he had just been at considerable pains to instal Canning
at the Foreign Office ; and, in any case, the policy of opposing
intervention in Spain was Wellington's as well as Canning's.
In reality he laboured to avert the war ; and if he failed, at least
he had succeeded in preventing a general explosion.

On minor matters he was still more successful. Russia was
checked in North America ; Austria was pressed discreetly to
repay war-time loans ; and he made some progress with the
abolition of the slave trade. Upon the question of the Spanish
colonies he served Canning as a loyal mouthpiece—" I shall of   *24*
course follow what is laid down in your despatch." But he
followed it with evident distaste, finding the rebels uncongenial
company and deploring undue haste—" I know that we must at
last recognise all these governments, but I would recognise them
when necessary, and only when really constituted and become
powers, instead of seeking for reasons for recognising them, and
by recognising them constitute them." This was rational ;
and he restated his position—" I consider it a point of honour   *25*
that we should not be in a hurry to recognise that independence,
and that the measure should be forced upon us by circumstances
rather than we should seek for occasions to adopt it. . . . I
therefore have always been for going as far as was necessary,
and never further." Canning recognised his fairness in a final
tribute to his work at Verona—" You have done, in respect to   *26*
that question (of Spanish America), all that could be desired ;
and upon the slave trade, more than could have been expected."

It had been a strange affair. The Congress of Verona with
its *parterre de rois*—two emperors, three kings, a cardinal, three
grand-dukes, twenty ambassadors, twelve ministers, and three
foreign secretaries—had been the last parade of a vanishing
Europe, where Metternich whispered his sharp asides and the

Duke moved in splendid profile through a lane of bowing gentle-men in stars. They had their relaxations too. There was the great Roman amphitheatre for their plays, and for lighter enter-tainment Dorothea Lieven and the Récamier with her echoes of Directoire *salons* and the distant days when Josephine was gay and General Bonaparte an awkward lover. A stranger echo hung about a stout and smiling archduchess, where Marie Louise, Duchess of Parma, played écarté with Wellington. As the cards fell between them, they settled their accounts in *napoléons* ; and when he dined with her, she told the Duke how sorry she was that she had failed to get his favourite roast mutton for him. For Napoleon's widow studied Wellington's tastes. He saw something of her son as well, finding him " a fine lad, educated just like the archdukes " ; and the Duke told someone later that " he was very civil to me." Then he was off to Paris by way of Milan and Lyon, having loyally applied the policy which enabled Canning to write triumphantly " For ' Alliance ' read ' England.' "

He had business in Paris, where he still hoped to check the French. Canning instructed him to offer British mediation ; the Duke, fearing a rebuff in Paris, delayed the offer ; Canning insisted ; and the Duke predicted gloomily that " the government have mistaken this case, and that the mediation will be rejected on the ground on which it was rejected at Verona." The Duke was right ; and Canning's insistence got nothing more for his country than " a parting blow." But Wellington had done his duty in Paris. Indeed, he had done more, since Lady Shelley had entrusted him with an important mission concerning a blouse. Less arduous than Mr. Canning's, he discharged it to a nicety and could report in triumph that " your blouse goes to you by the stage tomorrow. But mind ! You are to wear it the first time you dine with me, with the Tiranna ! " He took the road again and was at Apsley House for Christmas, 1822.

3

The new year opened pleasantly enough with house-parties at Stratfield Saye. The Duke of York came to shoot with the lugubrious Leopold ; he asked the Shelleys ; but their meeting was delayed, since a week later he was still pressing her to come with the Liverpools and Madame Lieven—and " mind you bring the blouse ! "—and when Neumann came, he found the Arbuthnots there with the Lievens and Prince Esterhazy. But Spain still filled his horizon, and he loyally seconded Canning's efforts to deter the French from intervention, even adding the unique resources of his personal position to the exiguous armoury of the Foreign Office. For in his character as a Grandee of Spain he sent Fitzroy Somerset to Madrid with sedative advice. Canning struck martial attitudes (he had already written gaily that the French tone " really stirs one's blood . . . in the good old constitutional way in which France and England used to hate and provoke each other ") and flung his thunderbolts about with a fine carelessness. He talked of his own " itch for war," made dashing speeches in the House of Commons, increased the Navy, and laid papers—the normal prelude of a declaration of war. In Canning's case, however, the free publication of diplomatic correspondence formed part of a design for invoking public opinion on matters of high policy and, perhaps, owed a little to the pardonable pride which literary men feel in their own compositions. These proceedings were unspeakably distasteful to the Duke, though they were still on friendly terms, Canning begging him expansively never to stand on ceremony in volunteering comments upon policy. But though Wellington defended his own action in the longest speech that he had yet delivered in the House of Lords, it was unpleasing to be dragged in Mr. Canning's foaming wake. He had misgivings now, warning Lord Liverpool that a draft of Canning's " would go to a break up of the Alliance ; and I don't believe that any of us, not even Mr. Canning himself, thinks that the affairs of Europe are in such a state that the Alliance provided in the Second Article of the Treaty of 1815 may not be necessary." Canning's pyrotechnics failed to exhilarate him :

> " We have given the Spaniards reason to believe that we should assist them, and we have shaken the confidence of France in our desire of maintaining peace for her sake as well as our own. Then at home, nobody knows what the policy of the Government is, and it will turn out at last that the country and Parliament will declare for neutrality before the government will have an opportunity of doing so ; and it will be believed that the government have been forced by the country to be neutral, their intentions having been to interfere in favour of Spain."

A series of false positions, however brilliant, was distasteful to the

37 Duke. He disliked the promiscuous publication of official documents ; and it was disconcerting to encounter the pitying regard of his Continental associates. For the French ambassador wrote
38 patronisingly that he was " *guerrier peu redoutable sur les champs de l'intrigue* " ; and Metternich, deep in Vienna, recorded with
39 regret, " *Quel dommage que Wellington soit si craintif, lui qui a un cœur si droit et une si honnête figure !* "

So he went the round of country houses in 1823, while Canning issued his challenges. The Duke moved from Stratfield Saye to Wherstead, from Wherstead to Maresfield, on to the Pavilion, and from Beaudesert to Hatfield. It was a stately progress ; and the red boxes followed him with their depressing tale of Canning's extravagances. There was no war with France ; no one had ever meant to have one ; and if they had, there was no time, since Spain collapsed before the French invasion with the most disconcerting suddenness and left Mr. Canning thundering in spite of everything to delighted crowds about the might of England.
40 It was far pleasanter to sit to Hayter in his cloak ; for Mrs. Arbuthnot had consented to Lady Shelley having a portrait of him, " provided the picture is not painted by Sir Thomas Lawrence, and is not so good as hers." So the Duke went his
41 social rounds and made a charming offer to Alava, exiled by the turmoil of Spanish politics, of a home with him in England.

But 1824 renewed his cares. He still maintained a correspondence upon foreign affairs with Metternich and with those embassies abroad where he had a brother or a friend ; and early
42 in the year he confessed to Henry Wellesley that " we are radically defective in our diplomatic head-quarters here." He disliked the hail of Blue-books, with which Canning sought to captivate his
43 countrymen ; for such publications seemed to lead inevitably to the renunciation of Cabinet control of foreign policy. Mr. Canning might prefer to have his policy debated in a wider circle than the *champ clos* of Downing Street, where ageing Tories sat round the table with disapproving faces ; but the Duke did not.
20 Trained in an older school, he valued secrecy—hardly for its own sake (though Madame Lieven hinted that he loved a secret), but for the greater freedom of manœuvre which secrecy confers. He was not greatly interested in evoking cheers. Besides, he disapproved the drift of Canning's policy, writing to Metternich that
44 " I feel as you do the *isolement* of the British government ; and I

am equally aware with you of the mischief which it does to us as well as to the world ; probably more to the world than to us." Canning might proclaim the dissolution of the Alliance in the gloating formula, " Every nation for itself, and God for us all." *45* But was it reasonable to expect the Duke to part from it without a pang ? The Allied ministers were men with whom he had worked in close confidence since the great days of 1815. They had shared common dangers, won wars together, and settled Europe in agreement. The endless conferences that followed Waterloo had left a certain *camaraderie* among them, which Wellington could not easily forget ; and, slow to make new friends, he was as slow at losing old ones. But his Continental ties were something more than personal. He had his principles, though they were less articulate than Mr. Canning's ; and it was wholly inevitable that his point of view should be more European. It was scarcely possible to be a Duke in four countries and a Marshal of every Continental army, to have served two emperors and half a dozen kings in command of an international army of occupation, to make an annual tour of inspection of the new Belgian fortresses—and to retain in its perfection that insularity which was now Mr. Canning's pride. Besides, the settlement of 1815 owed so much to his work. He had won Waterloo ; his diplomacy restored Louis XVIII ; the peace-treaty bore his signature ; the Reparations settlement was his personal achievement ; and if Canning could intimate in a celebrated flourish that he had called a New World into existence, it was almost as true that Wellington had called the Old.

The two were bound to clash. Canning owed his promotion almost wholly to the Duke's intervention ; but even gratitude will not enable oil to mix with water. Their views were poles apart ; their methods were discordant ; and what soldier relishes the sight of a civilian flourishing a sword ? Viewed by the Duke, the Foreign Secretary was hasty, ill-advised, and quite unbearably dramatic ; his popular appeals were most distasteful ; and—the uneasy question rose in Wellington—was he quite a gentleman ? These discontents found a sympathetic audience at Windsor, where his sovereign fished disconsolately in Virginia Water. He did not fish alone ; for Lady Conyngham was there, and they had week-end parties at the Cottage. The life was not conspicuously gay. The King breakfasted alone, the Duke with *46*

Lady Conyngham ; they met at three ; phaetons were at the door ; the guests paired off and drove—a gentleman and lady between each spinning pair of wheels—till five ; sometimes the royal drive was diversified by brandy and water at a park lodge ; then dinner in the pagoda, conversation until ten, and cards till midnight. But the 'Cottage Coterie'—a pair of Austrians, two Lievens, and the French ambassador—was anything but favourable to Mr. Canning ; and the Duke was admitted to their circle. He talked freely to them, though he was hardly a party to their drawing-room conspiracy " *de faire sauter M. Canning.*" But that autumn he involved himself in a dispute with Canning on the latter's plan of visiting Paris ; Canning suspected royal intrigues and retorted sharply that " it is high time to look about me, and to beware of what Burke calls ' traps and mines.' " The Duke was not a plotter ; but it was comforting to pour his views into receptive ears. He was distressed by Canning's eagerness to sanctify South American revolutionaries with British recognition, pleading in vain that " considering what is passing in Ireland, and what all expect will occur in that country before long, the bad with hope, the good with apprehension and dread, we must take care not to give additional examples in these times of the encouragement of insurrection, and we must not be induced by clamour, by self-interested views, by stock-jobbing, or by faction, to give the sanction of our approbation to what are called the governments of these insurgent provinces." The analogy of Ireland haunted him : how could Dublin Castle extend a hand to Buenos Ayres ? He reasoned lucidly that " if you hold that the people of Colombia have been guilty of no crime, and that Bolivar is a hero and no rebel, then you ought not to prosecute O'Connell." This was logical ; and in the last weeks of 1824 he carried his objections to the length of offering to resign. There were struggles in the Cabinet ; the King almost mutinied ; but Canning got his way. Lord Liverpool was on his side, and the Duke ultimately acquiesced, admitting to a foreign diplomat that he regretted having introduced Canning to the Cabinet, but that it was impossible to dismiss him. So the New World was duly conjured into being. Not that Canning's policy was a romantic gesture towards the great open spaces, since in its later phases it was partly inspired by a legitimate anxiety to forestall the United States ; " Spanish America," as he wrote gaily, " is free, and if we do not mismanage our affairs sadly she is English. The Yankees will shout in triumph, but it is they who lose most by our decision."

The Duke's skies were darkening. Madame Lieven wrote that " Mr. Canning poses as a Radical to please the populace— the other Ministers smile approvingly to keep their places. The Duke of Wellington alone is prepared to break a lance for the good cause." Ireland was full of menace, and the Roman Catholic question began to loom with unpleasant urgency. His shooting was improving, though ; and he could report a bag of fourteen rabbits, a dozen hares, a brace of pheasants, and a partridge. One theme alone seemed to inspire him with no misgivings ; for national defence found him as calm as ever—" I confess that I am one of those who do not much apprehend invasion. I think steam navigation has in some degree altered that question to our disadvantage. . . . But I confess that I think a solid invasion of the country . . . is out of the question." His nerves were always steady, and the soldier in him was still reassured ; but as he went to Windsor for Christmas, 1824, the statesman was distinctly uneasy. For the world was full of awkward problems. Portugal was in an uproar ; Byron had died at Missolonghi ; and British sympathy seemed to be solicited on behalf of revolutionaries in every hemisphere. Nearer home the Irish situation increased in gravity ; and the Duke corresponded copiously with Peel, who was now the guardian of public order at the Home Office. The two men drew together. Their convergence, as *Coningsby* diagnosed it, " was the sympathetic result of superior minds placed among inferior intelligences, and was, doubtless, assisted by a then mutual conviction, that the difference of age, the circumstance of sitting in different houses, and the general contrast of their previous pursuits and accomplishments, rendered personal rivalry out of the question." Besides, they both distrusted Canning. As 1825 wore on, the King surrendered to his Foreign Secretary ; but his colleagues surrendered none of their misgivings.

The Duke passed the year among his customary employments. The Ordnance Office kept him busy with revetments, counterscarps, and barracks at Bermuda ; he was consulted upon Indian affairs ; and his views about the Greeks were plainly expressed. " The establishment of a new Power in Europe, which must be founded on the principles of modern democracy, and therefore inimical to this country," filled him with no enthusiasm. Not that he loved the Turk, admitting frankly that " the Turkish government is so oppressive and odious to all mankind, that we could scarcely expect to carry the country with us in a course of policy . . . the result of which is to be to maintain by the exercise of our power that government at Constantinople." But he viewed the expansion of Russian influence with genuine concern. His minor interests were less absorbing. He defended spring guns in the House of Lords for the simple reason that they checked poachers, and he favoured Lady Shelley with a discourse on education :

" As for John, you must impress upon his mind, first, that he is coming into the world at an age at which he who knows nothing will be nothing. . . .

" If he means to rise in the military profession—I don't mean as high as I am, as that is very rare—he must be master of languages, of the mathematics, of military tactics of course, and of all the duties of an officer in all situations.

" He will not be able to converse or write like a gentleman . . . unless he understands the classics ; and by neglecting them, more-over, he will lose much gratification which the perusal of them will always afford him ; and a great deal of professional information and instruction.

" He must be master of history and geography, and the laws of his country and of nations. . . .

" Impress all this upon his mind ; and moreover tell him that there is nothing like never having an idle moment. . . ."

For he was still the young Colonel with a habit of private reading, who thirty years before had filled his trunk for India with im-proving books, who took his Blackstone with him and learned from Cæsar how to cross a river.

As he sat to Hayter, the tide of his impatience mounted. For portrait-painters were rapidly becoming one of the burdens of his life. They talked ; they borrowed all his clothes ; and, what was worse, they could not paint. Even Lawrence kept him standing for three hours with folded arms, and then produced a complete travesty of his sword. This must plainly be put right at once. The painter made excuses ; but the Duke insisted.

" Do it now."

" I must go to the Princess Augusta's."

" Oh no ; you must put my sword right. It is really bad."

After all, he had more experience of swords—and of portraits
—than most men.

In the last days of 1825 a diversion offered itself. For Alexander died at Taganrog, and the King and Canning tentatively
suggested (with profuse expressions of anxiety for the Duke's   *61*
health) that he should go to Russia on a special mission to the
new Emperor. The prospect was uninviting, since he was far
from well and the road from London to St. Petersburg in mid-
winter was long. Besides, it was proposed that he should do his
best to stop the Russians from going to war with Turkey in the
cause of Greek independence. Preventing wars was his *métier* ;
but this war could only be prevented if the Porte could be prevailed on to make concessions to the Greeks ; and it was doubtful
how far the Duke would relish being made an instrument of Greek
emancipation. Madame Lieven gleefully proclaimed that his
mission was " *une idée bouffonne et grande* . . . side by side with   *62*
the salaam the Duke is to make he should come to an understanding on the question of Greece." The ingenious Canning, she
thought, would thus contrive to " compromise him and mock him
at the same time—a double pleasure." But how could he refuse ?
" I don't see how I, who have always been preaching the doctrine   *63*
of going wherever we are desired to go, who had consented to go
and command in Canada, could decline to accept the offer of this
mission." So he announced himself " at all times ready and
willing to serve your Majesty in any station " and accepted.
Indeed, if Canning told the truth, he " not only accepted but   *62*
jumped at the proposal." But his alacrity is doubtful, since the
world whispered that Canning would not be inconsolable if this
Arctic journey proved too much for him ; and the Duke seemed
to share the world's misgivings. Rarely emotional, he took leave   *64*
of his friends with unusual tenderness ; Alava had never seen him
so profoundly moved ; he parted from his mother with emotion ;
and the tears streamed down his cheeks, as he left Lady Burghersh.

4

Wellington entered upon his Russian campaign in February,
1826. The journey was to take three weeks ; and to elude the
minor irritants of Polish inns he adopted the ingenious expedient
of a silk mattress ; silk, it was hoped, would be impenetrable to   *65*

invaders ; and he had chosen a light material, upon which they would be more conspicuous. Such ingenuity was not unworthy of a great tactician. Besides, there was a strong element of the White Knight in the Duke's composition. A lifetime in the field will often implant a taste for minor ingenuities ; for the exigencies of campaigning tend to stimulate such proclivities; and the returning veteran will sometimes carry them into the less exacting conditions of civilian life. Was he not the inventor of a patent finger-bandage, which he demonstrated incessantly ? Were not his later years delighted by the dual precaution of a sword-umbrella ? So the ingenuity of his travelling bed (explained with pride to Lady Shelley after his return) was quite in character.

He went by way of Berlin, where he called upon the King of Prussia and wrote to Canning five times in one day. He was frankly sceptical of his prospects of success in Russia; if the Russians chose to go to war with Turkey, he should not be able to stop them. But his major object was to localise the conflict, to prevent a scuffle in the Balkans from developing into a European war. "The question of Greek and Turk is trifling in comparison"; and he was infinitely less concerned with the brutalities of Pashas and the indomitable Ypsilanti than with the major problem of European peace. As to the Greeks, he was prepared for " an arrangement short of independence." But peace must be preserved in Europe ; and he agreed with Canning in believing that another Congress was the last way to preserve it. His carriage rumbled across Poland and the sad Livonian levels, and he reached St. Petersburg in the first week of March. That evening he saw Nesselrode and called upon the Emperor Nicholas on the next day. The Czar seemed eminently reasonable about the Greeks ; and Wellington plunged into a vortex of diplomacy, mitigated by that Russian official hospitality which consisted of "pallid asparagus and fœtid oysters." His nights, as someone wrote, were "nothing but blows-out for the Duke," his days all "politics and pipeclay." Stiff Russian guardsmen in tall shakoes and tight tunics presented arms ; stiffer generals raised fingers to preposterous cocked-hats ; the Czar gave him a regiment of infantry on the anniversary of the Allies' entry into Paris ; and he visited a stupendous girls' school, where he watched young ladies curtsey by platoons and heard twenty-five pianos in simultaneous action. He managed to survive it somehow, without even getting one of

his customary colds. Indeed, the chief thing that impressed the
Duke in Russia was that no one seemed to have a cold. He
drafted endless protocols and spoke his mind to Nicholas, warning
him " that he can fix the moment when, and the point at which   69
the first shot will be fired ; but that he may as well talk of stopping the course of the Neva as of fixing the limits of his operations
if once he goes to war." The Russians listened blandly ; but it is
doubtful how far his presence in St. Petersburg modified their
course. Indeed, he was a shade perplexed by the Byzantine
complications of palace politics, confessing to his brother that " it
is difficult to judge of matters here, and whether there is any
Minister or not, and who is the adviser. We have some great   70
diplomatic characters here, but I believe they are all as much in
the dark as I am." He worked assiduously to avert a Russo-
Turkish war or, at the worst, to localise it. That was his main
objective, and he succeeded in attaining it ; for there was no
European war. As to the Greeks, he was already reconciled to
seeing them with something short of independence ; and when
the persuasive Lievens represented that Russian policy was not
aimed at abetting revolutionaries, but at the re-establishment
of order in Greece—" a regular state of things, a hierarchical   71
discipline "—the Duke was charmed. His pen grew busy with
more drafts ; and a Protocol emerged which guaranteed to Greece
a qualified degree of independence under Anglo-Russian auspices. Canning was slightly rueful, since the Protocol committed
England to Greek independence far beyond his original instructions to the Duke. But Wellington was three weeks distant from
the Foreign Office and acted on his own discretion. Canning
could have no grievance, since the Duke followed lines that were
perfectly consistent with a disinterested support of Greek emancipation. Peace was preserved ; the world was spared the horrors
of another Congress ; and a ray of hope fell across Greece. The
Duke was moving with the times (though his critics have preferred to think that he was unaware of what he was doing) ; and
if the Russians rejoiced, it does not follow that British interests
had been betrayed. Imperial gratitude expressed itself, as
always, in terms of sables and malachite vases ; and at four
o'clock one April morning Wellington started for home again.
He might have stayed in Russia for the coronation ; but he preferred to leave. The work was over ; and Peel, who had acted

as his Cabinet correspondent, was pressing him not to delay his
72   return "a single day beyond absolute necessity." Once again
duty called ; this time it was his duty to the Tories. For his
Tory colleagues were uncomfortable without him. He travelled
73   by Warsaw and Berlin, where he stopped long enough to receive
the honour of a Prussian infantry regiment ; and before the
month was out, he was in Apsley House once more.

5

Wellington's Russian campaign was over. It had been a
picturesque interlude, and the walls of Stratfield Saye bore traces
of it in the form of innumerable engravings of high-collared
autocrats, of sleighs, of snowy scenes, of angry bears, of the tall
buildings of St. Petersburg. But no musical composer was ever
moved to celebrate his *1812*, no painter to depict him in the
snow. Yet, like Napoleon, he had returned without his army ;
but, unlike the Emperor, he had left home without it too.

Home was a trifle unattractive in April, 1826. Canning was
74   high in the ascendant, and the skies were darkened by "the three
C's," as Croker called them, "Corn, Currency, and Catholics."
The eager Huskisson must really be restrained from committing
ministers to repeal the Corn Laws. The Duke would go no
75   further than an undertaking that they should be "fairly considered" in the next session ; while the Government's nice
equipoise upon the Catholic question must be maintained. That
76   summer he found greater comfort in the past—in dining at the
Admiralty with Croker and the Duke of York and recalling how
the French cavalry at Waterloo in their cuirasses and jack-boots
"lay sprawling and kicking like so many turned turtles," and
regaling a house-party of Lord Hertford's with reminiscences of
Spain and Paris and the distant days of his campaign in Denmark.
But the unpleasing present still persisted ; red boxes followed
him with their distasteful reminders of the world of 1826 ; and
at sight of them he grew almost peevish. Canning was worse
77   than ever—"a most extraordinary man. Either his mind does
not seize a case accurately ; or he forgets the impressions which
ought to be received from what he reads, or is stated to him ; or
knowing and remembering the accurate state of the case, he dis-
torts and misrepresents facts in his instructions to his ministers
with a view to entrap the consent of the Cabinet to some principle

on which he would found a new-fangled system." The Foreign
Office papers failed to circulate for Cabinet approval ; and when
the British minister was suddenly withdrawn from Spain without
notice to the Cabinet, Wellington complained bitterly to the
Prime Minister :

> " Here we are with a step taken which will be considered as a   78
> signal of war throughout Europe . . . without any one of the
> ministers being aware of the existence even of discussion.
> " I am certain that Mr. Canning would not consent to such a
> proceeding by any other man.   There is no person who (with
> propriety, in my opinion) reserves to himself more frequently the
> right of judging for himself of the cases for which he is to be held
> responsible.   I am certain, likewise, that you will admit that this
> is not the mode in which the business of this country ever has been,
> or can be carried on."

But Canning was incorrigible.   His latest escapade was the
defence of Portugal—of Portugal lately turned constitutional
and acidly described by the Duke as " Constitutional Portugal,   79
I mean in the modern sense with licentious Chambers sitting in
Lisbon and publishing their debates and a licentious press."
This victim of repression failed to stir his sympathies.   It had
been one thing to rescue decorous Braganza Portugal and Bourbon
Spain from the revolutionary legions of the French ; but this was
quite another matter.   However, Mr. Canning and the Cabinet
thought otherwise.   A splendid declamation was pronounced
in the House of Commons—" We go to plant the Standard of
England on the well-known heights of Lisbon.   Where that
Standard is planted, foreign dominion shall not come . . . "—and
while Mr. Canning stirred members' pulses, the Duke conveyed
the same intelligence to the Lords in nine sentences.   Even the
prospect of a new war in the Peninsula failed to move him to
eloquence.   For Great Britain intervened at last—in the sacred
name of non-intervention—and when a brigade sailed for the
Tagus, Wellington dutifully acquiesced with notes for the com-   80
manding officer on the familiar topic of bullock-carts.

The year ended with a menace of still further change.   For the
Duke of York was dying, mourned by the tearful King in the
congruous lament, " Alas ! my poor brother ! "   He had com-   81
manded the army (with a brief interruption due to the vivacious
Mrs. Clarke) since the distant days when Arthur Wesley was a

Colonel ; and his broad figure formed an unchanging part of the
architecture of the Horse Guards. He died in the first week of
1827, and the world waited for a new Commander-in-Chief.
There was one soldier with transcendent claims. But Peel
warned the Duke that his sovereign contemplated taking the
command in person. Was it not a royal hallucination that he
had charged with the heavy cavalry at Salamanca ? Besides,
the post-war exercises of the British army had been mainly
sartorial ; and the King played a splendid part in military
tailoring. Wellington received the warning with a bitter intimation that he had been promised the succession, but that he always
viewed the royal promise, "like many others, as so many empty
and unmeaning words and phrases." The fancy passed, however ; and Wellington was duly installed as Commander-in-Chief,
taking command in a General Order consisting of a single sentence.

Now there could be no moi ˙ promotion. For he had reached
the very summit of his professio... How could he rise further ?
There were still politics, of course ; in civil life he was no more
than a mere minister ; but if a vacancy occurred, could a Commander-in-Chief hope to become Prime Minister ? Croker, at
any rate, thought not ; the way, he felt, was clear for Canning
now. The vacancy occurred within a month. For the Prime
Minister collapsed in February ; and the age, the interminable
age of Liverpool was over.

6

Who was to be Prime Minister ? There was an eager scurry ;
and the Duke spoke his mind at the breakfast-table at Apsley
House. The present Government, he said, must be kept together
for everybody's sakes—"After them comes chaos." Croker
agreed, adding that it would all have been so simple if he had not
become Commander-in-Chief, but that put him out of the question
as Prime Minister.

"Yes, yes, I am in my proper place, in the place to which I
was destined by my trade. I am a soldier, and I am in my place
at the head of the army, as the Chancellor, who is a lawyer, is in
his place on the woolsack. We have each of us a trade, and are
in our proper position when we are exercising it."

This was admirable ; but who was to be Prime Minister ?
Canning felt no uncertainties : his moment had arrived. But

even Canning required colleagues ; and his Tory colleagues were
frankly hostile to the notion of a Canning administration. For,
all else apart, his Catholic opinions scared them. They scared
the Duke as well, who could not bear his methods at the Foreign
Office and confessed to Arbuthnot (who passed it on to Peel) that   *85*
he detected " much of trickery ; he sees that the sons and relations of our most vehement opponents are taken into employ ;
and he cannot divest himself of the idea that, directly or indirectly,
there has been an understanding with some of the leaders of the
Opposition." If Canning was in league with the Whigs, it was
quite impossible for the Duke to serve under him. At any rate,
he did not mean to. Four years of Canning had made him a
Tory of the strictest sect. But he played scrupulously fair ; and
when the King summoned him to Brighton, Wellington sent word
that " he had nothing to say to him, and that it would not be fair   *86*
to his colleagues that he should see the King at such a moment."
But his own opinions were developing. For the ardent Pro-   *87*
testants besieged him with suggestions that he should manœuvre
Canning out of the new Cabinet ; the Duke, however, favouring
a continuance of the *status quo*, repelled them. They even proposed that he should take the Premiership himself ; but Wellington put by the crown, though he confessed that " circumstances
might be conceived under which it would be his duty to accept
the situation if he was called upon by the King to do so." His
views inclined, however, to the substitution of Mr. Robinson as
Prime Minister ; Canning, he thought, would be content to serve
under Mr. Robinson. Canning, however, was indisposed to
become the major ornament of a Robinson administration,
suspecting that " the Protestant part of the Government wished   *88*
to have me as *cheap* as possible, to task me to the utmost for
their support in the House of Commons and in the Foreign
Office . . . but to repress all higher aspirations as strictly as if
I were of another species than their Lordships." Perhaps he was.

The tension lasted from mid-February to the second week of
April. London buzzed with rumours ; Taper and Tadpole were   *89*
on tip-toe ; and Mr. Croker lived in an ecstasy of exclusive information. But perhaps George IV enjoyed this interlude more
than any of his subjects, except when agitated Tory magnates
addressed him in the most unbecoming terms. For the King
presided over the *imbroglio* in a mood that was positively Puckish.

He had suffered much from his ministers, and it was a treat for him to keep them dangling. Once, indeed, he asked the leading characters in the official comedy to Windsor. It was an uncomfortable house-party; and when Wellington passed the whole morning with the King, Canning aged visibly. Besides, the royal mood at lunch was plainly favourable to the Duke. After lunch the customary phaetons came. The royal Puck, with perfect malice, sent the Duke for a drive with Princess Lieven, a fervent Canningite, and kept Canning at home for a talk. The drive was trying; and it was painfully significant to find on their return that the impartial King had passed the entire afternoon with Canning. But nothing came of it. For when the rival statesmen met, each asked the other if he knew anything; but their elusive sovereign, deep in his delicious game of hide-and-seek, had said precisely nothing.

Yet even royal games must end at last; and Canning's firm refusal of any compromise won the trick. No Government could live without him; and if he could not have Tory colleagues, he should bring in the Whigs. A cold exchange of letters with the Duke ensued. His Grace's sincere and faithful servant, George Canning, advised him that he had his Majesty's commands to reconstruct the administration, that it was his wish to adhere to the principles on which Lord Liverpool's had so long acted together, and that his Grace's continuance as a colleague was essential. The Duke replied with a polite enquiry of his dear Mr. Canning who was to be Prime Minister. Canning responded in a didactic vein that he had believed it to be generally understood that the person charged with the formation of a Government was apt to be Prime Minister, that this course would be followed in the present instance, and that the King approved. The letters rang like pistol-shots on a frosty morning. The Duke was winged. One shot remained, however, and he fired it. Writing in a cold fury, he expressed his inability to believe that any Government of Canning's could follow the ancient ways of Lord Liverpool's, or that anyone would ever think so, or that its policy could serve either King or country. So he resigned. His resignation of the Ordnance, which was a Cabinet office, was natural. But he declined to serve Canning as Commander-in-Chief and resigned the Horse Guards too; and for the first time in forty years the Duke was out of place.

23

III

THE Duke was out ; and gleeful caricatures depicted *Achilles in the Sulks, or the Great Captain on the Stool of Repentance*, with a figure, angry and aquiline, sitting in Apsley House and exclaiming bitterly,

> " Here for brutal courage far renowned,
> I live an idle burden to the ground.
> (*Others* in *counsel* fam'd for nobler skill
> More useful to *preserve* than *I* to *kill.*) "

Lately Commander-in-Chief and Master-General of the Ordnance, he was now a comparatively private individual, a mere Field Marshal with marked Tory leanings. Opinion was a trifle shocked, although strict Protestants nodded approval when he resigned. A file of Tory colleagues followed. For the Duke's resignation was a signal to Peel and the older Tories. He was a party-leader now ; Peel was his aide-de-camp ; and the ranged nobility awaited his commands. For he had travelled far in the eight years since he accepted office from Lord Liverpool on an express understanding that he should not be bound to go into Opposition with his colleagues. That reservation had once served to mark him as a public servant still, to distinguish him from the humbler breed of politicians. But he was a politician now ; and, like any politician, he resigned.

The Duke was out ; and the King was left almost alone with Mr. Canning and the Whigs. This was a shade alarming, since the royal conscience was firmly opposed to Catholic Emancipation, and the sovereign was left feeling " very sore at his notion of desertion by those who forced Mr. Canning on him originally." The royal irritation was expressed in a curt acceptance of the Duke's double resignation. But how could he complain ? Wellington could scarcely be expected to serve in Mr. Canning's Cabinet. That disposed of the Ordnance. Could he retain the Horse Guards ? The office of Commander-in-Chief was not political. But Wellington chose to view Canning's second letter

1

2 as " a rebuke for which I had given no provocation, and in which the authority of the King's name was very unnecessarily introduced." His honour, the last refuge of an angry statesman, was involved. Besides, there would have to be frequent consultation
3 between Prime Minister and Commander-in-Chief ; questions were bound to arise on pay, on garrisons, on the troops in Portugal; and manifestly he did not possess the Prime Minister's confidence. The fact was that his dislike of Canning was too strong for any form of official co-operation. For he was writing vehemently of
4 " this charlatan " and the " foolish, insulting and indecent manner of his behaviour to me." Yet Wellington was not the man to act impulsively from motives of merely personal distaste. He saw a larger issue, to which his quarrel with Canning was only incidental. Was not the world of 1827 full of threats to the existing order ?

5 " Rely upon it, my dear Charles, the object of the great aristocracy, and of the *parti conservateur* of this country, is to secure the Crown from the mischief with which it is threatened, by moderation, by consistency, by firmness and good temper. Matters have been brought to the state in which they are by a man (for after all there is but one man) who does not possess a particle of any one of those qualities. The aristocracy must not aid his views. They must not render perpetual the unfortunate separation between the Crown and the party to which I have above referred. I earnestly recommend, then, moderation and temper, and above all, respect for the Crown and for the person of the King."

This had the firm tone of a party-leader—of the new leader of the *parti conservateur* and its natural allies, the aristocracy.
6 For though Mrs. Arbuthnot could still describe him as "of *no party*," Wellington was now the rising hope of the stern, unbending Tories.

The spring passed in irritable explanations, while the army lived under a confused interregnum with Lord Palmerston, that hermit of the War Department, for its temporary and civilian
7 Commander-in-Chief. The Duke made a reasoned statement on his resignation in the House of Lords, which compelled the praises of Lord Ashley for its manly virtue. How could their Lordships have supposed him capable of a desire to be Prime Minister—" a station, to the duties of which I was unaccustomed,

in which I was not wished, and for which I was not qualified ;
as it must be obvious to your Lordships, that not being in the
habit of addressing your Lordships, I should have been found,
besides other qualifications, incapable of displaying, as they ought
to be displayed, or of defending the measures of government as
they ought to be defended in this House, by the person thus
honoured by his Majesty's confidence ?   My Lords, I should have
been worse than mad if I had thought of such a thing." This
was putting it a trifle high.   Besides, his disclaimer gave awkward
hostages to the enemy if an opportunity of office should recur.
(" *En politique*," as a judicious Emperor remarked to an impulsive
politician, " *il ne faut point dire ' Jamais.' *")   But statesmen
are frequently carried away by their own abnegation, when they
disclaim their own ambitions.   There was an awkward inter-   8
change of correspondence with Canning, discontinued by the latter
from an anxiety (which seemed a shade belated) that it might not
" degenerate into controversy."   The King, a little nervous now,
intimated that the command of the new army was still open ; but
the Duke's frowns persisted.   His brother William was the bearer   9
of a furtive invitation (promptly disavowed to Canning by the
courageous monarch) to call at Windsor.   The Duke went at
duty's summons ; and London buzzed again.   The irrepressible
Creevey met him one afternoon coming out of Arbuthnot's front-   10
door in Parliament Street and promptly buttonholed him with
" Curious times these, Duke."   The Duke agreed, put his arm
through the inquisitive Whig's, swung him right round, and
marched him off towards the House of Lords.   He sent a civil
message through Creevey to Lord Grey and spoke with heat of
Canning, stopping at intervals to emphasise his points and very
nearly pulling the button off Creevey's coat in the process.   No
one, he said, could act with Canning ; and his temper was quite
sure to blow him up.   Others noticed it as well that summer, a
sharp American observer recording that " Mr. Canning's temper   11
has become most uncertain."   Canning, it seemed, was growing
odd ; office had broken stronger men ; and the Duke watched
him with genuine concern.   One evening the Prime Minister bore
down upon the American ambassador with an unprovoked tirade
against the aristocracy ; and Wellington drew up a chair between
Gallatin and Humboldt, looked anxious, and asked suddenly if
they found anything odd in Mr. Canning's manner.   He had seen

such things before ; could it be possible that Canning might be going the same way as Castlereagh ? While the Duke looked on,
12 he did not play an active part in Parliament, though he spoke once or twice on the Corn Bill with a clear repudiation of " any feeling of party or of faction, or of the least desire to embarrass His Majesty's Government." For he had not learnt—perhaps he never mastered—the ways of Opposition. He had served the State far too long to distinguish readily between Opposition and sedition. He might resign : that was permissible. But the Duke could rarely bring himself to oppose a Government, even if it was Mr. Canning's.

The House rose in July ; and the Prime Minister was far from well. He had never managed to throw off a cold contracted at the Duke of York's funeral in the previous winter, when they were all kept standing on cold pavements ; he had persuaded Eldon to stand on the Lord Chancellor's cocked-hat and written gaily to the
13 Duke that " Mr. Mash, or whoever filched the cloth or the matting from under our feet in the aisle, had bets or insurances against the lives of the Cabinet." He had been ailing all the summer ; and now the bet was almost won. For ' it was a rich, warm night at the beginning of August, when a gentleman enveloped in a cloak, for he was in evening dress, emerged from a club-house at the top of St. James' Street, and descended that celebrated eminence.' He paused, as readers of *Endymion* know, to impart the news that Mr. Canning was *in extremis*. That brief reign was over now ; it had lasted for three months. Strange how the Duke's customary allowance of power to his opponents was a Hundred Days.
14 His epitaph on Canning was laconic—" I hear that Dr. Farr says that it was Canning's temper that killed him." This was
15 unkind ; but he spoke kindly of him in company, admiring his rare gifts of speech and writing and the patience with which Canning had permitted him to " cut and hack " his drafts. But he deplored the ungovernable rages with which he often greeted differences in council ; and Canning impressed him as " one of the idlest of men." For industry of the Duke's order often suspects more rapid methods. Idle or not, Canning was gone ; and the King was left to find a new Prime Minister. There was a flutter among the expectant Tories. Would the Duke be sent for ? He was not ; for by a pleasing irony the King, averse to further changes and dreading the humiliation of a summons to the evicted

Tories, summoned the shadowy presence of Mr. Robinson, now ennobled as Lord Goderich, to keep Canning's Government together. That 'transient and embarrassed phantom' reigned *16* without distinction and with a growing personal discomfort, until he vanished like an uneasy spirit at cockcrow. To steer a course with a mixed crew of Whigs and Tory Canningites might have tasked stronger nerves than his ; and his nerves were anything but strong. A later age views nervous ailments with an indulgent eye. But to the full-blooded world of 1827 an intermittently lachrymose Prime Minister was merely comic. Lord Goderich whimpered through five months of office ; and when he made his final exit behind a borrowed royal handkerchief, a heartless world guffawed. Not much had been accomplished, though Wellington had been induced to resume his post as Commander-in-Chief. He took com- *17* mand "as of an Army in the Field" without political considera- tions, although his action was submitted for approval to his Tory *18* friends ; for the Duke felt his new position as a party-leader with responsibilities towards his political associates.

The reign of Goderich was a conscious interlude ; and Welling- ton watched from his Tory fastness. One day before the summer ended he strolled in to the 'Social Day' of a new sculptor's *19* exhibition. A respectful circle in the gallery marked the majestic presence of Mrs. Siddons in tow of an Academician. The Duke's air was less sublime ; Haydon, indeed, was positively disap- pointed and "never saw one whose air and presence were so unlike genius or heroism." But, thanks to the Elgin Marbles, Haydon's standards of the heroic were unduly elevated. He thought that Wellington "seemed embarrassed, and as if he felt he was un- popular." That was quite possible in a year in which he had endured distinct rebuffs. But he was not too embarrassed to admire the sculpture, stepping to the order-book and inscribing himself for a *Milo* and a *Samson*. One of the artist's friends came up to thank him. "He should go abroad," said the clear military voice. This sentence of exile sounding a little unpropitious, he added hastily, "Not to stay, but to see—eh—the—eh—great works as others have done." Then he wheeled briskly round, lifted a martial finger to his hat, and left the gallery, his duty to the arts accomplished. In the autumn he paid a round of visits in the north, and was triumphantly received, even Grey recording *20* that his "course has been one continued scene of rejoicing." The cheers melted his diffidence. He was a coming man once more, though he shot worse than ever. They were all at Stratfield 21 Saye ; the Duchess was unwell and kept her room, where Mrs. Arbuthnot bore with fortitude the tedium of her conversation. Downstairs Alava told his stories and Lady Jersey aired her charms, while the gentlemen expressed their sympathies with Turkey at the outrageous violence of Navarino. The Duke was in the grip of one of his tremendous colds ; the subject of catarrh 22 appeared to fascinate him, and he was apt to send detailed directions for its treatment to his relations, confiding sovereign remedies to diplomatic bags. They had lent Apsley House to the 23 Shelleys ; and poor Kitty wrote from Stratfield Saye begging Lady Shelley to stay on in London, adding, " I hope you like my Douro upon further acquaintance I Is he not the living image of his father ? " For she was still devoted to her alarming Duke.

Then he was back in London, while Lord Goderich, a tearful 24 Sisyphus, administered his country. Wellington's infrequent sense of family loyalty impelled him to press his brother Henry's claims to a peerage ; Henry's ambition was to figure as Lord Cowley, if that spelling of their former name was correct, although he had " a decided aversion to the name of Colley." His wish was gratified, and Lord Cowley joined the Duke, Lord Wellesley, and Lord Maryborough in the family peerage ; for with the sole exception of Gerald, who was in the Church, they were all peers now. The weeks went by ; Lord Goderich's outcries became more audible ; and as his tears flowed faster, he resigned.

The question, the eternal question which had haunted 1827, was raised again in the first week of 1828. Who was to be Prime 25 Minister ? There had been a notion of Lord Harrowby ; but he refused. Richard was even spoken of. But the King knew his own mind at last ; for nine months of keeping company with Whigs had roused his sleeping fervour for the Reformation, and he was now an ardent Protestant. That meant a Tory Government ; a Tory Government meant Wellington ; and the Duke 26 was sent for. His audience was highly unusual ; for the King was ill. A cheerful voice, owned by an unbecoming figure in a dirty silk jacket, exclaimed from the recesses of a royal bed, " Arthur, the Cabinet is defunct." The royal head was crowned by a singularly greasy turban ; and royal art proceeded to enliven the occasion with a perfect rendering of the deportment of his

late ministers.   His visitor was then requested to form a Govern-   27
ment upon the understanding that Catholic Emancipation should
form no part of Cabinet policy.   The Duke was guarded.   In
view of his position as Commander-in-Chief, he must consult his
friends.   He asked for time, but went so far as to elicit royal
wishes for and against individuals.   The King had no objections
except to Lord Grey ; the Government, he thought, should be
composed of persons of both opinions upon the Catholic question ;
and he repeated frequently that he desired nothing more than a
strong Government.   The Duke returned to town and sent for
Peel—Peel was his second-in-command—and he would speak to
nobody till Peel had been consulted.   Peel's advice was plain.
Their course, he felt, would be anything but simple, since the
Tories had been split by Canning and the tide of Catholic Emanci-   28
pation was rising.   But he was content to serve under Wellington
in a reunited Tory administration, and was decidedly of opinion
that the Duke should be Prime Minister.   Canning had once
objected to " the union of the whole power of the State, civil and   29
military, in the same hands " as being " a station too great for
any subject, however eminent, or however meritorious, and one
incompatible with the practice of a free constitution."   The Duke
himself had termed it madness.   But his view was changed.   He
could do better than Goderich.   Besides, the Tories looked to
him ; the King was quite subdued ; and was it not his duty to
accept public situations ?   So the Duke, at fifty-eight, became
Prime Minister.

> *The man of the age is clearly the Duke, the saviour of Europe, in the perfection of manhood, and with an iron constitution.*—ENDYMION.

I

HE was to govern England now ; and an expectant world took his success for granted. Wellington had never failed ; his long career had been a mere procession of success ; and what civilian task could find him wanting ? After all, he was no stranger to administration. Eight years in the Cabinet were a respectable apprenticeship ; he had once governed Ireland, to say nothing of his administrative experience in Portugal, Mysore, and France. Diplomacy could hold no mysteries for him, since he had attended Congresses with Castlereagh, conferred with kings and emperors on equal terms, and corresponded with half the Continent. It was an adequate equipment ; and the world was not in the least

1 surprised that, in *Endymion's* phrase, ' England should be ruled by the most eminent man of the age, and the most illustrious of her citizens.'

The task was formidable, though. The auguries were good—

2 ' the conviction that the Duke's government would only cease with the termination of his public career was so general, that, the moment he was installed in office, the Whigs smiled on him ; political conciliation became the slang of the day, and the fusion of parties the babble of clubs and the tattle of boudoirs.' But the task was formidable. Could he perform the duties of Prime Minister ? Pure administration had no terrors, since he knew his mind, could take decisions, and always answered letters. A slightly excessive sense of detail might, perhaps, encumber him. Soldiers are bred to detail, since there is nothing in the world (as Napoleon III once wrote to a War Minister) with so much detail about it as an army ; and the Duke's passion for exactitude was sometimes lost among *minutiæ*, as when he accompanied an offer to keep an appointment in Westminster Hall with the somewhat

3 exaggerated caution that " it will take me a quarter of an hour to go from the Ordnance to Westminster Hall ; and as much for the Man who is to go for me." He could face all the paper-work, since Wellington had been writing State papers for as long as his countrymen could remember. There would be public speaking

to be done, of course, and he was not a speaker. But the House of Lords must put up with his plain manner of debating, once described by Walter Scott as " slicing the argument into two or three parts and helping himself to the best." That would suffice ; for the world did not expect him to give performances like Mr. Canning's. His colleagues could do all the talking. But could he manage them ? That was, perhaps, more doubtful, since he was accustomed to the simple compliance of a staff ; and a staff is not a Cabinet. Staff officers can be trusted not to resign at awkward moments. But Cabinets require arts of management that are wholly unfamiliar to commanders in the field. Generals of division act upon instructions ; the Quartermaster-General is rarely troubled by his conscience in performing simple departmental duties ; but would Secretaries of State be equally reliable ? As he complained later, " One man wants one thing and one another ; they agree to what I say in the morning, and then in the evening up they start with some crotchet which deranges the whole plan. I have not been used to that in all the early part of my life. I have been accustomed to carry on things in quite a different manner : I assembled my officers and laid down my plan, and it was carried into effect without any more words."

But Cabinets work upon different lines. For Cabinets consist of colleagues; and the Duke was more accustomed to subordinates. Would he be happy as the head of such a republic ? There was his party, too. A lifetime in the field had trained him to expect obedience in the ranks ; they were not called on to concur, but merely to obey ; and he applied the same simple canons of duty to his political followers. " The party ! " he exclaimed with irritable emphasis. " What is the meaning of a party if they don't follow their leaders ? Damn 'em ! let 'em go ! " And it is hardly to be wondered at that they occasionally went. For even party men have been known to require something more than to be led.

These were the limitations of his splendid equipment for civilian office. Mechanically perfect, he was defective in the minor arts of persuasion. The defect was inherent in his nature and aggravated by his training. For he was anything but pliant ; and there had been no need for him to persuade anyone at Headquarters. If *Endymion's* glowing forecast of ' a dictatorship of patriotism ' was correct, all would be well. Few men were better qualified to be dictator. But if dictation failed, if a need arose to persuade colleagues or fellow-citizens that he was in the right, his prospects of success were questionable. He might, perhaps, succeed so long as operations were confined to the familiar political *terrain* over which he had manœuvred with Lord Liverpool and Mr. Canning. So long as politics remained a highly complicated game played by well-connected persons within the limits of the Parliamentary board, he played with tolerable skill. But when the board was suddenly enlarged and new pieces with strange moves appeared upon it, he was baffled. This was not politics as he had learnt them. For politics according to the rules were a genteel affair in which residents in Mayfair governed England by the simple process of making speeches to one another in Westminster. That was the old *terrain*, on which he could manœuvre with fair proficiency. But now the ground was unfamiliar ; Westminster had ceased to be the sole battlefield of politics, and operations were in progress all over England ; strange, unauthorised belligerents had elbowed the recognised players into corners ; and where once the game of politics had turned upon the evolutions of competing groups, it now depended on the incalculable appetites of crowds. The Duke was never at his best with crowds ; he had no taste for them, whether they cheered or hooted him ; besides, the best years of his life had been devoted to obstructing their desires. For a Chief Secretary learns to be indifferent to Irish crowds ; and the long war against the French was little more than an attempt to discipline the Paris mob. He had learnt a deep distaste for democracy in the dark, tumultuous years when murder was its leading argument and Thistlewood its chief apostle ; and if crowds were to be the arbiters of politics, the Duke would stand his ground. He was a shade bewildered, as he faced the new attack. There was no precedent (outside the unpleasing precedents of France) for politics on such a scale. For this was something wholly different from the orderly manœuvres of political parties. The rules of war were openly defied, and the *terrain* had been transformed out of all recognition. It seemed to have no limits now ; and where were the familiar mountain-ranges, which had once prescribed the course of operations ? He could not have been more at sea, if fate had suddenly transferred Headquarters from the Lines of Torres Vedras, where he could foresee with precision the direction

of the next French offensive, to Nelson's quarter-deck surrounded
by a shifting element and exposed to attack from every point of
the compass.

But the Duke stood his ground. Indeed, resistance was his
main conception of a statesman's duty. Not that his mind was
purely negative. But he had not been the chosen swordsman of
the *ancien régime* for nothing. What had he fought the French
for, if not to check the tide of change ? He had resisted change
at Busaco and Salamanca and Waterloo ; and it was too much
to hope that he would welcome it in England. He had lived half
a lifetime with the sound of the French guns in his ears ; he was
the saviour of Europe ; and was it reasonable to expect him to
applaud the principles from which he had saved it ? His country
must be saved again. The need to save it from the French had
passed ; but there were still the Whigs. For those misguided men
were on the path which led direct to the French Revolution ;
and it was vital at all costs to bar them out of office. So early
as 1821 he had urged Liverpool to pocket his official pride for the
compelling reason that the dread alternative was to " give up the   7
government to the Whigs and Radicals, or, in other words, the
country in all its relations to irretrievable ruin " ; in 1827, when
Liverpool collapsed and the Tory dams began to break, he had
told Croker that " after them comes chaos " ; and now the   8
Whigs were at the gates.

How to exclude them ? He was too intelligent to oppose a
front of mere negation. That was the Tory system ; but the
Duke was more than a mere ' pig-tail ' Tory. A master of
defensive strategy, he was well aware that at a certain stage
resistance becomes dangerous to the defenders. It had never
been his habit to defend positions after they had become inde-
fensible. That was the moment for a neat withdrawal to his
next position. When he commanded the last army of England
in the Peninsula, he stood to fight at Busaco, fell back to Torres
Vedras, and stood to fight again ; and he proposed to execute
the same manœuvre in defence of social order. He always said
that the best test of a great general was " to know when to   9
retreat, and to dare to do it " ; and statesmen might do worse
than learn the lesson. It would be madness to risk the safety of
the constitution in an affair of outposts ; that had always been
poor Craufurd's weakness, and the Duke found Tory braves

almost as uncontrollable. But they must choose their ground with care, defend a strong position as long as it could be defended, and then, if circumstances unfortunately turned it, fall back to the next. For a judicious strategy of retreat might, if persisted in, keep the Whigs perpetually in Opposition and save the State. That was his design. It would require a mobile force for its successful execution ; and his Cabinet, the Tory party, and the King were anything but mobile. Politicians had an awkward weakness for consistency, which inclined them to defend positions long after a retreat had become imperative ; and the King was now afflicted with an exceptionally trying conscience upon religious questions. But the Duke took command. He had led highly miscellaneous armies in his time ; and in 1828 he led another.

II

His methods of recruitment were simple but effective. All the
week he sat in Apsley House with Arbuthnot at his elbow inter-
viewing candidates for office and writing briefly to likely recruits.
Croker found him one day in the later stages, when his patience
was wearing a little thin. The Duke compared himself to a dog
with a can tied to its tail and pointed irritably to a formidable
mountain of red boxes and green bags. " There," he explained,
" is the business of the country, which I have not time to look at
—all my time being employed in assuaging what gentlemen call
their feelings." This was a novelty ; staff officers had had no
feelings. But politicians were less reasonable ; and he assumed
with evident distaste the unfamiliar task of persuading these
unmanageable creatures. His object was to repair the damage
done by Mr. Canning, to reunite the Tory party by retaining
Canning's misguided followers in a Tory administration. They
gave him endless trouble, since Mr. Huskisson, who led the little
group, was full of stipulations. First there were his leanings
towards fiscal freedom. Then, if he was to stay at the Colonial
Office, Lamb must remain Chief Secretary ; that would be a
guarantee that strict neutrality would be observed upon the
Catholic question. The cheerful Palmerston must be promoted
to the Cabinet. And was the Duke prepared to apply the principles of Mr. Canning in foreign affairs ? His recent treaty about
Greece went further than the Duke's Protocol of 1826. But
Wellington satisfied their scruples by declaring that " the King's
treaties must be observed " and appointing one of the group to
the Foreign Office. The Canningites were duly enlisted ; but
their inclusion involved sacrifices. For Tories of the older school
were dropped in order to make room for them ; but as he banished
them, Wellington wrote ruefully that " the King's service must
be carried on." He was less tender with the normal appetites
which beset Prime Ministers, informing one persistent applicant
for a peerage that as there had been twenty-six creations in the
last two years, it was his duty " to discourage and protest against

any more being created unless some public service of magnitude
or public emergency should require it. If this duty is not performed, either the House of Lords will become a democratic body
and a nuisance, or contemptible and useless. In either case the
constitution of the country will be overturned." Few party-
leaders can afford to tell their followers that the House of Lords
will be unduly adulterated by their ennoblement ; but the Duke
was never a master of the soft answer. He was prepared to
govern England and, for that purpose, to enlist a Government ;
but minor arts of management were far beyond him, and he totally
disdained the latest mode of popular conciliation. Canning had
always shown a weakness for the Press ; but the Duke was
frankly hostile. Journalists, in his experience, existed for the
propagation of falsehoods ; and he asked helplessly, " What can
we do with these sort of fellows ? We have no power over them,
and, for my part, I will have no communication with any of them."

The voyage opened with a further sacrifice. Pressure was put
on the Prime Minister to resign the office of Commander-in-Chief,
and he reluctantly acceded. Work crowded on him ; as he wrote
grimly to an apologetic correspondent, " If you were to see the
number of plans which I receive every day upon every description
of subject, all of which I am obliged to peruse, you would admit
there was no necessity for having any scruple about sending me
your plan for diminishing the pay of the army." Stray callers
were occasionally informed a shade ungraciously by letter that
the Prime Minister, having learnt the object of their unsuccessful
visit, did not regret not having seen them and must be acquitted,
never having heard of them, of any disrespect. But Creevey
found him " rising most rapidly in the market as a practical man
of business. All the deputations come away charmed with him.
But woe to them that are too late ! He is punctual to a second
himself, and waits for no man." He found little pleasure in his
situation, writing to the Prince of Orange that he was involved in
duties for which he was " not qualified, and they are very disagreeable to me " ; but he added in a more cheerful tone that
the Government was an unqualified success.

" There is in fact but little, if any, opposition to it. This state
of things cannot last, I know. But as the whole of the landed and
great commercial and monied interests of the country are decidedly
with us, I hope that, if the existing state of tranquillity in this

24

country should terminate, we shall remain still with a strong
government.

" Your Royal Highness would scarcely recognise England again
if you were now to come here. There is no party remaining. The
ladies and the youth of the country in particular are with us, and I
could almost count upon my fingers those who are hostile to the
government."

This was a glowing picture. But though beauty smiled upon the
Government, his colleagues did not always smile on one another.
The Canningites were fretful from the first ; groups of bereaved
politicians attached to statesmen recently deceased are rarely
enlivening companions. He was prepared to make concessions
about Corn ; but they found him unhelpful towards Greece.
This was embarrassing, since Greek independence was prominent
in the political testament of Mr. Canning ; Wellington had
assured the House of Lords that he must claim " the right of not   12
being included in the number of Mr. Canning's enemies," and introduced a Bill pensioning his family. But it was more questionable how far the Duke could be regarded as Mr. Canning's intellectual heir, since he displayed a strong distaste for the Greek
legacy. For Mr. Canning, they felt sure, would never have termed
Navarino an " untoward event " in the King's Speech. The
watchful Palmerston diagnosed strong anti-Russian leanings,   13
which he was inclined to attribute to the Duke's past encounters
with the Lievens and some imagined slight at St. Petersburg ;
besides, the energetic Dorothea was unpopular with Lady Jersey
and Mrs. Arbuthnot, the twin stars of the Duke's firmament.
There were endless Cabinets on Greece with " much discussion   14
and entire difference of opinion." Spring turned to summer, and
they continued uncomfortably " differing upon almost every
question . . . meeting to debate and dispute, and separating
without deciding." For the leaven of Mr. Canning's principles
was having difficulty with the Tory lump. His followers grew
still more restive. The Duke found them uneasy bedfellows,
confessing to Arbuthnot that he regretted their inclusion, and   15
complaining of " the manner in which the *four* hang together " to
Ellenborough, who confirmed his view with an unpleasing pano-
rama of the Canningite revolt—Palmerston " always *pecking*,"
Grant " obstinate and useless," and the innocuous Dudley incited
to rebellion by the more active Huskisson. Huskisson was

16 always trying ; Lord Palmerston was bad enough—the exasperated Prime Minister had once termed him a mutineer ; but
Huskisson was quite unbearable. Persons who believe themselves
possessed of an economic gospel are frequently distinguished by
an offensive air of conscious superiority. Besides, he was the
leader of the little group ; and as the vicar of Mr. Canning upon
earth he could scarcely hope to engage the Duke's affections.

Relief came from an unexpected quarter, as the long shadow
of Reform fell across the scene. That rock was, to all appearances,
one of the few on which the Cabinet was unlikely to split. For
Mr. Canning had opposed Reform ; the Duke was no Reformer ;
and, however they might disagree upon Corn, Portugal, and
Greece, they might reasonably be expected to maintain a united
front upon Reform. Indeed, the problem of Reform itself
appeared to be in a fair way towards solution by simpler methods
in the best English manner, since they were extremely practical
and quite devoid of logic. Thorough-paced Reformers argued
that the whole system of representation stood in need of drastic
overhaul ; but reasonable men, unwilling to admit the need, met
it unobtrusively. For as the more outrageous boroughs disqualified themselves by electoral misdeeds, their members were
inconspicuously transferred to the new industrial towns, a
practical device which robbed Reformers of their grievance whilst
enabling Tories to admire the incomparable outline of the existing
constitution. In the spring of 1828 East Retford was available
for redistribution, and the inheritance was disputed between
industry and agriculture ; for the Whigs wished to transfer its
member to Birmingham, while Tory ministers preferred to add
17 him to the county members. The matter was discussed in
Cabinet, where Huskisson regarded himself as committed by a
previous utterance to the Opposition view, and it appeared to be
agreed to leave it as an open question. Accordingly (not without
pressure from the enterprising Palmerston) he voted with the
Opposition. That night, seized with a pardonable scruple after
18 voting against his colleagues, Huskisson wrote to the Duke
offering his resignation and expecting that the offer would be
gracefully refused. But the Duke thought otherwise. Fine
shades were never to his taste ; and it was quite beyond him that
there were degrees of resignation. If a gentleman resigned,
Wellington assumed that he meant it. Besides, a resignation

from Huskisson was too good to be overlooked. Marmont had once exposed a flank to him at Salamanca ; and now Huskisson had done the same, and with similar results. For the Duke positively swooped.

After a decent interval he hurried to the King ; and the startled Huskisson, expecting to be pressed to stay, received instead a curt intimation that the sovereign had been made aware of his intentions. There was a flutter among the Canningites. Lord Dudley saw the Duke, who was blandly *19* unaware that there could be any mistake. Palmerston pursued him to the House of Lords and had half an hour's conversation. They paced up and down the Long Gallery, as Palmerston un-folded Huskisson's slightly involved apologia and Wellington stared at the ground. But the Duke insisted that the letter meant what it said ; that Peel had thought the same ; that this had been coming for some time ; and that such behaviour would soon bring him into as much discredit as Lord Goderich. Besides, he could not go upon all-fours to Mr. Huskisson and ask him to remain. (That was his ruling thought : if Canningites chose to resign, why should the Duke prevent them ?) Lord Palmerston was still plying him with arguments ; and when he intimated that he should feel bound to go out with Huskisson, the Duke raised his eyes, looked sharply at him, and resumed their walk. But they reached no conclusion.

Then Palmerston returned to his colleague ; and they con-cocted a second letter to the Duke, endeavouring to make him *20* responsible if Huskisson left office. A brief reply from Apsley House informed them that it was better to lose Huskisson than to submit to the humiliation of begging him to stay. For the Duke's *amour propre* was stirred. As he said afterwards, " I told Dudley and Palmerston that I had no objection, *21* nay, I wished, that they and Huskisson could get out of the scrape, but that I begged on my own part to decline taking a roll in the mud with them. This was not a very elegant expres-sion, but it was a sincere one." The *imbroglio* dragged on to an accompaniment of protracted explanations. But Wellington could not escape from his initial belief that a man must be taken to mean what he said. There was no difference of principle— *22* " There is not the idea of a principle in all these papers. . . . We hear a great deal of Whig principles, and Tory principles, and

Liberal principles, and Mr. Canning's principles ; but I confess that I have never seen a definition of any of them, and cannot make to myself a clear idea of what any of them mean." Political ideas were wholly irrelevant ; the simple point was that Huskisson had providentially resigned, and the Duke meant to hold him to it.

He was victorious, although the victory gave him a little trouble ; and in the middle of it all he had to dine at the Mansion House. A colleague found him looking " ill, and as if he had been annoyed ; but he was quite in good spirits with his reception, *elated.*" He rather enjoyed the duel and was quite determined not to submit to Huskisson ; as for Palmerston, he " did not choose to fire great guns at sparrows " ; and, to Ellenborough's eye, he was " completely roused, and seems to feel as he did at Waterloo." In the last days of May silence descended on the field ; the Canningites resigned ; and *Endymion's* lovely mother heard a Tory hostess exclaim in triumph, " They are all four out. . . . The only mistake was ever to have admitted them. I think now we have got rid of Liberalism for ever." It was a sweeping forecast.

III

His forces had begun to shrink. For the little group had been his Light Division, whose agility would have been of value if he desired to manœuvre towards the Left. Henceforward he was left with a residue of solid Tories, whose inclinations lay all towards the Right. The Canningites were gone, each to his destiny—for Palmerston a drift towards the Whigs, the Foreign Office, and a reign (nearly thirty years away) over Victorian England; for Lamb his father's coronet and the unaccustomed exercise of Melbourne's endless conversations with a schoolgirl Queen; and for Huskisson the fatal locomotive. Their simultaneous departure left the Duke undismayed. He was not sorry to be rid of them. Their presence had endangered Cabinet discipline; and in replacing them he took steps to remedy the defect. For two of the vacancies were filled by military men. Sir George Murray, a Peninsular veteran, went to the Colonial Office in succession to the fretful Huskisson; and Sir Henry Hardinge, who had been his *liaison* officer with Blücher, replaced Lord Palmerston. The Prime Minister found the change congenial, as his late Quartermaster-General was unlikely to waste valuable time in unnecessary disputation, though the Opposition found derisive things to say about a " military and aide-de-campish " Government; and when a minister said that their minds were a blank sheet upon some question, a House of Commons wit remarked that it must be cartridge-paper.[1]

But their prestige was unimpaired. For there was no effective Opposition; and the Duke exasperated Princess Lieven by saying, " I am the most popular Minister that England has ever seen; take my word for it, I am very strong."[2] It was not like him to be boastful; but when he saw Dorothea, he seemed to harp upon his popularity. She was a sounding-board; and it was just as well for St. Petersburg to understand that Wellington was firmly seated in office. For his policy had a distinctly anti-Russian flavour; and the Russians would be more respectful if they realised that his reign was more than a passing episode of politics.

3   He reigned securely now. His brother Henry, to whom he was
unlikely to exaggerate, was informed that " we are going on well
here. The government is very popular ; and indeed there is but
4   little opposition." His Chancellor found him an admirable man
of business, and Aberdeen, the new Foreign Secretary, worked
5   under his direction ; ' for almost every despatch of the following
years there is a draft memorandum, preserved in Wellington's
correspondence, and often embodied with just the necessary
diplomatic wrappings from which his own peculiar telegraphic
style was so refreshingly free.' Foreign affairs were a shade
trying, as he found the legacies of Canning's policy distinctly
embarrassing. Russia was at war with Turkey in spite of all his
efforts; the French were straining at the leash ; and the territorial
claims of Greece were growing every day. The Eastern Question
had passed momentarily beyond control ; and the Duke was
limited by circumstances to a glum acquiescence in the inevitable.
In Portugal he was compelled to witness the exact reverse of what
Mr. Canning had intended. The Portuguese declined to rally
to the constitution in defence of which Canning had struck his
splendid attitude. For the British standard had been duly
planted on the heights of Lisbon ; but no one seemed to mind.
This was a shade humiliating. Indeed, a flavour of humiliation
seemed to infect foreign affairs, as the rather ruffled birds of
Mr. Canning's policy came home to roost. But Mr. Canning, *felix
opportunitate mortis*, was not there to smooth them ; and it was
left to Wellington to put the best face upon a series of unpleasing
situations.

His hands were full that summer, and his friends found him
6   looking white and overworked. His days were arduous—the
Treasury at noon, business till five, and then the House of Lords,
followed by a dull dinner and more papers until bed. Even when
7   he dined with Mrs. Arbuthnot, " poor fellow ! the moment he
had some coffee he sat down and read, and wrote papers till past
twelve o'clock at night ! I told him he would soon have no eyes
left." But he got away to Cheltenham, when the House rose,
and recuperated in those decorous alleys. He sipped his water
every morning early and strolled in the Montpellier Gardens.
8   Each afternoon he took his bath ; this relaxation lasted an hour,
and he mitigated the tedium with an armful of newspapers.
(Always the White Knight, he had a frame put across the bath

to support his paper, thus solving a problem that has often baffled
meaner intellects.) The summer passed ; and the autumn Cabinets
came round with his autumn colds, though Mrs. Arbuthnot found
that he was " wonderfully improved by Cheltenham, has got a   *9*
brown, healthy colour, and seems to have got his head and
stomach quite right " ; and he was well enough to wing a keeper
of Lord Hertford's. They were still busy with the Eastern
Question ; and William, Duke of Clarence, afforded occasional
diversion by his vagaries as Lord High Admiral. For this
elderly eccentric, flown (as royal personages sometimes are) by
a titular dignity, endangered naval discipline by irregular exercises of authority. He was a royal duke and, what was more, the
next King of England ; but Wellington had faced more formidable foes and checked him with such firmness that his future
sovereign resigned.   Indeed, he simultaneously refused a favour
asked by the Duchess of Kent, now Queen-mother presumptive,   *10*
who was anxious to instal Sir John Conroy in an Ordnance job.
For Wellington was rarely prone to seek royal smiles.

The Prime Minister drafted indefatigably on every subject ;
as Dorothea Lieven bitterly observed, he was " the universal
man." His pen was busy with the problems of both hemispheres   *11*
—with the next war in North America, with the Persian Gulf
(where Bagdad and Persia should, he felt, be strengthened as out-   *12*
works of India against Russian aggression), with an offensive
classical quotation by which a legal luminary had once annoyed
the King, with a fantastic allegation in *The Times* that he was
selling gunpowder to Russia, and the vast burden of a correspondence affording him " the advantage which I possess in the
proffered assistance of nearly every gentleman in England, who
has nothing to do but to amuse himself, and is tired of his usual
amusements, and of reading the newspapers." The indomitable
Haydon, in the thick of " Eucles arriving with the news of
Marathon," wrote asking leave to dedicate a pamphlet upon
State encouragement of the nobler forms of art, and received a
prompt refusal " in his own immortal hand." A more detailed
proposal for the embellishment of the House of Lords with scenes
illustrative of constitutional principles alternating with portraits
of King Alfred, Bacon, Nelson, and the Duke failed to excite him,
since he responded with a bare acknowledgment and left Haydon
with a suspicion that he was " innately modest." Haydon, quite

undeterred, sent him a copy of his pamphlet (duly acknowledged), and proposed a public grant of £4,000 for historical paintings. The Duke's attitude was highly unpromising ; for he first asked for details and, when he got them, objected that the scheme was not officially before him and that, in any case, he was opposed " to the grant of any public money for the object." He read

13 everything and wrote voluminously ; even Marie Louise received a civil message from the Duke condoling with her on the illness of Count Neipperg (her first husband's death at St. Helena had caused him less concern) ; and, to make all things worse, his

14 London house was full of workmen. For they were reconstructing Apsley House upon a more majestic scale ; and in the midst of the confusion the Duke's mind was busy with the Catholics.

The problem had been looming for a generation, ever since Mr. Pitt fell back defeated by the conscience of George III. That was a formidable fortress ; and until it fell, the road to Catholic Emancipation was effectually blocked. Time had removed it now. But, strange to record, the royal conscience was inherited by George IV ; and those rococo battlements still barred the way. Would the Duke succeed where Pitt had failed ? It was not certain that he would make the attempt, since he had little taste for superfluous reforms ; though Creevey wrote at the very outset

15 of his term of office that " my sincere opinion is—and I beg to record it thus early—that the Beau *will* do something for the Catholics of Ireland." He knew his Beau ; the Beau knew his Ireland ; and if Catholic Emancipation became a practical necessity, he was quite capable of acting. The obstacles were grave, since the royal conscience and the Tory faith were equally opposed to it. But could Wellington be seriously asked to respect the scruples of a king who fished all day at Virginia

16 Water and came to Council meetings in a blue surtout covered with gold frogs in order to exchange racing tips with Greville behind a royal hand ? If he did not respect the royal person, he was unlikely to respect the royal scruples. The Tories were a graver obstacle, since the Government had been formed upon an express

17 understanding that " the Roman Catholic question should be considered as one not to be brought forward by the Cabinet." But troops embarked for one objective had very frequently been transferred to another ; after all, he had begun the war in the Peninsula (and won Vimeiro) with a force designed to operate in

Venezuela. The only doubt was how far his present command
would be capable of this manœuvre. The Tory mind was not
adaptable ; besides, there was the Tory past upon the Catholic
question. But the last thing that the Duke thought of was his
army's mind ; they were not asked to have one ; he did not invite the rank and file to make his plans ; that was his duty.
It might be awkward for them to have to contradict their former
speeches ; civilian politicians were apt to over-value consistency.
But a retreat was sometimes the soundest strategy ; he knew the
value of a well-timed retreat ; and if the situation called for one,
they must abandon the position.

His mind was quickened by the events of 1828. The air was
full of toleration. For the Whigs secured relief for Dissenters by
the repeal of the Test and Corporation Acts. The Duke had little
taste for Nonconformists ; Methodist conventicles in the Peninsula had evoked the slightly grudging comment that " the meeting   *18*
of soldiers in their cantonments to sing psalms, or to hear a sermon
read by one of their comrades is, in the abstract, perfectly innocent." But when the House of Commons chose to emancipate
them, he urged the Lords to concur, though his mind was still   *19*
adverse to the Catholic claims. That was in April. Events
moved swiftly in the summer, since the House of Commons positively carried a motion in favour of Catholic Emancipation by six
votes, and an Irish by-election resulted in the impressive march
of regimented voters headed by their parish priests to return a
Catholic for County Clare. O'Connell, though ineligible, was
elected ; and the Catholic claims became an urgent problem, if
Ireland was to be governed. Wellington spoke on the question in   *20*
June. His tone was guarded, and his sympathies were carefully
extended to both sides. Disclaiming all doctrinal objections, he
proclaimed the issue " to be a question entirely of expediency,"
an intimation with which politicians frequently preface a change
of front. He concentrated on the practical difficulties of devising
a *Concordat*, and hinted that something might be managed, if only
an arrangement could be found whereby " the King shall have
the power to control the appointment of the hierarchy, and their
intercourse with the See of Rome, and which shall connect the
Roman Catholic Church in Ireland with the Government." His
peroration was a *staccato* plea for calm reflection :

   " If the public mind was suffered to rest ; if the agitators of

Ireland would only be quiet ; if the difficulties of this question were not aggravated by these perpetual discussions ; and if men could have time to reflect upon the state of this question, they might become more satisfied, and it might then become more possible to discover the means of doing something."

So Mr. Creevey had been right. The Beau was perfectly prepared to do something for the Catholics, if only they would let him alone. It was a conversion as momentous (and far swifter in its consequences) than Mr. Gladstone's to Home Rule.

21   In August he approached the King for leave " to take into consideration the whole case of Ireland, with a view to the adoption of some measure to be proposed to Parliament for the pacification of that country." He faced the facts in his plain fashion :

> " The influence and the powers of Government in that country are no longer in the hands of the officers of the government, but have been usurped by the demagogues of the Roman Catholic Association ; who, acting through the influence of the Roman Catholic clergy, direct the country as they think proper. . . .
>
> " We have a rebellion impending over us in Ireland . . . and we have in England a Parliament which we cannot dissolve, the majority of which is of opinion, with many wise and able men, that the remedy is to be found in Roman Catholic emancipation, and they would unwillingly enter into the contest without making such an endeavour to pacify the country."

That was his notion. If the citadel of public order was to be defended, the advanced position from which Eldonian Tories still defied the Catholics must be abandoned. Peel had reached the same conclusion, although he felt compelled by his own record 22   as an uncompromising Protestant to warn the Duke " that it would not conduce to the satisfactory adjustment of the question, that the charge of it in the House of Commons should be committed to my hands." A reluctant convert, he proposed to 23   announce his own conversion and resign. The Duke wrestled stoutly with his scruples. He had lost his Light Division, when the Canningites resigned ; in all probability his next step would cost him a brigade of Tories ; Peel was his chief ally ; and his ally must be retained at all costs. But his next objective was 24   the royal conscience ; and all through the autumn his guns played upon that flimsy fortress. His policy was formulated in detail,

though he still maintained silence in public ; for secrecy must be
maintained on the eve of a retreat. He proposed to enfranchise
the Catholics and admit them to public life in exchange for a few
formal safeguards and the dissolution of their Association. A
hint of his intentions crept into a letter, which startled a Catholic
correspondent with an intimation that if the question could be
sunk " in oblivion for a short time . . . I should not despair of   25
seeing a satisfactory remedy," though he still professed to " see
no prospect of such a settlement." Such Delphic utterances
brought indignant charges of duplicity from angry Protestants
when the mine was fired in the next year ; and Wellington was
afterwards reduced to a blunt admission in debate that his letter
" had been better let alone. Indeed, I shall take care not to write   26
such a letter again to such an individual." But could he help
himself ? He was not yet authorised to formulate—much less to
announce—a policy ; and until the King released him, he was
bound to work on in silence.

A new year opened ; and in the first days of 1829 the Duke
was busy sounding Bishops, coaxing Peel, and managing the
King. He was successful in persuading Peel not to abandon the
ship in heavy weather. But if persuasion was a new art to him,
George IV gave him ample opportunities for learning it. The
Duke's system was simplicity itself—" I make it a rule never to   27
interrupt him, and when in this way he tries to get rid of a subject
in the way of business which he does not like, I let him talk himself out, and then quietly put before him the matter in question,
so that he cannot escape from it." For George IV, no more
amenable than Burgos to surprise attacks, required a siege *en
règle* ; and the Duke laid siege to him with infinite patience.
His parallels crept slowly towards the doomed fortress ; and one
by one the royal outworks fell, until the last remnant of the
King's conscience sought refuge in the citadel itself. It was
Ciudad Rodrigo over again ; for the unhappy King, whose favourite delusion was that he had fought in Spain, at least enjoyed the
rare distinction of a siege by Wellington. His pressure was relentless. In January he broke down the embargo on Cabinet
consideration of the problem. That month the King assented
gloomily—" Damn it, you mean to let them into Parliament ? "   28
—to a plain announcement of Catholic Emancipation in the
Speech from the Throne ; and in February the murder was out.

The Whigs, robbed of their leading grievance, were sulky ; for
the Duke had outmanœuvred them by falling back from an
untenable position.   But his Tory forces had little relish for the
manœuvre.   He spoke almost nightly in the House of Lords ;
and though a derisive Whig conjectured that his utterances could
be summarised as " My Lords ! Attention ! Right about face !
Quick march ! " he grew positively persuasive.   It was a new
experience for him ; there had been no need to persuade his
army to fall back to Torres Vedras ; but the Tories were more
troublesome, and even Mrs. Arbuthnot shewed signs of mutiny.
The storm broke in March.   Peel, who had honourably resigned
his seat at Oxford, was defeated by wild clergymen ; the King
was breathing treason to his circle ; but Wellington persisted
grimly.   As he told Arbuthnot, " I have undertaken this business,
and I am determined to go through with it. . . . I will succeed,
but I am as in a field of battle, and I must fight it out in my own
way."   His royal master whimpered about abdication, though
the audience was ended by a royal kiss (not, one feels, the least
distasteful of the Duke's official duties).   But a final plunge of
his galled charger almost unseated him.   For the King, positively
frantic with Protestant apprehension, refused the final jump.
He had been drinking brandy and water, when the Duke arrived
with Peel and Lyndhurst.   Their audience was painful, as the
King talked for six hours.   At intervals he took more brandy ;
at intervals they made an interjection.   But the racing stream
of royal indignation poured over their attentive heads.   He
should postpone the Bill—the Bishops must advise him—
besides, there was his oath.   He was not sure precisely what it
was ; but he had taken one ; and so the Bill must go.   They
intimated that the Government went with it.   But the interminable harangue proceeded with an uncomfortable echo of the
dreadful garrulity which had marked the onset of his father's
madness.   The Duke was quite convinced that he was mad ;
he hated to be cruel to a monarch in distress ; but resignation
was the only course that might restore the royal senses.   So
they resigned.   Three rigid backs were turned on Windsor,
and three gentlemen returned to London.   The cure was effica-
cious, as a prompt recantation followed them, with the affecting
postscript, " God knows what pain it costs me to write these
words. G.R."   The careful Premier extracted a more specific

statement of the royal approval, and the King complied. The long siege was over ; and the Duke's flag fluttered on the captured citadel.

It remained to pass the Bill. The King would march with him ; but could he discipline the Tory peers into a wise retreat ? His own authority was sadly shaken by the violence of Protestant attacks—" If my physician called upon me, it was for treasonable ³⁷ purposes. If I said a word whether in Parliament or elsewhere, it was misrepresented for the purpose of fixing upon me some gross delusion or falsehood." In fine, there was a distinct danger that the Duke himself would be discredited ; and if his name lost its magic, who would remain to give orders to a distracted nation ? Something must be done in order to restore his credit ; and in his sober way he made up his mind to do it. Among the most vociferous of his opponents was Lord Winchilsea, an unimportant ³⁸ peer distinguished by a loud voice, a mannerism of flourishing a large white handkerchief when making speeches, and the *abandon* of his Protestant invective. This zealot in an ecstasy of in- dignation composed a letter to the Press, in which he charged ³⁹ the Duke with a mean subterfuge contrived in order that he " might the more effectually, under the cloak of some outward show of zeal for the Protestant religion, carry on his insidious designs, for the infringement of our liberties, and the introduction of Popery into every department of the State." This was too much. He had resolved to make an example, and Lord Winchilsea would serve. The imputation of dishonest motives must be stopped—if necessary, by a challenge. Duelling was never to his taste ; he had discountenanced it strongly in the Peninsula, since he disapproved of officers on active service running unnecessary risks in private quarrels. He was on active service now ; but he reflected with complete detachment that a quarrel with Lord Winchilsea would serve a public end, since it might dispel the prevailing " atmosphere of calumny " and restore ³⁷ his personal authority. Then the Prime Minister proceeded to pick his quarrel. Lord Winchilsea was asked in a curt note if ³⁹ he was the author of the offending letter. When he admitted it, the Duke demanded an apology. The Secretary at War acted for him, thus demonstrating the utility of staff officers in a Government, when the Prime Minister proposes to in- dulge in affairs of honour. The correspondence followed its

appointed course : stiff gentlemen waited on one another ;
solemn memoranda were drawn up ; the Duke demanded
" that satisfaction . . . which a gentleman has a right to
require, and which a gentleman never refuses to give " ; and
in the mist of a March morning he rode out to Battersea.
40   The Duke was punctual, and his opponent kept him waiting.
A round-eyed doctor, fetched early out of bed, recognised his
formidable patient, who cheerfully remarked, " Well, I dare say
you little expected it was I who wanted you to be here." Then
they rode up and down till Winchilsea arrived ; and the little
party—four gentlemen, a doctor, and a case of pistols—proceeded
on foot to a quiet corner. The Duke turned to his second.

" Now then, Hardinge, look sharp and step out the ground.
I have no time to waste. Damn it ! don't stick him up so near
the ditch. If I hit him, he will tumble in."

There was a pause. The seconds had a final conference ; and
the Duke waited with a smile. Then Hardinge handed him a
pistol. He had been wondering all the morning whether to shoot
his man. It would be awkward if he killed him ; he supposed he
would have to go to prison until he could be tried ; so he resolved
to shoot him in the leg. A steady voice said " Fire " ; and the
Duke raised his pistol. But Winchilsea's was still pointing at the
ground. The Duke paused for an instant, fired, and hit his coat.
Then Winchilsea fired in the air. His second flourished a paper,
which contained a withdrawal of the offensive charge. The Duke
listened carefully. " This won't do," he said, " it is no apology."
Then someone pencilled in the mystic word ; the Duke distributed a chilly bow to each of his adversaries, lifted two fingers to
his hat, and rode away. He went straight to Mrs. Arbuthnot's ;
walked in upon her at breakfast, and startled her by asking what
she thought of a gentleman who had been fighting a duel ; and
41   later in the day he told the King at Windsor. " I have another
subject," he remarked, " to mention to your Majesty, personal
to myself. I have been fighting a duel this morning." His
sovereign graciously replied that he was glad of it. That mirror
of deportment told someone that he was delighted with the
Duke's conduct, that gentlemen must not stand upon their
privileges, and that he should have done the same himself (and
malice added that he would soon believe he had). But it elicited
42   a wail of horror from Jeremy Bentham, who favoured Wellington

with a strange effusion beginning " Ill-advised Man ! " dwelling
in gratifying terms on the disastrous consequences of his removal
from public life, and bleakly endorsed by the recipient, " Compliments. The Duke has received his letter." This prompt reply
stirred Bentham's gratitude, and evoked further warnings against
the perils of assassination, with slightly rambling reminiscences
of Aaron Burr, John Wilkes, and Nelson's signal at Trafalgar.

The duel served its purpose. His motives were unquestioned
now : " the system of calumny was discontinued. Men were
ashamed of repeating what had been told to them. . . . I am
afraid that the event itself shocked many good men. But I am
certain that the public interests at the moment required that I
should do what I did." The House of Lords resumed the Bill ;
and he argued manfully. They listened, and a respectful House
heard Wellington warn the extremists :

> " I am one of those who have probably passed a longer period of
> my life engaged in war than most men, and principally in civil war ;
> and I must say this, that if I could avoid, by any sacrifice whatever,
> even one month of civil war in the country to which I was attached,
> I would sacrifice my life in order to do it. . . ."

This was far more impressive than all his laboured disquisitions
on the Bill of Rights, the House of Stuart, and the *Concordat* of
Rhenish Prussia. But he debated endlessly against the sullen
legions of outraged Protestantism, until the Bill passed its final
stage. Then he allowed himself a modest *Te Deum* in the House
of Lords.

It was thirty-six years since Captain Wesley in a maiden speech
counselled the Irish House of Commons to use the Catholics with
moderation. The encyclopædic Croker disinterred the speech ;
but the Duke had quite forgotten it. For he was always more
anxious to be right than to be consistent ; though in the present
case he happened to be both.

IV

THE campaign of Catholic Emancipation was over. Its strategy
—the swift recognition that Ireland had become ungovernable,
the abandonment of an untenable position, and the bold retreat
—was eminently characteristic ; and it had ended, as the Duke's
campaigns were apt to end, in victory. Wellington had never
failed. Indeed, he was almost coming to believe in his own luck ;
for one day when Croker called, the Duke cheerfully remarked,
1 " Yes, 'tis all my good luck, my Fortunatus's cap," lifting a finger
to the small red Cossack cap that he wore indoors in cold weather.
Where Pitt had failed, where Canning had not even summoned
up courage for an attempt, Wellington had achieved success. The
Whigs were dished ; the House of Lords was silenced ; and the
King had been outflanked. The siege of Windsor was, perhaps,
the most brilliant of Wellington's campaigns ; for the victory was
single-handed. His personal authority had been his only weapon ;
and when the fortress of the King's elusive conscience fell, it
capitulated to one besieger. Small wonder that his sovereign
2 remarked sulkily that " Arthur is King of England, O'Connell
King of Ireland, and myself Canon of Windsor." A teasing
Guelph had done his best to irritate King George against the
3 Duke by terming him ' King Arthur ' ; and there was something
in the accusation. For in his lonely mastery of King and Lords
the Duke of Wellington came near to being a fourth estate of the
realm in his own person.

Successful in its outcome, his Catholic campaign had been less
satisfactory in its effect upon his followers. For discipline is
always strained by a retreat ; and the Tory squadrons had found
the retreat anything but enjoyable. Mobility was not their
forte ; designed by nature for the fixed defence of suitable
positions, they were as unhandy as fortress artillery in a sudden
evacuation ; and it was not surprising that some of the heavier
pieces had been left behind in the Duke's swift retreat. This was
distinctly awkward. Guns can be spiked ; but it is not so easy

to silence politicians ; and there was an uncomfortable possibility that some of his Tory artillery, fallen into the enemy's
hands, would be turned against his lines. For High Tories were
now leagued with Whigs in Opposition. The Duke's apostasy
had roused them to excesses of bitterness ; during the debates
some humorist imported a rat into the House of Lords ; and the
Duchess of Richmond adorned her drawing-room with an array
of stuffed rats under glass labelled with the names of leading
Protestant apostates. In such a mood there was not much
prospect of Tory unity, and the Duke's Parliamentary forces
were sadly diminished. He had already lost the Canningites ; the
solid Tories were departing now ; there was still Peel, of course.
Peel was an invaluable ally. But with his Light Division gone
and his main body wavering, could the Duke hope to win the
war with the Portuguese ?

Precarious in Parliament, the Duke's position was not greatly
strengthened in the country. Peel's adherence was an indication
that Wellington was allied with the new forces of industrial progress. But the alliance had not yet borne fruit in progressive
legislation. Besides, his main achievement was scarcely of a
nature to evoke English gratitude. He had emancipated the
Catholics, and grateful Irishmen passed glowing resolutions ;
O'Connell himself sat with a Catholic committee to raise funds
and decorate the Phœnix Park with a towering Wellington Testimonial. But Irish gratitude is an uncertain passport to British
affections. Few statesmen have survived after rendering a
service to Ireland. The bare attempt cost Mr. Gladstone his
career, and subsequently an all-powerful dictator fell from the
summit of his Coalition within a year of making peace in Ireland.
It would almost seem that acts of justice towards Ireland must be
their own reward ; for English politics hold no other.

2

He was just sixty now, a trim frock-coated figure with a head
growing frosty and the profile that political cartoonists loved to
draw. Coloured or plain, his eye was always sharp ; the splendid
hatchet of his nose was etched upon the background ; and his
tight-lipped smile was visible in whatever disguise the caricaturist's fancy had suggested—a mute's, a rat-catcher's, an
Egyptian mummy's, or the sporting hat and multitudinous capes

of *The Man wot drives the Sovereign*. The gentler pencil of H. B. began its work with him that year ; and the Duke, always recognisable, took the centre of the political stage. Even the grateful *Edinburgh* exclaimed " A greater than Cæsar is here, one who has not destroyed in peace the country he had saved by his sword."

The effort had been great. He had endured torrents of abuse, and done more public speaking on the Relief Bill than in the previous twenty years of his life. Abuse was a small matter ; but he found oratory an uncongenial exercise and derived little pleasure from addressing the House of Lords with a bad cold, to sink back into his seat and wrap his cloak tightly round him. It was some satisfaction to compose a lengthy memorandum on army discipline and to confront reformers with the grim apophthegm, " I know the British army, and I dare not." The old martinet had " always considered this desire to alter the system of discipline of the army as one of the morbid symptoms of the times. It is like the notion that thieves ought not to be punished . . ." ; and his conviction, that " the man who enlists into the British army is, in general, the most drunken and probably the worst man of the trade or profession to which he belongs, or of the village or town in which he lives," still burned as brightly as though Badajoz had been sacked a week before. But his real pride in the army appeared when he informed a correspondent that " its conduct in the field is unrivalled. Its officers are gentlemen, and moreover the gentlemen of England. . . ." His military duties cost him a fall that summer, when his horse threw him at a review in the Park. He was unhurt ; and as he rode off the ground, they cheered him to the echo, crowding round to shake his hand. The ubiquitous Creevey met him the same afternoon riding down a side street in the West End, and congratulated him upon his Irish achievement.

" You must have had tough work," said the pert little Whig, " to get thro'."

" Oh, terrible, I assure you," replied the unruffled Duke, and rode off down the street.

He could return to business now ; and, in all conscience, there was quite enough of it, with Ireland and the Russo-Turkish war and currency and Portugal and the London traffic problem. It was a relief for him to manage a Civil List pension for Miss Ponsonby, the Lady of Llangollen and his mother's friend ; for he

was capable of a friendly job at need.   Indeed, he took endless
trouble to do something for George Brummell.   That exquisite,
a stranger to the Duke, was languishing at Calais ; and Wellington had done his best to provide him with a post in the consular
service.   But his Foreign Secretaries were uniformly unhelpful ;   *12*
Dudley objected that the King would not like it ; the Duke
appealed to Cæsar, who remarked without sympathy that
Brummell was a damned fellow and had behaved very ill to him ;
but Wellington persisted, and his sovereign acquiesced.   Then
Dudley was obstructive ; and after him Aberdeen was nervous,
until the Duke assured him that he would take full responsibility.
So, thanks to Wellington, George Brummell got his post, though
with a final gesture of dandyism he subsequently recommended
that it should be suppressed as a sinecure.

He went his autumn rounds among the country houses, and
someone engineered a meeting with Huskisson at Lord Hertford's.   *13*
Would he take back the Canningites ?   That was an intriguing
question.   There was some evidence besides that the Whigs
themselves might join his forces ; and Arbuthnot, his intelligence   *14*
officer, was out taking soundings.   But, for the moment, he
continued with his force of Tories, though the appointment of a
Whig as Privy Seal indicated that he was prepared for a manœuvre towards the Left.   No party man, the Duke had strong
prejudices in favour of a national administration.   Indeed, his
Catholic policy had been undertaken with the sole object of
uniting all parties in support of firm government in Ireland.   But   *15*
politicians were unreasonable, and he found the King more
trying than ever.   The royal intellect was busy with alterations
in the Guards' uniform ; deep in the mysteries of tailoring,   *16*
George held a daily review of pattern coats.   His mind was full of
collars ; but it was not too full to make difficulties for the Prime
Minister.   The Duke retained his confidence that " nobody can   *17*
manage him but me," though once a bitter cry escaped him :

" If I had known in January 1828 one tithe of what I do now,   *18*
and of what I discovered in one month after I was in office, I should
have never been the King's minister, and should have avoided loads
of misery !   However, I trust that God Almighty will soon determine
that I have been sufficiently punished for my sins, and will relieve
me from the unhappy lot which has befallen me !   I believe there
never was a man suffered so much ; and for so little purpose ! "

The mood, which was unlike him, passed ; but whilst it lasted, he found less pleasure in his public duties than in going to the

19 play to see Fanny Kemble as *Juliet.* Foreign affairs were uninviting, since Canning's gay commitments had destroyed in advance the positions from which he might have made some resistance to

20 the advancing tide of Russia ; as he wrote ruefully, " Mr. Canning and Madame de Lieven have much to answer for ! " His mood was irritable, and his Greek policy was little more than a bad-

21 tempered rearguard action ; though a sudden gleam from Mr. Canning illumined him when a hint of a French monarchy in Colombia elicited from Wellington an unexpected echo of the

22 Monroe Doctrine, with a sardonic reservation in favour of the exportation of the Duke of Cumberland. His diplomacy was

23 firmly based upon the principle of non-intervention, by which (unlike its other exponents) he meant what he said, and not—in

24 Talleyrand's malicious phrase—" *un mot metaphysique et politique qui signifie à peu près la même chose qu'intervention.*" So the Duke kept the peace of Europe ; and as the year went out, the world passed into 1830.

3

The year 1830 opened uneventfully. The calendars announced a new decade ; but calendars were often wrong. The world, to all appearances, was very much what it had been since Waterloo. Canning and Castlereagh were gone ; but the Duke and Metternich remained. Europe was still a symphony in white—in France a white ground sprinkled with the lilies of the Most Christian King ; in Russia the white silence, mile after mile, where the Czar reigned behind the winter mists ; in Italy the white gleam of Austrian uniforms, as Uhlans jingled by and *Kaiserlicks* hummed airs from Schubert. England was chilled that winter ; and as it starved, the Duke sat answering his letters. Because he answered them in country houses, there was unkind comment

25 about " gadding about, visiting, and shooting while the country is in difficulty, and it is argued that he must be very unfeeling and indifferent to it all to amuse himself in this manner." But Greville, who noted it, termed the impression " most false and unjust," allowing that Wellington needed a little relaxation, and that, " all things considered, it is not extraordinary he should prefer other people's houses to his own." Besides, he never

missed his work, opening every letter and answering them all himself.   The miscellany was amazing—currency, a king for Greece,
screw steamers, agricultural distress, West Indians complaining
that they could no longer supply rum to the United States,
French designs on Algiers, low wages at Birmingham (with a
sample bag of assorted hardware), and a proposal that Bucking-
hamshire lace should be made compulsory at Court, eliciting the
grim reply that " if the use of lace is the fashion it will be worn   *26*
whether the King orders the use of it or not.   If it is not the
fashion it will not be worn, though the King might order the use
of it."   He seemed to have an eye for everything—even for the
exasperating swarm of inventors, " who speculate upon inventing   *27*
plans and projects for government when they have nothing else
to do.   There are thousands of them at present in England ; as
well as I believe elsewhere ; the offspring of the march of intellect.
Their object is money ; which, please God, they shall not get from
the Public Treasury."

The King's health was failing now ; and party politics were
in inextricable confusion.   For the Duke had split the Tories ;
the Whigs were split already ; and the Canningites hung impartially on the flank of either army.   Bewildered groups steered
intersecting courses in an endless saraband, and the Duke might
have his choice of partners for the Parliamentary dance.   He
could recall the Canningites ; but Huskisson was a distasteful
colleague.   Or he might beckon to Lord Grey and strengthen his
depleted ranks with a Whig reinforcement.   But he guessed that   *28*
" all these parties prefer the Government to any other," and made
no sign.   For, if the truth were known, he was not greatly interested in colleagues.   His Catholic campaign had shewn him that
he could manage the House of Lords ; and he was quite content
to leave the Commons to Peel.   The Government's position there
was frankly precarious, since Peel's majority depended upon casual   *29*
support ; and a derisive Opposition said scornful things about
" a good weak Government."   But what risk was there in an
unguarded flank in the absence of any enemy strong enough to
take advantage of it ?   That spring they were defeated twice
on unimportant questions, of which a Jews' Relief Bill provoked
Wellington to write that " this Christian community will not much   *30*
like to have Jewish magistrates and rulers. . . . It besides gives
a false colouring, and throws ridicule upon the great measures of

1828 and 1829, which it resembles only in name." For he was no friend of emancipation for its own sake. He had been perfectly prepared to emancipate the Catholics in order to ensure strong government in Ireland ; but Jews were quite another matter.

Spring turned to summer ; and the King, " very nervous but very brave," was dying by inches. Once he called for the *Racing Calendar*, and almost to the last he talked of horses. The Duke was often at his bedside ; and the prospect of a new sovereign

31   filled him with misgivings, since King William would probably suggest that they should take in Lord Grey. But Wellington was not inclined to admit him as a colleague—" I would infinitely prefer that he should be at the head of the Government to belonging to a Government of which he was a member." For he had little taste for Coalitions. He would not find it more congenial to sit in Cabinet with the Canningites. So it was probable that Whigs, Radicals, and Canningites would unite in Opposition under Grey. What would happen then ? The House of Commons would plainly be the main theatre of war ; and the Duke and Peel " must look not to what is personal to ourselves, but what is necessary for the King's service, and we must make sacrifices to provide for its security. I have long been of opinion that it is desirable that the power of the government should be concentrated in one hand, and that hand that of the leader of the House of Commons." So he pressed Peel to take his place, and offered to serve under him. Such abnegation was uncommon ;

32   but nothing came of it. The King died in June—" poor Prinney," as Creevey wrote, " is really dead "—and the Duke saw a faded ribbon round his neck tied to a miniature. The portrait was a woman's, and he recognised Mrs. Fitzherbert.

The world was changing now ; and he watched King William

33   with some apprehension, as he launched into a little speech at his accession Council. But it turned out to be nothing worse than a becoming epitaph upon his brother. The Duke breathed again. Perhaps his new master would prove more reasonable than his antecedents gave any grounds to hope. The streets, at any rate,

34   were still for Wellington, since he was " much cheered by the people " ; and King William seemed to share their views. For the Duke told Greville that he found him both reasonable and

35   tractable, and that he could do more business with him in ten minutes than with George IV in ten days. He had his weaknesses,

of course. For it was highly disturbing to receive twelve hours'
notice that the King proposed to bring the King and Queen of   *36*
Wurtemberg to dine at Apsley House. And the festivity itself
was more disturbing still. The royal guests were late, to start
with ; but, once at Apsley House, King William threw himself
into the entertainment with terrifying zest. For an unsuspected
appetite for after-dinner speaking developed under the Duke's
hospitality. The least felicitous of his allusions was a warm
panegyric on the married virtues, highly flattering to the Queen
of Wurtemberg but inappropriate to Wellington. Then he
desired the band to play, *See the conquering hero comes*, and
addressed himself to his embarrassed host. The theme inspired
him. He spoke of Marlborough, Queen Anne, Vimeiro, and the
defeated French ; then, with a sudden memory that the French
ambassador was present, he argued with creditable ingenuity that
the Duke's victories were not over the armies of his ally and
friend, the King of France, but over those of a usurper. Refreshed by this excess of royal tact (quite wasted on the French
ambassador, who did not know a word of English and was
restrained with difficulty from bowing his acknowledgments), he
returned to the main theme, spoke once more of Marlborough,
and closed with an expansive vote of royal confidence in the
present administration, which had been, he thought, and would
be highly beneficial to the country, and should retain his confidence
as long as he was on the throne. Such tributes were unusual
from such a quarter ; and the Duke's reply was brief. A startled
company dispersed to set the clubs buzzing with the story.
Happy the nation with an impromptu speaker for its king ; but
less happy its Prime Minister.

Things might have been far worse, though. For the eccentric
monarch gave no sign of Whig opinions, and the Duke was left
undisturbed in office. But his Parliamentary weakness persisted ; and before the summer ended, he signalled to the Canningites for reinforcements. Lord Melbourne was approached, and   *37*
intimated that he could not join without Grey and Huskisson.
This was too much for Wellington ; Huskisson might be endured,
but he declined to swallow Grey. So there were no Canningite
recruits. A demise of the Crown involved a General Election, and
he faced the contest with undiminished confidence. His team
was weak enough (even Greville wrote contemptuously of " the   *38*

Duke's awkward squad ") ; but the issues were unexciting. For
it was improbable that feelings would run high upon economy and
slavery. The contest opened quietly ; but as it proceeded, a long
shadow fell across the hustings. For strange news began to come
from France. The Paris streets had risen in the last days of July;
the troops were helpless ; Marmont tasted the flavour of defeat once
more ; and Charles X was off to England. This was revolution.
All its familiar badges reappeared—the National Guard, M. de La
Fayette, and the tricolour. Was 1830 to revisit the familiar scenes
of 1789 ? One thing was certain : the world was changing fast.

4

The Duke still went about his business in a changing world.
He recognised the change, writing quietly to the Prince of Orange
that " it will be scarcely possible that we can all feel the same
confidence in the duration of peace hereafter, as we have done
heretofore from the year 1815 up to the 25th of last month."
The age of Waterloo was ending ; but he kept his head. The
last revolution in Paris had cost Europe twenty years of war.
But Wellington had no wish to see another. A word from him
might have set armies on the move from Poland to the Rhine.
Louis Philippe had made his revolution ; and Europe, if its leaders
chose, might oblige him with his Valmy, his campaign of France,
his Waterloo. The Duke need only raise a finger. Metternich
would not be unwilling ; for Metternich lived in the age of
Waterloo. But Wellington, oddly enough, had quite outlived it.
For his main desire was to preserve the peace of Europe, and
he was prepared to do so at any reasonable cost. The chastise-
ment of France, which had once been his leading accomplishment,
had no attractions for him now. In consequence the Duke was
rigidly opposed to intervention, informing Greville that " we
should not take any part, and that no other Government ought or
could." There must be no war ; he wrote to Aberdeen that
" there are some bitter pills to swallow. . . . However, the best
chance of peace is to swallow them all." For he was disinclined
to treat the settlement of 1815 as sacrosanct, concluding that
" good policy requires that we should recognise the Duc d'Orléans
as King at an early period." Few men are reconciled so easily to
the destruction of their own handiwork ; and his self-control
endured a further strain in August, when a Brussels mob streamed

out of a theatre and rioted against the Dutch connection. For the waves of revolution, spreading beyond France, threatened the counter-revolutionary dykes erected in 1815. If anything was the Duke's own creation, it was the Kingdom of the Netherlands, the child of Waterloo. Its armies had served under him ; its Barrier fortresses along the French frontier had been his own peculiar charge ; and now its southern province was in insurrection. There was every temptation to rush to the rescue. But the Duke resisted it. For his belief in peace was still stronger than his belief in the peace-treaties of Vienna.

Europe was changing round him, and he kept his head. But the change in Europe found an uncomfortable echo nearer home. England was polling in those summer weeks ; and as the news came in from France, the tone of the elections changed. There was a sudden sense that the old order was passing away ; Reform, *43* of which little had been heard in the opening phases, became a leading issue ; and Palmerston wrote gleefully that " this event is decisive of the ascendancy of Liberal Principles throughout Europe. . . . The reign of Metternich over and the days of the Duke's policy might be measured by algebra, if not by arithmetic." Besides, there was an odd belief that Wellington was somehow identified with the fallen Polignac, whose crude efforts at reaction had provoked the July Revolution. Progressive persons whispered that the Duke had caused Charles X to appoint him, and had even written to prescribe the due reactionary lines which he should follow. But Grey doubted the story ; Wellington told *44* Lady Jersey that he had not written to King Charles since his accession ; and his denial in a letter to Alava was explicit.

" *Por lo que toca á mi nombramiento del ministerio de Polignac,* *45* *creo que no está en Europa hombre político que tiene ménos que yo á decir á ese asunto. Jamas me habló Polignac sobre sus intenciones. Jamas le he escrito, ni al Rey, despues del nascimiento del Duque de Bordeaux, ni al Duque d'Angoulême ; ni he comunicado con ninguno en Francia sobre las cosas internas.*"

This was plain enough ; but an untrue belief is frequently as influential as the truth itself. Besides, the fact remained that a Paris mob had challenged law and order with undeniable success and reversed the immutable decrees of 1815. The Duke was the embodiment of law and order ; he was 1815 incarnate ; and if these things could be done in France, why not in England ?

The fall of Polignac was promptly echoed beyond the Channel in an unpleasing change of temper. The impassive *Place* recorded that " the impression the events in Paris made on even the least intelligent of the people was such as will never either be effaced or to any extent forgotten by them " ; an *Edinburgh* reviewer cried that " the battle of English liberty has really been fought and won at Paris " ; Cobbett was in *staccato* raptures ; and Brougham thundered before Yorkshire crowds. If 1830 was to be a year of revolutions, English Radicals would not be left behind ; and the Whigs followed at a more becoming pace. For the near prospect of office had its customary effect on a divided Opposition, and the Whig party was reforming its disunited ranks. The skies began to darken, and the gloomy Eldon predicted " a storm for changes here, especially for Reform in Parliament." If there was to be an English Revolution, that was its most likely theme.

Reform was looming nearer now. Detained for years upon the fringe of politics, it had been a topic for occasional declamations by Parliamentary faddists and a dangerous toy for Radicals to play with. But in 1830 it took the centre of the stage, and every candidate who had a real constituency was forced to talk Reform. How would the Duke regard it ? Canning had opposed Reform : that was one thing in its favour. But Wellington was hardly likely to tamper with the constitution. Democracy, even in the comparatively blameless form of a proposal to enfranchise the middle class, was not to his taste. He had small respect for elected persons, and was not greatly interested in the constituencies by which they might be elected. He had seen Parliamentary democracy at close range in Cadiz ; and the example of Spain was not encouraging. For her colonies had gone, and he was inclined to think that " no country in what is now called a modern constitutional state can keep a dependency." This was unpromising for England. Besides, the times were scarcely propitious for constitutional experiments, with open revolution in the streets of Paris and Brussels in a heady uproar. Indeed, the troubles on the Continent hardened his inclination to resist Reform and induced a fatal mood of complacency. For in a document suspiciously resembling a draft for a newspaper article he painted an unpleasing picture of events abroad, concluding that these facts, " if viewed in their true light, will give the people of this

country fresh reason every day to be satisfied with their own
institutions." This comfortable temper was unfriendly to
Reform ; and an ugly stir among the agricultural labourers sent
him still further to the Right. For there was rioting that autumn
in sixteen counties ; the invisible ' Captain Swing ' summoned
his rustic followers ; the Oldham colliers were out ; and the new
cotton towns were seething. Was it a moment for concessions ?
The Duke thought not. Misled by Catholic Emancipation, his
critics have enquired why he did not concede Reform. But he
never made concessions for their own sake. Catholic Relief had
been undertaken in order to unite responsible opinion in support of
strong government in Ireland. His whole administration was a
campaign in defence of social order ; and the concession to the
Catholics had been no more than a deft withdrawal to a stronger
position in rear. But if his troops fell back before Reform and
admitted democracy to Parliament, what would remain ? There
was no further retreat possible, and he resolved to hold his ground.
For 1829 had been his Busaco. Now he had reached Torres
Vedras. The sea was at his back ; and he must stand to fight.

He took his own decision in his own solitary fashion. There
were no Cabinets upon Reform, and Peel was not consulted.
Peel, indeed, was understood to complain that the Prime Minister
was never influenced by men—only by women, and those invari-   50
ably silly. The Duke's little *camarilla*, whom Greville impolitely
termed " the women and the toad-eaters," were not Reformers ;
and no influences checked his drift towards the Right. His mind
was thoroughly made up, and a later letter to a colleague shews
how impossible it was for him to repeat the brilliant manœuvre
of Catholic Emancipation :

" I have not leisure to discuss Parliamentary Reform either in   51
writing or in conversation. I confess that I doubt whether it will
be carried in Parliament.

" If it should be carried it must occasion a total change in the
whole system of that society called the British Empire ; and I don't
see how I could be a party to such changes, entertaining the opinions
that I do.

" To tell you the truth I must add that I feel no strength excepting in my character for plain manly dealing. I could not pretend
that I wished sincerely well to the measures, which I should become
not merely a party but the principal in recommending.

" I shall sincerely lament if I should be mistaken, and that

Parliament should adopt the new course proposed. I foresee nothing but a series of misfortunes for the country in all its interests, and even affecting its safety. I cannot be a party in inflicting those misfortunes."

It is impossible to say that he misjudged the moment for retreat, since he would have regarded the retreat itself as an inadmissible surrender. For Reform in 1830 was a subject on which he was incapable of compromise. The brilliant opportunism of Catholic Emancipation could not be repeated; and there was no alternative to resistance.

What other course was open? Crowds were on the move, and he instinctively resisted crowds. Gentlemen could be bargained with; but crowds must be resisted. He had resisted them before. The age of Castlereagh had been a generous education in resistance, and the Duke had served his apprenticeship as a Cabinet minister under the beneficent rule of the Six Acts. If it was to be 1819 over again, he knew the method; and he was soon provisioning his garrisons and warning officers against the narrow streets of Manchester as though he were still Lord Liverpool's Master-General of the Ordnance. The age of Cato Street seemed to return, as warnings reached him of plots against his life. He informed a young colleague that " I never neglect and never believe these things," and had bolts put inside his carriage doors. Quite undeterred, he went to the unruly North. It might have a good effect if the Duke shewed himself in Lancashire. There was a railway to be opened between Liverpool and Manchester; and Huskisson, who was the local member, was a shade resentful that " the Great Captain is to be there with all his tail. Of course, one object is to throw me into the background." But Huskisson, alas! retained the centre of the stage. The Duke's train was a sumptuous affair, crowned with a canopy that could be lowered for tunnels. Wellington arrived wearing his Spanish cloak, entrained at Liverpool, and laughed heartily at his unusual situation. A vast company rose to receive him; the band played *See the conquering hero comes*; a gun boomed; and his strange conveyance rumbled majestically into the tunnel. After a dreadful interval the train emerged, and anxious multitudes observed its progress through the cuttings until " the flying machines sped through the awful chasm at the speed of 24 miles an hour." (Even the Duke with his sharp eyes could

not read the mile-stones.) This breathless flight could scarcely
be maintained ; and they halted at Parkside for water. The
halt was pleasingly diversified by a march-past of trains, which
were reviewed by Wellington from his state carriage. Gentlemen
got down to stretch their legs, and the Prime Minister shook hands
with Huskisson from his door. They were both talking to Mrs.
Arbuthnot, when there was a sudden cry. The " Rocket " was
approaching. Men ran to safety from the monster ; but the
unhappy Huskisson, who lost his head, limped helplessly all ways
at once and clung to a carriage door in panic. The engine swept
him off ; and a dispirited procession reached Manchester, where
they feasted in a dismal hush. But the Duke was cheered to the
echo, and both his hands were nearly shaken off.

So Huskisson was gone ; and within a fortnight Wellington
renewed his signals to the Canningites. For the elections had
increased his weakness in the House of Commons. The Whigs
appeared to be united now ; and it was no longer safe to leave his
Parliamentary flank uncovered. Peel was clamouring for reinforcements. Besides, the Canningites would be more palatable
without poor Huskisson. So he sent somebody to Palmerston
with a direct offer ; but Palmerston refused to join without his   56
Canningite associates and the Whig leaders. This was too much
for Wellington, and Palmerston went off to Paris. For the
Duke, quite prepared to re-enlist his Light Division, could scarcely
be expected to take in the enemy as well. A final effort was no
more successful, when Lord Palmerston spent six minutes at
Apsley House, insisted on a thorough reconstruction of the
Government, and was bowed out.

The Duke was still busy with the peace of Europe, insisting
that a Conference about the Netherlands should meet in London ;   57
and his letter-bag still yielded a fair number of communications
from Mr. Haydon, who was pressing indomitably for a State
subsidy for art. Wellington responded bleakly that "no
minister could go to Parliament with a proposition for a vote for
a picture to be painted," and left poor Haydon (who was quite
overwhelmed by tradesmen, babies, and a colossal canvas of
Xenophon arriving in sight of the sea) convinced that "impossibility, from Wellington's mouth, must be impossibility
indeed." As for Reform, he spoke his mind upon it in the House
of Lords :

58   " I never read or heard of any measure up to the present moment which in any degree satisfies my mind that the state of the representation can be improved. . . . I am fully convinced that the country possesses at the present moment a Legislature which answers all the good purposes of legislation, and this to a greater degree than any Legislature ever has answered in any country whatever. I will go further, and say, that the Legislature and the system of representation possess the full and entire confidence of the country. . . . I will go still further, and say, that if at the present moment I had imposed upon me the duty of forming a Legislature for any country, and particularly for a country like this, in possession of great property of various descriptions,—I do not mean to assert that I could form such a Legislature as we possess now, for the nature of man is incapable of reaching such excellence at once,—but my great endeavor would be, to form some description of Legislature which would produce the same results. The representation of the people at present contains a large body of the property of the country, and in which the landed interest has a preponderating influence. Under these circumstances, I am not prepared to bring forward any measure of the description alluded to by the noble Lord. And I am not only not prepared to bring forward any measure of this nature, but I will at once declare that, as far as I am concerned, as long as I hold any station in the government of the country, I shall always feel it my duty to resist such measures when proposed by others."

This was plain speaking. As he sat down, the Duke turned to
59 Aberdeen.

" I have not said too much, have I ? "

His colleague guardedly replied that he would hear of it. But the cautious Foreign Secretary gave a more significant summary of the Duke's speech to an enquirer—" *He said that we are going out.*"

Their weakness in the House of Commons was a real menace now. For he had openly defied Reform, and Reformers were in
60 a majority there. He still professed to think that things might do, and said to Lady Jersey, " Lord, I shall not go out—you will see we shall go on very well," while Mrs. Arbuthnot echoed him faithfully. He trusted that his enemies—Whigs, Radicals, High Tories, and Canningites—were too divided to combine against him. Besides, the country gave him something more serious to think about than Parliamentary manœuvres. Tempers were rising now, and London did its best to behave like Paris.

Excited meetings roared every evening in the Rotunda, Black-
friars ; informers scrawled their apprehensions to the Home
Office ; and the new Police, with every hair on end, found *caches*
of tricolour cockades. The Duke was in his element, took pistols   *61*
with him in his carriage, and drafted operation orders for the
defence of Apsley House with armed men at every window and
one in poor Kitty's bath-room. But, all things considered, it
would be just as well to postpone the royal visit to the City.
The King was to have gone in state to the Lord Mayor's Dinner ;   *62*
but there was evidence that Wellington was to be attacked. He
was quite equal to attempts upon his life. But a disorderly
attack on the procession in the King's presence was quite another
matter ; and the Duke, by what Lord Wellesley termed a little
bitterly " the boldest act of cowardice he had ever known,"
decided to postpone it. The postponement was a grave humiliation ; stocks fell ; and an Opposition bard chanted derisively,

> "Charles the Tenth is at Holie-Rode,   *63*
>   Louis Philippe will sone be going ;
>   Ferdinand wyse and Miguel good
>   Mourne o'er the dedes their people are doing ;
>   And ye Kynge of Great Britain, whom Godde defende,
>   Dare not go out to dine with a frende."

Outnumbered in the House of Commons, the Government had
now confessed its inability to preserve the normal life of London.
Hats were still raised to Wellington as he rode down to Whitehall,   *64*
though a few boys hooted him. But his Government was a
doomed fortress ; its guns were silent now ; and the garrison
waited behind battered walls for the last assault. Reform was
looming in the Commons ; but before they reached it, ministers
were defeated on the Civil List. The Duke was frankly startled.   *65*
He had a dinner at Apsley House that evening (it was November
15) ; an excited gentleman came in with the news ; and the
Prime Minister, who was no feminist, said, " Do not tell the
women."
     He took a night to think it over and resigned. If they stayed
in, Brougham's motion on Reform would be carried against them ;   *66*
but a timely resignation served to postpone it—"indeed it was with
that view that I thought it best to lose no time in sending it."
Forced to abandon his position, he could still fire a shot against
Reform from his retreating rearguard. But the Duke was out.

" What is the best test of a great general ? "
" To know when to retreat, and to dare to do it."—WELLINGTON.

I

THE Duke, a private gentleman once more, surveyed the unpleasing scene, while Grey assembled the incongruous elements of the first Whig administration since the distant days of Fox. As he sat musing by the fire at Mrs. Arbuthnot's, they overheard him thinking aloud.

1 " They want me to place myself at the head of a faction ; but I say to them, I have now served my country for forty years—for twenty I have commanded her armies, and for ten I have sat in the Cabinet—and I will not now place myself at the head of a faction."

For he was disinclined to lead the Opposition ; the old gamekeeper could not turn poacher. A life of public service is an indifferent training for the Opposition, since he had served the King too long to acquire the habit of obstructing the King's ministers ; and Rogers, who was listening, would take his message to Lord Grey. A private gentleman once more, he was still the leading gentleman in England ; and gentlemen in 1830 had work to do. County magistrates and Yeomanry must maintain order in the countryside, where something unusual was brewing.

2 Wellington was Lord-Lieutenant of Hampshire ; he had already sent all the Hampshire gentlemen out of town ; and the deep voice still rumbled on.

1 " When I lay down my office to-morrow, I will go down into my county and do what I can to restore order and peace. And in my place in Parliament, when I can, I will approve ; when I cannot, I will dissent ; but I will never agree to be the leader of a faction."

3 A rare mood of despair was on him. " Bad business," was his verdict in Peel's drawing-room, " devilish bad business " ; and he looked so grave as he walked out of Downing Street and stepped into his cabriolet that Greville (though he got his customary nod)

4 did not like to speak to him. The times were out of joint. For he was quite convinced that the French meant to go to war, and there was every sign of an impending revolution. The French,

of course, were at the bottom of it—" I entertain no doubt that
there exists a formidable conspiracy. . . .   I am inclined to think
that the operations of the conspirators in this country are conducted by Englishmen.   But that the original focus is at Paris."
French gold enabled agitators to flit about in gigs ; and the Duke
waited grimly for the explosion.   He was inclined to blame himself for allowing " a licentious press to repeat *usque ad nauseam*
the misrepresentations of all parties."   But what hope was there
that a misguided public could be preserved by Grey and his Whig
colleagues ?   " The gentlemen now in power are committed to
Revolution by the applause with which, as private persons, they
greeted those in Paris and Brussels."   Besides, their policies were
a delirious and conflicting blend of Opposition pledges.   And
there was little salvation to be hoped for from the Crown.   He
had once said that where kings can ride on horseback and inflict
punishment, revolution is impossible.   Russia, perhaps, enjoyed
that happy state ; but it was evident that such feats of equitation
were far beyond William IV.

What was to be done ?   The Duke performed his county duties
and returned to town.   His first reluctance to lead his friends in
Opposition was passing now ; and he gave fifty of his late colleagues a dinner at Apsley House.   They dined in the great
gallery among his Spanish pictures ; and when the Duke of Richmond proposed his health with the sentiment that he hoped their
host would soon give them the word of command " As you were,"
Wellington replied almost cheerfully, " No, not as you were, but
much better."   This was a trifle more encouraging, though he
still counselled his retreating followers " to remain quiet till they
see real cause to take an active part."   For in rearguard actions
unnecessary conflicts were to be discouraged.   So they fell
slowly back, as 1830 went out.

2

The world in 1831 was not more cheerful ; and Mr. Croker
found the Duke " in very low spirits about politics," though he
still could not see his way to open fire as leader of an organised
Opposition.   But when the Reform Bill was produced, he knew
his mind clearly enough, opining that the measure would, " by
due course of law, destroy the country," while the disfranchise-
ment of existing boroughs would give " a shake . . . to the

property of every individual in the country." For he was more interested in the sanctity of vested interests than in the forms of Parliamentary representation. But party discipline presented irritating problems. It had already been revealed to him that a Prime Minister's authority over his followers is considerably less than that of a commander in the field; and he now discovered that an Opposition leader's is more slender still, complaining bitterly that "nobody does anything but what he likes, excepting myself. We are all commanders, and there are no troops. Nobody obeys or ever listens to advice but myself. Then I am abused because things do not go right." Even the faithful Peel—" that fellow in the House of Commons "—was trying. " One can't go on without him ; but he is so vacillating and crotchetty that there's no getting on with him. I did pretty well with him when we were in office, but I can't manage him now at all. . . ." Wellington was determined to defeat the Bill and had little patience with half-measures. His views were plainly stated; but his popularity seemed almost unimpaired. For one day in February he was thrown from his horse at Oxford Circus ; they took him to a shop, where he announced that he was not seriously injured and requested that the mud might be removed from his clothes ; a cab was called ; and as he entered it, the Duke was loudly cheered. But he still argued stoutly in the House of Lords that Reform involved " the downfall of the constitution," contending shrewdly that Whig declamations on the toiling masses should be discounted because nobody proposed to enfranchise them, and that it was wise " to consider what a House of Commons ought to be, and not what the constituents ought to be " (a devastating test by which to judge some later extensions of the franchise). His strategy was simple—" to reject the Reform Bill, if only to gain time "—and in order to render their defensive tactics effective he was urging the divided Tories to close their ranks. In April a Government defeat in the House of Commons was followed by a dissolution. There was an afternoon of wild confusion in the Lords; peers shook their fists and bawled abuse at one another; the Lord Chancellor bounded about the Chamber ; and guns boomed the tidings that King William had left his palace for the House.

But the Duke was absent. He was at Apsley House by Kitty's bedside. For poor, faded Kitty was sadly ailing. An Irish friend, who saw her early in the year, was shocked to find

her on a sofa, " paler than marble . . . a miniature figure of herself in wax-work." A tiny head on a big pillow, she stirred a little
as her visitor arrived ; and a familiar voice said faintly, " O !
Miss Edgeworth, you are the truest of the true—the kindest of the
kind." A thin white hand stole out to greet her, and a faint
touch of colour returned with the shadow of a smile. She lay on
the ground-floor of his great London house among the trophies—
glass cases full of china given by respectful monarchs, stupendous
candelabra from the Portuguese, and the Homeric shield, gift of a
grateful City. Her visitor stared at them ; and a faint voice
behind her murmured, " All tributes to merit ! there's the value,
all pure, no corruption ever suspected even. Even of the Duke
of Marlborough that could not be said so truly." For her Duke
was perfect, though he could never bear it when she told him so.
He alarmed her sometimes. But then great men were bound to
be alarming ; and her brother's boys used to run up the back-   *18*
stairs, when they came to see her, for fear of an encounter with
their terrifying uncle. He was gentle with her now and positively
wrote to Alava about her health. She seemed to rally in the   *19*
spring ; but he still sat with her. Her thin fingers strayed inside
his sleeve and found a circlet fastened on his arm years before by   *20*
Kitty Pakenham. The guns were booming for King William now
across the Park. That afternoon the House of Lords was full of
agitated peers ; but her Duke was there beside her, as his poor,
faded Kitty died.

Parliament had been dissolved, and London illuminated for
Reform. A cheerful mob paraded Piccadilly on the look-out for
recalcitrant householders. Dark windows meant a Tory occu-
pant ; and the great house at Hyde Park Corner with its tall
portico stood out against the summer night in sombre outline.
Mourning apart, the Duke was the last man in London who was
likely to put candles in his windows for Reform in order to oblige
a mob ; and presently the stones began to crash into the silent   *21*
rooms (one did some damage to a picture), until a servant on the
roof let off a blunderbuss, and the crowd moved off to draw Park
Lane for Tories.

3

The twin scourges of Reform and cholera strode on through
1831. Reform was grave enough ; but the Duke was not afraid

22   of cholera—" the only thing I am afraid of is fear. . . . If three
or four hundred *Notables* were to leave London for fear of it, they
would be followed by three or four hundred thousand, and then
this country would be plunged into greater confusion than had
been known for hundreds of years." But Reform was a more
23   formidable menace. His fears of violent revolution had vanished
now ; but he was frankly alarmed by the prospect of a measure
which " totally alters all the existing political interests of the
country, creates one-fourth entirely new interests . . . and this
at the most critical period in the history of the world." He was
inclined to blame himself for the destructive power of the press—
24   " I allowed my contempt for the newspapers—a contempt
founded upon the experience of a long life, of their utter inefficiency to do an individual any mischief . . . —to influence my conduct in respect to the press, when I was in office. The press is an
engine of a very different description, when it attacks individuals,
and when it attacks the institutions of the country. It is powerful in respect to the latter, and no man can blame my own neglect
more than I do." Meanwhile, deluded citizens were voting
steadily for Reform ; there would be a majority of Reformers in
the new House of Commons ; and what was to be done ? It
might be comforting to sit at Walmer talking of old times to
Alava and Croker. But what was he to do ? Reform was a
25   chimera menacing the " last asylum of peace and happiness,"
where great towns with no members of Parliament enjoyed " the
benefit of being governed by the system of the British constitution
without the evil of elections " and an eccentric franchise secured
the Parliamentary services of steady persons whose presence
" constitutes the great difference between the House of Commons
and those assemblies abroad called Chambers of Deputies." His
contempt for the new members was profound—" they dare not
vote according to the suggestions of their own judgment after
discussion ; they are sent as delegates for a particular purpose
under particular instructions, and not members of Parliament
sent to deliver it *de arduis regni.*" He was acting on the defensive
now ; and the first necessity was to unite his forces. This was
26   achieved by midsummer. Peel was still enigmatic ; but the
Tories were aligned behind the Duke. Even Lord Winchilsea was
reconciled, and Wellington went over to inspect his Yeomanry.
    Their course in Parliament was plain. The Bill must be

defeated, though the Duke retained his old reluctance to declare
a general war upon the Whigs—" I could not be a party to any　*27*
violent or factious opposition against any government named by
the King." For he was a public servant ; and his services were
at Lord Grey's disposal upon matters of foreign policy. He even
waited on the Prime Minister in Downing Street, and wrote long
memoranda for his guidance. But he was quite unbending on
Reform. If the Commons passed the Bill, the Lords must throw
it out. For time, he felt convinced, was on their side ; rejection　*28*
meant delay ; and under cover of delay sanity might yet prevail.
He was in town that autumn ; Greville attended a great dinner
at Apsley House, where the Duke told him stories about George　*29*
IV and all the trinkets they had found in his belongings—gloves,
gages d'amour, and women's hair of every colour with the powder
and pomatum still upon it—and what a trial the Duchess of
Kent had been with her commanding ways. But with Reform
impending it was impossible for him to find a refuge in talk about
old times. The Tory peers must be convened, and he wrote
argumentative letters in all directions. That autumn his old
mother died at eighty-nine, having seen her incomparable pair
of Gracchi on every eminence in two continents. The Opposition
leaders met at Apsley House, and Eldon came in after dinner,　*30*
post-prandial in the extreme. If the Bill passed the Commons,
the Lords must do their duty. Wellington informed his peers
that Reform was synonymous with democracy—" this fierce
democracy "—and that democracy involved an immediate
onslaught upon property :

> " A democracy has never been established in any part of the　*31*
> world, that it has not immediately declared war against property—
> against the payment of the public debt—and against all the principles
> of conservation, which are secured by, and are in fact the principal
> objects of the British Constitution, as it now exists. Property and
> its possessors will become the common enemy. . . ."

The Spanish precedent still haunted him ; for he insisted that
Reform would paralyse " the strength which is necessary to
enable his Majesty to protect and keep in order his foreign
dominions, and to ensure the obedience of their inhabitants. We
shall lose these colonies and foreign possessions, and with them
our authority and influence abroad." Four days later angry

Reformers read in black-edged newspapers that the Bill was
dead, rejected by the House of Lords. An undergraduate was
32 driving back to Christ Church in the Oxford coach, and confided
to his diary Gladstone's impressions of his first debate.

The Bill was dead ; but, with the country in an ugly ferment,
33 it might rise again. The Duke's windows suffered once more ;
and when he went to Walmer, six gentlemen, headed by a fighting
Army chaplain, rode as his escort. It was November now, and
Wellington drove in his britzka—that open carriage in which
everyone caught colds—with an armed servant on the box and
a brace of double-barrelled pistols by his side. The Arbuthnots
were at the Castle ; and his tone was frankly pessimistic. Then
Croker and a house-party arrived ; Lord Stanhope began asking
him questions about the Peninsula, retiring to his room to write
down all his answers ; and they found the Duke looking grave.
34 He faced the facts about Reform, announcing that " the dis-
franchisement of any place is a painful thing to swallow. I don't
mean that we shan't be obliged to swallow it—but it is a monstrous gulp." The closing sentence of his speech had urged the
Lords to leave the door open :

31 " In recommending to your Lordships to vote against this Bill,
I earnestly entreat you to avoid pledging yourselves, whether in
public or private, against any other measure that may be brought
forward. I recommend to you to keep yourselves free to adopt any
measure upon this subject which shall secure to this country the
blessings of a government."

This was the strategy of retreat once more : the enemy were
pressing hard, and it might be necessary to fall back to the next
ridge. But warfare extended now far beyond the walls of
Parliament ; for crowds were on the move in every quarter of
the kingdom, and Wellington's first instinct was to repress them.
35 Crowds almost invariably warped his judgment. He sent his
sovereign a warning letter on the subject of the Political Unions ;
they were reported to be arming now, and he advised their prompt
suppression, pointing his advice with the alarming precedents of
36 the National Guard and the Irish Volunteers. The letter conveyed a hint that Wellington was prepared to take the helm
again, rescue the King from his Whig captors, fight a General

Election upon the issue of public order, and restore England to her senses. But his bewildered sovereign was unresponsive.

To restore public order was the main problem now. As the Duke wrote, "that once done, the reform of the Parliament might be considered with honour and safety, if not with advantage. Till these unions are put down, it does not much signify, in reality, what course is taken." In this mood he was frankly indifferent to the negotiations in progress between ministers and the more cautious of his Tory followers in the House of Lords. What did the details of Reform matter, if revolution went unchallenged on its way? But the Duke could see that events had made Reform quite inevitable—"the King has . . . pronounced himself for Reform, and it would not be easy to govern in his name without Reform. But the more gentle and more gradual the reform, the better for the country. . . ." His mind was moving towards a fresh stage in the long retreat; but he must not be hurried.

4

The next attack would come in 1832. For the Bill was passing through the Commons for the third time. How was it to be received when it reached the House of Lords? That fortress was not quite impregnable, since it was generally known that Grey proposed to spike its slightly antiquated guns by a creation of sufficient peers to pass the Bill; and in January one enthusiast was pressing Wellington to see the King, advise him to refuse this exercise of the prerogative, form a Tory Government, and go to the country. But the Duke refused. He always thought of details; and one detail of Parliamentary routine stood in the way. For this exhilarating programme would leave no time for Parliament to renew the Mutiny Act before a dissolution. Besides, he doubted how far the King would play his part. He had every reason to, since when he had been prepared to act on similar lines in the autumn, the King hung back and the moment for the *sortie* passed. Now there was nothing to be done except to stand on the defensive; and he waited for the Bill behind the ramparts of the House of Lords.

An unwise "endeavour to bully slight colds" had ended in a temperature, and shooting gave him bad headaches before Christmas; but he was soon restored, out in the saddle through six hours of February rain, and riding sixty miles a day to hounds.

As for the situation, he was past tactics now. A gloomy certainty
40   possessed him that " we are governed by the mob and its organ—
a licentious press . . . the mob and Mr. Place the tailor ! "
41   Convinced that " the monarchy . . . approaches its termination," he was averse from ingenious manœuvres designed to
avert the creation of Whig peers. Indeed, he rather welcomed
this expedient, since its very ruthlessness would expose Grey's
42   *coup d'état* in all its nudity and spare noblemen the degradation
of changing their minds. The King might still prevent it—" the
43   King of this country is a tower of strength "—but Wellington
would put no pressure on him.

The Bill reached the House of Lords in March, and Wellington
fired a warning shot from the battlements. Even Greville, who
had been busy in the negotiations for a compromise, found his
44   tone " fair and gentlemanlike . . . a speech creditable to himself, useful and becoming . . . a very handsome speech." He
45   opposed the second reading at length, though in a tone of marked
restraint. But months of negotiation between Whig ministers
and ' Waverers ' had weakened his defences ; and the Bill passed
its second reading. The enemy had penetrated his position
now ; for the Lords' vote admitted that there was to be a Reform
Bill of some sort, and the Duke faced the uncomfortable fact
46   —" my own opinion is, that we shall not escape a Reform Bill on
the principle of that now in the House of Lords, and that the
efforts of all ought to be directed to render that bill as little
noxious as possible." The threatened fortress was quite indefen-
sible, and the heroic gesture of a last stand among the ruins made
no appeal to Wellington. Always practical, he was prepared to
abandon the position and fall back fighting. But he had few
illusions as to the final outcome, since he was frankly sceptical of
the value of any possible amendments of the Bill. What else
was there to do, though, unless the King came to his senses ?
The world was more than usually out of joint ; for Wellington
could scarcely take a ride in London without hearing angry cries,
47   though Croker was consoled to notice " with what respectful, I
should say *increased* attention he is received by every well-dressed
person, and even by a vast majority of the lower orders." But his
48   health was glaringly omitted from a long toast-list at the King's
dinner to the East India directors. The skies were dark indeed ; and
49   the Duke ruefully confessed that " I am out of the whole affair."

Grey's temper changed the situation. The Bill was in committee now ; and when the House of Lords shewed signs of independence in the first week of May, the Prime Minister posted off to Windsor with a peremptory demand for the creation of fifty peers. This was too much for his much-enduring sovereign, who refused to give the required assurances. The Government resigned ; King William sent for Lyndhurst ; and, in *Endymion's* gleeful narrative, 'the bold chief baron advised His Majesty to   *50* consult the Duke of Wellington.'

5

Was he to be Prime Minister again ? He had his chance ; and this was the precise situation for which he had played in November, 1831—the King at bay, the Whigs dismissed, and loyal subjects to the rescue. But the *sortie*, which might have saved the fortress six months before, was now little more than a forlorn hope. For it was 1832. However, it might still serve a useful purpose ; for Wellington was thoroughly alive to " the advantage   *51* of taking the King out of the hands of the Radicals—that is, in reality—of giving the country the benefit of some government " —and taking the sting out of the Reform Bill.

It was a Thursday when Lord Lyndhurst saw him, and they   *52* went off in search of Peel. The three men met at Apsley House ; Croker was there as well, and asked who was to be Prime Minister. Lyndhurst nodded towards Peel, and said that he must tell them. Peel spoke with unaccustomed emphasis : if the new Government proposed to carry a Reform Bill, he could not and would not have anything to do with it. He had already made a *volte face* on Catholic Relief, and was quite determined not to repeat the experience. Croker suggested that Lord Harrowby, who had been prominent among the ' Waverers,' might fill the part ; but the Duke disliked the idea, doubting if Harrowby would be acceptable to the Tory peers. That night he wrote a note to Lyndhurst :

" I shall be very much concerned indeed if we cannot at least   *53* make an effort to enable the King to shake off the trammels of his tyrannical Minister. I am perfectly ready to do whatever his Majesty may command me. I am as much averse to the Reform as ever I was. No embarrassment of that kind, no private consideration, shall prevent me from making every effort to serve the King."

So he was prepared to abandon his defensive strategy and lead the forlorn hope ; and on Friday Lyndhurst went down to Windsor and informed the King.

Croker saw the Duke again on Saturday, and found him grim, but not uncommunicative. " Well," he remarked, " we are in a fine scrape, and I really do not see how we are to get out of it." Harrowby, he said, had declined ; so had the Speaker ; and if no one else would act, he must form a Government himself. As the Duke remarked to Croker, he had passed his whole life in troubles and was now in troubles again, but it was his duty to stand by the King. That was his leading thought ; the royal summons was a command to Wellington ; and he pressed Croker to let Peel know that he would serve with him or under him or in any way that Peel might think best for the common cause. But Peel had little taste for a second recantation followed by a second martyrdom, and kept carefully aloof. That day the printers were at work on Place's wily placard, " To stop the Duke, go for Gold " ; a general run on the banks might paralyse the new Tory Government ; and windows in Birmingham already displayed the threat, " No taxes paid here until the Reform Bill is passed." But though the King was hissed as he drove up from Windsor, a crowd cheered Wellington outside the palace. He told the King that, " happen what would, he would stand by him and endeavour to extricate him from the difficulty in which he was placed." But he must have colleagues ; and the King, who took a hand in the Duke's game, had no success with Peel or the Speaker. That afternoon Wellington interviewed a long procession of reluctant Tories ; but none of them would serve except his military stalwarts, Murray and Hardinge. For the Tory intellect was not equal to the Duke's conception of a rearguard action in politics, his incessant series of retreats to the next ridge in rear ; and their civilian weakness for consistency was strangely troubled by the prospect of helping to pass Reform after resisting it so long. But they all dined together at the Carlton Club that night. The Duke was in the chair and listened to innumerable speeches, followed by a long session with the reluctant Speaker.

More interviews filled Sunday. His patience was beginning to wear a little thin, since he observed to Croker (who was hanging back) that in such a crisis, if a man put himself on the shelf, it might not be so easy to take him off the shelf when he perhaps might desire it.   That night he saw the Speaker once again without success ;   for that dignitary's eloquence, repressed by his official situation, found release in a disquisition that lasted for three hours, led nowhere, and provoked from Lyndhurst the disrespectful comment that his prospective colleague was " a damned tiresome old bitch."   The Speaker asked for time ;   but on Monday night the House of Commons intervened with a debate, which proved conclusively that the Duke's forces were inadequate. He faced the facts at once, and informed the King on Tuesday morning that he could not form a Government.

The *sortie*, which lasted for five breathless days, had failed ; and the long siege was nearly over.   For Wellington had failed to break the Whig blockade of the House of Lords.   The Whigs were back again in office ;   and the peers, surrounded by a hostile Government and an angry House of Commons, were bound to capitulate.   But it had been a gallant effort, though *Coningsby* conjectures that ' the future historian of the country will be perplexed to ascertain what was the distinct object which the Duke of Wellington proposed to himself in the political manœuvres of May 1832,' and concludes disapprovingly that ' this premature effort of the Anti-Reform leader to thrust himself again into the conduct of public affairs . . . savoured rather of restlessness than of energy.'   But did it ?   His objectives were plain enough—to form a Tory Government which would preserve public order and pass a moderate Reform Bill.   If he failed, it was because his followers permitted him to fail.   Opponents of Reform, they were unable to share his willingness to pass the Bill.   For they viewed it as good partisans were bound to view it :   Reform was not a Tory measure, and what Tory could square his principles with voting for it ?   The Duke took another view.   Never a good party man, he was prepared to sacrifice Tory orthodoxy in a crisis. Indeed, he did not regard himself as a mere party leader—" I was not acting for any body of men, but for the King."   That was the key to all his actions.   The King was in difficulties, and must be rescued ;   the King had summoned Wellington, and Wellington had eaten the King's salt.   However desperate the adventure, he could not refuse.   He did not spare himself, offering to serve under Peel and enduring endless interviews with his reluctant followers.   But persuasion was not his *forte* ;   and if his followers

56

thought more of Tory principles than of the King's dilemma, the Duke was not to blame.

Reform rolled on implacably ; and Wellington, determined to avert the final ignominy of a wholesale creation of Whig peers by an unwilling King, withdrew his opposition to the Bill ; his followers ' skulked in clubs and country houses,' whilst it passed through its remaining stages ; and on a summer afternoon Whigs crowded to the House of Lords to hear the royal assent recited to the empty benches opposite.

6

One June morning he rode out of Apsley House to give a sitting to Pistrucci at the Mint.   An ugly crowd collected in the City to wait for him on his return, and a magistrate offered his assistance.   The Duke's reply was practical.

" You can do nothing.   The only thing you can help me in is to tell me exactly the road I am to take to get to Lincoln's Inn ; for the great danger would be in my missing my way and having to turn back on the mob."

He started with his groom, and the mob followed them. They tried to drag him from his horse in Fenchurch Street ; but two Chelsea pensioners appeared, whom he stationed at each stirrup with orders to face about whenever he was forced to halt. There was some stone-throwing in Holborn ; and when he saw a coal-cart in the distance, " Hillo ! " said the Duke in a grim aside, " here's the Artillery coming up ; we must look out."   But an obliging gentleman, who drove a tilbury behind him for some time, gave valuable cover, and earned the Duke's esteem by " never looking towards me for any notice."   Two policemen joined the little party ; and the Duke disposed them at his horse's head as an advance guard.   When they reached Lincoln's Inn, the mob was still at his heels.   He surveyed the situation and enquired if there was another exit.   It seemed there was. " Then be so good," said the Duke, " as to shut the gate."   The enemy detained by this simple stratagem, he rode out into Lincoln's Inn Fields ; but the mob was after him again.   His horse was walking, and an excited gentleman named Martin Tupper leapt on the steps of Surgeons' Hall, exclaiming loudly, " Waterloo, Waterloo ! "   The mob was slightly awed ; the Duke raised two fingers to his hat ; and the strange ride went on, " the cast-

metal man " (as Carlyle wrote to his mother) " riding slowly five
long miles all the way like a pillar of *glar* ! " He had a little
escort now, as they went up the Strand and along Pall Mall ;
gentlemen in club windows saw him staring straight between his
horse's ears. They rode up Constitution Hill ; but the mob
headed him by a dash across the Park ; and they were waiting
outside Apsley House to hoot, as he reached home at last. It
was June 18. " An odd day to choose," the Duke said to
somebody. " Good morning."

II

THE new world, where Reform was law and Mr. Creevey boarded his first omnibus, filled Wellington with grave misgivings. He was quite convinced that the revolution had begun, and waited for the end with dignity. The least of troubles was his personal unpopularity. An emblem of opposition to Reform, he was continually hooted ; but he had grown accustomed to the mob outside his house, and even to the groans of village Radicals as he rode home from hunting. He faced it in his quiet way, reporting calmly that " I think that I have got the better of the mobs in London by walking about the town very quietly, notwithstanding their insults and outrages. It is certain that the better class are ashamed of them, and take pains upon all occasions to testify every mark of respect for me." But the prospect was dark— " the government of England is destroyed "—and his mind ran on revolutionary precedents. The monarchy might still survive, if only the army remained sound ; but the Jacobins were in the saddle, and he might live to see a National Guard. He even detected symptoms of the Great Rebellion—" the times are much more similar to those of Charles I than people are aware of. The same parties, almost under the same denominations, are *en presence. . . .*" But the French precedents unnerved him ; for it was 1789 over again. The road had forked once more towards safety or revolution ; and when his countrymen made the wrong choice, how could the old duellist of the *ancien régime* feel anything but dark forebodings ? " Our wise rulers prefer the course which faction suggested forty years ago to that of wisdom, of experience, and reflection. God knows what will happen to the world."

His course was clear, though. A Tory clergyman, who was inclined to emigrate from his ungrateful country, had asked for the Duke's advice.

" You have, I understand, a cure of souls. Can you abandon your post in a moment of crisis and dangers for worldly objects ?

Your flock ought to provide for your decent and comfortable sub-
sistence ; and they not only do not perform that duty, but they
persecute you ! Still, ought you to abandon them ? Is it not your
duty to remain at your post ? Expect better times. Make every
exertion, every sacrifice to enable you to do justice by everybody,
including your family ; but I confess, if I was in your situation, I
would not quit my post."

The parable applied as plainly to himself : he could not quit his
post. For though the Duke was out of office, he was keenly
aware that, politics apart, he was a public institution. As the
late King's executor, he had assumed peculiar and delicate duties
towards the Crown. Besides, the world conspired to regard him
as a universal dispensary of good advice. "Every man," as he   6
once wrote, "has one resource only ; that is, to apply to the Duke
of Wellington." A mannerism grew upon him of alluding to
himself in the third person. Cæsar had done the same ; but in
Cæsar's case the habit was a mere convenience for narrative.
In Wellington's it served to indicate an odd dualism. For
he seemed to recognise two persons in himself—an ageing gentleman of modest tastes who could be happy in congenial society,
and a public figure whose requirements were often more majestic.
In this mood of queer detachment he wrote to Croker of his own
state appearance as Chancellor of Oxford, "I am the Duke of   7
Wellington, and, *bon gré mal gré,* must do as the Duke of Wellington doth." That was his duty for the future. It was far pleasanter, no doubt, to sit gossiping about the past in the low rooms at
Stratfield Saye, or to pace the sunny flagstones of his battlements
at Walmer eluding Stanhope's endless questions. But there was
his duty to be done. He could not quit his post ; the splendid *rôle*
must be played out to the end.

The new Parliament met early in 1833 ; and Wellington
returned from a stroll into the House of Commons to view the
children of Reform with the chilly verdict, "I never saw so many   8
shocking bad hats in my life." He feared the worst, informing
Greville that his first consideration was to keep a roof over his   9
head, the next to support Grey as the sole alternative to anarchy ;
for "I consider Lord Grey's Government as the last prop of the
Monarchy." Besides, Opposition had never been his *forte*—
"I have been in office, and have served the King throughout my   10
life ; and I know all the difficulties in which the Government are

placed." But since the revolution was over and the House of
Lords had ceased to count, he saw no reason for regular attendance. Now he was almost irresponsible, and wrote cheerfully
that " I have been here generally amusing myself with the
Foxhounds," gaily attired in a scarlet coat, strapped trousers,
and a lilac waistcoat. But he was in the Lords sometimes ; and
the devoted Haydon watched him speaking with such a manly
air or deliberately fetching out his glasses to read a quotation
He was in calmer water now ; and someone who rode with him in
St. James's Park noticed how everyone got up and all hats came
off at his approach. He was still convinced that " we are going,
but I think it will be gradually. There will be no catastrophe ;
we are not equal to one. We shall be destroyed by the due course
of law, unless the Virgin of the Pillar or some miracle saves us."
But the process was comfortingly gradual ; and when the King
came to his Waterloo banquet that year, he had his windows
mended for the occasion.

Not that he mitigated his despair, writing to Stanhope that
he would " do anything to be able to quit this unfortunate and
unhappy country." But how could he ? There was nothing for
it but to visit country houses, attend the House of Lords, and
instal a novel system of warming Stratfield Saye by hot-water
pipes. (He was a domestic pioneer, even achieving triumphs
in the uncharted field of household sanitation.) This mild routine
carried him through 1833, until the University of Oxford brought
him upon the stage again as Chancellor. The honour pleased
him, though he protested that he " knew no more of Greek and
Latin than an Eton boy in the remove." H. B. poked pleasant
fun at *A Great Doctor of Cannon Law*, and the Duke conjectured gaily that " I shall get to the Woolsack at last." In
June, 1834, he went to Oxford for his installation. It was a great
occasion, with the Sheldonian packed to receive him and Mrs.
Arbuthnot there to share his triumph. The Oxford Tories took
him to their bosoms ; Eldon was there as well, and the Duke
gave a degree to his old adversary, Winchilsea. He had learnt
with some apprehension that a speech in Latin was expected—
" Now, any speech is difficult, but a Latin one was impossible ;
so in this dilemma I applied to my physician, as most likely, from
his prescriptions, to know Latin, and he made me a speech, which
answered very well. I believe it was a very good speech, but I

did not know much of the matter." His Latin quantities were uncertain, and a shocked university heard its heroic Chancellor affront the rules by mispronouncing *Jacobus* as three short syllables. This was encouraging for the prospects of *Carolus* ; but the incalculable Latinist defied convention once again with a protracted ' o.' False quantities were all forgiven, when a tactful prizewinner declaimed the Newdigate and reached the apostrophe,

" And the stern soul the world could scarce subdue
Bowed to thy Genius, Chief of Waterloo."

The packed Sheldonian rose at the Chancellor, roaring its homage ; caps waved, feet stamped, and an impassive figure was seen rigid in its seat through a haze of dust. He noticed them at last, lifted his tasselled cap, and signalled to the poet to proceed ; and then the cheerful uproar broke out again.

The Arbuthnots went off to Woodford. They were to meet again as usual in the autumn ; but she died with dreadful suddenness in August. " Only think," wrote Mr. Creevey in his unpleasant idiom, " of the Beau's flirt, Mrs. Arbuthnot being dead ! " He was at Hatfield, when the news arrived. The letter fell from his hand, and he flung himself down on a sofa ; then he rose on the verge of sobs and paced the room. That night he thought of poor Arbuthnot. They had both loved her ; and the Duke felt that he must go to him. Early the next morning he posted off to console the widower. But the loss was Wellington's. For he had lost the only home that he had ever had. An exile until middle life, he had returned at fifty to his two big houses where poor, fluttered Kitty muddled accounts and failed to recognise his guests. That had been nothing like a home. But he was always at his ease in his chair at Mrs. Arbuthnot's. They had met first in Paris, when it was no novelty for Wellington to meet handsome women. Harriett Arbuthnot was quite as handsome as the rest, and far more sensible. She listened well, entered into politics, and could be trusted not to talk. She did not gush over him in public ; and her slight tendency to order him about was an agreeable change for an authoritative man. Besides, her husband was an invaluable subordinate with vast official knowledge ; and Wellington could always find sanctuary at her house in Parliament Street. All this was ended now ; there would be no more talks beside her fire, no more little jokes about the implacable *Tiranna* and her Slave. There was still Arbuthnot ; and the two lonely men drew silently together. He had once shared Arbuthnot's home with him, and now the Duke gave Arbuthnot a shelter. They would be widowers together. But when the world watched him speaking calmly in the House of Lords that week, it thought him hard. For the world knew nothing of his stricken letters to Frances Shelley, who had once shared their jokes—all ended now.

2

An ageing, lonely man, he had his work, his friends, and his interminable correspondence. His friends receded now behind the distances which separate deaf men from the world ; their voices came to him across the silence, and he answered loudly from the farther shore. But his contact with the world was principally maintained on paper ; and he had little reason to complain of any lack of it. For everybody wrote to him ; and from a constitutional inability to ignore a letter he wrote back to everyone. Stray correspondents invariably received the Duke's compliments and a full, if occasionally acid, statement of his point of view. Remedies for ailments from which he did not suffer were civilly returned ; and unsolicited precautions for his spiritual welfare received due acknowledgment. For he was never frivolous about religion. A faithful Churchman, he was no church-goer in London because " in point of fact, I never hear more than what I know by heart of the Church service, and never one word of the sermon " ; besides, the precious remnants of his hearing would be imperilled by sitting " for two hours every week uncovered in a cold church." He had tried St. James's, Piccadilly, and found it too chilly for him. But he invariably attended divine worship at Stratfield Saye and Walmer, where " my presence at church can operate as an example." He explained, for his correspondent's benefit, that he was not " a person without any sense of religion. If I am so, I am unpardonable ; as I have had opportunities to acquire, and have acquired a good deal of knowledge upon the subject. . . . I am not ostentatious about anything. I am not a ' Bible Society man ' upon principle, and I make no ostentatious display either of charity or of other Christian virtues."

His correspondent in this instance was a zealous bishop. But he had other correspondents upon spiritual themes. Early in 1834 he received an exhortation from a young lady much *22* addicted to good works and playing on the harp, who had been encouraged by her success with a convicted murderer to try her hand upon the Duke. Exhorted to spiritual rebirth by a total stranger, he answered promptly. Two blots, an error, and the circumstance that he misdated his reply convinced her that the Duke was overwhelmed by his emotions, although the month was January when the most hardened sinners frequently mistake the year without spiritual commotion, and he had made precisely the same error when writing to the King about his Cabinet in *23* January, 1828. Heartened by this conviction, Miss Jenkins called at Apsley House and left a Bible. The Duke resisted the temptation to present his compliments and acquaint Miss Jenkins that there were several in the house already. Indeed, he made no reply, although the gift was accompanied by a " suitable *24* note." This was in April ; and Miss Jenkins' note remained unanswered for four months. But Mrs. Arbuthnot died in the first week of August ; and before the month was out, the Duke's mind had turned to his religious correspondent, who received an answer (addressed to ' Mrs. Jenkins ') acknowledging her gift and asking whether he might have the pleasure of meeting her. It was most unlike him to wait four months before answering a letter or, having waited so long, to answer it at all. But in the interval something had gone out of his life with Mrs. Arbuthnot ; was it possible that Mrs. Jenkins might replace her ? Her reply enlightened him, revealing that, though willing to receive him, she was *Miss* Jenkins after all. The young evangelist had reached this great decision in consultation with her friend, Mrs. L., " a perfect woman of the world." The Duke, a little startled, rejoined that he was not " in the habit of visiting young unmarried *25* ladies with whom he is not acquainted " ; but he proposed to call, when he was next in town.

He called upon her in November. Miss J. was fortified by prayer for the ordeal, " praying to God to be with me every moment of the time, directing even my dress." Divine guidance had indicated her old dark green merino as most suitable for the occasion ; and as she went downstairs to receive her formidable guest, dear Mrs. L. cried after her, " Now if the Lord should send

His arrow into his soul ! " The Duke was standing by the fire ; and she was quite surprised to notice that he had " such a beauti- ful silver head, such as I always from my childhood admired." Her mission would, it seemed, be less distasteful than she had feared. " This," she remarked, " is very kind of your Grace." He took her hand without a word ; and the odd pair sat in two chairs on each side of the little fire. Miss Jenkins rose, exclaim- ing, " I will show you *my Treasure* " ; the Duke got up politely ; and his hostess returned to her seat clasping an enormous Bible. Then she began to read, announcing that her reading was from the third chapter of the Gospel according to St. John :

> " There was a man of the Pharisees, named Nicodemus, a ruler of the Jews : The same came to Jesus by night, and said unto him, Rabbi, we know that thou art a teacher come from God : for no man can do these miracles that thou doest, except God be with him. Jesus answered and said unto him, Verily, verily, I say unto thee, Except a man be born again, he cannot see the kingdom of God. Nicodemus saith unto him, How can a man be born when he is old ? can he enter the second time into his mother's womb, and be born ? Jesus answered, Verily, verily, I say unto thee, Except a man be born of water and of the Spirit, he cannot enter into the kingdom of God. That which is born of the flesh is flesh ; and that which is born of the Spirit is spirit. Marvel not that I said unto thee, Ye must be born again. . . ."

As she reached these words, Miss Jenkins emphasised her Scripture lesson by pointing at the Duke. His reply was slightly unex- pected, since he promptly clasped her outstretched hand and said with emphasis, " Oh, how I love you ! how I love you ! " Some arrow, as Mrs. L. had hoped upstairs, had pierced him ; but was it quite the arrow for which Mrs. L. had hoped ? His hearing was imperfect, and it may be doubted whether he had caught the sacred words. But his sight was unimpaired ; and he could see a pretty girl in a green dress.

He left, saying that he should call again, and made Miss Jenkins promise to write to him. She made several attempts, but finally desisted from this arduous composition, " considering such was not the will of God." The weeks went by, and his time was fully occupied. For the Whigs were out ; Sir Robert Peel was on his way from Rome ; and the Duke held the fort, acting temporarily as Prime Minister and all three Secretaries of State. These

administrative exercises would have kept most men busy at sixty-five. But though the Duke was the entire Cabinet in his own person, he found time in those crowded weeks for a note to Miss   26
Jenkins asking the reason of her silence and proposing to visit her again. Her silence was unbroken ; but the Duke persisted. He called one Sunday afternoon and seemed a little flurried. It appeared that he was going on a visit to the King, on hearing which his pious hostess expressed a wish that it had been to the King of Kings. His conversation was exciting, since he alluded once more to his feelings for her and exclaimed : " This must be for life ! " Indeed, he said it twice, and positively asked her if she felt sufficient for him to be with him a whole life. Miss Jenkins, who was quite prepared to be a Duchess, modestly replied : " If it be the will of God." He left her hurriedly and was a shade annoyed to find on his return that she had locked the door. Her explanation, which he received in silence, was that she had shut herself in to pray. He asked her why she had not written ; and when she pleaded divine guidance, he was silent again. A doubt was growing on him. Locked doors, excessive piety, devotions at unseasonable moments, and a tendency to confuse the King of Kings with William IV—these were disturbing symptoms. Was Miss Jenkins all that the Duke had hoped ?

He kept his distance for a fortnight ; and as the days went by, a dreadful doubt grew on Miss J. as well. Was she to be a Duchess after all ? A newspaper (for she did not disdain earthly means of intelligence) informed her that he was in town ; and she put the matter to the test by a note entreating him to cease his visits.   27
Her love for him was candidly avowed ; she was fully aware that his intentions could not be otherwise than strictly honourable ; but for religious reasons (which were set out at length) it was advisable that their meetings should remain purely spiritual. The Duke's reply conveyed (in three sentences) his entire con-   28
currence. Miss J. was horrified. His answer had confirmed her worst suspicions, and her racing pen bombarded him with texts. Page after page informed him of his degradation and excused her own prompt acceptance of his proposal by her firm conviction—how could he have ever doubted it ?—that Miss Jenkins would " confer as high an honour on a Prince in bestowing my hand on him as he would on me in receiving it." He answered almost humbly :

29   " I beg your pardon if I have written a line or used an expression
which could annoy you. Believe me ; it is the thing of all others
that I would wish to avoid ! And that there is nobody more strongly
impressed than I am with veneration for your Virtues, attainments,
and Sentiments ! "

But though his tone was highly apologetic, there was nothing here
about marriage. Quite undeterred, Miss Jenkins received his
letter with the raptures appropriate to a repentant sinner. For a
Duke penitent might be a Duke redeemed, a Duke set on the right
path and looking for a Duchess. That was her dream ; she never
30 wavered in her faith that Providence had " influenced the Duke
of Wellington to love me above every other lady upon earth from
the first moment he beheld me." Her devoted Mrs. L. was of
the same opinion ; and how could Mrs. L.—" a perfect woman of
the world in her early life "—be wrong ?

There was an interval from January to June, 1835 ; and then
the extraordinary couple resumed their comedy—she still convinced of her power to elevate him (as well as his to do the same
for her), and he anything but reluctant to continue his association
with a pretty girl. For the attentions of twenty-one are flattering
to sixty-six. Besides, if she was so uncompromisingly good, she
would at least be safe. Letters written to Miss J. would hardly
find their way into the newspapers ; she was unlikely to divert
31 the town (like Miss Harriette Wilson) by publishing her reminiscences ; and he could meet her without fear of awkward consequences. So by midsummer their meetings were resumed. She
had been writing letters to him without posting them ; he asked
to see them and was favoured with the loan of much improving
literature. He seemed to enjoy her narratives of conversation
with irreligious strangers in stage coaches, discussed the merits of
a preacher whose ministrations she enjoyed at Ramsgate, and
was almost meek in his request that her more voluminous epistles
should (in view of excess postage) be confided to several envelopes.
He asked to see her ; but the adroit Miss Jenkins practised with
skill the tactics of the flying nymph. He took pleasure in
their correspondence. For it was always to his taste to be
treated without undue deference ; Mrs. Arbuthnot had continually
ordered him about ; and Miss Jenkins, with all Scripture at her
back, was nothing if not authoritative. Indeed, her habits of command impelled her to rebuke him for ceasing to seal his notes with

a coronet and signing them with a bare initial. This was gross
disrespect—she should return his letters and receive none from him
in future unless they bore his full insignia. It was years since
anyone had dared to question the Duke's conduct ; and he replied
with the familiar irony that he had " always understood that the
important parts of a Letter were its Contents. I never much considered the Signature ; provided I knew the handwriting ; or the
Seal provided it effectually closed the Letter." But he accepted
the rebuke and undertook that future letters should be " properly
signed and sealed to your Satisfaction," noting with some relief
that she proposed to send him back his letters and adding help-
fully that he would save her the trouble of burning them. Before
this olive-branch appeased her, a second furious epistle sped from
Miss J. to Apsley House. This was too much for Wellington,
who took refuge in his chilliest third person, presented compliments, repeated his apology, and gave detailed instructions for the
return of his letters. Miss Jenkins was distracted. Should she
abandon her letters and her Duke ? The tactics of the flying
nymph had yielded excellent results ; she had sixty letters from
him ; and she spread them out before the Lord, asking His
guidance as to their disposal. Her prayer was answered when
Mrs. L., always the woman of the world, advised her not to part
with them. It was His will ; for had not Miss J. " asked the
Lord to put it into her heart to advise me agreeably to His will " ?
So Mrs. L. prevailed ; Miss Jenkins kept her letters ; and an irritated Duke informed her coldly that " it is a matter of Indifference
whether Miss J. has burnt the Letters ; or kept them ; or sent
them back."

They corresponded still ; for Wellington lived in the grip of a
nervous inability to refrain from answering letters. Composing
suitable replies was, with him, an automatic reaction. But he
was chilly now, regretting bleakly that " Miss J. is not satisfied
with the formal style of his Notes. She was not satisfied when he
wrote to her in a form more consistent with familiarity. . . . The
Duke assures Miss J. that he can reply to any letter which she
may think proper to address the Duke as fully in one form as the
other." When she asked him to return one of her letters, he
replied coldly that as " they are in general long and they succeed
each other rapidly," it was his practice to destroy them. She
pelted him with tracts and hymns in manuscript adorned with

32

four distinct grades of underlining ; on one sublime occasion she ran to " nineteen sides of paper under three covers " ; each family bereavement brought him her consolations ; and she formed an irritating habit of entrusting him with bulky letters for transmission to royal personages on the subject of Sunday observance, the rates of Marlborough House (upon which she had some texts unfamiliar to rating lawyers), and more eternal themes. They
33 met once in 1836, with Mrs. L. safely ensconced behind the folding doors. But this time there were no scenes ; and the female Polonius heard little more than her fearless friend admonishing the Duke ; though when Miss Jenkins asked about the trouble in his knee, he seemed quite gratified, drawing his chair a little nearer, " which of course met with the withdrawal on my part due to Christianity."

They did not meet again for years, although the nymph was
34 now pursuing. She sent him wipers for his spectacles and for his pens ; she offered him a Bible in large print, which elicited the cautious answer that " that which I now have answers perfectly, and I will not deprive you of another." For he was wary now and less inclined to notify her of his movements. By 1840, faint but pursuing, she was offering to come and nurse him ; but he assured her of his perfect health, adding defensively that " he has no reason to believe that he will have occasion to trouble her upon any subject whatever." For she was quite unbearable, writing with alarming frequency and getting little in return beyond bare acknowledgments, until " the Duke would recommend [her] to save herself from such anxiety in future by omitting to write to him." His last shot was still more final—" to avoid disappointment he now tells her that he will write no more."

Was this the end ? Plainly, if Wellington had anything to do with it. But four years of silence were too much for Miss J. ; and in 1844 she opened fire again. His replies at first were passive
35 —he was obliged for her kind enquiries, reluctant to embark upon religious topics, and relieved to learn that her misunderstanding
36 with Mrs. L. was at an end. But that year he called on her again and, on leaving, found quite a crowd round his horses. Indeed, he sent her his sole recorded present—a wax impression of his features on half a ducal visiting-card. This treasure left her in grave doubt as to its ultimate disposal—whether it should repose for ever in the British Museum or be realised in order that

its proceeds might be spent upon the thankless task of propagating the Gospel among the Jews. More visits followed ; and his notes grew friendlier again, though they were mainly filled with brave assertions of his rude health and the intolerable burden of affairs. (Her new *rôle* as the Lady with the Lamp must be repelled at all costs.) But she soon grew exacting, expecting him to answer every letter. This was bad enough ; but when she wrote a rambling story about money troubles, his patience finally ran out :

> " I will give her any reasonable assistance she may require from   37
> me ; when she will let me know in clear distinct Terms what is the
> Sum she requires.
>   " But I announce again ; that I will never write upon any other
> Subject."

Such brutality sent her into apocalyptic transports ; she even contemplated returning the precious seal and a lock of his hair. But Mrs. L., still worldly, pressed her to keep them both ; and the Duke, sternly apprised that he had totally misunderstood, was unexpectedly apologetic—" P.S.," wrote Wellington, " I never   38 will offend again in any manner." His humility was quite astonishing. He had been humouring his fractious correspondent for twelve years, and her most extravagant *boutades* seemed powerless to exasperate him into a final breach. He made one attempt in 1847, in which " Field Marshal the Duke of Wellington   39 presents his Compliments. . . . He declines to [write] anything further to Miss J., being convinced that as usual any correspond-ence will end in his giving her Offence, however much he may desire and endeavour to please her." But this attempted *Nunc dimittis* elicited no more than a stern intimation that his corre-spondent " cared no more for his Field Marshalship than his Generalship " ; and within three months they were both corre-sponding hard, the Duke complaining helplessly that " you write   40 at great length ; with much celerity, in light coloured Ink." He seemed to find distraction in the taming of this spiritual shrew. It was such a change to encounter someone who stood up to him ; he always liked commanding women. Besides, he was not far off eighty ; and the solicitude of thirty-three for his welfare was dis-tinctly gratifying. But when she favoured him with letters for transmission to Miss Coutts and Sir Robert Peel, he sent them back with a sharp intimation that " I am not the Post Man !   41 nor the Secretary of Sir Robert Peel nor your Secretary ! " His patience was evaporating once again, and in a *cri de cœur* he wrote that " to read one letter from you is as much as I can do."

A gleam of hope appeared in 1850, when she announced her impending departure to the United States, and the Duke eagerly enquired her new address. But she stayed on relentlessly ; and with exaggerated caution for her health he begged her to avoid fatiguing herself by excessive letter-writing. His request was vain ; for shortly afterwards he received a wild farrago, in which her pen wandered distractedly among her symptoms, linseed poultices, the cost of jellies, and the inadequacy of her income, the whole richly decorated with appropriate texts. He asked how much she needed and what was her banker's name—" all this *legibly written* ! " But she answered him with more texts. The Duke was helpless ; and when Miss Jenkins grew reproachful, he bowed himself out with awful courtesy in a note concluding, " He thus finally takes his Leave ! "

But he did nothing of the kind. Involved in her epistolary toils, he was as helpless as Laocoon. When she informed him of her health, the force of habit was too strong for him, and he replied. The stern pietist was soon rebuking him for regular attendance at earthly ceremonies ; but he answered (with fervent requests that she should write no more) that he " considers it his Duty to serve the Public to the best of his Ability." That was in March, 1851. She never heard from him again, though he heard frequently from her. Indeed, a letter to the Duke was waiting on her table to be posted when the doctor called eighteen months later. He was always so kind about posting her letters. " That," she remarked, " is for the Duke." But he informed her gently that there was no Duke to read it. He had eluded her at last ; and she departed for New York, to qualify still further for her heavenly crown by writing up her Journal, re-reading his three hundred and ninety letters, and reposing in the happy consciousness of a Duke very nearly saved from the burning.

III

It was still 1834, and the Duke stared about him in the uncomfortable world created by Reform. But there were compensations; for the Whigs were breaking fast. First, Lord Grey resigned; Melbourne succeeded him; but when Lord Spencer died, removing Althorp to the Lords, there was a sudden buzz.

" ' It is an immense event,' said Tadpole.   *1*

' I don't see my way,' said Taper.

' When did he die ? ' said Lord Fitz-Booby.

' I don't believe it,' said Mr. Rigby.

' They have got their man ready,' said Tadpole.

' It is impossible to say what will happen,' said Taper.

' Now is the time for an amendment on the address,' said Fitz-Booby.

' There are two reasons which convince me that Lord Spencer is not dead,' said Mr. Rigby."

But Mr. Rigby was wrong as usual. Spencer was dead beyond a doubt; Althorp succeeded to the title; and Lord Melbourne must find someone else to lead the House of Commons. His sovereign made difficulties and, with a sudden access of resolution, dismissed his ministers. For there were still the Tories; and the King sent for Wellington. The Duke was at Stratfield Saye. He was up early that November morning; for he was going *2* hunting. But the King's letter came at six o'clock. His hunters countermanded, he ordered post-horses, was off by eight, and by dinner-time had seen the King at Brighton. His sovereign asked him to form a Government; but he " told his Majesty that the *3* difficulty of the task consisted in the state of the House of Commons, and that all our efforts must be turned to get the better of these difficulties, that I earnestly recommended to his Majesty to choose a Minister in the House of Commons," and that Peel should be his choice. This was rare unselfishness, since their relations had been a little strained by Peel's refusal to join him in the forlorn hope of 1832. But the Duke's mind was quite made up that Peel must be Prime Minister; Arbuthnot had con-

veyed as much to Sir Robert in the summer ; and now Wellington
informed the King. But where was Peel ? With rare improvidence he was abroad. For Sir Robert had gone off to Italy. He
must be sent for. Meanwhile, the Duke and Lyndhurst could
govern England until he returned. Lyndhurst was to be Lord
Chancellor, and the Duke calmly assumed all the remaining offices
of state, writing gleefully that " I am in harness again ; and I
have sent to bring home Sir Robert Peel."

He was indeed in harness ; for that week, " after much
fumbling for his spectacles," he was sworn in as First Lord of
the Treasury, Home Secretary, Foreign Secretary, and Secretary
of State for War and the Colonies. He was the government of
England. H. B. portrayed a solitary figure at the head of the
Cabinet table asking two lines of empty chairs, " How is the
King's Government to be carried on ?—that is the question " ;
whilst a rival caricaturist depicted *The United Administration*,
all clean-shaven, trim, and aquiline—Wellingtons to a man—
in red, in blue, in black, in wig and gown, in capes, frock-coats,
and robes, voting with splendid unanimity and encouraged by
their sovereign's exclamation, " Now, my chosen friends and
Ministers, I sincerely hope there will be none of those dissensions
and disputes between you there were with the last." Their
offices and titles filled the margin of this pleasing scene :

First Lord of the Treasury .	. DUKE OF WELLINGTON
Home Secretary .	. DUKE OF VITTORIA
Foreign Secretary .	. PRINCE OF WATERLOO
War and Colonies .	. DUKE OF CIUDAD RODRIGO
Lord Privy Seal .	. COUNT VIMIERA
First Lord of the Admiralty .	. BARON DOURO
Chancellor of the Exchequer .	. ARTHUR WELLESLEY
Lord High Chancellor .	. VISCOUNT WELLINGTON

And for three flurried weeks the charge was very nearly true.
Taking possession as Home Secretary before his predecessor's
papers had been cleared away, he was reported by scared officials
to have " fixed his headquarters at the Home Office, and occasionally roves over the rest." His policy was simple : " all that he
knew, which he told in his curt, husky manner, was, that he had
to carry on the King's government." This was an infinite relief
after the crotchets of the Whigs ; and the world shared Lady

Salisbury's consciousness that " it was really a moment worth   *8*
living for to see that great man once more where he ought to be,
appreciated as he deserves by his King, and at the head of this
great country." For there could be few finer sights than the
industrious old hero in temporary charge of England.

But Mr. Hudson reached Rome at last ; Sir Robert raced
across the Alps, ' the great man in a great position, summoned   *7*
from Rome to govern England ' ; and the Duke subsided into
the Foreign Office, where he soon impressed ambassadors that
" thirty minutes with him suffice to transact what can never be   *9*
accomplished in as many hours with our wavering ministers of
France." For Wellington was still as punctual and decisive as
ever. But administrative virtues could not win General Elections, and the future of Peel's Government depended on the polls.
Electioneering was hardly the Duke's province, though echoes of
the distant warfare sometimes came his way. A young gentleman   *10*
with slightly fluctuating principles, who had once asked him
(without success) to accept the dedication of an epic poem, wrote
imploring his support at High Wycombe. But nothing came of
it ; his correspondent was at the bottom of the poll once more,
exclaiming darkly that he was now a cipher and chivalrously
assuring the Duke that he might always count on the support of
Benjamin Disraeli.

The elections went against them ; and Wellington was soon
assuring country neighbours that, " whatever way the Cats jump   *11*
in this Quarter," he would not miss his hunting in the autumn of
1835. They had been five months in office ; they would be out
again at any moment ; and when Peel was threatened with a
final defeat in the House of Commons, an obliging colleague
offered to send news of the division to Apsley House. But the   *12*
Duke was perfectly prepared to wait until the morning.

" I am quite satisfied to have it when the newspapers come
in at ten o'clock. If I could do any good by having it earlier, I
would ; but as I can't, I'd just as soon wait."

A friend interposed, remarking that he took it coolly and
enquiring if anxiety ever kept him awake.

" No," said the Duke, " I don't like lying awake ; it does no
good. I make a point never to lie awake."

IV

THE brief interlude of Tory government worked wonders with the Duke's popularity. Oxford in 1834 had marked his readmission to the canon of Tory saints ; but the next year restored him to a wider circle of good graces. Not that the world of 1835 had any wish to be governed by the Tories. But it was profoundly touched by the spectacle of Wellington in harness once again. His obvious good faith, his chivalry towards Peel, his willingness to serve under a younger man were in vivid contrast with the normal appetites of party politics ; and the old man resumed his place in popular regard as a national institution. He went to Cambridge in the summer and was triumphantly received by town, gown, and Yeomanry ; Vauxhall shouted itself hoarse when he appeared ; and roaring crowds greeted him at a Hyde Park review. His pessimism had begun to melt.

2   "It is very bad," he observed to somebody at dinner, "but I consider the country on its legs again."

"Do you ? " said Greville. "I am glad you think so."

"Oh yes," the Duke replied, "I think that, however this may end ; I think the country is on its legs again."

Even his Parliamentary authority was recovering. The House of Lords had never lost its habit of attending to his simple arguments ; as young Disraeli allowed, "there is a gruff, husky sort of a downright Montaignish naïveté about him, which is quaint, unusual, and tells." But when he silenced Brougham, the Boanerges of the new era, in mid-flight by lifting a warning forefinger and murmuring across the House, "Now, take care what you say next," it was a veritable triumph. For he had come into his own again. Young men of promise in 1836 noted signs of his approval with avidity, Disraeli writing gleefully that the Duke had told somebody at dinner that his Aylesbury speech was "the most manly thing done yet" and positively asked, "When will he come into Parliament ? " And the less ardent Gladstone, who met him at Sir Robert Peel's and noted that "he receives remarks made to him very frequently with no more than ' Ha ! '

a convenient suspensive expression, which acknowledges the
arrival of the observation and no more," commented favourably
on his mental powers.

His life was easier again ; and he could return to his normal
occupations. The past absorbed him now ; for Gurwood was
editing his *Dispatches*, and the Duke turned over old papers to
elucidate doubtful points. Then there were endless sittings to be
given to portrait-painters. Indeed, the reckless Haydon had laid   7
siege to him whilst he was still in office ; but Wellington refused
to sit. Quite undeterred, the painter called at Apsley House,
borrowed his clothes, and asked the Duke to look at the completed picture. This was too much. The indignant hero had
" no objection to any gentleman painting any picture of me that
he may think proper ; but if I am to have anything to say to the
picture, either in the way of sitting or sending a dress, I consider
myself, and shall be considered by others, as responsible for it. . . .
Paint it, if you please, but I will have nothing to say to it. To
paint the Emperor Napoleon on the rock of St. Helena is quite a
different thing from painting me on the field of battle of Waterloo.
The Emperor Napoleon did not consent to be painted. But I
am to be supposed to consent ; and moreover, I on the field of
battle of Waterloo am not exactly in the situation in which
Napoleon stood on the rock of St. Helena." This was discouraging ; but Haydon urged that with six children to support he
could scarcely ignore a good commission. The Duke, who felt
that Haydon had made free with his wardrobe, was obdurate,
though he consented rather sulkily to the persistent artist
" painting and engraving a picture of me in any way you please,
and in any costume."

But his defence was not always so successful ; and in his later
years artists became a plague. Indeed, the pestilence was almost
endemic. As he wrote helplessly from Walmer, " I did not . . .   8
ask you to come here . . . as I expected a descent of artists. I
have had one ; some still remain, and more are coming—two
from Scotland. I literally lead the life of the subaltern officer of
a regiment. I parade, dressed for duty, at nine in the morning,
and again once or twice a day. There is not a moment of
the day or night that I can call my own. These gentlemen
are at breakfast, dinner, and supper, and all the evening my
existence is at their pleasure ; I cannot move along the

passage, or on the staircase, or the ramparts, without meeting them. . . ."

He had his public duties, too—meetings of Tory peers at Apsley House, dinners at Kensington with Princess Victoria and her overpowering mamma, his correspondence with Sir Robert on Opposition tactics, and regular attendance in the House of Lords where he spoke twenty-one times in 1836 upon every topic from insolvent debtors to railways. His course in politics was slightly complicated by his leader ; for he had a leader now. Peel was sometimes a little trying, though the Duke was on better terms with him and took his hunting-coat to Drayton with a gay intimation that he was " prepared to do whatever you please." But Sir Robert's aptitude for chilling followers was impressive ; even Wellington complained that " our leader does not excite enthusiasm " ; and their relations sometimes resembled an exchange of signals between passing icebergs. But it was no time for dashing tactics, as the Tory rearguard receded slowly before Melbourne's languid advance. It was the dawn of a new age, although the dawn crept imperceptibly up the sky, until the apprehensive gaze of Wellington grew almost accustomed to the change of colouring.

A new age was dawning, although Greville wrote comfortably that " *nothing* will happen, because, in this country, *nothing* ever does." Familiar outlines of the night began to vanish. Beaux of the Regency crept silently away ; royal uncles receded ; and Mrs. Fitzherbert died among her memories. The Duke appeared in Tilney Street. He was the late King's executor, and Mrs. Fitzherbert's papers had presented problems of unusual delicacy which he had dealt with while she was still alive. Some had been sealed up and sent to Coutts' Bank ; but the grate received a generous supply ; and as the fire roared up, Wellington said grimly to his companion, " I think, my lord, we had better hold our hand for a while, or we shall set the old woman's chimney on fire." A new day was climbing up the sky ; and as Kensington flushed in the summer dawn of 1837, two kneeling men informed a sleepy girl that she was Queen of England.

APOTHEOSIS

O good gray head which all men knew.
ODE ON THE DEATH OF THE
DUKE OF WELLINGTON.

I

THE past receded now—the legendary past, where Nelson walked his quarter-deck and Mr. Pitt, sharp-nosed among the candles of Guildhall, urged England to save Europe, and a trim frock-coated figure cantered along the lines to lift a low cocked-hat and point through the thinning smoke towards the French. The past receded into a middle distance hazy with patriotic folklore, a region of soldiers' tales and steel engravings. But one figure held the foreground still, where Wellington lingered indomitably on the bright Victorian scene. A hero of the last reign but two, he was the past incarnate. Men saw his profile and heard the guns of Badajoz; a spare, familiar figure brought back forgotten echoes; and the deep voice took them into their fathers' memories of days before Reform, before Waterloo, before Vimeiro, before . . . His walks abroad became a progress, upon which the London streets turned respectfully to watch the past go by. Every hat came off; genteel persons made excuses to stop and stare; across the way young surgeons crowded on the steps of St. George's Hospital to watch him pass; and as he turned slowly in at Apsley House, the butcher's boy pulled up his cart to see. Not that he was a passive spectacle. A cheering crowd once followed him up Constitution Hill until he reached his gate; he turned in the saddle, pointed to the iron shutters on the windows that they had broken once, swept them a bow, and then rode in without a word. The roads near Walmer knew him well, driving a pair-horse phaeton from the left-hand seat in order that his companion might have his good ear. His driving was a little wild, but his talk was always on the target—economy, dockyard employment as a method of reducing the poor-rate, the futility of supposing that England would be the workshop of the world for ever, foreign markets, means of securing them by lower costs of manufacture (they were just driving into Ramsgate and stopped at the first draper's shop, where he bought a white cotton handkerchief with red spots, emerging with the sage reflection that it had only cost a shilling and was an article which, one would think,

439

might find a market anywhere), and so back to Walmer, dinner at
seven o'clock, a little talk, and candles at eleven.   For the Duke
lived on, half national monument, half Delphic oracle.

I

His talk was never better than in those later years.   It had
lost nothing of its astringent quality ;   yet somehow it was
mellower.   For he could be almost genial with the omniscient
Croker, stepping in from the battlements at Walmer with a
sardonic intimation that " I've just been receiving a lecture from   *4*
Croker on fortification," and protesting amiably at the dinner-
table, " My dear Croker, I can yield to your superior information
on most points, and you may perhaps know a great deal more of
what passed at Waterloo than myself ;   but, as a sportsman, I will
maintain my point about the percussion caps."

This was the epoch of his briefest sayings.   Uttered in his
distinct voice, these oracles were patiently collected, not infrequently improved upon, and assembled like Sibylline leaves to
form a canon of *staccato* wisdom.   Debt, discretion, habits of
industry, and early rising were among his austere themes ;   his
views were obstinately normal, and his conclusions wholly to the
taste of the age of Samuel Smiles.   If he spoke at any length, it
was generally about the past.   Respectful interlocutors headed
him firmly in the direction of the Peninsula and pelted him with
questions.   Stanhope was quite incorrigible in this vein, making
a torment of his evenings, when the old man would have so much
preferred a quiet hour between his candles with a paper.   But the
implacable inquisitor nightly perched beside him on his reading-   *5*
table, until a thoughtful lady piled it high with books.   Quite
undeterred, the relentless Stanhope took them off and installed
himself as usual.

" I don't think much of your fortifications," said a deep
voice from the Duke's armchair.

Not that his topics were exclusively martial.   For one day he   *6*
read them the report of *Bardell* v. *Pickwick* ;   and he was occasionally engaged by deeper themes provided by his religious correspondents.   Someone found him deep in a forbidding work by   *7*
Habershon upon the Prophecies, and he was known to recommend
a learned publication which proved (by the aid of Scripture) that
the aboriginal population of America had originally come from

Tyre. He found it quite convincing and regarded their successful navigation of the Atlantic without compasses as conclusive evidence of the activities of a higher Power. Then he talked of old times in India, told stories about Talleyrand, and went off on the campaign of Vimeiro. For it was more comforting to recall the past than to contemplate a present where O'Connell was haranguing crowds. Crowds always irritated him ; as he thought of them, a little rhyme came back to him—

> " *Pour la canaille*
> *Faut la mitraille* "

and he murmured it quite lovingly as they went in to dinner. But his old despairs had very nearly vanished, since his countrymen showed sense enough to discard the Whigs ; and though there were difficulties in sight, " I do not conceive them to be insurmountable, and I have good hopes for the future." For though the world was changing fast, perhaps it would not change too much.

2

The customary scene was Walmer, though the big house at Hyde Park Corner and the long rooms at Stratfield Saye still knew their master. But his most frequent setting in those later years was the low, castellated house beside the Kentish sea. Its aspect, like the Lord Warden's, was strictly military. But time had made them both civilians ; its port-holes were bedroom windows now, its platform a verandah, and the moat performed the peaceful office of a kitchen-garden. No less civilian, the Duke, white-trousered and blue-coated, emerged at six o'clock, tramped up and down his battlements, enjoyed the morning sun, and reappeared at breakfast. A morning with his papers, a ride to Dover in the afternoon, another turn upon the flagstones, dinner, a quiet evening (unless Stanhope was in the house), and a bowed figure with a silver head lit the flat candlesticks and wished them all good-night.

His life was easy there, though he had his Cinque Ports business, giving the countersign to the Dover garrison each day and walking through Walmer in procession with the pilots when his Court was held. He was a friendly neighbour, strolling unasked into Deal lodging-houses in order to invite a wholly unimportant stranger to shoot his woodcock, or sending somebody at Dover his garden key. Stray visitors with children found themselves miraculously asked to dinner ; and when someone in the neighbourhood complained of the devastations of the Castle rooks, he replied meekly that they should be destroyed. He had his sterner moments, though, when a female was summarily deported from the neighbourhood ; and a letter asking him to make some charitable award to a young lady, who pleaded that she was eligible for an annuity bequeathed to Kentish girls and that her father (whom she supported by dressmaking) was seventy-eight, provoked the Duke's compliments and his desire " that she will specify in clear and distinct terms what is the benefit in the way of annuity which is in the gift of the Duke ; which he has the power of conferring on young ladies *seventy-eight years old* of the County of Kent."

He had his garden ; though he was no gardener, admitting to an applicant for employment who had confessed that he knew nothing of gardening, " No more do I, but you can learn." His grounds were full of robins, because the wintry old man had quite a feeling for them. But a slow walk up and down the ramparts was his invariable resource. He tramped them with Arbuthnot ; and an indulgent housekeeper enjoyed the sight of " our two dear old gentlemen so happy together." The Duke, however, was the younger, and on occasion youth would assert itself. For sometimes as they paced the path along the beach at dusk, the younger man halted.

" Now, Arbuthnot," said a deep voice, " you've been out long enough. The dew is falling and you'll catch cold ; you must go in."

So Arbuthnot, slightly protesting, went back to the Castle ; and the Duke tramped on alone.

A cloud of witnesses observed him, but none more eagerly than Haydon. The preliminaries of his visit were much as usual. A Liverpool committee had commissioned a large picture of the Duke musing on the field of Waterloo. True, he had never mused there ; but the sublime in art is not easily discouraged, and Haydon leapt at the canvas with a muttered prayer that he might be no less victorious than his heroic subject. In the intervals of lecturing all over the country and designing a Nelson monument, he painted hard. Would the Duke sit to him ? There was a

chance. Meanwhile, the busy painter improved the occasion
by writing to him on the subject of the Nelson project (eliciting
the slightly ominous reply that Wellington was " not the committee, nor the *secretary to the committee* ; and, above all, not the
corresponding secretary "). He painted hard, borrowed a sketch
of " Copenhagen," and traced his saddler ; and when that
deserving tradesman revealed that he had made all the Duke's
saddles from Salamanca to Waterloo, this information " so
increased my reverence I offered him my arm." Small wonder
that he glowed over the discovery of a small niece of Wellington's
who called her uncle, ' Dukey.' " The terror of Napoleon—
Dukey to his niece ! " But there were still the elusive clothes.
The Duke remained inexorable and " hopes that he will have
some cessation of note-writing about pictures. The Duke knows
nothing about the picture Mr. Haydon proposes to paint. At
all events, he must decline to lend to anybody his clothes, arms
and equipments." Was this the end ? In spite of everything
his picture grew ; D'Orsay called at the studio one day, sublime
in scented gloves, white greatcoat, blue cravat, and " hat of the
primest curve and purest water," picked up a brush and gave a
touch. This would never do—" a Frenchman touch Copenhagen ! "—and the indignant patriot rubbed out the sacrilegious
brushwork. The Duke's clothes still defeated him. But not
for long, since the indomitable Haydon had traced his tailor and
ordered himself a pair of trousers of the Duke's own pattern,
" so that I shall kill two birds with one stone,—wear 'em and
paint 'em. So, my Duke, I *do* you in spite of you."

Not quite in spite of him ; for one October day the postman
brought an invitation to go down to Walmer. The eager guest
set off by way of Ramsgate ; the Castle bell was sounded when he
arrived ; and he met the party at dinner. He found them
gossiping about a circus lady, coast erosion, and Napoleonic
personages. The Duke averred that the French system was
" bullying and driving—they robbed each other, and then poured
out on Europe to fill their stomachs and pockets by robbing
others." So much for the French. As for Don Carlos, he was
" a poor creature." Mankind in general, it seemed, was not much
better, since that evening Wellington was of the opinion that the
natural state of man was plunder ; society was founded upon
property, and that was going fast. The talk strayed, as usual,

to Spain—how they had burnt houses for fuel and how the British soldier must always have a home to go to at night.

" Your Grace," Haydon courageously remarked, " the French always bivouac."

" Yes," said the Duke, " because French, Spanish and all other nations lie anywhere. It is their habit. They have no homes."

Arbuthnot nodded in his chair ; Haydon was studying the Duke's head, until the hero gave a tremendous yawn and rang for candles. He lighted two and gave one to his latest guest. " God bless your Grace," said Haydon, and retired to struggle with the inspiring consciousness of the greatest man on earth asleep just through the wall.

They breakfasted at ten. " Which will ye have," asked Wellington, " black tea or green ? " Six children clamoured at the windows. " Let them in," said Wellington. The invading hordes arrived, charging the Duke with cries of " How d'ye do, Duke ? how d'ye do, Duke ? " One urchin clamoured thirstily, " I want some tea, Duke."

" You shall have it, if you promise not to slop it over me, as you did yesterday."

The speaker hugged them, three a side ; and then they all romped wildly up and down the ramparts, with the Duke in full cry after a small girl. " I'll catch ye," said the Duke, " ha, ha, I've got ye."

He went out hunting in the morning ; and after hunting he sat to Haydon, " like an eagle of the gods who had put on human shape, and had got silvery with age and service." His ride had made him " rosy and dozy " ; and after dinner he read the *Standard* until bedtime. The next day was Sunday ; and Haydon very nearly sat in the Duke's pew, profoundly affected by the spectacle of the conqueror in church. That night he read his paper again. He seemed a little aged when he sat again on Monday, " like an aged eagle beginning to totter from his perch." But a Russian diplomat appeared at lunch ; and the Duke " put on a fine dashing waistcoat " for the occasion. More sketching in the afternoon with Lady Burghersh to keep his subject talking. But he was done at last.

" It's very fine," said Lady Burghersh.

" Is it though ? " said the Duke. " I'm very glad." He

never looked at it. But Arbuthnot and Lady Burghersh both
begged Haydon not to alter it, as he had caught the likeness.
One more evening at the Castle ; then candles and a loud good-
night, and Haydon ended his last day at Walmer.

But sometimes they had statelier visitors. The Duke always
prided himself that he possessed " the most charming marine
residence he had ever seen—that the Queen herself had nothing
to be compared with it." And one day in 1842 he received an
intimation of the royal pleasure to visit him in force. The preparations were extensive ; Pitt's room was hastily partitioned off
and gaily papered to form a royal dining-room ; the village
carpenter put up a little shelf to hold a timepiece in view of the
royal bed (understood to be required for Albert's full happiness) ;
and their careful host gave detailed directions for the guard of
honour to parade " at a distance from the road and the Castle ;
so as not to frighten the Queen's horses." The Duke himself
removed to the Ship Hotel at Dover. Even his laundry, evacuated by the Duke's mangle, became a royal guard-room ; and
H. B. depicted him surrendering his fortress and retreating with
Lady Douro and his humble belongings. It was all a great
success. The Duke rode over every day ; the royal couple read
Hallam's *Constitutional History* (varied with doses of St. Simon
by way of light refreshment) or went out for excursions. But
they found the house a little draughty ; the Queen caught a cold ;
and it was three weeks before the Duke got back his Castle.
Someone remarked that they had knocked about his rooms a little.
" Yes," he replied with a little smile, " yes, oh yes, they have
rather. Cut up Mr. Pitt's room and turned it into a dining-room,
but it don't signify, I'll soon knock all that down again."

For it was not so easy to displace the past at Walmer.

3

His thoughts were much in the past. With Arbuthnot dozing
in his chair and Alava's endless Spanish chatter, how could he
escape the past ? Not that his life was a mere retrospect, since
it was full of children. They came to stay with him, made havoc
of his breakfast, played hide-and-seek with him along the ramparts, and bombarded him with cushions in the drawing-room.
The *rôle* was most unlikely ; but, as he wrote, " it is my fate to be
all things to all men, women, and children." Indeed, a small boy,

interrupted in a raid upon the Walmer fruit-trees, paid him an unusual compliment—" Never mind, let's go to the Duke ; he always allows everything and gives you what you like directly."

He had been fond of children in the East ; the war deprived him of the nursery days of his own sons ; and when he was restored to them, they were too old for him to do much more than give directions to their tutors, pay their bills, and send their *23* Latin verses to Richard for that connoisseur's approval. But his later years were bright with children. Dickens once saw him at Vauxhall " in a bright white overcoat " with two little girls and *24* Lady Douro ; grave visitors to Stratfield Saye were slightly embarrassed at being received by an old gentleman on all-fours *25* among the crumbs under the dining-table ; and a staid individual who warned a fellow-traveller on the Deal steam-boat that he *26* should really tell his little girl not to romance, as she had just told him that she had a pillow-fight with the Duke of Wellington, was pained to learn that it was the strictest truth. When children stayed with him, he sometimes wrote them letters to arrive by *27* post ; his bulletins to anxious parents were rich in detail—" Bo was indisposed while I was away. He says himself that his *28* Indisposition was occasioned by his eating too much dinner ; which is not unlikely." He shipped them off to France with the precautions appropriate to a well-timed invasion ; and when he wrote to them, he was particularly careful not to write to their parents by the same post, " as I recollected that it was necessary *29* that a letter should be brought for herself by the Postman in order to produce all the Satisfaction that it was capable of producing." His evening pillow-fight (known as the ' battle of Waterloo,' con- *30* ducted in the drawing-room and usually opened by a judicious cushion hurled through his newspaper) was almost a ritual ; and he had a pleasing habit of carrying a store of shillings hung on red and blue ribbons for distribution to stray children. " Are you for *31* Navy," asked the Duke, " or Army ? " Intending sailors got a blue ribbon and soldiers scarlet, though in one disastrous instance a small child, to whom he had promised a commission in the Guards, objected loudly : " But I am a dirl, Mr. Dook." It was all, as Dickens wrote, " good, and aged, and odd." *32*

There was a saving streak of oddity about him. With strongly individual tastes and personal requirements he ran largely to unusual contraptions ; and his mind, as fertile as the

White Knight's in strange devices of his own invention, soared
far beyond the commonplace in household and personal appoint-
33 ments. The lives of visitors were darkened by a teapot perched
in some complicated way on a hot-water jug, which appeared to
possess no merit except that of capsizing more easily than usual ;
he loved to demonstrate his patent finger-bandage ; a supply of
sword-umbrellas afforded him protection against assassins in wet
weather ; and he gratified his fancy by appearing on the road in
queer, boat-like conveyances of personal design. Strange clothing fascinated him in later years. Always susceptible to colds,
he had a weakness for unusual cloaks and mufflers ; overalls of
strange construction seemed to appeal to him ; and he had been
known to appear on horseback with a fur collar and an umbrella.
His passion for such ingenuities had made him a domestic
pioneer. Guests at Stratfield Saye were nearly suffocated by his
novel heating system ; and, born a century before his time, he
was a sanitary enthusiast.

His tastes were simple. A modest standard of barrack-room
discomfort satisfied him, though he was conscious of the arts.
The windfall of King Joseph's coach at Vitoria gave him the
nucleus of a picture gallery, supplemented by judicious purchases
in Paris. He was still buying Dutch and Italian pictures ; and
occasionally he took a fancy to commission a particular scene.
34 Wilkie's *Chelsea Pensioners* originated in one of his ideas, and he
had the notion of setting Landseer to paint a dramatic moment
in a lion-tamer's exhibition. But he was more at home in music.
His guests were firmly led off to the Ancient Concerts, where he
was sometimes gratified by hearing his father's compositions ;
35 Grisi was brought down to sing at Walmer ; and he arranged his
programmes with precision—a selected vocalist and instrumentalists to taste (" If they want the horn I'll have Puzzi. I used to
like the violincello ").

So he lived on amongst his friends. Douro was married to a
charming young lady, of whom he saw a great deal ; and sometimes there were additions to his circle, when Alava made him
36 receive " Mons. Merimée . . . a sort of lion." But strange
faces were infrequent among his grown-up visitors ; for his taste
in acquaintances was formed. He had a home at last, a refuge
from the innumerable contacts of his official life. The world
complained that he did not surround himself with Peninsular

veterans. But why should he? He had lived half his life among them ; and it was far pleasanter to gossip to his little court. Gossip, alas ! was not so easy across the silence of his deafness ; and he turned increasingly to paper, writing innumerable little notes to privileged young ladies about his garden and the weather and the vexations of his public life. Almost indecipherable now, those scribbled pages, where a rose-leaf or a lock of his white hair is often pressed, hold in their trivialities the brave secret of his long struggle against loneliness and silence.

But he could still be formidable. The uneasy figure of John Gurwood moved in the outer circle of his intimates. Brought into early prominence by reckless gallantry at Ciudad Rodrigo, his subsequent career failed to live up to his own expectations. A slight display of temperament before Waterloo was scarcely helpful ; and he spent the next few years in almost constant disappointments and the gloomy survey of *Gazettes* in which his name did not appear. An obscure love-affair assisted his decline, and so early as 1823 his nerves were gravely shaken by a hold-up in Spain. But the Duke, on taking over at the Horse Guards, promptly promoted him ; and Gurwood responded by publishing his master's *General Orders*. This led him to a larger project, and he prepared to edit the entire *corpus* of Wellington's *Dispatches*. Close association with the Duke made him a devotee ; and when the work concluded, the Duke reciprocated by obtaining him a pension and the post (after a struggle with Macaulay) of Deputy-Lieutenant of the Tower. Gurwood expanded in the sunshine of success. It was extremely pleasant to frequent the little circle at Stratfield Saye—so pleasant that he consented to be seen there without his wife. For Mrs. Gurwood's antecedents would hardly bear the strict examination to which pedigrees were subjected in the Duke's social neighbourhood. A bright Parisian *brunette*, she was unlikely to associate on easy terms with Lady Douro. First heard of as the widow of an invisible M. Mayer, deceased (it was charitably supposed) in Africa, Fanny Gurwood, *née* Kreilssamner, of Mulhouse, had two sisters of whom one worked at a Paris dressmaker's, while the other enjoyed the less arduous protection of the Director of the *Comédie Française* ; and it was Gurwood's practice to accept the Duke's invitations as a bachelor. But in spite of everything his nerves continued to grow worse ; and they were not improved by a sharp controversy with Napier, in which his Peninsular laurels were impugned. As years went by, he had recourse to mediums ; animal magnetism fascinated him ; and he dabbled in the new wonders of mesmerism. His work grew heavier than ever, as he was now deep in an enlarged edition of the *Dispatches*. Mountains of documents confronted him, all clamouring to be copied out, arranged in order, printed, and indexed. At last he finished them ; but the index was too much for him. Sleep left him ; he was dreadfully depressed, spending a good deal of his time burning his precious papers ; and the Duke gave him leave to go to Brighton, where he sat brooding in his lodgings until one afternoon he cut his throat. The Duke's consolations to his widow included a request for papers ; for Wellington, it seemed, had heard from somebody that Gurwood had kept notes of his conversation. But Fanny answered that the unhappy man had destroyed all his documents " from an overstrained sense of delicacy towards Your Grace." The Duke replied with a detailed reiteration of the story :

> " A few days after the funeral of the lamented Colonel Gurwood, the Duke was informed by different persons, by some verbally, by others in writing, that the Colonel had been in the habit, when associating with him, of retiring to his room early at night, or as soon as possible, in order to write down a memorandum of what the Duke had said. . . .
> " The Duke does not believe that there is an instance in history of a similar act. It is anti-social ; it puts an end to all the charms of society, to all familiar and private communication of thought between man and man ; and, in fact, it places every individual in familiar society in the situation in which he puts himself in a publick assembly, with a gentleman of the press to report what he says. . . ."

Sublimely unaware that Stanhope had been doing the same thing for years, the Duke continued in a tone of stern reproof. He was at pains to demonstrate the depravity of such a practice in order to establish that the notes had better be destroyed for Gurwood's sake. This was too much for Fanny Gurwood, who answered hotly. Wellington, quite unabashed, restated his position at length, reminding Mrs. Gurwood a shade unkindly that " he was in the habit of daily intercourse with the Colonel, that he has had the pleasure of receiving him at his house in Hampshire, and at Walmer Castle, to both of which he was

29

constantly invited, and always welcome whenever he chose to come, and that he did come frequently ; but the Duke had never had the honour of receiving Mrs. Gurwood, excepting at balls, concerts, or publick breakfasts " ; and that, in consequence, she was without sufficient knowledge of her late husband's practice when in contact with the Duke. He was still painfully explicit upon the story which had reached him and the iniquity, if credible, of such proceedings. It was all a trifle heavy-handed, although Fanny had given quite as good as she got. But the calm waters of his later years were rarely ruffled ; and his letters dealt more frequently with less exciting themes, as the sea-wind rattled his windows and the sun crept along his battlements.

The long procession of public life went slowly by, and the Duke rode with it. Indeed, he rode in the procession now rather than at its head. His juniors tasted the doubtful joys of leadership, whilst he played to perfection the *rôle* of Elder Statesman. It was a rewarding part, invariably greeted by rounds of affectionate applause. For they cheered him now. Cæsar's Commentaries were unfavourably compared with his *Dispatches*, and ' Atticus '
1   wrote respectful things about " the aquiline supremacy of the Cæsars " in a prose style that bore a strong resemblance to Disraeli's. Dispraise of him was out of fashion ; only perverse persons like Mr. Borrow, who had once used his fists upon a Radical in the Duke's defence, were goaded into finding fault
2   with him for being overrated and with " the loathsome sycophantic nonsense which it has been the fashion to use with respect to Wellington these last twenty years." Even the sharp eye of
3   Jane Carlyle was melted by his " dear kind face " ; and her formidable mate, who once heard him for a quarter of an hour in
4   the House of Lords, confessed that " Wellington hawking, haing, humming—the worst speaker I had ever heard—etched and scratched me out gradually a recognisable *portrait of the fact*, and was the only noble lord who had *spoken* at all." Indeed, a glimpse of Wellington, seen at a ball of Lady Ashburton's in 1850,
5   moved Carlyle to rhapsodies—" Truly a beautiful old man ; I had never seen till now how beautiful, and what an expression of graceful simplicity, veracity, and nobleness there is about the old hero when you see him close at hand. His very size had hitherto deceived me. He is a shortish slightish figure, about five feet eight, of good breadth however, and all muscle or bone. His legs, I think, must be the short part of him, for certainly on horseback I have always taken him to be tall. Eyes beautiful light blue, full of mild valour, with infinitely more faculty and geniality than I had fancied before ; the face wholly gentle, wise,

valiant, and venerable. The voice too, as I again heard, is
'aquiline,' clear, perfectly equable—uncracked, that is—and
perhaps almost musical, but essentially tenor or almost treble
voice—eighty-two, I understand. He glided slowly along,
slightly saluting this and that other, clear, clean, fresh as this
June evening itself, till the silver buckle of his stock vanished into
the door of the next room and I saw him no more."

He was sometimes a spectator now, watching the young
Queen at her first Council and telling somebody that if she had
been his own daughter he could not have desired to see her   6
perform her part better, watching her Coronation, and watching
her reviews a shade derisively—" Much better come in her
carriage." What was a young lady doing on horseback " sur-   7
rounded only by such youths as Lord Hill and me, Lord Albe-
marle and the Duke of Argyll—and if it rains and she gets wet,
or if any other *contretemps* happens, what is to be done ? All
these things sound very little, but they must be considered in a
display of that sort. As to the soldiers, I know *them ;* they won't
care about it one sixpence. It is a childish fancy, because she
has read of Queen Elizabeth at Tilbury Fort ; but *then* there was
threat of foreign invasion, which was an occasion calling for
display ; what occasion is there now ? " Such was the chilly
welcome offered by one legendary figure to its successor.

He watched her hanging on Lord Melbourne's words and drew
the sage conclusion that "she does nothing without consulting him,   8
even up to the time of quitting the table after dinner and retiring
to bed at night." But he was disinclined to active Opposition,
though he assured Arbuthnot that " I have always been and shall
always be in front of the Battle. I cannot hold back." He could
not, if by holding back he meant retirement into private life.
For the Duke of Wellington, that public character which he sustained with an increasing effort, still made demands upon him
which were not to be denied. He must continue to speak his
mind in public and, in that sense, to stand in the forefront of the
battle. The only doubt that Tories sometimes felt was upon
which side he was fighting. The Duke had never been a good
Tory. Indeed, his hostility to all the arts of party was frankly
expressed—" There is nobody who dislikes, so much as I do, and
who knows so little of Party Management. I hate it. . . ."   9
Such prejudices were a rare handicap to leadership in Opposition.

Besides, he often had his doubts; and Opposition leaders who give way to doubts are lost. There was so much to be said for a Government supported by all moderate men. Not that he had the slightest taste for Coalitions; Canning had formed a Coalition once; and "the truth is that *Coalitions* have a bad name!" But, from his point of view, there were worse fates than being governed by Lord Melbourne; and it would be extremely awkward to impose the Tories on the House of Commons, the country, and the Queen. His sense of public duty always kept him in close relations with the Government, writing memoranda for their guidance on Canada and Indian defence. Indeed, he often felt himself obliged to intervene in their support. This was exasperating to eager Tories, who muttered angrily about his failing powers; for what could be more distressing to the Greeks than to observe their great Achilles in a constant posture of defence over the body of a Whig Patroclus? But the Whigs acclaimed his statesmanship; and even from a Tory standpoint there was something to be said for his magnanimity, if England was to be preserved by perpetuating Melbourne and averting a dark future ruled by O'Connell and the Radicals.

The past engaged him too, when Soult came to London for the Coronation and the Duke tactfully postponed publication of the Toulouse volume of his *Dispatches*. The long pursuit across the Pyrenees was ended in a drawing-room at Buckingham Palace, when Wellington came up with Soult at last; and Soult even went to Apsley House. The Duke was civil; but when somebody proposed that he should give the health of the French army, " Damn 'em," he said, " I'll have nothing to do with 'em but beat 'em."

2

He was just seventy, when his course was sharply interrupted. The failing Whigs resigned in 1839, and Melbourne advised his sovereign to send for the Duke. They spoke about his deafness, and Lord M. impressed her to be sure that the old man understood what she said to him. She talked to Wellington for twenty minutes and found him kind. He received her news with concern; but when she asked him to form a Government, the Duke replied that he had no power over the House of Commons, that they were sure to contradict him, and that she had better send for Peel. Then she expressed a hope that Wellington would take a place in the Cabinet.   He made objections, saying that he was old and deaf and unfit for discussion, but that if he could serve her comfort, he should accept.   She mentioned something about the Household ; but he advised her not to make stipulations before anything was proposed.   Then she saw Peel ; and " the Queen don't like his manner after—oh ! how different, how dreadfully so, to that frank, open, natural and most kind, warm manner of Lord Melbourne."   Their interview was highly unpromising, with Sir Robert stiff and shy and the Queen shy and petulant.   When she announced that she should not part with her Ladies, he started visibly and said that he must consult the Duke.   They both returned on the next afternoon, and Wellington tried his hand with her alone.   She had been pressing Peel to make him drop his notion of joining the Cabinet as leader in the House of Lords without office and become Foreign Secretary instead.   She asked the old man thoughtfully whether it would not be too much for him.

" I'm able to do anything," he said in his decided way.

Then they discussed her Ladies ; and the Duke repeated all his arguments—how their opinions were of no significance, but the principle involved had some importance.   The Queen was obdurate ; the Duke, not unaccustomed to young ladies, was less persuasive than usual ; they failed to solve the problem ; and Conservatism subsided once more into Opposition, ' brained ' (in   *13* Disraeli's figure) ' by a fan,' whilst H. B. was moved to unusual bitterness and Alava remarked derisively, " *Je croyais que c'était seulement en Espagne que ces sortes de choses arrivaient.*"

They were all at a Palace ball on the next evening, and their triumphant sovereign wrote that " Peel and the Duke of Welling-   *12* ton came by looking very much put out."   But were they ? Not Wellington, at any rate ; for that day he had been writing gleefully to countless applicants for office that he " found himself   *14* under the necessity of declining to undertake the Commission with which the Queen was pleased to offer to entrust me and recommended that it should be entrusted to Sir Robert Peel. Thank God !   He has resigned the same. . . ."

3

The old man resumed his sentry-go over the Queen, her ministers, and his innumerable charges.   It was a weary round.

15 " Rest ! " he cried bitterly that autumn. " Every other animal —even a donkey, a costermonger's donkey—is allowed some rest, but the Duke of Wellington never ! There is no help for it. As long as I am able to go on, they will put the saddle upon my back and make me go." The load grew heavier—or did it only seem
16 heavier now ? " It is like everything else," he wrote. " Nobody else will do it. The Duke of Wellington *must*." That *rôle* absorbed him, when he would gladly have subsided into leisure.
17 " I am the Duke of Wellington," as he confessed, " and an officer of the army. But there is not an affair of any kind in which I am not required to be a party. And each of these cases is attended by consequences. I am now required to be a party to the establishment of a college in Kent to teach agriculture. . . ." This was too much ; his ordinary business included giving brides away, the House of Lords, Cinque Ports matters, and writing
18 sympathetic letters to maiden ladies who enquired about the weight of baggage carried by soldiers on the march. But agriculture was really quite outside his province ; and with his customary ardour of exposition he took several pages to say so. That was his Achilles' heel : he could not resist answering his letters. Such fatal regularity breeds correspondence ; and as his wrist grew more rheumatic, the notion spread that there was no topic in the world upon which a letter to the Duke would be out of place,
19 until he was left protesting angrily that " they forget that the Duke of Wellington has only one pair of eyes, and only a certain number of hours in the day like other people," or (more touch-
20 ingly) " that which people will not understand is that the whole labour and business and ceremony and everything else of the world cannot be thrown upon one man, and that an old one ! ! "

He was unequal to it now. At seventy his health began to fail
21 under his incorrigible abstemiousness. Indeed, a breakfast of dry bread was a poor preparation for a morning ride on a November day, enlivened by showers of icy rain and conversation on bimetallism. Chilled to the bone, he sat down to his papers, munched half an Abernethy biscuit, and collapsed. But his collapse was brief. In a few hours the still figure on the little bed was up and giving orders once again ; in a few days he answered letters as usual, paid the household bills, attended to his charities, tramped up and down the drawing-room urging a visitor to " tell them at Dover that you have seen me walking—and well—instead

of lying speechless at your feet," and posted off in his open britzka
for an eight hours' drive to London, where he sat in Council to
hear his sovereign announce that she proposed to marry Prince
Albert of Saxe-Coburg-Gotha.   But the attacks recurred in 1840
and 1841 ; for he was ageing now, and his austerity impaired his   *22*
powers of resistance.   Did not Mr. Greville notice how loosely the
clothes hung on him and think him " only a ruin " ?   His face   *23*
grew thinner, and he stooped noticeably ; he was a little apt to
drop asleep over the fire ; his step was firm enough, but he swayed
in the saddle (*Punch* turned a kindly eye upon " the neat white-
haired old gentleman, whom we have all seen rolling upon his horse   *24*
in the Park and Pall Mall—a wonder to all bystanders that he did
not topple over," and one eye-witness recalls him in the saddle at
a perilous tilt, the crop in his right hand rising and falling in a
continuous salute all down the Row).   There was no more hunting
now ; and as it tried his eyes to read without his spectacles, he
could not hope to shoot.   His recreations were all gone.   Even
music failed to entertain him, as the silence of his deafness
deepened ; and, once a connoisseur of Grisi and Tamburini, he
seemed listless now and rarely called for his favourite airs.
" One by one," as an observant neighbour wrote, " all his   *23*
pleasures have dropped from him like leaves from a tree in
winter."   For it was winter now, and the bare boughs of Wellington stood in bleak outline.

He still cast a shadow on the House of Lords, speaking
assiduously on topics of all dimensions from foreign policy to
penny postage and the comparative futility of Indian missions.
His vast knowledge was fortified by an extensive correspondence
with contemporary observers.   Mr. Raikes had constituted himself the Duke's Paris correspondent (rewarded by an unsuccessful   *25*
effort to get him Consular employment) and elicited his comments on the shifting phases of Palmerstonian diplomacy.   The
Duke was frankly sceptical of the advantages of international
controversy conducted "for the same cause as those who quarrel in   *26*
Billingsgate ; that is for language rather than substance."   His
aims were simpler—" to bring the French government back into
its real and beneficial position in the councils of Europe."   For
splendid isolation was little to his taste—" I have no confidence
in the system of *isolement*.   It does not answer in social life for
individuals, nor in politics for nations.   Man is a social animal.

I have still less confidence in *paix armée*. I will do everything that a private individual can do to conciliate and procure peace."
27 (Had he not informed the House of Lords that he was " one of those who consider that the greatest political interest of this country is to remain at peace and amity with all the nations of the world " ?) His comments ranged over the distant past, as
28 he recalled " our absurd declaration of the independence of the colonies of Spain " or thought of Portugal, which once " was not only sound, but, with our assistance, formidable : it was the basis on which the machinery was founded which finally overturned the world."

But the past was very distant now ; and the Duke almost felt that he belonged to it. For when news arrived of armed insurrection in the Welsh mining valleys and shooting in the streets of Newport, he raised two hands in helpless protest and
29 exclaimed, " Oh ! if I were only twenty years younger ! " That would have made him only fifty ; at fifty he had helped Liverpool and Castlereagh to tame democracy ; but he was seventy—and
30 times had changed. " In these times," as he noted later, " and since the Reform Act, a Tory Government is not to be expected." Schedule A and the extended franchise had done their work, and politics appeared to be reduced to a mere scramble between democracy and property, in which no single individual counted for anything and ministers were under the degrading necessity " of taking their course, not according to their notions of what may be wise for the country ; but of what they may be able to carry through both Houses of Parliament." In such a world what place was there for Wellington ? He could still do his military duty and assist in the smooth operation of the House of Lords ; but he found the part increasingly distasteful.

It was some consolation, when Peel brought the Conservatives to power in 1841. Lord M. departed, and Sir Robert took his place. This time there was no suggestion that the Duke should
31 form a Government, although he was still bravely willing " to do anything, go anywhere, and hold any office, or no office, as may be thought most desirable or expedient for the Queen's
32 service." Indeed, the King of Prussia had enquired during the alarums of Palmerston's Egyptian crisis in 1840 if Wellington would command the German armies against France ; and the old man replied that, subject to the Queen's consent, he felt as

equal to the task as ever. But when Peel formed his Government, the Queen recognised that Wellington's health was "too uncertain, *33* and himself too prone to sleep coming over him—as Peel expressed it—to admit of his taking an office in which he would have much to do." So he joined the Cabinet with the less arduous responsibility of leading the House of Lords. His health had rallied, *34* and Greville found him in better trim. But the fresh burden of official business told upon his temper. His duties were discharged ; but their discharge was painful now, and his tired fancy magnified them, until he thought himself too busy to see anyone and refused interviews with terrifying rudeness.

He laboured through the years of Peel's administration. Indeed, when Hill died in 1842, he resumed the post of Commander-in-Chief, adding the Horse Guards to his cares at seventy-three. State ceremonies still engaged him—he received the King of Prussia in his Prussian uniform and the Czar in his Russian *35* kit ; the Queen came to Stratfield Saye ; and when the Prince of Wales was christened, he bore the Sword of State. The return to duty seemed to revive him ; for in 1843 he "spoke *36* with extraordinary vigour, and surprised everybody. He is certainly a much better man in all respects this year than he was two years ago, mind and body more firm." His private comments were as tart as ever ; and he received the news of Ellenborough's Indian enthronement among scenes of Curzonian magnificence with the grim observation that "he ought to sit *37* upon it in a strait waistcoat." The Cabinet was almost tender with him, each minister rising from his place when he had anything to say and going to the chair beside the Duke in order that *38* his views might be audible to their old colleague. He had strong opinions of his own on national defence, which were accentuated by the rising temper of the French ; and among graver problems the proposal for a Peninsular medal recurred. He had never reconciled himself to the notion of a general award of medals. But when his sovereign deftly combined it with a suggestion *39* that his veterans would value a memento of the Duke, he was outmanœuvred ; and forty years after Vimeiro a medal was issued to all survivors of the war, bearing on its reverse a figure of Wellington kneeling to Queen Victoria.

But home affairs absorbed them, when the rains of 1845 destroyed the Irish crop. Peel's mind moved rapidly towards

40 Free Trade. The Duke was sceptical. " Rotten potatoes,"
he remarked without enthusiasm, " have done it all ; they have
put Peel in his d——d fright." He was an old Protectionist ;
but caring less for Protection than for national stability, he
41 argued stoutly that " a good government for the country is more
important than the Corn Laws or any other consideration."
Unlike the Prime Minister, he was no convert to Free Trade—
42 " My position is not the Corn Law ; but it is to maintain a Government in the country." This faith made him a loyal Peelite ;
43 long afterwards he wrote that " having in 1834 brought Sir
Robert Peel from Rome and handed over to him the government
of the country, and having once found that he possessed the
confidence of the sovereign, of Parliament, and of the country,
and thinking that a *government* is of more importance than any
measure or particular law, since the passing of the Reform Act—
I have been most anxious that Sir Robert Peel shall retain power
in his hands ; and I did everything in my power on the one hand
to induce him to modify his proposed measures, and to take time
for carrying them into execution, in order that they might
satisfy those who supported his Government, and on the other
to persuade his colleagues in office to go on."

That was his simple reasoning, when he informed the Cabinet
44 in 1846 that " the Corn Law was a subordinate consideration."
The major problem was the government of England ; and when
Croker bombarded him with Protectionist orthodoxy, he replied
45 majestically, " I am the *retained* servant of the Sovereign of this
empire," and refused to be distracted from the larger issue. Who
was to govern England ? His angry correspondent would prefer
the Corn Laws to be repealed, if they must, by Mr. Cobden.
That was politician's logic. But the Duke would have none of it.
He had seen the fatal consequences of permitting Whigs and
Radicals to carry Reform in 1832 instead of letting Tories do it
with a slight sacrifice of consistency ; and he was not prepared
for a repetition of the same mistake in 1846—" I will not be
instrumental in placing the Government in the hands of the
League and the Radicals." That was his guiding principle. It
was his old strategy of retreat—the deft withdrawal to the next
position in rear, which would keep safe men in office and leave
dangerous characters in Opposition. He had employed it with
success on Catholic Emancipation ; his own supporters failed

him, when he applied it to Reform ; and it was his guide along
the twisting path that led towards Free Trade. He faced with
equanimity the prospect of separation from a large section of
the Tory Party—" I have . . . put an end to the connection   46
between the Party and me." Party loyalties were a secondary
matter, if the country was to be saved from the dubious embraces
of Mr. Cobden. Better Free Trade, he reasoned, with Sir Robert
Peel than Free Trade and the mob. Free Trade was quite inevitable either way ; and, as in 1829, he gave his orders to the House
of Lords—' My Lords ! Attention ! Right about face ! March ! '
They wheeled obediently and repealed the Corn Laws at the
Duke's command. It was the last and most beneficent of his
retreats. The Bill was passed ; and as the old man left the
House in the summer dawn, a little crowd began to cheer. " God   47
bless you, Duke," a workman shouted. " For Heaven's sake,
people," the gruff answer came, " let me get on my horse."

4

Peel fell within the month, and the Duke was out again. But
Opposition was no place for him ; he had never shewn the
slightest aptitude for it ; and his position was now more anomalous
than ever. His views were still Conservative ; but it was quite
impossible for him to " act with a party in Parliament," since he   48
was Commander-in-Chief to a Whig Prime Minister. Lord John
was tactful ; and the watchful Greville noted that " it is curious   49
to see what good terms he is on with the Duke of Wellington, who
is much more cordial and communicative with him than he was
with his former colleagues." They corresponded freely on India   50
and army matters ; and the Duke's letters almost relaxed the
customary stiffness of his official tone. Not that his approval
was extended to all John Russell's colleagues. Lord Palmerston
was at the Foreign Office ; and the livelier excursions of Palmerstonian diplomacy failed to commend themselves to Wellington,
who was profoundly shocked by spirited interventions on behalf
of British tourists :

> " Only conceive calling upon an independent Sovereign to   51
> punish one of his subjects *severely* for anything ! . . . What we
> require is to be able to flatter up the vanity of the sovereign people !
> to be cried up by their vile Press as a Government bullying the world
> in protection of the sole amusement and habits of each thirty-

millionth part of the sovereign people wandering about in search of amusement."

The Duke, it is evident, would not have indulged in heroics over Don Pacifico. His patriotism, though, burned brightly still. For he was quite obsessed by national defence; Arbuthnot reported that " it haunted the Duke of Wellington, and deprived him of rest, and night and day he was occupied with the unhappy state of our foreign relations, the danger of war, and the defenceless state of our coasts." His views were vigorously expressed to the Prime Minister; and a letter to the Inspector-General of Fortifications, dwelling in harrowing detail upon the dangers of invasion and closing with a prayer " that the Almighty may protect me from being the witness of the tragedy, which I cannot persuade my contemporaries to take measures to avert," occasioned general alarm. This document was confidential; but the recipient showed it to Lady Shelley, who lent copies to half the House of Lords. It reached a newspaper; and the Duke's annoyance was extreme. His indignation smouldered for two years, until he met her husband out one evening.

" Good evening, Duke," said Shelley. " Do you know, it has been said by someone, who must have been present, that the cackling of geese once saved Rome. I have been thinking that perhaps the cackling of my old goose may yet save England."

The Duke stared at him and laughed. " By God, Shelley," he said, " you are right. Give me your honest hand." And an old friendship had been saved.

He still had his friends, his walks upon the Walmer battlements, and his correspondence. Mr. Haydon still left little notes at Apsley House asking for an authentic hat to paint from. An application to the Duke elicited the stern reply that " those to whom he gives his hats and clothes know best what to do with them "; but a sympathetic valet heard the painter's prayer and succumbed to a sovereign (of which poor Haydon had few to spare); and the triumphant hero-worshipper " carried off a genuine hat—the glorious hat which had encircled the laurelled head of Wellington! I trusted it to nobody; I took it in the hat-box, called a cab, and gloried in it." The Duke's life was a protracted triumph now. Warned by the dismal fate of Marlborough, he watched his dignity with care—" The Duke of Marlborough, because he was an old man, was treated like an old

woman. I won't be." No problem caused him more anxiety
than his own statue. In the beginning he had viewed it with a
fine indifference, asking " to be considered as *dead* upon all   56
matters relating to the statue," and writing that " the Duke is the
man of all men in England who has the least to do with the
affair." When it was erected on the arch opposite his house,
Arbuthnot wrote almost shyly to him that " it seems as if it would   57
be a Gala day in London." But when it was proposed (on purely
æsthetic grounds) to move it, he took legitimate offence. Even
the Queen, it seemed, took sides against him. More sensitive
than anybody seemed to realise, he felt as though the world was
all united in execration of him, " as . . . in 1808, when I was   58
persecuted by all factions, out of doors as well as in Parliament ;
and the Lord Mayor and the City of London, wishing to treat
a general officer according to the precedent of Admiral Byng,
petitioned the King George III, in my own presence, to bring me
by name to trial before a general court-martial. I faced them
all. . . ." The topic became dangerous ; even the Prime   59
Minister asked Greville nervously if he should mention it at
Apsley House ; and it provoked the Duke to a rare degree of
self-consciousness. Reminding Croker that " more than forty   60
years ago Mr. Pitt observed that I talked as little of myself or my
acts as if I had been an assistant-surgeon of the army," he
launched into a vigorous protest against the fancied slight. The
Prime Minister received a fuller version of the same theme, in   61
which indignation moved him to unusual eloquence—" Without
conviction or trial for offence, or complaint alledged, or even
whispered or suspected ; displeasure is marked with my conduct,
as according to the Hypothesis stated in this letter will be the
opinion founded on the removal of the Statue from its pedestal "
—and he came near threatening to resign the command of the
army. His thunderbolts prevailed ; the Queen surrendered ;   62
and the Duke continued to ride sedately on his arch.

5

He was not far off eighty when the warning bells of 1848
began to clang. Half Europe was in flames ; and a dull glare
on the sky warned London, where half a million Chartists were
on the march. The Duke was studiously calm and did his best to
steady nervous ministers, beckoning one across the House of   63

Lords to inform him that " we shall be as quiet on Monday as we are at this hour, and it will end to the credit of the Government and the country." It did ; but not without his help. For when the Cabinet decided to stop the Chartist march on Westminster, the Duke was sent for. This was a military matter ; and military matters were plainly for the Duke. The old man came promptly ; returns were called for ; maps were unfolded on the Cabinet table ; and as he gripped the problem, his swift decisions put courage into them all. Macaulay was profoundly impressed and thought it the most interesting spectacle that he had ever witnessed. (He told somebody that he should remember it to his dying day ; but then Macaulay remembered everything.) The Duke made his plan on Sunday. If London was to be defended, he was a master of the defensive. He had the Guards, some guns, and three regiments of foot. But it had never been his way to shew the enemy his strength. Besides, the military were a last resource ; for the police might be sufficient. On Monday there was nothing to be seen about the streets except police and special constables (a nephew of the Emperor was on a beat in Piccadilly). Somewhere behind them the troops were waiting, as they had waited behind the slope at Salamanca and the long ridge of Waterloo. But they were never needed ; for the great demonstration melted before a few police inspectors, and revolution drove respectfully to Westminster with its petition in a four-wheeled cab.

But the storms of 1848 brought shipwrecked mariners for consolation to the Duke. The Prince of Prussia came to stay at Stratfield Saye ; and when Wellington got back to London, he called every day on Metternich at the Brunswick Hotel in Hanover Square. The exiles from Vienna came to Apsley House to see the table laid for his Waterloo banquet ; and when Radetzky thrashed the Italians, the Duke wrote to congratulate him. The world was sadly changed, and universal revolution had made havoc of the settlement of 1815 ; but it was some consolation to visit the Metternichs on Richmond Green (and give the Prince a little overcoat of his peculiar design). It was a most disturbing time, when France resumed the tricolour and Lamartine sent pacific messages to Wellington and Lord Palmerston had questionable dealings with the most revolutionary governments ; but though the world was changed, the Duke lived bravely on.

III

A NEW decade—his ninth—was opening. His ninth ? In one sense it was the tenth decade that Wellington had seen. For his eyes had opened in 1769 ; and here was 1850. He was past eighty now ; and time had left the old man almost alone upon an emptying stage. They were all gone ; his colleagues waited for him in stiff, marble attitudes upon their monuments ; the Emperor was at the Invalides, watched by a silent circle of tall Caryatids ; Lord Liverpool was gone, with Castlereagh and Canning ; and now his juniors were going. Melbourne flickered out ; a sudden accident took Peel ; and when the old man spoke a few sentences about him in the House of Lords, his voice was broken. He was a lonely figure ; and as he stood beside his brother Richard's open grave in Eton Chapel, his mouth quivered. Even the faithful Arbuthnot deserted him at last. The Duke saw the doctor in his little room at Apsley House and drew a chair close to catch his words.

" No, no," he said, taking the doctor's hand between his own and rubbing it, " he's not very ill, not very bad—he'll get better."

The old man stared hopefully into the doctor's eyes. " It's only his stomach which is out of order," he suggested. " He'll not die."

But there was no hope. Arbuthnot died with his hand in Wellington's, " quite tranquil " (the Duke wrote), " as a flame extinguishes when the substance which keeps it alive is consumed " ; and the last echo of Harriett Arbuthnot died with him.

His life was full of dying echoes now—of lost ladies and forgotten ministers and his poor fluttered Kitty in her white muslin without jewellery sitting apart and talking to her boys' tutor instead of to the guest of honour, pausing at intervals to gaze with embarrassing devotion in his own direction. One echo pleased him ; for though he had worn mourning for his friend at Hatfield, he took pleasure now in writing little notes to a new Lady Salisbury. Sometimes she shared his daily tramp along the Piccadilly side of the Green Park ; and she was always glad

to have his letters. She told him so, and he was no less glad to
7   write them. " They amuse me," he wrote, " as they do you,
and I laugh while writing them, thinking of the amusement they
will afford you." So she heard all about his minor worries and
affairs of state and local politics at Walmer and cures for colds
and Palmerston's iniquities and the deplorable irregularity of
brides' mothers who expected him to give away their daughters
without informing him whether to meet them at the hotel or at
St. George's, Hanover Square, and if at the church, whether at
the door or in the vestry. His daily gossip with her was a real
pleasure to him. For the deaf talk freely on paper ; and as the
silence deepened round him, the little scribbled notes became his
only form of conversation.

8   His correspondence was still a burden, though. " It is quite
curious," he noted, " with what a number of Insane persons I am
in relation. Mad retired Officers, Mad Women . . ." But he
was gradually learning to elude his persecutors, announcing with
9   an air of discovery that " some write in order to get an answer
which they shew." Indeed, he speculated innocently whether
Cæsar and Hannibal had been exposed to the same form of persecution. He was to blame, he felt, for letting it be thought that
he was " a good-natured Man, with whom Persons may venture
to take liberties, and what the French call serviceable." (Serviceable indeed to the widowed lady at Boulogne who asked him for
five pounds to get her back to England and, when he sent it, asked
five more because his unexpected bounty had moved her to break
a looking-glass with a large piece of statuary.) Small wonder
the Mendicity Society was invoked for his protection and made
matters worse by advertising the extent to which he had been
imposed upon ; for a migratory troop of beggars followed him
about and encamped before his doors. The White Knight was
still strong in him ; and he was fascinated by the new electric
10 cable at Dover, though slightly troubled by the problem of
avoiding injury from passing ships by fastening it securely to
the bottom of the sea. A terrifying machine, known as the
' Jump Baby ' or ' Baby Jumper ' engaged him deeply ; and
Lady Salisbury received a gift of one with profuse instructions
how to screw it to the nursery ceiling and no less than three
reminders that Lord Salisbury or the house carpenter should test
it before a small Cecil was entrusted to this " delightful instru-

30

ment." He had less taste for large-scale inventions, since the
railway failed to commend itself to Wellington, who felt that it
was fraught with peculiar perils for ladies. " I cannot bear,"   *11*
he wrote, " seeing or hearing of ladies going alone by the Trains
on the Rail Roads. It is true that you have with you your
children. But still the protection of a Gentleman is necessary."
The gentry, he conceived, had allowed themselves " to be cheated
and bustled . . . out of the best system and establishment for
travelling that existed in any part of the World. England did
not require Rail Roads." But, however uncalled for, they
had come ; and though he used them on occasion, he remained
gravely impressed with their mysterious menace to England's
womanhood—" If I could attain the object, no lady should ever
go by a Train, at all events without protection. It is horrible
altogether." His greatest heights of ingenuity were reserved, as
usual, for sartorial invention. Lady Salisbury, whose taste in
costume was unusual, received consignments of his waistcoats   *12*
with detailed instructions for their adaptation ; and when the
polite world giggled discreetly over Mrs. Bloomer's epoch-making
innovation, the Duke was highly interested. " I am vastly
amused," he wrote, " by the Bloomer discussions ! I understand
them, being somewhat of a Taylor." But the contemplated
revolution in female apparel was too much for him; and he
concluded that " it is impossible that the Costume should be
adopted ! "
    The roar of public life receded. But when patriotic draymen
mobbed the unpleasant Haynau, he commented grimly that
" the travellers of the Bull family will suffer for it." He made a   *13*
strenuous attempt to induce Prince Albert to be his successor at
the Horse Guards. Not that he had the least intention of resigning ;   *14*
for he told the Prince that he was, thank God, very well and
strong and ready to do anything. But he was nearly eighty-one ;
and it was most desirable, he felt, that the Crown should control
the army in these democratic times—" the democrats would
blow me up if they could, but they find me too heavy for them."
He said the same thing to the Queen, who countered that Albert
already acted as her private secretary and worked far harder than
she liked, and that these extra duties might be too much for him.
There were more conferences ; memoranda were exchanged ;
but the proposal dropped. A livelier business occupied him,

when a prince was born on May 1, 1850. The lyre was struck
by Thackeray :

15

" To Hapsly Ouse next day
    Drives up a Broosh, and for,
A gracious prince sits in that Shay
    (I mention him with Hor !)

" They ring upon the bell,
    The Porter shows his Ed
(He fought at Vaterloo as vell,
    And vears a Veskit red).

" To see that carriage come
    The people round it press :
' And is the galliant Duke at ome ? '
    ' Your Royal Ighness, yes.'

" He stepps from out the Broosh,
    And in the gate is gone ;
And X, although the people push,
    Says wery kind, ' Move hon.'

" The Royal Prince unto
    The galliant Duke did say,
' Dear Duke, my little son and you
    Was born the self-same day.

" ' The Lady of the land,
    My wife and Sovring dear,
It is by her horgust command
    I wait upon you here.

" ' That lady is as well
    As can expected be ;
And to your Grace she bids me tell
    This gracious message free.

" ' That offspring of our race
    Whom yesterday you see,
To show our honour for your Grace,
    Prince Arthur he shall be.

" ' You fought with Bonypart,
     And likewise Tippoo Saib ;
   I name you then with all my heart
     The Godsire of this babe.' "

Albert recorded their selection with a less sprightly pen, reporting
for the eye of Stockmar that " his first name is in compliment   *16*
to the good old Duke, on whose eighty-first birthday he first saw
the light.   Patrick is in remembrance of our recent visit to Ireland ; William, of the Prince of Prussia, whom we shall ask to
be godfather, and also in remembrance of poor Queen Adelaide,
on whose account we have also selected the Duchess Ida of Saxe-
Weimar as godmother.   My name the Queen insists on retaining
by way of *coda*.   I hope you will approve the arrangement.
The Exhibition is making good progress. . . ."

The Duke had his cares as Ranger of Hyde Park.   For his
territory had been invaded by a determined female, who was   *17*
unlawfully established in a hut by the Serpentine and was suspected of intent to sell cakes and oranges.   " We must proceed,"
he wrote, " with caution and Regularity " ; and he rode out to
reconnoitre her position as thoroughly as though she had been
Masséna.   He viewed the ground with care ; but before his
offensive could develop, the enemy decamped, leaving the Duke
victorious again.   He had one more victory in 1851, when the
Great Exhibition glittered in the Park.   The watchful Commons
had insisted that no trees should be cut down.   A dreadful
consequence ensued.   For when the marvels of art and industry
were exposed to view, the lively sparrows began to spoil them.
The dilemma was agonising, since it was impossible to shoot the
sparrows without breaking half the glass in the great building.
What was to be done ?   His country turned, as usual, to Wellington.   The Duke was sent for ; and the Queen herself explained
the difficulty.   " Try sparrow-hawks, Ma'am," he replied.   It was
Wellington's last victory.

He found the Exhibition a great resource, rode up to see it
every day, talked to the stall-keepers, made appointments to meet   *18*
ladies in " the Glass Palace," and bought Miss Coutts a bracelet
there.   That summer he met Thiers and " had to make him some   *19*
phrases about the Emperor Napoleon."   There was a fancy ball
in Queen Anne costume, to which he dutifully went in powder   *20*
and three-cornered hat, remembering to show the children how to

walk a minuet before he went. Politics were a receding murmur
now, though early in the year he had been called on to advise the
Queen, when John Russell resigned and nobody would form a
21 Government. The Duke was sent for and advised his sovereign
to try Lord John again. Not that he had turned Whig, since he
called on Derby afterwards to express his satisfaction and said,
" Well, they are in the mud, and now you can look about you."
He was quite right ; for the Conservatives came in the next year.
He sat beside the new Prime Minister in the House of Lords ; and
as he strained to catch the unfamiliar names of the new Cabinet (a
Mr. Disraeli was to be Chancellor of the Exchequer), the old man
22 kept asking Derby, " Who ? Who ? " So somebody nicknamed
the Government of 1852 ' the Who ? Who ? Ministry.'

The slow weeks of 1852 went by ; and Wellington still went
23 his rounds. That summer he made quite a long speech in the
House of Lords on the Militia Bill ; and when the stooping figure
24 rose at the Academy banquet, they heard him speak of the admirable discipline which had prevailed on board the sinking *Birken-*
25 *head.* He spoke a final sentence on the same subject in the House
of Lords. Then the House rose for the recess, and England went
on holiday. The Duke, as usual, was at Walmer, pacing slowly
26 up and down his battlements or writing letters in his little room.
(His standing-desk stood in the recess that looked towards the sea
and caught the morning sun ; and his camp-bed, with the silk
mattress which he had devised for Russia in 1825, was in the
corner of the room.) A Grand-Duchess and her husband came
27 to stay, and there were moments when their host could " wish my
Imperial Royalties were in Russia." But he saw them off from
Dover and returned to his little fortress with relief. That was the
28 worst of being deaf—" one gets bored in boring others, and one
becomes too happy to get home." Deafness apart, he had little
fault to find with life at eighty-three—" I really believe that there
is not a youth in London who could enjoy the world more than
myself . . . but being deaf, the spirit, not the body, tires ! "
The body, indeed, was strictly mortified by his remarkable
régime, which comprised systematic starving and massage with
vinegar and water.

September came ; and he rode into Dover and caught the
29 train to Folkestone for a call on Mr. Croker. They told him at
the station that the house was only half a mile away. So the

Duke started out to walk there and discovered that it was a three-mile walk ending with a climb up a steep hill ; and at the end of it he found that Croker had gone into Dover. He started home again, ordered a fly to take him to the station, but positively walked part of the way until his conveyance overtook him. A meeting was arranged with more success a few days later ; and the two old men sat gossiping about the past. They talked of old Irish Office Bills which he had left in Croker's charge when he went out to take command in the Peninsula, of the forgotten Parliament on College Green, of his horse " Copenhagen," and the endless complexities of Reparations in 1818. The Duke began to tell a story about a Spanish lady at Salamanca who had hidden some papers about herself, and broke off to spare Mrs. Croker's blushes. Then he explained to her that " all the business of war, and indeed all the business of life, is to endeavour to find out what you don't know by what you do ; that's what I call ' guessing what was at the other side of the hill.' " The talk ran on French generals, and he said reminiscently that the Emperor was the best of them all. His own success in Spain had come, he thought, because he was " a *conquérant sans ambition.* I had for a time a sovereign power there, but no one suspected me of any design to become King of Spain or Portugal, like Joseph or Soult or Junot. I *was* almost King of Spain. . . ." The time slipped by ; and when his carriage came, the Duke walked slowly down the steps counting them aloud for Croker's guidance. A slightly intoxicated Irishman with a Peninsular medal besieged him at the station and received the invariable sovereign. Then the Duke went back to Walmer.

He was not lonely, though ; for his son Charles was at the Castle with his children. Besides, there was his correspondence—eight pages of Spanish in pale ink from Ciudad Rodrigo about a local grievance, his daily gossip with Lady Salisbury, and all his begging letters. His mind was running on the past ; and he wrote off a long account of the mob that followed him through London in 1832, and how pleased the King had been when Oxford made him Chancellor. He had a letter from a madman, who proposed to call with a message from the Lord. But he was expecting more normal visitors ; for Lady Burghersh was due to arrive on Tuesday and Lady Salisbury on Wednesday. He seemed quite well on Monday ; and when his servant went to him on Tuesday

morning (it was September 14), he ordered his carriage for a drive
to Dover. But a little later he felt unwell and, methodical as
ever, said: " I feel very ill; send for the apothecary." It
was his last order; for the Duke never spoke again. He had
been born beside the sea, where the long tide crept slowly round
the bay from Dalkey to the hill of Howth; and the sea whispered
still beyond the windows of his silent room, as the tide ebbed
slowly and the Duke sat on, a huddled figure in a high-backed
chair.

IV

ALL through the long November night it rained. The rain fell relentlessly, and London waited for the dawn with gleaming pavements. The Park trees stood dripping in the downpour outside a shuttered house at Hyde Park Corner. It drummed on the Great Hall at Chelsea, where two hundred thousand people had trooped by candlelight for five days past a still pageant of black velvet and silver stars, watched by immobile sentries resting stiffly on their arms reversed. Eastwards across the darkness a gilded cross dripped in the winter night on the Cathedral dome that waited for the day with all its windows darkened ; and midway the hours chimed slowly from the Horse Guards. Outside on the parade the water stood in pools, and the rain whispered round the tent where men were working all night long on the great car. The night was paling now ; and as it turned to grey, a darker mass was etched upon it, where the long lines of troops moved into place. There was a steady tramp of marching feet ; cavalry went jingling by ; words of command hung on the chilly morning air ; and as the pale winter day came up, the rain checked. For the Duke was riding out again ; and it was his way to ride out after rain. (Had it not rained that night before he rode to Waterloo ?) It was broad daylight now. A gun thudded in the Park. The ranks stiffened ; and as the bands wailed out the slow refrain, his last ride began.

Duke of Wellington, Marquis of Wellington, Marquis of Douro, Earl of Wellington in Somerset, Viscount Wellington of Talavera, Baron Douro of Wellesley, Prince of Waterloo in the Netherlands, Duke of Ciudad Rodrigo in Spain, Duke of Brunoy in France, Duke of Vittoria, Marquis of Torres Vedras, Count of Vimiero in Portugal, a Grandee of the First Class in Spain, a Privy Councillor, Commander-in-Chief of the British Army, Colonel of the Grenadier Guards, Colonel of . . .

The minute-guns spoke slowly from the Park ; and the car—

twenty-seven feet of assorted allegory—" rolled," in its proud
creator's words, " majestically forth." It was a triumph in its
way—a triumph over Banting, the undertaker, who had submitted
drawings made (*proh pudor !*) by a Frenchman ; a triumph for
the new superintendent of the Department of Practical Art, whose
modest sketch had drawn from Prince Albert the rapturous
exclamation, " This is the thing." Small wonder that this sublime vehicle, all black and gold, was generously adorned with
lions' heads, with sabres, with laurel wreaths ; and in case its
delicate symbolism should be missed, a thoughtful hand had
added an immense trophy of real swords and muskets. One
witness might observe a trifle bleakly that something in its outline
recalled a railway truck. But *The Times'* enraptured eye was
fastened on " the magnificent dolphins, symbolical of maritime
supremacy, playfully wrought out along the spokes . . . the
sumptuous pall, powdered with silver embroiderings—and the
not less superb canopy of silver tissue, after an Indian pattern,
manufactured with unexampled rapidity and skill by Keith &
Co., of Wood-street." Nor was the *Illustrated London News*
blind to the marvels of the canopy's supports, since they were
halberts—no ordinary halberts, though, but halberts rising from
ornamental tripods and " lowered by machinery in passing
through Temple Bar," itself surmounted by vases burning incense
and transformed into the semblance of a proscenium arch for some
sepulchral pantomime. This portent had a stormy birth. Competing Government Departments hung like rival fairies above
its cradle. The Lord Chamberlain was gravely exercised ; the
Board of Works had a word to say ; the War Department
intervened ; and for some occult departmental reason the Board
of Trade conceived the matter to be its own sole concern. Six
foundries struggled with the castings ; the ladies of the School of
Art stitched with demented fingers ; and in three weeks this
monument of art and industry rumbled across the Horse Guards.
It rumbled, to be more precise, into the Mall ; and there, just
opposite the Duke of York's column, it gave a dreadful lurch
and stayed. For the sodden roadway had collapsed under its
weight, and the great wheels were buried up to the lions on their
axles. Twelve dray-horses, sublime with funeral feathers,
strained vainly at the traces. But five dozen constables leaned on
a cable ; and the stupendous hearse staggered once more into

motion. The slow march resumed ; and from the Park the
minute-guns still thudded on the damp morning air—

> . . . *Field-Marshal of Great Britain, a Marshal of Russia,*
> *a Marshal of Austria, a Marshal of France, a Marshal of Prussia,*
> *a Marshal of Spain, a Marshal of Portugal, a Marshal of the*
> *Netherlands, a Knight of the Garter, a Knight of the Holy Ghost,*
> *a Knight of the Golden Fleece, a Knight Grand Cross of the Bath,*
> *a Knight Grand Cross of Hanover, a Knight of the Black Eagle,*
> *a Knight* . . .

The Queen was waiting at the Palace with a melancholy conviction that " we shall soon stand sadly alone ; Aberdeen is almost
the only personal friend of that kind we have left. Melbourne,
Peel, Liverpool—and now the Duke—*all* gone ! " The news
had reached them in the Highlands on an excursion from Allt-na-
Giuthasach, whilst they were " sitting by the side of the Dhu
Loch, one of the severest, wildest spots imaginable " ; and her
pen promptly underlined his epitaph—" the pride and the *bon
génie*, as it were, of this country. He was the GREATEST man this
country ever produced, and the most *devoted* and *loyal* subject,
and the staunchest supporter the Crown ever had. He was to
us a true kind friend and most valuable adviser. . . . Albert is
much grieved. The dear Duke showed him great confidence and
kindness." Even his small godson, Arthur of Connaught, kept
murmuring, " The Duke of Wellikon, little Arta's Godpapa " ;
for the pair of them had rambled through the big rooms at
Apsley House together, when the Queen sent the baby round for
the last anniversary of Waterloo. Small wonder that the long
procession and the silent crowds made " a deep and *wehmütige*
impression," as the old man passed her Palace windows for the
last time. Albert rode with his mournful thoughts in the *cortège*.
He felt the loss as well, " as if in a tissue a particular thread
which is worked into every pattern was suddenly withdrawn."
Stockmar responded with a thoughtful analysis of human greatness, concluding with a slightly condescending estimate—" His
intellect was not many-sided and mobile, but with all its one-
sidedness it was always clear and sound, so that although the
principles which lay at the foundation of his character were not
of the noblest kind, still they contained a good sprinkling of prac-

tical truth, justice, and honesty." His object, it would seem, was to incite his princely pupil " to replace the Duke for the country and the world." The country was less ardent to accept the substitute ; and a notion that the Prince might be Wellington's successor as Commander-in-Chief occasioned general alarm. But he retained his sober predilection for " *silent* influence," and drove sedately in a mourning carriage. Half England rode in the procession, watched by the silent pavements. There was no sound along the route except a sudden, scattered cry of " Hats off " above the rolling of the wheels, the wail of military bands, the thud of muffled drums, the slow beat of hoofs, and the dull pulse of tramping men.

> . . . *Knight of the Sword of Sweden, a Knight of St. Andrew of Russia, a Knight of the Annunciado of Sardinia, a Knight of the Elephant of Denmark, a Knight of Maria Theresa, a Knight of St. George of Russia, a Knight of the Crown of Rue of Saxony, a Knight of Fidelity of Baden, a Knight of Maximilian Joseph of Bavaria, a Knight of St. Alexander Newsky of Russia, a Knight of St. Hermenegilda of Spain, a Knight of the Red Eagle of Brandenburgh, a Knight of St. Januarius, a Knight of the Golden Lion of Hesse-Cassel, a Knight of the Lion of . . .*

Still they went by. Three thousand foot brought on the slow *cortège* ; eight squadrons followed, and three batteries of guns clanked past. It was the strangest medley of his long career slowly passing by. East India Directors ; one rigid private of every British regiment with arms reversed ; Chelsea Pensioners marching a little stiffly ; then the civilians—the Bench, the Cabinet, and Mr. Disraeli in a mourning coach wishing that his memory of Thiers' obituary of a French Marshal had not been quite so perfect as to obtrude itself almost *verbatim* into his funeral oration. The new Laureate, whose *Ode* was out that morning, watched from a window and was " struck with the look of sober manhood in the British soldier," as he marched to bury the great Duke ; and by the strangest irony of all a son of the Emperor was waiting gravely at St. Paul's in diplomatic uniform. For when Walewski hesitated, the Prince-President had sent him orders to attend ; and Napoleon's son mourned Wellington by order of Napoleon's nephew, his bland Russian colleague en-

couraging him with " *Mon cher, si nous allions* ressusciter *ce
pauvre duc, je comprends que vous pourriez vous dispenser d'assister
à cette cérémonie; mais puisque nous sommes invités pour
l'enterrer.* . . ." Mr. Carlyle, much tried by " all the empty
fools of creation " crowding to Chelsea, mourned " the one true
man of official men in England, or that I know of in Europe,"
from a second-floor in Bath House. Generous to " the *last*
perfectly honest and perfectly brave public man," he was highly
disrespectful to the car—" of all the objects I ever saw the abom-
inably ugliest, or nearly so. An incoherent huddle of expensive
palls, flags, sheets, and gilt emblems and cross poles, more like
one of the street carts that hawk door-mats than a bier for a
hero . . . this vile *ne plus ultra* of Cockneyism ; but poor Wellington lay dead beneath it faring dumb to his long home." That
thought almost stifled Lord Shaftesbury's austere disapproval
of so much secular magnificence—" fine, very fine, but hardly
impressive ; signs of mortality but none of resurrection ; much
of a great man in his generation, but nothing of a great spirit in
another ; not a trace of religion, not a shadow of eternity. . . .
Stupendously grand in troops and music. It was solemn, and
even touching ; but it was a show, an eye-tickler to 999 out of
every thousand—a mere amusement." Perhaps. Yet the
crowds watched bareheaded all through the winter morning
(outside St. Paul's they were so closely packed that the lamp-
lighters never reached the street-lamps, and the lights burned all
day above the silent throng) ; and as the long procession passed,
band after band caught up the slow refrain—

. . . *The Lord High Constable of England, the Constable
of the Tower, the Constable of Dover Castle, Warden of the Cinque
Ports, Chancellor of the Cinque Ports, Admiral of the Cinque
Ports, Lord-Lieutenant of Hampshire, Lord-Lieutenant of the
Tower Hamlets, Ranger of St. James's Park, Ranger of Hyde
Park, Chancellor of the University of Oxford* . . .

The long lines went by, wound slowly through the Park and past
the blind windows of his empty house, down the long hill towards
the City, until the trumpets died away.

AUTHORITIES

THE EDUCATION OF ARTHUR WESLEY

I

1. LECKY, W. E. H.: *History of Ireland in the Eighteenth Century*, 1892, I, 289–90.

2. GEORGIAN SOCIETY: *Records of Eighteenth-Century Domestic Architecture and Decoration in Ireland*, 1909–13, V, 65.

3. WALPOLE, HORACE: *Letters* (ed. Paget Toynbee), 1903–25, VIII, 256.

4. GEORGIAN SOCIETY: *op. cit.*, V, *passim*.

5. LECKY, W. E. H.: *op. cit.*, I, 285–6. 6. *Ibid.*, III, 413.

7. *Ibid.*, I, 293. 8. *Ibid.*, I, 282. 9. *Ibid.*, II, 188.

10. GEORGIAN SOCIETY: *op. cit.*, I–IV, *passim*.

11. WALPOLE, HORACE: *op. cit.*, III, 209. 12. *Ibid.*, V, 129.

13. LECKY, W. E. H.: *op. cit.*, II, 22.

14. DUBLIN MERCURY: April 29–May 2, 1769.

15. Assignment of 6 Merrion Street by Earl of Antrim to Earl of Mornington for £2,697. August 16, 1769, Registry of Deeds, Dublin.

16. GEORGIAN SOCIETY: *op. cit.*, I, 13–14, 37, Plates XXXIX–XL.

17. MURRAY, J.: *Lost Escutcheon*, 1850; *Birthplace of Wellington*, 1852; *Wellington : the Place and Day of his Birth*, 1852. BURKE, SIR B.: *Rise of Great Families*, 1873, 94–107. NOTES AND QUERIES, *4th Series*, X, 443; *7th Series*, XI, 35. THE TIMES, June 3, 4, 7, 8, 10, 19, 1926.

A. BIRTHPLACE.—The following have been suggested :

    (*i*) Mornington House, 6 Merrion Street (now 24 Upper Merrion Street), Dublin.

    (*ii*) Grafton Street, Dublin.

    (*iii*) Dangan, co. Meath.

    (*iv*) Trim, co. Meath.

    (*v*) Mornington, co. Meath.

    (*vi*) Athy, co. Kildare.

    (*vii*) Between Dangan and Dublin.

    (*viii*) At sea off Dublin.

All except (*i*) are disposed of by the fact that the four contemporary Irish newspapers which record the event place it " in Merrion Street " (*Dublin Gazette*, May 2–4 ; *Dublin Mercury*, May 4 ; *Pue's Occurrences*, May 6 ; *Public Register or Freeman's Journal*, May 6, 1769). Merrion Street being established as the locality, there is little uncertainty as to the actual house. A shadowy tradition founded on oral evidence and recorded in *Complete Peerage*, places the event in an unidentified house belonging to Provost Andrews, of Trinity College, which is stated to have been lent to the Morningtons whilst their new residence was getting ready. But it

seems hardly likely that an unmarried Provost was still in possession of a
house in Merrion Street in addition to his official residence at a date ten
years after his own appointment.   No lease of it in his name is to be found
in the Registry of Deeds, and contemporary Directories are unanimous in
giving Trinity College as his sole address.   There is, however, a bare possibility that the event occurred during a brief tenancy of these premises, of
which no tangible evidence exists.   But, on the whole, it is reasonable to
assume that Lord Mornington's occupation of No. 6 preceded his formal
acquisition of the house on Aug. 16, 1769 ; and (i) may therefore be
adopted with confidence.

    B. DATE OF BIRTH.—Two dates have been suggested :
        (i) April 29.
        (ii) May 1.

    (i) is supported by (a) notice of birth on April 29 in *Exshaw's Gentle-
man's Magazine*, May, 1769 ; (b) entry of baptism on April 30 in Register
of St. Peter's, Dublin ; and (c) copy of prescription by Sir Fielding Ould,
M.D., dispensed by Messrs. Evans, 9 Dawson Street, Dublin, on April 30
for Lady Mornington and " the young child."

    (ii) is supported by (a) Lord Mornington's attestation of April 1, 1779
(Lord's Entries, Office of Arms, Dublin Castle) ; (b) Lady Mornington's
statement of April 6, 1815 (MURRAY, W. : *The Place and Day of his Birth*,
20) ; and (c) W.'s lifelong belief.

    The evidence in support of (i) is scarcely satisfactory, since the pre-
scription for " the young child " proves on examination to have been
wholly unsuited to a new-born infant, and was therefore written for his
sister Ann, then twelve months old.   As to the notices in *Exshaw* and St.
Peter's Register, the former was a monthly magazine of frequent inac-
curacy, and Irish parish registers of this period are unreliable as to dates.
If, moreover, both are accepted as correct, it would follow that W. was
baptised on the day following his birth, a circumstance which presupposes
that the infant was thought to be in danger of immediate death.   But
there is no trace whatever of this remarkable fact either in tradition (though
it is not easy to believe that so precarious an opening of so long and
eminent a career could have passed wholly unnoticed) or in the chemist's
books, since Arthur's first medicine (and that a mere lotion) was not made
up until July 1, 1769.

    In the absence, therefore, of reliable evidence in support of (i), I
incline to (ii), which rests upon the belief of W. and of both his parents,
and is supported by the father's sworn evidence in a public document of
great formality.

II

    1. DELANY, MRS. : *Autobiography and Correspondence*, 1861, I, 348–9.
    2. *Ibid.*, I, 406.   3. *Ibid.*, I, 361.   4. *Ibid.*, I, 345.
    5. BARRINGTON, D. : *Miscellanies*, 1781, 317.
    6. DELANY, MRS. : *op. cit.*, I, 409.   7. *Ibid.*, II, 501.
    8. BARRINGTON, D. : *op cit.*, 318–19.
    9. DELANY, MRS. : *op. cit.*, III, 546.   10. *Ibid.*, III, 535.

11. GEORGIAN SOCIETY : *op. cit.*, III, 75.
12. DELANY, MRS. : *op. cit.*, III, 514–15.   13. *Ibid.*, III, 539.
14. *Ibid.*, III, 540, 546.
15. PUBLIC GAZETTEER : June 21, 1760.
16. DELANY, MRS. : *op. cit.*, 531–2.
17. LECKY, W. E. H. : *op. cit.*, I, 342.
18. BARRINGTON, D. : *op. cit.*, 320.

III

1. WALPOLE, HORACE : *op. cit.*, VII, 197.   2. *Ibid.*, VII, 293.
3. *Ibid.*, VIII, 317–18.
4. GEORGIAN SOCIETY : *op. cit.*, II, 205.
5. DELANY, MRS. : *op. cit.*, V, 408.
6. Information supplied by Mr. Reginald Blunt. The school was at 185 King's Road, Chelsea, on the south side, a little west of the present Town Hall.
7. MORNINGTON, EARL OF : *Letter to Dublin agent*, Oct. 7, 1780. In the possession of Lord Gerald Wellesley.
8. LYNDON, W. : *Letter to Lord Wellesley*, undated. In the possession of Lord Gerald Wellesley. Cf. Mortgage £1,000 of March 4, 1774, by Earl of Mornington to C. P. Leslie and S. Gardiner. Registry of Deeds, Dublin.
9. Account for funeral expenses of Lord Mornington. In the possession of Lord Gerald Wellesley.
10. THACKERAY, W. M. : *Lines on a Late Hospicious Ewent*, 1850.

IV

1. Mortgage of Laracor, Great Ginnetts, Little Ginnetts, Clonemeath, and Doolestown, co. Meath, by Earl of Mornington to Rt. Hon. D. La Touche, of Dublin, for £8,000, July 4, 1781. Registry of Deeds, Dublin.
2. MAXWELL LYTE, H. C. : *History of Eton College*, 1889, 334.
3. ETON COLLEGE REGISTER, 1921.
4. MAXWELL LYTE, H. C. : *op cit.*, 323.
5. ETON COLLEGE LISTS, 1678–1790. Ed. R. A. Austen-Leigh, 1907.
6. MAXWELL LYTE, H. C. : *op. cit.*, 300–1.
7. FRASER, SIR W. : *Words on Wellington*, 1900, 122, 161.
8. MAXWELL LYTE, H. C. : *op. cit.*, 305.
9. MAXWELL, SIR H. : *Life of Wellington*, 1899, I, 4.
10. VILLEBIOT, G. DE LA : *L'Académie d'Équitation et les Origines de l'enseignement équestre à Angers*, (Angers) 1909.
11. STANHOPE, EARL : *Conversations with the Duke of Wellington*, 1888, 164–7.
12. BRIALMONT AND GLEIG : *Life of Wellington*, 1858, I, 6.
13. MAXWELL, SIR H. : *op. cit.*, I, 5–6.
14. Mortgage of Dangan, Ballymaglasson, Mornington, Laracor, Oldrath, Great Ginnetts, Little Ginnetts, Clonemeath, Doolestown, and

31

Moygare to Hon. R. Annesley and H. Gorges, of Dublin, for £10,000. May 24, 1785. Registry of Deeds, Dublin.

15. DICTIONARY OF NATIONAL BIOGRAPHY : *s.v.* Wellington.

V

1. CROKER, J. W.: *Correspondence and Diaries*, 1885, I, 337.
2. MORNINGTON, COUNTESS OF: *Letter to Miss Butler and Miss Ponsonby*, Llangollen, Nov. 26, 1787. In the possession of C. Hamilton, Esq., Hamwood, Dunboyne, co. Meath.
3. MORNINGTON, COUNTESS OF: *Letter to Miss Butler and Miss Ponsonby*, Llangollen, Dec. 17, 1787. *Ibid.*
4. *The Hamwood Papers of the Ladies of Llangollen* (ed. Bell), 1930, 72.
5. FRASER, SIR W.: *op. cit.*, 206.
6. GRIFFITHS, A.: *Wellington, his Comrades and Contemporaries*, 1897, 3.   7. *Ibid.*, 4–5.
8. MAXWELL, W. H.: *Life of Wellington*, 1839, I, 12.
9. WELLINGTON: *Bond for £100*, Dec. 1789, *Apsley House Papers*.
10. WESLEY, ANNE: *Letter to Miss Butler*, Llangollen, Sept. 15, 1789. In the possession of C. Hamilton, Esq. *Ibid.*
11. LECKY, W. E. H.: *op. cit.*, II, 209.   12. *Ibid.*, II, 252.
13. WELLINGTON: *Letter to Earl of Mornington*, March 20, 1790, *Apsley House Papers*.
14. WELLINGTON: *Letter to Earl of Mornington*, June 14, 1790, *Apsley House Papers*.
15. WELLINGTON: *Letter to Earl of Mornington*, June 18, 1790, *Apsley House Papers*.
16. PARLIAMENTARY REGISTER, XI, Dublin, 1791.
17. LECKY, W. E. H.: *op. cit.*, II, 408–9, 430 ; III, 3, 79.
18. WELLINGTON: *Letter to Page*, Ap., 1792, *Apsley House Papers*.
19. MAXWELL, W. H.: *op. cit.*, I, 10–11.
20. LECKY, W. E. H.: *op. cit.*, III, 194.
21. 82 Grafton Street : *Apsley House Papers*.
22. WELLESLEY PAPERS, 1914, I, 121.
23. PEARCE, R. R.: *Memoirs and Correspondence of Richard, Marquess Wellesley*, 1846, I, 44.
24. WELLINGTON: *Letter to Page*, Oct. 1792, *Apsley House Papers*.
25. LECKY, W. E. H.: *op. cit.*, III, 7.
26. WELLINGTON: *Letter to Page*, Sept. 1792, *Apsley House Papers*.
27. MORNINGTON, EARL OF: *Letter to Sir Chichester Fortescue*, June 20, 1796. In the possession of Lord Gerald Wellesley (partly printed in *Supplementary Despatches*, XIII, 3).
28. PARLIAMENTARY REGISTER (IRELAND), 1793, XIII, 5.
29. LECKY, W. E. H.: *op. cit.*, III, 140.
30. PARLIAMENTARY REGISTER (IRELAND), XIII, 313.
31. FORTESCUE, HON. J.: *Wellington*, 1925, 12.
32. CROKER, J. W.: *op. cit.*, I, 337.

33. ELLESMERE, EARL OF: *Personal Reminiscences of the Duke of Wellington*, 1904, 79–80 ; CROKER, J. W. : *loc. cit.*

34. FRASER, SIR W. : *op. cit.*, 32–3 ; GLEIG, G. R. : *Personal Reminiscences of the Duke of Wellington*, 1904, 283.

35. FRASER, SIR W. : *op. cit.*, 10.

VI

1. ROSE, J. HOLLAND : *William Pitt and the Great War*, 1911, 32.

2. *Ibid.*, 118.

3. GIBBON, E. : *Autobiography* (ed. Everyman's Library), 178.

4. WRIGHT, T. : *Caricature History of the Georges*, 1867, 479.

5. MAXWELL, SIR H. : *op. cit.*, I, 8.

6. FORTESCUE, HON. J. : *History of the British Army*, IV, 354.

7. WILSON, HARRIETTE : *Memoirs* (ed. Davies), 1929, 1.

8. HUGO, V. : *Quatrevingt-Treize* (ed. Nelson), 159.

9. WRIGHT, T. : *op. cit.*, 380.

10. Conveyance of Dangan by Earl of Mornington to T. Burrowes for £25,000, Sept. 18, 1793. Registry of Deeds, Dublin.

11. CARLYLE, T. : *French Revolution* (ed. J. Holland Rose), 1902, III, 254.

12. GRIFFITHS, A. : *op. cit.*, 7.

13. Regimental accounts, Dublin, Nov. 1793, *Apsley House Papers*.

14. BRIALMONT AND GLEIG : *op. cit.*, I, 12.

15. MAXWELL, W. H. : *op. cit.*, I, 13–14.

16. FORTESCUE, HON. J. : *British Army*, IV, 141, 145, 154–5, 157.

17. W.O. : 12, 4804, *Public Record Office*.

18. Regimental accounts, Cork, April 1794, *Apsley House Papers*.

19. Regimental accounts, Cork, May 1794. *Ibid.*

20. FORTESCUE, HON. J. : *Wellington*, 13 ; *British Army*, IV, 282.

21. STANHOPE, EARL : *op. cit.*, 111.

22. MAXWELL, SIR H. : *op. cit.*, I, 11.

23. BUNBURY, SIR H. : *Narratives of Some Passages in the Great War with France* (ed. Fortescue), 1927, 29.

24. WELLINGTON : *Letter to Mornington*, Sept. 19, 1794, B.M. Add. MSS. 37308, f. 15.

25. STANHOPE, EARL : *op. cit.*, 182.

26. WELLINGTON : *Letter to General Cunninghame*, Yzendoom, Nov. 19, 1794, *Apsley House Papers*.

27. *Supplementary Despatches*, 1871, XIII, 2.

28. Regimental accounts, Dec. 1794. In W.'s writing, *Apsley House Papers*.

29. FORTESCUE, HON. J. : *British Army*, IV, 320–2.

30. *MS. General and Brigade Orderly Book*, Feb. 16–April 11, 1795. In the author's possession.

31. WELLINGTON : *Letter to Earl Camden*, June 26, 1795 : " . . . as I told you in London " (BRIALMONT AND GLEIG, *op. cit.*, I, 22). Camden entered Dublin March 31, 1795 (LECKY, W. E. H. : *op. cit.*, III, 325). It follows that W.'s London interview with him took place between his

appointment as Lord-Lieutenant and his departure for Ireland—both in March, 1795.

VII

1. BRIALMONT AND GLEIG : *op. cit.*, I, 22–3.
2. Bill £14 12s. 1d. for cloth supplied by Lucas, Dublin, 1795. Paid May 30, 1807, *Apsley House Papers.*
3. WELLINGTON : *Letter to Earl Camden,* April 29, 1795, *Camden Papers.*
4. MORNINGTON, EARL OF : *Letter to Earl Camden,* April 24, 1795. *Ibid.*
5. PARLIAMENTARY REGISTER (IRELAND) : 1795, XV, 376–81.
6. *Ibid.*, 381.
7. WELLINGTON : Fragment of letter to Earl Camden. Undated (for date cf. " the expedition to the Coast of France will not last for ever " and FORTESCUE : *British Army,* IV, 416–18), *Camden Papers.*
8. IRISH ALMANACK, 1795.
9. CAMDEN, EARL : *Letter to Lt.-Col. Wesley,* Sept. 15, 1793, *Apsley House Papers* (Copy in *Camden Papers*).
10. Prescription, *Apsley House Papers.*
11. FORTESCUE, J. : *British Army,* IV, 477–81.
12. MAXWELL, SIR H. : *op. cit.*, I, 18.
13. MORNINGTON, EARL OF : *Letter to Sir Chichester Fortescue,* June 20, 1796. (Partly printed in *Supplementary Despatches,* XIII, 3.) In the possession of Lord Gerald Wellesley.
14. CAMDEN, EARL : *Letter to W.,* June 5th, 1796, *Apsley House Papers.*
15. CAMDEN, EARL : *Letter to Earl Mornington,* undated (misplaced in 1795), *Apsley House Papers.*
16. LECKY, W. E. H. : *op. cit.*, III, 322.
17. PAGE : *Letter to W.,* June, 1796, *Apsley House Papers.*
18. Account of R. Faulder, June 6, 1796, *Apsley House Papers.*
19. MORNINGTON, EARL OF : *Letter to Sir Chichester Fortescue,* August 5, 1797. In the possession of Lord Gerald Wellesley.
   List of books in W.'s writing, endorsed in another hand " August 1798," and (more faintly) ". . . from Calcutta to Madras," *Apsley House Papers.*
21. LLOYD, W. : *History of the Late War in Germany between the King of Prussia and the Empress of Germany and her Allies,* 2 vols. (Vol. I bound in 2 parts), 1781–90. Vol. I, part II, 46.   22. *Ibid.*, 44.
23. *Ibid.*, 51–2.
24. OMAN, C. W. C. : *Wellington's Army,* 1912, 82–6 ; *Column and Line in the Peninsular War,* 17.
25. CARLYLE, T. : *Frederick the Great* (Centenary Edition), VI, 72–3 ; 273.
26. HART, B. H. LIDDELL : *Great Captains Unveiled,* 1927, 37–74.
27. SAXE, MAURICE COMTE DE : *Les Reveries ou Memoires sur l'Art de la Guerre,* 1758, 22.   28. *Ibid.*, 28.   29. *Ibid.*, 49.
30. BOURRIENNE, L. A. F. DE : *Memoires sur Napoléon,* 1831, II, 231–3.
31. NAPOLÉON : *Correspondance,* No. 2458.

SEPOY GENERAL

1. MUIR, RAMSAY : *Making of British India*, 1915, 301.
2. THACKERAY, W. M. : *Adventures of Philip*, 1862, cap. xvi.
3. BUSTEED, H. E. : *Echoes from Old Calcutta*, 1897, 110–51.

I

4. ELERS, G. : *Memoirs* (ed. Monson and Leveson-Gower), 1903, 46–7.
5. *Ibid.*, 55–6.
6. WELLINGTON : *Letter to General Cunninghame*, March 9, 1797, *Apsley House Papers.*
7. PEARCE, R. R. : *op. cit.*, I, 308.
8. HICKEY, W. : *Memoirs*, 1913–23, IV, 154.
9. BUSTEED, H. E. : *op. cit.*, 127.
10. HICKEY, W. : *op. cit.*, IV, 155–8.   11. *Ibid.*, IV, 160–1.
12. *Supplementary Despatches*, I, 1–3.   13. *Ibid.*, I, 4–5.
14. WELLINGTON : *Letter to Earl of Mornington*, April 17, 1797, *Apsley House Papers* (printed incomplete, without indication of omissions, in *Supplementary Despatches*, I, 4–6).
15. *Supplementary Despatches*, I, 12–17.
16. MORNINGTON, EARL OF : *Letter to Sir Chichester Fortescue*, July 5, 1797. In the possession of Lord Gerald Wellesley.
17. MORNINGTON, EARL OF : *Letter to Sir Chichester Fortescue*, Aug. 5, 1797. *Ibid.*
18. MORNINGTON, EARL OF : *Letter to Sir Chichester Fortescue*, Oct. 14, 1797. *Ibid.*
19. *Supplementary Despatches*, XIII, 3 (misdated May 1, 1797 ; original in the possession of Lord Gerald Wellesley, dated May 2, 1797).
20. *Ibid.*, I, 18.   21. *Ibid.*, I, 9–12.   22. *Ibid.*, I, 19–24.
23. HICKEY, W. : *op. cit.*, 171–2.
24. WELLINGTON : *Letter to Page*, Prince of Wales's Island, Sept. 10, 1797, *Apsley House Papers.*
25. *Supplementary Despatches*, I, 24–34.
26. HICKEY, W. : *op. cit.*, IV., 190–1.
27. *Supplementary Despatches*, I, 34–49.
28. BRIALMONT AND GLEIG : *op. cit.*, I, 29.
29. CURZON, MARQUESS : *British Government in India*, 1925, I, 208.
30. MORNINGTON, EARL OF : *Letter to Sir Chichester Fortescue*, Nov. 30, 1796. In the possession of Lord Gerald Wellesley.
31. *Supplementary Despatches*, I, 51–2.

II

1. *Supplementary Despatches*, I, 52–83.
2. *Ibid.*, I, 67.   3. *Ibid.*, I, 57.
4. List of books in W.'s writing, endorsed Aug. 1798 (cf. *Education of Arthur Wesley*, VII, *n.* 20), *Apsley House Papers.*   For W.'s later reference

to his study of Cæsar, see ROGERS, SAMUEL : *Recollections*, 1859, 227–8,
ELLESMERE, EARL OF : *op. cit.*, 97.

    5. HICKEY, W. : *op. cit.*, IV, 201.

    6. *Supplementary Despatches*, I, 84–5.   7. *Ibid.*, I, 96, 112–13.

    8. ELERS, G. : *op. cit.*, 63–4.

    9. ROBERTS, P. E. : *India under Wellesley*, 1929, 41–6.

    10. PEARCE, R. R. : *op. cit.*, I, 178–80.

    11. *Supplementary Despatches*, I, 52–5.   12. *Ibid.*, I, 86, 118.

    13. ROBERTS, P. E. : *op. cit.*, 48.

    14. *Supplementary Despatches*, I, 87.   15. *Ibid.*, I, 95.

    16. *Ibid.*, I, 97.   17. *Ibid.*, I, 126.   18. *Ibid.*, I, 111–12.

    19. *Ibid.*, I, 110.   20. *Ibid.*, I, 118–19.   21. *Ibid.*, I, 140.

    22. *Genealogist* : New Series, XXI, 101 ; HICKEY, W. : *op. cit.*,
III, 99.

    23. PEARCE, R. R. : *op. cit.*, I, 217, 245, 248.

    24. WELLESLEY, MARQUESS : *Dispatches*, 1840, I, 454.

    25. ROBERTS, P. E. : *op. cit.*, 50.

    26. *Supplementary Despatches*, I, 107.

    27. *Ibid.*, XIII, 4.   28. *Ibid.*, I, 167.

    29. ELERS, G. : *op. cit.*, 83–5 ; *Supplementary Despatches*, I, 160–5.

    30. *Supplementary Despatches*, I, 203.   31. *Ibid.*, I, 73, 215.

    32. *Ibid.*, I, 200.   33. *Ibid.*, I, 192.   34. *Ibid.*, I, 187–8.

    35. *Ibid.*, I, 153.   36. *Ibid.*, I, 195–6.   37. *Ibid.*, I, 206.

    38. *Ibid.*, I, 208.

    39. ELERS, G. : *op. cit.*, 101–3.

    40. MAXWELL, SIR H. : *op. cit.*, I, 32–3 ; 404. MS. Diary of Capt.
J. Malcolm, B.M. Add. MSS. 13664, f. 45.

    41. FORTESCUE, J. : *British Army*, IV, 736.

    42. *Supplementary Despatches*, I, 209.

    43. FORTESCUE, J. : *British Army*, IV, 738.

    44. MAXWELL, W. H. : *op. cit.*, I, 62–3.

    45. HUTTON, W. H. : *Marquess Wellesley*, 1893, 33.

    46. CROKER, J. W. : *op. cit.*, II, 102–3.

    47. ELERS, G. : *op. cit.*, 103.

    48. PEARCE, R. R. : *op. cit.*, I, 307–14, 425–31.

    49. MAXWELL, SIR H. : *op. cit.*, I, 36.

III

    1. ELERS, G. : *op. cit.*, 99–100.

    2. *Dispatches*, I, 36–8 ; *Supplementary Despatches*, I, 213.

    3. *Supplementary Despatches*, I, 215.   4. *Ibid.*, I, 250–1.

    5. ROBERTS, P. E. : *op. cit.*, 70–1.

    6. PEARCE, R. R. : *op. cit.*, I, 335–8.

    7. *Supplementary Despatches*, I, 245–6.   8. *Ibid.*, I, 278.

    9. *Ibid.*, I, 419–21, 440.   10. *Ibid.*, I, 403.

    11. *Ibid.*, I, 258–72.   12. *Ibid.*, I, 226.

    13. FORTESCUE, J. : *British Army*, IV, 750–2.

    14. *Supplementary Despatches*, I, 376–7.

15. *Dispatches*, I, 125–7.   16. *Ibid.*, I, 129–30.
17. *Ibid.*, I, 133–4.   18. *Ibid.*, I, 135.
19. ROBERTS, P. E. : *op. cit.*, 75.
20. *Supplementary Despatches*, I, 433–4, 480.   21. *Ibid.*, I, 529.
22. FORTESCUE, J. : *British Army*, IV, 753–9.
23, ROBERTS, P. E. : *op. cit.*, 68.
24. *Supplementary Despatches*, II, 174–81.   25. *Ibid.*, II, 109.
26. *Ibid.*, II, 255–6.   27. *Ibid.*, II, 263.
28. *Ibid.*, II, 315.   29. *Ibid.*, II, 284–9.

IV
1. *Dispatches*, I, 275 ; *Supplementary Despatches*, II, 331.
2. *Supplementary Despatches*, II, 315.
3. *Ibid.*, II, 318–22.
4. *Dispatches*, I, 281–3.
5. *Supplementary Despatches*, II, 333, 356–7.   6. *Ibid.*, II, 364.
7. *Dispatches*, I, 305–6.
8. *Ibid.*, I, 307.   9. *Ibid.*, I, 321.
10. STANHOPE, EARL : *op. cit.*, 103.
11. *Dispatches*, I, 313–19.
12. *Supplementary Despatches*, II, 332, 350, 356, 362.

V
1. *Supplementary Despatches*, II, 368.
2. ELERS, G. : *op. cit.*, 116–17.
3. *Ibid.*, 119.   4. *Ibid.*, 122.
5. *Supplementary Despatches*, II, 364.
6. *Ibid.*, 409.   7. *Ibid.*, 501.
8. ELERS, G. : *op. cit.*, 120–1.
9. ERCK, J. C. W. : *History of the 83rd Wallajahbad Light Infantry* (Cannanore), 1910, 65–6.
10. ELERS, G. : *op. cit.*, 116, 124.   11. *Ibid.*, 126.
12. *Supplementary Despatches*, II, 489.   13. *Ibid.*, II, 592.
14. *Ibid.*, III, 239.   15. *Ibid.*, II, 405, 439–41, 456, 520.
16. *Ibid.*, II, 594.   17. *Ibid.*, II, 631.
18. *Dispatches*, I, 52–3.
19. *Supplementary Despatches*, II, 451.
20. *Ibid.*, II, 614.   21. *Ibid.*, II, 625.
22. *Ibid.*, III, *passim* ; FORTESCUE, J. : *Wellington*, 40–1.
23. *Ibid.*, III, 109.   24. *Ibid.*, III, 15–16.
25. *Ibid.*, III, 65.   26. *Ibid.*, III, 185.   27. *Ibid.*, III, 501.
28. Account of Hope, Reynolds, & Griffiths, Madras, Ap. 1802, *Apsley House Papers*.
29. CURZON, MARQUESS : *op. cit.*, I, 43, 64.
30. MACAULAY, LORD : *Essay on Warren Hastings*, 1841.
31. CURZON, MARQUESS : *op. cit.*, I, 208.   32. *Ibid.*, I, 241.
33. HICKEY, W. : *op. cit.*, IV, 329–30.   34. *Ibid.*, IV, 287.
35. CURZON, MARQUESS, *op. cit.*, I, xvi.   36. *Ibid.*, I, 71.

37. *Supplementary Despatches*, III, 150.

38. ROBERTS, P. E.: *op. cit.*, 178.

39. OWEN, S. J.: *Selection from the Despatches, Memoranda, and other Papers relating to India of Field-Marshal the Duke of Wellington*, 1880, xlvi.

40. ROBERTS, P. E.: *op. cit.*, 182–208; MUIR, RAMSAY: *op. cit.*, 201–5, 239–40.

41. *Supplementary Despatches*, III, 386–7.

42. *Dispatches*, I, 357–65.

43. GRIFFITHS, A.: *op. cit.*, 16.

44. *Supplementary Despatches*, III, 432–3.

45. *Dispatches*, I, 367–83.   46. *Ibid.*, I, 393–5.

47. *Supplementary Despatches*, III, 461.

48. *Dispatches*, I, 432–3, 467–9.

49. FORTESCUE, J.: *British Army*, V, 7–9.

50. *Dispatches*, I, 464.

51. *Ibid.*, I, 506–9.   52. *Ibid.*, I, 595–6.

53. *Supplementary Despatches*, IV, 97.

54. *Dispatches*, I, 520–1.   55. *Ibid.*, I, 484–7.

56. *Supplementary Despatches*, IV, 117.

57. *Dispatches*, II, 21–2.

58. *Supplementary Despatches*, IV, 126–7.   59. *Ibid.*, IV, 143.

60. *Dispatches*, II, 91.

61. *Ibid.*, II, 98.   62. *Ibid.*, II, 179.

63. FORTESCUE, J.: *British Army*, V, 13–19.

64. *Dispatches*, II, 257.

65. *Supplementary Despatches*, IV, 153.

66. *Dispatches*, II, 309.   67. *Ibid.*, II, 222.

68. FORTESCUE, J.: *British Army*, V, 22–34; MAXWELL, SIR H.: *op. cit.*, I, 55–60.

69. *Dispatches*, II, 356.   70. *Ibid.*, II, 219.

71. *Supplementary Despatches*, IV, 187–8.   72. *Ibid.*, IV, 289.

73. *Dispatches*, II, 457.

74. *Supplementary Despatches*, IV, 205.

75. FORTESCUE, J.: *British Army*, V, 39–41.

76. STANHOPE, EARL: *op. cit.*, 57.

77. *Dispatches*, II, 647.   78. *Ibid.*, II, 700.

79. FORTESCUE, J.: *British Army*, V, 73; CROKER, J. W.: *op. cit.*, II, 232–3; BRIALMONT AND GLEIG: *op. cit.*, I, 123–4.

80. *Dispatches*, II, 514.

81. *Ibid.*, III, 144–8; DOUGLAS, J.: *Bombay and Western India*, 1893, II, 26.

82. WELLINGTON: *Letter to Mrs. Gordon, Bombay*, May 18, 1804. In the possession of C. A. Oliver, Esq.

83. WELLINGTON: *Letter to Mrs. Gordon, Bombay*, dated May 18, 1804, but written at Chinchore, which W. did not reach until June 4, 1804. *Ibid.*

84. Accounts of Bombay tradesmen, May–Sept. 1804, *Apsley House Papers*.

85. *Supplementary Despatches*, IV, 334–7.   86. *Ibid.*, IV, 385.
87. *Dispatches*, III, 168.   88. *Ibid.*, III, 193.
89. *Ibid.*, III, 444.   90. *Ibid.*, III, 339.
91. Receipt of R. Home, *Apsley House Papers*.
92. Accounts of Calcutta tradesmen, Sept. 1804, *Ibid.*
93. *Supplementary Despatches*, IV, 466.
94. *Dispatches*, III, 462.
95. WELLINGTON : *Letters to Mrs. Gordon*, Dec. 7 and 20, 1804.   In the possession of C. A. Oliver, Esq.
96. *Dispatches*, III, 593–4.
97. *Supplementary Despatches*, IV, 479 ; *Dispatches*, III, 631, 648–50.
98. *Supplementary Despatches*, IV, 487.
99. *Ibid.*, IV, 489, 493 ; *Dispatches*, III, 673.
100. *Ibid.*, IV, 500 ; *Dispatches*, III, 663.
101. WELLINGTON : *Letter to Lord Wellesley*, Feb. 17, 1805.   In the author's possession (cf. *Dispatches*, III, 683).
102. *Supplementary Despatches*, IV, 496.
103. Account of Miss Hope, Madras, March 1, 1805, *Apsley House Papers*.
104. ELERS, G. : *op. cit.*, 173–5.
105. *Supplementary Despatches*, IV, 503.   106. *Ibid.*, IV, 497.
107. STANHOPE, EARL : *op. cit.*, 130.
108. *Dispatches*, III, 686 ; *Supplementary Despatches*, IV, 507–11.
109. STANHOPE, EARL : *op. cit.*, 259.
110. YOUNG, N. : *Napoleon in Exile : St. Helena*, 1915, I, 95.

DUBLIN CASTLE

I

1. *Supplementary Despatches*, IV, 514–20.
2. *Ibid.*, IV, 520–32.   3. *Ibid.*, IV, 512.
4. CROKER, J. W. : *op cit.*, II, 233–4.
5. MOORE, SIR J. : *Diary* (ed. Maurice), 1904, I, 367.
6. *Supplementary Despatches*, IV, 533–41.
7. STANHOPE, EARL : *op. cit.*, 117–18.
8. MAXWELL, SIR H. : *op. cit.*, I, 75.
9. SWINTON, J. R. : *Sketch of the Life of Georgiana, Lady de Ros*, 1893, 173.
10. ROSE, J. H. : *op. cit.*, 556.
11. FORTESCUE, J. : *British Army*, V, 285–99.
12. CASTLEREAGH, VISCOUNT : *Correspondence*, VI, 93–4, 97.
13. *Supplementary Despatches*, IV, 587.
14. *Dispatches*, IV, 2.
15. *Supplementary Despatches*, XIII, 279.
16. EDGEWORTH, MARIA : *Life and Letters* (ed. Hare), 1894, I, 151.
17. *Ibid.*, I, 145.

18. BURKE, SIR B. : *Peerage*, 1929, *s.v.* Gosford ; *Landed Gentry*, 1921, *s.v.* Bence.

19. MAXWELL, SIR H. : *op. cit.*, I, 78.

20. GEORGIAN SOCIETY : *op. cit.*, III, 106.

21. EDGEWORTH, MARIA : *op. cit.*, I, 150.

22. WELLINGTON : *Letter to Page*, April 8, 1806, *Apsley House Papers*.

23. *Apsley House Papers*, 1806.

24. *Return of Members of Parliament*, 1213–1874, 1878, II. (W. returned for Rye, April 1, 1806.)

II

1. COBBETT, W. : *Parliamentary Debates*, April 18, 1806.

2. *Ibid.*, April 22, 1806.   3. *Ibid.*, April 28, 1906.

4. WELLINGTON : *Letter to Page*, 14 Clifford Street, May 3, 1806, *Apsley House Papers*.

5. COBBETT, W. : *op. cit.*, May 8, 12 ; June 5, 20, 1806.

6. *Ibid.*, July 10, 1806.   7. *Ibid.*, July 14, 1806.

8. SWINTON, J. R. : *op. cit.*, 179.

9. *Supplementary Despatches*, IV, 587.   10. *Ibid.*, IV, 546–86.

11. WELLINGTON : *Letter to Marquess Wellesley*, Hastings, Sept. 14, 1806, B.M. Add. MSS. 37415, f. 15.

12. MACLEOD, COL. : *Letter to W.*, July 7, 1806, *Apsley House Papers*.

13. OMAN, C. W. C. : *Wellington's Army*, 78.

14. FORTESCUE, J. : *British Army*, V, 366.

15. *Ibid.*, V, 313, 375–7.

16. WELLINGTON : *Letter to Marquess Wellesley*, Oct. 3, 1806, B.M. Add. MSS. 37415, f. 17.

17. *Supplementary Despatches*, VI, 35–8

18. WELLINGTON : *Letter to Marquess Wellesley*, Oct. 3, 1806, B.M. Add. MSS. 37415, f. 19.

19. WELLINGTON : *Letter to Marquess Wellesley*, Oct. 22, 1806, B.M. Add. MSS. 37415, f. 21.

20. WELLINGTON : *Letter to Marquess Wellesley*, Oct. 26, 1806, B.M. Add. MSS. 37415, f. 23.

21. *Supplementary Despatches*, VI, 50.   22. *Ibid.*, VI, 51.

23. *Return of Members of Parliament*, 1213–1874, II. (W. returned for Michael Midshall, Jan. 15, 1807.)

24. WELLINGTON : *Letters to Windham*, 11 Harley Street (renumbered 24 Harley St. in 1866), Jan. 25, Feb. 16, 1807, B.M. Add. MSS. 37852, ff. 15, 24. *Supplementary Despatches*, VI, 55–61.

25. COBBETT, W. : *Parliamentary Debates*, Feb. 26, 1807.

26. *Supplementary Despatches*, IV, 590.

27. WELLINGTON : *Letter to Marquess Wellesley*, March 27, 1807, B.M. Add. MSS. 37415, f. 39. Cf. *Supplementary Despatches*, XIII, 285–6.

III

1. *Third Report of the Committee on Finance*, 1808.

2. *Supplementary Despatches*, V, 33.   3. *Ibid.*, VII, 353.

4. LARPENT, F. S. : *Private Journal*, 1854, 75.
5. *Supplementary Despatches*, V, 5.   6. *Ibid*., V, 18–19, 22.
7. LEVER, C. : *Charles O'Malley, the Irish Dragoon* (ed. 1905), 61.
8. *Supplementary Despatches*, V, 67, 69.   9. *Ibid*., V, 52, 61.
10. *Ibid*., V, 21, 48 ; *Return of Members of Parliament*, 1213–1874, II (W. returned for Newport, Isle of Wight, May 8'; returned for Tralee, May 21 ; elects to sit for Newport, July 27, 1807) ; NAMIER, L. B. : *Structure of Politics at the Accession of George III*, 1929, 386 *n*.
11. SWINTON, J. R. : *op. cit*., 118.
12. *Supplementary Despatches*, V, 69–71, 75, 82.
13. *Ibid*., V, 28–36.   14. *Ibid*, V, 71.   15. *Ibid*, V, 66–7.
16. *Ibid*., V, 79.   17. *Ibid*., V, 86.   18. *Ibid*., V, 126.
19. COBBETT, W. : *Parliamentary Debates*, June 29, July 1, 9, 16, 1807.
20. *Supplementary Despatches*, V, 108, 124.   21. *Ibid*., V, 92.
22. *Ibid*., V, 125.   23. *Ibid*., V, 129.   24. *Ibid*., V, 132, 135.

IV

1. ROSE, J. H. : *Life of Napoleon I*, 1903, II, 140–3 ; *Napoleonic Studies*, 1904, 133–65.
2. CROKER, J. W. : *op. cit*., I, 342–3.
3. *Supplementary Despatches*, VI, 1.
4. *Ibid*., VI, 3 ; HARRIS, RIFLEMAN : *Recollections* (ed. Davies), 1928, 11.
5. FORTESCUE, J. : *British Army*, VI, 70–2.
6. *Supplementary Despatches*, VI, 15.   7. *Ibid*., VI, 9.
8. CROKER, J. W. : *op. cit*., II, 120.
9. *Supplementary Despatches*, VI, 12–13, 18–19, 25.
10. *Dispatches*, IV, 5.
11. *Supplementary Despatches*, VI, 24.
12. MAXWELL, W. H. : *op. cit*., I, 230.

V

1. CASTLEREAGH, VISCOUNT : *Correspondence*, VI, 186–8.
2. WYATT, B. : *Letter to Sir E. Littlehales*, Oct. 1, 1807, *State Paper Office, Dublin Castle*.
3. *Supplementary Despatches*, XIII, 288.   4. *Ibid*., V, 139.
5. *Ibid*., V, 150, 167.   6. *Ibid*., V, 151.   7. *Ibid*., V, 185.
8. *Ibid*., V, 200–1.   9. *Ibid*., V, 192, 202–3.
10. *Ibid*., V, 214.   11. *Ibid*., V, 247.
12. *Hibernian Magazine*, Jan. 1808.
13. *Supplementary Despatches*, V, 317.
14. COBBETT, W. : *Parliamentary Debates*, Feb. 1, 9, 23, 25, 29, 1808.
15. *Ibid*., April 14, 1808.
16. STANHOPE, EARL : *op. cit*., 68–9.
17. *Supplementary Despatches*, VI, 65–6.   18. *Ibid*., V, 341.
19. CASTLEREAGH, VISCOUNT : *Correspondence*, VI, 230–1.
20. *Supplementary Despatches*, IV, 592–601.

21. *Supplementary Dispatches*, V, 330. 22. *Ibid.*, V, 405.
23. COBBETT, W. : *Parliamentary Debates*, May 11, 1808.
24. *Supplementary Despatches*, V, 442-3. 25. *Ibid.*, V, 444.
26. OMAN, C. W. C. : *History of the Peninsular War*, 1902-22, I, 1-56 ;
ROSE, J. H. : *Napoleon I*, II, 159-68.
27. FORTESCUE, J. : *British Army*, VI, 148-50.
28. *Supplementary Despatches*, V, 405.
29. COBBETT, W. : *Parliamentary Debates*, April 26, 1808.
30. *Supplementary Despatches*, V, 406.
31. COBBETT, W. : *Parliamentary Despatches*, May 16, 1808.

VI

1. *Dispatches*, IV, 31.
2. *Supplementary Despatches*, V, 462. 3. *Ibid.*, VI, 80-2.
4. *Ibid.*, VI, 68. 5. *Ibid.*, V, 444. 6. *Ibid.*, VI, 73.
7. STANHOPE, EARL : *op. cit.*, 69.
8. Commission to Sir A. Wellesley, June 14, 1808, *Apsley House Papers*.
9. CROKER, J. W. : *op. cit.*, I, 12-13.
10. *Supplementary Despatches*, V, 453. 11. *Ibid.*, V, 365, 447.
12. MOORE, SIR J. : *op. cit.*, II, 239, 250.
13. CROKER, J. W. : *op. cit.*, I, 343.
14. WELLINGTON : *Letter to Marquess Wellesley*, Windsor, June 17, 1808, B.M. Add. MSS. 37415, f. 42.
15. *Supplementary Despatches*, V, 454.
16. STANHOPE, EARL : *op. cit.*, 227.
17. *Ibid.*, 291 ; SWINTON, J. R. : *op. cit.*, 149-50.
18. NAPIER, W. F. P. : *History of the War in the Peninsula*, 1828, I, 42.
19. *Supplementary Despatches*, V, 457.
20. *Dispatches*, IV, 16-19. 21. *Ibid.*, IV, 16.
22. *Ibid.*, IV, 25.
23. FORTESCUE, J. : *British Army*, VI, 188-9.
24. *Dispatches*, IV, 20, 24.
25. *Supplementary Despatches*, VI, 89.

PENINSULAR

1. GRIFFITHS, A. : *op. cit.*, 16.

I

2. *Supplementary Despatches*, VI, 89. 3. *Ibid.*, V, 473.
4. *Dispatches*, IV, 47.
5. *Supplementary Despatches*, V, 473-4.
6. *Dispatches*, IV, 50.
7. MOORE, SIR J. : *op. cit.*, II, 239, 250.
8. FORTESCUE, J. : *British Army*, VI, 192-9.
9. CASTLEREAGH, VISCOUNT, *op. cit.*, VI, 385.

10. *Dispatches*, IV, 31 *n*.
11. CROKER, J. W.: *op. cit.*, I, 343–4.
12. *Dispatches*, IV, 59.
13. *Supplementary Despatches*, VI, 91–2.
14. *Dispatches*, V, 134–5.
15. LARPENT, F. S.: *op. cit.*, 4.
16. TOMKINSON, W.: *Diary of a Cavalry Officer*, 1894, 12 ; SCHAUMANN, A. L. F.: *On the Road with Wellington*, 1924, 9, 11.
17. FORTESCUE, J.: *British Army*, VI, 206 ; OMAN, C. W. C.: *Peninsular War*, I, 236.
18. *Ibid.*, VI, 207–14 ; I, 237–40.
19. *Ibid.*, VI, 214–34 ; I, 242–62.
20. *Dispatches*, IV, 107.
21. *Supplementary Despatches*, VI, 122.
22. *Proceedings upon the Inquiry relative to the Armistice and Convention, &c. made and concluded in Portugal, in August, 1808, between the Commanders of the British and French Armies*, 1809, 87.
23. CROKER, J. W.: *op. cit.*, II, 122.   24. *Ibid.*, 89.
25. *Ibid.*, 16.   26. *Ibid.*, 56–9.
27. *Supplementary Despatches*, VI, 122–4.
28. *Inquiry*, 39.
29. *Supplementary Despatches*, VI, 132–3.
30. MOORE, SIR J.: *op. cit.*, II, 256–9.
31. *Dispatches*, IV, 156–7.
32. MOORE, SIR J.: *op. cit.*, II, 264–6.
33. *Supplementary Despatches*, VI, 134.
34. *Ibid.*, VI, 143 ; *Dispatches*, IV, 146.
35. MOORE, SIR J.: *op. cit.*, II, 261.
36. *Despatches*, IV, 142–4.
37. LARPENT, F. S.: *op. cit.*, 318.
38. MOORE, SIR J.: *op. cit.*, II, 205.
39. *Dispatches*, IV, 158–9.   40. *Ibid.*, IV, 147.
41. CROKER, J. W.: *op. cit.*, II, 123.

II

1. BYRON, LORD: *Childe Harold's Pilgrimage*, 1812, I, xxvi.
2. WORDSWORTH: *Concerning the Relations of Great Britain, Spain, and Portugal, to each other, and to the Common Enemy, at this Crisis ; and specifically as affected by the Convention of Cintra : The whole brought to the Test of those Principles, by which alone the Independence and Freedom of Nations can be Preserved or Recovered*, 1809 (ed. Dicey, 1915), 50–1.
3. BYRON, LORD: *op. cit.*, I, xxv. Suppressed stanzas.
4. *Supplementary Despatches*, VI, 149.   5. *Ibid.*, VI, 148.
6. *Dispatches*, IV, 157.
7. WELLINGTON: *Letter to Marquess Wellesley*, London, Oct. 5, 1808, B.M. Add. MSS. 37415, f. 47.
8. CREEVEY, T.: *Papers* (ed. in 1 vol.), 1912, 89–90.

9. MORNINGTON, LADY : *Letter to Marquess Wellesley*, Sept. 3, 1808, B.M. Add. MSS. 37315, f. 56.

10. WELLESLEY, LADY : *Letter to Marquess Wellesley*, Phœnix Park, Aug. 13, 1808, B.M. Add. MSS. 37315, f. 54.

11. *Supplementary Despatches*, VI, 150–1.

12. CROKER, J. W. : *op. cit.*, I, 344.

13. STANHOPE, EARL : *op. cit.*, 243 ; OMAN, C. W. C. : *Peninsular War*, I, 292–4.

14. *Inquiry*, 5.

15. *Supplementary Despatches*, VI, 153, 169, 184 ; XIII, 310.

16. *Inquiry*, 12. 17. *Ibid.*, 15–17.

18. *Supplementary Despatches*, VI, 153.

19. *Inquiry*, 59.

20. MOORE, SIR J. : *op. cit.*, II, 303.

21. *Inquiry*, 120–1. 22. *Ibid.*, 122.

23. HARPER, G. M. : *William Wordsworth*, 1916, 174, 176–8.

24. WORDSWORTH, W. : *op. cit.*, xxxii.

25. LOCKHART, J. : *Life of Scott*, II, 226 (quoted in MAXWELL, SIR H. : *op. cit.*, I, 127).

26. SMITH, SIR HARRY : *Autobiography* (quoted in ROBINSON, MAJOR-GEN. C. W. : *Wellington's Campaigns*, 1914, I, 66).

27. *Supplementary Despatches*, V, 525.

28. *Ibid.*, VI, 196–200 ; V, 526. 29. *Ibid.*, V, 536.

30. COBBETT, W. : *Parliamentary Debates*, Jan. 27, 1809.

31. EDGEWORTH, M. : *op. cit.*, I, 160.

32. COBBETT, W. : *op. cit.*, Feb. 6, 1809.

33. *Ibid.*, Feb. 21, 22, 1809. 34. *Ibid.*, March 28, 1809.

35. FORTESCUE, J. : *British Army*, VI, 319.

36. CASTLEREAGH, VISCOUNT : *op. cit.*, VII, 39–41 ; FORTESCUE, J. : *British Army*, VII, 125–8 ; *Dispatches*, IV, 261–3.

37. CASTLEREAGH, VISCOUNT : *op. cit.*, VII, 43–4.

38. WELLINGTON : *Letter to C. Flint*, April 14, 1809. In the possession of F. M. Guedalla, Esq.

39. *Supplementary Despatches*, V, 643 ; VI, 209.

40. *Ibid.*, VI, 222–4.

41. BRETT, O. : *Wellington*, 1928, 60–1.

III

1. Information supplied by Georgiana, Viscountess Gough.

2. *Pakenham Letters, 1800–1815* (privately printed), 1914, 45.

3. *Dispatches*, IV, 267–8.

4. FORTESCUE, J. : *British Army*, VII, 146. 5. *Ibid.*, VII, 149.

6. OMAN, C. W. C. : *Wellington's Army*, 82–6.

7. GUILLON, E. : *Les Complots Militaires sous le Consulat et l'Empire*, 1894, 48–144 ; OMAN, C. W. C. : *Peninsular War*, II, 315, 321, 632–9 ; CASTLEREAGH, VISCOUNT : *op. cit.*, VII, 64–8.

8. *Dispatches*, IV, 276. 9. *Ibid.*, IV, 308.

10. TOMKINSON, W. : *op. cit.*, 3.

11. FORTESCUE, J.: *British Army*, VII, 158–63.

12. WELLINGTON: *Letter to C. Flint*, May 7, 1809. In the possession of F. M. Guedalla, Esq.

13. *Supplementary Despatches*, VI, 270.

14. *Dispatches*, IV, 371.

15. *Ibid.*, IV, 374.   16. *Ibid.*, IV, 380.

17. *Ibid.*, IV, 373–4 ; FORTESCUE, J.: *British Army*, VII, 202.

18. *Ibid.*, IV, 412.

19. FORTESCUE, J.: *British Army*, VII, 207 ; OMAN, C. W. C.: *Peninsular War*, II, 471.

20. *Dispatches*, IV, 430.

21. FORTESCUE, J.: *British Army*, VII, 215–16.

22. *Dispatches*, IV, 526.   23. *Ibid.*, IV, 524–5, 528.

24. FORTESCUE, J.: *British Army*, VII, 222.

25. SCHAUMANN, A. L. F.: *op. cit.*, 182.

26. FORTESCUE, J.: *British Army*, VII, 226–7.

27. *Ibid.*, VII, 232–61.

28. *Dispatches*, IV, 543.   29. *Ibid.*, IV, 544–6.

30. *Ibid.*, V, 15.   31. *Ibid.*, V, 31.   32. *Ibid.*, V, 73.

33. *Ibid.*, V, 59.   34. *Ibid.*, V, 82–5.

35. BYRON, LORD : *Childe Harold's Pilgrimage*, I, xvi, xlvii.

36. *Supplementary Despatches*, VI, 373.

37. FORTESCUE, J.: *Wellington*, 112.

38. *Dispatches*, V, 3.

39. *Supplementary Despatches*, VI, 332.   40. *Ibid.*, VI, 360–1.

IV

1. *Dispatches*, V, 158.

2. *Supplementary Despatches*, XIII, 377.

3. FORTESCUE, J.: *British Army*, VII, 372–5.

4. *Supplementary Despatches*, VI, 383.

5. BYRON, LORD : *Childe Harold's Pilgrimage*, I, lxxxvii (suppressed stanza).

6. GUEDALLA, P.: *Palmerston*, 1926, 60.

7. *Supplementary Despatches*, VI, 401–2.

8. WELLINGTON : *Letter to C. Flint*, Dec. 7, 1809   In the possession of F. M. Guedalla, Esq.

9. *Dispatches*, V, 89.   10. *Ibid.*, V, 234–9.

11. *Ibid.*, V, 215–16.   12. *Ibid.*, V, 247.

13. *Ibid.*, V, 245.   14. *Ibid.*, VI, 9.

15. OMAN, C. W. C.: *Peninsular War*, III, 107.

16. *Supplementary Despatches*, VI, 388.   17. *Ibid.*, XIII, 396–7.

18. OMAN, C. W. C.: *Peninsular War*, III, 185 (citing *Continuation of Vertot*, II, 51).

19. *Dispatches*, V, 37.   20. *Ibid.*, V, 563.

21. CROKER, J. W.: *op. cit.*, I, 24.

22. *Supplementary Despatches*, VI, 434.

23. *Dispatches*, V, 403.

24. *Dispatches,* V, 331-2.　　　25. *Ibid.,* V, 384.
26. COLE, LOWRY : *Letter to Hon. Henrietta Cole,* Guarda, Feb. 28, 1810, *Lowry Cole Papers.*
27. *Dispatches,* V, 515.　　　28. *Ibid.,* V, 500.
29. *Ibid.,* V, 611.　　　30. *Ibid.,* V, 466, 473.
31. *Ibid.,* V, 475.
32. STANHOPE, EARL : *op. cit.,* 20.
33. *Dispatches,* VI, 6-9.
34. *Ibid.,* VI, 200, 287, 417, 429.　　　35. *Ibid.,* VI, 33.
36. *Supplementary Despatches,* VI, 588.　　　37. *Ibid.,* VI, 582.
38. *Ibid.,* VI, 515.　(Names inserted from original in *Apsley House Papers.*)　　　39. *Ibid.,* VI, 564.
40. WELLINGTON : *Letter to C. Flint,* Aug. 29, 1810.　In the possession of F. M. Guedalla, Esq.
41. FORTESCUE, J. : *British Army,* VII, 506-32 ; OMAN, C. W. C. : *Peninsular War,* III, 359-86.
42. MAXWELL, SIR H. : *op. cit.,* I, 202.
43. *Dispatches,* VI, 494.
44. WELLINGTON : *Letter to C. Flint,* Oct. 20, 1810.　In the possession of F. M. Guedalla, Esq.
45. FORTESCUE, J. : *British Army,* VII, 547.
46. *Supplementary Despatches,* VI, 612.
47. *Dispatches,* VI, 555.
48. *Supplementary Despatches,* VII, 1-2.
49. *Dispatches,* VII, 7.
50. *Supplementary Despatches,* XIII, 526.
51. COLE, LOWRY : *Letter to Hon. Henrietta Cole,* Nov. 3, 1810, *Lowry Cole Papers.*

V

I

1. *Dispatches,* VII, 59-60.　　　2. *Ibid.,* VII, 392.
3. *Supplementary Despatches,* VII, 43.
4. *Dispatches* (cited in ROBINSON, C. W. : *Wellington's Campaigns,* I, 177).
5. *Dispatches,* VII, 428.
6. FORTESCUE, J. : *British Army,* VIII, 110, 116.
7. SCHAUMANN, A. L. F. : *op. cit.,* 306.
8. FORTESCUE, J. : *British Army,* VIII, 142 ; *Dispatches,* VII, 490-6.
9. FORTESCUE, J. : *British Army,* VIII, 153-75.
10. *Supplementary Despatches,* VII, 176-7.
11. *Ibid.,* VII, 123 ; *Dispatches,* VII, 547.
12. NAPIER, W. F. P. : *op. cit.,* III, 540-1.
13. *Dispatches,* VII, 583.
14. FRASER, SIR W. : *op. cit.,* 164.
15. *Dispatches,* VIII, 232-3.
16. *Supplementary Despatches,* VII, 245.

2

1. *Peninsular*, IV, *n.* 51.
2. STANHOPE, EARL : *op. cit.*, 29.
3. ROGERS, S. : *Recollections*, 204.
4. TOMLINSON, W. : *op. cit.*, 108.
5. STANHOPE, EARL : *op. cit.*, 71.
6. LARPENT, F. S. : *op. cit.*, 96.
7. LEVER, C. : *Charles O'Malley* (ed. 1905), 571.
8. LARPENT, F. S. : *op. cit.*, 357.
9. *Supplementary Despatches*, VII, 43.
10. FORTESCUE, J. : *British Army*, VII, 420.
11. SIMMONS, G. : *A British Rifle Man*, 1899, 305.
12. TOMKINSON, W. : *op. cit.*, 117.
13. SCHAUMANN, A. L. F. : *op. cit.*, 317.
14. LEVER, C. : *op. cit.*, 554.
15. OMAN, C. W. C. : *Wellington's Army*, 295.
16. *Dispatches*, VIII, 378–9.
17. GLEIG, G. R. : *Personal Reminiscences of the Duke of Wellington*, 1904, 19.
18. LARPENT, F. S. : *op. cit.*, 403.   19. *Ibid.*, 68.
20. *Dispatches*, VII, 587.   21. *Ibid.*, VII, 202.
22. STANHOPE, EARL : *op. cit.*, 14.   23. *Ibid.*, 18.
24. *General Orders* (ed. Gurwood), 1837, xxv.
25. WELLINGTON : *Letter to C. Flint*, May 7, 1809. In the possession of F. M. Guedalla, Esq.
26. *Dispatches*, VII, 406.   27. *Ibid.*, VII, 641.
28. LEVER, C. : *op. cit.*, 277.
29. WELLINGTON : *Letter to Major-General Stopford*, Freneda, Nov. 9, 1811. In the possession of Lord Gerald Wellesley.
30. *Dispatches*, VII, 198.   31. *Ibid.*, IX, 75.
32. *Ibid.*, VII, 393.
33. *Supplementary Despatches*, VII, 171–2.   34. *Ibid.*, VII, 5.
35. ROGERS, S. : *op. cit.*, 207.
36. LARPENT, F. S. : *op. cit.*, 52–3, 75.
37. ROGERS, S. : *op. cit.*, 217.

VI

1. CROKER, J. W. : *op. cit.*, I, 339–40 ; II, 285–6 ; FRASER, SIR W. : *op. cit.*, 183.
2. GLEIG, G. R. : *Personal Reminiscences of Wellington*, 388.
3. STANHOPE, EARL : *op. cit.*, 9.
4. *Dispatches*, VIII, 557.
5. FORTESCUE, J. : *British Army*, VII, 349–68 ; FRASER, SIR W., *op. cit.*, 165.
6. *Dispatches*, VIII, 650.   7. *Ibid.*, VIII, 581–6, 656–8, 661–3.

32

8. *Supplementary Despatches*, VII, 307.

9. FORTESCUE, J. : *British Army*, VIII, 393–410.

10. *Dispatches*, IX, 173.

11. TOMKINSON, W. : *op. cit.*, 162.

12. FORTESCUE, J. : *British Army*, VIII, 462.

13. TOMKINSON, W. : *op. cit.*, 165.

14. FORTESCUE, J. : *British Army*, VIII, 471.

15. *Ibid.*, VIII, 473–80.

16. STANHOPE, EARL : *op. cit.*, 51–2.

17. FORTESCUE, J. : *British Army*, VIII, 480-513 ; OMAN, C. W. C. : *Peninsular War*, V, 418–74.

18. *Dispatches*, IX, 310.

19. CROKER, J. W. : *op. cit.*, II, 120.

20. D'URBAN, B. : *Peninsular Journal* (ed. I. J. Rousseau), 1930, 274.

21. *Pakenham Letters*, 170.

22. GOYA, F. LUCIENTES Y : *Drawing of Wellington*, British Museum, Department of Prints and Drawings ; BERUETE, A. DE : *Goya as Portrait Painter* (tr. S. Brinton), 1922, 147 ; *Dispatches*, IX, 299 (for W.'s presence " On the heights near Alba de Tormes," July 23, 1812) ; ROGERS, S. : *Recollections*, 204 (for W.'s habit of shaving overnight) ; FORTESCUE, J. : *British Army*, VIII, 506 (for W.'s wound).

The following is the text of the note appended by a member of Goya's family to the British Museum drawing :

Un dibujo hecho en Alba de Tormes despues de la batalla de Arapiles de Duque de Wellington por el que se hizo el retrato.

It appears to follow that Goya's three oil paintings of W. (equestrian portrait painted for W., now at Stratfield Saye ; portrait with hat, formerly in the possession of Alava, now in U.S.A. ; portrait without hat in the possession of Duke of Leeds, now in National Portrait Gallery) were founded on the British Museum drawing. If this view is accepted, the agreeable anecdotes of Goya's violent onslaughts on W. during a sitting at Madrid must be dismissed.

23. ROUSSEAU, I. J. : *Unpublished Letters of Wellington, July–August, 1812*, Cambridge Historical Journal, III, i, 99.

24. *Dispatches*, IX, 351.

25. ROGERS, S. : *op. cit.*, 195.

26. OMAN, C. W. C. : *Peninsular War*, V, 514–5.

27. *Supplementary Despatches*, VII, 406, 414.

28. *Ibid.*, VII, 432 ; *Dispatches*, IX, 378, 432.

29. *Dispatches*, IX, 398.   30. *Ibid.*, IX, 434.

31. ROBINSON, C. W. : *op. cit.*, II, 281.

32. *Dispatches*, IX, 465.

33. *Supplementary Despatches*, VII, 443.

34. *Dispatches*, IX, 479.

35. *Supplementary Despatches*, VII, 478.

36. *Dispatches*, IX, 574.

37. FORTESCUE, J. : *British Army*, VIII, 572–91.

38. *Ibid.*, VIII, 608.

39. D'URBAN, B. : *op. cit.*, 301.
40. *Dispatches*, IX, 582–5.
41. *Pakenham Letters*, 185.

VII

1. OMAN, C. W. C. : *Peninsular War*, VI, 244–6.
2. FORTESCUE, J. : *British Army*, IX, 75 ; *Dispatches*, X, 26–7.
3. *Dispatches*, X, 19 ; cf. *Sepoy General*, II, *n.* 32.
4. *Ibid.*, X, 53–4, 63–5.
5. WARD, C. H. DUDLEY : *A Romance of the Nineteenth Century*, 1923, 82.
6. LARPENT, F. S. : *op. cit.*, 75, 82, 98.   7. *Ibid.*, 56.
8. *Ibid.*, 71–4.
9. SCHAUMANN, A. L. F. : *op. cit.*, 365–6.
10. LARPENT, F. S. : *op. cit.*, 60, 229.
11. *Dispatches*, X, 73, 371.
12. *Ibid.*, X, 209, 231 ; LARPENT, F. S. : *op. cit.*, 80 ; COLE, SIR G. LOWRY : *Letters to Wellington*, March 22, 26, 1813, *Lowry Cole Papers*.
13. *Dispatches*, X, 117.   14. *Ibid.*, X, 322.
15. Cf. *Sepoy General*, V, *n.* 46.
16. *Dispatches*, X, 334.
17. *Ibid.*, X, 429 ; Playbill, Light Division Theatre, Gallegos, Feb. 4, 1813, *Lowry Cole Papers*.
18. LARPENT, F. S. : *op. cit.*, 112.
19. MAXWELL, SIR H. : *op. cit.*, I, 310.
20. SCHAUMANN, A. L. F. : *op. cit.*, 369–70.
21. LARPENT, F. S. : *op. cit.*, 148.
22. CROKER, J. W. : *op. cit.*, I, 336 ; II, 307.
23. WELLINGTON : *Letter to C. Flint*, June 10, 1813. In the possession of F. M. Guedalla, Esq.
24. WELLINGTON : *Orders to Sir G. Lowry Cole*, June 19, 1813, *Lowry Cole Papers*.
25. FORTESCUE, J. : *British Army*, IX, 162–94 ; OMAN, C. W. C. : *Peninsular War*, VI, 384–450.
26. CROKER, J. W. : *op. cit.*, II, 232.
27. TOMKINSON, W. : *op. cit.*, 254 ; MAXWELL, SIR H. : *op. cit.*, I, 322.   28. *Ibid.*, 253.
29. BEATSON, F. C. : *With Wellington in the Pyrenees*, 1914, 2 ; ROSE, J. H. : *Life of Napoleon I*, II, 321.
30. CROKER, J. W. : *op. cit.*, I, 337 ; II, 307.

VIII

1. *Dispatches*, X, 496.
2. FORTESCUE, J. : *British Army*, IX, 199.
3. *Pakenham Letters*, 217.
4. *Dispatches*, X. 539.   5. *Ibid.*, X, 613–14.
6. *Ibid.*, X, 524 ; *Supplementary Despatches*, VIII, 17.
7. *Ibid.*, X, 532 ; *Supplementary Despatches*, VIII, 95.

8. LARPENT, F. S.: *op. cit.*, 227, 242; BEATSON, F. C.: *op. cit.*, 158; FORTESCUE, J.: *British Army*, IX, 272; OMAN, C. W. C.: *Peninsular War*, VI, 662.

9. *Dispatches*, X, 602.   10. *Ibid.*, X, 596.

11. *Ibid.*, X, 593; LARPENT, F. S.: *op. cit.*, 183, 229.

12. *Ibid.*, X, 612–15.   13. *Ibid.*, X, 639–40.

14. OMAN, C. W. C.: *Wellington's Army*, 295, 301.

15. *Dispatches*, XI, 35.

16. *Supplementary Despatches*, VIII, 626–7.

17. *Dispatches*, XI, 306, 309.

18. MAXWELL, SIR H.: *op. cit.*, I, 373.

19. ROBINSON, C. W.: *op. cit.*, II, 372.

20. FORTESCUE, J.: *British Army*, IX, 396–407.

21. *Ibid.*, IX, 422–42.

22. *Dispatches*, XI, 275; MAXWELL, SIR H.: *op. cit.*, I, 357; CROKER, J. W.: *op. cit.*, I, 340.

23. *Ibid.*, XI, 230.   24. *Ibid.*, XI, 301.

25. CROKER, J. W.: *op. cit.*, I, 341.

26. *Dispatches*, XI, 304–6.

27. *Supplementary Despatches*, VIII, 411.

28. LARPENT, F. S.: *op. cit.*, 307; GLEIG, G. R.: *op. cit.*, 21.

29. FORTESCUE, J.: *British Army*, IX, 449–72.

30. LARPENT, F. S.: *op. cit.*, 357–60.   31. *Ibid.*, 385.

32. *Ibid.*, 382.   33. *Ibid.*, 398.

34. *Ibid.*, 422, 425; MAXWELL, SIR H., *op. cit.*, I, 366; STANHOPE, EARL: *op. cit.*, 184.   35. *Ibid.*, 428.

36. *Dispatches*, XI, 586; *Supplementary Despatches*, VIII, 707.

37. *Dispatches*, XI, 547.   38. *Ibid.*, XI, 607.

39. LARPENT, F. S.: *op. cit.*, 476.

40. *Supplementary Despatches*, VIII, 725.

41. BROUGHTON, LORD: *Recollections of a Long Life*, 1909, I, 190.

42. LARPENT, F. S.: *op. cit.*, 485–8.

IX

1. LARPENT, F. S.: *op. cit.*, 496–7, 500.   2. *Ibid.*, 508–9.

3. *Supplementary Despatches*, IX, 58.

4. *Dispatches*, XI, 681.   5. *Ibid.*, XI, 668.

6. *Supplementary Despatches*, IX, 74.

7. BROUGHTON, LORD: *op. cit.*, I, 111–14; *Supplementary Despatches*, IX, 64.

8. *Supplementary Despatches*, IX, 29.   9. *Ibid.*, IX, 100.

10. LARPENT, F. S.: *op. cit.*, 529.

11. CROKER, J. W.: *op. cit.*, I, 334.

12. *Dispatches*, XII, 28, 38, 44.

13. CROKER, J. W.: *op. cit.*, I, 333; MAXWELL, SIR H.: *op. cit.*, I, 379.

14. *Dispatches*, XII, 62.

15. ELERS, G.: *op. cit.*, 272–4; CROKER, J. W.: *op. cit.*, III, 280.

16. BYRON, LORD: *Don Juan*, IX, vi.

17. LARPENT, F. S. : *op. cit.*, 227.

18. *Dispatches*, XII, 51.

19. BRIALMONT AND GLEIG : *op. cit.*, II, 355 ; SHELLEY, FRANCES LADY : *Diary* (ed. Edgcumbe), 1912–13, I, 61, 66 ; *The Courier*, June 24, 1814.

20. *Dispatches*, XII, 66–9 ; CREEVEY, T. : *op. cit.*, 102–5.

21. SHELLEY, FRANCES LADY : *op. cit.*, 67–71.

22. BROUGHTON, LORD : *op. cit.*, I, 156–7 ; *The Star*, July 2, 1814.

23. WELLINGTON : *Letter to Earl of Longford*, Brussels, May 22, 1815. In the possession of Lord Longford.

24. *Dispatches*, XII, 123–9.

25. *Supplementary Despatches*, XIV, 537.

26. *Dispatches*, XII, 77.

27. *Ibid.*, XII, 95, 107–8, 114 ; *Supplementary Despatches*, IX, 228.

28. *Dispatches*, XII, 138, 181, 208.   29. *Ibid.*, XII, 199.

30. BROUGHTON, LORD : *op. cit.*, I, 258 ; *Dispatches*, XII, 218.

31. *Supplementary Despatches*, IX, 241.

32. *Dispatches*, XII, 9.

33. *Supplementary Despatches*, IX, 467.   34. *Ibid.*, IX, 405–6.

35. GEORGE, PRINCE REGENT : *Letter to Earl Bathurst*, Brighton, Nov. 19, 1814. Catalogue No. 90 (1926), H. Sotheran & Co., London.

36. *Supplementary Despatches*, IX, 422–3, 425–6.

37. GALLATIN, T. : *A Great Peace Maker* (ed. Gallatin), 1914, 34–5.

38. *Supplementary Despatches*, IX, 434–7, 439.

39. *Ibid.*, IX, 459.   40. *Ibid.*, IX, 517–19.

1815

1. *Supplementary Despatches*, IX, 552, 582, 588.

2. *Ibid.*, IX, 586–7.

3. METTERNICH, PRINCE DE : *Mémoires, Documents et Écrits Divers*, 1880, I, 205–6 ; STANHOPE, EARL : *op. cit.*, 25–6 ; *Supplementary Despatches*, IX, 583–4.

4. *Supplementary Despatches*, XIV, 539 ; HOUSSAYE, H., *1815*, 1911, I, 202, *n.* 2.

5. *Dispatches*, XII, 268.

6. *Supplementary Despatches*, XIV, 539–40.

7. SHELLEY, FRANCES LADY : *op. cit.*, 112.

8. ROGERS, S. : *op. cit.*, 214.

9. CREEVEY, T. : *op. cit.*, 225.   10. *Ibid.*, 215, 226–7.

11. *Dispatches*, XII, 324.

12. FORTESCUE, J. : *British Army*, X, 238, 243–8, 430.

13. *Ibid.*, X, 233, 237.

14. *Supplementary Despatches*, X, 18.

15. FORTESCUE, J. : *British Army*, X, 239–42 ; *Supplementary Despatches*, X, 219 ; EDMUNDS, BRIG.-GEN. SIR J. : *Wellington's Staff at Waterloo* (unpublished note).

16. *Dispatches*, XII, 291–2.   17. *Ibid.*, XII, 358.

18. *Despatches*, XII, 346.   19. *Ibid.*, XII, 378.
20. CREEVEY, T. : *op. cit.*, 228.
21. *Dispatches*, XII, 375–6.
22. *Supplementary Despatches*, X, 183, 244.
23. MERCER, C. : *Journal of the Waterloo Campaign* (ed. Fortescue), 1927, 91–2.   24. *Ibid.*, 107.
25. *Dispatches*, XII, 433, 438, 472.   26. *Ibid.*, XII, 435.
27. MAXWELL, SIR H. : *op. cit.*, II, 10.
28. *Dispatches*, XII, 462.
29. FORTESCUE, J. : *British Army*, X, 278–83 ; *Supplementary Despatches*, X, 509–10 ; MAXWELL, SIR H. : *op. cit.*, II, 13–14 ; CREEVEY, T. : *op. cit.*, 223, 229 ; FRASER, SIR W. : *op. cit.*, 257–310 ; SWINTON, J. R. : *op. cit.*, 133.
30. FORTESCUE, J. : *British Army*, X, 289–325 ; STANHOPE, EARL : *op. cit.*, 109 ; CREEVEY, T. : *op. cit.*, 230 ; OMAN, C. W. C. : *Wellington's Army*, 81 ; HOUSSAYE, H. : *op. cit.*, II, 211 ; ELLESMERE, EARL OF : *op. cit.*, 170.
31. MAXWELL, SIR H. : *op. cit.*, II, 27.   32. *Ibid.*, II, 37–8.
33. *Supplementary Despatches*, XII, 512.
34. FORTESCUE, J. : *British Army*, X, 332–3.
35. MERCER, C. : *op. cit.*, 147–53.   36. *Ibid.*, 157.
37. FRASER, SIR W. : *op. cit.*, 2–4.   38. *Ibid.*, 35.
39. *Dispatches*, XII, 476–7 ; *Supplementary Despatches*, X, 501.
40. HOUSSAYE, H. : *op. cit.*, II, 318–20.
41. OMAN, C. W. C. : *Wellington's Army*, 81.
42. FORTESCUE, J. : *British Army*, X, 352–4.
43. STANHOPE, EARL : *op. cit.*, 110.
44. MAXWELL, SIR H. : *op. cit.*, II, 57.
45. *Dispatches*, XII, 529.
46. MAXWELL, SIR H. : *op. cit.*, II, 67, 75.
47. STANHOPE, EARL : *op. cit.*, 221.
48. SHELLEY, FRANCES LADY : *op. cit.*, I, 169.
49. MERCER, C. : *op. cit.*, 171.
50. FRASER, SIR W. : *op. cit.*, 80–1.
51. PALMERSTON, VISCOUNT : *Selections from Private Journals of Tours in France in 1815 and 1818*, 1871, 54.
52. FORTESCUE, J. : *British Army*, X, 380.
53. *Ibid.*, X, 389.   54. *Ibid.*, X, 392.
55. STANHOPE, EARL : *op. cit.*, 245.
56. FORTESCUE, J. : *British Army*, X, 394 ; MAXWELL, SIR H. : *op. cit.*, II, 92 ; *Supplementary Despatches*, X, 531 ; ELLESMERE, EARL OF : *op. cit.*, 172 ; SHELLEY, FRANCES LADY : *op. cit.*, I, 103.
57. *Dispatches*, XII, 478.
58. CREEVEY, T. : *op. cit.*, 236–7.
59. *Dispatches*, XII, 441.   60. *Ibid.*, XII, 493.
61. *Supplementary Despatches*, XI, 24–5.
62. *Ibid.*, X, 147.   63. *Ibid.*, X, 169, 231.
64. *Dispatches*, XII, 502.   65. *Ibid.*, XII, 534.

66. *Supplementary Despatches*, XI, 21.
67. *Dispatches*, XII, 558.   68. *Ibid.*, XII, 581.
69. *Ibid.*, XII, 597–9.   70. *Ibid.*, XII, 601.
71. *Ibid.*, XII, 623.
72. *Supplementary Despatches*, XI, 130.
73. MERCER, C. : *op. cit.*, 284.
74. *Supplementary Despatches*, XI, 47.
75. *Dispatches*, XII, 516.
76. SHELLEY, FRANCES LADY : *op. cit.*, I, 105.
77. *Supplementary Despatches*, XI, 55.
78. CROKER, J. W. : *op. cit.*, I, 332.
79. *Supplementary Despatches*, X, 553–4.
80. MOLÉ, COMTE : *Mémoires*, 1922, I, 266–7.
81. *Supplementary Despatches*, X, 275.
82. CROKER, J. W. : *op. cit.*, I, 61.
83. SIMPSON, J. : *Paris after Waterloo*, 1853, 129.
84. GRANVILLE, HARRIET COUNTESS : *Letters* (ed. Leveson Gower) 1894, I, 62.
85. SHELLEY, FRANCES LADY : *op. cit.*, I, 96, 102–3, 106, 125, 127, 129.
86. *Dispatches*, XII, 529.
87. GRANVILLE, HARRIET COUNTESS : *op. cit.*, I, 68.
88. *Ibid.*, I, 74, 109.
89. SHELLEY, FRANCES LADY : *op. cit.*, I, 112–13, 116, 128, 133–5, 137, 145–6 ; II, 9.
90. SIMPSON, J. : *op. cit.*, 192–7 ; LOCKHART, J. G. : *Life of Sir Walter Scott*, V, 82–4, 91 ; SCOTT, SIR W. : *Paul's Letters to his Kinsfolk*.
91. *Dispatches*, XII, 590.   92. *Ibid.*, XII, 610.
93. *Supplementary Despatches*, XIV, 619.   94. *Ibid.*, X, 507.
95. *Dispatches*, XII, 691.
96. PALMERSTON, VISCOUNT : *op. cit.*, 33–5.
97. *Dispatches*, XII, 668.
98. PALMERSTON, VISCOUNT : *op. cit.*, 12–16.
99. *Supplementary Despatches*, XI, 175–80 ; PHILIPS, W. ALISON, *Confederation of Europe*, 1914, 123–56 ; WEBSTER, C. K. ; *Pacification of Europe, 1813–1815*, in *Cambridge History of British Foreign Policy*, 1922, I, 514–17.

OCCUPIED TERRITORY

1. PHILLIPS, W. ALISON : *op. cit.*, 126.
2. BURGHERSH, LADY : *Correspondence with the Duke of Wellington* ed. Weigall), 1903, 16.
3. EDGEWORTH, MARIA : *op. cit.*, I, 265.
4. BERRY, M. : *op. cit.*, III, 78.

I

5. *Dispatches*, XII, 694–6 ; *Supplementary Despatches*, XI, 231–8 ; WEBSTER, C. K. : *op. cit.*, in *Cambridge History of British Foreign Policy*, I, 506–7.

6. GLEIG, G. R. : *op. cit.*, 309.
7. BYRON, LORD, *Don Juan*, IX, i.
8. *Supplementary Despatches*, XI, 305.
9. *Ibid.*, XI, 273, 301, 309–10, 313–16.
10. SHELLEY, FRANCES LADY : *op. cit.*, I, 196–205.

II

1. SHELLEY, FRANCES LADY : *op. cit.*, 205.
2. CURZON, MARQUIS : *British Government in India*, 1925, II, 180–1.
3. SHELLEY, FRANCES LADY : *op. cit.*, I, 229–30.
4. WELLESLEY, LORD GERALD : *Cheltenham Spa* in *Country Life*, Jan. 16, 1926.
5. WELLINGTON, DUCHESS OF : *Letter to Lady Eleanor Butler and Miss Ponsonby, Cheltenham*, July 18 (year omitted, but evidently 1816 from references to W.'s health and temporary absence from Cheltenham. Cf. SHELLEY, FRANCES LADY : *op. cit.*, I, 229). In the possession of C. Hamilton, Esq., Hamwood, Dunboyne, co. Meath.
6. GLEIG, G. R. : *op. cit.*, 275.
7. *Supplementary Despatches*, XI, 434, 449.
8. *Ibid.*, XI, 458–9.   9. *Ibid.*, XI, 427, 441–2.
10. HAYDON, B. R. : *Autobiography* (ed. Davies), 1926, I, 245–7.

III

1. *Supplementary Despatches*, XI, 513, 533.
2. SHELLEY, FRANCES LADY : *op. cit.*, I, 308–9.
3. CREEVEY, T. : *op. cit.*, 277.
4. SWINTON, S. R. : *op. cit.*, 142–6.
5. BURGHERSH, LADY : *op. cit.*, 16.
6. *Supplementary Despatches*, XI, 561.   7. *Ibid.*, XI, 564.
8. WEBSTER, C. K. : *Foreign Policy of Castlereagh, 1815–1822*, 1925, 82–6 ; *Supplementary Despatches*, XI, 751–2 ; XII, 13–17, 119, 156–74, 190–1, 193.
9. *Supplementary Despatches*, XI, 745.
10. *Ibid.*, XI, 500 ; XIV, 655.   11. *Ibid.*, XI, 687.
12. *Dictionary of National Biography*, s.v. WARD, JAMES : *Art Journal*, 1849 ; WARD, J.: *The Battle of Waterloo in an Allegory painted for exhibiting at the Egyptian Hall, Piccadilly*, 1821.
The oil sketch for the large picture (afterwards hung in Chelsea Hospital), now in the writer's possession, is reproduced as Frontispiece.
13. BURGHERSH, LADY : *op. cit.*, 21 ; *Supplementary Despatches*, XII, 118.
14. *Supplementary Despatches*, XII, 92.   15. *Ibid.*, XII, 183.
16. *Ibid.*, XII, 213.   17. *Ibid.*, XII, 261.
18. *Ibid.*, XII, 289–90.
19. *Ibid.*, XII, 271 ; MAXWELL, SIR H. : *op. cit.*, II, 115.
20. *Ibid.*, XII, 285, 302.
21. WELLINGTON, DUCHESS OF : *Letter to Lord Wellesley* (undated), B.M. Add. MSS. 37315, f. 256.

22. WELLINGTON, DUCHESS OF : *Letter to Lord Wellesley* (undated), B.M. Add. MSS. 37316.

23. *Supplementary Despatches*, XII, 325–6, 333–4.

24. *Ibid.*, XII, 430.   25. *Ibid.*, XII, 513.

26. *Ibid.*, XII, 547–8.

27. CREEVEY, T. : *op. cit.*, 276–88.

28. *Ibid.*, 288–9 ; *Supplementary Despatches*, XII, 678.

29. *Supplementary Despatches*, XII, 722.

30. PALMERSTON, VISCOUNT : *op. cit.*, 46, 49, 53 ; *Supplementary Despatches*, XII, 735.

31. *Supplementary Despatches*, XII, 848.

32. *Ibid.*, XII, 874, 879.   33. *Ibid.*, XII, 776.

34. *Ibid.*, XII, 813.

THE CABINET

I

1. SHELLEY, FRANCES LADY : *op. cit.*, I, 71, 106.

2. MAXWELL, SIR H. : *op. cit.*, II, 260.

3. SHELLEY, P. B.: *Mask of Anarchy*, ii; *Song to the Men of England*, i.

4. DISRAELI, B. : *Coningsby*, 1844, II, i.

5. DISRAELI, B. : *Whigs and Whiggism* (ed. Hutcheon), 1913, 379.

6. *Dispatches, New Series*, I, 96.   7. *Ibid.*, I, 7, 13, 66, 69.

8. *Ibid.*, I, 80–1.

9. *Ibid.*, I, 56 ; cf. HALÉVY, É : *History of the English People* (tr. Watkin), 1926, II, 72, for a romantic inference that W. favoured military dictatorship.   This picturesque suggestion is neatly contradicted by W. himself in the continuation of the passage quoted by Prof. Halévy.

10. *Ibid.*, I, 89.   11. *Ibid.*, I, 87.

12. SHELLEY, FRANCES LADY : *op. cit.*, II, 65–6.

13. *Dispatches, New Series*, I, 101.

14. WELLINGTON : *Letter to Baron Vincent*, Jan. 5, 1820, *Apsley House Papers*.

15. NEUMANN, P. VON : *Diary* (ed. Beresford Chancellor), 1928, I, 13.

16. GREVILLE, C. C. F. : *Journal of the Reigns of King George IV and King William IV*, 1875, I, 23.

17. NEUMANN, P. V. : *op. cit.*, I, 18 ; GREVILLE, C. C. F. : *op. cit.*, I, 26–7 ; MAXWELL, SIR H. : *op. cit.*, II, 150–1 ; OMAN, C. W. C. : *The Unfortunate Colonel Despard and other Studies*, 1922, 22–48.

18. SHELLEY, FRANCES LADY : *op. cit.*, II, 86.

19. RUSSELL, G. W. E. : *Collections and Recollections*, 1898, 22.

20. CREEVEY, T. : *op. cit.*, 337.   21. *Ibid.*, 312.

22. SHELLEY, FRANCES LADY : *op. cit.*, II, 104.

23. STANHOPE, EARL : *op. cit.*, 92.

24. GREVILLE, C. C. F. : *op. cit.*, I, 37.

25. *Dispatches, New Series*, I, 131–2.   26. *Ibid.*, I, 128.

27. *Ibid.*, I, 97–8, 101.   28. *Ibid.*, I, 116–21.

29. NEUMANN, P. V.: *op. cit.*, I, 30.

30. SHELLEY, FRANCES LADY: *op. cit.*, II, 139.

31. LIEVEN, PRINCESS: *Diary* (ed. Temperley), 1925, 43.

32. ELLESMERE, EARL OF: *op. cit.*, 80–1.

33. NEUMANN, P. V.: *op. cit.*, I, 48.

34. SHELLEY, FRANCES LADY: *op. cit.*, II, 34, 37.

35. *Ibid.*, II, 49.   36. *Ibid.*, II, 66–8, 73–6, 81.

37. *Ibid.*, II, 93–113.

38. *Hamwood Papers*, 352.

39. WELLINGTON: *Letter to Sir T. Lawrence*, Oct. 20, 1820, B.M. Add. MSS. 12102; *Dictionary of National Biography, s.v.* SIR T. LAWRENCE.

40. *Dispatches, New Series*, I, 150–3.

41. GREVILLE, C. C. F.: *op. cit.*, I, 43; NEUMANN, P. V., *op. cit.*, I, 50–1.

42. *Dispatches, New Series*, I, 154–5.

43. PARKER, C. S.: *Sir Robert Peel from his Private Papers*, 1891, I, 83; *Parliamentary Debates*, Dec. 10, 1819.

44. *Dispatches, New Series*, I, 155–6.   45. *Ibid.*, I, 192–6.

46. *Parliamentary Debates*, Jan. 25, 1821.

47. HAYDON, B. R.: *Autobiography* (ed. Davies), I, 313–4.

48. SHELLEY, FRANCES LADY: *op. cit.*, II, 110; BRIALMONT AND GLEIG, *op. cit.*, III, 115.

49. STANHOPE, EARL: *op. cit.*, 44, 289.

50. *Parliamentary Debates*, Feb. 9, 1822.

51. *Dispatches, New Series*, I, 241.

52. CROKER, J. W.: *op. cit.*, I, 225.

53. CUNNINGHAM, A.: *Life of Sir David Wilkie*, 1843, II, 73; WELLINGTON, EVELYN DUCHESS OF: *op. cit.*, I, 83.

54. ASHTON, J.: *Hyde Park*, 1896, 268.

55. GREVILLE, C. C. F.: *op. cit.*, I, 54–5; CROKER, J. W.: *op. cit.*, I, 224.

56. STANHOPE EARL: *op. cit.*, 126; *Dispatches, New Series*, I, 255–8.

57. CROKER, J. W.: *op. cit.*, I, 226; BYRON, LORD: *Occasional Pieces*; NEUMANN, P. V.: *op. cit.*, I, 102; *Dispatches, New Series*, I, 263.

II

1. *Dispatches, New Series*, I, 264.

2. CROKER, J. W.: *op. cit.*, I, 230.

3. PHILLIPS, W. ALLISON: *George Canning*, 1903, 60.

4. HALÉVY, É.: *op. cit.*, II, 156.

5. TEMPERLEY, H. W. V.: *Foreign Policy of Canning*, 1925, 28.

6. HALÉVY, É.: *op. cit.*, II, 157; CREEVEY, I.: *op. cit.*, 386.

7. *Dispatches, New Series*, I, 192.

8. NEUMANN, P. V.: *op. cit.*, I, 102–3.

9. GREVILLE, C. C. F.: *op. cit.*, I, 51.

10. *Dispatches, New Series*, I, 273–9.

11. PARKER, C. S.: *op. cit.*, I, 336; NEUMANN, P. V.: *op. cit.*, I, 103.

12. TEMPERLEY, H. W. V.: *op. cit.*, 45.

13. BYRON, LORD: *The Age of Bronze*, xiii, xvi.

14. *Dispatches, New Series,* I, 116–21.   15. *Ibid.,* I, 304.
16. *Ibid.,* I, 344, 559.   17. *Ibid.,* I, 541.
18. *Ibid.,* I, 460.   19. *Ibid.,* I, 290.
20. LIEVEN, PRINCESS : *op. cit.,* 111.
21. NEUMANN, P. V. : *op. cit.,* I, 30.
22. CREEVEY, I. : *op. cit.,* 406.
23. TEMPERLEY, H. W. V. : *op. cit.,* 483–6.
24. *Dispatches, New Series,* I, 384–5.
25. *Ibid.,* I, 516–7.   26. *Ibid.,* I, 621.
27. STANHOPE, EARL : *op. cit.,* 232–3.
28. TEMPERLEY, H. W. V. : *Foreign Policy of Canning* in *Cambridge History of British Foreign Policy,* II, 60.
29. *Dispatches, New Series,* I, 626, 638–9, 649, 654, 671.
30. SHELLEY, FRANCES LADY : *op. cit.,* II, 114–15.
31. NEUMANN, P. V. : *op. cit.,* I, 113.
32. *Dispatches, New Series,* I, 657.   33. *Ibid.,* II, 34.
34. *Parliamentary Debates,* April 24, 1823.
35. *Dispatches, New Series,* II, 79.
36. *Ibid.,* II, 64.   37. *Ibid.,* II, 74.
38. TEMPERLEY, H. W. V. : *op. cit.,* 90.
39. METTERNICH, PRINCE DE : *op. cit.,* IV, 8.
40. SHELLEY, FRANCES LADY : *op. cit.,* II, 119.
41. *Dispatches, New Series,* II, 179.   42. *Ibid.,* II, 221.
43. *Ibid.,* II, 228–9.   44. *Ibid.,* II, 222.
45. PHILLIPS, W. ALISON : *George Canning,* 122.
46. SHELLEY, FRANCES LADY : *op. cit.,* II, 146–7.
47. TEMPERLEY, H. W. V. : *op. cit.,* 240–7 ; LIEVEN, PRINCESS : *op. cit.,* 61–74.
48. *Dispatches, New Series,* II, 317–25.   49. *Ibid.,* II, 277.
50. *Ibid.,* II, 385.   51. *Ibid.,* II, 364–6.
52. TEMPERLEY, H. W. V. : *op. cit.,* 147 ; *Cambridge History of British Foreign Policy,* II, 74.
53. LIEVEN, PRINCESS : *Letters during her Residence in London* (ed. Robinson), 1902, 71.
54. SHELLEY, FRANCES LADY : *op. cit.,* II, 122.
55. *Dispatches, New Series,* II, 382.
56. DISRAELI, B. : *Coningsby,* II, i.
57. *Despatches, New Series,* II, 570–1.
58. *Parliamentary Debates,* March 7, 1825.
59. SHELLEY, FRANCES LADY : *op. cit.,* II, 128.
60. *Ibid.,* II, 124–5 ; HAYDON, B. R. : *op. cit.,* I, 375.
61. *Dispatches, New Series,* III, 53–6.
62. LIEVEN, PRINCESS : *Diary,* 110–11 ; TEMPERLEY, H. W. V., *op. cit.,* 352 ; CRAWLEY, C. W. : *Greek Independence,* 1930, 54–5.
63. *Dispatches, New Series,* III, 113.
64. GREVILLE, C. C. F. : *op. cit.,* I, 79.
65. SHELLEY, FRANCES LADY : *op. cit.,* II, 143.
66. ELLESMERE, EARL OF: *op. cit.,* 77 ; FRASER, SIR W.: *op. cit.,* 34.

67. *Dispatches, New Series*, III, 113–38.

68. *Ibid.*, III, 142–50, 222 ; BUCHAN, S. : *The Sword of State : Wellington after Waterloo*, 1928, 90.

69. *Ibid.*, III, 159.   70. *Ibid.*, III, 220.

71. LIEVEN, PRINCESS : *Diary*, 112–13.

72. *Dispatches, New Series*, III, 145.   73. *Ibid.*, III, 302.

74. CROKER, J. W. : *op. cit.*, I, 321.

75. *Dispatches, New Series*, III, 314, 343.

76. CROKER, J. W. : *op. cit.*, I, 330, 332–45.

77. TEMPERLEY, H. W. V. : *op. cit.*, 415–16.

78. *Dispatches, New Series*, III, 417–18.   79. *Ibid.*, III, 376.

80. *Ibid.*, III, 491–5.   81. *Ibid.*, III, 500.

82. *Ibid.*, III, 531–2.   83. *Ibid.*, III, 566.

84. CROKER, J. W., *op. cit.*, I, 363.

85. PARKER, C. S., *op. cit.*, I, 452–3.

86. GREVILLE, C. C. F., *op. cit.*, I, 91–2.

87. WELLESLEY PAPERS : I, 164–5 ; *Dispatches, New Series*, III, 611.

88. *Ibid.*, I, 156–7.

89. TEMPERLEY, H. W. V. : *op. cit.*, 418–29.

90. *Dispatches, New Series*, III, 628–31.

III

1. *Dispatches, New Series*, III, 631.

2. *Ibid.*, IV, 34.   3. *Ibid.*, IV, 10.

4. TEMPERLEY, H. W. V. : *op. cit.*, 431–2.

5. *Dispatches, New Series*, III, 655.

6. SHELLEY, FRANCES LADY : *op. cit.*, II, 166.

7. *Parliamentary Debates*, May 2, 1827 ; *Dispatches, New Series*, IV, 16.

8. *Dispatches, New Series*, IV, 35–7.   9. *Ibid.*, IV, 63–70.

10. CREEVEY, T. : *op. cit.*, 463–4.

11. GALLATIN, J. : *op. cit.*, 269.

12. *Parliamentary Debates*, June 1, 12, 25, 1827.

13. *Dispatches, New Series*, III, 574.   14. *Ibid.*, IV, 76.

15. GREVILLE, C. C. F., *op. cit.*, I, 107–8.

16. DISRAELI, B. : *Endymion*, III.

17. *Dispatches, New Series*, IV, 97 ; *Letter to Lord Westmorland*, Aug. 17, 1827. In the author's possession.   18. *Ibid.*, IV, 102.

19. HAYDON, B. R. : *op. cit.*, I, 413–14.

20. SHELLEY, FRANCES LADY : *op. cit.*, II, 159, 166 ; LIEVEN, PRINCESS : *Correspondence with Earl Grey*, I, 61.

21. SHELLEY, FRANCES LADY, *op. cit.*, II, 167–9.

22. BURGHERSH, LADY : *op. cit.*, 39–41.

23. SHELLEY, FRANCES LADY : *op. cit.*, II, 171–2.

24. *Dispatches, New Series*, IV, 162–4, 167.

25. GREVILLE, C. C. F. : *op. cit.*, I, 116 ; *Dispatches, New Series*, IV, 169 ; CROKER, J. W. : *op. cit.*, I, 399, 401.

26. RAIKES, T. : *Journal*, 1858, II, 371.

27. *Dispatches, New Series*, IV, 183–4.
28. PARKER, C. S.: *op. cit.*, II, 28, 30.
29. *Dispatches, New Series*, IV, 20.

PRIME MINISTER

I

1. DISRAELI, B.: *Endymion*, III.
2. ID.: *Sybil*, I, iii.
3. WELLINGTON: *Letter to Colonel Stanhope*, Dec. 10, 1819. In the author's possession.
4. LOCKHART, J.: *op. cit.*, VII, 182.
5. MAXWELL, SIR H.: *op. cit.*, II, 194. 6. *Ibid.*, II, 240.
7. *Dispatches, New Series*, I, 195.
8. CROKER, J. W., *op. cit.*, I, 363.
9. FRASER, S. W.: *op. cit.*, 35.

II

1. *Dispatches, New Series*, IV, 201.
2. CROKER, J. W.: *op. cit.*, I, 404.
3. BULWER, SIR H.: *Life of Lord Palmerston*, 1870, I, 215–20.
4. *Dispatches, New Series*, IV, 209. 5. *Ibid.*, IV, 221.
6. CROKER, J. W.: *op. cit.*, I, 397.
7. *Dispatches, New Series*, IV, 253.
8. *Ibid.*, IV, 321. 9. *Ibid.*, IV, 268–9.
10. CREEVEY, T.: *op. cit.*, 498.
11. *Dispatches, New Series*, IV, 335.
12. *Parliamentary Debates*, Feb. 25, June 6, 1828.
13. BULWER, SIR H.: *op. cit.*, I, 226, 249. 14. *Ibid.*, I, 246, 250.
15. ELLENBOROUGH, LORD: *Political Diary*, 1828–1830, 1881, I, 98, 104. 16. *Ibid.*, I, 107.
17. BULWER, SIR H.: *op. cit.*, I, 253–8.
18. *Dispatches, New Series*, IV, 449.
19. BULWER, SIR H.: *op. cit.*, I, 259–66.
20. *Dispatches, New Series*, I, 450.
21. CROKER, J. W.: *op. cit.*, I, 423.
22. *Dispatches, New Series*, IV, 453.
23. ELLENBOROUGH, LORD: *op. cit.*, I, 112. 24. *Ibid.*, I, 116.
25. DISRAELI, B.: *Endymion*, V.

III

1. BUCHAN, S.: *op. cit.*, 130; BULWER, SIR H.: *op. cit.*, I, 286.
2. LIEVEN, PRINCESS: *Letters from London*, 157, 163.
3. *Dispatches, New Series*, IV, 499.
4. GREVILLE, C. C. F.: *op. cit.*, I, 135.
5. CRAWLEY, C. W.: *op. cit.*, 109.
6. ELLENBOROUGH, LORD: *op. cit.*, I, 167.

7. SHELLEY, FRANCES LADY : *op. cit.*, II, 177.
8. WELLESLEY, LORD G. : *Cheltenham Spa in Country Life,* Jan. 16, 1926.
9. SHELLEY, FRANCES LADY : *op. cit.*, II, 180 ; NEUMANN, P. v. : *op. cit.*, I, 192.
10. *Dispatches, New Series,* IV, 683.
11. LIEVEN, PRINCESS : *Letters from London,* 146.
12. *Dispatches, New Series,* V, 70, 117–19, 153, 184–5 ; HAYDON, B. R. : *Autobiography,* II, 453–7.
13. BURGHERSH, LADY : *op. cit.*, 44.
14. *Dispatches, New Series,* V, 244.
15. CREEVEY, T. : *op. cit.*, 494.
16. GREVILLE, C. C. F. : *op. cit.*, I, 142, 148, 156.
17. *Dispatches, New Series,* IV, 194.
18. OMAN, C. W. C. : *Wellington's Army,* 326.
19. *Parliamentary Debates,* April 28, 1828.
20. *Ibid.,* June 10, 1828.
21. *Dispatches, New Series,* IV, 564–70.
22. PARKER, C. S. : *op. cit.*, II, 56.
23. *Dispatches, New Series,* V, 44–5.
24. *Ibid.,* V, 133–6, 252–68.   25. *Ibid.,* V, 326.
26. *Parliamentary Debates,* Feb. 10, 1829.
27. GREVILLE, C. C. F. : *op. cit.*, I, 217.
28. ELLENBOROUGH, LORD : *op. cit.*, I, 325.   29. *Ibid.,* I, 337.
30. MAXWELL, SIR H. : *op. cit.*, II, 230–1.
31. GREVILLE, C. C. F. : *op. cit.*, I, 171.   32. *Ibid.,* I, 188.
33. ELLENBOROUGH, LORD : *op. cit.*, I, 368.
34. *Ibid.,* I, 376–7.   35. *Ibid.,* I, 374.
36. *Dispatches, New Series,* V, 518.   37. *Ibid.,* V, 585–6.
38. GREVILLE, C. C. F., *op. cit.*, I, 198.
39. *Dispatches, New Series,* V, 527, 531, 533–8.
40. *Ibid.,* V, 539–45 ; ELLENBOROUGH, LORD : *op. cit.*, I, 403 ; GREVILLE, C. C. F. : *op. cit.*, I, 192–3 ; MAXWELL, SIR H. : *op. cit.*, II, 234.
41. ELLENBOROUGH, LORD : *op. cit.*, I, 404 ; CREEVEY, T., *op. cit.*, 542 ; GREVILLE, C. C. F. : *op. cit.*, I, 195 ; SHELLEY, FRANCES LADY : *op. cit.*, II, 188.
42. *Dispatches, New Series,* V, 546–7, 554–5.
43. *Parliamentary Debates,* April 2, 1829.
44. *Ibid.,* April 10, 1829.
45. CROKER, J. W. : *op. cit.*, II, 11.

IV

1. CROKER, J. W. : *op. cit.*, II, 4.
2. LIEVEN, PRINCESS : *Letters from London,* 187.
3. GREVILLE, C. C. F. : *op. cit.*, I, 222.
4. CROKER, J. W. : *op. cit.*, II, 15.
5. *MS. Proceedings of the Wellington Testimonial Committee,* April, 1829. In the possession of Lord Gerald Wellesley.

6. HALÉVY, É. : *op. cit.*, I, 276.

7. ELLENBOROUGH, LORD : *op. cit.*, II, 14.

8. *Dispatches, New Series*, V, 592-7.   9. *Ibid.*, VI, 248.

10. GREVILLE, C. C. F. : *op. cit.*, I, 209 ; CREEVEY, T. : *op. cit.*, 543.

11. *Hamwood Papers*, 381.

12. GREVILLE, C. C. F. : *op. cit.*, I, 253.   13. *Ibid.*, I, 238.

14. *Dispatches, New Series*, VI, 198-9.   15. *Ibid.*, VI, 20.

16. GREVILLE, C. C. F. : *op. cit.*, I, 250.   17. *Ibid.*, I, 252.

18. *Dispatches, New Series*, VI, 294.

19. NEUMANN, P. v. : *op. cit.*, I, 200.

20. *Dispatches, New Series*, VI, 34.

21. CRAWLEY, C. W. : *op. cit.*, 165-73.

22. *Dispatches, New Series*, VI, 28.

23. BEALES, A. C. F. : *Foreign Policy of Wellington*, 1828-30 (unpublished thesis, University of London, 1927).

24. RAIKES, T. : *op. cit.*, I, 64.

25. GREVILLE, C. C. F. : *op. cit.*, I, 262, 266.

26. *Dispatches, New Series*, VI, 527.

27. *Ibid.*, VI, 529.   28. *Ibid.*, VI, 533.

29. GREVILLE, C. C. F. : *op. cit.*, I, 275 ; HALÉVY, É. : *op. cit.*, II, 300.

30. PARKER, C. S. : *op. cit.*, II, 154-6.

31. *Dispatches, New Series*, VII, 106-8.

32. CREEVEY, T. : *op. cit.*, 553 ; BRETT, O. : *op. cit.*, 228.

33. CREEVEY, T. : *op. cit.*, 554.

34. ELLENBOROUGH, LORD : *op. cit.*, II, 280.

35. GREVILLE, C. C. F. : *op. cit.*, II, 3.   36. *Ibid.*, II, 13-16.

37. BULWER, SIR H. : *op. cit.*, I, 361.

38. GREVILLE, C. C. F. : *op. cit.*, II, 42.

39. *Dispatches, New Series*, VII, 153.

40. GREVILLE, C. C. F. : *op. cit.*, II, 21.

41. *Dispatches, New Series*, VII, 157.   42. *Ibid.*, VII, 165.

43. HALÉVY, É. : *op. cit.*, III, 5 ; GUEDALLA, P. : *Palmerston*, 1926, 145.

44. GREVILLE, C. C. F. : *op. cit.*, II, 94-5 ; LIEVEN, PRINCESS : *Correspondence with Earl Grey*, I, 257-8, 261, 274.

45. *Dispatches, New Series*, VII, 12. (" As to my nomination of the Polignac ministry, I think there is no public man in Europe who has less to say to this event than I. Polignac never spoke to me of his intentions. I have never written to him, nor to the King, since the birth of the Duc de Bordeaux, nor to the Duc d'Angoulême ; nor have I communicated with anyone in France upon internal affairs.") Cf. *Parliamentary Debates*, March 28, 1831.

46. BUTLER, J. R. M. : *Passing of the Great Reform Bill*, 1914, 85-9.

47. *Ibid.*, 90.

48. *Dispatches, New Series*, I, 207.   49. *Ibid.*, VII, 226.

50. GREVILLE, C. C. F. : *op. cit.*, II, 94 ; RAMSAY, A. A. W. : *Sir Robert Peel*, 1928, 134.

51. *Dispatches, New Series*, VII, 352-3.

52. *Dispatches*, New Series, VII, 300–1, 322.
53. ELLESMERE, EARL OF : *op. cit.*, 62 ; ELLENBOROUGH, LORD : *op. cit.*, II, 417.
54. RAMSAY, A. A. W. : *op. cit.*, 135.
55. *The Times*, Sept. 13, 1930 ; SHELLEY, FRANCES LADY : *op. cit.*, II, 202 ; ELLENBOROUGH, LORD : *op. cit.*, II, 370.
56. *Dispatches, New Series*, VII, 281, 328 ; MAXWELL, SIR H. : *op. cit.*, II, 252–3 ; BULWER, SIR H. : *op. cit.*, II, 362–4 ; LIEVEN, PRINCESS : *Letters from London*, 262.
57. *Dispatches, New Series*, VII, 307–9 ; HAYDON, B. R. : *Autobiography*, II, 496–7.
58. *Parliamentary Debates*, Nov. 2, 1830.
59. RAMSAY, A. A. W. : *op. cit.*, 136.
60. ELLENBOROUGH, LORD : *op. cit.*, II, 417 ; GREVILLE, C. C. F. : *op. cit.*, II, 54–5.
61. *Dispatches, New Series*, VII, 354–5.
62. ELLENBOROUGH, LORD : *op. cit.*, II, 418–22.
63. BUTLER, J. R. N. : *op. cit.*, 102.
64. ELLENBOROUGH, LORD : *op. cit.*, II, 423.
65. LIEVEN, PRINCESS : *Letters from London*, 277 ; GREVILLE, C. C. F. : *op. cit.*, II, 61 ; LADY DOVER : *Letter to Lady C. Lascelles*, Nov. 18, 1830. In the possession of Mrs. Lascelles, Woolbeding ; DUCHESS OF SUTHERLAND : *Letter to Lady C. Lascelles*, Nov. 18, 1830. *Ibid.*
66. *Despatches, New Series*, VII, 361.

REARGUARD ACTION

I

1. ROGERS, S. : *op. cit.*, 220.
2. *Dispatches, New Series*, VII, 368.
3. LIEVEN, PRINCESS : *Letters from London*, 277.
4. GREVILLE, C. C. F. : *op. cit.*, II, 63.
5. *Dispatches, New Series*, VII, 373–5.
6. *Ibid.*, VII, 382–5 ; GLEIG, G. R. : *op. cit.*, 50–3.
7. LIEVEN, PRINCESS : *Letters from London*, 82.
8. CROKER, J. W. : *op. cit.*, II, 80–1 ; GREVILLE, C. C. F. : *op. cit.*, II, 80.
9. *Dispatches, New Series*, VII, 387.
10. CROKER, J. W. : *op. cit.*, II, 104 ; *Dispatches, New Series*, VII, 399–400.
11. *Dispatches, New Series*, VII, 409–10.
12. BURGHERSH, LADY : *op. cit.*, 51.
13. MAXWELL, SIR H. : *op. cit.*, II, 257.
14. *Observer*, Feb. 20, 1831.
15. *Parliamentary Debates*, March 24, 28, 1831.
16. *Dispatches, New Series*, VII, 425–8.
17. EDGEWORTH, M. : *op. cit.*, II, 174–6.

18. Information supplied by Georgiana, Viscountess Gough.

19. *Dispatches, New Series,* VII, 432.

20. ARBUTHNOT, P. : *Memories of the Arbuthnots,* 1920, 224.

21. *Dispatches, New Series,* VII, 557–8.

22. STANHOPE, EARL : *op. cit.,* 13.

23. *Dispatches, New Series,* VII, 470, 530.

24. GLEIG, G. R. : *op. cit.,* 59.   25. *Ibid.,* 68–82.

26. GREVILLE, C. C. F. : *op. cit.,* II, 153–4.

27. *Dispatches, New Series,* VII, 436 ; GREVILLE, C. C. F. : *op. cit.,* II, 159, 185.

28. *Dispatches, New Series,* VII, 493.

29. GREVILLE, C. C. F. : *op. cit.,* II, 189–92.   30. *Ibid.,* II, 197–9.

31. *Parliamentary Debates,* Oct. 4, 1831.

32. MORLEY, J. : *Life of Gladstone,* 1903, I, 75.

33. *Dispatches, New Series,* VII, 561 ; GLEIG, G. R. : *op. cit.,* 102–3.

34. STANHOPE, EARL : *op. cit.,* 32.

35. *Dispatches, New Series,* VIII, 30–4.   36. *Ibid.,* VIII, 143–5.

37. *Ibid.,* VIII, 71.   38. *Ibid.,* VIII, 98–9.

39. *Ibid.,* VIII, 147, 213 ; NEUMANN, P. v. : *op. cit.,* I, 263, 268–9.

40. *Ibid.,* VIII, 157–8.   41. *Ibid.,* VIII, 155.

42. *Ibid.,* VIII, 153.   43. *Ibid.,* VIII, 169.

44. GREVILLE, C. C. F. : *op. cit.,* II, 272.

45. *Parliamentary Debates,* April 10, 1832.

46. *Despatches, New Series,* VIII, 280.

47. CROKER, J. W. : *op. cit.,* II, 150.

48. RAIKES, T. : *op. cit.,* 16–17.

49. *Dispatches, New Series,* VIII, 289.

50. DISRAELI, B. : *Endymion,* viii.

51. *Dispatches, New Series,* VIII, 340.

52. CROKER, J. W. : *op. cit.,* II, 154–69 ; GREVILLE, C. C. F. : *op. cit.,* II, 294–304, 340–1 ; DISRAELI, B. : *Coningsby,* I, vii ; *Endymion,* viii.

53. *Dispatches, New Series,* VIII, 304.

54. BUTLER, J. R. M. : *op. cit.,* 396–7.

55. RAIKES, T. : *op. cit.,* I, 19.

56. *Dispatches, New Series,* VIII, 322.

57. STANHOPE, EARL : *op. cit.,* 176 ; SWINTON, J. R. : *op. cit.,* 166–8 ; FRASER, SIR W. : *op. cit.,* 21–3, 206 ; RAIKES, T. : *op. cit.,* I, 33 ; TUPPER, M. : *My Life as an Author,* 1886, 66 ; FROUDE, J. R. : *Carlyle's Early Life* (ed. 1896), II, 305 ; MAXWELL, SIR H. : *op. cit.,* II, 271 ; *Dispatches, New Series,* VIII ; ROGERS, S. : *op. cit.,* 224–5.

II

1. MAXWELL, SIR H. : *op. cit.,* II, 270–1, 273 ; *Dispatches, New Series,* VIII, 380–1.

2. *Dispatches, New Series,* VIII, 361, 367–8.

3. *Ibid.,* VIII, 492.   4. *Ibid.,* VIII, 435.

5. *Ibid.,* VIII, 472–3.   6. *Ibid.,* VIII, 357.

33

7. CROKER, J. W. : *op. cit.*, II, 224.

8. FRASER, SIR W. : *op. cit.*, 11.

9. GREVILLE, C. C. F. : *op. cit.*, II, 363 ; MAXWELL, SIR H. : *op. cit.*, II, 274.

10. MAXWELL, SIR H. : *op. cit.*, II, 276.   11. *Ibid.*, II, 275, 277.

12. HAYDON, B. R. : *Autobiography*, II, 560.

13. GREVILLE, C. C. F. : *op. cit.*, II, 372.

14. RAIKES, T. : *op. cit.*, I, 104.

15. GREVILLE, C. C. F. : *op. cit.*, II, 380.

16. STANHOPE, EARL : *op. cit.*, 36.   17. *Ibid.*, 48.

18. MAXWELL, SIR H. : *op. cit.*, II, 289 ; SHELLEY, FRANCES LADY : *op. cit.*, II, 231.

19. SHELLEY, FRANCES LADY : *op. cit.*, II, 253 ; ELLESMERE, EARL OF : *op. cit.*, 46 ; FRASER, SIR W. : *op. cit.*, 159–61 ; CROKER, J. W. : *op. cit.*, II, 227–8 ; RAIKES, T., *op. cit.*, II, 373.

20. CREEVEY, T. : *op. cit.*, 628 ; MAXWELL, SIR H. : *op. cit.*, II, 296 ; GREVILLE, C. C. F. : *op. cit.*, III, 116 ; SHELLEY, FRANCES LADY : *op. cit.*, II, 252–7 ; LIEVEN, PRINCESS : *Correspondence with Earl Grey*, III, 2.

21. *Dispatches, New Series*, VIII, 147–9.

22. *Letters of the Duke of Wellington to Miss J.* (ed. C. T. Herrick), 1924, 39, 41 ; cf. MOORE, GEORGE : *Le Revers d'un Grand Homme* in *Impressions and Opinions* (ed. 1913).

23. MAXWELL, SIR H. : *op. cit.*, II, 210–11.

24. *Letters to Miss J.*, 42.   25. *Ibid.*, 43–7.

26. *Ibid.*, 49.   27. *Ibid.*, 51–2.   28. *Ibid.*, 53.

29. *Ibid.*, 59–60.   30. *Ibid.*, 44, 63.   31. *Ibid.*, 65–90

32. *Ibid.*, 91, 95, 103.   33. *Ibid.*, 105–6.

34. *Ibid.*, 118, 120, 122, 129–32.   35. *Ibid.*, 134–6.

36. *Ibid.*, 141–2.   37. *Ibid.*, 164.   38. *Ibid.*, 168.

39. *Ibid.*, 171.   40. *Ibid.*, 173.   41. *Ibid.*, 182–4.

42. *Ibid.*, 194–207.   43. *Ibid.*, 214.   44. *Ibid.*, 215–16.

III

1. DISRAELI, B. : *Coningsby*, II, iii.

2. STANHOPE, EARL. : *op. cit.*, 230.

3. PARKER, C. S. : *op. cit.*, 252.

4. STANHOPE, EARL : *op. cit.*, 62.

5. GREVILLE, C. C. F. : *op. cit.*, III, 149.   6. *Ibid.*, III, 155.

7. DISRAELI, B. : *Coningsby*, II, iv.

8. MAXWELL, SIR H. : *op. cit.*, II, 303.

9. RAIKES, T. : *op. cit.*, I, 235–6.

10. WELLINGTON : *Letter to B. Disraeli*, Jan. 3, 1835, *Apsley House Papers* ; MONYPENNY, W. F. : *Life of Disraeli*, 1910, I, 246–7, 275.

11. WELLINGTON : *Letter to Fellows*, March 23, 1835, *Apsley House Papers*.

12. MAXWELL, SIR H. : *op. cit.*, II, 306.

IV

1. RAIKES, T. : *op. cit.*, I, 294–5.
2. GREVILLE, C. C. F. : *op. cit.*, III, 216.
3. DISRAELI, B. : *The Young Duke*, V, vi.
4. GREVILLE, C. C. F. : *op. cit.*, III, 232.
5. MONYPENNY, W. F. : *op. cit.*, I, 335.
6. *Gladstone Papers*, 1930, 23.
7. HAYDON, B. R. : *Autobiography* (ed. Davies), II, 579–84.
8. SWINTON, J. R. : *op. cit.*, 157–8.
9. PARKER, C. S. : *op. cit.*, II, 321.
10. BURGHERSH, LADY : *op. cit.*, 73.
11. GREVILLE, C. C. F. : *op. cit.*, III, 403.
12. *Ibid.*, III, 396 ; CREEVEY, T. : *op. cit.*, 662 ; BRETT, O. : *op. cit.*, 250.

APOTHEOSIS

I

1. ELLESMERE, EARL OF : *op. cit.*, 177.
2. RAIKES, T. : *op. cit.*, II, 378.
3. GLEIG, G. R. : *op. cit.*, 285–7.
4. SWINTON, J. R. : *op. cit.*, 146 ; RAIKES, T. : *op. cit.*, I, 455.
5. GRANT DUFF, SIR M. E. : *A Victorian Vintage : Selections from Diaries* (ed. A. Tilney Bassett), 1930, 103.
6. FRASER, SIR W. : *op. cit.*, 203 ; SWINTON, J. R. : *op. cit.*, 147.
7. RAIKES, T. : *op. cit.*, II, 373–4, 380–6.   8. *Ibid.*, II, 369.
9. *Ibid.*, II, 386–7 ; CONWAY, SIR M. : *Walmer Castle* in *Country Life*, Nov. 1, 8, 1919.
10. CURZON, MARQUESS : *Personal History of Walmer Castle and its Lords Warden*, 1927, 181, 256–7.
11. WELLINGTON : *Letter to Townshend*, Dec. 29, 1848. In the author's possession ; *Letter to S. S. Curling*, April 24, 1844. *Ibid.* ; CURZON, MARQUESS : *op. cit.*, 177.
12. WELLINGTON : *Memoranda to Capt. Watts*, Nov. 1838, *Walmer MSS. ; Letter to Miss Edwards*, Aug. 11, 1847. *Ibid.*
13. CURZON, MARQUESS : *op. cit.*, 253.
14. *Ibid.*, 173.   15. *Ibid.*, 227.   16. *Ibid.*, 188.
17. HAYDON, B. R. : *Autobiography*, II, 644–65.
18. WELLINGTON, EVELYN DUCHESS OF : *Catalogue of Pictures and Sculpture at Apsley House*, 1901, II, 376.
19. BRIALMONT AND GLEIG : *op. cit.*, IV, 148.
20. CURZON, MARQUESS : *op. cit.*, 214–19.
21. WELLINGTON : *Memorandum*, Nov. 19, 1842 ; *Walmer MSS.*
22. CURZON, MARQUESS : *op. cit.*, 195.
23. BRIALMONT AND GLEIG : *op. cit.*, IV, 162–3, 166–7.
24. FORSTER, J. : *Life of Charles Dickens* (ed. Everyman's Library), II, 81.

33*

25. KERR, MARK : *Land, Sea, and Air*, 1927, 345.

26. CURZON, MARQUESS : *op. cit.*, 176.

27. STANHOPE, EARL : *op. cit.*, 107-8.

28. WELLINGTON : *Letter to Lady Robert Grosvenor*, Walmer, Sept. 19, 1839. In the possession of Hon. Mrs. Maurice Glyn.

29. WELLINGTON : *Latter to Lady Robert Grosvenor*, Dec. 30, 1839. *Ibid.*

30. SWINTON, J. R. : *op. cit.*, 153.

31. CURZON, MARQUESS : *op. cit.*, 177 ; GRANT DUFF, SIR M. E. : *op. cit.*, 58.

32. FORSTER, J. : *op. cit.*, I, 409.

33. MAXWELL, SIR H. : *op. cit.*, II, 374 ; FRASER, SIR W. : *op. cit.*, 34 ; ELLESMERE, EARL OF : *op. cit.*, 77-8.

34. ELLESMERE, EARL OF : *op. cit.*, 174.

35. BURGHERSH, LADY : *op. cit.*, 83, 113.   36. *Ibid.*, 131.

37. WARD, D. : *A Romance of the Nineteenth Century*, 77-183 ; *cf.* GLEIG, G. R. : *op. cit.*, 290-3.

II

1. DISRAELI, B. : *Whigs and Whiggism* (ed. Hutcheon), 379.

2. BORROW, G. : *The Romany Rye*, 1857, Ap., chap. x.

3. WILSON, D. A. : *Carlyle at his Zenith*, 1927, 286.

4. FROUDE, J. A. : *Carlyle's Life in London* (ed. Silver Library), II, 413.   5. *Ibid.*, II, 48-9.

6. GREVILLE, C. C. F. : *op. cit.*, III, 408.

7. MAXWELL, SIR H. : *op. cit.*, II, 312.   8. *Ibid.*, II, 316.

9. *Ibid.*, II, 315.   10. *Ibid.*, II, 313.   11. *Ibid.*, II, 332.

12. VICTORIA, QUEEN : *Girlhood*, 1912, II, 163-75.

13. DISRAELI, B. : *Sybil*, IV, xiv ; STANHOPE, EARL : *op. cit.*, 140.

14. WELLINGTON : *Letters to Lady Shelley and others*, May 10, 1839, *Apsley House Papers.*

15. STANHOPE, EARL : *op. cit.*, 194.

16. BURGHERSH, LADY : *op. cit.*, 139.

17. STANHOPE, EARL : *op. cit.*, 133.

18 . WELLINGTON : *Letter to Miss C.* . . . May 2, 1846. In the author's possession.

19. STANHOPE, EARL : *op. cit.*, 296.

20. BURGHERSH, LADY : *op. cit.*, 143.

21. STANHOPE, EARL : *op. cit.*, 197-213.

22. CROKER, J. W. : *op. cit.*, II, 358-9 ; GREVILLE, C. C. F. : *op. cit.*, 267-9, 271.

23. *Ibid.*, 236-7, 264, 283.

24. *Punch*, IX (1845), quoted in MAXWELL, SIR H. : *op. cit.*, II, 335 ; information supplied by Miss Redgrave.

25. ABERDEEN, EARL OF : *Letter to Wellington*, Oct. 26, 1841, *Raikes Papers, Pierpoint Morgan Library. New York* ; GREVILLE, C. C. F. : *op. cit.*, II, 59.

26. RAIKES, T. : *Private Correspondence with the Duke of Wellington*, 1861, 161, 196–7, 262–3.

27. *Parliamentary Debates*, April 6, 1840. 28. *Ibid.*, 62, 375.

29. STANHOPE, EARL : *op. cit.*, 195.

30. RAIKES, T. : *op. cit.*, 384–5.

31. PARKER, C. S. : *op. cit.*, II, 461.

32. GREVILLE, C. C. F. : *op. cit.*, II, 34.

33. VICTORIA, QUEEN : *Letters*, I, 389.

34. GREVILLE, C. C. F. : *op. cit.*, II, 58–9.

35. *Ibid.*, II, 77, 243 ; VICTORIA, QUEEN : *Letters*, I, 472.

36. GREVILLE, C. C. F. : *op. cit.*, II, 145. 37. *Ibid.*, II, 139.

38. *Ibid.*, II, 223.

39. VICTORIA, QUEEN : *Letters*, II, 130-5.

40. GREVILLE, C. C. F. : *op. cit.*, II, 351.

41. MAXWELL, SIR H. : *op. cit.*, II, 341.

42. CROKER, J. W. : *op. cit.*, III, 39.

43. *Ibid.*, III, 113.

44. VICTORIA, QUEEN : *Letters*, II, 74.

45. CROKER, J. W. : *op. cit.*, III, 52–5.

46. MAXWELL, SIR H. : *op. cit.*, II, 351. 47. *Ibid.*, II, 352.

48. *Ibid.*, II, 355.

49. GREVILLE, C. C. F. : *op. cit.*, II, 417.

50. WELLINGTON : *Letters to Lord John Russell*, 1846–50, *Pierpoint Morgan Library, New York ; Russell Papers, Public Record Office.*

51. BURGHERSH, LADY : *op. cit.*, 197–8.

52. GREVILLE, C. C. F. : *op. cit.*, III, 75–6.

53. SHELLEY, FRANCES LADY : *op. cit.*, II, 272–89, 410–11.

54. HAYDON, B. R. : *Letter to Kendall* (undated). In the author's possession ; *Autobiography*, II, 777.

55. HAYDON, B. R. : *op. cit.*, II, 684.

56. *Ibid.*, II, 642 ; CROKER, J. W. : *op. cit.*, III, 124.

57. ARBUTHNOT, C. : *Letter to Wellington*, Sept. 24, 1846. In the author's possession.

58. CROKER, J. W. : *op. cit.*, III, 126.

59. GREVILLE, C. C. F. : *op. cit.*, III, 91.

60. CROKER, J. W. : *op. cit.*, III, 128.

61. WELLINGTON : *Letter to Lord J. Russell*, July 10, 1847. In the possession of the Marquess of Lansdowne.

62. VICTORIA, QUEEN : *Letters*, II, 145–6.

63. MAXWELL, SIR H. : *op. cit.*, II, 368–70.

64. METTERNICH, PRINCE DE : *Mémoires*, VIII, 16–19, 24, 33, 51.

III

1. PARKER, C. S. : *op. cit.*, III, 546.

2. FRASER, SIR W. : *op. cit.*, 6.

3. BRIALMONT AND GLEIG : *op. cit.*, IV, 151–2.

4. BURGHCLERE, LADY : *A Great Man's Friendship : Letters of the*

Duke of Wellington to Mary, Marchioness of Salisbury, 1850–1852, 1927, 73; BURGHERSH, LADY: *op. cit.*, 193.

5. SHELLEY, FRANCES, LADY: *op. cit.*, II, 312–13.

6. BURGHCLERE, LADY: *op. cit.*, 6.   7. *Ibid.*, vii.

8. *Ibid.*, 131.   9. *Ibid.*, 76, 80, 122, 321.

10. *Ibid.*, 86–7, 226–8.   11. *Ibid.*, 93, 112, 127.

12. *Ibid.*, 68–9, 208, 228.   13. *Ibid.*, 111.

14. MARTIN, SIR T.: *Life of the Prince Consort*, 1876, II, 253–62.

15. THACKERAY, W. M.: *Lines on a Late Hospicious Ewent*, 1850.

16. MARTIN, SIR T.: *op. cit.*, II, 265.

17. BURGHCLERE, LADY: *op. cit.*, 130–3, 135–7, 150.

18. *Ibid.*, 181.   19. *Ibid.*, 200.   20. *Ibid.*, 194.

21. GREVILLE, C. C. F., : *op. cit.*, III, 389; VICTORIA, QUEEN: *Letters*, II, 371–3; MONYPENNY, W. F., AND BUCKLE, G. E.: *op. cit.*, III, 295–6.

22. MONYPENNY, W. F., AND BUCKLE, G. E.: *op. cit.*, III, 348.

23. *Parliamentary Debates*, June 15, 1852.

24. BURGHCLERE, LADY: *op. cit.*, 270.

25. *Parliamentary Debates*, June 22, 1852.

26. CURZON, MARQUESS: *op. cit.*, 255.

27. BURGHCLERE, LADY: *op. cit.*, 311.

28. *Ibid.*, 312–15.

29. *Ibid.*, 318–20; CROKER, J. W.: *op. cit.*, III, 272–80.

30. *Ibid.*, 325–6, 329–30.

31. *Ibid.*, 331; BURGHERSH, LADY: *op. cit.*, 201–2.

32. MAXWELL, SIR H.: *op. cit.*, II, 386.

IV

Official Programme of the Public Funeral of the late Field-Marshal, Arthur Duke of Wellington, K.G., as issued by the authority of the Earl-Marshal, 1852; *Order of Proceedings and Ceremonies observed in the Public Funeral of the late Field-Marshal, Arthur Duke of Wellington, K.G.*, 1852; *The Times*, Nov. 11–19, 1852; *Illustrated London News*, Nov. 20, 1852; FROUDE, J. A.: *op. cit.*, II, 135–6; HODDER, E.: *Life of Lord Shaftesbury*, 1886, II, 337–8; MALMESBURY, EARL OF: *Memoirs of an Ex-Minister* (ed. in 1 vol.), 1885, 278–9; MARTIN, SIR T.: *op cit.*, II, 464–72; MONY-PENNY, W. F., AND BUCKLE, G. E.: *op. cit.*, III, 393–4, 578–80; RED-GRAVE, F. M.: *Richard Redgrave*, 1891, 100–4; STANLEY, LADY AUGUSTA: *Letters, 1849–1863* (ed. Baillie and Bolitho), 1927, 46; TENNYSON, A.: *Ode on the Death of the Duke of Wellington*, 1852; TENNYSON, H.: *Alfred Lord Tennyson* (ed. in 1 vol.), 1905, 302; VICTORIA, QUEEN: *Letters*, II, 478–9, 487.

INDEX